# THE FRAGMENTARY CLASSICISING HISTORIANS
# OF THE LATER ROMAN EMPIRE

## II

# ARCA
## Classical and Medieval Texts, Papers and Monographs

## 10

**General Editors**
Neil Adkin (University of North Carolina, Chapel Hill)
Francis Cairns (The Florida State University)
Robin Seager (University of Liverpool)
Frederick Williams (Trinity College Dublin)
*Assistant Editor*: Sandra Cairns

ISSN 0309–5541

# THE FRAGMENTARY CLASSICISING HISTORIANS OF THE LATER ROMAN EMPIRE

## EUNAPIUS, OLYMPIODORUS, PRISCUS AND MALCHUS

### II
Text, Translation and Historiographical Notes

## R. C. BLOCKLEY

FRANCIS CAIRNS

Published by Francis Cairns (Publications) Ltd
PO Box 296, Cambridge, CB4 3GE, Great Britain

First published 1983
Paperback reprint 2007

**British Library Cataloguing in Publication**
A catalogue record for this book is available from the British Library

ISBN 978 0905205 15 1 (Hardback)
ISBN 978 0905205 49 6 (Paperback)

Printed and bound by
CPI Antony Rowe, Eastbourne

# CONTENTS

# INTRODUCTION

The second volume of *The Fragmentary Classicising Historians of the Later Roman Empire* contains texts, translations and notes to the fragments of Eunapius, Olympiodorus, Priscus and Malchus (excluding the material preserved by Zosimus). To these, for completeness, have been added Candidus and some substantial articles from the *Suda* which have been on occasion attributed to one or more of these authors.

This second volume was undertaken, at the request of the publisher, after the first volume had been completed. As a result, the views set out there have been tested by a close and careful study of the texts and their language. In general I have found no reason to modify my views, although the following two qualifications must be made, both concerning Eunapius. First, in common with most commentators, I underestimated the tone of bitter sarcasm in the History, which in places I misread as nothing more than rhetorical pomposity. Once recognised, this sarcasm is very evident, especially at the end of *Fr.* 37 (on which see n.81), in the first part of *Fr.* 42 and in *Fr.* 56. Second, Eunapius' superficial and hysterical judgements and the usual lack of detailed information, when taken together with the remarks at the end of *Fr.* 1 and in *Fr.* 15 about the pressure which Julian's admirers placed upon him to write his History and with the comments in *Fr.* 42 (p.62) on the current condition of the cities of Thrace, now suggest to me that the first two parts of the History published (part 1 to the death of Julian, part 2 to 378 – see vol. I pp.3-5) were written very soon after the events which they describe. This lends support to Barnes' view (which I was reluctant to accept in vol. I pp.24f.) that Eunapius' work, which I am here categorising almost as 'instant history', appeared before Ammianus' more detailed, sophisticated and better considered narrative.

Other substantive changes are: the transfer of all the passages of the *Epit. de Caes.* assigned to Eunapius (except 41,22-23 = *Fr.* 11,2) to the category of 'possible'; the shortening of some passages from *Vit. Soph.* to exclude material, usually of a religious or biographical nature, which was almost certainly not in the History (e.g. at *Vit. Soph.* 8,1,11 - 2,3 = Eunapius *Fr.* 64,3); the transfer of *Suda* I 368 from Priscus *Fr.* 57 to the *Anonyma e Suda*; and the withdrawal of the following passages which had been categorised as 'possible': Philostorgius *HE* 7,15 (at Eunapius *Fr.* 58), Jordanes *Get.* 50,264-66 (at Priscus *Fr.* 25), *Get.* 56,285 (at Priscus *Fr.* 60), Nicephorus Callistus *HE* 15,11 (at Priscus *Frr.* 32, 36, 38) and Procopius *Wars* 3,5,8-17 (at Priscus *Fr.* 53). Minor errors and omissions which I have discovered have been corrected in the notes.

Of the seven anonymous articles from the *Suda* grouped at the end of the text, all but E 3770 (and possibly A 783) seem to have come from the same pen. Malchus was certainly not their author, and there are insufficient grounds for attributing them to Candidus. The style and contents of Z 84, B 164 and E 2494 (= Malchus *Frr.* 8; 9,3; 10) suggest that these articles, too, should be attributed to this anonymous author and not to Malchus. I have not transposed them to the 'Anonymus' simply to avoid disturbing the correlation of the fragments with the numbering of the conspectus in volume I.

Although the texts of the fragments are eclectic, they are based upon the best editions available to me. These are as follows:

> *Chronicon Paschale*, ed. L. Dindorf, in *CSHB* XVI-XVII.
>
> *Epitome de Caesaribus*, in Sextus Aurelius Victor, *De Cae-saribus*, ed. Fr. Pichlmayr, corr. R. Gruendel, Leipzig (1966) pp.131-76.
>
> Eunapius, *Vitae Sophistarum*, ed. J. Giangrande, Rome (1956).
>
> Evagrius, *Ecclesiastical History*, ed. J. Bidez and L. Parmentier, London (1898).
>
> *Excerpta de Insidiis Iussu Imp. Constantini Porphyrogeniti Confecta*, ed. C. de Boor, Berlin (1905).
>
> *Excerpta de Legationibus Iussu Imp. Constantini Porphyro-geniti Confecta*, ed. C. de Boor, Berlin (1903).
>
> *Excerpta de Sententiis Iussu Imp. Constantini Porphyrogeniti Confecta*, ed. U. Ph. Boissevain, Berlin (1906).
>
> *Excerpta de Virtutibus et Vitiis*, I ed. U. Ph. Boissevain, Berlin (1908), II ed. A.G. Roos, Berlin (1910).
>
> Jordanes, *Romana et Getica*, ed. Th. Mommsen, in *MGH*, *A.A.* VI, 1.
>
> Malalas, *Chronicon*, ed. L. Dindorf, in *CSHB* XV.
>
> Nicephorus Callistus, *Historia Ecclesiastica*, in *PG* CXLV-CXLVI.
>
> Philostorgius, *Kirchengeschichte*, ed. J. Bidez, Leipzig (1913).

Photius, *Bibliotheca*, ed. R. Henry, I-II, Paris (1959).
Procopius, *Bella*, ed. J. Haury, corr. G. Wirth, 2 vols., Leipzig (1962).
Sozomenus, *Kirchengeschichte*, edd. J. Bidez and G.C. Hansen, Berlin (1960).
Suidas [*Suda*], *Lexicon*, ed. A. Adler, 6 vols., Leipzig (1928-35).
Theophanes, *Chronographia*, ed. C. de Boor, 2 vols, Leipzig (1883).
Zonaras, *Annales*, ed. M. Pinder, in *CSHB* XLIV-XLVI.

As in volume I, those fragments categorised as 'probable' or 'possible' are enclosed in square brackets. References after a fragment indicate that the passages there cited repeat material in the fragment, usually *verbatim* or almost so. An asterisk after one of these citations indicates that there the historian to whom the passage has been assigned is named as the source of the material.

The apparatuses to the text are abbreviated, containing only significant manuscript variants and noteworthy conjectures not admitted into the text. More recent work, of which there is not a great deal, has been incorporated where appropriate, with reference to the bibliography in volume I or to the supplementary bibliography at the end of the present volume. The manuscript designations used in the base editions have been followed where necessary; the term 'edd.' indicates that a reading is found in a plurality of the older editions; no designation means that a reading is found in all the manuscripts or in all of those not identified as sources of alternative readings. In the Greek text no attempt has been made to homogenise the spelling from author to author, since the text provided is not, e.g., of Olympiodorus, but of Sozomen, Philostorgius and so on using Olympiodorus.

In the translations I have attempted to express clearly, but in reasonably literal and elegant English, what, in my view, the writers wished to communicate. I have attempted neither to homogenise the style throughout the volume nor to remove all the awkwardnesses, especially in Eunapius, Photius' summaries and many of the articles from the *Suda*. On the other hand, while following (with some hesitation) Mommsen's presentation of Jordanes' spelling and grammar, I have made the English translation rather more elegant (I hope) than the original. At points in a few passages, especially of Eunapius, I am not sure what the writer was trying to say, and, I suspect, the writer was not always sure himself. In rendering names of peoples and places I have usually followed the form given in the text, whereas in discussion in the notes I have usually followed the form preferred today, unless I have reason to reject it. I have not sought consistency where different authors are involved (e.g. Arnegisclus, Argagisclus) or where the author might himself have been inconsistent (e.g. Akatiri, Akatziri in Priscus).

The purposes of the notes, which are complementary to, and should be read with, those to the conspectuses in volume I, are to clarify the texts and translations and to provide further commentary upon the historiography. They are not intended to offer even a partial historical or linguistic commentary (which would require another volume, possibly two), and, thus, references to modern work on the language of the writers and the history of the period have been kept to a minimum. When references are necessary I have preferred to cite, wherever possible, readily accessible works such as Bury and *PLRE*.

Since the numbering of the fragments in this volume differs from that of the earlier collections, I have provided at the end an index cross-referencing my collection with the earlier ones which are the most in use. A short bibliography supplements that of volume I. Finally, acknowledgement is due to Sandra Cairns, for editorial patience, and to Dr Frederick Williams, for vigilant and learned proof-reading of both volumes.

*R.C. Blockley*                              *Carleton University, Ottawa*
                                                            *1983*

# EUNAPIUS

**Text and Translation**

# EUNAPIUS

# TESTIMONIA

# 1

(Photius *Bibl. Cod.* 77, I pp.158-60)

Ἀνεγνώσθη Εὐναπίου χρονικῆς ἱστορίας τῆς μετὰ Δέξιππον,
νέας ἐκδόσεως, ἐν βιβλίοις τεσσαρεσκαίδεκα. ἄρχεται μὲν τῆς
ἱστορίας ἀπὸ τῆς Κλαυδίου βασιλείας, ἐς ὃν Δεξίππῳ ἡ ἱστορία
καταλήγει, ἀποτελευτᾷ δὲ εἰς τὴν Ὀνωρίου καὶ Ἀρκαδίου τῶν
Θεοδοσίου παίδων βασιλείαν, ἐκεῖνον τὸν χρόνον τέλος τῆς ἱστορίας          5
ποιησάμενος ὃν Ἀρσάκιος μὲν τοῦ χρυσοῦ τῆς ἐκκλησίας στόματος
Ἰωάννου ἀπελαθέντος εἰς τὸν ἀρχιερατικὸν θρόνον ἀνηγμένος
ἱεράτευεν, ἡ δὲ τοῦ βασιλεύοντος Ἀρκαδίου γυνὴ κατὰ γαστρὸς
ἔχουσα καὶ ἀμβλώσασα τὸν βίον ἀπέλιπεν.

Οὗτος ὁ Εὐνάπιος Σαρδιανὸς μὲν γένος ἐστί (τὰς γὰρ ἐν Λυδίᾳ          10
Σάρδεις ἔσχε πατρίδα), δυσσεβὴς δὲ τὴν θρησκείαν ὤν (τὰ
Ἑλλήνων γὰρ ἐτίμα), τοὺς μὲν εὐσεβείᾳ τὴν βασιλείαν κοσμήσαντας
παντὶ τρόπῳ καὶ ἀνέδην κακίζων διασύρει, καὶ μάλιστά γε τὸν
μέγαν Κωνσταντῖνον, ἐξαίρει δὲ τοὺς δυσσεβεῖς, καὶ τῶν ἄλλων
πλέον Ἰουλιανὸν τὸν παραβάτην, καὶ σχεδόν τι τὸ τῆς ἱστορίας αὐτῷ          15
εἰς τὸ ἐκείνου ἐγκώμιον συντεθὲν ἐξεπονήθη.

Ἔστι δὲ καλλιεπὴς τὴν φράσιν, εἰ περιέλοι τις αὐτοῦ τῶν
λόγων τὸ ἀλεκτρυονῶδες καὶ ἐλαφωδέστερον καὶ συωδέστερον καὶ
δὴ καὶ τοὺς ἱερακώδεις καὶ κορακώδεις καὶ πιθηκώδεις, καὶ τὸ
ποταμῶδες δάκρυον, καὶ τὰ ὅμοια· τούτοις γὰρ καὶ τὴν ἄλλην τῶν          20
ὀνομάτων περιλυμαίνεται καὶ διανοθεύει εὐγένειαν. καὶ τροπαῖς μὲν
κέχρηται παραβόλως, ὅπερ ὁ τῆς ἱστορίας οὐκ ἐθέλει νόμος· ἀφαι-
ρεῖται δὲ τὸ λυποῦν ἡ τῆς λέξεως ἔμφασις τὰ πολλὰ καὶ ἀστειότης.
τῇ συνθήκῃ δὲ καὶ τῷ σαφεῖ πρὸς ἱστορίαν καὶ ταῖς περιόδοις
συμμέτρως καὶ οἰκείως ἔχει· πλὴν ἐνιαχοῦ δικανικώτερον μᾶλλον ἢ          25

19 δὴ καὶ edd [δέκα codd., Henry

2

# EUNAPIUS

## TESTIMONIA

### 1

(Photius *Bibl. Cod.* 77, I pp.158-60)

Read the second edition of Eunapius' *Chronicle after Dexippus* in fourteen books. He begins his narrative after the reign of the Emperor Claudius, the point at which Dexippus' History ends, and finishes it in the reigns of Honorius and Arcadius, the sons of Theodosius. He makes the point of termination the date when Arsacius was raised to the episcopal throne upon the deposition of John Chrysostom and when the wife of the Emperor Arcadius died after a miscarriage.

This Eunapius, whose place of origin was Sardis in Lydia, was impious in his beliefs, being a pagan. He slanders the Emperors who adorned their reigns with Christian piety, disparaging them continually and in every way, especially Constantine the Great. He praises the impious, particularly Julian the Apostate. Indeed, he has worked up his history almost into an encomium of that ruler.

He is an elegant stylist, if you ignore words like 'cockerelish',[1] 'more hindlike', 'more porcine', and also the 'hawkish's', the 'corvine's', the 'monkeyish's', and the 'tears-like-a-river', and so on. For with these expressions he spoils and debases the nobility of the rest of his vocabulary. In his use of figures of speech he is reckless in a manner inappropriate for a historical style, but the usual smoothness and urbanity of the writing masks the unpleasantness. His organisation and clarity are suitable for history, and his periods are well-balanced and appropriate, except that in some places he uses overblown circumlocutions more

ἱστορικώτερον μεστοῖ καὶ περιβάλλει τὸν λόγον. νεωτερίζει δ᾽ οὐκ
ὀλίγα καὶ περὶ τὰς συντάξεις, πλὴν οὐκ εἰς τὸ ἄχαρι οὐδ᾽ εἰς τὸ ταῖς
μεθόδοις λαβὴν ἐπιδοῦναι. Δύο δὲ πραγματείας τὴν αὐτὴν περιέχουσας ἱστορίαν συνεγράψατο, πρώτην καὶ δευτέραν. καὶ ἐν μὲν τῇ πρώτῃ πολλὴν κατὰ      30
τῆς καθαρᾶς ἡμῶν τῶν Χριστιανῶν πίστεως κατασπείρει βλασ-
φημίαν, καὶ τὴν Ἑλληνικὴν ἀποσεμνύνει δεισιδαιμονίαν, πολλὰ τῶν
εὐσεβῶν βασιλέων καθαπτόμενος· ἐν δὲ τῇ δευτέρᾳ, ἣν καὶ νέαν
ἔκδοσιν ἐπιγράφει, τὴν μὲν πολλὴν ὕβριν καὶ ἀσέλγειαν, ἣν κατὰ τῆς
εὐσεβείας ἐσκέδαξεν, ὑποτέμνεται, τὸ δὲ λοιπὸν τῆς συγγραφῆς      35
σῶμα συνείρας νέαν ἔκδοσιν, ὡς ἔφημεν, ἐπιγράφει, ἔτι πολλὰ τῆς
ἐκεῖσε λύσσης ὑποφαίνουσαν.

Ἀμφοῖν δὲ ταῖς ἐκδόσεσιν ἐν παλαιοῖς ἐνετύχομεν βιβλίοις,
ἰδίως ἑκατέραν ἐν ἑτέρῳ τεύχει καὶ ἑτέρῳ συντεταγμένην· ἐξ ὧν
αὐτῶν καὶ τὴν διαφορὰν ἀναλεξάμενοι ἔγνωμεν. συμβαίνει οὖν ἐν τῇ      40
νέα ἐκδόσει πολλὰ τῶν χωρίων διὰ τὰς γεγενημένας τῶν ῥητῶν
περικοπὰς ἀσαφῶς ἐκκεῖσθαι, καίτοι φροντιστής ἐστι τοῦ σαφοῦς·
ἀλλ᾽ ὅτῳ τρόπῳ λέγειν οὐκ ἔχω, μὴ καλῶς κατὰ τὰς περικοπὰς
ἁρμόσας τοὺς λόγους ἐν τῇ δευτέρᾳ ἐκδόσει τὸν νοῦν λυμαίνεται τῶν
ἀναγνωσκομένων· ἐν οἷς καὶ τὸ τέλος.      45

39 ἑκατέρᾳ . . . συντεταγμένῃ Goulet (1980) p.68

2

(Photius *Bibl. Cod.* 98, II p.66)

Εἴποι δ᾽ ἄν τις οὐ γράψαι αὐτὸν ἱστορίαν, ἀλλὰ μεταγράψαι
τὴν Εὐναπίου, τῷ συντόμῳ μόνον διαφέρουσαν, καὶ ὅτι οὐχ, ὥσπερ
ἐκεῖνος, οὕτω καὶ οὗτος Στελίχωνα διασύρει· τὰ δ᾽ ἄλλα κατὰ τὴν
ἱστορίαν σχεδόν τι ὁ αὐτός, καὶ μάλιστα ἐν ταῖς τῶν εὐσεβῶν βασιλέων διαβολαῖς. δοκεῖ δέ μοι καὶ οὗτος δύο ἐκδόσεις, ὥσπερ      5
κἀκεῖνος, πεποιηκέναι. ἀλλὰ τούτου μὲν τὴν προτέραν οὐκ εἶδον· ἐξ
ὧν δὲ ἦν ἀνέγνωμεν ἐπέγραψε "νέας ἐκδόσεως" συμβαλεῖν ἦν καὶ
ἑτέραν αὐτῷ, ὥσπερ καὶ τῷ Εὐναπίῳ, ἐκδεδόσθαι. σαφὴς δὲ
μᾶλλον οὗτος καὶ συντομώτερος, ὥσπερ ἔφημεν, Εὐναπίου, καὶ ταῖς
τροπαῖς, εἰ μὴ σπάνιον, οὐ κεχρημένος.      10

6-7 ἐξ ὧν δὲ ἦν [ ἦν δὲ et ἐξ ὧν post ἐκδόσεως transp. edd.

suitable for forensic oratory than for history. He often innovates, especially in syntax, but not so as to cause inelegance or arouse criticism of his methods.

He produced two works which covered the same period, a first and a second. Throughout the first he scatters a great deal of blasphemy against our pure Christian faith, glorifying the superstition of the pagans and frequently assailing the pious Emperors. In the second, which he entitles 'New Edition', he removes the excessive and arrogant insolence which he directed against Christian piety, and, patching together the rest of his material, he calls it, as I have said, a 'New Edition'. But it still shows many traces of the distemper of the first.

I have come across both editions in old collections; in one case each was separate, in another on the same roll.[2] It was from these, as I read, that I realised the difference between the two. The result, therefore, is that, although Eunapius aims at clarity, many passages of the 'New Edition' are obscure because of excisions in the text. How this was allowed to happen I do not know, but because in the second edition he has not properly adjusted the language in the light of the excisions, he destroys the import of his words. End.

2

(Photius *Bibl. Cod.* 98, II p.66)

One might say that [Zosimus] did not write a history, but rather copied out Eunapius, differing only in that he condenses his source and does not, unlike Eunapius, attack Stilicho. For the rest his history is almost identical, especially in the criticisms of the pious Emperors. It appears to me that Zosimus, like Eunapius, published two editions, although I have not seen the first. But from the fact that he entitled the one which I have read 'New Edition' one can conjecture that he, like Eunapius, produced another.[3] He is clearer and, as I have said, briefer than Eunapius and he does not use figures of speech, or only rarely.

# FRAGMENTA

## Liber I

### 1

(*Exc. de Sent.* 1)

Δεξίππῳ τῷ Ἀθηναίῳ κατὰ τοὺς Ἀθήνησιν ἄρχοντας, ἀφ᾿ οὗ παρὰ Ἀθηναίοις ἄρχοντες, ἱστορία συγγέγραπται, προσαριθμου- μένων καὶ τῶν Ῥωμαϊκῶν ὑπάτων, καὶ πρό γε αὐτῶν τῶν ὑπάτων τε καὶ ἀρχόντων ἀρξαμένης τῆς γραφῆς. τὸ δὲ ἓν κεφάλαιον τῆς ἱστορίας τὰ μὲν ἀνωτέρω καὶ ὅσα τὸ ποιητικὸν νέμεται γένος ἐφεῖναι    5 καὶ ἐπιτρέψαι τῷ πιθανῷ καὶ μᾶλλον ἀναπείθοντι τὸν ἐντυγχάνοντα, τὰ δὲ προϊόντα καὶ ἐπὶ πλέον μαρτυρούμενα συνενεγκεῖν καὶ κατα- κλεῖσαι πρὸς ἱστορικὴν ἀκρίβειαν καὶ κρίσιν ἀληθεστέραν. βιάζεται γοῦν καὶ συναριθμεῖται τὸν χρόνον ἔς τε τὰς ὀλυμπιάδας περι- γράφων καὶ τοὺς ἐντὸς ἑκάστης ὀλυμπιάδος ἄρχοντας. πρόθυρα δὲ    10 κάλλους ἀνάμεστα προθεὶς τῆς συγγραφῆς καὶ προϊὼν τά τε ἔνδον ἐπιδείξας σεμνότερα, τὸ μὲν μυθῶδες καὶ λίαν ἀρχαῖον ἀφαιρεῖ καὶ ἀφίησιν ὥσπερ φάρμακον παλαιὸν καὶ ἀδόκιμον ἐς τοὺς συντε- θεικότας· Αἰγυπτίους δὲ χρόνους ἀναλεγόμενος καὶ συνωθούμενος ἐπὶ τὰ πρῶτα καὶ τελεώτερα τῶν παρ᾿ ἑκάστοις ἀρχῶν, τοὺς    15 ἡγεμόνας καὶ πατέρας τῆς ἱστορίας ἐκτίθησιν, ἔνδηλος ὢν καὶ σχεδόν τι μαρτυρόμενος ὅτι τῶν ἀπιστουμένων ἕκαστον ἕτερος προλαβὼν εἴρηκεν. καὶ περιφέρει γε τὴν ἱστορίαν ἐκ πολλῶν καὶ παντοδαπῶν τῶν ταῦτα εἰρηκότων ὥσπερ ῥῶπόν τινα ποικίλον καὶ χρήσιμον εἰς ἓν μυροπώλιον τὴν ἰδίαν ἐξήγησιν κατακεκλειμένην καὶ    20 συνηγμένην. πάντα δέ, ὅσα πρός τε τὸ κοινὸν ἁπάντων ἀνθρώπων ἀξιόλογα καὶ κατ᾿ ἄνδρα δι᾿ ἀρετὴν περιττοῦ τινος ὀνόματος τετυχη- κότα, λάβρως ἐπιδραμὼν καὶ διαθέμενος τῷ λόγῳ, τελευτῶν ἐς Κλαύδιον καταλύει τὴν συγγραφήν, καὶ Κλαυδίου τῆς βασιλείας ἔτος τὸ πρῶτον, ἐς ὃ δὴ καὶ τῆς βασιλείας ἤρχετο καὶ ἐτελεύτα, ἐνιαυτὸν    25 ἄρξας Ῥωμαίοις ἕνα· οἱ δὲ καὶ ἕτερον αὐτῷ χαρίζονται. εἶτα ὀλυμ- πιάδας καταλογίζεται τόσας καὶ τόσας καὶ ὑπάτους καὶ ἄρχοντας ἐπὶ ταύταις, τὴν χιλιάδα τῶν ἐτῶν ὑποβάλλων, ὥσπερ ἀγωνιῶν, εἰ μὴ πολλῶν λίαν ἐτῶν ἀποδοίη λόγον τοῖς ἐντυγχάνουσιν.

Ἐγὼ δὲ ὁ τοῦτο τὸ ἔργον εἰς νοῦν βαλόμενος, ὑπ᾿ αὐτοῦ    30 Δεξίππου ταῦτα ἔχων ἐκδιδάσκεσθαι καὶ συλλαμβάνειν ὅσος καὶ ἡλίκος ὁ κίνδυνος κατὰ τὸν ἐνιαυτὸν ἕκαστον ἱστορίαν γράφειν, καὶ πρὸς τοὺς ἐντυγχάνοντας ὁμολογεῖν ὅτι ταῦτα οὐκ ἔστιν ἀληθῆ κατὰ

---

15 τελεώτερα [παλαιότερα Bekker        18 παραφέρει Dindorf
19 τινα [τι καὶ edd.

# FRAGMENTS

## Book I

### 1

(*Exc. de Sent.* 1)

Dexippus of Athens organises his History under Athenian archons, from the date when archons were instituted, adding also the names of the Roman consuls, although the work begins before the institution of either archons or consuls.[4] The guiding principle of the History is to avoid the earlier material and that which is more congenial to poets, leaving it to those plausible writers who are more inclined to *persuade* the reader as to what happened. Dexippus himself brings together the later, better evidenced events and organises them with an accuracy appropriate for history and with a reliability of judgement. He gives his narrative shape and chronology by dividing it up by Olympiads and archons within each Olympiad. He provides his History with a preface full of beauty[5] and, as he proceeds, he imparts great stateliness to the body of the work by omitting material which is mythological or excessively ancient, returning it like an old and discredited medicine to those who mixed it. As he surveys the Egyptian period[6] and presses on to the foundation and the major achievements[7] of the states amongst each people, he notes the leaders and the fathers of history, making it clear and almost producing evidence to prove that every unhistorical fact had been set down before him by another writer. He draws his history from many, varied sources, making a compact and coherent narrative which is like a perfumery store that carries a variety of useful goods. All events which men in general regard as important or which are connected with a particularly distinguished person are rapidly surveyed and arranged in the text.

Dexippus closes his History with the reign of the Emperor Claudius (II), his first year in which he both ascended the throne and died. (He thus ruled for one year, although others give him a second.) Then he tabulates such-and-such a number of Olympiads and co-ordinates with them the consuls and archons. He even indicates the years by the thousand, as if he were in agony unless he set before his readers a catalogue comprising an enormous number of years.[8]

Having studied this work, I have gained from Dexippus himself an understanding of the extent and the nature of the danger in writing history as a yearly chronicle. For he himself admits to his readers that

τοὺς χρόνους, ἀλλὰ τῷ μὲν οὕτως, τῷ δὲ ἑτέρως ἔδοξε, καὶ περιφανῶς ἑαυτοῦ κατηγορεῖν, ὥσπερ ἐκεῖνος, ὅτι χρονικὴν ἱστορίαν      35
γράφων πλανωμένην τινὰ καὶ μεστὴν τῶν ἀντιλεγόντων, ὥσπερ
ἀπρόεδρον ἐκκλησίαν, ἐκτίθησι τὴν γραφήν, ὀξέως δὲ καὶ τῆς
Βοιωτίας ἀκούων παροιμίας, ὅτι οὕτως αὐλεῖν οὐ πρέπει, κἀκεῖνα
προσελογιζόμην ὅτι τέλος ἱστορίας καὶ σκοπὸς ἄριστος τὰ πραχθέντα
ὅτι μάλιστα δίχα τινὸς πάθους ἐς τὸ ἀληθὲς ἀναφέροντα γράφειν, οἱ      40
δὲ ἀκριβεῖς λογισμοὶ τῶν χρόνων, ὥσπερ ἄκλητοι μάρτυρες, αὐτο-
μάτως ἐπεισιόντες ἐς ταῦτα ὠφελοῦσιν οὐδέν. τί γὰρ Σωκράτει
πρὸς σοφίαν καὶ Θεμιστοκλεῖ πρὸς δεινότητα συντελεῖται παρὰ τῶν
χρόνων; ποῦ δὲ ἐκεῖνοι καλοὶ κἀγαθοὶ διὰ θέρος ἦσαν; ποῦ δὲ τὰς
ἀρετὰς ἐφ' ἑαυτῶν, καθάπερ τὰ φύλλα, πρὸς τὴν ὥραν τοῦ ἔτους      45
αὐξανομένας καὶ ἀπορρεούσας παρείχοντο; ἀλλ' ἴσως ἕκαστος αὐτῶν
τὸ γοῦν ἐς φύσιν καὶ δύναμιν ἀγαθὸν διαρκῶς καὶ συνεχῶς ἐν ταῖς
ἐνεργείαις ἀπεδίδου καὶ διέσωζεν. τίς οὖν λόγος πρὸς ἱστορίας τέλος
εἰδέναι καὶ γινώσκειν ὅτι τὴν ἐν Σαλαμῖνι ναυμαχίαν ἐνίκων οἱ
Ἕλληνες κυνὸς ἐπιτέλλοντος; τί δ' ὄφελος ἦν τοῖς ἐντυγχάνουσιν εἰς      50
ὠφέλειαν ἱστορικῆς χρείας, εἰ κατὰ ταύτην ἐτέχθη τὴν ἡμέραν ὁ
δεῖνα, καὶ μελοποιὸς ἀνέσχεν ἢ τραγῳδὸς ἄριστος; εἰ γὰρ ἔσχατος
ὅρος τῶν περὶ τὴν ἱστορίαν καλῶν τὸ πολλῶν καὶ ἀπείρων πραγμάτων ἐν ὀλίγῳ χρόνῳ καὶ διὰ βραχείας ἀναγνώσεως πεῖραν λαβεῖν
καὶ γενέσθαι γέροντας ἔτι νέους ὄντας δι' ἐπιστήμην τῶν προ-      55
γεγονότων, ὥστε τίνα μὲν φευκτέον, τίνα δὲ αἱρετέον, εἰδέναι,
τοὐναντίον ἔμοιγε δοκοῦσι ποιεῖν οἱ περιττοῖς καὶ ἀπηρτημένοις
ἐπεισοδίοις ὥσπερ ξενικοῖς ἡδύσμασι τὸ τῆς ἱστορίας ἐδώδιμον καὶ
χρήσιμον ἀνατρέποντες καὶ διαφθείροντες ἁλμυρῷ λόγῳ πότιμον
ἀκοήν. κωλύει μὲν γὰρ ἴσως οὐδὲν καὶ περιττόν τι μαθεῖν, βλαβερὸν      60
δὲ ὁμολογουμένως περιττοῦ τινος ἕνεκεν τὸ χρήσιμον μὴ μαθεῖν,
ἄλλως τε, ὥς φησιν αὐτὸς Δέξιππος, τῶν μὲν χρονικῶν ἢ πάντων
ἢ τῶν πλείστων διαπεφωνημένων, τῶν ⟨δὲ⟩ ὑπερόρων καὶ φανερῶν
πράξεων συμπεφωνημένων καὶ ὡμολογημένων. τίς γὰρ οὕτω περι-
βόητος ἅπασιν ὅσοι λόγων ἥψαντο καὶ κατέλιπον λόγους ὡς      65
Λυκοῦργος ὁ Λακεδαιμόνιος; ἐς ὃν καὶ ἡ τοῦ θεοῦ μαρτυρία διὰ
στόματος ἅπασι θεὸν ἄντικρυς ἀνακαλοῦντος ἐπὶ τῷ θεῖναι τοὺς
νόμους. τίς δὲ τῶν ταῦτα εἰρηκότων ἑτέρῳ συμφέρεται περὶ τῶν
ἡνίκα ἐτίθει τοὺς νόμους χρόνων; ἀλλὰ πάντες, ὥσπερ οἰκίαν ἢ
στῦλον δοκιμάζοντες ἤ τι τῶν ὁμοίων, ὅτι μὲν ἔστι καὶ γέγονε συν-      70
τίθενται καὶ κατανεύουσι, περὶ δὲ τοῦ πότε παντοδαπῇ ⟨ἀπορίᾳ⟩ ἐμ-
πεπλήκασι τὰ βιβλία. ὁπότε καὶ Θουκυδίδης ὁ πάντων ἀκριβέστατος

63 δὲ add. Niebuhr      ὑπερόρων [ὑπερώρων Dindorf ὑπερόχων Kuiper
67 στόματος Dindorf [στόμασιν cod.      71 ἀπορίᾳ add. Niebuhr

often the dating is uncertain and subject to different opinions, and he actually makes an explicit charge against himself that in following the chronographical method he has produced a work which is like an un-chaired meeting, full of errors and contradictions. I can clearly hear the Boeotian proverb, "This is not the way to play the flute". Further-more, I have been reflecting that whereas the highest aim and function of history is to record events with a minimum of subjectivity and in the light of the truth, the details of chronology, intruding irrelevantly like uncalled witnesses, are of no help in this. For what do dates contribute to the wisdom of Socrates or the acuity of Themistocles? Were they great men only during the summer? Did one see them growing and shedding their virtues like leaves according to the time of the year? Rather, both alike exhibited and preserved their virtues and their skills repeatedly and continually. Of what relevance was it to the aim of history to learn that the Greeks won the sea-battle at Salamis when the dog-star was rising? Of what use was it for the readers' historical edu-cation to learn that on a particular day so-and-so was born, who later became a leading poet or playwright? If the most important of the benefits of history is that concisely and in a short space of time we can become familiar with many, indeed a countless number, of facts and, through a knowledge of past events, gain the experience of old age while still young, so that we know what is to be avoided and what sought after — if this is so, they seem to me to do the opposite who, by introducing an excessive amount of extraneous material, spoil the nourishing and beneficial part of the feast of history with their foreign spices and ruin its sweet draught with their bitter style. Perhaps there is no objection to the pursuit of excessive learning as such, but one must agree that harm is done if this pursuit results in a failure to absorb what is beneficial. This is especially so since, as Dexippus himself points out, while all, or the majority, of chronologies are discrepant, there is ab-solute agreement over the famous events that are of more than local importance. For who is so well known to all readers and producers of literature as Lycurgus the Lacedaemonian? Everyone can tell of the tes-timony of the god to him, declaring him divine on account of his work in legislation. Yet who, when he has recited this, agrees with anyone else upon the date of that legislation? They are all like those critics of a building or a column or some such thing, who, although they are in perfect agreement that it exists, nevertheless have filled books with a multitude of arguments upon the date of its construction. Thucydides, the most accurate of all the historians, tells how that great and famous

τὸν μέγαν καὶ πολυύμνητον ἐκεῖνον πόλεμον ἀρχήν τινα καὶ προφάσεις φησὶ λαβεῖν πρὸς δευτέραν κίνησιν ἐκ διαφορᾶς ἡμερῶν, ἢ
περὶ πόλεων ἁλώσεως αὐτοῖς ἐγένετο, καὶ οὐδὲ αὐτὸς ἔχει διαιτᾶν    75
σαφῶς καὶ ἀκριβῶς τίνες ἐπεκάλουν δικαιότερον, ἀλλ' ἐπὶ τὰς
ἡμέρας ἐλθὼν ὑποδηλοῖ καὶ παραδείκνυσιν ὅτι κενή τις σπουδὴ καὶ
ἀχρεῖος ἡ περὶ τοὺς χρόνους διατριβὴ καὶ σχολή.

Τοιαῦτά τινα καὶ πλείω ἕτερα πρὸς ἐμαυτὸν ἐκκλησιάσας καὶ
βουλευσάμενος, καὶ τοῖς ἐς τὰ χρονικὰ σπεύδουσιν καὶ ἀνεστηκόσιν    80
ὅμοιά τινα παρεγγυῶν, ὡς ἡ περὶ τὰς ὥρας καὶ ἡμέρας ἀκρίβεια
πλουσίων οἰκονόμοις τισὶ καὶ λογισταῖς πρέπει, καὶ νὴ Δία γε τοῖς ἐς
τὰ οὐράνια κεχηνόσι, καὶ ὅσοι πρὸς ἀριθμῷ φανερῶς κάθηνται,
αὐτὸς δὲ προαγορεύων πόρρωθεν τοῖς ἐντυγχάνουσιν ὅτι πιστεύσας
ἐμαυτῷ δύνασθαι γράφειν ⟨τὰ⟩ γεγονότα τε καὶ γινόμενα πρὸς τόδε    85
τὸ ἔργον ὥρμησα, τὸ μὲν κατ' ἐνιαυτὸν καὶ καθ' ἡμέραν ὥσπερ ἀπ-
ροσδιόνυσόν τινα ῥῆσιν παραιτησάμενος, τὸ δὲ κατὰ χρόνους, οἳ τοῖς
βασιλεῦσι περιγράφονται, κρίνας ἀληθέστερον. ἀναγνώσεται γοῦν
τις ὅτι ταῦτα ἐπὶ τοῦδε τοῦ βασιλέως ἢ τοῦδε ἐπράττετο· καθ' ὃν δὲ
ἐνιαυτὸν καὶ ἡμέραν, ἕτερος ἐς τὴν ἀπάτην χορευέτω τις· ἐγὼ δὲ    90
κατὰ τὸ πιστεύειν ἐμαυτῷ γράφω, ἀνδράσιν ἑπόμενος, οἳ τοῦ καθ'
ἡμᾶς βίου μακρῷ προεῖχον κατὰ παιδείαν καὶ διατεταμένως ἐνῆγον
μὴ σιωπᾶν τὰ κοινὰ τῶν ἔργων καὶ ὅσα ὁ καθ' ἡμᾶς ἔφερε χρόνος
καὶ τὰ πρὸ ἡμῶν μετὰ τὴν Δεξίππου γραφὴν οὔπω λόγου τε καὶ
ἱστορίας ἐμφανοῦς τετυχηκότα. ἐγίνετο δὲ ἐκείνοις τε κἀμοὶ κοινὸν    95
τὸ ἔργον τόδε, καὶ πάντα γε ἐς τὸν Ἰουλιανὸν ἀναφέρειν ἐδόκει, ὃς
ἐβασίλευσε μὲν ἐφ' ἡμῶν, τὸ δὲ ἀνθρώπινον αὐτὸν ὥσπερ τινὰ θεὸν
προσεκύνουν ἅπαντες. λόγου δὲ ἦν ἄξιον ⟨καὶ⟩ καλῶς ἔχειν ἐδόκει,
καθάπερ τοῖς ἕνεκεν ἐρωμένης ⟨ἀργαλέον καθεστῶτα πόλεμον
ὑμνοῦσι ποιηταῖς γενομένοις ἀρίστοις, οὕτω καὶ ἡμῖν ἀρχήν τινα καὶ    100
γένεσιν προθεμένοις τὴν θείαν . . . .

81 παρεγγυῶ Bekker    84 προαγορεύω Bekker    πιστεύω Boissevain
85 δύναμαι van Herwerden    τὰ add. Boissevain    90 χορεύεται Mai et edd.
(ut corruptum)    91 κατὰ Niebuhr [καὶ cod.    98 καὶ add. Mai
99 ⟨ἀργαλέον καθεστῶτα πόλεμον ὑμ⟩νοῦσι add. Boissevain [ἀργαλέον . . .
νοῦσι cod.    101 τὴν θείαν scripsi [ θ̄ν cod. τὸν θεὸν Boissevain    post θεὸν
ap. Boissevain xxvii vv. sequuntur quorum pauca modo verba et litterae
leguntur et qui finem primi et secundum excerptum continuerant.


2

[ (Suda Σ 199)

Σελευκίς· ὄρνεόν ἐστιν εὔπεπτον καὶ ἀκόρεστον καὶ πανοῦργον
καὶ τὰς ἀκρίδας χανδὸν λαφύσσον.]

war which he described flared up anew, the reason being a dispute over the dates upon which some cities were captured.[9] He himself is unable to decide clearly and certainly which claims were the more justified; and so, when he comes down to a matter of days, he demonstrates clearly that to spend one's time in the study of chronology is a display of useless and irrelevant zeal.

Reflecting upon these and other considerations (and I recommend a similar procedure to those with a passion for chronology), I concluded that concern for precision in recording seasons and days is appropriate for the managers and accountants of the rich, and, of course, those who gape at the heavens and all others who obviously apply themselves to counting. But I declare to my readers here and now that I have approached this work confident in my own ability to write about the past and the present and have declined to date events by the year or the day on the ground that the practice is irrelevant, preferring as more accurate to use the reigns of Emperors as my time-divisions. My reader will learn that a certain action was performed during the reign of a certain Emperor, but I leave it to others to dance off into the delusion of dating by year and day.

I write with confidence in myself since I am following the advice of those who were by far the most cultivated men of our age. They earnestly besought me not to allow to pass in silence those events of general importance, both of our own time and of the period between now and the end of Dexippus' History, which have not yet found an historian of note.[10] This work was the common concern of themselves and myself; and we judged all to reach a climax in the Emperor Julian, who reigned in our day and whom all men revered as some divinity. Just as for the poets who sang of the toilsome war which arose over a loved one and who reached the pinnacle of their craft, their enterprise brought fame and seemed worthwhile, so for us, who have described an origin and a reign which was divine, . . ..[11]

## 2

[(*Suda* Σ 199)

Seleucis: a bird with a good digestion and a large appetite, omnivorous and especially fond of locusts.]

12    Eunapius: Text

(Zosimus 1,47-62)

3

[(Zosimus 1,63)]

4

[(Zosimus 1,64-71)]

5

1. (*Suda* K 391)

Καρῶνος, Κάρου τοῦ βασιλέως υἱός, γενόμενος ἐν ἐξουσίᾳ καὶ βουλήσεως κύριος, ἀνέδραμε τηλικοῦτον κακὸν ἐς τυραννίδα, ὥστε ἀπέδειξε χρυσὸν τοῖς πειραθεῖσι τὴν τραγῳδουμένην τυραννίδα· οὕτω καὶ τοὔνομα τοῖς ἔργοις μακρῷ παρῆλθε. παίδων μὲν γὰρ εὖ γεγονότων ὕβρεις διὰ τὸ σύνηθες οὐδὲ ὕβρεις ἐνομίσθησαν, ἀλλ' ἦν     5
ἐγκύκλιον αὐτῷ καὶ πρόχειρον τοιαῦτα ἁμαρτάνειν. ὁ δὲ ἐγκλήματά τε ἀνέπλαττε καὶ ἐδίκαζε τοῖς ἀδικουμένοις καὶ τῶν δικαζομένων οὐδεὶς ἐσώζετο· ὅπου γε πολλῆς οὔσης καὶ ἀδιηγήτου τῆς φθορᾶς, παρανηλίσκοντό τινες τῶν εὐδαιμόνων, ὥσπερ ἐν κοινοῖς δείπνοις ἀλεκτορίδες· ἐς τὴν Καρῶνου τρυφήν. μεμνῆσθαι δὲ τῶν κατακοπ-     10
τομένων ἔφασκε, τῶν μὲν ὡς οὐκ ἐπήνεσαν αὐτοῦ τὸ κάλλος, τῶν δέ, ὅτι λέγοντα, ὅτε ἦν μειράκιον, οὐκ ἐθαύμασαν ὡς ἐβούλετο· ἀπώλλυντο δέ τινες καὶ γελάσαντες ἐναντίον αὐτοῦ ποτε, καὶ πάντα ἦν αὐτοῦ βαρύτερα διοσημείας, καὶ ἐλύττα ἐν μέσοις τοῖς ὑπηκόοις.
(Cf. Δ 1205*, E 133*, M 83*, Υ15*)

4 εὖ Casaubon, Wolfflin [οἱ codd.     10 τροφήν V

2. (John of Antioch *Fr.* 162 = *Exc. de Virt.* 51)

Ὅτι Καρῶνος ὁ τοῦ Κάρου υἱὸς βασιλεύσας πρᾶγμα μὲν εἰς κοινὸν ὄφελος φέρον οὐδὲν εἰργάσατο, τρυφῇ δὲ καὶ ἐκδεδιῃτημένῳ βίῳ τὰ καθ' ἑαυτὸν παραδοὺς παρανάλωμα τῆς τρυφῆς ἐποιεῖτο φόνους οὐδὲν ἠδικηκότων ἀνθρώπων κατά τι προσκεκρουκέναι νομισθέντων αὐτῷ, βαρυνομένων δὲ πάντων ἐπὶ τῇ πικρᾷ τυραννίδι     5
συναναμιχθείσῃ νεότητι, καὶ πάντα ἐκμελῶς καὶ δίχα λογισμοῦ πράττοντος ⟨οὐ πολλῷ ὕστερον δίκην ἔδωκε⟩. (Cf. *Suda* K 391, Π 401)

2 φέρον Suda K 391 [φέρων Exc.     3 παραδοὺς [ἐκδοὺς Mendelssohn
7 οὐ πολλῷ ὕστερον δίκην ἔδωκε addidi [ξήτει ἐν ταῖς περὶ ἀρετῆς καὶ κακίας
add. Müller *FHG* IV p.601 ξήτει ἐν τῷ περὶ ἐπιβουλῶν Mendelssohn.

(John of Antioch *Fr.* 163 = Zosimus 1,73)

(Zosimus 1, 47-62)

3

[(Zosimus 1,63)]

4

[(Zosimus 1,64-71)]

5

1. (*Suda* K 391)

Carinus, the son of the Emperor Carus, having come to power and being free to act as he wished, quickly embarked upon a reign of such evil that he made the tyrannies of tragedy seem benign to those who endured it, by so much did he outstrip the name of tyrant in his actions. His sexual abuse of high-born children was, because of its frequency, not held to be abuse; for this kind of criminal behaviour was habitual and commonplace with him. He both fabricated charges against persons and himself tried his victims; none of those brought to trial escaped. Amongst this multiplicity of indescribable deaths some of the nobles were slaughtered, like cockerels at public banquets, for the amusement of Carinus. As they were being cut down he said of some that they had not praised his good looks, of others that, when he was giving a speech as a youth, they had not expressed the admiration that he wished; some died because they had once laughed at him. Everything that he did was worse than the portents had foretold as he raged like a madman amidst his subjects. (Cf. Δ 1205*, E 133*, M 83*, Υ 15*)


2. (John of Antioch *Fr.* 162 = *Exc. de Virt.* 51)

When Carinus, the son of Carus, was Emperor he performed no action for the common good. He devoted all of his resources to his dissipated and undisciplined life, one of the excesses of his dissipation being the murder of innocent men whom he considered to have caused him some offence. Since all were oppressed by this bitter tyranny compounded by the youthfulness of one who did everything inappropriately and without reflection, <he was killed shortly afterwards>.[12]

(Cf. *Suda* K 391, Π 401)


(John of Antioch *Fr.* 163 = Zosimus 1,73)

6

(Zosimus 2,1-7)

7

[1. (*Epit. de Caes.* 40,20)

Alexander fuit Phryx origine, ingenio timidus, inferior adversus laborem vitio senectae aetatis.]

[2. (*Epit. de Caes.* 41,2)

Constantinus, Constantii imperatoris et Helenae filius, imperavit annos triginta. hic dum iuvenculus a Galerio in urbe Roma religionis specie obses teneretur, fugam arripiens atque ad frustrandos insequentes publica iumenta, quaqua iter egerat, interfecit et ad patrem in Britanniam pervenit; et forte iisdem diebus ibidem Constantium parentem fata ultima perurgebant.]    5

(Zosimus 2,8-17)

8

[(*Epit. de Caes.* 41,4)

Hic sororem suam Constantiam Licinio Mediolanum accito coniungit; filiumque suum Crispum nomine, ex Minervina concubina susceptum, item Constantinum iisdem diebus natum oppido Arelatensi Licinianumque, Licinii filium, mensium fere viginti, Caesares effecit.]    5

(Zosimus 2,18-28)

9

1. (*Suda* K 2285)

Κωνσταντῖνος ὁ μέγας βασιλεύς. περὶ οὗ ἔγραψεν Εὐνάπιος φληνάφους καὶ παρῆκα αὐτὰ αἰδοῖ τοῦ ἀνδρός.

2. (*Vit. Soph.* 6,3,8)

Κωνσταντῖνος μὲν οὖν καὶ Ἀβλάβιον τιμῶν ἐκολάζετο, καὶ ὅπως γε ἐτελεύτα ἐν τοῖς περὶ ἐκείνου γέγραπται.

[3. (Philostorgius 2,4)

Ὅτι φησὶ τὸν Κωνσταντῖνον ἀνελεῖν τὸν ἴδιον παῖδα Κρίσπον, διαβολαῖς τῆς μητρυιᾶς συναρπασθέντα· κἀκείνην δὲ πάλιν φωραθεῖσάν τινι τῶν κουρσώρων μοιχωμένην, τῇ τοῦ λουτροῦ ἀλέᾳ

1 Κρῖσπον Gothofredus [Πρίσκον codd.

**6**

(Zosimus 2,1-7)

**7**

[1. (*Epit. de Caes.* 40,20)

Alexander was a Phrygian by birth, fearful by nature, and unequal to toil because of the infirmity of his advanced years.[13] ]

[2. (*Epit. de Caes.* 41,2)

Constantine, the son of the Emperor Constantius and Helena, ruled for thirty years. As a young man he was detained at Rome by Galerius as a hostage, although the excuse was a religious obligation. He took flight and, in order to frustrate his pursuers, killed the mounts of the public post along the roads which he travelled. He reached his father, Constantius, in Britain, and the latter happened to die at about the same time.[14] ]

(Zosimus 2,8-17)

**8**

[(*Epit. de Caes.* 41,4)

He [Constantine] summoned Licinius to Milan and married his sister, Constantia, to him. He made Caesars his son Crispus, born of a concubine Minervina, and Constantine, who was born at that time at the city of Arles, and the son of Licinius, who was about twenty months old.[15] ]

(Zosimus 2,18-28)

**9**

1. (*Suda* K 2285)

Constantine, the great Emperor. There is much rubbish about him in Eunapius, which I have passed over out of respect for the man.

2. (*Vit. Soph.* 6,3,8)

Constantine, then, favoured Ablabius, but was punished for it. The manner of the Emperor's death I have described in the part of my History devoted to him.

[3. (Philostorgius 2,4)

Constantine put to death his son Crispus, being deceived by the false accusation of the latter's stepmother. When she, in her turn, was caught in adultery with one of the *cursores*,[16] he ordered that she be

ἐναποπνιγῆναι προστάξαι. καὶ τῷ παιδίῳ τοῦ ξίφους διδοῦντα Κωνσταντῖνον τὴν δίκην, μετ᾽ οὐ πολὺν χρονὸν ὑπὸ τῶν ἀδελφῶν φαρ-    5
μάκοις κατὰ τὴν Νικομήδειαν διατρίβοντα ἀναιρεθῆναι.]

[4. (Sozomen 1,5)

Οὐκ ἀγνοῶ δέ, ὡς Ἕλληνες λέγουσι, Κωνσταντῖνον ἀνελόντα
τινὰς τῶν ἐγγυτάτω τοῦ γένους, καὶ τῷ θανάτῳ Κρίσπου τοῦ ἑαυτοῦ
παιδὸς συμπράξαντα, μεταμεληθῆναι, καὶ περὶ καθαρμοῦ κοινώ-
σασθαι Σωπάτρῳ τῷ φιλοσόφῳ, κατ᾽ ἐκεῖνο καιροῦ προεστῶτι τῆς
Πλωτίνου διαδοχῆς· τὸν δὲ ἀποφήνασθαι, μηδένα καθαρμὸν εἶναι    5
τῶν τοιούτων ἁμαρτημάτων. ἀδημονοῦντα δὲ τὸν βασιλέα ἐπὶ τῇ
ἀπηγορεύσει, περιτυχεῖν ἐπισκόποις, οἳ μετανοίᾳ καὶ βαπτίσματι
ὑπέσχοντο πάσης αὐτὸν ἁμαρτίας καθαίρειν· ἡσθῆναί τε τούτοις
κατὰ σκοπὸν εἰρηκόσι, καὶ θαυμάσαι τὸ δόγμα, καὶ Χριστιανὸν
γενέσθαι, καὶ τοὺς ἀρχομένους ἐπὶ τοῦτο ἀγαγεῖν.]    10

(Zosimus 2,29-38)

**10**

[(Philostorgius 3,1)

Ὅτι Κώνσταντά φησιν, ὃς ἦν πρεσβύτερος τῶν Κωνσταντίνου
παίδων, ἐπιβουλεῦσαι τῷ ἀδελφῷ Κωνσταντίνῳ· καὶ μάχῃ τοῖς
στρατηγοῖς αὐτοῦ συρραγέντα διαφθαρῆναί τε καὶ τὴν μοῖραν τῆς
ὑπ᾽ αὐτὸν ἀρχῆς εἰς τὴν Κώνσταντος ἀνακοινωθῆναι.]

1. Κώνσταντά codd. [Κωνσταντῖνόν Tillemont    2 Κωνσταντίνῳ codd.
[Κώνσταντι Tillemont

(Zosimus 2,39-41)

**11**

1. (*Vit. Soph.* 10,1,1)

Περὶ Προαιρεσίου καὶ προλαβοῦσιν ἱκανῶς εἴρηται, καὶ ἐν τοῖς
ἱστορικοῖς κατὰ τὴν ἐξήγησιν ὑπομνήμασι.

[2. (*Epit. de Caes.* 41,22-23)

Constans vero venandi cupidine dum per silvas saltusque
erraret, conspiravere aliquanti militares in eius necem, auctoribus
Chrestio et Marcellino simulque Magnentio: qui ubi patrandi negotii
dies placuit, Marcellinus natalem filii simulans plerosque ad cenam
rogat. itaque in multam noctem convivio celebrato Magnentius quasi    5
ad ventris solita secedens habitum venerabilem capit. ea re cognita
Constans fugere conatus apud Helenam, oppidum Pyrenaeo
proximum, a Gaisone cum lectissimis misso interficitur anno tertio

drowned in a hot bath. Not long afterwards Constantine, while staying at Nicomedia, was poisoned by his brothers and so paid the penalty for the execution of Crispus.[17] ]

[4. (Sozomen 1,5)

I am not ignorant of the pagan claim that Constantine, repenting the murder of some of his closest relatives, and particularly the support which he gave to the murder of Crispus, his own son, approached Sopater the philosopher, at that time the head of the school of Plotinus, about purification. Sopater replied that no one could be purified of such sins. The Emperor was dismayed by this reply, but happened to meet some bishops who promised to cleanse him of all sin upon repentance and baptism. He, being pleased with their words, which were to his purpose, and delighted with their teaching, became a Christian and encouraged his subjects to do likewise.]

(Zosimus 2,29-38)

## 10

[((Philostorgius 3,1)

Constans, who was the eldest of the sons of Constantine, plotted against his brother Constantine. The latter, meeting his brother's generals in battle, was destroyed, and his part of the Empire was incorporated into that of Constans.[18])]

(Zosimus, 2,39-41)

## 11

1. (*Vit. Soph.* 10,1,1)

Concerning Prohaeresius I have said sufficient, both above in this text and in the narrative of my History.

[2. (*Epit. de Caes.* 41,22-23)

While Constans, in his passion for hunting, was off wandering through the woods and dales, some of the military, under the leadership of Chrestius, Marcellinus and Magnentius, plotted to kill him. When they had settled upon the day for doing this, Marcellinus, pretending that it was his son's birthday, invited a large number of people to a banquet. When the feasting had been prolonged far into the night, Magnentius left as if to relieve himself and donned the imperial regalia. When he learned this, Constans tried to flee to Helena, a town very close to the Pyrenees. There he was killed by Gaiso, who had been sent after him with picked

18     Eunapius: Text

decimo Augustae dominationis (nam Caesar triennio fuerat), aevi
septimo vicesimoque.]                                                  10

(Zosimus 2,42)

## 12

[(*Epit. de Caes.* 42,2)
Magnentius quoque Decentium consanguineum suum trans
Alpes Caesarem creavit.]

(Zosimus 2,45-54)

## 13

(*Exc. de Sent.* 3)
    ... ἀλλ᾽ ἡ μὲν παροιμία φησὶ τὸ θέρος ἐπὶ τῇ καλάμῃ φαί-
νεσθαι· τότε δὲ ὁ Κωνστάντιος ἐδείκνυ τοῦ πατρὸς ὤν.

2 ὤν cod. [ἦν Boissevain    post ὤν add. γνήσιος υἱός van Herwerden, παιδίον
Meineke

(Zosimus 2,55)

## 14

1. (*Exc. de Sent.* 4)
    Ὅτι κατὰ τὸν Ἰουλιανὸν τὸν Καίσαρα δοκούντων τῷ Κωνσταν-
τίῳ βεβουλεῦσθαι καλῶς ὁ χρόνος τὴν πεῖραν ἐς τὸ ἐναντίον
ἔστρεφε, ταῖς τοῦ Καίσαρος ἀρεταῖς συνενθουσιώσης ἤδη τῆς τύχης,
καὶ σχεδὸν ἑκάστης ἡμέρας ξένα καὶ ποικίλα φερούσης τῷ βασιλεῖ
διηγήματα· ἐφ᾽ οἷς ὁ Κωνστάντιος δακνόμενος ἤδη καὶ δυσφορῶν      5
ὑπὸ φθόνου, τοὺς ἡγουμένους τῶν φύσει πολεμίων ἐπετείχιζε τῷ
Καίσαρι, καὶ τὴν ἑαυτοῦ προσετίθει τοῖς ἐχθροῖς δύναμιν, μόνα ὁρῶν
τὰ ⟨ἑαυτῷ⟩ ἡδέα, καὶ τὸ οἰκεῖον ξένον ὑπολαμβάνων, εἰ σὺν τῷ
Καίσαρι σώζοιτο, καὶ τὸ ξένον οἰκεῖον, εἰ καταλύοι μεθ᾽ ἑαυτοῦ τὸν
Καίσαρα· ὥστε ὁ πόλεμος εἰς τὸ ὕπουλον μεταβαλὼν καὶ τὸ φύσει   10
πολέμιον ἐποίει σύμμαχον.

1 δοκούντων τῷ cod. [δοκοῦν τῷ αὐτῷ edd.    8 ἑαυτῷ add. Boissevain
9 καταλύοι Niebuhr [καταλύει cod.

2. (*Vit. Soph.* 7,3,8)
    Πεμφθεὶς δὲ Καῖσαρ ἐπὶ Γαλατίας οὐχ ἵνα βασιλεύῃ τῶν
ἐκείνῃ μόνον, ἀλλ᾽ ἵνα ἐν τῇ βασιλείᾳ διαφθαρῇ, παρὰ δόξαν ἅπασαν
ἐκ τῆς τῶν θεῶν προνοίας ἀνήνεγκεν, πάντας μὲν λανθάνων ὅτι
θεραπεύει θεούς, πάντας δὲ νικῶν ὅτι ἐθεράπευε θεούς, καὶ τόν τε

soldiers, in the thirteenth year of his reign as Augustus (he had already been Caesar for three) and in the twenty-seventh year of his life.[19]

(Zosimus 2,42)

## 12

[(*Epit. de Caes.* 42,2)

Magnentius, too, made his blood-relative, Decentius, Caesar beyond the Alps.[20]]

(Zosimus 2,43-54)

## 13

(*Exc. de Sent.* 3)

... but, as the proverb says, the ear shows itself upon the stalk; and on that occasion Constantius showed himself his father's son.[21]

(Zosimus 2,55)

## 14

1. (*Exc. de Sent.* 4)

Although it seemed to Constantius that he had arranged things well in the case of the Caesar Julian, time turned his plans upside down. For by this time Fortune was filled with admiration for Julian's virtues, and almost every day brought new and varied reports to the Emperor. These gnawed at Constantius and weighed him down with envy, and he raised up the leaders of our natural enemies against Julian. Seeing only his personal interests, he lent his power to the enemy, regarding what was his own as foreign, if it were to be saved together with the Caesar, and what was foreign as his own, providing only it destroyed the Caesar along with himself. Thus the war became a concealed sore in which the natural enemy became an ally.[22]

2. (*Vit. Soph.* 7,3,8)

He was sent to Gaul as Caesar, not that he should rule those there, but that he should be destroyed while ruling. But against all expectation because of the providence of the gods he emerged unscathed, concealing from all that he worshipped the gods and conquering all because of this devotion. He crossed the Rhine and destroyed or enslaved

Ῥῆνον ἐπεραιώθη, καὶ πάντα ὅσα ὑπὲρ ἐκεῖνον ἔθνη βάρβαρα          5
συνελὼν καὶ δουλωσάμενος, πολλῶν ἐπιβουλῶν καὶ μηχανημάτων
πλεκομένων αὐτῷ (ὡς ἐν τοῖς περὶ ἐκεῖνον ἀναγέγραπται) . . . .
(Zosimus 3,1,1 - 2,1)

## Liber II

## 15

*(Exc. de Sent.* 5)

Τὰ μὲν οὖν ἀπὸ τῆς Δεξίππου συγγραφῆς ἐς τοὺς Ἰουλιανοῦ
καθήκοντα ⟨καιροὺς⟩ ὡς ἐνῆν μάλιστα διὰ τῶν ἀναγκαίων ἐπι-
τρέχουσιν ἱκανῶς ἐν τοῖς ἔμπροσθεν δεδήλωται· φέρεται δὲ ἐντεῦθεν
ὁ λόγος ἐφ᾿ ὅνπερ ἐφέρετο ἐξ ἀρχῆς, καὶ ἀναγκάζει γε τοῖς ἔργοις
ἐνδιατρίβειν ὥσπερ τι πρὸς αὐτὸν ἐρωτικὸν πεπονθότας, οὔτι μὰ Δία     5
τεθεαμένους ἢ πεπειραμένους· κομιδῇ γὰρ ἦν ὁ γράφων τάδε παῖς,
ἡνίκα ἐβασίλευσεν· ἀλλὰ δεινόν τι χρῆμα καὶ ἀπαραίτητον εἰς ἔρωτα
τὸ κοινὸν ἀνθρώπων ἁπάντων πάθος καὶ τὸ τῆς ἐπ᾿ αὐτῷ δόξης
ἀστασίαστον. πῶς γὰρ ἦν σιωπᾶν ὑπὲρ ὧν οὐδεὶς ἔφερε σιωπᾶν,
πῶς δὲ μὴ λέγειν ὅσα καὶ οἱ μὴ δυνάμενοι λέγειν ἀπὸ στόματος     10
ἔφραζον, ἐς γλυκεῖάν τινα καὶ χρυσῆν διατριβὴν τὴν ἐκείνου μνήμην
ἀναφέροντες; καὶ ὁ μὲν πολὺς ἄνθρωπος ταῦτα πάσχοντες ὅμως
ἔλαττον ἐς τὸ γράφειν ἐξεβιάζοντο· τὸ δὲ ἐξαίρετον καὶ ὅ τιπερ ἦν ἐν
παιδείᾳ γνωριμώτατον, οὐδὲ ἀφιέντα ἠφίεσαν, ἀλλ᾿ ἐνέκειντο παρα-
θαρσύνοντες ὡς συνεπιληψόμενοι τοῦ πόνου. ὁ δὲ ἐς τὰ μάλιστα     15
γεγονὼς αὐτῷ γνώριμος, ὁ Περγαμηνὸς ἀνὴρ Ὀριβάσιος, ἐκ φυσικῆς
φιλοσοφίας ἰατρικὴν ἐπιτάττειν ἄριστος καὶ δρᾶν ἔτι θειότερος, καὶ
ἀσεβήσειν ἐβόα περιφανῶς, εἰ μὴ συγγράφοιμι· καὶ τῶν γε πράξεων
(πάσας δὲ ἠπίστατο παρὼν ἁπάσαις) μάλα ἀκριβῶς ὑπόμνημα
συνετέλει πρὸς τὴν γραφήν· ὥστε οὐκ ἦν ἀναβολὴ καὶ βουλομένῳ     20
ῥαθυμεῖν.

1 in marg. ΠΡΟΟΙΜΙΟΝ ΤΟΥ Β ΛΟΓΟΥ    2 καιροὺς add. Mai [aut χρόνους
Boissevain    8 ἐπ᾿ αὐτῷ Bekker [ἐφ᾿ αὐτῷ cod. ἐφ᾿ ἑκάστῳ Kuiper
15 συνεπιληψόμενοι Bekker [ἐπιληψόμενοι cod.

## 16

1. *(Exc. de Sent.* 6)

Τοῦτο ἐγένετο τὸ εὐτύχημα, καὶ πάντα ὥσπερ ὀστράκου
μεταπεσόντος ἐπὶ τὸ βέλτιον ἐχώρησε Ῥωμαίοις.

all the barbarian tribes there, despite the many plots and schemes woven against him, as I have described in the parts of my History devoted to him . . ..

(Zosimus 3,1,1 - 2,1)

## Book II
## 15

(*Exc. de Sent.* 5)

In the preceding chapters the history from the end of Dexippus' work to the time of Julian has been summarised as adequately as possible, with a concentration on the most important events. Henceforth my narrative centres upon the one who was its object from the beginning, and, feeling the love that I do for him, I am compelled to turn my attention to his achievements. Of course, I never saw him or personally knew him; for when he was Emperor, the writer of this History was just a child. But the general affection of all mankind for him and the universal high repute in which he is held are a marvellous and irresistible inspiration to love. How could one be silent about those things upon which no one could endure to be silent? How not speak of those great deeds which even those who had no skill in speaking described, remembering his age as one of sweetness and gold? The majority, while holding these sentiments, were, nevertheless, under less compulsion to write them down. But the outstanding and most famous figures of the world of learning would not excuse me, even though I declined, and they pressed me with their encouragement and promises that they would help me in the task. Oribasius of Pergamum, the most intimate of Julian's companions and, as a result of his training in natural philosophy, the most eminent medical expert and a still more inspired practitioner, declared openly that I should be committing a sin if I did not write my History. Furthermore, he composed for my use in writing a detailed memorandum of the deeds of the Emperor; for he was familiar with all, having been present at them. Thus, I had no excuse for delay, even had I wished to shirk the task.

## 16

1. (*Exc. de Sent.* 6)

This turned to success, and everything, as if heads followed tails, changed to the better for the Romans.[23]

[2. (*Suda* E 1771)
Ὁ οὖν Μάρκελλος κύριος ἦν τῶν πραγμάτων, ὀνόματος μόνου
καὶ σχήματος τῷ Ἰουλιανῷ ἐξιστάμενος, τὴν δὲ ἀληθεστέραν αὐτὸς
ἀρχὴν μεταχειριζόμενος. (Cf. O 719*)]

(Zosimus 3,2,2 - 3,2)

## 17

(*Exc. de Sent.* 7)
Ὅτι φησὶν ὁ Εὐνάπιος περὶ τοῦ παραβάτου Ἰουλιανοῦ· τῆς δὲ
στρατείας ταύτης σφοδροτάτης τε ἅμα καὶ κλεινοτάτης τῶν πρὸ
αὐτῆς γενομένων τὴν διήγησιν ἐς τήνδε τὴν γραφὴν ἐντείνοντες οὐ
πεισόμεθα ταὐτὸν τοῖς ἐν ἡμέρᾳ δᾷδας ἀνασχοῦσιν, ἵνα τι κρυπ-
τόμενον ἀνεύρωσιν, οὐδὲ ὑπὲρ ὧν ἱκανῶς ἅμα καὶ ουνενθουσιῶν    5
τοῖς ἑαυτοῦ καλοῖς βιβλίδιον ὅλον τῇδε ἀναθεὶς τῇ μάχῃ διῆλθεν ὁ
βασιλικώτατος καὶ ἐν λόγοις Ἰουλιανός, αὐτοὶ παραβαλούμεθα καὶ
συνεκθήσομεν ἑτέραν γραφὴν τὰ αὐτὰ σημαίνουσαν, ἀλλὰ τοῖς μὲν
βουλομένοις τὸ μέγεθος τῶν ἐκείνου λόγων τε καὶ ἔργων ἀνα-
σκοπεῖν τὸ περὶ τούτων βιβλίον <ἀναγινώσκειν> ἐπιτάξομεν, καὶ    10
πρὸς ἐκείνην φέρεσθαι τὴν ἀκτῖνα τῆς συγγραφῆς. ἐκ τῆς ἐνεργείας
τῶν τότε ὑπ' αὐτοῦ πραχθέντων ἐπὶ τὴν τοῦ λόγου δύναμιν ἀπορ-
ρυεῖσαν καὶ διαλάμψασαν· αὐτοὶ δὲ ὅσον οὐ πρὸς ἅμιλλαν μειρακι-
ώδη καὶ σοφιστικήν, ἀλλ' εἰς ἱστορικὴν ἀκρίβειαν ἀναστῆσαι καὶ
διαπλάσαι τὸν λόγον, ἐπιδραμούμεθα τὰ γεγενημένα, συνάπτοντες    15
τοῖς εἰρημένοις τὰ ἐχόμενα.

6 βιβλίον Cobet         10 ἀναγινώσκειν add. Niebuhr

(Zosimus 3,3)

## Liber III
## 18

1. (*Exc. de Sent.* 8)
Ὅτι Ἰουλιανὸς τοὺς ἀρχομένους καὶ τοὺς πολεμίους ἐδίδασκεν
ἅμα τίσι δοκεῖ τὸν ὄντως βασιλέα κρατεῖν, καὶ ὡς ἀνδρείᾳ μὲν καὶ
ῥώμῃ καὶ χειρῶν κράτος πρὸς τοὺς ἀνθεστηκότας μόνον τῶν
πολεμίων χρήσιμα, δικαιοσύνη δὲ μετ' ἐξουσίας ὥσπερ πηγή τις
οὖσα τῶν ἀρετῶν καὶ τοὺς μὴ παρόντας χειροήθεις τε ποιεῖν καὶ    5
δουλοῦσθαι πέφυκε. τοιαύτας ὑποτέων ἀρετὰς καὶ σπέρματα

2 δοκεῖ [δεῖ Bekker      5 τε ποιεῖν Bekker [ἐμποιεῖ cod.
6 ἀρετὰς [ἀρχὰς Meineke

[2. (*Suda* E 1771)

Therefore Marcellus was really in charge of affairs, conceding to Julian only the name and regalia of Caesar and keeping the real power in his own hands.[24]   (Cf. O 719*)]

(Zosimus 3,2,2 - 3,2)

## 17

(*Exc. de Sent.* 7)

This expedition was more violent and renowned than those that preceded it. While I shall incorporate an account of it in my narrative, I shall not be persuaded to the same course as those who hold up torches in daylight to search for something hidden. Furthermore, the most noble Emperor Julian, enthused by his own achievements, adequately described in his own words these events in a pamphlet which he dedicated to the battle; and so I shall not produce another narrative with the same contents for comparison with his work. Rather, those who wish to observe the greatness of his words and his deeds I shall direct to turn to his pamphlet on these events and to the splendours of his account, whose brightness has been reflected from the real experience of his achievements into the power of his words. For my part, since I am building and shaping my account not for the purpose of competing in a youthful or sophistic manner with Julian's but with a view to historical accuracy, I shall skim over what happened in the battle, adding what followed after the events that he describes.[25]

(Zosimus 3,3)

## Book III
## 18

1. (*Exc. de Sent.* 8)

Julian taught both the men under his command and the enemy with what qualities he thought the true king ruled: that courage, strength and physical force were only of use against those of the enemy in the field, whereas justice combined with authority was like some fountain-head of virtues, which made even those far away manageable and obedient. Proclaiming from his tribunal these virtues and principles of his philosophy to those under his command, he ordered the Romans to harm none of the Salii nor to ravage or plunder their territory. He told

φιλοσοφίας ἐς τοὺς ὑπηκόους ἅπαντας ἀπὸ βήματος ἐπέταττε Ῥωμαίοις μηδένα Σαλίων ἀδικεῖν μηδὲ δηοῦν ἢ οἴνεσθαι τὴν ἰδίαν χώραν.
ἰδίαν δ' ἀπέφαινε πᾶσαν αὐτοὺς δεῖν ὑπολαμβάνειν, ἣν ἄνευ μάχης καὶ πόνων ἔχουσιν· ὡς ἀναγκαῖον εἶναι πολεμίαν τὴν τῶν πολεμούντων  10
ἡγεῖσθαι καὶ νομίζειν, οἰκείαν δὲ τὴν τῶν παρακεχωρηκότων.

2. (Exc. de Sent. 9)
Ὅτι εἰώθει Ἰουλιανὸς ἀρχὴν νίκης, οὐ πολέμου τίθεσθαι.

[3. (Suda Γ 264)
Ἐδόκει γὰρ τό τε σῶμα γιγαντώδης εἶναι καὶ τὸν θυμὸν θηριώδης, καὶ ἐς ἀγχίνοιαν τῶν συλληστευόντων ἁπάντων πολυπλοκώτερος.]

1. (Exc. de Sent. 10)
Τοῦτον δεξάμενος ἑταῖρον ἐφ' ἑαυτῷ συνιστάμενον εἶχεν· εἶτ' ἄλλος προσῄει, καὶ πλῆθος ἦν· καὶ καθάπερ οἱ Πυθαγόριοί φασι, μονάδος ἐπὶ δυάδα κινηθείσης οὐκέτι τὴν τῶν ἀριθμῶν ἠρεμεῖν φύσιν, ἀλλὰ διαχεῖσθαι καὶ ῥεῖν ἐς πολύ, οὕτω Χαριέττονος Κερκίωνα προσλαβόντος αἵ τε πράξεις ἐπὶ πολὺ προῄεσαν καὶ ὁ τῶν συν-  5
ισταμένων ὄχλος ἀνὰ λόγον ἠκολούθει ταῖς πράξεσιν.

[5. (Suda Α 2395)
Χαριέττων μὲν οὖν καὶ πρὸ τούτου φανερός τις ὢν καὶ ἀνυπόστατος τῷ τε πλεονάζοντι τοῦ δραστηρίου φοβῶν ἀνεῖχεν ἀπὸ λῃστείας ἅπαντας.]

6. (Exc. de Leg. Gent. 1)
Ὅτι τοῦ Ἰουλιανοῦ ἐς τὴν πολεμίαν χωροῦντος, καὶ τῶν Χαμάβων ἱκετευόντων φείδεσθαι καὶ ταύτης ὡς οἰκείας, ὁ Ἰουλιανὸς συνεχώρει, καὶ τὸν βασιλέα σφῶν προελθεῖν κελεύσας, ἐπειδὴ προῆλθε, καὶ ἐπὶ τῆς ὄχθης εἶδεν ἑστηκότα, ἐπιβὰς πλοίου (τὸ πλοῖον ἐκτὸς ἔχων τοξεύματος), ἑρμηνέα ἔχων διελέγετο τοῖς  5
βαρβάροις. ἐκείνων δὲ πάντα ποιεῖν ὄντων ἑτοίμων, ὁρῶν εὐπρόσωπόν τε ἅμα καὶ ἀναγκαίαν αὐτῷ τὴν εἰρήνην (Χαμάβων γὰρ μὴ βουλομένων ἀδύνατόν ἐστι τὴν ἐκ τῆς Βρεττανικῆς νήσου σιτοπομπίαν ἐπὶ τὰ Ῥωμαϊκὰ φρούρια διαπέμπεσθαι), καμπτόμενος ὑπὸ τῆς χρείας χαρίζεται τὴν εἰρήνην, καὶ ὅμηρα ᾔτει λαβεῖν πίστεως  10
ἕνεκεν. τῶν δὲ ἱκανοὺς εἶναι αἰχμαλώτους λεγόντων, ἐκείνους ἔφη τὸν πόλεμον αὐτῷ δεδωκέναι· καθ' ὁμολογίαν γὰρ μὴ λαβεῖν· νυνὶ δὲ ζητεῖν παρ' αὐτῶν τοὺς ἀρίστους, εἰ μὴ τεχνάζουσι περὶ τὴν εἰρήνην. τῶν δὲ ἱκετευόντων καὶ ἀξιούντων εἰπεῖν οὓς βούλεται,

5 ἐκτὸς ἔχων τοξεύματος Niebuhr [οὖν ἔχων τοξεύματος A ἣν ἐκτὸς τ. Müller ἔξω ἔχων τ. Dindorf ἀνέχων τ.ἐκτὸς de Boor

them that they should understand that all the land which they had won without fighting and toil was theirs: thus, while they must regard as enemy territory that which belonged to those at war with them, they must treat as their own that which belonged to those who had submitted to them.[26]

2. (*Exc. de Sent.* 9)

It was Julian's custom to lay the beginning of a victory rather than of a war.[27]

[3. (*Suda* Γ 264)

He was reputed to have a gigantic stature and a fierce temper and to be more clever and cunning than all his fellow brigands.[28] ]

4. (*Exc. de Sent.* 10)

Receiving him as an ally, he kept him by his side, and then another came, and soon there was a crowd. But just as, according to the Pythagoreans, a monad, when it is moved towards a dyad, loses its nature as a single number and divides up and becomes many, so, when Charietto took up Cercio, their activities increased and the number of their allies multiplied in proportion with their achievements.[29]

[5. (*Suda* A 2395)

Since Charietto was well known even before this, invincible and terrifying because of his many deeds of daring, he stopped them all from brigandage.[30]]

6. (*Exc. de Leg. Gent.* 1)

When Julian entered the enemy's territory, the Chamavi begged him to treat this land, too, as if it were his own. Julian agreed and ordered their king to come to him. When the king came and Julian saw him standing on the bank,[31] the Caesar embarked in a boat and, keeping the boat out of arrow range, spoke to the barbarians through an interpreter. They were willing to do all that he demanded, and since he saw that peace was obviously desirable, indeed necessary for him (for without the acquiescence of the Chamavi it is impossible to transport the supplies of grain from the island of Britain to the Roman garrisons),[32] guided by his own advantage, he granted peace, demanding hostages as a pledge. When they said that those whom the Romans had captured were sufficient, Julian replied that he held them as a result of the fighting, not by agreement: now he was seeking their best men, lest they use deceit in respect of the peace-agreement. They agreed and

26    Eunapius: Text

μεταλαβὼν αὖθις τὸν τοῦ βασιλέως αὐτῶν αἰτεῖται παῖδα, πλαττό-   15
μενος, ὃν εἶχεν αἰχμάλωτον, ὥσπερ οὐκ ἔχων. ἐνταῦθα ὅ τε βασιλεὺς
αὐτῶν καὶ οἱ βάρβαροι πρηνεῖς ἐκταθέντες οἰμωγῇ τε ἀφθόνῳ καὶ
ὀλοφύρσει προσεκέχρηντο δεόμενοι μηδὲν ἀδύνατον ἐπιτάττεσθαι·
ἀδύνατον δὲ αὐτοῖς εἶναι καὶ τοὺς πεσόντας ἀναστῆσαι καὶ ὁμήρους
δοῦναι τοὺς τετελευτηκότας. γενομένης δὲ σιωπῆς, ὁ τῶν βαρβάρων   20
βασιλεὺς ἀναβοήσας μέγιστον ὅσον· εἴθε ἔζη μοι, ἔφη, ὁ παῖς, ἵνα σοὶ
δοθεὶς ὅμηρος, ὦ Καῖσαρ, δουλείαν ηὐτύχει τῆς ἐμῆς βασιλείας εὐ-
δαιμονεστέραν. ἀλλ᾽ ὑπὸ σοῦ τέθνηκεν ἀτυχήσας ἴσως καὶ τὸ
ἀγνοηθῆναι. πολέμῳ γὰρ ἐπίστευσε τὸ σῶμα νέος ὤν, ὃν σὺ μόνον
ἀντάξιον εἰρήνης ὑπολαμβάνεις. καὶ νῦν, ὦ βασιλεῦ, σὺ μὲν ἐξαιτεῖς   25
ὡς ὄντα, ἐγὼ δὲ ἄρχομαι θρηνεῖν συνορῶν τίνα οὐκ ἔχω. παῖδα γὰρ
ὀδυρόμενος ἕνα καὶ κοινὴν εἰρήνην τῷ παιδὶ συναπολώλεκα. κἂν
μὲν πιστεύσῃς τοῖς ἐμοῖς ἀτυχήμασιν, παραμυθίαν ἔχει μοι τὸ πάθος
ὡς ὑπὲρ ἁπάντων ἠτυχηκότι· ἂν δὲ ἀπιστήσῃς, καὶ πατὴρ ἀτυχὴς
καὶ βασιλεὺς ὀφθήσομαι. τοῖς γὰρ ἐμοῖς κακοῖς οὐκ ἀκολουθήσει μὲν   30
ὁ παρὰ τῶν ἄλλων ἔλεος, ὅσπερ ἅπασιν ὀφείλεται τοῖς ἐν τοιούτοις
καθεστηκόσιν, προσκείσονται δὲ αἱ κοιναὶ συμφοραί. καὶ οὐ παραιτή-
σομαι τοὺς ἄλλους ἀτυχιῶν, ἀλλὰ κοινωνεῖν ἐμοὶ τῶν δεινῶν
ἀναγκάσω, τοσοῦτον ἀπολαύων τῆς βασιλικῆς ἐξουσίας ὅσον ἀτυχεῖν
μόνος μὴ δύνασθαι. τούτων ἀκούων ὁ βασιλεὺς τήν τε ψυχὴν ἔπαθε   35
καὶ τοῖς λεγομένοις εὐπαθῶς ἐπεδάκρυσε· καὶ καθάπερ ἐν τοῖς
δράμασιν, ὅτ᾽ ἂν εἰς ἄπορον καὶ δύσλυτον αἱ τῶν ὑποκειμένων ἔργων
πλοκαὶ τελευτήσωσιν, ὁ καλούμενος ἀπὸ μηχανῆς θεὸς ἐπεισόδιος
εἰς μέσον ἕλκεται πάντα συμπεραίνων καὶ καταστρέφων ἐπὶ τὸ
σαφέστερον καὶ εὔκριτον, οὕτω καὶ αὐτὸς ἐπὶ πράγμασιν ἀμηχάνοις   40
καὶ δυσεξόδοις, μετ᾽ οἰμωγῆς ἁπάντων τὴν μὲν εἰρήνην αἰτούντων,
τὸν δὲ ἐπιζητούμενον ὅμηρον ἀπαγορευόντων μὴ ἔχειν, τόν τε νεανίσκον παραγαγὼν ἅπασιν ἔδειξε βασιλικῶς παρ᾽ αὐτῷ διαιτώμενον
καὶ διαλεχθῆναι τῷ πατρὶ κελεύσας ὅσα ἐβούλετο περιεσκόπει τὸ
πραχθησόμενον. τὰ δὲ ἐπὶ τούτοις ἦν ἄξια τούτων. οὐκ ἔτεκεν ὁ   45
ἥλιος τοιαύτην ἡμέραν, οἵαν τότε ἐξῆν τοῖς παροῦσιν ὁρᾶν καὶ
ἱστορεῖν. οἱ μὲν γὰρ ἀπὸ θορύβου καὶ θρήνων ἐκπλήξει καὶ θάμβει
συνδεθέντες ἐς τὸ ἀκίνητον ἐπάγησαν, ὥσπερ Ἰουλιανοῦ δείξαντος
αὐταῖς οὐ τὸν νεανίσκον, ἀλλ᾽ εἴδωλον, ὁ δὲ βασιλεύς, ἐπεὶ ἡσυχία
μυστηρίων ἁπάντων ἐγένετο σταθερωτέρα, βαρὺ φθεγξάμενος εἰς   50
μέσον· τοῦτον, εἶπεν, ὁ μὲν ὑμέτερος, ὡς ὑμεῖς ὑπολαμβάνετε,

31 τοιούτοις Niebuhr [τούτοις A   33 τοὺς ἄλλους ἀτυχιῶν Niebuhr [τοῖς ἄλλοις
ἀτυχῶν A   34 ἀναγκάσω Niebuhr [ἀναγκάσαι A   36 εὐπαθῶς Cantoclar
[ἀπαθῶς A συμπαθῶς Dindorf   ἐξεδάκρυσε edd.   43 αὐτῷ Dindorf
[αὐτοῦ A

begged him to name whom he wished. In reply he demanded the king's son, whom he held as a prisoner, pretending that he did not have him. Thereupon the barbarians and their king threw themselves on their faces and with plentiful groans and lamentations besought Julian not to enjoin what they could not carry out: they were unable to raise up the fallen and deliver the dead as hostages.[33]

When silence was restored, the barbarian king declared at the top of his voice, "Would that my son were alive so that, as a hostage with you, Caesar, he might enjoy a bondage more blessed then my kingly power. But he has been killed by you, perhaps with the ill-luck to die unrecognised. For, though young, he risked his life in war. He alone you value as a fair pledge for peace, and now, O Emperor, you demand him as if he were alive, while I begin to grieve, seeing the vision of the one whom I have lost. My only son I mourn, and with him I have lost peace for us all. If you believe my tale of woe, my grief has the consolation for me that I have suffered for us all; but if you do not, my misfortune will be clear both as a father and as a king. For not only will others feel no pity for my loss (which is the due of all in such circumstances), but my people will suffer disaster also. Being unable to protect the others from misfortune, I shall compel them to share my sorrows. Such is the privilege of kingly power, that I am not allowed to suffer alone!"

When the Emperor heard this, his heart was saddened and he readily wept tears at the words. Just as when, in a play, the complications of the plot come to an inextricable impasse, the so-called *deus ex machina* is adventitiously dragged onto the stage, bringing everything around to a clear and satisfactory conclusion, so, too, Julian in a situation of either stalemate or disaster, amidst the lamentations of all the barbarians, as they begged for peace and swore that they did not have the hostage demanded, brought forward the young man whom he had treated as befits royalty, and showed him to them all. Then, having told him to say whatever he wished to his father, Julian returned to consider the business in hand.

What followed this was a fitting sequel. Those present would never be able to witness and describe a day like this. The Chamavi, turned from groaning and lamentation to stunned amazement and consternation, were struck motionless, as if Julian had showed them not the young man, but his ghost. When a silence had fallen, more profound than at all the Mysteries, the Emperor addressed them all in a deep voice:[34] "This boy, whom your aggression had destroyed, as you

πόλεμος ἀπολώλεκε, θεὸς δὲ ἴσως καὶ τὸ Ῥωμαίων σέσωκε φιλ-
άνθρωπον. ἔξω δὲ αὐτὸν ὅμηρον, οὐ παρ᾽ ὑμῶν καθ᾽ ὁμολογίαν,
ἀλλὰ παρὰ τοῦ πολέμου λαβὼν καὶ τῷ κρατεῖν ἀρκούμενος. καὶ
οὗτος μὲν οὐδενὸς ἀτυχήσει τῶν καλλίστων ἐμοὶ ξυνών, ὑμεῖς δὲ    55
πειρώμενοι παραβαίνειν τὰς συνθήκας ἀποτεύξεσθε πάντων. φημὶ
δὲ οὐχ ὅτι κολάσομαι τὸν ὅμηρον, ὃν οὐδὲ ἐνέχυρον παρ᾽ ὑμῶν εἴληφα
τῆς εἰρήνης, ἀλλ᾽ ἀνδρείας ἀπόδειξιν καθ᾽ ὑμῶν ἔχω· ὃ καὶ ἄλλως
ἄνισον καὶ θεομισὲς τοὺς οὐδὲν ἀδικοῦντας ὑπὲρ τῶν ἀδικούντων
δάκνειν καὶ σπαράττειν, ὥσπερ τὰ θηρία τοὺς ἀπαντῶντας, ὅτ᾽ ἂν    60
ὑφ᾽ ἑτέρων διώκηται· ἀλλ᾽ ὅτι πρῶτον μὲν ἄρξετε χειρῶν ἀδίκων,
οὗ μείζων ὄλεθρος οὐκ ἔστιν ἀνθρώποις, κἂν δοκῶσι πρὸς τὸ βραχὺ
καὶ παρὸν ἐπιτυγχάνειν· δεύτερον δὲ ὅτι πρὸς Ῥωμαίους ὑμῖν ὁ λόγος
ἔσται κἀμὲ τὸν ἄρχοντα τούτων, ὃν οὔτε πολεμοῦντες οὔτε εἰρήνην
αἰτοῦντες ἐνικήσατε. προσεκύνησαν ἐπὶ τούτοις ἅπαντες καὶ ἀνευ-    65
φήμουν θεόν τινα ἐπὶ τοῖς λόγοις ἡγούμενοι. σπεισάμενος γοῦν καὶ
τὴν τοῦ Νεβισγάστου μητέρα μόνον αἰτήσας, ἐκείνων ὁμολογη-
σάντων τε ἅμα καὶ δόντων, ἀνέζευξεν ἐπὶ τοιαύταις πράξεσιν, μετ-
οπώρου τε ἑστηκότος καὶ χειμῶνος ἤδη συνισταμένου καὶ δια-
ψύχοντος. (Cf. Petrus Patricius *Fr.* 18)

52 σέσωκε Bekker [δέδωκε A    57 εἴληφα Hoeschel [εἴλημα A    61 ἄρξετε
Boissonade [ἄρξηται A

(Zosimus 3,4,1 - 8,1)

## 19

(*Exc. de Leg. Gent.* 2)

Ὅτι Βαδομάριός τις δυνάμει καὶ τόλμῃ προεῖχε Γερμανῶν
καὶ εἰς τοῦτο ὑπετύφετο μεγαλαυχίας, ὥστε ἐτύγχανε μὲν ὅμηρον τὸν
ἑαυτοῦ δεδωκὼς υἱόν, ἕως ἂν ἀποδῷ τοὺς αἰχμαλώτους, οὓς ἐκ τῆς
καταδρομῆς εἶχε συνηρπασμένους, τούτους δὲ οὐκ ἀποδιδοὺς ἀπήτει
τὸν ὅμηρον, πολλὰ ἀπειλῶν, εἰ μὴ λάβοι. ἀποπέμπει δὴ τοῦτον    5
Ἰουλιανὸς αὐτῷ τοσοῦτον ἐπιθείς, ὡς οὐκ ἔστιν ἀξιόπιστον ἐν
μειράκιον ὑπὲρ πολλῶν εὐγενεστέρων ὁμηρεῦον παρ᾽ αὐτῷ, ἀλλ᾽ ἢ
τοὺς αἰχμαλώτους ἀποδιδόναι προσῆκον ὄντας ὑπὲρ τρισχιλίους τοῖς
αὐτίκα ἥξουσι πρέσβεσιν, ἢ ἀδικοῦντα εἰδέναι. ταῦτα ἔγραφέ τε καὶ
τὴν πρεσβείαν ἔστελλεν, καὶ αὐτὸς εἵπετο τῇ πρεσβείᾳ ἀπὸ Νεμέτων    10
ἄρας ἐπὶ τὸν Ῥῆνον. ἤδη τε ἦν πρὸς τοῖς Ῥαυράκοις, ὅ ἐστι φρούριον.

thought, God, allied with the philanthropy of the Romans, has saved. I shall keep him as a hostage, not handed over by you under agreement, but taken in war; for I am satisfied with my victory. He will lack nothing of the best while he is with me, but you, if you attempt to break the treaty, shall suffer everything. I do not say that then I shall punish the hostage, whom I have not received from you as a pledge of peace, but whom I hold as proof of our bravery against you. Besides, it is unfair and ungodly to rend and tear to pieces those who are innocent in the place of those who do harm, as wild beasts do to those in their path when they are being pursued by others. But I do say that you shall be the first to raise hands to injustice, the most self-destructive act that men can perform, even if in the short term it brings apparent gain. And secondly, I remind you that you will have to reckon with the Romans, and me, their ruler, whom you have never bested either in war or when seeking peace."

At this all the Chamavi threw themselves down and blessed him, thinking him a god for these words. So Julian made peace, demanding only the mother of Nebisgastes,[35] and the barbarians straightway ratified the peace and handed her over. When these things had been accomplished, the Emperor broke camp, since it was now late autumn and the cold of winter was already beginning.[36]
(Cf. Petrus Patricius *Fr.* 18)

(Zosimus 3,4,1 - 8,1)


## 19

(*Exc. de Leg. Gent.* 2)
A certain Vadomar was outstanding amongst the Germans for strength and daring. He burned with such a measure of arrogance that, when he had handed over his own son as hostage until he returned the captives whom he had taken in his raid, he demanded the return of the hostage even though he had not restored the captives, making many threats if this were not done. Julian returned the son to Vadomar, adding only that in his eyes one youth was not a worthwhile hostage for so many better-born persons; but he should either hand over the captives (more than 3,000 in number) to the envoys who would come to him straightway, or he would be taught that he was acting unjustly. Julian wrote this and sent the embassy, and he himself followed the envoys from Speier to the Rhine. For Vadomar at the time was opposite the fortress of Augst.[37]

## 20

1. (*Exc. de Sent.* 11)

Ὅτι φησὶν ὁ Εὐνάπιος περὶ Ἰουλιανοῦ· ἐνταῦθα δὲ γενομένους μεμνῆσθαι προσήκει ὡς νῦν ἡ γραφὴ περιέχει τὰ τοῦ Καίσαρος ἔργα, ταῦτα δὲ ἐγώετο Κωνσταντίου βασιλέως βασιλεύοντος·
ὥσπερ οὖν ἐν τοῖς κατὰ Κωνστάντιον ἀμφοτέρων μεμνημένη τὰ τοῦ
προκειμένου Κωνσταντίου μᾶλλον εἶλκεν καὶ παρῆγεν εἰς τὸν λόγον,    5
οὕτως ἐπειδὴ τὸν λόγον ἐκ τῆς γενέσεως εἰς Ἰουλιανὸν ἐλθόντα τὸν
Καίσαρα νῦν ἀναγράφει, ἐπιμνήσεται πάλιν, ἐς ὅσον ἂν ἐγχωρῇ αὖ,
τῶν κατὰ τοὺς παραπίπτοντας καιροὺς εἰς τὸν Καίσαρα Κωνσταντίῳ
συντεθειμένων τε καὶ μεμηχανημένων.

2 προσήκει van Herwerden [προσῆκεν cod.    7 αὖ, τῶν Bekker [αὐτῶν cod.
τῶν Dindorf

2. (*Vit. Soph.* 6,3,8)

Ἀβλαβίῳ δὲ τὸν παῖδα κατέλιπε Κωνστάντιον, συμβασιλεύ-
σαντα μὲν αὐτῷ, διαδεξάμενον δὲ τὴν ἀρχὴν τοῦ πατρὸς σὺν Κωνσταντίνῳ καὶ Κώνσταντι τοῖς ἀδελφοῖς. ἐν δὲ τοῖς κατὰ τὸν θειότατον
Ἰουλιανὸν ἀκριβέστερον ταῦτα εἴρηται.

3. (*Vit. Soph.* 7,1,6)

Οὗτος, πάντων ἀνῃρημένων ὑπὸ τοῦ Κωνσταντίου (ταῦτα δὲ ἐν
τοῖς κατὰ Ἰουλιανὸν ἀκριβέστερον γέγραπται), καὶ ψιλωθέντος τοῦ
γένους Ἰουλιανοῦ, περιελείφθη μόνος, δι' ἡλικίαν περιφρονηθεὶς καὶ
πραότητα.

3 Ἰουλιανοῦ Giangrande [Ἰουλιανός codd., exp. Cobet.

4. (*Exc. de Sent.* 12)

Ὁ μὲν γὰρ Ῥωμαῖος Μάριος τὸν ἀντίπαλον Σύλλαν διπλοῦν
θηρίον ἀποκαλῶν, ἀλώπεκα καὶ λέοντα, μᾶλλον ἔφασκε φοβεῖσθαι
τὴν ἀλώπεκα· Κωνσταντίῳ δὲ λέων μὲν οὐδεὶς παρῆν πολλαὶ δὲ
ἀλώπεκες κύκλῳ περιτρέχουσαι διεθορύβουν τὸν Καίσαρα.

5. (*Exc. de Sent.* 13)

Πᾶσα δὴ βία τὴν γραφὴν κατὰ μικρὰ καὶ ἐπὶ Κωνστάντιον
φέρεσθαι καὶ τῶν ὑπ' ἐκείνου πραττομένων ἕκαστον ἀναγαγεῖν ἐπὶ
τοὺς καιροὺς καθ' οὓς ἐγίνετο καὶ συνέπιπτεν. τότε δὴ ὁ Κωνστάντιος ἐφ' οἷς <χαίρειν> ἔδει δυσφορῶν καὶ ὅσα ἔπραττεν Ἰουλιανὸς
ἔλεγχον τῆς ἰδίας βασιλείας ὑπολαμβάνων, τάς τε δηλουμένας ἐπι-    5
νικίους ἑορτὰς εἰς πένθος καὶ συμφορὰν μετέβαλλε καὶ διοιστρούμενος
ὑπὸ φθόνου καὶ λύσσης πρὸς τὸν ἐμφύλιον ἐξώγκωτο πόλεμον.

1 δὴ van Herwerden [δ' ἡ cod.    4 χαίρειν add. Niebuhr    ᾔδει Mai

## 20

1. (*Exc. de Sent.* 11)

Having reached this point, I should declare that now my History deals with the deeds of the Caesar and that these took place while Constantius was Emperor. Therefore, just as in the sections on Constantius, although the actions of both were mentioned, those of Constantius, as the more important character, received more space and emphasis in the narrative, so now, since the narrative deals with Julian from his birth to his promotion to Caesar, I shall describe again, as far as repetition is permissible and in their appropriate places, the plots which Constantius laid against the Caesar.

2. (*Vit. Soph.* 6,3,8)

To the care of Ablabius he [Constantine I] left his son Constantius, who had been co-ruler with him[38] and who shared his father's Empire with his brothers Constantine and Constans. These things I have set out in more detail in the part of my History on the most holy Julian.

3. (*Vit. Soph.* 7,1,6)

When all of his relatives had been destroyed by Constantius (as I have described in more detail in the sections of my History on Julian) and his family had been stripped of its property, Julian alone was left alive, being scorned because of his youth and his mild disposition.

4. (*Exc. de Sent.* 12)

The Roman Marius used to call his rival Sulla two wild beasts in one, a fox and a lion, and said that he feared the fox more. There was no lion by Constantius, but many foxes, circling around him and barking at the Caesar.[39]

5. (*Exc. de Sent.* 13)

It is absolutely necessary that for a short while the narrative turn to Constantius' court to recall each of the things that he did at the time when it occurred. Certainly, at that period Constantius was aggrieved at what he should have rejoiced over and he viewed Julian's achievements as a refutation of his own kingship. The Caesar's triumphs, as they were reported, he viewed as grievous misfortunes and, stung by jealousy and rage, he began to work himself up to civil war.[40]

(Zosimus 3,8)

## 21

1. (*Vit. Soph.* 7,3,8)

... τὸν ἱεροφάντην μετακαλέσας ἐκ τῆς Ἑλλάδος καὶ σὺν
ἐκείνῳ τινὰ μόνοις ἐκείνοις γνώριμα διαπραξάμενος, ἐπὶ τὴν καθ-
αίρεσιν ἠγέρθη τῆς Κωνσταντίου τυραννίδος. ταῦτα δὲ συνῄδεσαν
Ὀρειβάσιος ἐκ τοῦ Περγάμου, καί τις τῶν ἐκ Λιβύης, ἣν Ἀφρικὴν
καλοῦσι Ῥωμαῖοι κατὰ τὸ πάτριον τῆς γλώττης, Εὐήμερος. ταῦτα δὲ    5
πάλιν ἐν τοῖς κατὰ Ἰουλιανὸν βιβλίοις ἀκριβέστερον εἴρηται.

2. (*Vit. Soph.* 21,1,4)

Ἐκ μειρακίου δὲ ἐπιφανὴς γενόμενος, Ἰουλιανὸς μὲν αὐτὸν εἰς
τὸν Καίσαρα προϊὼν συνήρπασεν ἐπὶ τῇ τέχνῃ, ὁ δὲ τοσοῦτον ἐπλε-
ονέκτει ταῖς ἄλλαις ἀρεταῖς, ὥστε καὶ βασιλέα τὸν Ἰουλιανὸν
ἀπέδειξε· καὶ ταῦτά γε ἐν τοῖς κατ᾽ ἐκεῖνον ἀκριβέστερον εἴρηται.

1 post δὲ Giangrande add. οὕτω ex A²

3. (*Exc. de Sent.* 14)

Ἔοικε μὲν οὖν καὶ ἄλλως ὁ χρόνος ἐν ταῖς μακραῖς περιόδοις
καὶ κινήσεσι πολλάκις ἐπὶ τὰ αὐτὰ καταφέρεσθαι συμπτώματα,
καθάπερ οἵ τε Δαρείῳ συστάντες ἐπὶ τοὺς μάγους ἦσαν ἑπτὰ καὶ οἱ
πολλοῖς ὕστερον χρόνοις Ἀρσάκῃ κατὰ Μακεδόνων συνεγερθέντες
ἴσοι τὸν ἀριθμὸν ἔτυχον.    5

2 τὰ αὐτὰ cod. [τοιαῦτα edd.

(Zosimus 3,9,1-4)

## 22

(Zosimus 3,9,5 - 10,1)

## 23

1. (*Exc. de Sent.* 15)

Συνορῶσι δὲ ὅτι θερμότητος μὲν [καὶ] δεῖται καὶ ὁρμῆς τὸ
ἀσφαλές· τὸ γὰρ τῆς ἀνάγκης παρὰ πόδας <ἐστὸς> ἐπίσκεψιν
ἥκιστα ἐνδεχόμενον προχειρότερον ἀπαιτεῖ τὸν κίνδυνον.

1 καὶ exp. Mai    2 ἐστὸς add. Bekker

2. (*Exc. de Sent.* 16)

Ὅτι περὶ τῆς στρατείας τῆς κατὰ Δαρδάνων πολυτρόπου γενομένης ἐκτίθησι μὲν αὐτὸς Ἰουλιανός, ἄλλα δὲ ἀλλαχοῦ καὶ πρὸς

1 Δαρδάνων scripsi [Ναρδινῶν cod. Ἀλαμανῶν Bekker Ναρισκῶν Müller
Χονοδομαρίου Thompson

(Zosimus 3,8)

## 21

1. (*Vit. Soph.* 7,3,8)

Having summoned the hierophant from Greece and having performed with him certain rites known only to themselves, he gathered his strength to destroy the tyranny of Constantius. His fellow conspirators in this were Oribasius of Pergamum and a certain Euhemerus from Libya, which the Romans call Africa in their native tongue. But again these things have been described in more detail in the books of my History on Julian.

2. (*Vit. Soph.* 21,1,4)

From his youth [Oribasius] was famous, and Julian, when he was promoted to Caesar, carried him off to make use of his [medical] skill. But he had other virtues so outstanding that he actually made Julian Emperor. These things have been described in more detail in the sections of my History on Julian.[41]

3. (*Exc. de Sent.* 14)

Therefore, it also seems that as time passes, over long periods the same phenomena recur. Thus, those who conspired with Darius against the Magi numbered seven, and, at a much later time, those who rebelled with Arsaces against the Macedonians were the same in number.[42]

(Zosimus 3,9,1-4)

## 22

(Zosimus 3,9,5 - 10,1)

## 23

1. (*Exc. de Sent.* 15)

They observe that safety is guaranteed by commitment and speed of action. For Necessity, most impatient of leisurely planning, treads at the heels and calls danger still closer.[43]

2. (*Exc. de Sent.* 16)

Julian himself speaks about the much-travelled expedition down into Dardania, writing various things in different places in his letters to

πολλοὺς ἀναφράζων ἐν ἐπιστολαῖς . πρός τινα γοῦν Κυλλήνιον καὶ
ταῦτα ἐξηγούμενον τὰ μὲν ἐπιτιμῶν ὡς διαμαρτάνοντα τῆς ἀληθείας
φαίνεται, καὶ παρεκτίθησί γε τὰ πραχθέντα ὅπως γέγονε · φάσκων         5
δὲ μὴ δεῖσθαι τοῦ τὰ ἔργα λέγοντος (οὐδὲ γὰρ Παλαμήδην Ὁμήρου
προσδεηθῆναί φησιν εἰς δόξαν), καὶ τὰς ἀλλοτρίας συγγραφὰς τῶν
ἰδίων ἔργων ὑπὸ μεγαλοψυχίας παραιτούμενος, αὐτὸς ὅμως διὰ
μέγεθος τῶν πεπραγμένων πρὸς τὸ λέγειν αὐτὰ κατασειόμενος, οὐδὲ
συγγραφὴν ἁπλῆν, ἀλλ' ἔπαινον νεανικόν τινα καὶ λαμπρὸν ἑαυτοῦ     10
διέξεισιν αὐτοκέλευστος, καὶ πρὸς πολλοὺς αὐτὰ διὰ τῶν ἐπιστολῶν
ὑμνῶν.

8 τό post διὰ add. Boissevain    10 νεανικόν [ἱστορικόν Niebuhr ἀκριβῆ Müller

3. (Exc. de Sent. 17)
    Ὅτι κρατεῖν ὡς ἐπίπαν εἴωθεν ἐν μὲν τοῖς ἀπείροις τὸ πλέον,
ἐν δὲ τοῖς ἐπιστήμοσι τὸ γεγυμνασμένον · οὐ γὰρ ἐν τοῖς μετὰ τέχνης
ἀπαντᾷ τὸ παράλογον τῆς τύχης, ἀλλ' ἐν τοῖς ἀτέχνοις χώραν ἔχει τὸ
αὐτόματον, ὥσπερ κἂν ταῖς ἄλλαις ἐπιστήμαις ὁρῶμεν τὸ προτεθὲν
οὐχ ὑπὸ τῶν ἀπείρων, ἀλλ' ὑπὸ τῶν μελετησάντων ἐκτελούμενον.     5

4 προτεθὲν Niebuhr [προστεθὲν cod.

4. (Exc. de Sent. 18)
    Ὅτι πᾶν ἔργον κρεῖττον ἀπορρήτως στρατηγούμενον · ὅστις δὲ
ἐν πολέμῳ κρύπτει τὰ πλείονα, κρείττων ἐστὶν ἢ ὁ μετ' ἔργων
θρασύτητος φανερῶς ἐπιών.

(Zosimus 3,10,1 - 11,2)

## Liber IV
## 24

(Exc. de Leg. Gent. 3)
    Ὅτι μετὰ τὴν Ἰουλιανοῦ τῆς βασιλείας ἀναγόρευσιν πρεσβεῖαι
πανταχόθεν συνέβαινον καὶ στέφανοι πολλοὶ χρυσοῖ [οἳ] αὐτῷ παρὰ
τῶν ἐθνῶν ἀνεκομίζοντο. ἐνταῦθα καὶ οἱ τὴν Ἰωνίαν οἰκοῦντες
ἔτυχον ὅσων ἐδεήθησαν, καὶ πλειόνων ἢ ἐλασσόνων, Λυδοὶ δὲ καὶ
εὐχῆς κρεῖττον ἔπραττον, Εὐναπίου μὲν τοῦ ῥήτορος ὑπὲρ αὐτῶν       5
πρεσβεύοντος, εὐημερήσαντος δὲ οὕτω κατὰ τὴν πρεσβείαν ὥστε καὶ
δίκῃ τινὶ περιμαχήτῳ συνειπεῖν, ᾗ ὁ βασιλεὺς αὐτὸν ἐκέλευεν · ὁ δὲ
ἐνίκα καὶ τὴν δίκην. καὶ ἐκ Κλαζομενῶν δὲ Πείσων εὐδοκίμει λέγων.

2 οἳ add. Niebuhr

(Zosimus 3,11,2)

many people. Thus, writing to a certain Cyllenius, who was explaining these events, he both censures him for distorting the truth and describes what really happened. He says that his achievements do not lack one to report them, pointing out that Palamedes did not need Homer to gain him fame, and, in his pride, criticises others' accounts of his own deeds. Nevertheless, impelled to describe them himself by the greatness of what was done, he produces of his own accord not a simple narrative, but a high-spirited and brilliant encomium of himself. He also celebrates these things in his letters to many persons.[44]

3. (*Exc. de Sent.* 17)
    It is always the case that amongst ignorant people numbers prevail, whereas with the knowledgeable it is training. For those who have skill are not confronted by unforeseen happenings, whereas for the unskilled accidents infest the terrain, just as in other disciplines we observe the ignorant missing their goal and those who are practised achieving it.

4. (*Exc. de Sent.* 18)
    Every action is better planned by the generals in secret. In war whoever conceals more is stronger than one who is over-bold in his actions and makes his advance known to all.[45]

(Zosimus 3,10,1 - 11,2)

## Book IV
## 24

(*Exc. de Leg. Gent.* 3)
    After Julian had been proclaimed Augustus embassies came to him from everywhere, and many golden crowns were brought to him from the provinces. On that occasion the inhabitants of Ionia had all their requests granted both large or small, and the Lydians achieved more than they had sought. The latters' envoy was the rhetor Eunapius, and he was so successful with his embassy that, at the Emperor's command, he also spoke on behalf of a contentious lawsuit and won that too. Moreover, Piso from Clazomenae won fame for his speech.[46]

(Zosimus 3,11,2)

25

[1. (*Suda* I 437)

Ἐπὶ τὸν Ἰουλιανὸν πολλαὶ δίκαι ἐχώρουν, χανδὸν ἐμφορου-
μένων τῶν ἀνθρώπων τῆς δικαιοσύνης τοῦ κρίνοντος· ἀναβολαί τε
οὐκ ἦσαν ἐπ' αὐταῖς, ὅσαι νόμιμον ἐκ τῶν συνήθων γραμμάτων τὸ
ἄδικον ἴσχουσιν εἰς βοήθειαν τῶν ἀδικούντων καὶ προειληφότων·
ἀλλ' ἢ παραχρῆμα ἔδει τὸ ἴσον ἐλέγχεσθαι κατὰ φύσιν, ἢ τὸ μέλλον    5
καὶ διωθούμενον εἰς τὸν χρόνον ὕποπτον ἦν. βαρὺς μὲν οὖν καὶ
λυπηρὸς ἐτύγχανε, καὶ ἐπὶ τοῖσδε καὶ τὸ τῶν πονηρῶν ἔθνος καὶ
ἀδικούντων διηγείρετο· οὐ γὰρ ἀδικεῖν ἐξῆν, οὐδὲ λανθάνειν ἀδι-
κοῦσι. βαρύτερον δὲ αὐτὸν ἀπεδείκνυε τοῖς μοχθηροῖς καὶ τὸ εὐ-
πρόσοδον. οἷα γὰρ προϊόντος μὲν πολλάκις διὰ τὰς ἱερομηνίας καὶ    10
θυσίας, ἡμέρου δὲ φύσει πρὸς πᾶσαν ἔντευξιν τυγχάνοντος, ἀκώλυτον
τοὺς δεομένους λόγου τυχεῖν. ὁ μὲν οὖν ἐλάχιστον τῆς ὑπὸ τῶν
πονηρῶν ταύτης βλασφημίας τε καὶ ὀργῆς ἠσθάνετο καὶ ἐφρόντιζε.]

2. (*Vit. Soph.* 9,1,3)

Τουσκιανοῦ δὲ μνησθῆναι καλόν. καὶ γὰρ οὗτος ἐκείνου μετέσχε
τῆς ὁμιλίας, ἀλλὰ τούτου μὲν καὶ ἐν τοῖς κατὰ Ἰουλιανὸν ἐμνήσθημεν
διεξοδικοῖς.

3. (*Exc. de Sent.* 19)

Ὅτι <ὁ> κυνικὸς Ἡράκλειος ἀκροασόμενον ἐκάλει τὸν Ἰουλιανὸν ὡς ἐς τὴν βασιλείαν ὠφελήσων αὐτόν. ὁ δὲ θαυμάσας τὸ τῆς
ὑποσχέσεως ὕψος ἑτοίμως ὑπήκουσεν. ἐπεὶ δὲ παρὰ δόξαν ἀπήν-
τησεν, ὁ Ἰουλιανὸς ἀντιγράψας λόγον τὴν ἑαυτοῦ δύναμιν ἐξέφηνε
καὶ τὸ τῆς φύσεως ἀνυπέρβλητον. οἱ δὲ ἀκούσαντες καταπλαγέντες    5
τὴν δύναμιν τοῦ λόγου καθάπερ θεοῦ προσεκύνησαν τὴν φιλανθρω-
πίαν, ὅτι τὸν βασιλικὸν θυμὸν διέλυσε λογικῇ φιλοτιμίᾳ. ὁ δὲ καὶ
ἑτέρῳ λόγῳ τὸν αὐτὸν κυνικὸν ἐτίμησεν.

1 ὁ add. Dindorf    Ἡράκλειος Mai (cf. *Fr.* 34,3) [Ἡράκλειτος cod.

4. (*Suda* Υ 175)

Εὐνάπιος· Μάξιμός τε καὶ Πρίσκος λόγου μὲν μετεχέτην, τῆς
δὲ τῶν κοινῶν καὶ ὑπαίθρων πραγμάτων πείρας ἐλάχιστον.

[5. (*Suda* Σ 63)

Ὅτι Σαλούστιος, ὁ τῆς αὐλῆς ἔπαρχος ἐπὶ Ἰουλιανοῦ, ἀνὴρ
ἦν διαφερόντως περιττὸς εἰς φιλανθρωπίαν· ᾧ γε τοσοῦτον ἡμερό-
τητος καὶ πραότητος ὑπῆρχεν εἰς ἅπαντας, ὥστε καὶ τὸν Μάρκελλον

## 25

[1. (*Suda* I 437)

Many lawsuits were brought before Julian, because men eagerly enjoyed his fairness as a judge. There were no deferrals granted on those grounds which, using the usual rescripts to confer legality upon an injustice, help those who have illegally taken prior possession of another's property. But either the natural justice of the case had to be proven immediately or an attempt for deferral to a future date was regarded with suspicion. Therefore he was a harsh and grievous judge, and the tribe of villains and criminals was agitated by these things. For they were not permitted to commit wrong, and, if they did, they did not escape punishment. Moreover, his accessibility was even more troublesome for evil-doers. For instance, since he often went out amongst the public during festivals and sacrifices, and since he was naturally affable to all whom he met, those who needed to speak with him could do so unhindered. He took very little notice of, or thought for, the angry curses of the wrongdoers which resulted from this practice.] [47]

2. (*Vit. Soph.* 9,1,3)

It is proper that mention be made of Tuscianus, since he, too, was one of the group around [Julian of Cappadocia]. But I have already remarked him in the narrative on [the Emperor] Julian in my History.[48]

3. (*Exc. de Sent.* 19)

The Cynic Heracleius invited Julian to attend his lecture, saying that he would help Julian as Emperor. Julian was amazed at this high promise and readily went to hear him. But when his expectations were disappointed, he wrote a speech against Heracleius demonstrating his own powers and his unsurpassed natural gifts. Those who listened to the speech were awed by its power and they worshipped his clemency as if it were divine, in that he had sated his royal anger by taking revenge in a speech. Julian punished the same Cynic in another speech also.[49]

4. (*Suda* Υ 175)

Maximus and Priscus both had their share of wisdom, but very little experience of politics and public affairs.

[5. (*Suda* Σ 63)

Salustius, the pretorian prefect [of the East] under Julian, was a man of outstanding and remarkable clemency. He was so kindly and merciful to all that when that Marcellus, who had behaved so high-

ἐκεῖνον, τόν, ἡνίκα ἦν Καῖσαρ, ὑβριστικῶς αὐτῷ χρησάμενον, πάνυ
περιδεᾶ ὄντα διὰ τὰ προγεγενημένα, καίτοι τοῦ παιδὸς ἐλεγχθέντος    5
ἐπανίστασθαι διὰ τὴν πρὸς Κωνστάντιον φιλίαν, τῷ νεανίσκῳ τὴν
δίκην ἐπέθηκε, τὸν δὲ Μάρκελλον καὶ διαφερόντως ἐτίμησε.
(Cf. Π 1326)]

(Zosimus 3,11,3)

## 26

1. (*Vit. Soph.* 16,1,9)
Μνήμην μὲν οὖν αὐτῷ τὴν πρέπουσαν κἀν τοῖς βιβλίοις τοῖς
κατὰ τὸν Ἰουλιανὸν ἡ γραφὴ πεποίηται, τὰ δὲ καθ᾽ ἕκαστον νῦν
ἐπεξελεύσεται.

[2. (*Suda* Λ 486)
Ὁ δὲ Ἰουλιανὸς καίπερ τοσούτοις ἐμβεβηκώς, τῆς τε περὶ
λόγους ἥπτετο φιλοτιμίας, καὶ τὸν τῆς Ἀντιοχείας σοφιστήν, ᾧ
Λιβάνιος ὄνομα, διαφερόντως ἐθαύμασε, τὰ μὲν ἴσως ἐπαινῶν, τὰ δὲ
ὅπως λυποίη τὸν μέγαν σοφιστὴν Προαιρέσιον, προτιμῶν ἕτερον.
Ἀκάκιος γοῦν τις αὐτῷ τῶν περὶ τὴν ῥητορικὴν δεινῶν καὶ ὁ ἐκ    5
Φρυγίας Τουσκιανὸς ἀεὶ πρὸς ταῦτα ἐπεκάλουν καὶ διεμέμφοντο τὰς
κρίσεις.    (Cf. A 784, Π 2375, T 835)]

(Zosimus 3,11,3-5)

## Liber V
## 27

1. (*Exc. de Sent.* 20)
Ὅτι τῷ Ἰουλιανῷ ἤκμαζεν ὁ πρὸς Πέρσας πόλεμος, τάς τε
Σκυθικὰς κινήσεις ὥσπερ ἐν κωφῷ κρυπτομένας ἔτι κύματι συνετίθει πόρρωθεν ἢ θεοκλυτῶν ἢ λογιζόμενος. λέγει οὖν ἐπιστέλλων,
"Σκύθαι δὲ νῦν μὲν ἀτρεμοῦσιν, ἴσως δὲ οὐκ ἀτρεμήσουσιν". ἐς
τοσόνδε ἐξικνεῖτο χρόνον ἡ τῶν μελλόντων αὐτῷ πρόνοια ὥσθ᾽ ὅτι    5
τὸν ἐπ᾽ αὐτοῦ μόνον καιρὸν ἡσυχάσουσι προγινώσκειν.

2-3 συνετίθει [συνενόει Boissevain

2. (*Suda* Οι 183)
Εὐνάπιος· οἱ δὲ τῶν Πάρθων οἰσυΐνας ἀσπίδας ἔχοντες καὶ
κράνη οἴσυϊνα πλοκήν τινα πάτριον πεπλεγμένα.

3. (*Exc. de Sent.* 21)
Ὅτι <τὸ> πρὸ Κτησιφῶντος πεδίον ὀρχήστραν πολέμου

1 τὸ add. Niebuhr

handedly towards him when he had been Caesar, was now altogether panic-striken over what he had done, although his son had been proven guilty of plotting rebellion as a supporter of Constantius, while condemning the young man to death, he honoured Marcellus highly.[50] (Cf. Π 1326)]

(Zosimus 3,11,3)

### 26

1. (*Vit. Soph.* 16,1,9)

Although the books on Julian in my History offered a fitting notice on [Libanius], I shall now run through his career in detail.

[2. (*Suda* Λ 486)

Julian, although he was busy with such important matters, had a strong desire for a reputation as a speaker. He expressed great admiration for the Antiochene sophist, Libanius. On the one hand, his praise was perhaps genuine, but, on the other, his purpose was to grieve the great sophist Prohaeresius by expressing preference for another. At any rate, Acacius, a man skilled in rhetoric, and the Phrygian Tuscianus always accused him of this and criticised his opinions.
(Cf. A 784, Π 2375, T 835)]

(Zosimus 3,11,3-5)

### Book V
### 27

1. (*Exc. de Sent.* 20)

In the middle of his war with the Persians Julian, either as a result of asking the gods or by using his own reasoning, foresaw from afar the Scythian disturbances, which were still concealed, as it were, in murky water. He says to someone in a letter, "The Scythians are now quiet, perhaps they will not remain quiet". His foreknowledge reached so far into the future that he knew that they would only keep quiet during his time.[51]

2. (*Suda* Οι 183)

Some of the Parthians, having wicker shields and helmets woven after the native fashion . . ..[52]

3. (*Exc. de Sent.* 21)

Having made the plain before Ctesiphon a dance-floor of war, to

πρότερον ἀποδείξας, ὡς ἔλεγεν Ἐπαμινώνδας, Διονύσου σκηνὴν
ἐπεδείκνυ Ἰουλιανός, ἀνέσεις τινὰς τοῖς στρατιώταις καὶ ἡδονὰς
ποριζόμενος.

[4. *(Suda Γ 484)*
Ὁ δὲ Ἰουλιανὸς ἐν Πέρσαις ὢν γυμνικοὺς ἀγῶνας ἦγε.
*(Cf. E 322, H 45)*]

5. *(Exc. de Sent. 22)*
Ὅτι τοσαύτη ἐν τοῖς προαστείοις Κτησιφῶντος ἀφθονία τῶν
ἐπιτηδείων ἦν ὥστε τὴν περιουσίαν κίνδυνον τοῖς στρατιώταις
φέρειν μήποτε ὑπὸ τρυφῆς διαφθαρῶσιν.

6. *(Exc. de Sent. 23)*
Ὅτι ἔοικε τὸ ἀνθρώπινον καὶ ἄλλως ἐπίφορον εἶναι καὶ
κάταντες πρὸς τὸ βάσκανον. καὶ οἱ στρατιῶται οὐκ ἔχοντες ὅπως
ἐπαινῶσιν ἀξίως τὰ πραττόμενα, "τοὺς Ἀχαιούς" φασώ "ἔκρινον
ἀπὸ τοῦ πύργου", στρατηγικός τις καὶ περιττὸς εἰς φρόνησιν ἕκαστος
εἶναι βουλόμενοι. καὶ τοῖς μὲν ὕλη τις ὑπῆν φλυαρίας· ὁ δὲ τῶν ἐξ      5
ἀρχῆς ἐχόμενος λογισμῶν ἐπὶ τὴν οἰκείαν ἀνέστρεφεν.

3 φασίν Niebuhr [φησί cod.

[7. *(Suda I 437)*
Ἔστι δὲ καὶ ὁ χρησμὸς ὁ δοθεὶς αὐτῷ, ὅτε περὶ Κτησιφῶντα
διῆγεν·
Γηγενέων ποτὲ φῦλον ἐνήρατο μητίετα Ζεύς,
ἔχθιστον μακάρεσσιν Ὀλύμπια δώματ' ἔχουσι.
Ῥωμαίων βασιλεύς, Ἰουλιανὸς θεοειδής,      5
μαρνάμενος Περσῶν πόλιας καὶ τείχεα μακρὰ
ἀγχεμάχων διέπερσε πυρὶ κρατερῷ τε σιδήρῳ,
νωλεμέως δὲ δάμασσε καὶ ἔθνεα πολλὰ καὶ ἄλλα,
ὅρρα καὶ ἑσπερίων ἀνδρῶν Ἀλαμανικὸν οὖδας
ὑσμίναις πυκιναῖσιν ἑλὼν ἀλάπαξεν ἀρούρας.      10
*(Cf. Anth. Pal. 14,148)*]

8. *(Suda I 311)*
Εὐνάπιος· τότε δὲ ἴλη τῶν καταφράκτων ἱππέων ὑπὲρ τοὺς
υ΄ ἐς τοὺς ὀπισθοφύλακας κατερράγη.

*(Zosimus 3,19-29)*

## 28

1. *(Exc. de Sent. 24)*
Ὥσπερ δὲ ἐν πολέμῳ καὶ τοσούτων ἐπικειμένων ἄρχοντος
δεόμενον τὸ στρατόπεδον τὴν αἵρεσιν περιεσκόπει. καὶ καθάπερ

use Epaminondas' phrase, Julian then put on a Dionysian scene, providing the soldiers with relaxation and enjoyment.[53]

[4. (*Suda* Γ 484)
Julian, while in Persia, gave athletic games.[54]
(Cf. E 322, H 45)]

5. (*Exc. de Sent.* 22)
The great abundance of supplies in the suburbs of Ctesiphon raised the danger that the soldiers would be ruined by excess.

6. (*Exc. de Sent.* 23)
It seems, besides, that mankind is prone to envy. The soldiers, not having the wherewithal to give due praise to what was being done, "Judged the Achaeans", as they say, "from the tower", each wishing to seem a man of strategy and extraordinary wisdom; and they found evidence to support their foolishness. But he, holding to the calculations which he had made at the beginning, turned back towards home territory.[55]

[7. (*Suda* I 437)
There is also the oracle which was given to him in the neighbourhood of Ctesiphon:
"Once all-wise Zeus slew the race of the Earth-born
Most hateful to the blessed gods who live on Olympus.
The king of the Romans, god-like Julian,
Warring at close quarters with the cities of the Persians
And their long walls, has destroyed them with fire
And strong steel, and has ceaselessly conquered
Many tribes and others. And often in battles
Seizing the lands of the men of the West,
He has ravaged the fertile fields of the Alamanni."
(Cf. *Anth. Pal.* 14,148)]

8. (*Suda* I 311)
Then a squadron of heavy cavalry over four hundred strong crashed into the rearguard.[56]

(Zosimus 3,19-29)

## 28

1. (*Exc. de Sent.* 24)
Since the army, in the middle of a war and confronted by such grave dangers, needed a leader, they began to consider their choice. Just

<οἵ> ἰατρικοί φασι καταδήλων γενομένων δυεῖν ἀλγημάτων τὸ
ἔλαττον ὑπὸ τοῦ σφοδροτέρου λύεσθαι, οὕτω καὶ τότε θεωρεῖν ἐξῆν
ὡς τὴν ὑπεροχὴν τοῦ κατὰ τὸν βασιλέα πάθους ὁ τοῦ πολέμου φόβος     5
παρὰ πόδας ἑστὼς καταμαραίνων ἀπήμβλυνεν. τὸ μὲν γὰρ γεγενημένον ἦν φανερόν, τὸ δὲ ὅπως εἴκαζε μὲν ἄλλος ἄλλως, ἠπίστατο
δὲ οὐδὲ εἷς. πλὴν ἐν τοῦτό γε ᾔδεσαν ὡς αἱρεῖσθαι προσῆκέν σφισιν
ἄρχοντα. εἰ δὲ καὶ πλῆθος ἦσαν, τοῦτο γοῦν ἠπίσταντο σαφῶς ὅτι
ἄρχοντος μὲν εὐπορήσουσι, τοιοῦτον δέ, οὐδὲ εἰ πλάττοι θεός, εὑ-     10
ρήσουσιν, ὅς γε διὰ φύσεως ἐξουσίαν καὶ τὸ ἰσομέγεθες τῷ θείῳ
ἀγωγῆς τε ἀνάγκην ἐξεβιάσατο πρὸς τὸ χεῖρον ἕλκουσαν, καὶ ἐκ
τοσούτων ἀνενεγκὼν κυμάτων οὐρανόν τε εἶδε καὶ ἐπέγνω τὰ ἐν
αὐτῷ καλά, τοῖς τε ἀσωμάτοις ὡμίλησε σῶμα ἔχων ἔτι, καὶ βασιλείας τε ἔτυχεν οὐχ ὅτι καὶ ἦρα βασιλείας, ἀλλ' ὅτι τὸ ἀνθρώπειον     15
ἑώρα δεομένους βασιλεύεσθαι, φιλοστρατιώτης τε ἦν διαφερόντως,
οὐχ ὅτι ἐβούλετο δημαγωγεῖν, ἀλλ' ὅτι τοῦτο ἠπίστατο τοῖς κοινοῖς
συμφέρειν.

3 καταδήλων Niebuhr     [καταδύτων Mai     κατὰ ταὐτὸν van Herwerden
κατα . . . ὼν legit Boissevain     9 ἄρχοντα Boissevain [ἄρχοντας cod.

## 2. (Exc. de Sent. 25)

Ὅτι πρὸς τὸν Ὀριβάσιον εἰπόντα ὡς οὐ χρὴ τὸν θυμόν, κἂν
ἐπεισπέσῃ, διὰ τῶν ὀμμάτων καὶ τῆς φωνῆς ἐκφορεῖσθαι, "ὅρα
τοίνυν" εἶπεν "ἐπειδὴ καλῶς λέγεις, εἰ τοῦτο ἐγκαλέσεις ἔτι
δεύτερον".

2 ἐπεισίῃ edd.

## 3. (Exc. de Sent. 26)

Ὅτι φασὶν Ἀλεξάνδρου θειάζοντος ἑαυτὸν ἐκ Διὸς Ὀλυμπιάδα
θρυπτομένην φάσκειν, "οὐ παύσεται τὸ μειράκιον διαβάλλον με πρὸς
τὴν Ἥραν;"

## 4. (Exc. de Sent. 27)

Ὅτι προσαγορεύων ὁ θεὸς τὸν Ἰουλιανόν φησιν,
ὦ τέκος ἀρμελάταο θεοῦ, μεδέοντος ἀπάντων.

## 5. (Exc. de Sent. 28)

Ὅτι ὁ Ἰουλιανὸς ἐν ταῖς ἐπιστολαῖς ἴδιον <πατέρα> ἀνακαλεῖ
τὸν ἥλιον, οὐχ ὥσπερ Ἀλέξανδρος διαβάλλεσθαι φάσκων πρὸς τὴν
Ἥραν ὅτι Ὀλυμπιὰς αὐτὸν ἐκ Διὸς ἀνελομένη τοῦτο οὐκ ἀπεκρύ-
πτετο, ἀλλ' οὗτός γε ἐπὶ ταῖς τοῦ θεοῦ μαρτυρίαις αἰωρούμενος ἐς
τὸν Πλάτωνα ὑποφέρεται, ὥσπερ ὁ ἐκείνου Σωκράτης φησί "μετὰ     5

1 πατέρα add. Mai     2 διαβάλλεται edd.

as, according to doctors, when two pains appear the lesser is eased by
the worse, so then, too, one could observe how fear of the enemy, who
was at their heels, weakened and dulled the enormous grief they felt for
their Emperor. What had happened was clear. How it happened, there
were various theories; no one knew. But this one thing they knew, that
they had to choose a leader. Even though they were an ignorant mob,
they at least realised clearly that though they would have plenty of
leaders they would not find an equal of Julian, even if God created one
for them. For he, through the strength of his personality and his
stature, as great as that of God, extirpated from himself that governing
force of life which drags men down and, raising himself up from deep,
deep waters, beheld the heavens and the beauty therein and, though
himself clothed in flesh, held converse with the incorporeal spirits.
He became Emperor not because he really lusted after kingship but
because he observed that mankind needed a ruler; and he was exceedingly solicitous for his soldiers not because he sought common
popularity but because he knew that this was to the advantage of the
state.[57]

## 2. (*Exc. de Sent.* 25)

Oribasius said to him that even if he felt anger he should not
show it in his eyes or his voice, to which Julian replied, "You are right.
See if you will have to criticise me again".[58]

## 3. (*Exc. de Sent.* 26)

They say that when Alexander proclaimed that he was Zeus' son,
Olympias quailed and said, "Will this boy not stop slandering me before
Hera?"

## 4. (*Exc. de Sent.* 27)

They say that the god spoke thus to Julian:
  "O child of the charioteer god, ruler of all".

## 5. (*Exc. de Sent.* 28)

Julian in his letters calls the Sun his own father, not in the sense
that Alexander made his false claim, saying to Hera that Olympias,
having conceived him of Zeus, did not conceal the fact. But, relying
upon the evidence of the god, he looks towards Plato and says, like
Plato's Socrates, "We are with Zeus, others are with another god".

μὲν Διὸς ἡμεῖς, ἄλλοι <δὲ> μετ᾽ ἄλλου του θεῶν᾽᾽, ταύτην καὶ
αὐτὸς εἰς τὴν ἡλιακὴν βασιλείαν τινὰ καὶ χρυσῆν σειρὰν ἀναφέρων
καὶ συναπτόμενος.

6. δὲ add. Niebuhr e Plat. *Phaedr.* 250B

### 6. (*Exc. de Sent.* 29)

Ἀλλ᾽ ὁπότε σκήπτροισι τεοῖς Περσήιον αἷμα
ἄχρι Σελευκείης κλονέων ξιφέεσσι δαμάσσης,
δὴ τότε σὲ πρὸς Ὄλυμπον ἄγει πυριλαμπὲς ὄχημα
ἀμφὶ θυελλείῃσι κυκώμενον ἐν στροφάλιγξι,
λυσάμενον βροτέων ῥεθέων πολύτλητον ἀνίην.        5
ἥξεις δ᾽ αἰθερίου φάεος πατρώιον αὐλήν,
ἔνθεν ἀποπλαγχθεὶς μεροπήιον ἐς δέμας ἦλθες.

τούτοις ἀρθέντα τοῖς ἔπεσιν αὐτὸν καὶ λογίοις μάλα ἡδέως φησὶν
ἀπολιπεῖν τὸ θνητὸν καὶ ἐπίκαιρον. πρόκεινται δὲ τῶν λογίων ἄλλαι
τινὲς εὐχαί τε καὶ θυσίαι περὶ τοὺς θεούς, ἃς ἐκείνῳ μὲν δρᾶν ἀναγ-        10
καῖον ἦν ἴσως, ἐς δὲ ἱστορικὸν τύπον καὶ βάρος φέρειν οὐκ ἦν εὔ-
λογον· τὸ γὰρ καθ᾽ ἕκαστα <γράφειν> οὐκ ἦν ἀλήθειαν τιμῶντος,
ἀλλὰ διὰ πολυπραγμοσύνην εἰς λῆρον ἀποφερομένου καὶ παρολισ-
θάνοντος. (Cf. *Suda* I 437)

1 ὁπόταν Suda I 437        4 θυελλίῃσι Suda    στροφάλιγξι Suda
[στροφαλιξι Exc.    5 λυσάμενον [ῥίψαντα Suda    ῥεθέων Suda [ῥοθέων Exc.
9 ἐπίκαιρον [ἐπίκηρον Dindorf        12 γράφειν add. Niebuhr

### 7. (*Vit. Soph.* 7,4,10)

Ὡς δὲ τὰ πράγματα συντόνως ἀπὸ τῶν μεγάλων ἐκείνων καὶ
λαμπρῶν ἐλπίδων ἐς τὸ ἀφανὲς καὶ ἄμορφον κατερράγη καὶ διω-
λίσθησεν, ὡς ἐν τοῖς διεξοδικοῖς τοῖς κατὰ Ἰουλιανὸν εἴρηται . . . .

2 κατερράγη codd. [κατερρύη Cobet

(Zosimus 3,29,1 - 30,1)

## 29

[1. (*Suda* I 401)

Οὗτος μετὰ Ἰουλιανὸν ἦρξεν· ὃς ἡνίκα Ἰουλιανὸς αἵρεσιν τοῖς
στρατευομένοις ἐτίθει, θύειν ἢ ἀποστρατεύεσθαι, μᾶλλον τὴν ζώνην
ἀποθέσθαι ἐβούλετο. ἐλθὼν δὲ ἐς Νίσιβιν πόλιν πολυάνθρωπον δύο
μόνον ἡμερῶν ἐνδιατρίψας αὐτῇ, ὅσα περ εἶχε χρήματα κατανάλωσε
τοῖς ἐνοικοῦσι μηδενὸς μεταδοὺς ἢ λόγου φιλανθρώπου ἢ πράξεως        5
ἀγαθῆς· ἄνθρωπος οὐ δι᾽ ἀρετὴν οἰκείαν, ἀλλὰ διὰ τὴν τοῦ πατρὸς
δόξαν ἐς τοσοῦτον ἀρχῆς προελθών. ἦν μὲν γὰρ οὐδὲ παντάπασιν
ἀσθενὴς τὸ σῶμα οὔτε πολεμικοῖς ἔργοις ἀγύμναστος· ἀμελέτητος
δὲ ὢν καὶ ἄγευστος παιδεύσεως, καὶ ἦν εἶχε φύσιν διὰ ῥαθυμίαν

This is the golden chain which he casts up and attaches to the kingdom of the Sun.[59]

6. (*Exc. de Sent.* 29)

"But having driven the Persian race headlong with your
Back to Seleucia conquered by your sword,        [sceptre
A fire-bright chariot whirled amidst storm-clouds
Shall take you to Olympus freed from your body
And the much-enduring misery of man.
Then you shall come to your father's halls
of heavenly light, from which you wandered
Into a human frame of mortality."

They say that, elated by these words and their prophecy, he most eagerly abandoned this mortal and transitory existence. This prophecy was preceded by certain other prayers and sacrifices to the gods, which it was perhaps necessary for him to perform, but which are not appropriate for inclusion in a serious formal history. For to include every detail is not the action of one who respects the truth, but of one who is carried away by idle curiosity and slips into empty prattle.[60]
(Cf. *Suda* I 437)

7. (*Vit. Soph.* 7,4,10)

But when the expedition after its high and bright hopes suddenly collapsed into obscurity and shapelessness and slipped away, as I have described in the narrative on Julian in my History . . ..

(Zosimus 3,29,1 - 30,1)

## 29

[1. (*Suda* I 401)

He [Jovian] reigned after Julian. When Julian gave the soldiers the choice of sacrificing to the gods or leaving the army, he preferred to resign.[61] Coming to Nisibis, a rich and populous city, he remained there only for two days, using up all its resources and having neither a kindly word nor a good deed for the inhabitants.[62] He was a man who had been made Emperor not as a result of his own qualities but because of the reputation of his father. For although he was not wholly lacking in bodily strength or experience in war, he was untrained and uneducated, and by his laziness he obscured and impaired what natural

ἡμαύρου καὶ ἠράνιζεν. οὗτος μετὰ Ἰουλιανόν, ὡς εἴρηται, τῆς    10
Ῥωμαίων βασιλείας ἐγκρατὴς γενόμενος, πάντων καταφρονήσας
ἐσπούδαξε τοῦ συμβάντος αὐτῷ ἀξιώματος ἀπολαῦσαι, καὶ φεύγων
ἐκ Περσίδος ἔσπευδε γενέσθαι τῶν Ῥωμαϊκῶν ἐθῶν ἐντὸς εἰς
ἐπίδειξιν τῆς τύχης, καὶ τὴν Νίσιβιν πόλιν τοῖς Πέρσαις, πάλαι
Ῥωμαίοις οὖσαν κατήκοον, ἐκδίδωσιν. ἀπέσκωπτον οὖν αὐτὸν ᾠδαῖς    15
καὶ παρῳδίαις καὶ τοῖς καλουμένοις φαμώσσοις, διὰ τὴν τῆς Νισί-
βιδος προδοσίαν. ὁ δὲ Ἰοβιανός, ἐκ τῆς γυναικὸς αὐτοῦ κινηθεὶς τὸν
ὑπὸ Ἀδριανοῦ τοῦ βασιλέως κτισθέντα ναὸν χαριέστατον ἐς ἀπο-
θέωσιν τοῦ πατρὸς Τραϊανοῦ, παρὰ δὲ τοῦ Ἰουλιανοῦ κατασταθέντα
βιβλιοθήκην εὐνούχῳ τινὶ Θεοφίλῳ, κατέφλεξε σὺν πᾶσιν οἷς εἶχε    20
βιβλίοις, αὐτῶν τῶν παλλακίδων ὑφαπτουσῶν μετὰ γέλωτος τὴν
πυράν. οἱ δὲ Ἀντιοχεῖς ἠγανάκτησαν κατὰ τοῦ βασιλέως . . . καὶ τὰ
μὲν ἀπέρριπτον τῶν βιβλίων ἐς τὸ ἔδαφος, ὥστε ἀναίρεσθαι τὸν
βουλόμενον καὶ ἀναγινώσκειν, τὰ δὲ τοῖς τοίχοις προσεκόλλιξον.
ἦν δὲ τοιαῦτα· ἤλυθες ἐκ πολέμου, ὡς ὤφελες αὐτόθ᾽ ὀλέσθαι· καί,    25
Δύσπαρι, εἶδος ἄριστε· καὶ τὰ ἑξῆς. καί, εἰ μὴ ἐγώ σε λαβὼν ἀπὸ
μὲν φίλα εἵματα δύσω, χλαῖνάν τ᾽ ἠδὲ χιτῶνα, τά τ᾽ αἰδῶ ἀμφι-
καλύπτει, αὐτὸν δὲ κλαίοντα θοῶς ἐπὶ Πέρσας ἀφήσω. γραῦς δέ τις
μέγαν καὶ καλὸν αὐτὸν θεασαμένη μαθοῦσά τε ἀνόητον εἶναι ἐφθέγ-
ξατο· ὅσον μῆκος καὶ βάθος ἡ μωρία. καὶ ἄλλος δὲ ἰδιώτης ἀπο-    30
τολμήσας, μεγάλῃ τῇ φωνῇ βοήσας ἐν τῷ ἱπποδρομίῳ γέλωτα
παρέσχε πᾶσιν εἰπὼν κενὰ καὶ ψυχρὰ τῇ ἡλικίᾳ αὐτοῦ. καὶ ἐπράχθη
ἂν ἄτοπα, εἰ μὴ Σαλούστιός τις ἔπαυσε τὴν στάσιν. ὁ δὲ Ἰοβιανὸς
χειμῶνος ὄντος ὡδοιπόρει ἐπὶ Κιλικίαν καὶ Γαλατίαν καὶ ἐν Δαδαστάνοις ἀπέθανε μύκητα πεφαρμαγμένον φαγών. κατὰ δὲ τὴν ἡγε-    35
μονίαν κοινὸς καὶ ἐλευθέριος ἔδοξεν εἶναι.
(Cf. Φ 64; John of Antioch *Fr*. 181 = *Exc. de Virt*. 63)]
22 lacunam indicavi

[2. (*Suda* M 1306)
    Μουσώνιος, ἐπὶ Ἰοβιανοῦ ἦν βασιλέως. πάντα, ὅσα ἦν ἄριστα,
μικρὰ ἐφαίνετο πρὸς τὸν ὄγκον Μουσωνίου καὶ τὴν σὺν τῷ δραστηρίῳ
τῆς γνώμης βαθύτητα· δι᾽ ἃ κατὰ λόγον εὐδοκιμῶν τήν τε ἀλιτενῆ
χώραν τῆς Ἀσίας ἐπῆλθε, καὶ ὁ τὴν ἀνθύπατον καὶ μείζονα ἔχων
ἀρχὴν πρὸς τὰς ἐπιδημίας ἐξίστατο, κἀκεῖνος ἅπαντα ἐπιὼν ἐν    5
ὀλίγαις ἡμέραις τὴν θάλασσαν ἐπλήρωσε τῶν ἀπὸ τῆς Ἀσίας
εἰσφορῶν. ἐπεκάλει δὲ οὐδεὶς ἄδικον οὐδὲν τοῖς γινομένοις· ἀλλὰ
παιδιά τις ἦν ἅπασι τοῖς καταβάλλουσι τὰ εἰσφερόμενα· Εὐνάπιος
γὰρ ὁ ἐκ Φρυγίας ῥήτωρ ἐπεστάτει τοῖς πραττομένοις.]

(Zosimus 3,30,2 - 35,3)

talent he had. When, as I have said, he became Emperor of the Romans after Julian, ignoring everything else in his eagerness to enjoy the rank that had devolved upon him, he fled from Persia,[63] hurried to reach the Roman provinces in order to publicise his elevation, and handed over to the Persians the city of Nisibis, which had long been subject to the Romans. Therefore, they[64] mocked him in ditties, parodies and in the so-called *famosi* (lampoons) because of the abandonment of Nisibis. Hadrian the Emperor had built a beautiful temple for the worship of his father Trajan, which at Julian's orders the eunuch Theophilus had made into a library. Jovian, at the urging of his wife, burned the temple with all the books in it, his concubines laughing and setting the fire. The Antiochians were angered at the Emperor . . .[65] and some of the pamphlets they threw on the ground so that whoever wished could pick them up and read them, others they pasted up on walls. These said such things as, "You came back from the war. You should have perished there", and, "Ill-omened Paris, most handsome to look at", and so on, including, "If I do not take you and strip your clothes from you, your cloak and your tunic, which hide your shame, and send you off in haste wailing to the land of the Persians".[66] A certain old woman, observing that he was tall and handsome, but learning that he was stupid, declared, "How high and deep is folly". In the hippodrome to the amusement of all, another daring individual shouted out empty and insipid remarks about his age, and trouble would have ensued had not a certain Salustius[67] stopped the disturbance. Although it was winter, Jovian took to the road to Cilicia and Galatia and died at Dadastana after eating a poisoned mushroom.[68] As a leader he seems to have been affable and open-handed.
(Cf. Φ 64; John of Antioch *Fr.* 181 = *Exc. de Virt.* 63)]


[2. (*Suda* M 1306)
    Musonius, during the reign of the Emperor Jovian. Everything that was best seemed diminished by comparison with the profundity and liveliness of his thought. Therefore, since he was justifiably esteemed, he came to the coastal region of Asia, and the proconsul, though he was the senior, stood aside for Musonius to make the official visits. Musonius went to every place and within a few days filled the sea with the contributions from Asia. No one alleged injustice against what was happening, but all who paid the contributions found them child's play. The rhetor Eunapius the Phrygian oversaw the transactions.[69]]

(Zosimus 3,30,2 - 35,3)

48    *Eunapius: Text*

## Liber VI
## 30
(*Exc. de Sent.* 30)
Ὅτι φησὶν ὁ Εὐνάπιος· περὶ μὲν οὖν τῶν παλαιοτέρων καὶ ὅσα πρὸ ἡμῶν ἀνάγκη συγχωρεῖν τοῖς γράψασιν ἢ τοῖς περὶ ἐκείνων λόγοις εἰς ἡμᾶς κατὰ μνήμην ἄγραφον εἰς διαδοχὴν περιφερομένοις καὶ καθήκουσιν· ὅσα δὲ ἐφ᾽ ἡμῶν αὐτῶν γέγονεν, ἀλήθειαν τιμῶντι, καθά φησιν ὁ Πλάτων, παραδοτέον τοῖς ἐντυγχάνουσιν.          5

2 περὶ Niebuhr [πρὸ cod.

## 31
1. (*Exc. de Leg. Gent.* 4)
Ὅτι Βαλεντινιανοῦ ἀνάρρησις ἐν Νικαίᾳ τῆς Βιθυνίας γίνεται, πρεσβεῖαί τε ὅσαι συνεπεφοιτήκεσαν ἐπὶ τοῦτον τοὺς χρυσοῦς ἔχουσαι στεφάνους πρὸς ἐκεῖνον ἀνεφέροντο. καὶ πρὸς πάσας ἀπεφαίνετο μὲν οὐδὲν ἐπιτρέχων ῥᾳδίως οὑτωσὶ καὶ συντόμως, ἐπηγγέλλετο δὲ ἅπασιν ὡς ποιήσων αὐτίκα μάλα.          5

2 τοῦτον codd. [τοῦτο de Boor          4 ἐπηγγέλλετο Niebuhr [ἀπήγγελλέ τι codd. ἐπηγγέλλετό τι de Boor, ἐπηγγέλλετο ... ὥς τι Müller

(Zosimus 3,36,1 - 4,1,1)

## 32
(Zosimus 4,1,1 - 2,2)

## 33
(Zosimus 4,2,2 - 3,5)

## 34
1. (*Exc. de Sent.* 31)
Ὅτι Φίλιππος ὁ Μακεδὼν τὸ μέτρον ἰδὼν τοῦ σφετέρου σώματος (ἐν παλαίστρᾳ γὰρ ἐπεπτώκει), διαναστὰς ἀπὸ τοῦ πτώματος σώφρονα ἀφῆκε λόγον ὡς ὀλίγην κατασχήσων γῆν εἶτα ἐπιθυμοίη τῆς ἁπάσης.

2. (*Exc. de Sent.* 32)
Ὅτι τὸν Θησέα φασὶν οἱ παλαιοὶ ζηλωτὴν Ἡρακλέους γενόμενον μικρὰ τῆς μιμήσεως ἐκείνης ἀποκερδᾶναι.

**Book VI**

**30**

(*Exc. de Sent.* 30)

In the case of persons and events before our generation, we must defer to the written authorities or to the reports about them which memory passes down to us via an oral tradition. But contemporary events we must hand down to posterity with due regard for truth, as Plato says.[70]

**31**

1. (*Exc. de Leg. Gent.* 4)

Valentinian was acclaimed at Nicaea in Bithynia, and the embassies which had set out bearing golden crowns for [Jovian] now brought them to him. To all he revealed nothing, so quickly and summarily did he deal with them, and he declared to all that he would very quickly take action.[71]

(Zosimus 3,36,1 - 4,1,1)

**32**

(Zosimus 4,1,1 - 2,2)

**33**

(Zosimus 4,2,2 - 3,5)

**34**

1. (*Exc. de Sent.* 31)

Philip of Macedon after a fall in the *palaestra* observed the size of his own body and, when he had gotten up from the fall, remarked wisely that though he now aimed to possess the whole earth, he would one day possess only a tiny part of it.[72]

2. (*Exc. de Sent.* 32)

The ancients say that Theseus, becoming the imitator of Heracles, reaped only a small benefit from this imitation.[73]

3. (*Exc. de Sent.* 33)

Ὅτι τοῦ Προκοπίου τοῦ συγγενοῦς Ἰουλιανοῦ στασιάσαντος καὶ τυραννίδι ἐπιθεμένου Ἡράκλειος ὁ κυνικὸς προσελθὼν αὐτῷ καὶ κατακροτήσας εὖ μάλα τῇ βακτηρίᾳ τοὔδαφος, "ἄλκιμος ἔσσο" φησίν "ἵνα τίς σε καὶ ὀψιγόνων εὖ εἴπῃ".

3 ἔσσο Dindorf [ἔσο cod.

4. (*Exc. de Sent.* 34)

Ὥσπερ οὖν οἱ φυσικοί φασι πάσης κινήσεως εἶναι τέλος ἀκι-νησίαν, ἣ ταῖς ἄλλαις κινήσεσι τὸ κινεῖσθαι δίδωσιν αὐτὴ μένουσα, οὕτως ἄν τις ὑπέλαβε καὶ τότε τὸν πρεσβύτην Ἀρβιτίονα παρα-τυχόντα τὴν τοῦ βασιλέως ἄτακτον καὶ κυματώδη φορὰν εἰς ὁμαλὸν καὶ λεῖον καταστορέσαι τοῦ λογισμοῦ πάθος· μικροῦ γὰρ ἐξέστη διὰ    5
δειλίαν τῶν κοινῶν πραγμάτων.

5. (*Suda* X 108)

Εὐνάπιος· ὁ δὲ Προκόπιος τοὺς χαριεστέρους ἀναλαβών, ἐπὶ τὸν βασιλέα Οὐάλεντα διὰ Φρυγίας συνηπείγετο.

2 συνηπείγετο Niebuhr [συνήπτετο codd.

[6. (*Suda* Π 380)

Παραλλάττουσι δὲ ἀλλήλους τῷ διαστήματι τῶν ὁδῶν ψευσ-θέντες ὅ τε Προκόπιος καὶ Οὐάλης ὁ βασιλεύς.]

[7. (*Suda* E 936)

Ἐμβάλλουσι δὲ ὁ μὲν βασιλεὺς ἐς Λυδίαν ὁ δὲ Προκόπιος ἐς Φρυγίαν τὴν ἄνω.]

8. (*Suda* M 1048)

Καὶ Εὐνάπιος· μικροῦ τὰ πράγματα μετακινήσαντος Ὁρμίσθου τοῦ Πέρσου.    (Cf. M 1056)

9. (*Exc. de Sent.* 35)

Μεγαλόψυχον γὰρ καὶ λίαν θεοειδὲς τὸ καὶ τῶν αἰτίων φεί-δασθαι, οὐκ ἔξω δὲ τῆς ἀνθρωπίνης φύσεως τὸ μὴ καὶ τῶν ἀναιτίων. τὸ μὲν γὰρ ξένον τῆς τιμωρίας λόγῳ γίνεται τῆς ἀρχῆς, ἵνα φόβῳ συνέχηται τὸ ἀρχόμενον· τὸ δὲ ὑπεροπτικὸν τῆς κολάσεως δι᾽ ἀρετῆς ὑπεροχὴν γίνεται, ὡς τῆς βασιλικῆς ἀρχῆς διὰ μέγεθος καὶ ὄγκον    5
ἀρκούσης ἑαυτῇ καὶ ἄνευ τιμωρίας. ἀλλὰ ταῦτα μέν, ὅπη γνώμης ἔχει τις καὶ κρίνει, οὕτως ἐχέτω.

10. (*Exc. de Sent.* 36)

Ὅτι ὁ Ποσειδόνιος ἔλεγεν ἀπελθόντος Ἀλεξάνδρου τὸ στρατό-πεδον ἐοικέναι τῶν Μακεδόνων ἐκτετυφλωμένῳ τῷ Κύκλωπι.

3. (*Exc. de Sent.* 33)

When Procopius, the kinsman of Julian, was in rebellion and aiming at usurpation, Heracleius the Cynic came before him and, striking the ground hard with his staff, said, "Be bold, so that someone of future generations might praise you".[74]

4. (*Exc. de Sent.* 34)

Just as, according to the natural philosophers, the end of all movement is rest, which itself by its immobility imparts movement to other motions, so you might suppose that on that occasion the old Arbitio, who happened to be present, soothed the Emperor's state of mind from erratic indecision to calm and orderly rationality. For as a result of his timidity [Valens] was only a little way from losing his throne.[75]

5. (*Suda* X 108)

Procopius, receiving the more accomplished of them, moved through Phrygia to do battle with Valens.

[6. (*Suda* Π 380)

Procopius and the Emperor Valens, mistakenly taking different roads, missed each other.]

[7. (*Suda* E 936)

The Emperor moved into Lydia, Procopius into Upper Phrygia.]

8. (*Suda* M 1048)

Hormisdas the Persian almost turned things around.[76]
(Cf. M 1056)

9. (*Exc. de Sent.* 35)

It is magnanimous and very much a characteristic of God to spare even the guilty, while it is within human nature to condemn even the innocent. For the inflicting of unusual punishment springs from the rationale of power whose purpose is to constrain the subject by fear, whereas the omission of punishment derives from great virtue, in that the kingly power, in its greatness and majesty, depends upon itself without resort to punishment. But on these matters let each man judge for himself.[77]

10. (*Exc. de Sent.* 36)

Poseidonius said that when Alexander died the Macedonian army was like the blinded Cyclops.[78]

35

(Suda Αι 179)

Αἰλιανός. οὗτος ἐπὶ Οὐάλεντος ἐστρατήγησεν· ἦν δὲ ἐκ
Συέδρων, ἐλεύθερος ἄγαν καὶ ἀνεστηκὼς ἐκ παιδὸς τὴν ψυχὴν
γενόμενος, ἀφθόνως ἐχορηγήθη τὰ παρὰ τοῦ σώματος. τὰ γὰρ
ὄργανα συνεπεπήγει καὶ ἐνέτρεχε τοῖς τῆς ψυχῆς κινήμασιν, ὥσθ᾽
ἅμα τι πρᾶξαι ἐδέδοκτο καὶ ἐπέπρακτο· καὶ παιδείας οὔτε ἐντὸς ἦν    5
οὔτε ἄμοιρος, ἀλλ᾽ ἦν ἀγροικότερος, καὶ τὸ θηριῶδες τοῦ θυμοῦ καὶ
ἄγριον οὐκ ἐξημέρωτο καὶ κατείργαστο ὑπὸ τοῦ λόγου.
(Cf. A 2329*, Σ 1316)

3 παρὰ AGT [περὶ IVM        4 ἐνέτρεχε AFVM [ἐπέτρεχε GIT

36

(Zosimus 4,9)

37

(Exc. de Leg. Gent. 5)

Ὅτι τῷ βασιλεῖ Οὐάλεντι ἡσυχίαν ἀπὸ τῶν οἰκείων καὶ τῶν
ὀθνείων ἄγοντι τὸ ἐπίλεκτον ἀγγέλλεται τῶν Σκυθῶν στράτευμα
πλησίον ἤδη που τυγχάνειν, οὓς ὁ Προκόπιος εἰς συμμαχίαν ἐξεκε-
κλήκει παρὰ τοῦ Σκυθῶν βασιλέως. γαύρους εἶναι τὰ φρονήματα
ἔλεγον τοὺς προσιόντας καὶ περιφρονητικοὺς τῶν ὁρωμένων,    5
ὀλιγώρους τε πρὸς τὸ ἀκόλαστον μεθ᾽ ὕβρεως καὶ πολὺ τὸ ἀγέρωχον
καὶ θερμὸν ἐπὶ πᾶσιν ἔχοντας. ὁ δὲ βασιλεὺς συντόμως αὐτοὺς ἀποτεμὼν τῆς ἐπὶ Σκύθας ὑποστροφῆς κατεῖχεν ἐντὸς ἀρκύων καὶ τὰ
ὅπλα παραδοῦναι κελεύσας. οἱ δὲ ἔδοσαν τὴν τῆς γνώμης ὑπεροψίαν
μέχρι τοῦ κινῆσαι τὰς κόμας ἐπιδειξάμενοι. διασπείρας οὖν αὐτοὺς    10
κατὰ τὰς πόλεις ἐν ἀδέσμῳ κατεῖχε φρουρᾷ, καὶ καταφρόνησιν ἐνε-
ποιεῖτο τοῖς θεωμένοις αὐτῶν τὰ σώματα πρός τε μῆκος ἀχρεῖον
ἐλαυνόμενα καὶ βαρύτερα τοῖς ποσίν, κατά τε τὸ μέσον διεσφιγμένα,
ἤπέρ φησιν Ἀριστοτέλης τὰ ἔντομα. δεχόμενοι δ᾽ οὖν αὐτοὺς εἰς τὰς
οἰκίας οἱ τὰς πόλεις οἰκοῦντες καὶ πειρώμενοι τῆς ἀσθενείας τὴν    15
ἑαυτῶν ἐξαπάτην γελᾶν ἠναγκάζοντο. τούτους ἀπῄτει τοὺς γενναίους
ὁ Σκυθῶν βασιλεύς. καὶ ἦν τὸ πρᾶγμα δριμὺ καὶ πρὸς τὸν τοῦ
δικαίου λόγον οὐκ εὐδιαίτητον. ὁ μὲν γὰρ ἔφασκε βασιλεῖ δεδωκέναι
κατὰ συμμαχίαν καὶ ὅρκους· ὁ δὲ ἀπέφασκε βασιλέα μὴ τυγχάνειν
καὶ αὐτὸν οὐκ ὀμωμοκέναι. ἐκείνου δὲ προστιθέντος τὸν Ἰουλιανόν,    20

5 ὁρωμένων [Ῥωμαίων Bekker ὡρισμένων de Boor   10 κώμας Wyttenbach
14 δ᾽ οὖν Valesius [δοῦναι A

## 35

(*Suda* Aι 179)

Aelianus. He was general under Valens. From Syedrae, he was a generous man, noble-spirited even from childhood and well-endowed with physical gifts. His body was so well co-ordinated and responsive to his will, that no sooner had he decided to do something than it was done. He was neither well- nor un-educated, but he was a rough-hewn man, and his natural ferocity and wildness were not fully under the control of his reason.[79]

(Cf. A 2329*, Σ 1316)

## 36

(Zosimus 4,9)

## 37

(*Exc. de Leg. Gent.* 5)

When the Emperor Valens was enjoying a respite from domestic and foreign problems, it was announced to him that the levy of Scythians, which Procopius had summoned to his aid from the Scythian king, was now close at hand. The reports said that their attitude as they advanced was one of arrogance and contempt towards everyone whom they espied, and since this behaviour was only encouraged by failure to call them to account, all suffered from their riotousness and indiscipline. The Emperor, speedily cutting off their retreat to Scythia, caught them in a trap and commanded them to surrender their weapons. This they did, but they showed their arrogance even in the shaking of their hair. Valens dispersed them around the cities, keeping them in free custody, and aroused the scorn of those who observed their physique, which was excessively tall, too heavy for their feet to bear, and pinched at the waist like the insects that Aristotle describes. When the inhabitants of the cities received them into their homes and realised their feebleness, they were forced to laugh at their own mistake.[80] These wondrous men the king of the Scythians demanded back. The issue was a contentious one and not easily to be settled with justice. The Scythian king claimed that he had sent his men to the Emperor under the terms of the treaty, to which Valens replied that neither was Procopius Emperor nor was there a treaty between him and the Scythians. The king then justified his sending of assistance to Procopius on the ground of the latter's

καὶ ὅτι διὰ τὴν ἐκείνου δεδώκει συγγένειαν, . . . καὶ τὰ τῶν πρέσβεων ἀξιώματα προστιθέντος, ὁ βασιλεὺς ἀντεφώνει, τούς τε πρέσβεις ἔχειν τὴν δίκην καὶ τοὺς παρόντας ὡς πολεμίους κατέχεσθαι πολεμίῳ πρὸς συμμαχίαν ἥκοντας. ἐκ τούτων δὲ τῶν προφάσεων ὁ Σκυθικὸς ἀνεγείρεται πόλεμος, τῷ μὲν ἀξιώματι τῶν συνιόντων  25
ἐθνῶν καὶ τοῖς μεγέθεσι τῶν παρασκευῶν ἐπὶ μέγα προβήσεσθαι
καὶ χωρήσειν πολυτρόπων συμφορῶν καὶ ἀτεκμάρτου τύχης προσ-
δοκηθείς, τῇ δὲ τοῦ βασιλέως ὀξύτητι καὶ προνοίᾳ κατενεχθεὶς
ἐπὶ τὸ σταθερὸν καὶ ἀσφαλέστερον.
(Cf. *Suda* A 4332*, Σ 982*)

21 lac. unius fere pag. in A

(Zosimus 4,10-11)

## 38
(Zosimus 4,12)

## 39
1. (*Exc. de Sent.* 37)
     Ὁ δὲ Θεόδωρος ὁ κατειλεγμένος τοῖς νοταρίοις ἐν δίκῃ
ἐτιμᾶτο παρὰ τοῦ βασιλέως · τό τε γὰρ εὖ γεγονέναι προσῆν αὐτῷ
καὶ τὸ εὖ πεφυκέναι πρὸς ἀρετὴν ἅπασαν, τό τε σῶμα συνήνθει ταῖς
ἀρεταῖς, καὶ τὸ ἐπαφρόδιτον ἐν ταῖς συνουσίαις κόσμος ἐδόκει τῶν
ἀρετῶν ἐμμελής τις εἶναι καὶ παναρμόνιος. ἀλλ' ἔλαθεν, ἥ φησιν   5
Ὅμηρος, ὑπὸ τῶν ἰδίων διαφθαρεὶς καλῶν. τὸ γὰρ ἀνθρώπινον, καὶ
ὅσοι περὶ στρατείας ἐπὶ τὰ κέρδη καὶ τὰς κοινὰς τύχας ἐπτοημένοι
καὶ κεχηνότες, τὴν ἡμερότητα καταμαθόντες αὐτοῦ καὶ τὸ πρὸς τὰς
ὁμιλίας εὔκρατες καὶ πρόχειρον, ταχὺ μάλα τὴν ἄμαχον καὶ φοβερὰν
καὶ τοῖς νοῦν ἔχουσι κολακείαν ὑποδύντες καὶ προβαλόμενοι καθάπερ   10
ἑλέπολίν τινα καὶ μηχανὴν ἄφυκτον, ἐξέωσαν τῶν ἀσφαλῶν καὶ
σωτηρίων λογισμῶν τὸν νεανίσκον καὶ κατέσεισαν εἰς τὸν μανιώδη
καὶ σφαλερὸν τῆς βασιλείας ἔρωτα.

[2. (*Suda* I 14)
     Ἰάκωβος · οὕτως πίων φάρμακον ἐπὶ Οὐάλεντος ἐτελεύτησεν.
ἦν δὲ ὁ συμβουλεύσας αὐτῷ πιεῖν τὸ φάρμακον Λιβάνιος σοφιστής,
διὰ τὸ ἐπιζητῆσαι τίς ὁ διαδεξόμενος τὴν βασιλείαν Οὐάλεντος.]

[3. (*Suda* E 3448)
     Εὐετήριος · οὗτος ἦν ἐπὶ Ἰοβιάνου βασιλέως, ὃς διὰ μὲν παιδείαν
καὶ φύσεως ὑπερβολὴν οὐδέν τι τῶν ἀρχαίων ἀποδέων, διὰ δὲ μαλα-

kinship with Julian and also raised the issue of his envoys' immunity. Valens countered that the envoys were suffering due punishment and that the reinforcements which had arrived were being held as enemies because they had come as allies of his enemy. From these causes arose the Scythian war which, because of the fame of the peoples involved and the size of their forces, was expected to become a large-scale conflict proceeding with fluctuations of fortune and unexpected developments, but which was brought by the decisiveness and foresight of the Emperor to a calm and safe conclusion.[81]
(Cf. *Suda* A 4332\*, Σ 982\*)


(Zosimus 4,10-11)

## 38
(Zosimus 4,12)

## 39

1. (*Exc. de Sent.* 37)
    Theodorus, one of the notaries, was justly honoured by the Emperor. For he had high birth and a natural proclivity to every virtue, his physical beauty matched his virtues, and his charm in company seemed a suitable and wholly appropriate ornament for his other qualities. But, as Homer says, "his virtues destroyed him unawares".[82] For civilian elements and those civil servants[83] who lusted after wealth and public office, learning of his easy-going nature and his relaxed and approachable social manner, quickly worked up their flattery, a weapon irresistible and fearful even to rational people, wheeled it up like some fatal siege-engine, and, turning the young man away from safe and salutary ideas, aroused in him a crazy and dangerous desire to become Emperor.[84]


[2. (*Suda* I 14)
    Jacobus. He died by drinking poison during the reign of Valens. He was advised to do this by the sophist Libanius because he had enquired about the identity of Valens' successor.]

[3. (*Suda* E 3448)
    Eueterius. He lived during the reign of the Emperor Jovian. Because of his education and outstanding natural talents he lacked none of

κίαν ψυχῆς καὶ ἁπλότητα πολλοὺς τῶν οὐκ αἰτίων ἐς κρίσιν κατέδησεν.]

[4. (Suda I 292)

Ἱλάριος ὁ ἐκ Φρυγίας, ἐπὶ Ἰοβιανοῦ βασιλέως Ῥωμαίων. κατὰ παιδείαν μὲν ἦν ἀνὴρ οὐ γνώριμος, κοινωνεῖν δὲ αὐτῷ θεὸς ἐδόκει τῆς κοινωνίας τοῦ μέλλοντος, ὥστε ἦν μάντις ἄριστος.]

[5. (Suda Π 792)

Πατρίκιος· οὗτος ἤκμασεν ἐπὶ Ἰοβιανοῦ βασιλέως· ἦν δὲ ἐκ Λυδίας· ὃς τῆς ἀπὸ τῶν φαινομένων ἢ καὶ παρατρεχόντων σημείων τεκμάρσεως ἀκριβὴς ἦν ἐξεταστής.]

[6. (Suda Σ 445)

Σιμωνίδης· οὗτος ἦν ἐπὶ Ἰοβιανοῦ τοῦ βασιλέως διὰ φιλοσοφίαν πᾶσιν ἐπισημότατος.]

7. (Vit. Soph. 7,6,5)

Καὶ ταῦτα ἔσχεν οὕτως, καὶ ἐν τοῖς διεξοδικοῖς ἀκριβέστερον γέγραπται.

[8. (Suda Φ 279)

Φῆστος. οὗτος περὶ τοὺς χρόνους Οὐάλεντος εἰς τὴν Ἀσίαν ἐκπέμπεται ἀνθύπατος· τὴν δὲ βασιλικὴν γλῶσσαν ἐπεπίστευτο. πέμπεται δὲ ὅμως, τὸν ποιητικὸν καὶ μυθώδη Ἔχετον, καὶ εἰ δή τις ἄλλος ἐκ Σικελίας ἢ Θετταλίας τοιοῦτος, χρυσὸν ἀποδείξων καὶ πανήγυριν. ἦν δὲ ἡ μανία οὐ θύραθεν, ἀλλ' ἔνδοθεν ἐλύσσα καὶ    5
ἐμαίνετο, ἀνὴρ φύσει πονηρὸς καὶ ἐξουσίαν ἔχων καὶ τὴν ἐν ταῖς κολάσεσιν ἀγριότητα καταλιπὼν εὐδοκιμοῦσαν ἐν τοῖς βασιλείοις, οὐκ ἔστιν ὅ τι παρανομίας ἀπέλειπε καὶ ἀσελγείας, ἀλλ' ἐπὶ τοσόνδε παραφορᾶς ἐρρύη καὶ φόνων, ὥστε καὶ Μάξιμον ξίφει διέφθειρε, Κοίρανον Αἰγύπτιον ἐπισφάξας αὐτῷ· καὶ ἔτι θερμὸς ὢν καὶ ζέων    10
τῷ λύθρῳ πάντας συνανήρει καὶ κατέφλεγε.
(Cf. Γ 301, Ε 3996, Θ 599)]

9. (Exc. de Sent. 38)

Ὅτι φιλοχρηματίαν φασὶ πηγήν τινα πάσης κακίας τυγχάνειν, οὐδὲ τῇ κακίᾳ πότιμόν τε καὶ χρήσιμον· ἐξ ἐκείνης γὰρ τῆς ἀρχῆς καὶ ἀπὸ τῆς τῶν χρημάτων περιττῆς ἐπιθυμίας τὸ τῆς ψυχῆς ἄλογον ἀρδόμενον ἔριν τ' ἀνέφυσεν ἀνθρώποις καὶ μάχην· ἔρις δὲ αὐξηθεῖσα πολέμους ἀνεβλάστησε καὶ φόνους· φόνων δὲ ὁ φυόμενος    5
καρπὸς φθορὰ τοῦ γένους καὶ ὄλεθρος· ἃ δὴ καὶ ἐπὶ Οὐάλεντος συνεπράττετο.

(Zosimus 4,13,3 - 15,3)

the ancient qualities. But because of his softness of spirit and frankness he caused many of the innocent men to be brought to judgement.[85] ]

[4. (*Suda* I 292)

Hilarius from Phrygia, during the reign of the Emperor Jovian. He was not famous for his education, but God appears to have given him a share in foreknowledge, so that he was an excellent prophet.]

[5. (*Suda* Π 792)

Patricius. He flourished under the Emperor Jovian. He was from Lydia. He was an excellent diviner both from celestial bodies and from chance portents.]

[6. (*Suda* Σ 445)

Simonides. He was a very famous philosopher during the reign of the Emperor Jovian.[86]]

7. (*Vit. Soph.* 7,6,5)

Thus these things turned out, which I have described in more detail in my History.[87]

[8. (*Suda* Φ 279)

Festus. During the reign of Valens he was sent to Asia as proconsul. He had been master of the rolls. Nevertheless, he was sent off to prove that, by comparison with himself, the poet's fabled Echetus (and any other murderous tyrant of Sicily or Thessaly) was pure gold and a holiday. He showed no external signs of his madness, but it raged deep within. He was a man naturally wicked and, when he gained authority, he went beyond the savagery of punishment which was the palace's policy and practised every manner of lawlessness and wanton violence. His deranged blood-lust was such that he decapitated Maximus himself, and after him killed Coeranus the Egyptian. But since he was still seething for blood, he killed all his victims together and burned their bodies.[88]    (Cf. Γ 301, E 3996, Θ 599)]

9. (*Exc. de Sent.* 38)

They say that love of money is a spring from which flow all evils, yet one that is neither drinkable nor usable for evil itself. The irrational part of the mind, drinking from this source and from excessive eagerness for wealth, begets strife and aggression amongst mankind. Strife, when it has grown, brings forth war and murder, and the children of murder are ruin and destruction of the human race. Precisely these things were perpetrated during Valens' reign.[89]

(Zosimus 4,13,3 - 15,3)

40

(Zosimus 4,16-19)

41

1. (*Exc. de Sent.* 39)

Τὰ μὲν οὖν πρῶτα τῆς συγγραφῆς, οὐδενὸς οὐδὲν σαφὲς λέγειν
ἔχοντος ὅθεν τε ὄντες οἱ Οὖννοι ὅπῃ τε κείμενοι τὴν Εὐρώπην πᾶσαν
ἐπέδραμον καὶ τὸ Σκυθικὸν ἔτριψαν γένος, ἐκ τῶν παλαιῶν συν-
τιθέντι κατὰ τοὺς εἰκότας λογισμοὺς εἴρηται, τὰ δὲ ἐκ τῶν ἀπαγγελλομένων δοξάζοντι πρὸς τὸ ἀκριβές, ὡς ἂν μὴ πρόσω τοῦ πιθανοῦ    5
τὴν γραφὴν ἀπαρτήσαμεν μηδὲ παραφέροι, πρὸς τὴν ἀλήθειαν ὁ
λόγος. ἡμεῖς δὲ οὐ ταὐτὸν πάσχοντες τοῖς ἐκ παίδων οἰκίαν μικρὰν
καὶ φαύλην οἰκήσασιν, εἶτα διὰ τύχης εὕροιαν μεγάλων καὶ λαμπρῶν
ἐπιλαβομένοις οἰκοδομημάτων ὅμως διὰ συνήθειαν τὰ ἀρχαῖα θαυ-
μάζουσι καὶ περιστέλλουσιν, οὕτως αὐτοὶ τὰ προειρημένα γεγράφθαι    10
συγχωρήσαντες ἑτέρων ἁπτόμεθα πάλιν, ἀλλὰ μᾶλλον ὥσπερ οἱ
κατά τινα θεραπείαν σώματος τὰ πρῶτα χρησάμενοί τινι φαρμάκῳ
δι᾿ ὠφελείας ἐλπίδα, κατὰ τὸ κρεῖττον πείρᾳ δοκιμάσαντες ἐπ᾿ ἐκεῖνο
μεθίστανται καὶ ῥέπουσιν, οὐ τῷ δευτέρῳ τὸ πρότερον ἀναιροῦντες,
ἀλλὰ τῷ δεδοξασμένῳ κακῶς τὸ ἀληθὲς ἐπεισάγοντες, καὶ καθάπερ    15
φῶς ἀπὸ λαμπάδος διὰ τῆς ἡλιακῆς ἀκτῖνος ἀφανίζοντες καὶ ἀμβλύ-
νοντες, ὁμοίως ἐπιθήσομεν τοῖς εἰρημένοις τὰ ἀληθέστερα, κἀκεῖα
διὰ τὴν ἱστορικὴν δόξαν συγχωρήσαντες μένειν καὶ ταῦτα διὰ τὴν
ἀλήθειαν ἐφελκυσάμενοι καὶ παραξεύξαντες.

1 τὰ μὲν οὖν Boissevain (legens τι μεν in cod.)   [⟨κατὰ⟩ μὲν οὖν Mai  κατὰ μὲν
οὖν ⟨τὰ⟩ Niebuhr    1-2 λέγειν ἔχοντος van Herwerden [ἔχειν λέγοντος cod.
3 ἔτριψαν van Herwerden [ἔρριψαν cod.    5 πρόσω Kuiper [πρϱσ cod.  ἀπὸ
Mai πέρα Polak    11 ἁπτόμεθα scripsi [ἅπτομε .. cod. (sec. Boissevain)
ἅπτομεν Jordan  ἀψόμεθα Boissevain  ἀποστε⟨ρούμεθα⟩ Mai

2. (*Suda* K 11)

Εὐνάπιος· οἱ δὲ Οὖννοι πλατὺ καγχάσαντες ᾤχοντο.

(Zosimus 4,20,3-4)

42

(*Exc. de Leg. Gent.* 6)

Ὅτι τῶν Σκυθῶν ἡττηθέντων καὶ ὑπὸ τῶν Οὖννων ἀναιρεθέντων καὶ ἄρδην ἀπολλυμένων τὸ πλῆθος, οἱ μὲν ἐγκαταλαμβα-
νόμενοι σὺν γυναιξὶ καὶ τέκνοις διεφθείροντο, καὶ οὐδεμία φειδὼ τῆς

2 τὸ πλῆθος secl. Müller

## 40

(Zosimus 4,16-19)

## 41

1. (*Exc. de Sent.* 39)

The first accounts of the history of the Huns, written at a time when no one had anything clear to say about their place of origin and where they were living when they overran Europe and crushed the Scythian nation, I have collected from the ancient authors and set down according to the criterion of probability. For the material drawn from oral reports I have used the criterion of accuracy, in order that my account not fall short in reliability and my narrative not do violence to the truth. My attitude is not the same as those who, after a childhood spent in a poor and humble house, although later through abundant good fortune they come into possession of a large and eminent mansion, nevertheless out of habit still idealise and cherish their old home. Though I have consented to include the older records on the Huns, I have joined them to other material. This I have done in the spirit of those who, when caring for an ailment, initially use a medicine which they hope will help, but, when they have tried and found a better one, change over to that. For I have not omitted the earlier information for the sake of the later reports, but have subjoined the true version to the erroneous opinions, dulling and obscuring the latter like the gleam of a lamp under the rays of the sun. So I shall add the truer version to that in the records, allowing the latter to remain as a tradition sanctified by history, while joining to it the former for the sake of the truth.[90]

2. (*Suda* K 11)

The Huns went off laughing uproariously.

(Zosimus 4,20,3-4)

## 42

(*Exc. de Leg. Gent.* 6)

The Scythians had been defeated and destroyed and were being utterly extirpated. Those who were captured were massacred with their wives and children. There was no limit to the savagery employed

περὶ τοὺς φόνους ἦν ὠμότητος. τὸ δὲ συναλισθὲν καὶ πρὸς φυγὴν
ὁρμῆσαν πλῆθος μὲν οὐ πολὺ τῶν εἴκοσι μυριάδων ἀποδέον, συν-      5
ῆλθον ἐς <τὸν Ἴστρον οἱ ἐς> τὸ μάχιμον ἀκμάζοντες ἄνδρες καὶ
ταῖς ὄχθαις ἐπιστάντες χεῖράς τε ὤρεγον πόρρωθεν μετὰ ὀλο-
φυρμῶν καὶ βοῆς καὶ προέτεινον ἱκετηρίας, ἐπιτραπῆναι τὴν διάβασιν
παρακαλοῦντες καὶ τὴν σφῶν συμφορὰν ὀδυρόμενοι καὶ προσθήκην
τῇ συμμαχίᾳ παρέξειν ἐπαγγελλόμενοι. οἱ δὲ ταῖς ὄχθαις ἐπιτεταγ-     10
μένοι Ῥωμαίων οὐδὲν ἔφασαν πράξειν ἄνευ βασιλέως γνώμης. ἐντεῦθεν ἀναφέρεται μὲν ἐπὶ τὸν βασιλέα ἡ γνῶσις· πολλῆς δὲ ἀντι-
λογίας γενομένης, καὶ πολλῶν ἐφ᾽ ἑκάτερα γνωμῶν ἐν τῷ βασιλικῷ
συλλόγῳ ῥηθεισῶν, ἔδοξε τῷ βασιλεῖ. καὶ γὰρ ὑπῆν τι ζηλοτυπίας
αὐτῷ πρὸς τοὺς συμβασιλεύοντας, οἳ παῖδες μὲν ἦσαν ἀδελφοῦ (καὶ    15
γέγραπται οὕτω πρότερον), τὴν βασιλείαν δὲ διῃρῆσθαι κατὰ σφᾶς
ἐδόκουν, τὴν διανομὴν οὐκ <ἀν>ενεγκόντες ἐπὶ τὸν θεῖον. τούτων
δὴ ἕνεκα, καὶ ὡς μεγάλη προσθήκη τὸ Ῥωμαϊκὸν αὐξήσων, δεχ-
θῆναι κελεύει τοὺς ἄνδρας τὰ ὅπλα καταθεμένους.

Πρὶν δὲ τὴν διάβασιν ἐκ βασιλέως ἐπιτραπῆναι, Σκυθῶν οἱ      20
τολμηρότατοι καὶ αὐθάδεις βιάσασθαι τὸν πόρον ἔγνωσαν, καὶ βιαζόμενοι κατεκόπησαν. οἱ δὲ διαφθείραντες τὸν ἀποδασμὸν τοῦτον τῆς
τε ἀρχῆς παρελύθησαν καὶ περὶ τοῖς σώμασιν ἐκινδύνευσαν, ὅτι
πολεμίους διέφθειραν, οἵ τε παραδυναστεύοντες βασιλεῖ καὶ δυνάμενοι
μέγιστον κατεγέλων αὐτῶν τὸ φιλοπόλεμον καὶ στρατηγικόν, πολι-    25
τικοὺς δὲ οὐκ ἔφασαν εἶναι. ὁ μὲν γὰρ βασιλεὺς ἐξ Ἀντιοχείας ἐπέτρεπεν αὐτοῖς τὴν ἀχρεῖον ἡλικίαν πρῶτον ὑποδεξαμένοις καὶ
παραπέμψασιν εἰς τὴν Ῥωμαϊκὴν ἐπικράτειαν καὶ ταύτην ἐς ὁμηρείαν
ἀσφαλῶς κατέχουσιν ἐπιστῆναι ταῖς ὄχθαις, καὶ μὴ πρότερον τοὺς
μαχίμους δέξασθαι διαβαίνοντας μηδὲ τὰ πλοῖα παρασχεῖν ἐς τὴν    30
περαίωσιν, εἰ μὴ τὰ ὅπλα καταθέμενοι γυμνοὶ διαβαίνοιεν. οἱ δὲ
ταῦτα ἐπιτραπέντες, ὁ μὲν ἐκ τῶν διαβεβηκότων ἤρα παιδαρίου τινὸς
λευκοῦ καὶ χαρίεντος τὴν ὄψιν, ὁ δὲ ἥλω ἐκ γυναικὸς εὐπροσώπου
τῶν αἰχμαλώτων, ὃς δὲ ἦν αἰχμάλωτος ὑπὸ παρθένου, τοὺς δὲ τὸ
μέγεθος κατεῖχε τῶν δώρων τά τε λωᾶ ὑφάσματα καὶ τὸ τῶν      35
στρωμάτων ἐπ᾽ ἀμφότερα θυσανοειδές· ἕκαστος δὲ ἁπλῶς αὐτῶν
ὑπελάμβανε καὶ τὴν οἰκίαν καταπλήσειν οἰκετῶν καὶ τὰ χωρία
βοηλατῶν καὶ τὴν ἐρωτικὴν λύσσαν τῆς περὶ ταῦτα ἐξουσίας. νικηθέντες δὲ ὑπὸ τούτων νίκην αἰσχίστην καὶ παρανομωτάτην, ὥσπερ
τινὰς εὐεργέτας καὶ σωτῆρας παλαιοὺς μετὰ τῶν ὅπλων ἐδέξαντο.    40

5-6 ἀποδέον, συνῆλθον ἐς ‹τὸν Ἴστρον οἱ ἐς› τὸ μάχιμον ἀκμάζοντες ἄνδρες
scripsi [ἀποδέουσαι συνῆλθον ἐς τὸ μάχιμον ἀκμαζούσας κινηθέντες A. ἀποδέον,
ὅσοι pro ἀποδέουσαι et ἀκμαζόντων pro ἀκμάζοντας coni. Müller    νικηθέντες
pro κινηθέντες Hoeschel    17 ἀν- add. Müller    33 ἥλω ἐκ de Boor
[ἠδέει A  ἥλω Wyttenbach

in the killings. After a multitude, almost two hundred thousand in number, had gathered together and turned to flight, the males who were especially fit for war gathered at the Danube[91] and, standing on the bank, stretched out their hands from afar with cries and lamentations, begging for pity and asking to be allowed to cross, and, as they bewailed their misfortunes, they promised the Romans that they would provide reinforcements for their auxiliary forces. The Romans in charge of the bank said that they could do nothing without the consent of the Emperor. When the report reached the Emperor, there was a considerable debate. After many arguments had been aired on both sides in the imperial consistory, the Emperor decided to admit the Scythians. For he was rather chagrined at his fellow Emperors who, being sons of his brother (as I have noted earlier), had decided to divide up their Empire between themselves without referring the division to their uncle. Because of this and in order that the Roman forces might be greatly increased, he ordered that the men should be received, after first surrendering their weapons.

Before the Emperor had given permission for the crossing, the boldest and most daring of the Scythians planned to force an entrance, and were cut down as they attempted to do so. The officers who had destroyed this group were cashiered and came into danger of their lives because they had destroyed our enemies. Those who enjoyed great influence and power at court mocked their military attitude with its eagerness for war, saying that they had no sense of politics. From Antioch the Emperor ordered them first to receive those persons who were too young for war and to distribute them throughout the Roman dominion, holding them securely as hostages; and they were to guard the bank, allowing none of the warriors to cross and supplying no boats for the crossing, unless they laid down their weapons and crossed unarmed. These were their orders. But one was smitten by a fair and pretty boy amongst those who had crossed, another was taken by the beautiful wife of one of the captives, another was captivated by some maiden, and they were all mesmerised by the valuable gifts given them, linen shirts and coverlets fringed on both sides. Quite simply, each of them had decided that he would fill his house with domestics and his farm with herdsmen and sate his mad lust through the licence which he enjoyed. Overpowered by the Scythians in this disgraceful and criminal manner, they received them with their weapons as if they were some long-standing benefactors and saviours. Having achieved this considerable

62     Eunapius: Text

οἱ δὲ τοσοῦτον ἀκονιτὶ πρᾶγμα διαπεπραγμένοι καὶ τὴν οἴκοι συμφορὰν εὐτυχήσαντες, οἵ γε ἀντὶ τῆς Σκυθῶν ἐρημίας καὶ τοῦ
βαράθρου τὴν Ῥωμαϊκὴν ἀρχὴν ἀπελάμβανον, εὐθὺς πολύ τι βάρβαρον ἐν τῷ παρασπόνδῳ καὶ ἀπίστῳ διέφαινον.
    Ἡ μὲν γὰρ ἄχρηστος ἡλικία προλαβοῦσα κατὰ τὴν διάβασιν      45
μετὰ βαθείας σπουδῆς καὶ φροντίδος τῶν ταῦτα βεβουλευμένων εἰς
τὰ ἔθνη κατεχεῖτο καὶ διεσπείρετο. οἰκέται δὲ καὶ γυναῖκες καὶ
παῖδες ἐκείνων, οἱ μὲν βασιλικὰ παράσημα ἔχοντες, τὰς δὲ ἦν
ἁβροτέρας ὁρᾶν ἢ κατὰ αἰχμάλωτον. παῖδες δὲ αὐτῶν καὶ τοῦ
οἰκετικοῦ πρός τε τὴν εὐκρασίαν τῶν ἀέρων ἀνέδραμον καὶ παρὰ      50
τὴν ἡλικίαν ἥβησαν, καὶ πολὺ τὸ ἐπιφυόμενον ἦν πολέμιον γένος. οἱ
μὲν οὖν παλαιοὶ μῦθοι λέγουσι περὶ τὴν Βοιωτίαν καὶ τὴν Κολχίδα
δρακοντείων ὀδόντων κατασπαρέντων ἐνόπλους ἅμα τῷ σπόρῳ
τοὺς ἄνδρας ἀναπάλλεσθαι· ὁ δὲ καθ' ἡμᾶς χρόνος καὶ τὸν μῦθον
τοῦτον εἰς φῶς καὶ ἔργον συνήγαγε καὶ ὀφθῆναι κατηνάγκασεν. οὐ      55
γὰρ ἔφθασαν τοῦ Σκυθικοῦ γένους εἰς τὴν ἐπικράτειαν τὴν Ῥωμαϊκὴν οἱ παῖδες ὥσπερ ὀδόντες διασπαρέντες, καὶ πάντα ἦν μεστὰ
θυμοῦ καὶ μανίας καὶ φόνων, ἀνελθόντων αὐτῶν ἐς ἡλικίαν μάχιμον
παρὰ τὸν χρόνον. τὸ δὲ ἀκμάζον τῆς Σκυθικῆς ἀλκῆς καὶ γενναιό-
τατον τοῖς ὑποδεξαμένοις ἀντὶ τῶν ἐκβεβληκότων ἐς ἐπανάστασιν      60
εὐθὺς ἐγερθὲν καὶ μαχόμενον πολὺ δεινότερα καὶ τραγικώτερα συν-
ετόλμησεν ὧν ἔπαθεν. ἡ μὲν γὰρ Θρᾴκη πᾶσα καὶ ἡ συνεχὴς αὐτῇ
χώρα Μακεδονία καὶ Θεσσαλία τοιαύτη τίς ἐστι καὶ οὕτω πολυ-
ύμνητος, ὥστε οὐδὲ εἷς κατὰ ταῦτα ἀναγράφειν λόγος ἦν. τοσαύτην
δὲ οὖσαν αὐτὴν καὶ οὕτω πολυάνθρωπον εὐδαίμονά τε ἅμα καὶ εὔ-      65
ανδρον ἡ τῶν Σκυθῶν ἄπιστος καὶ παράλογος ἐπανάστασις ἐξαπιναίως καὶ παραχρῆμα τῆς διαβάσεως συντολμηθεῖσα καὶ ἀνοιδήσασα
κατεστόρεσεν ἐς τοσόνδε καὶ καθημάξευσε ταῖς συμφοραῖς, ὥστε
χρυσὸν ἀποδειχθῆναι πρὸς τὰ Θρᾴκια πάθη τὴν Μυσῶν παροιμιώδη
λείαν. δόξαν <δ'> αὐτοῖς στασιάζειν ἀξιομάχου μὴ παρούσης δυνά-      70
μεως ἐς ἄμυναν, τῷ τε πλήθει πρὸς ἀνθρώπους ἀφυλάκτους καὶ
ἀνόπλους ἐφάνησαν φοβερώτατοι καὶ τῷ φονικωτάτῳ πρὸς τὸ
κρατούμενον πάντα ἀνδρῶν ἐχήρωσαν. περιειστήκει δὲ ἐς ἴσον
λόγον καὶ Σκύθας Οὔννων μὴ φέρειν ὄνομα καὶ Ῥωμαίους Σκυθῶν.
πόλεις γοῦν εὐαρίθμητοι καὶ ὀλίγαι τινὲς διεσώθησαν καὶ ἔτι σῴζον-      75
ται τειχῶν ἕνεκεν καὶ οἰκοδομημάτων· ἡ δὲ χώρα καὶ τὸ πλεῖστον
ἀπανάλωται, καὶ ἔστιν ἀοίκητον καὶ ἄβατον διὰ τὸν πόλεμον.
    Βασιλεὺς δὲ ἐπειδὴ τούτων ἐπύθετο τῶν ἀδιηγήτων κακῶν,
πρὸς μὲν τοὺς Πέρσας ἀναγκαίαν εἰρήνην συνθέμενος, ἑαυτῷ δὲ

43 ἀπελάμβανον Niebuhr [ὑπελάμβανεν A ὑπελάμβανον Hoeschel   49-50 τοῦ
οἰκετικοῦ Wyttenbach [τὸν οἰκετικόν A τὸ οἰκετικὸν Hoeschel 71 δ' add. Müller

goal without effort and turned their misfortunes at home to their own advantage (for instead of the desert of deepest Scythia they were beginning to take over the Roman Empire), they immediately revealed the degree of their barbarism by faithlessly breaking their agreements.

Those too young for war, who had been the first to cross, were scattered thinly across the provinces through the utmost care and wisdom of those who had planned this: their domestics, their wives, their children, boys wearing the badges of royalty, the women (as one could observe) living more splendidly than appropriate for captives. In our favourable climate their children and those of their domestics developed and matured beyond their years – the enemy nation was growing fast! The ancient tales say that when the serpent's teeth were sown in Boeotia and Colchis, armed men sprang up at the very moment of sowing. Our age brought this tale to life and forced us to watch it. For no sooner had the children of the Scythian race been sown in the Roman Empire like teeth, than every place was filled with anger and madness and killing as they came prematurely to warlike age. The flower of Scythian strength and nobility immediately rose up in insurrection and made war, not upon those who had driven them out, but upon those who had received them, and they inflicted sufferings more terrible than they had endured. The whole of Thrace and the neighbouring parts of Macedonia and Thessaly are so beautiful and far-famed that no one description does justice to them. Such it was, so populous, so rich and full of men, when the treacherous and unexpected revolt of the Scythians, a venture which suddenly developed immediately after the crossing, reduced it to such a state and crushed it under such misfortunes that the proverbial plundering of Mysia was heaven compared with the sufferings of Thrace.[92] When they decided to revolt, there was in the vicinity no force strong enough to contain them. Their numbers caused great panic in the unprotected and unarmed civilian population, and the areas which they overran were depopulated as a result of their murderous behaviour. As a result the Romans feared the name of the Scythians no less than the Scythians feared that of the Huns. A few cities, easy to count, were protected (as they still are) by their walls and fortifications, but the countryside was for the most part devastated and it remains uninhabited and untravelled as a result of the war.[93]

The Emperor Valens, when he learned of these indescribable catastrophes, of necessity made peace with the Persians and, repenting that

πολεμήσας ἐπὶ μεταγνώσει τῆς ὑποδοχῆς, τῷ θυμῷ τε ὑπερέξεσε    80
καὶ πρὸς τὸν πόλεμον ἐντείνων ἑαυτὸν προκαταπέμπει τὸ Σαρακηνῶν
ἱππικὸν ὡς ἀντισχῆσον τοῖς βαρβάροις. ἤδη γὰρ καὶ τὴν Κωνσταντινούπολιν κατέτρυχον καὶ τοῖς τείχεσιν ἠνώχλουν περικαθήμενοι,
πολέμιόν τε οὐδὲν ὁρῶντες ἐς ἀντίπαλον μάχην καὶ τοῖς φρονήμασιν
ἐς πᾶσαν ὕβριν ὠλισθηκότες. ὃ δὴ καὶ περιφανῶς ἔδοξε κάλλιστα    85
στρατηγῆσαι κατὰ τὸν καιρὸν ἐκεῖνον ἡ τύχη.

(Zosimus 4,20,5 - 22,3)

## 43

1. (*Exc. de Sent.* 40-41)
    Ὅτι Μαρκιανὸς ἀνὴρ ἐς ἀρετὴν ἅπασαν ὥσπερ τις κανὼν
ἠκριβωμένος. φιλόκαλος γὰρ ὢν καὶ φιλάγαθος ὁ Μουσώνιος τοὺς
πανταχόθεν καθεῖλκεν παρ᾽ ἑαυτόν, ὥσπερ ἡ μαγνῆτις λίθος τὸν
σίδηρον. οὐκ ἦν δὲ βασανίζειν ὁποῖός τις ὁ δεῖνα, ἀλλὰ Μουσωνίου
φίλον ἀκούσαντα ὅτι καλὸς ἦν εἰδέναι.    (Cf. *Suda* M 208)    5

2 ἀπηκριβωμένος *Suda*    3 εἷλκε *Suda*    λίθος om. *Suda*

2. (*Exc. de Sent.* 42)
    Ὅτι συνηρῆσθαι τοῦ πολέμου δοκοῦντος Μουσώνιος ἵππου
ἐπιβὰς ἐξῄει τῶν Σάρδεων. καὶ ὁ Θεόδωρος τὸν συγγραφέα μεταπεμψάμενος ἐδάκρυσε τὴν ἔξοδον, καὶ ἀνδρὶ τἆλλα γε ἀτεράμονι καὶ
ἀτέγκτῳ δάκρυα κατεχεῖτο τῶν παρειῶν ἀκρατέστερον.

1 συνηρτῦσθαι van Herwerden    συνηρτῆσθαι Niebuhr

3. (*Exc. de Sent.* 43)
    Ὅτι τὸ ἐπὶ Μουσώνιον ἐπίγραμμα τὸ παρὰ Θεοδώρου τοι-
οῦτόν ἐστιν·

    ἔνθα μὲν Αἴας κεῖται ἀρήιος, ἔνθα δ᾽ Ἀχιλλεύς,
    ἔνθα δὲ Πάτροκλος θεόφιν μήστωρ ἀτάλαντος,
    ἔνθα δ᾽ ἐπὶ τρισσοῖσι πανείκελος ἡρώεσσι    5
    ψυχὴν καὶ βιότοιο τέλος Μουσώνιος ἥρως.

4. (*Exc. de Sent.* 44)
    Ὅτι οἱ Ῥωμαῖοι κατεκόπησαν παρὰ Ἰσαύρων, καὶ τούτῳ
ὥσπερ δράματι μεγάλῳ καὶ τραχεῖ τὸ κατὰ Μουσώνιον ἐπεισόδιον
οὐκ ἔλαττον ὁ δαίμων ἐπήνεγκεν. ἐνταῦθά που τῆς συγγραφῆς
ἀφώρισται τὸ πραχθέν, ὅτι τοῖς χρόνοις παρέτεινε καὶ συγκατέ-
στρεψεν ἐπὶ τὰ προειρημένα, ὥστε τοῖς καιροῖς μὴ πολὺ παραλ-    5
λάττειν ἐς τὸ τέλος τὴν γραφήν.

(Cf. *Suda* Δ 1498*, Ε 2143*)

he had received the Scythians, blaming himself and seething with rage, concentrated all his efforts upon the war. He sent ahead the Saracen cavalry to confront the barbarians, who were already attacking Constantinople and, settling down to a siege, were beginning to make attempts on the walls, since they saw none of the enemy coming out to fight them and were already slipping into over-confidence. Under the circumstances fortune seems to have planned this very advantageously for the Romans.[94]

(Zosimus 4,20,5 - 22,3)

## 43

1. (*Exc. de Sent.* 40-41)
    ... Marcianus was like a perfect model of every virtue. For Musonius, being a lover of beauty and goodness, attracted all to himself from all sides as a magnet attracts iron. One did not need to enquire after the character of someone, but if he were called a friend of Musonius', one knew that he was good.[95]     (Cf. *Suda* M 208)

2. (*Exc. de Sent.* 42)
    When the hostilities seemed to have been ended, Musonius mounted a horse and left Sardis. Theodorus summoned the historian and wept at Musonius' departure, and the tears poured uncontrollably down the cheeks of a man who was otherwise tough and unbending.[96]

3. (*Exc. de Sent.* 43)
    The following is Theodorus' epigram upon Musonius:
> "There warlike Ajax lies, there lies Achilles,
> There lies Patroclus, a god-like counsellor,
> There lies the hero, alike in all ways
> To all three in his soul and the end of his life,
> Musonius".

4. (*Exc. de Sent.* 44)
    The Romans were butchered by the Isaurians, and to this, as if to some great and savage tragedy, the god joined the no less terrible affair of Musonius. I have inserted this event at this point in my narrative, because it linked up with and found its conclusion at the time of the actions I earlier described, with the result that chronologically my account ends up more or less at the same point.[97]
(Cf. *Suda* Δ 1498*, E 2143*)

66     Eunapius: Text

5. (Vit. Soph. 10,7,13)
    Ἐπανέστη δὲ αὐτῷ ὁ Μουσώνιος, εἰς σοφιστικὴν ὁμιλητὴς ὢν
αὐτοῦ (περὶ οὗ πολλὰ διὰ τὰς ἄλλας <πράξεις> ἐν τοῖς διεξοδικοῖς
γέγραπται).

2 πράξεις add. Giangrande [αἰτίας add. Junius

(Zosimus 4,20,1-2)

44

1. (Exc. de Sent. 45)
    Ὅτι ὁ βασιλεὺς Οὐάλης κατὰ τὸν καιρὸν ἡνίκα οἱ Σκύθαι
τὴν Μακεδονίαν ἐπέτρεχον παρελθὼν εἰς τὴν πόλιν τὰς πανταχόθεν
δυνάμεις συνήγειρεν, ὡς μέγα τι καὶ παράδοξον ἐργαζόμενος. ὅσον
δὲ παιδεία ἀναγνώσεως ἰσχύει πρὸς τοὺς πολέμους καὶ ἡ διὰ τῆς
ἱστορίας ἀκριβὴς θεωρία πρὸς ἄμαχόν τινα καὶ γραμμικὴν ἔκβασιν     5
τελευτῶσι καὶ συνηναγκασμένην καὶ τότε ὁ χρόνος ἀπέδειξεν.
πολλῶν γὰρ ἐπὶ πολλοῖς μαρτυρούντων, καὶ τῆς πείρας πόρρωθεν
βοώσης ὅτι οὔτε πολλοῖς οὔτε ὀλίγοις μάχεσθαι προσῆκεν ἀπε-
γνωκόσιν ἑαυτῶν καὶ πρὸς κίνδυνον ἑτοίμως ἔχουσιν, ἀλλ᾽ ὅτι τοιαῦτα στρατόπεδα καταλύειν συμφέρει χρόνῳ τρίβοντα τὸν πόλεμον     10
καὶ περικόπτοντα τὰς ἀφορμὰς τῶν ἐπιτηδείων, ὅπως ὑφ᾽ ἑαυτῶν
πολεμῶνται δι᾽ ἔνδειαν πολλοὶ τυγχάνοντες, καὶ μὴ πρὸς τύχην ἀπο-
κινδυνεύωσιν, ἀλλ᾽ ἐν ἀπόρῳ καὶ τὸ κινδυνεύειν ἔχωσιν, ἐπὶ τοῖς
ἐναντίοις οὔσης τῆς ἐπιχειρήσεως.

3 ἐργαζόμενος cod. [ἐργασόμενος edd.        10 χρονοτριβοῦντα Dindorf
12 πολεμῶνται van Herwerden [πολεμοῖντο cod.

2. (Exc. de Sent. 46)
    Ὡς δὲ ἦν τοιούτων ἀρετῶν κτῆσις ... σπανιώτερον δὲ οὐδὲν
ἀρετῆς ἐν βίοις διεφθαρμένοις καὶ ἀγωγαῖς ἐπὶ τὸ χεῖρον προκατ-
ειλημμέναις.

lac. post κτῆσις indicant edd.

[3. (Suda Σ 177)
    Σεβαστιανός. οὗτος ἐπὶ Οὐάλεντος ἦν· ἐγένετο δὲ ἐπὶ τούτου
ἀνδρῶν πολεμικῶν ζήτησις· εὑρέθη δὲ οὗτος ὁ ἀνὴρ πάσης ἐλπίδος
κρείττων, οὐδεμᾶς ἀρετῆς ἀποδέων· οὐδενὸς γὰρ μὴ ὅτι τῶν καθ᾽
αὐτὸν ἀνθρώπων <ἐλείπετο>, ἀλλὰ καὶ τοῖς παλαιοῖς δίκαιος ἦν
παραβάλλεσθαι, καὶ τούτων τοῖς ἄγαν εὐδοκιμοῦσιν εἰς ἅπαντα. ὃς     5
γε φιλοπόλεμος μὲν ὤν, ἥκιστα φιλοκίνδυνος ἦν, οὐ δι᾽ ἑαυτόν, τῶν

4 ἐλείπετο add. Bernhardy

5. (*Vit. Soph.* 10,7,13)

His [Eusebius' of Alexandria] adversary was Musonius, who was a fellow student of the sophistic art, about whom, because of his other activities, I have written much in my History.

(Zosimus 4,20,1-2)[98]

## 44

1. (*Exc. de Sent.* 45)

At the time when the Scythians were overrunning Macedonia, the Emperor Valens arrived at Constantinople and was collecting his forces from all sides since he was facing a great and unexpected task. That occasion illustrated how a literary education has value in war and how those who aim at a goal directly, economically and without a fight are aided by the experience of events gained through reading history. For there is much evidence from many occasions, and experience from olden times shouts out, that one ought not, with forces either large or small, do battle with those who have come to despair of their lives and are ready to face danger. Rather one should destroy such armies by dragging out the war and by cutting off their sources of supplies, so that as a result of starvation their own numbers become their enemy, and they are unable to gamble on fortune, since to risk battle is not an option for them, that initiative lying with their opponents.[99]

2. (*Exc. de Sent.* 46)

Since the possession of such virtues was ... there is nothing rarer than virtue in lives which have been ruined and conduct which already inclines to evil.[100]

[3. (*Suda* Σ 177)

Sebastianus. He lived during Valens' reign. During this reign there was a search for good soldiers, and this man was discovered, who exceeded all expectations since he had all the virtues. He fell short of none of his contemporaries and was justly compared even with the most highly and widely esteemed of the ancients. He loved war but refused to take risks, not for his own sake but for that of his men. He

ἀρχομένων δὲ ἕνεκεν. χρημάτων δὲ αὐτῷ πλήθους ἔμελεν, ὅσα τὸ
σῶμα διὰ τῶν ὅπλων κοσμήσειν ἔμελλε· τροφὴν δὲ προῄρειτο
σκληρὰν καὶ τραχεῖαν, καὶ ὅση καμόντι ἤρκει, καὶ ὁρμωμένῳ πρὸς
κάματον οὐκ ἦν κώλυμα. φιλοστρατιώτης δὲ ὢν διαφερόντως,      10
στρατιώταις οὐκ ἐχαρίζετο, ἀλλὰ πᾶσάν τε ἀφῄρει πλεονεξίαν τὴν
ἀπὸ τῶν οἰκείων, καὶ τὸ ἁρπακτικὸν ἐπὶ τοὺς πολεμίους ἔτρεπεν·
ἐκόλαζε δὲ ἰσχυρῶς τοὺς παραβαίνοντας ταῦτα, καὶ τοῖς πειθομένοις
εἰς τὸ εὐπορεῖν συνηγωνίζετο. ἁπλῶς δὲ εἰπεῖν, ὑπόδειγμα καὶ
χαρακτῆρα παρεῖχεν ἑαυτὸν ἀρετῆς. γεγονὼς δὲ ἐπὶ μεγάλαις καὶ     15
λαμπραῖς στρατηγίαις, ὥσπερ ὁ Ῥοδίων κολοσσός, διὰ μέγεθος
καταπληκτικὸς ὤν, οὐκ ἔστιν ἐράσμιος, κἀκεῖνος διὰ τὸ ἀφιλοχρή-
ματον θαυμαστὸς ὤν, οὐκ ἔσχε χάριν· προσκεκρουκὼς δὲ διὰ
γνώμης ὀρθότητι τοῖς κατακοιμισταῖς εὐνούχοις τῶν βασιλέων,
εὔκολος ὢν διὰ πενίαν καὶ κοῦφος εἰς μετανάστασιν, διεδέχθη τῆς     20
στρατηγίας.   (Cf. K 1947, Π 2723)]

14 εὐπορεῖν M. Schmidt [εἶναι codd.      19 τοῦ βασιλέως Π 2723

4 (*Exc. de Sent.* 47)
    Ὅτι Σεβαστιανὸς τὴν ἡγεμονίαν παρὰ τοῦ βασιλέως Οὐάλεντος
εἰληφὼς παρὰ τὴν πάντων ὑπόνοιαν δισχιλίους ᾔτησεν ὁπλίτας. τὴν
δὲ ἐξουσίαν τῆς αἱρέσεως αὐτὸς ἐπιτραπείς, τοῦ βασιλέως καὶ χάριν
προσομολογήσαντος, ὅτι κινδυνεύσει περὶ δισχιλίους, εἶτα ἐρομένου
τὴν αἰτίαν, δι' ἣν ὀλίγους αἰτοίη, τὰ λοιπὰ ὁ Σεβαστιανὸς ἔφη τὸν      5
πόλεμον εὑρήσειν· τοῖς γὰρ εὖ πράττουσι πολλοὺς προσθήσεσθαι·
πλῆθος δὲ μετακαλεῖν ἐξ ἀναγωγίας δύσκολον· ὀλίγων δὲ ἀρχομένων
ἐς τὸ καλὸν μεταπλασθέντων, καὶ τῆς ἀγωγῆς ἐπιτυγχανούσης, τοὺς
κατὰ μικρὸν προσιόντας ῥᾴδιον ἐπὶ τὸ κρεῖττον ἐνταθήσεσθαι.

[5. (*Suda* E 374)
    Ὁ δὲ Οὐάλης ἐκβακχευθεὶς ἐπὶ τοὺς πολεμίους ἀθρόαν παρ-
ήγγειλεν ἔξοδον.]

(Zosimus 4,22,4 - 24,2)

# Liber IX
## 45

1. (*Suda* Π 444)
    Καὶ Εὐνάπιος· πολὺ διεστῶτας ἀλλήλων χωρεῖν ἐκέλευεν,
ὅπως μὴ δουποίη τὰ ὅπλα, μήτε τῷ παραστάτῃ θλιβόμενα, μήτε τῷ
φέροντι διὰ τὸν συνωθισμὸν περικτυπούμενα.

desired wealth only sufficient to equip himself with excellent weapons. He preferred an austere and simple diet, enough to revive his strength but not enough to hinder him at the start of a task. Although he was exceedingly fond of his men, he did not pander to the troops, but erased all of their eagerness to plunder the provincials and directed their rapacity against the enemy. Those who disobeyed these ordinances he punished severely, those who obeyed he helped to become wealthy.[101] In a word, he himself was an exemplar of virtue. He held high and illustrious commands, but just as the Colossus of Rhodes, though striking because of its size, is not loved, so he, though an object of wonderment because of his lack of greed, did not inspire affection. His uprightness annoyed the imperial eunuch-chamberlains, and, because his poverty made him good-natured and easy to remove, he was replaced in his command.[102]   (Cf. K 1947, Π 2723)]

4. (*Exc. de Sent.* 47)
When Sebastianus received his command from the Emperor Valens, against all expectations he asked for only two thousand soldiers. He was given leave to choose those whom he wished, and when the Emperor declared himself grateful that he would enter the war with only two thousand men and asked why he had chosen so few, Sebastianus replied that the war itself would discover the rest. "For", he said, "many will join those who enjoy success. But it is a hard task to recall a large number from bad habits. If at first a few are retrained to good discipline and their training brings success, those who gradually join them will easily be improved".[103]

[5. (*Suda* E 374)
Valens in a fury ordered the whole army to march against the enemy.]

(Zosimus 4,22,4 - 24,2)

# Book IX
## 45

1. (*Suda* Π 444)
He ordered them to advance in very loose order, so that their weapons should not make a noise, either through swinging against the next man or through clanging against themselves.[104]

2. (*Suda* Σ 1019)

Καὶ Εὐνάπιος· ὁ δὲ φέρων γράμματα ἐν χαλκῷ, στέατι περι-
πεπλασμένα, καθεὶς ἐν πήρᾳ, ἐπιθεὶς τε καὶ ἄλλους ἄρτους ὁμοίους,
ὡς μή τινα γνῶναι τὸ ἀπόρρητον.  (Cf. A 2202, K 67)

1-2 παραπεπλασμένα GM      2 ὁμοίως GM

3. (*Suda* Π 2351)

Εὐνάπιος· ὁ δὲ βασιλεὺς τούτους δεξάμενος· κτήματά τε αὐτοῖς
καὶ χώραν ἀπένειμε, καὶ προβόλους τε ὑπελάμβανε γενναίους καὶ
ἀδαμαντίνους ἔχειν πρὸς τὰς ἐκείνῃ τῶν Οὔννων ἐμβολάς.

(Zosimus 4,24,3 - 26,9)

## 46

1. (*Exc. de Sent.* 48)

Ὁ δὲ βασιλεὺς Θεοδόσιος, παραλαβὼν τοσαύτην ἀρχὴν καὶ
βασιλείαν, συνεμαρτύρησε τοῖς παλαιοῖς ἡλίκον ἐστὶ κακὸν ἐξουσία
καὶ ὅτι πρὸς τὰ πάντα στεγανόν τι καὶ μόνιμον πλὴν εὐτυχίας ἄνθρωπος. οὐ γὰρ ἔφθασε παρελθὼν ἐπὶ τὴν ἀρχήν, καὶ καθάπερ
μειράκιον νεόπλουτον πατρὸς ἐπὶ πολλῷ χρόνῳ πολλὰ χρήματα    5
σεσωρευκότος διὰ σωφροσύνην καὶ φειδώ, ἀθρόως κυριεῦσαν τῶν
πραγμάτων σφοδρόν τινα καὶ παντοῖον ὄλεθρον κατὰ τῶν εὑρε-
θέντων μαίνεται, οὕτω καὶ τότε ἦν ὁρῶντα ἐπισκοπεῖν ὥσπερ ἐκ
περιωπῆς, τόν γε ἔμφρονα, μηδένα τρόπον ἀμελούμενον κακίας καὶ
ἀκολασίας ἐς τὴν κοινὴν τῶν πραγμάτων διαφθοράν.    10

2. (*Suda* P 294)

Εὐνάπιος· τοσαύτη τις ἦν ἡ πρὸς τὸ ἀσελγέστερον ῥύμη τε καὶ
φορά, ὥστε οἱ ἄρχοντες τῶν πολεμίων ἦσαν πολεμιώτεροι.

3. (*Suda* Σ 478)

Εὐνάπιος· ὥστε ὁ σιρομάστης μᾶλλον εὐδοκίμει τοῦ δόρατος.

4. (*Exc. de Sent.* 49)

Ἀπορία γὰρ πρὸς εἰσφορὰς ἀκίνδυνον.

(Zosimus 4,27,1 - 29,2)

## 47

1. (*Exc. de Sent.* 50)

Οἱ δὲ Νικοπολῖται τῶν ἄλλων Θρακῶν κατεγέλασαν, οἳ τῷ
φόβῳ τῆς βασιλείας τὰ δεινὰ ἔπασχον, τὸ μὲν βοηθῆσον ἀεὶ δι᾽
ἐλπίδος λεπτῆς εἰκάζοντες, τὸ δὲ τῶν κινδύνων ἐνεστηκὸς πείρᾳ καὶ

2. (*Suda* Σ 1019)

He carried a letter graven on a bronze tablet, covered with dough and placed in a pouch with other similar cakes to prevent the discovery of the secret message.[105]    (Cf. A 2202, K 67)

3. (*Suda* Π 2351)

The Emperor received them and gave them supplies and land in the expectation that they would be an excellent and unyielding bulwark against the Hunnic inroads in that area.

(Zosimus 4,24,3 - 26,9)

## 46

1. (*Exc. de Sent.* 48)

When Theodosius became Emperor over such a large territory, he provided proof of the old adages that power is a great evil and that man is a creature steadfast and unyielding in the face of everything except good fortune. For no sooner had he become Emperor than he behaved like a youth who is heir to new wealth accumulated over a long time by the foresight and thrift of his father and who, when he has suddenly come into his inheritance, is seized by a violent desire to dissipate it in every way. Thus, at that time a wise observer could see as if from a watchtower that the Emperor was using every manner of wickedness and excess towards the ruin of the state.

2. (*Suda* P 294)

So strong was the impulse and inclination to excess, that the governors were more hostile than our enemies.

3. (*Suda* Σ 478)

. . . so that the pit-probe was more esteemed than the spear.

4. (*Exc. de Sent.* 49)

For penury is immune to taxation.[106]

(Zosimus 4,27,1 - 29,2)

## 47

1. (*Exc. de Sent.* 50)

The inhabitants of Nicopolis laughed at the rest of the Thracians, who, because they feared the power of the Emperor, were suffering terribly, persistently clinging to a slender hope of help in the future,

ὄψει διὰ μαλακίαν ὑπομένοντες. οὔτε γοῦν αὐτοὶ φρουράν τινα στρατιωτικὴν πεμφθήσεσθαι προσεδόκησαν οὔτε ἐν ἑτέροις ἔθεντο     5 τὴν σωτηρίαν, ἀλλὰ τῶν μὴ δυναμένων ἑαυτοῖς ἀμύνειν περιφρονή-σαντες ἐς ἐλευθερίαν ἐπικίνδυνον ἀπέστησαν.

5 οὔτε Dindorf [οὐδὲ cod.

2. (Exc. de Sent. 51)
    Ὅτι ἐπὶ Θεοδοσίου οἱ βάρβαροι τὴν Θράκην ἐδῄωσαν κατὰ μικρόν.

[3. (Suda E 2040)
    Τοιαῦτα καὶ τοσαῦτα ἐπέκλυσεν κακά, ὥστε χρυσὸς ἦν αὐτοῖς καὶ λευκή τις ἡμέρα κρατῆσαι τοὺς βαρβάρους.]

(Zosimus 4,30,1 - 33,2)

## 48

1. (Exc. de Sent. 52)
    Τοιοῦτον δέ τι ἱστόρηται γενέσθαι κατὰ τὴν Νέρωνος βασι-λείαν, ἀλλὰ περὶ μίαν πόλιν. φασὶ γὰρ τραγῳδόν τινα διὰ τὴν Νέρωνος εἰς ταῦτα φιλοτιμίαν ἐκπεσόντα τῆς Ῥώμης εἶτα πλανᾶσθαι, δόξαν αὐτῷ <εἰς ..> καὶ τὸ τῆς φωνῆς πλεονέκτημα πρὸς ἀν-     
θρώπους ἡμιβαρβάρους ἐπιδεικνύναι, καὶ παρελθεῖν εἰς τοιαύτην     5 μεγάλην πόλιν καὶ πολυάνθρωπον, συναγεῖραί τε αὐτοὺς εἰς θέατρον. καὶ συνελθόντων τὴν μὲν πρώτην ἡμέραν σφαλῆναι τῆς ἐπιδείξεως · οὐδὲ γὰρ τὴν ὄψιν ὑπομείναντας τοὺς θεατάς, ἅτε ἄρτι καὶ πρῶτον ἑωρακότας, φεύγειν θλιβομένους περὶ ἀλλήλοις καὶ πατουμένους. ὡς δὲ ὁ τραγῳδὸς ἰδίᾳ τοὺς πρώτους αὐτῶν ἀπολαβὼν τήν τε τοῦ     10 προσωπείου φύσιν ἐδείκνυ καὶ τοὺς ὀκρίβαντας, ὑφ' ὧν τὸ μέγεθος εἰς ὕψος παρατείνεται, καὶ συνέπεισεν οὕτως ἀνασχέσθαι καὶ τλῆναι τὴν ὄψιν, τότε παρελθὼν εἰς ἀνθρώπους καὶ ὡς μόλις ὑφισταμένους τὴν θέαν, τὸ μὲν πρῶτον ἐπιεικῶς καὶ μετρίως τῆς φωνῆς αὐτοῦ διέγευσε καὶ τοῦ μέλους (Εὐριπίδου δὲ τὴν Ἀνδρομέδαν ὑπεκρίνετο),     15 προϊὼν δὲ σφοδρότερόν τε ἤχησε καὶ ὑφῆκεν αὖθις, εἶτα ἐπήγαγεν ἁρμονίαν σύντονον, ἐπὶ ταύτῃ δὲ πάλιν εἰς τὴν γλυκεῖαν περιήνεγκεν. ὥρα δὲ ἦν θέρους ὅ τι περ ἀκμαιότατον καὶ τὸ θέατρον κατείχετο. καὶ ὁ τραγῳδὸς ἀναπαυσαμένους ἠξίου σφᾶς φοιτᾶν ἐπὶ τὴν ἀκρόασιν περὶ λήγουσαν καὶ ἀποψύχουσαν ἡμέραν · οἱ δὲ πρὸ τῶν ποδῶν     20 πεσόντες καὶ καλινδούμενοι πάσας ἀφίεσαν φωνὰς μήποτε αὐτοὺς

4 εἰς addidi et lacunam indicavi (fortasse Ἄβδηραν in lac.)     5 τοιαύτην [Ταρσὸν Niebuhr Ἴσπαλιν Bernhardy     14 αὐτοῦ scripsi [αὐτοῦ cod. αὐτοὺς Niebuhr     20 πρὸ Niebuhr [πρὸς cod.

while for the present they weakly endured the dangers which they saw and suffered. The Nicopolitans neither expected a military garrison to be sent to them nor did they rely on others for their safety, but, scorning those who were unable to defend themselves, opted for a precarious independence.[107]

2. (*Exc. de Sent.* 51)
    During the reign of Theodosius the barbarians gradually devastated Thrace.

[3. (*Suda* E 2040)
    So many woes of this kind beset them that they thought it a blessed and happy day if the barbarians conquered them.[108] ]

(Zosimus 4,30,1 - 33,2)

## 48

1. (*Exc. de Sent.* 52)
    It is said that something similar happened in Nero's reign, but in only one city. For they say that a certain tragic actor, having been exiled from Rome by Nero out of his jealousy in these matters, decided to go off <to . . .> and to exhibit his outstanding voice to men who were half barbarian; and he came to this great and populous city and invited them to the theatre.[109] When they gathered on the first day the performance was a failure, since the audience could not endure the sight, which they then saw for the first time, but fled, crushing and trampling each other in the process. But when the actor had taken the leading men aside and showed them the nature of the mask and the boots which increased his height, he persuaded them in this way to endure the sight and he came on stage again. Since the people could still hardly bear the spectacle, he at first very properly gave them a mild taste of his voice and its repertoire (he was performing Euripides' *Andromeda*) and as he proceeded he increased his volume, then lowered it, then introduced a severe song, and concluded with a sweet melody. It was summer and the hottest part of the day, and the theatre was full. The actor told them to take a rest and return to the recital at evening when it was growing cooler, but they threw themselves grovelling at his feet and entreated him in every way not to deprive them of such blessed

74     *Eunapius: Text*

ἀποστερῆσαι τοιαύτης μακαριότητος καὶ ἡδονῆς. ἐνταῦθα ὁ τραγῳδὸς
ἀφεὶς ἑαυτὸν ἐπὶ τὴν σκηνὴν καὶ τὸ πάθος, – καίτοι γε τὰ πλεῖστα
περιῄρητο τῆς τραγῳδίας πρὸς ἀνθρώπους ἀξυνέτους, ὄγκος τε καὶ
βαρύτης λέξεων καὶ τὸ περὶ ταῦτα εἶδος καὶ ἡ τοῦ μέτρου χάρις τό τε        25
τῶν ἠθῶν ἐναργές, ὀξύτατόν τε καὶ ἐπιφορώτατον εἰς ἀκοῆς κίνησιν,
καὶ πρὸς τούτοις τὸ γινώσκεσθαι τὴν ὑπόθεσιν, – ἀλλ᾽ ὅμως τούτων
ἁπάντων γεγυμνωμένος ἐς τοσόνδε τῇ τε εὐφωνίᾳ καὶ τῷ μέλει
μόνῳ κατεκράτησεν ὥστε οἱ μὲν ἀνεχώρουν προσκυνοῦντες ὡς θεὸν
καὶ τὰ ἐξαίρετα τῶν παρὰ σφίσιν αὐτῷ δῶρα ἐκόμιζον, καὶ τὸν        30
πλοῦτον ὁ τραγῳδὸς ἐβαρύνετο. μετὰ δὲ τὴν ἑβδόμην τῆς ἐπιδείξεως
ἡμέραν νόσημα κατέσκηψεν εἰς τὴν πόλιν, καὶ πάντες οὐ τὰς λέξεις
σαφῶς, ἀλλὰ τὸ μέλος, ὡς ἕκαστος εἶχε δυνάμεως καὶ φύσεως,
ἐκβοῶντες, καὶ διαρροίας ἀκρατοῦς ἅμα ἐπιπιπτούσης ἐν τοῖς
στενωποῖς παρεθέντες ἔκειντο, κακῶς ὑπὸ τῆς Ἀνδρομέδας ἐπι-        35
τριβόμενοι, καὶ ἐχηρώθη τε ἀνδρῶν καὶ γυναικῶν ἡ πόλις, ὥστε ἐκ
τῶν προσοίκων ἐποικισθῆναι. ἀλλ᾽ ἐπ᾽ ἐκείνων μὲν εὐφωνίαν τε ἦν
αἰτιάσασθαι καὶ ἀέρος ὑπερβάλλουσαν θερμότητα, ἢ τὸ μέλος διὰ
τῆς ἀκοῆς ἐπὶ τὰ κύρια τῶν ψυχικῶν ὀργάνων συνέτηξε καὶ διέ-
καυσεν· ἐπὶ δὲ τῶν καθ᾽ ἡμᾶς ἀνθρώπων αἱ μὲν αἰτίαι τοῦ πάθους        40
εὐθεώρητοι· περὶ τὰ ἔντερα γὰρ ἦσαν ἅπασαι καὶ ὑπὸ γαστέρα· τὸ
δὲ καί τινας τῶν οὐκ ἀνοήτων πρὸς τοῦτο ὠλισθηκέναι οὐκ εἰς
φυσικὴν ἄν τις εἰκότως, ἀλλ᾽ εἰς θειοτέραν ἀνενέγκοι κίνησιν, ὡς
ποινηλατεῖσθαι σαφῶς τὸ ἀνθρώπινον.

25 εἶδος [ἦδος Meineke    30 αὐτῷ Meineke [αὐτοῖς cod.    33 μέλος Dindorf
[γένος cod.

## 2. (*Exc. de Sent.* 53)

Φυλαὶ μὲν γὰρ τῶν πολεμίων <εἰς> τὴν ἀρχὴν διεβεβήκεσαν
ἄπειροι, καὶ πλείους ἐπιδιέβαινον, οὐδενὸς κωλύοντος· ἀλλ᾽ ἐν τοσούτοις κακοῖς κέρδος αὐτοῖς ἐδόκει γνήσιον τὸ δωροδοκεῖσθαι παρὰ
τῶν πολεμίων. εἶχε δὲ ἑκάστη φυλὴ ἱερά τε οἴκοθεν τὰ πάτρια συν-
εφελκομένη καὶ ἱερέας τούτων καὶ ἱερείας· ἀλλὰ στεγανή τις ἦν λίαν        5
καὶ ἀδαμάντινος ἡ περὶ ταῦτα σιωπὴ καὶ τῶν ἀπορρήτων ἐχεμυθία.
ἡ δὲ εἰς τὸ φανερὸν προσποίησις καὶ πλάσις εἰς τὴν τῶν πολεμίων
ἀπάτην διηρτυμένη καὶ συντεθειμένη, Χριστιανοί τε εἶναι πάντες
ἔλεγον καί τινας ὡς ἐπισκόπους αὐτῶν ἐς τὸ θαυμαζόμενον σχῆμα
καταστολίσαντες καὶ περικρύψαντες, καὶ πολλῆς αὐτοῖς τῆς ἀλώ-        10
πεκος ἐπιχέαντες, εἰς τὸ μέσον προηφίεσαν, πανταχοῦ τὸ ἀφύλακτον
διὰ τῶν καταφρονουμένων ὅρκων παρ᾽ ἐκείνοις, παρὰ δὲ τοῖς βασιλεῦσι σφόδρα φυλαττομένων, ὑποτρέχοντες καὶ κατασκευάζοντες.

1 εἰς addidi    7 τὸ [τι Boissevain

enjoyment. Thereupon the actor returned to the stage and launched into a passionate piece. Although most of the qualities of the tragedy — the dignity and profundity of the words and the form used to this purpose, the charm of the metre, the clarity of characterisation, the sharpness and suitability of the tone, and in addition a comprehension of the plot — were lost upon these ignorant people, nevertheless, having worked himself up to this performance, he won them by his melodious singing alone, so that when they left the theatre they worshipped him as a god and brought him as gifts the choicest of their possessions, and the actor was weighed down with riches. On the seventh day after the performance disease fell upon the city, and, since it brought with it an uncontrollable diarrhoea, they all lay about feebly in the streets, singing not the actual words but the tunes, as best they could. Thus they were horribly destroyed by the *Andromeda*, and the city was denuded of its men and women, so that it had to be repopulated from the neighbourhood. In their case the melodiousness was to blame and the excessive warmth of the air which caused the singing to dissolve through the ears and burn into the seat of the vital organs. But in the case of our contemporaries the causes of the ailment were easy to see in that they were all centred upon the intestines and the parts below the belly; although the fact that some people who were by no means fools fell into this would reasonably be ascribed not to natural causes but to divine agency, to make it clear that mankind was under attack by the Furies.[110]

## 2. (*Exc. de Sent.* 53)

For countless tribes had crossed into the Empire and more followed, since there was no one to prevent them. But in so desperate a situation they [i.e. the barbarians] considered it legitimate gain to accept gifts from the enemy. Each tribe had brought along from home its ancestral objects of worship together with their priests and priestesses, but they kept a deep and impenetrable silence upon these things and spoke not a word about their mysteries. What they revealed was fiction and sham designed to fool their enemies. They all claimed to be Christians and some of their number they disguised as their bishops and dressed them up in that respected garb and, providing for them, as it were, a large fox-skin,[111] brought them forward. Thereby they were able to get access to and appropriate what they rendered unguarded by swearing oaths which they held in contempt but which the Emperors

ἦν δέ τι καὶ τῶν καλουμένων μοναχῶν παρ' αὐτοῖς γένος, κατὰ
μίμησιν τῶν παρὰ τοῖς πολεμίοις ἐπιτετηδευμένον, οὐδὲν ἐχούσης τῆς    15
μιμήσεως πραγματῶδες καὶ δύσκολον, ἀλλὰ ἐξήρκει φαιὰ ἱμάτια
σύρουσι καὶ χιτώνια πονηροῖς τε εἶναι καὶ πιστεύεσθαι. καὶ τοῦτο
ὀξέως συνεῖδον οἱ βάρβαροι τὸ θαυμαζόμενον παρὰ 'Ρωμαίοις ῥαδίως
ἐς παραγωγὴν ἐπιτηδεύσαντες, ἐπὶ τά γε ἄλλα μετὰ βαθύτητος καὶ
σκέπης ὅτι μάλιστα στεγανωτάτης τῶν ἀπορρήτων τὰ παρὰ σφίσιν    20
ἱερὰ γεννικῶς τε καὶ ἀδόλως φυλάττοντες. οὕτω δὲ ἐχόντων τούτων,
ὅμως ἐς τοσαύτην ἄνοιαν ἐξεπεπτώκεσαν ὥστε συμπεπεῖσθαι
σαφῶς καὶ ἀμάχως τοὺς δοκοῦντας νοῦν ἔχειν ὅτι Χριστιανοί τέ εἰσι
καὶ πάσαις ταῖς τελεταῖς ἀνέχοντες.

15 ἐπιτετηδευμένον Niebuhr [ἐπιτετηδευμένων cod.   19 ἐπὶ scripsi [ἐπεὶ cod.
καίτοι Boissevain   21 post φυλάττοντες add. διετέλουν Niebuhr
24 ἀνέχοντες Dindorf [ἀνεχον... cod. ἐνέχονται Boissevain

3. (*Exc. de Sent.* 54)

Ὅτι ἐπὶ Θεοδοσίου τοῦ βασιλέως ἐς τοῦτο ἤδη συνέπεσεν
ἅπαντα καὶ περιηνέχθη κατά τινα βίαν ἀπαραίτητον καὶ ἀνάγκην
ἀνυπόστατον καὶ θεήλατον ὡς καὶ τὸ τῶν ὄνων γένος, μὴ ὅτι τῶν
ἵππων, ἀλλὰ καὶ τῶν ἐλεφάντων γενέσθαι τιμιώτερον. ὁ μὲν οὖν
Μακεδὼν Φίλιππος καταζευγνύναι μέλλων περὶ ἑσπέραν ἤδη, εἶτα    5
πυθόμενος ὡς οὐ δυνατόν, εἰπόντων τῶν κωλυόντων χιλὸν οὐχ ὑπάρχειν ἱκανὸν τοῖς ὑποξυγίοις, ἀνέζευξε τοῦτ' ἐπειπών, ὡς οὐδὲν
βασιλέως ἀτυχέστερον, ὃς καὶ πρὸς τὸν τῶν ὄνων καιρὸν ζῆν ἀναγκάζεται. ὁ δὲ καθ' ἡμᾶς χρόνος ἐκινδύνευσεν ὅλος ἐπὶ τοῖς ὄνοις
σαλεύειν.    10

(Zosimus 4,33,3-4)

## 49

(Zosimus 4,34,1 - 35,1)

## 50

(*Exc. de Sent.* 55)

Τοῦ βασιλέως δὲ Γρατιανοῦ τὰ μὲν καθ' ἕκαστον καὶ οἷός τις
ἦν οὔτε δυνατὸν ἦν περιεργάζεσθαι (τὰ γὰρ ἐν τοῖς βασιλείοις ἐπι-
κρύπτεται καὶ μάλα στεγανῶς) οὔτε πολυπραγμονοῦντι συμμαθεῖν·
τὰ γὰρ ἀπαγγελλόμενα παρ' ἑκάστου, πολλὰς καὶ πολυμόρφους τὰς
διαφορὰς ἔχοντα, μόνην τὴν ἀλήθειαν ὥσπερ τινὰ θησαυρὸν ἀπόρ-    5
ρητον οὐ διεγύμνου καὶ ἀπεκάλυπτεν. ὥσπερ οὖν τοῖς γράφουσι τὰς
εἰκόνας καὶ τὸ δοθὲν παράδειγμα χαρακτηρίζουσιν ἐπιτείνει τὴν περὶ
τὸ πρόσωπον ὁμοιότητα μικρά τινα τῶν ὑποκειμένων συμβόλων, καὶ

greatly respected. They also had with them some of the tribe of so-called 'monks', whom they had decked out in imitation of the monks amongst their enemies. The imitation was neither laborious nor difficult, but it sufficed for them to trail along grey cloaks and tunics to both become and be accepted as evildoers. The barbarians used these devices to deceive the Romans, since they shrewdly observed that these things were respected amongst them, while the rest of the time, under cover of the deepest secrecy, they worshipped the holy objects of their native rites with noble and guileless intent. Although the situation was such, the Romans had fallen into such folly that even those who appeared to be sensible persons were clearly and readily persuaded that they were Christians and bound by all Christian rites.[112]

3. (*Exc. de Sent.* 54)

In the reign of the Emperor Theodosius the whole situation was adverse and unstable under some unavoidable compulsion and inexorable necessity brought on by the gods, so that even asses were more valuable, not only than horses, but even than elephants. When Philip the Macedonian wished at evening to halt his army and when he learned that he could not because, as those who were advising to the contrary pointed out, there was not enough pasture for the draught animals, he ordered the army to move on, adding that nothing was more unfortunate than a king who was forced to regulate his life according to the convenience of asses. Our age seemed totally to ride upon the backs of asses.[113]

(Zosimus 4,33,3-4)

## 49

(Zosimus 4,34,1 - 35,1)

## 50

(*Exc. de Sent.* 55)

Despite a diligent enquiry I was unable to make a full investigation and gain information on the individual actions of the Emperor Gratian and the qualities he showed therein, since these things were extremely closely guarded secrets in the palace. The reports passed on by individuals contained many and various discrepancies and did not reveal the simple truth, but rather concealed it like some forbidden treasure. A parallel is offered by the portrait painter who seeks to capture the sitter before him. The likeness of the face is captured through some of its

ἢ ῥυτὶς ἐπὶ τοῦ μετώπου διακεχαραγμένη ἤ τις ἴονθος παρανατέλλων
παρὰ τὸ γένειον ἢ τοιοῦτό τι μικρὸν καὶ παρημελημένον τῶν κατὰ    10
τὴν ὄψιν, ὃ παροφθὲν μὲν οὐχ ὑπογράφει τὸ εἶδος, ἀκριβωθὲν δὲ
μόνον αἴτιον τῆς ὁμοιότητος γίνεται, οὕτως ἔξεστι καὶ ἐπὶ τοῦδε τοῦ
βασιλέως συλλαμβάνειν οἷός τις ἦν, νέος τε ὢν καὶ ἐν ἐξουσίᾳ βασιλικῇ τραφεὶς ἐκ παιδὸς καὶ μὴ μεμαθηκὼς οἷον τὸ ἄρχον καὶ οἷον τὸ
ἀρχόμενον· τοῦτο γὰρ μάλιστα διαφαίνει τὸ τῆς φύσεως μέγεθος,    15
ὅταν τὴν προτεθεῖσαν ἀγωγὴν καὶ συνήθειαν ἡ φύσις ἐπὶ τὸ κρεῖττον
ἐξώσῃ καὶ βιάσηται. ἔξεστι δὲ λαβεῖν ἐκ τῶν ὑποκειμένων παρα-
δειγμάτων, εἰς ἃ συνωμολόγουν ἅπαντες καὶ ἀντέλεγεν οὐδὲ εἰς τῶν
ληρεῖν συνειθισμένων καὶ τὸν κοινὸν φλήναφον ἠσκηκότων.

9 ἢ Boissevain [η cod. ἡ edd.      14 ἄρχον Meineke [ἄρχειν cod.      17 λαβεῖν
Boissevain [μαθεῖν Mai      19 ληρεῖν Boissevain [λέγειν edd.

(Zosimus 4,35,2-6)

**51**

(Zosimus 4,37)

**52**

(Zosimus 4,38-40)

**53**

(Zosimus 4,41)

**54**

(Zosimus 4,42-47)

**55**

(*Exc. de Sent.* 56)

  Ὅτι ἐπὶ Θεοδοσίου τοῦ Μαξίμου στασιάσαντος καὶ βαρβάρων
κατὰ Ῥωμαίων ἐκστρατευσάντων φήμη κατέσχε τοῖς βαρβάροις ὡς
οἱ Ῥωμαῖοι στρατὸν ὅτι πλεῖστον συλλέγουσι. καὶ συλλογισάμενοι τὸ
δεινὸν οἱ βάρβαροι ἐπὶ τὸ σύνηθες ἀνέδραμον σόφισμα, καὶ κατέδυσαν
ἐπὶ τὰς Μακεδονικὰς λίμνας. καὶ συμφανές γε ἅπασι κατέστη ὡς ἡ    5
Ῥωμαίων βασιλεία, τρυφὴν μὲν ἀρνουμένη, πόλεμον δὲ αἱρουμένη,
οὐδὲν ἀφίησι τῆς γῆς τὸ ἀνήκοον καὶ ἀδούλωτον. ἀλλὰ δεινόν γέ τι
χρῆμα ταῖς τῶν ἀνθρώπων φύσεσιν ὁ θεὸς ἐγκατέμιξεν, ὥσπερ τοῖς
ὀστακοῖς τὴν ἐπικίνδυνον χολὴν καὶ τοῖς ῥόδοις ἀκάνθας, οὕτω ταῖς

2 τοῖς βαρβάροις Mai      7 τὸ cod. [ἔτι Kuiper

minor characteristics – a deep furrow on the brow, prominent side-
burns, or some similar insignificant detail of the features, which, if
overlooked, causes the portrait to fail, but if rendered accurately, is the
sole reason why the likeness has been caught. Just so, in the case of this
Emperor, one can infer what kind of man he was, since, though still
young, he had been Emperor from childhood, and yet had learned
neither how to rule nor how to be ruled. For greatness of character is
especially shown when one's natural virtue overcomes the conduct and
mores that have been implanted in one and forces them to grow better.
It is possible to draw a portrait of Gratian from the available examples
of his behaviour upon which all agree to a man, even those whose habit
it is to spread the usual idle gossip.[114]


(Zosimus 4,35,2-6)

## 51
(Zosimus 4,37)

## 52
(Zosimus 4,38-40)

## 53
(Zosimus 4,41)

## 54
(Zosimus 4,42-47)

## 55
(*Exc. de Sent.* 56)

During the reign of Theodosius, when Maximus had rebelled and
the barbarians had launched an attack on the Romans, a report reached
the barbarians that the Romans were gathering their largest possible
army. The barbarians, contemplating the danger to themselves, resorted
to their usual plan and hid in the marshes of Macedonia. It was clear to
all that if the Roman state rejected luxury and embraced war, it would
conquer and enslave all the world. But God has set a deadly trait in
human nature, like the poisonous gall in a lobster or thorns on a rose.

ἐξουσίαις συγκατασπείρας τὴν ἡδονὴν καὶ ῥαθυμίαν, δι᾽ ἥν, πάντα    10
ἐξὸν εἰς μίαν μεταστῆσαι πολιτείαν καὶ συναρμόσαι τὸ ἀνθρώπινον,
αἱ βασιλεῖαι τὸ θνητὸν σκοποῦσαι πρὸς τὸ ἡδὺ καταφέρονται, τὸ τῆς
δόξης ἀθάνατον οὐκ ἐξετάζουσαι καὶ παρεκλέγουσαι.

13 παρεκλέγουσαι cod. [παραβλέπουσαι van Herwerden

(Zosimus 4,48-50)

## 56

(*Vit. Soph.* 6,11,1-7)

Οὐ γὰρ ἔφθανεν ἐκεῖνος ἐξ ἀνθρώπων ἀπιών, καὶ ἥ τε θεραπεία τῶν κατὰ τὴν Ἀλεξάνδρειαν καὶ τὸ Σαραπεῖον ἱερῶν διεσκε-
δάννυτο· οὐχ ἡ θεραπεία μόνον, ἀλλὰ καὶ τὰ οἰκοδομήματα, καὶ
πάντα ἐγίνετο καθάπερ ἐν ποιητικοῖς μύθοις, τῶν Γιγάντων κεκρα-
τηκότων. καὶ τὰ περὶ τὸν Κάνωβον ἱερὰ ταὐτὸ τοῦτο ἔπασχον, Θεο-    5
δοσίου μὲν τότε βασιλεύοντος, Θεοφίλου δὲ προστατοῦντος τῶν
ἐναγῶν, ἀνθρώπου τινὸς Εὐρυμέδοντος
        ὅς ποθ᾽ ὑπερθύμοισι Γιγάντεσσιν βασίλευεν,
Εὐαγρίου δὲ τὴν πολιτικὴν ἀρχὴν ἄρχοντος, Ῥωμανοῦ δὲ τοὺς κατ᾽
Αἴγυπτον στρατιώτας πεπιστευμένου· οἴτινες, ἅμα φραξάμενοι κατὰ    10
τῶν ἱερῶν καθάπερ κατὰ λίθων καὶ λιθοξόων θυμόν, ἐπὶ ταῦτα
ἀλλόμενοι, πολέμου δὲ μήτε ἀκοὴν ὑφιστάμενοι, τῷ τε Σαραπείῳ
κατελυμήναντο καὶ τοῖς ἀναθήμασιν ἐπολέμησαν, ἀνανταγώνιστον
καὶ ἄμαχον νίκην νικήσαντες. τοῖς γοῦν ἀνδριάσι καὶ ἀναθήμασιν ἐς
τοσόνδε γενναίως ἐμαχέσαντο, ὥστε οὐ μόνον ἐνίκων αὐτά, ἀλλὰ καὶ    15
ἔκλεπτον, καὶ τάξις ἦν αὐτοῖς πολεμικὴ τὸν ὑφελόμενον λαθεῖν. τοῦ δὲ
Σαραπείου μόνον τὸ ἔδαφος οὐχ ὑφείλοντο διὰ βάρος τῶν λίθων, οὐ
γὰρ ἦσαν εὐμετακίνητοι· συγχέαντες δὲ ἅπαντα καὶ ταράξαντες, οἱ
πολεμικώτατοι καὶ γενναῖοι, καὶ τὰς χεῖρας ἀναιμάκτους μέν, οὐκ
ἀφιλοχρημάτους δὲ προτείναντες, τούς τε θεοὺς ἔφασαν νενικηκέναι,    20
καὶ τὴν ἱεροσυλίαν καὶ τὴν ἀσέβειαν εἰς ἔπαινον σφῶν αὐτῶν κατε-
λογίζοντο.

Εἶτα ἐπεισῆγον τοῖς ἱεροῖς τόποις τοὺς καλουμένους μοναχούς,
ἀνθρώπους μὲν κατὰ τὸ εἶδος, ὁ δὲ βίος αὐτοῖς συώδης, καὶ ἐς τὸ
ἐμφανὲς ἔπασχόν τε καὶ ἐποίουν μυρία κακὰ καὶ ἄφραστα. ἀλλ᾽    25
ὅμως τοῦτο μὲν εὐσεβὲς ἐδόκει, τὸ καταφρονεῖν τοῦ θείου· τυραννικὴν
γὰρ εἶχεν ἐξουσίαν τότε πᾶς ἄνθρωπος μέλαιναν φορῶν ἐσθῆτα, καὶ
δημοσίᾳ βουλόμενος ἀσχημονεῖν· ἐς τοσόνδε ἀρετῆς ἤλασε τὸ ἀνθρώπινον. ἀλλὰ περὶ τούτων μὲν καὶ ἐν τοῖς καθολικοῖς τῆς ἱστορίας
συγγράμμασιν εἴρηται.    30

9 Εὐαγρίου Seeck [Εὐετίου codd.

For in high authority he has implanted love of pleasure and ease, with the result that, while they have all the means with which to unite mankind into one polity, our Emperors in their concern for the transient turn to pleasure while neither pursuing nor showing interest in the immortality which is brought by glory.

(Zosimus 4,48-50)

## 56

(*Vit. Soph.* 6,11,1-7)

For as soon as he [Antoninus] departed from mankind the cults of the gods at Alexandria and at the Serapeum were destroyed, and not only the cults but the temples also, and it was all as in the myths of the poets when the Giants had won; and the temples at Canobus suffered exactly the same fate. Theodosius was then Emperor, and Theophilus was the leader of the defiled ones, a man who was a sort of Eurymedon,
who once ruled the overweening Giants,
and Evagrius was the civil governor of Egypt, and Romanus the military commander. These men, girding their anger at the holy objects for a battle against stones and stone-masons and hearing not a sound of war, fell upon these things, wreaked destruction on the Serapeum, fought with its votive offerings, and won a victory without facing an enemy or fighting a battle. They fought so nobly against the statues and the votive offerings that they not only conquered but stole them also, leaving only the floor of the Serapeum because of the weight of the stones, which were difficult to move. Their strategy in this war was that the thief should avoid detection, and when they had thrown everything into turmoil and confusion, these most warlike and noble men raised their hands, stained not by blood but by money, and declared that they had defeated the gods and held their temple-robbery and impiety a matter for praise.

Then they brought into the holy places the so-called 'monks', men in appearance but swine in their way of life, and they both permitted and themselves performed openly thousands of unspeakable indignities, thinking it pious, however, to show contempt for things divine. For at that time whoever wore a black cloak and wished to behave disgracefully in public had the power of a tyrant, to such a height of virtue had mankind come. But these things I have described in the general narrative of my History.

57

(*Exc. de Sent.* 57)

Ὅτι ὀλισθηρόν, ὡς ἔοικε, καὶ σφαλερώτερον ἄνθρωπος πρὸς τιμὴν ἢ συμφοράν. θεραπεύσαντες γὰρ τὸν Τατιανὸν οἱ περὶ τὸν βασιλέα Θεοδόσιον, τιμάς τε ὑπερφυεῖς ἐκ τοῦ βασιλέως καὶ μεταγνώσεις ἐπὶ τοῖς γεγενημένοις ἐνσπόνδους ποιησάμενοι, καὶ περὶ τῶν μελλόντων οὐρανομήκεις ἐλπίδας ὑποσπείραντες, τοῦτον παρέ-     5
πεισαν ἀγαγεῖν τὸν υἱὸν αὐτοῦ Πρόκλον τοὔνομα· ὃν εἰς τὸ δεσμωτήριον συνέκλεισαν, καὶ τὸν Τατιανὸν ἐπὶ Λυκίας ἀπέπεμψαν τοῦ παιδὸς χηρώσαντες.

5 ὑποσπείραντες Boissevain [ὑποτείναντες edd.

(Zosimus 4,51-52)

58

[1. (*Suda* A 81)

Ἀβρογάστης. Φράγγος, ὃς κατὰ ἀλκὴν σώματος καὶ θυμοῦ τραχύτητα φλογοειδὴς ἦν, δευτεραγωνίστης τυγχάνων Βαύδωνος. ἄλλως τε ἦν καὶ πρὸς σωφροσύνην πεπηγώς τε καὶ διηρθρωμένος, καὶ πρὸς χρήματα πόλεμον πολεμῶν ἄσπονδον. διέφερε γοῦν τῶν εὐτελῶν στρατιωτῶν ὅσον γε εἰς πλοῦτον οὐδέν. καὶ διὰ τοῦτο ἐδόκει     5
τῷ βασιλεῖ Θεοδοσίῳ χρήσιμος, ὅς γε πρὸς τὸν Οὐαλεντινιανοῦ τρόπον, ἀρρενωπὸν ὄντα καὶ δίκαιον, καὶ τὸ παρ' ἑαυτοῦ βάρος ἐπετίθει, καθάπερ ὀρθὸν καὶ ἀστραβῆ τινα κανόνα τοῖς βασιλείοις, πρὸς τὸ μηδὲν τῶν περὶ τὴν αὐλὴν παραβλάπτεσθαι ἢ ἁμαρτάνεσθαι.]

[2. (John of Antioch *Fr.* 187 = *Exc. de Ins.* 79)

Ὅτι ἐπὶ Θεοδοσίου τοῦ βασιλέως Οὐαλεντινιανὸς ὁ νέος βασιλεὺς ἀγγέλλεται ἐξ ἐπιβουλῆς τοιᾶσδε τεθνηκέναι. ὁ τούτου πατὴρ Οὐαλεντινιανὸς γυναιξὶ πλείοσιν ἐχρήσατο παρὰ τοὺς διατεταγμένους Ῥωμαίων νόμους. ἡ τοίνυν τούτου δευτέρα γυνὴ θυγάτηρ μὲν ἐλέγετο γεγενῆσθαι Ἰούστου, Μαγνεντίου δὲ γυνὴ τοῦ τυραννήσαντος κατὰ     5
τοὺς Κωνσταντίου χρόνους, διὰ νεότητά τε οὐ τυχοῦσα τέκνων ἐξ ἐκείνου χηρεύουσα καὶ ἐγκρατευομένη διετέλει. ἧς διὰ κάλλους ὑπερβολὴν ἐρασθεὶς ὁ βασιλεὺς ἄγεται ταύτην κατὰ δεύτερον γάμον. ἐξ ἧς Οὐαλεντινιανὸς ὁ νέος ὁ Θεοδοσίῳ συμβασιλεύσας ἐτέχθη, καὶ Γάλλα ἡ Θεοδοσίῳ συναφθεῖσα μετὰ τὴν Φλακίλλης τελευτήν, καθ'     10
ὃν καιρὸν τόν τε Μάξιμον ἐνίκα καὶ τὸν Οὐαλεντινιανὸν ἔσωζεν· ὥστε ὑπῆρχεν αὐτῷ πρὸς τὰ κοινὰ τῆς βασιλείας καὶ ἡ τῆς κηδείας συνάφεια.

Τότε δὴ οὖν τῆς τοῦ Οὐαλεντινιανοῦ ἀναιρέσεως διαγγελθείσης, μέγιστον κατεῖχε πένθος αὐτόν τε τὸν βασιλέα τῆς ἕω καὶ     15

## 57
(*Exc. de Sent.* 57)

Man is a creature more likely to slip and fall in the face of honour than of misfortune. For those around Theodosius paid court to Tatianus, promising him that the Emperor would forget the past and confer upon him extraordinary honours, and, by offering him sky-high hopes for the future, they persuaded him to bring along his son Proculus. The latter they threw into gaol and they exiled Tatianus to Lycia after depriving him of his son.[115]


(Zosimus 4,51-52)


## 58
[1. (*Suda* A 81)

Abrogastes, a Frank, second-in-command to Baudo, and one whose physical strength and fierce temper made him like an inferno. Otherwise, his temperance was firm and complete, and he waged an endless war on corruption. His wealth was no more than that of a common soldier. For this reason he seemed to the Emperor Theodosius to be an ideal person to reinforce with his own gravity the habits of Valentinian, which were manly and just, and, as a model of rectitude in the palace, to ensure that no criminal acts or injuries be committed at court.[116]]

[2. (John of Antioch *Fr.* 187 = *Exc. de Ins.* 79)

During the reign of the Emperor Theodosius news came that the young Emperor Valentinian had been killed as the result of a plot, the manner of which was as follows. His father Valentinian had a number of wives contrary to Roman law. His second wife was said to have been the daughter of Justus and the wife of Magnentius who had usurped during the reign of Constantius [II]. Because of her youth she had had no children by Magnentius and was at the time living as a celibate widow. The Emperor fell in love with her because of her great beauty and made her his second wife. Her children were the younger Valentinian, co-Emperor with Theodosius, and Galla, who was married to Theodosius after the death of Flacilla, at the time when he defeated Maximus and saved Valentinian. Thus they were co-Emperors and related by marriage.[117]

When the murder of Valentinian was reported, great grief fell upon the Emperor of the East and the dead man's sister, the Empress

84   Eunapius: Text

τὴν ἀδελφὴν τοῦ τετελευτηκότος βασιλίδα Γάλλαν, μεγάλη τε
ἐμελετᾶτο τοῦ πολέμου σπουδὴ κατὰ τοῦ τὸν φόνον ἐργασαμένου.
Ἀρβωγάστης δὲ ἦν, ἐκ τοῦ Φράγκων γένους, Βάνδωνος τοῦ πρὸς
Γρατιανοῦ τοῦ βασιλεύσαντος τὴν στρατοπεδαρχικὴν ἐξουσίαν ἐπι-
τραπέντος υἱός, φλογοειδής τε καὶ βάρβαρος τὴν ψυχήν, ὃς τὸν     20
Οὐαλεντινιανὸν βιασάμενος εἰς τὴν τοῦ πατρὸς παρῆλθε στρατη-
λασίαν· οὐ γὰρ ἦν ἀντιλέγειν αὐτῷ διὰ τὴν ἐν τοῖς πολέμοις ῥώμην.
οὗτος γοῦν πολλοὺς τῶν ἐν ἀξιώμασι παρὰ τὴν τοῦ βασιλέως βουλὴν
διεχειρίζετο, καὶ τούτους οὐ μόνον ἀγνοοῦντος τοῦ κρατοῦντος, ἀλλὰ
καὶ κωλύοντος· ἐν οἷς καὶ τὸν Ἁρμόνιον, ὃς Ταύρου μὲν ἦν παῖς τοῦ     25
τὴν ὕπατον διέποντος, ἐπειδή τι τὸν Ἀρβωγάστην ἐλύπησεν, ὁ μὲν ἐπὶ
τὸ ξίφος τὴν χεῖρα ἔτρεψεν, ὁ δὲ Ἁρμόνιος τῷ βασιλεῖ τὸ σῶμα
παραδοὺς σὺν τῇ ἁλουργίδι κατετέμνετο· ἐκ τούτου τε πολλὴ πρὸς
τὸν στρατοπεδάρχην καὶ τὸν βασιλέα γέγονεν ἡ ὑπόνοια. καὶ ὁ μὲν
Οὐαλεντινιανὸς τὴν Θεοδοσίου λάθρα μετεπέμπετο συμμαχίαν, ὡς     30
μὴ δυνάμενος φέρειν τὴν τοῦ τυράννου θρασύτητα· πλὴν ὥς τι σοφὸν
κατὰ τοῦ τυράννου πράττειν ἡγούμενος γραμματεῖον αὐτῷ τῆς διαδοχῆς ἐπὶ τοῦ συνεδρίου δίδωσιν. ὅπερ δεξάμενος ὁ βάρβαρος καὶ
ἀναγνοὺς παραχρῆμα τοῖς ὄνυξι διεσπάραξεν, λεοντώδει δὲ τῇ φωνῇ
κατὰ τοῦ βασιλέως ὀργισθείς, ἀπῄει πρόκωπον ἔχων τὸ ξίφος.     35
πολέμιος τοίνυν ἀπεδείχθη φανερὸς τῇ Ῥωμαίων ἀρχῇ. καὶ ὁ μὲν
Οὐαλεντινιανὸς ἐβούλετο παραχρῆμα πρὸς τὸν Θεοδόσιον ἐξιππεύ-
σασθαι, ὁ δὲ βάρβαρος τὴν κατ' αὐτοῦ κίνησιν ἐπιτείνας, πρός τι
πολισμάτιον Ἰταλικὸν Βέρναν λεγόμενον διατρίβοντι καὶ ῥᾳθυμό-
τερον περὶ τὴν τοῦ πολιχνίου φρουρὰν διαγενομένῳ προσπεσὼν καὶ     40
ἀφύλακτον τοῦτον εὑρὼν ξίφει διεχρήσατο. οὕτω μὲν οὖν Οὐαλεντινιανὸς ὁ νέος βιώσας ἔτη κ', βασιλεύσας δὲ ἔτη η', καταστρέφει
τὸν βίον.

Ὁ δὲ Ἀρβωγάστης, Εὐγένιον αὐτῷ ἐπὶ σοφιστικὸν ἐγκαθή-
μενον θρόνον, καὶ ὑπὸ γλώττης εὐδοκιμοῦντα, ὁ θεῖος ἐπέστη Ῥιχο-     45
μήριος, ἡνίκα παρὰ τὸν Θεοδόσιον μετὰ τὴν Μαξίμου νίκην ἐν τοῖς
ἑῴοις βασιλείοις ἀπήγετο. καὶ ὁ μὲν Ῥιχομήριος τὸ σῶμα καμὼν
ἐτελεύτα κατὰ τὴν Κωνσταντίνου· τὸν δὲ Εὐγένιον ὁ βάρβαρος
βασιλέα τῶν ἑσπερίων ἀποδείξας ἄκοντί γε περιτίθησι τὸ σχῆμα.
ὅστις εὐθέως πρεσβείαν πρὸς τὸν Θεοδόσιον ἔστειλε πειρώμενος, εἰ     50
ὁμολογοίη φίλος εἶναι καὶ δέχοιτο αὐτὸν βασιλεύοντα.]

23 οὗτος M [οὕτω PS   γοῦν [γὰρ edd.   26 τι PS [δὲ M   ἐλύπησεν M
[ἐλύπτησεν PS   45-46 et 47 Ῥιχομήριος M [Σεριχομήριος PS

(Zosimus 4,53-55)

Galla, and they became very eager for war against the murderer. This was Arbogast, a Frank and a man of fiery and barbarous spirit, the son of Baudo, who had been appointed master of the soldiers by the Emperor Gratian. Arbogast through his warlike prowess compelled Valentinian to allow him to succeed his father as general.[118] He slew many persons of high standing in the Emperor's council, not merely without the Emperor's knowledge but despite his attempts to prevent it. Amongst these was Armonius, the son of Taurus the consul. When he annoyed Arbogast and the latter reached for his sword, Armonius fled to the Emperor for protection, but was run through together with the imperial robe. As a result there was much suspicion between the general and the Emperor. Valentinian secretly sought the active assistance of Theodosius, saying that he could not endure the forwardness of his tyrannical general. However, thinking to outmanoeuvre the tyrant, Valentinian in a council-meeting handed him a rescript announcing his removal from office. The barbarian took it, read it and tore it to shreds with his fingers,[119] and, having roared out his rage at the Emperor, walked out with drawn sword. Thus he showed himself an overt enemy of the Roman state, and Valentinian wished immediately to ride off to Theodosius. The barbarian set out against Valentinian and fell in with him as he was staying at a small town of Italy called Verna[120] and relaxing with the garrison of the tiny place. Catching him unawares, he cut him down with his sword. Thus died the younger Valentinian, having lived for 20 years and reigned for eight.

Arbogast was introduced to Eugenius, who held a sophistic chair and had a high reputation for eloquence, by his uncle Richomer at the time when the latter was leaving to join Theodosius at the eastern court after the victory over Maximus. Richomer fell sick and died at Constantinople, whereas the barbarian made Eugenius Emperor of the western Romans, clothing him in the imperial regalia against his will. Eugenius immediately sent an embassy to Theodosius to inquire whether the latter was willing to be his friend and accept him as Emperor.]

(Zosimus 4,53-55)

## 59

(*Exc. de Leg. Gent.* 7)

Ὅτι ἐπὶ Θεοδοσίου τοὺς πρώτους χρόνους τῆς βασιλείας τοῦ
Σκυθῶν ἔθνους ἐξελαυνομένου τῆς χώρας ὑπὸ τῶν Οὔννων διεβεβήκεσαν τῶν φυλῶν ἡγεμόνες ἀξιώματι καὶ γένει προήκοντες.
οὗτοι ταῖς τιμαῖς τοῦ βασιλέως ἐξωγκωμένοι καὶ πάντα ἐφ᾽ ἑαυτοῖς
ὁρῶντες κείμενα στάσιν ἐν ἀλλήλοις οὐ μικρὰν ἤγειραν, οἱ μὲν          5
ἀγαπᾶν καὶ δέχεσθαι τὴν παροῦσαν εὐδαιμονίαν κελεύοντες, οἱ δὲ τὸν
οἴκοι γεγονότα φυλάττειν ὅρκον αὐτοῖς καὶ μὴ παραβαίνειν ἐκείνας
τὰς συνθήκας. αὗται δὲ ἦσαν ἀσεβέσταται καὶ βαρβαρικὸν ἦθος εἰς
ὠμότητα παρατρέχουσαι, παντὶ τρόπῳ Ῥωμαίοις ἐπιβουλεύειν καὶ
πάσῃ μηχανῇ καὶ δόλῳ τοὺς ὑποδεξαμένους ἀδικεῖν, κἂν τὰ μέγιστα          10
ὑπ᾽ αὐτῶν εὖ πάσχωσιν, ὡς ἂν τῆς ἐκείνων ἁπάσης χώρας ἐγ-
κρατεῖς γένωνται. περὶ τούτου μὲν οὖν ἦν αὐτοῖς ἡ στάσις, καὶ δια-
νεμηθέντες ἀλλήλων ἀπερράγησαν, οἱ μὲν τὰ χείρω προθέμενοι τῆς
βουλῆς, οἱ δὲ τὰ εὐσεβέστερα, ἐπικρύπτοντες δὲ ἑκατέρα στάσις τὴν
πρόφασιν τῆς ὀργῆς ὅμως. καὶ ὁ βασιλεὺς τιμῶν οὐκ ἔληγεν, ἀλλ᾽          15
ὁμοτραπέζους εἶχε καὶ ὁμοσκήνους, καὶ πολὺ τὸ φιλόδωρον ἐς αὐτοὺς
ἦν· οὐδαμοῦ γὰρ ἐξεφέρετο καὶ παρεγυμνοῦτο τὰ τῆς φιλονεικίας. ἦν
δὲ ἡγεμὼν τῆς μὲν θεοφιλοῦς καὶ θείας μερίδος Φράβιθος, ἀνὴρ νέος
μὲν κατὰ τὴν ἡλικίαν, γεγονὼς δὲ εἰς ἀρετὴν καὶ ἀλήθειαν ἁπάντων
ἀνθρώπων κάλλιστος. θεούς τε γὰρ ὡμολόγει θεραπεύειν κατὰ τὸν          20
ἀρχαῖον τρόπον καὶ οὐδεμίαν ὑπέστη πλάσιν εἰς ἀπάτην καὶ διάκρουσιν, ἀλλὰ γυμνὴν καὶ καθαρὰν διέφαινε τὴν ψυχὴν περὶ τοῦ βίου,
ἐχθρὸν ὑπολαμβάνων

ὁμῶς Ἀΐδαο πύλῃσιν
ὅς χ᾽ ἕτερον μὲν κεύθῃ ἐνὶ φρεσίν, ἄλλο δὲ εἴπῃ.          25

γυναῖκα οὖν ᾔτησε Ῥωμαίαν εὐθύς, ἵνα μηδὲν ὑβρίζῃ διὰ σώματος
ἀνάγκην. καὶ ὁ βασιλεὺς ἐπέτρεψε τὸν γάμον, καὶ ὁ πατὴρ τῆς κόρης
(ἐτρέφετο γὰρ ὑπὸ πατρὶ) καὶ τὸ πρᾶγμα ἐθαύμασε μακάριον ἑαυτὸν
ὑπολαμβάνων, εἰ τοιοῦτον ἔχοι γαμβρόν. τῶν μὲν οὖν ὁμοφύλων
ὀλίγοι τινὲς τὴν εὐσέβειαν καὶ ἀρετὴν ἀγασθέντες τοῦ νεανίσκου          30
πρὸς τὴν ἐκείνου γνώμην ἐχώρησαν καὶ συνεστήκεσαν, οἱ δὲ πολλοὶ
καὶ δυνατώτεροι τῶν δεδογμένων ἐξ ἀρχῆς ἀπρὶξ εἴχοντο καὶ πρὸς
τὴν ὠδῖνα τῆς ἐπιβουλῆς σφαδάζοντες ἐμεμήνεσαν· ὧν ἦρχεν Ἐρί-
ουλφος, ἀνὴρ ἡμμανὴς καὶ τῶν ἄλλων λυσσωδέστερος. συμποσίου
δὲ προτεθέντος αὐτοῖς παρὰ τοῦ βασιλέως ἁδροτέρου καὶ πολυ-          35
τελεστέρου, τὴν παροιμίαν ἀποδείξαντες ἀληθῆ τὴν λέγουσαν· οἶνος

1-2 τοῦ . . . ἔθνους de Boor [τὸ . . . ἔθνος codd.          ἐξελαυνομένου scripsi
[ἐξελαυνόμενοι codd.    21-22 διάκρουσιν Dindorf [διακράτησιν A διακρότησιν
Classen

## 59

(*Exc. de Leg. Gent. 7*)

During the early years of the reign of the Emperor Theodosius, when the Scythian nation was being driven from its lands by the Huns, the leaders of the tribes who were paramount in reputation and nobility crossed over to Roman territory.[121] They, being loaded with honours by the Emperor and observing that everything was theirs for the taking, came into considerable conflict among themselves. One side said that they should rejoice in and accept their present good fortune, the other that they should keep the oaths that they had sworn at home and not break their pledge. This pledge, a most unholy one that went beyond the normal savagery of the barbarians, was that, even if they were to receive the greatest kindnesses from the Romans, they would plot against them in every way and use every treacherous device to harm those who had taken them in, in order that they might gain possession of all their territory. This was the subject of their conflict and, since they held different views, they split apart, some holding to the worse plan, others to the more honourable, although both factions concealed the cause of their animus. The Emperor continued to honour them, inviting them to dine at his table and visit his rooms, and he gave them many gifts, for no single detail of their quarrel came to light. The leader of the virtuous and god-fearing party was Fravitta, a man young in years but the most remarkable of all in his virtue and honesty. He openly declared that he worshipped the gods after the ancient fashion and he had no inclination towards deceit and evasion, but in his way of life revealed a soul that was transparently pure, holding him an enemy

like the gates of Death
who hides one thing in his heart and speaks another.[122]

He straightway asked for a Roman wife, lest the needs of the body force him to violence. The Emperor permitted him the marriage, and the father of the girl (who was still living at home) was delighted at the match and thought himself lucky to have such a son-in-law. A minority of Fravitta's fellow-tribesmen applauded the young man's honourable and virtuous conduct and adopted the same point of view. The larger and more powerful faction, however, clung fast to their initial opinion and were striving furiously to bring their plot to fruition. Their leader was Eriulf, a half-madman who raged more wildly than the rest. At a very grand and costly banquet thrown for them by the Emperor they showed the truth of the proverb *in vino veritas*. For on that occasion

καὶ ἀλήθεια τοῦ Διονύσου, καὶ τότε ῥήξαντος αὐτοῖς παρὰ πότον τὴν
ἐπικρυπτομένην στάσιν, διαλύεται μὲν τὸ συμπόσιον ἀτάκτως, καὶ διὰ
θυρῶν ἐχώρουν τεθορυβημένοι καὶ παρακεκινηκότες· ὁ δὲ Φράβιθος
δι' ἀρετῆς ὑπερβολὴν τὸ καλὸν καὶ δίκαιον κάλλιον ἅμα καὶ θεο-        40
φιλέστερον ὀφθήσεσθαι νομίζων, εἰ προσθείη τάχος, οὐ περιμείνας
ἕτερον καιρόν, ἀλλὰ σπασάμενος τὸ ξίφος τῆς πλευρᾶς Ἐριούλφου
διήλασεν. καὶ ὁ μὲν ἔκειτο πεσών, ὀνειροπολήσας τὴν ἄδικον ἐπι-
βουλήν· οἱ δὲ .... (Cf. *Exc. de Sent.* 58)

39 παρακεκινηκότες [παρῳνηκότες Classen    41 προσθείη [προσείη Niebuhr

(Zosimus 4,56)

## 60

[1. (John of Antioch *Fr.* 187 = *Exc. de Ins.* 79)

Οὓς δὴ ὁ Θεοδόσιος ποικίλοις διακρουσάμενος λόγοις καὶ φιλ-
ανθρώποις ἀποκρίσεσι δελεάσας ἀπεπέμψατο. αὐτὸς δὲ Ῥωμαϊκὸν
μὲν τὸν Τιμάσιον, Σκυθικὸν δὲ τὸν Γαϊνάν, ἐξ Ἀλανῶν δὲ τὸν Σαοὺλ
ἄρχοντας τῶν στρατοπέδων παραλαβών, ἅμα δὲ καὶ Στελίχωνα τοῖς
στρατεύμασιν ἐπιστήσας (ὃς ἦν μὲν καὶ αὐτὸς ἀνέκαθεν τοῦ Σκυθικοῦ     5
γένους, τῆς δὲ τοῦ βασιλέως ἀδελφῆς Σερήνης αὐτῷ προσγαμηθείσης, βασιλέως οὐδὲν ἀπελείπετο), πολλούς τε τῶν Θρακίων
Οὔννων σὺν τοῖς παρεπομένοις φυλάρχοις διαναστήσας εἴχετο τῆς
πρὸς τὴν Ἰταλίαν πορείας, ὡς ἂν τὸν Εὐγένιον μηδέν τι προσ-
δοκῶντα ἀπαράσκευον καταλάβοι. ἐξιόντι δὲ αὐτῷ τῆς αὐλῆς ἡ       10
βασίλισσα τελευτᾷ.

Ὁπηνίκα δὲ τοῖς τῆς Ἰταλίας προσῆλθεν ὅροις, τῷ παραλόγῳ
τῆς ὀξύτητος καὶ τῷ τάχει τῆς ἀφράστου διαδρομῆς ὁ Εὐγένιος
ἔπτηξεν, ἀνὴρ ἄπειρος πολέμου καὶ σάλπιγγος. ὁ δὲ Ἀρβωγάστης
ἀντεμάνη ἐπιθυμῶν πολέμου καὶ μάχης καὶ φόνων καὶ πολὺ τῆς     15
ἡμέρας διαγωνισάμενος· καθ' ἣν ὁ ἥλιος ἀφανὴς ἐγένετο τοῖς
ἀνθρώποις περὶ μέσην τῆς ἡμέρας ὥραν, ὥστε καὶ ἀστέρας φανῆναι,
καὶ νυκτομαχοῦντες ἅπαντες ἀνηλίσκοντο συνδαπανώμενοι ξίφεσιν.
ἄχρι μὲν οὖν περὶ τρίτην φυλακὴν τῆς νυκτὸς ἐν τούτοις τὰ τῶν
στρατοπέδων ὑπῆρχεν. ἐπειδὴ δὲ Θεοδόσιος, τότε μὲν ὑπαναχωρήσας,     20
τὸν δὲ θεὸν ἱκετεύσας, καθεύδουσι τῇ ἑξῆς τοῖς ἐναντίοις ἐπιπίπτει,
τὸ μὲν πλεῖστον ἐν ταῖς εὐναῖς, τὸ δὲ ἀνιστάμενον τῶν ὅπλων γε-
γυμνωμένον διεχειρίζετο, αὐτόν τε τὸν Εὐγένιον ζωγρήσας τῆς
κεφαλῆς ἀποτέμνει, καὶ μακρῷ δόρατι περιπήξας ἐν ὅλοις τοῖς τῆς
Ἰταλίας ὅροις διεπόμπευσεν, ὡς ἅπαν τὸ τῶν πολεμίων πλῆθος πρὸς     25

6 post ἀδελφῆς add. θυγατρὸς Müller    6-7 προσγαμηθείσης Müller [προσ-
μανείσης codd.

Bacchus with his wine brought into the open the hidden dissension,[123] and the banquet broke up in confusion as they rushed out of the room shouting in their excitement. But Fravitta, realising that the party of justice and right would seem even more just and righteous if he acted quickly, did not wait for another opportunity, but drew his sword and plunged it into Eriulf's side. And he fell down and lay there, having dreamed in vain of his unjust plot. But the . . . .

(Cf. *Exc. de Sent.* 58)

(Zosimus 4,56)

## 60

[1. (John of Antioch *Fr.* 187 = *Exc. de Ins.* 79)

Theodosius tricked [Eugenius' envoys] with a friendly response to their requests, giving them evasive replies, and sent them home. In command of the forces he placed the Roman Timasius, the Scythian Gainas and the Alan Saul, and he also made Stilicho general, a man who was himself of Scythian descent but enjoyed power equal to the Emperor since he was married to Serena, Theodosius' sister;[124] he also summoned many of the Huns of Thrace, who served under their tribal chieftains. Then he set out for Italy in order to catch Eugenius, who was expecting no move, unawares. As he was leaving the palace the Empress died.

When Theodosius reached the borders of Italy, Eugenius, a man unused to the blast of war, was alarmed by the Emperor's unexpected swiftness and the speed of his advance, which had gone unobserved. But against him raged Arbogast, who was eager for war and fighting and slaughter, and he fought on for the whole of the day. In the middle of the day the sun was eclipsed and the stars appeared, so that the soldiers, fighting a night-battle, were all cut down, the loss of life being great on both sides.[125] This was the situation until about the third watch of the night, when Theodosius withdrew from the battle and prayed to God. Then on the next day he fell upon the enemy while they were asleep, slaughtering the majority in their beds and cutting down unarmed those who leapt up to face him. Eugenius he captured alive and, having cut off his head, stuck it on a long spear and paraded it throughout the territory of Italy, so that all the enemy soldiers came to the victor and

τὸν νενικηκότα χωρεῖν καὶ τοῖς αὐτοῦ πείθεσθαι διατάγμασιν. ὁ δὲ
Ἀρβωγάστης, ἐν τούτῳ τε τὸ μανικὸν τῆς βαρβάρου φύσεως ἀποδείξας, αὐτοχειρίᾳ διεφθάρη τῷ σφετέρῳ περιπεσὼν ξίφει. ἐπὶ
τούτοις τε θρίαμβοι κατὰ τὴν Ῥώμην ἐγένοντο, καὶ στεφανηφορεῖν
τὴν ἁπανταχοῦ τῶν ὑπηκόων γῆν ἐδόκει καὶ πανηγυρίζειν ἐπὶ τῇ      30
καθαιρέσει τοῦ τυράννου.]

[2. (Suda E 2180)
Ὁ δὲ Θεοδόσιος τὴν βασίλισσαν θανοῦσαν ἐπ᾿ ἤματι σχεδόν τι
ἐδάκρυσεν. ἀνάγκη γάρ, καὶ ὁ προκείμενος πόλεμος συνεσκίαζεν
αὐτῷ τὸ περὶ τὴν γυναῖκα πάθος.]

(Zosimus 4,57-58)

61

[(Philostorgius 11,2)
Ταῦτα λέγων ὁ δυσσεβὴς περὶ τοῦ εὐσεβεστάτου Θεοδοσίου,
οὐκ αἰσχύνεται κωμῳδεῖν αὐτὸν ἐπ᾿ ἀκρασίᾳ βίου καὶ τρυφῆς ἀ-
μετρίᾳ, δι᾿ ἣν αὐτὸν ἁλῶναι γράφει καὶ τῷ τοῦ ὑδέρου νοσήματι.]

(Zosimus 4,59)

62

1. (Exc. de Sent. 59)
Ὅτι οἱ παῖδες Θεοδοσίου ἐπὶ τῆς βασιλείας αὐτοῦ ἔστησαν. εἰ
δὲ τὸ ἀληθέστερον, ὅπερ ἐστὶ σκοπὸς ἱστορίας, προστιθέναι δεῖ τοῖς
γεγενημένοις, τὸ μὲν ὄνομα ἦν τῶν βασιλέων, τὸ δὲ ἔργον τῶν μὲν
κατὰ τὴν ἑῴαν Ῥουφίνου, τὰ δὲ ἑσπέρια Στελίχωνος εἰς ἅπασαν
ἐξουσίαν· οὕτω γοῦν οἱ μὲν βασιλεῖς ἐπετάττοντο παρὰ τῶν ἐπι-     5
τροπευόντων τὰς ἀρχάς, οἱ δὲ ἐπιτροπεύοντες ἀεὶ πρὸς ἀλλήλους
ἐπολέμουν ὥσπερ βασιλεύοντες, φανερῶς μὲν οὐκ ἐναντίας χεῖρας
καὶ ὅπλα ἀράμενοι, κρύφα δὲ ἀπάτης καὶ δόλου μηδὲν ὑπολείποντες·
διὰ γὰρ μαλακίαν καὶ ἀσθένειαν ψυχῆς τὸ διέρπον καὶ ὕπουλον τῶν
μηχανημάτων αὐτοῖς ὡς ἀνδρεῖον . . ..                              10

10 post ἀνδρεῖον duae paginae desiderantur in cod.

2. (Suda P 240)
Ῥουφῖνος· οὗτος ἐπὶ Θεοδοσίου ἦν, βαθυγνώμων ἄνθρωπος καὶ
κρυψίνους. ἦσαν δὲ οὗτός τε καὶ Στελίχων ἐπίτροποι τῶν Θεοδοσίου
παίδων. ἄμφω τὰ πάντα συνήρπαζον, ἐν τῷ πλούτῳ τὸ κράτος
τιθέμενοι, καὶ οὐδεὶς εἶχεν ἴδιον οὐδέν, εἰ μὴ τούτοις ἔδοξε. δίκαι τε

obeyed his commands. Meanwhile Arbogast showed his native barbarian madness by falling on his sword and killing himself. A triumph was held for this victory at Rome, and all the provinces were wreathed in celebration of the destruction of the usurper.]


[2. (*Suda* E 2180)
Theodosius mourned the dead Empress for about one day. For the demands of the impending war overshadowed his grief for his wife.]


(Zosimus 4,57-58)

## 61

[(Philostorgius 11,2)
Although he says these things about the most pious Theodosius, the impious historian [i.e. Philostorgius] is not ashamed to criticise him for intemperate living and excessive luxury which, he says, was the cause of his dropsy.[126]]

(Zosimus 4,59)

## 62

1. (*Exc. de Sent.* 59)
The sons of Theodosius succeeded him as Emperor. But to give the truer interpretation of the situation (which is the goal of history), they had the name of Emperors whereas the real and absolute power lay with Rufinus in the East and Stilicho in the West. After this manner the Emperors were controlled by the guardians of their regimes, while the guardians themselves, as if they were Emperors, were continually at war with each other, not in open armed conflict but utilising every clandestine device of deceit and treachery. Because their spirits were soft and feeble these furtive and cancerous stratagems <seemed> to them manly . . ..[127]


2. (*Suda* P 240)
Rufinus. A secretive and inscrutable man who lived during the reign of Theodosius. He and Stilicho were the guardians of Theodosius' sons. Since they both held wealth to be power they plundered everything, and no one kept any of his possessions unless these men permitted

92    *Eunapius: Text*

ἅπασαι πρὸς τούτων ἐδικάζοντο, καὶ πολὺς ἦν ὄχλος τῶν περιθεόν-    5
των, εἴ πού τινι χωρίον ὑπάρχοι παντομιγές τε καὶ εὔκαρπον· καὶ ὁ
δεσπότης εὐθὺς συνήρπαστο, κατηγορίας πεπλασμένης εὐλόγου διά
τινων ὑφειμένων ἐνηδρευμένος. καὶ ὁ ἀδικούμενος ἠδικεῖτο, τοῦ
ἀδικοῦντος κρίνοντος. ἐς τοῦτο δὲ ὁ Ῥουφῖνος ἐχώρησεν ἀμετροκάκου
πλεονεξίας, ὥστε καὶ ἀνδράποδα δημόσια ἀπημπόλει, καὶ ὅσα δημόσια    10
δικαστήρια Ῥουφίνῳ πάντες ἐδίκαζον. καὶ ὁ τῶν κολάκων περὶ
αὐτὸν ὄχλος ἦν πολύς. οἱ δὲ κόλακες χθὲς μὲν καὶ πρώην δεδρακότες
τοῦ καπηλείου καὶ τοῦ τὰ βάθρα καλλύνειν καὶ τοὔδαφος κορεῖν, ἄρτι
δὲ χλαμύδας τάς τε εὐπαρύφους ἐνδεδυκότες καὶ περόναις χρυσαῖς
διαπεπερονημένοι καὶ σφραγῖσι χρυσοδέτοις διεσφιγμένοι. τὰ δὲ    15
πολλὰ κατὰ Ῥουφίνου εὕροις ἐν τῇ τοῦ Σαρδιανοῦ Εὐναπίου Χρονο-
γραφίᾳ.     (Cf. A 1562, B 30 and 31, K 269, Π 240 and 1362, Σ
1032; John of Antioch *Fr.* 188 = *Exc. de Virt.* 67)

5 τούτων Kuster [τούτοις codd.    8 ἐνηδρευμένος edd. [ἐνηδρευμένης codd.
15 post διεσφιγμένοι lacunam indicat Müller

3. (*Suda* A 1569)
    Εὐνάπιος· οὕτως ἀμείλικτοι ἦσαν ἄμφω κατὰ τὴν ἀλήθειαν,
καὶ τὸ ἔργον ἐχώρει περιφανέστερον.

[4. (*Suda* M 203)
    Μάρκελλος, μάγιστρος Ἀρκαδίου τοῦ βασιλέως, κόσμος ἀρετῆς
ἁπάσης ἤ, τό γε ἁρμονικώτερον εἰπεῖν, ἀρετή τις ἔμψυχος.

(Zosimus 5,1-3)

63
(Zosimus 5,4)

64
[1. (John of Antioch *Fr.* 190 = *Exc. de Ins.* 80)
    Ὅτι Ῥουφῖνος ὁ ἐπίτροπος Ἀρκαδίου ἐξ ἐπιβουλῆς Εὐτροπίου
τοῦ προκοίτου τῆς Ἀρκαδίου διήμαρτε κηδείας· ἀλλ' ὅμως τῇ πλεονεξίᾳ καὶ τῇ χαλεπότητι τῶν τρόπων πᾶσιν ὑπέροπτος ἦν, τόν τε
βασιλέα οἰκειότητι τῶν βαρβάρων καταπλήττων καὶ βαρεῖαν ἐπι-
τιθεὶς ἀνάγκην πρὸς τὸ κοινωνῆσαι τῆς ἁλουργίδος αὐτῷ· ποτὲ δὲ    5
καὶ πλῆθος βαρβάρων εἰσαγαγών, ὧν Ἀλάριχος ἡγεῖτο, πᾶσαν ὁμοῦ
τὴν Ἑλλάδα καὶ τὰ περὶ τὴν Ἰλλυρίδα διεπόρθει, ὡς καὶ δῆλος
ἅπασι γενέσθαι τῇ τῆς τυραννίδος ἐπιβουλῇ.

2 κηδείας de Boor [κηδίας codd.

it. Since all lawsuits were referred to them, many persons raced around
the Empire to see if anyone owned an estate that was fertile and bore
many different crops. Its owner was immediately arrested[128] and en-
snared by a plausible charge laid by someone who had been suborned
for the purpose; and the victim of this injustice was condemned, since
its originator was also the judge. Rufinus became so excessively greedy
that he sold the public slaves, and everyone gave verdicts in the public
courts to suit Rufinus. He was surrounded by a great crowd of flatterers,
who yesterday and the day before were runaway tavern-servants and
bench-cleaners and floor-sweepers, but who now had put on robes with
lovely purple borders pinned up with golden pins, their fingers squeezed
with signets set in gold. You can find many attacks upon Rufinus in
the Chronography of Eunapius of Sardis.
(Cf. A 1562, B 30 and 31, K 269, Π 240 and 1362, Σ 1032; John of
Antioch *Fr.* 188 = *Exc. de Virt.* 67)


3. (*Suda* A 1569)
    In truth so cruel were they, and the reality of this became more
obvious.[129]

[4. (*Suda* M 203)
    Marcellus, *magister* of the Emperor Arcadius, a paragon of all
virtues or, to speak more accurately, virtue personified.[130]]

(Zosimus 5,1-3)

## 63
(Zosimus 5,4)

## 64
[1. (John of Antioch *Fr.* 190 = *Exc. de Ins.* 80)
    Rufinus the guardian of Arcadius was foiled in the marriage[131]
through the plotting of Eutropius, Arcadius' chamberlain. But because
of his greedy and cruel ways he despised everyone and terrified the
Emperor by his close relations with the barbarians. Bringing heavy
pressure to bear upon Arcadius to make him co-Emperor, Rufinus on
one occasion actually introduced a force of barbarians led by Alaric
and ravaged the whole of Greece and the regions near to Illyria. As a
result it was clear to all that he was plotting usurpation. He secretly

Ὁ μὲν γὰρ ὑπέχαιρε καὶ τὸν κοινὸν ὄλεθρον ἰδίαν κρηπῖδα τῆς
βασιλείας ὑπελάμβανεν· ὁ δὲ βασιλεὺς ἐν ἀφασίᾳ διετέλει. οὐ μὴν καὶ    10
ὁ Στελίχων ἐνταῦθα ὅμοιος ἦν, ἀλλὰ διέπλευσε μὲν αὐτὸς ἐς τὴν
Ἑλλάδα, καίτοι μηδὲν προσήκουσαν τοῖς τῆς ἑσπερίας τέρμασι, τὰς
τῶν ἐνοικούντων οἰκτείρας συμφοράς· καὶ τοὺς βαρβάρους σπάνει
τῶν ἀναγκαίων διαφθείρας ἔπαυσε τῆς τῶν ἐπιχωρίων ὁρμῆς.
συγκαλεσάμενος δὲ Γαϊνάν, ὃς τότε τῶν ἑσπερίων στρατοπέδων    15
ἔξαρχος ἦν, ἀρτύει τὴν κατὰ Ῥουφίνου σκευήν· ὅτε δὴ καὶ ὁ τοῦ
Ἀρκαδίου στρατὸς ἔκ τε τῆς Εὐγενίου καθαιρέσεως καὶ τῆς τῶν
βαρβάρων τῶν κατὰ τὴν Ἰλλυρίδα διώξεως ἐπὶ τὴν Κωνσταντίνου
πόλιν ἐχώρει. ὁ μὲν γὰρ βασιλεὺς κατὰ τοὺς παλαιοὺς νόμους εἰς
ὑπάντησιν τῶν στρατοπέδων ἐκ τῆς πόλεως προῆλθεν, καὶ ὁ Γαϊνὰς    20
αὐτὸν ἐφρούρει, πᾶσα δὲ ἦν ἀνάγκη καὶ τὸν τῆς αὐλῆς ἔπαρχον
συνεξιέναι· Ῥουφῖνός τε ἦν καὶ ἅμα τε ὁ βασιλεὺς ὑπὸ τῶν στρατοπέδων Αὔγουστος ὀνομάζεται, καὶ Ῥουφῖνος κατετέμνετο, ταύτης τε
ἔτυχε τῆς τελευτῆς. παῖδες δὲ αὐτοῦ καὶ γαμετὴ πρὸς τὴν ἐκκλησίαν
κατέφυγον, διηρπάζοντο δὲ ἀκωλύτως ἅπαντα ὅσα κατὰ τὴν δυνασ-    25
τείαν ἐκτήσατο.]

16  κατὰ secl. edd.          22  τε ἦν PS [δὲ ἦν M  τις ἦν Cramer

## 2. (*Vit. Soph.* 7,3,4)

Καὶ ταῦτά γε οὕτως· ἅμα τε γὰρ ὁ ἐκ Θεσπιῶν ἐγίνετο, πατὴρ
ὢν τῆς Μιθριακῆς τελετῆς, καὶ οὐκ εἰς μακρὰν πολλῶν καὶ ἀδιη-
γήτων ἐπικλυσθέντων κακῶν, (ὧν τὰ μὲν ἐν τοῖς διεξοδικοῖς τῆς
ἱστορίας εἴρηται, τὰ δέ, ἐὰν ἐπιτρέπῃ τὸ Θεῖον, λελέξεται), ὅ τε
Ἀλλάριχος ἔχων τοὺς βαρβάρους διὰ τῶν Πυλῶν παρῆλθεν, ὥσπερ    5
διὰ σταδίου καὶ ἱπποκρότου πεδίου τρέχων.

1  ἐκ Θεσπιῶν codd. [aut ἐκ Θεσπιῶν aut ἐκ Θεσπίσεων Giangrande  Ἀγόριος
Οὐέττιος Cumont    2  post μακρὰν lacunam indicat Boissonade      4  ὅ τε
scripsi [ὅτε codd.  ὁ [τε] Giangrande

## 3. (*Vit. Soph.* 8,1,10 - 2,3)

Τοῖς τῆς Ἑλλάδος ἱερεῖς, εἰς μακρόν τι γῆρας ἀνύσας, ὅς γε ἦν
ὑπὲρ τὰ ἐνενήκοντα, συναπώλετο· πολλῶν καὶ ἄλλων ἐν τῷδε τῷ
χρόνῳ τῶν μὲν διὰ λύπην προϊεμένων τὸν βίον, οἱ δὲ ὑπὸ τῶν βαρβάρων κατεκόπτοντο . . . . καὶ ταῦτα μὲν ἐν τοῖς διεξοδικοῖς, ἐὰν τῷ
δαίμονι δόξῃ, γραφήσεται, οὐ τὸ καθ᾽ ἕκαστον ἔχοντα, ἀλλὰ τὸ κοινὸν    5
ἐκεῖ σαφέστερον λελέξεται.

(Zosimus 5,5-7)

rejoiced and regarded the universal destruction as the starting point of his own attempt on the throne. The Emperor remained incapable of action, but Stilicho adopted a different policy in these circumstances. Out of pity for the misfortunes of the inhabitants of Greece he sailed there, even though it was not part of the western Empire, and having destroyed the barbarians by starvation, he withdrew from his assault upon the inhabitants.[132] Summoning Gainas, who was at the time a general of the western army, he made ready his plot against Rufinus. When Arcadius' army on its return from the destruction of Eugenius and the pursuit of the barbarians in Illyria was approaching Constantinople, the Emperor, following the ancient custom, went out from the city to greet the army, and Gainas guarded him; and it was absolutely necessary that the praetorian prefect (which Rufinus was) accompany the Emperor. At one and the same time the Emperor was hailed Augustus by the army and Rufinus was cut down; and this was his end. His wife and children fled to the church, and they[133] seized for themselves without hindrance all that he had accumulated during his period of power . . ..[134] ]

2. (*Vit. Soph.* 7,3,4)

These things turned out as [the hierophant] said. For as soon as the man from Thespiae, who was the father of the Mithraic ritual, became hierophant, shortly afterwards many indescribable disasters swept over the land (some of which I have described in the narrative of my History and others will be set down, if God permits), and Alaric with his barbarians passed through Thermopylae as if he were racing over a running track or a plain flat enough for horses.[135]

3. (*Vit. Soph.* 8,1,10 - 2,3)

Having lived to a great age (he was over ninety) [Priscus] perished at the same time as the temples of Greece. At this time there were many who threw away their lives out of grief, and others were cut down by the barbarians . . . . If the divine power permits, I shall set these things down in the detailed narrative of my History, where they will be clearly described not as they affected individuals but as they affected the state.[136]

(Zosimus 5,5-7)

65

1. (*Suda* E 3776)

Εὐτρόπιος ὁ εὐνοῦχος, ἐπίτροπος Θεοδοσίου τοῦ βασιλέως. καί
φησιν Εὐνάπιος· ὁ μὲν γὰρ Ῥουφῖνος ἀνήρ τε ὢν ἢ δοκῶν, καὶ ἐν
ἀξιώμασι γεγονώς, καὶ ποικίλαις ὁμιλήσας τύχαις, οὐ παρὰ λόγον
οὐδὲ τοῦ πρέποντος ἐκτὸς ἐδόκει κατεξανίστασθαι τῆς νεωτερι-
ζούσης ἅπαντα τύχης. ὁ δὲ θαλαμηπόλος εὐνοῦχος, παραλαβὼν τὸ      5
ἐκείνου κράτος, ἐς τοσόνδε κατέσεισεν ἅπαντα καὶ κατεβρόντησεν,
ὥστε οὐ μόνον Ῥουφῖνος ἦν αὐτός, ἀλλ' ὁ τοῦ μύθου Σαλμωνεὺς
μικρόν τι χρῆμα πρὸς αὐτὸν ἦν, ὅς γε ὢν εὐνοῦχος, ἀνὴρ εἶναι κατε-
βιάζετο. καὶ οἱ μὲν μῦθοί φασι τὴν Γοργόνα φανεῖσαν ἅμα τε
φαίνεσθαι καὶ τοὺς ἰδόντας μεταβάλλειν εἰς λίθον· ὁ δὲ καθ' ἡμᾶς      10
βίος λῆρόν τινα περιττὸν καὶ φλήναφον τὸν μῦθον ἀπέδειξε. καὶ
πολὺν καταχέει διασυρμὸν ὁ ἱστορικὸς τουτουὶ τοῦ εὐνούχου, τοῦ βίου
αὐτοῦ ἐπάξιον.    (Cf. X 473*)

[2. (*Suda* Π 1293)

Ὁ δὲ εὐνοῦχος κατεκράτει τῶν βασιλείων, καὶ περισπειρα-
σάμενος τὰς αὐλὰς συνέσφιγγεν ἅπαντα, καθάπερ τις γενναῖος ὄφις,
καθελίττων εἰς τὴν ἑαυτοῦ χρείαν. περὶ Εὐτροπίου λέγει.]

3 χείαν Toup [χρείαν codd.

[3. (*Suda* T 597)

Τιμάσιος. οὗτος ἐπὶ Θεοδοσίου τοῦ βασιλέως ἦν· ὃν ὁ Εὐτρόπιος ἐπιστῆσαι τοῖς πράγμασι βουλόμενος, ἐκ τῆς Ἀσίας μετε-
καλεῖ πρὸς τὰ βασίλεια. ὁ δὲ γαῦρός τε ἀνὴρ ὢν καὶ ἀγέρωχος καὶ
στρατείαις ὡμιληκώς, καὶ τοῦτο πρῶτον ἀγαθὸν ἡγούμενος τῶν ἐν
ἀνθρώποις, τιμὴν καὶ δόξαν καὶ πλοῦτον ἐπικλύζοντα, καὶ τὸ ἔχειν      5
ἑαυτῷ ὅ τι βούλοιτο κεχρῆσθαι καὶ ἀδεῶς, διά τε μέθην νύκτα καὶ
ἡμέραν οὐκ εἰδέναι, οὔτε ἀνατέλλοντα καὶ δυόμενον καθορᾶν ἥλιον,
ἴσα καὶ οὐρανοῦ εἶναι νομίσας τὴν μετάκλησιν, ἐκ τῶν ἀλύπων καὶ
διακεχυμένων πρὸς ὀλιγωρίαν διατριβῶν ἀπορρήξας ἑαυτὸν καὶ
κατατείνας τὴν ψυχὴν εἰς φιλοδοξίαν, βαρὺς ἀναστὰς ἐκ Παμφυλίας      10
ἐπὶ Λυδίαν ἀνέστρεφεν, ὡς ἂν δή τις βασιλεύων ἢ τόν γε βασιλέα καὶ
τὸν εὐνοῦχον κατὰ πάρεργόν τι παιδιὰν θησόμενος, εἰ βούλοιτο.
(Cf. Γ 78, Π 855)]

2-3 μετεκαλεῖτο V

4. (*Exc. de Sent.* 60-61)

.... μασε καθάπερ ἐξ οὐρανοῦ πρὸς τὴν γῆν διενεχθὲν καὶ
καταπέσον ἐς τὰ ἀνθρώπινα. ὁ μὲν οὖν Βάργος τὴν ἀρχὴν πιστευθεὶς

1 .... μασε Boissevain [.. . ρασε edd. 2 καταπέσον cod. [κατὰ τοῦτον edd.

## 65

1. (*Suda* E 3776)

Eutropius the eunuch, guardian of the Emperor Theodosius.[137] Eunapius says: Rufinus was a man, or seemed to be. Having held high office and having experienced various ups and downs, not unexpectedly and (as it seemed) properly he strove against fortune as she changed everything. But the eunuch bedroom-attendant, when he inherited Rufinus' power, shook and demolished everything to such an extent that not only Rufinus but also the mythical Salmoneus were insignificant compared with him; and though he was an eunuch, he strove to be a man. The myths say that when the Gorgon appeared, those who looked at her turned to stone immediately. But our age proved that the myth is so much trash and nonsense.[138] The historian pours much ridicule upon this eunuch, appropriate for the life he lived. (Cf. X 473*)

[2. (*Suda* Π 1293)

The eunuch held power in the palace and, coiling around through the halls, like a true serpent seized everything and dragged it off to his lair.]

[3. (*Suda* T 597)

Timasius. He lived during the reign of the Emperor Theodosius. Eutropius wished to place him in charge of affairs and summoned him from Asia to court. He was an arrogant and haughty man and an experienced soldier, who held that the greatest blessings of mankind were honour, fame and abundant wealth, to have whatever he wanted and to enjoy it in security, to be so drunk as not to distinguish night and day, and never to see the rising or the setting of the sun. Regarding the summons as a message from heaven, he tore himself away from his life of idleness and dissipation verging on neglect of duty and steeled his heart for glory. Full of self-importance he set out from Pamphylia and journeyed to Lydia in the manner of a king or one who would, if he wished, treat the Emperor and the eunuch as mere incidental child's-play.     (Cf. Γ 78, II 855)]

4. (*Exc. de Sent.* 60-61)

. . . as if sent from heaven to earth and falling amongst mankind.[139] Bargus, having been entrusted with the command, went off

παρὰ τοῦ εὐνούχου ἐξήει μάλα φαιδρὸς καὶ γεγηθὼς ἐπὶ τὴν ἀρχήν,
ὡς ἂν ἀρχὰς ὑποθησόμενος ἑαυτῷ τινας πάλιν, καὶ μετὰ πολλῶν καὶ
διεφθαρμένων στρατιωτῶν, πρὸς τὸ πολεμεῖν τοῖς εὐεργέταις· τῷ    5
γὰρ περιόντι τῆς τόλμης καῖ τῷ μεγέθει τῶν ἐγχειρουμένων πολλοὺς
ἤδη περιπεφευγὼς κινδύνους, ἐς τὸ ἀκίνδυνον ἤδη πρὸς ἅπαντας καὶ
λίαν εὐτυχὲς τὴν τόλμαν ἐξεβιάζετο. συνετώτερος δ᾽ ὢν κατὰ πόδας
ᾔει πρὸς τὴν ἐπιβουλήν. καὶ δῆτα γυνὴ συνῴκει τῷ Βάργῳ· ταύτην
διὰ καθειμένων ἀνθρώπων πάλαι πρὸς τὸν ἄνδρα τὸν λεγόμενον    10
ἀλλοτρίως ἔχουσαν διά τινος ἠρτυμένης καὶ συνεσκιασμένης ἐπιβουλῆς, ἐπὶ τὸν ἄνδρα ὥσπερ ἔχιδναν νωθρὰν καὶ ὑπὸ κρύους κατε-
ψυγμένην ταῖς ὑποκειμέναις ἐπαγγελίαις ἀνέστησαν καὶ ὤρθωσαν.
καὶ τέλος φυγὼν καὶ συλληφθεὶς τὴν τῶν ἀχαρίστων ὑπέσχε δίκην.
καὶ ὁ μὲν ἑαυτὸν μανικώτατον καὶ τὸν εὐνοῦχον φρονιμώτατον <ἀπο-    15
δείξας> ἔκειτο μαρτυρῶν ἡλίκον ἐστὶ τὸ τῆς ἀχαριστίας παρὰ θεῷ
ἔγκλημα.

11 ἠρτυμένης καὶ συνεσκιασμένης Niebuhr [ἠρτημένης καὶ συσκιασμένης
15-16 ἀποδείξας add. Niebuhr

[5. (Suda X 80)
Ὁ δὲ Εὐτρόπιος καιροῦ καὶ τύχης ἀμέτρως τε καὶ χανδὸν
ἀρυόμενος, καὶ κατεμφορούμενος καὶ πολυπραγμονῶν, ὥστε οὐκ
ἔλαθε πατὴρ παῖδα μισῶν, ἢ ἀνὴρ γυναῖκα, ἢ μήτηρ τέκνον· ἀλλ᾽
ἐξηκοντίζετο ἅπαντα πρὸς τὴν ἐκείνου γνώμην.]

4 ἐξηκοντίζετο ἅπαντα Bernhardy [ἐξηκοντίζετο ἅπαντας codd.

[6. (Suda Δ 326)
Πάντες δειμαίνοντες τοῦ εὐνούχου Εὐτροπίου τὴν ἀκοὴν ἐξε-
στήκεσαν, καθάπερ οἱ μνηστῆρες τὸν Ὀδυσσέα γυμνωθέντα τῶν
ῥακίων ἰδόντες.]

3 ῥακίων codd. [ῥακέων Gaisford

[7. (Suda Σ 897)
Ὅτι ἐπὶ Εὐτροπίου τοῦ εὐνούχου, τοῦ ἐπιτρόπου Θεοδοσίου τοῦ
βασιλέως, τὸ τῶν εὐνούχων ἔθνος διὰ τὴν ἐκείνου βαρύτητα καὶ
δυναστείαν ἐς τοσοῦτον ἐπέδωκε καὶ παρετάθη πλήθους, ὥστε τινὲς
ἤδη καὶ τῶν γενειάδας ἐχόντων, εὐνοῦχοι βουληθέντες καὶ Εὐτρόπιοι
γενέσθαι προσελπίζοντες τῆς ψυχῆς ἀφηρέθησαν σὺν τοῖς ὄρχεσι,    5
τὸ τοῦ Εὐτρόπιου ἀπολαύσαντες. χρυσοῖ τε ἀνδριάντες ἀνίσταντο
πανταχοῦ, καὶ οἰκοδομήματα διηγείρετο καὶ κατελαμπρύνετο παρ᾽
αὐτοῦ σεμνότερα τῆς ὅλης πόλεως.]

6 τὸ τοῦ Εὐτρόπιου ἀπολαύσαντες scripsi [τὸν Εὐτρόπιον ἀπολέσαντες codd.,
del. Kuster τοῦτο τοῦ Ε. ἀπολαύσαντες Toup

to take it up beaming with joy and happiness, thinking to lay the
groundwork for another assault on his benefactors, this time with the
help of a large number of corrupted soldiers. Since he had escaped
many dangers as the result of his growing daring and the enormity of
his undertakings, he forced this daring upon the erstwhile impunity and
great good luck that he had enjoyed in his dealings with everyone. But
Eutropius was cleverer and followed hard upon Bargus' heels with his
own plot.[140] Bargus had a wife who, being long alienated from her
husband, was like a torpid snake chilled by the cold. Some men, sent
for this purpose following a secret plan that had already been laid,
roused her to action against her husband by promising rewards. The
upshot was that Bargus tried to flee, was captured and paid the penalty
for his ingratitude; and, having shown that he was the more crazy and
the eunuch the cleverer, he bore witness to how serious the crime of
ingratitude was in the eyes of God.

[5. (*Suda* X 80)
    Eutropius made endless and eager use of his opportunities and
good fortune and he immersed himself so much in his meddling that if
a father hated his son, a husband his wife, a mother her daughter, none
escaped his notice. Everything flew swiftly to his knowledge.]

[6. (*Suda* Δ 326)
    All in fear shrank from the prying ears of Eutropius, as the suitors
did from Odysseus when they saw him stripped of his rags.[141]]

[7. (*Suda* Σ 897)
    In the time of Eutropius the eunuch, the guardian of the Emperor
Theodosius,[142] because of the former's importance and power the tribe
of eunuchs became so numerous that even some persons who had
beards, in their eager haste to become eunuchs and Eutropiuses, lost
their wits and their testicles, enjoying the advantages of Eutropius.
Golden statues of him were set up everywhere, and he built splendid
palaces more magnificent than the whole city.]

8. (*Exc. de Sent.* 62)

Ὅτι ὁ εὐνοῦχος τοῦτον τοσοῦτον ὄντα καὶ τηλικοῦτον ἐκβαλὼν
τοῦ βίου, εὐνοῦχος ἄνδρα καὶ [ὁ] δοῦλος ὕπατον καὶ θαλαμηπόλος τὸν
ἐπὶ τοῖς στρατοπέδοις γεγενημένον, μέγα δή τι καὶ ὑπὲρ ἄνδρας
ἐφρόνει· καὶ μή τίς γε τὸ Ἀβουνδαντίου πάθος, κἀκείνου τελέσαντος
ἐς ὑπάτους . . . .                                                                      5

2 ὁ exp. Mai        5 post ὑπάτους lacunam indicant edd.

(Zosimus 5,8-10)

## 66

1. (*Exc. de Sent.* 63)

Ἀπίθανον μὲν γὰρ τὸ γραφόμενον· πλὴν εἴ τις ἕτερος αὐτὰ
γράφειν ἱκανός ἐστι, θαυμάζω αὐτὸν ἔγωγε τῆς ἀνδρείας, καὶ
ἀνδρεῖος ἀποφαινέσθω μοι τῆς ἀνεξικακίας χάριν. ἀλλ᾿ εἰκὸς μὲν
τοὺς τὰ ἀκριβέστερα γράψαντας κατὰ χρόνους καὶ κατὰ ἄνδρας καὶ
προσποιουμένους ἀσφαλῶς τι λέγειν, ἔς τε χάριν καὶ ἀπέχθειαν ἀνα-      5
φέρειν τὴν συγγραφήν· τῷ δὲ ταῦτα γράφοντι οὐ πρὸς ταῦτα ἔφερεν
ἡ ὁδός, ἀλλ᾿ ὡς ὅτι μάλιστα ἀνατρέχοι καὶ στηρίζοιτο πρὸς ἀλήθειαν.
ἐπεὶ καὶ κατὰ τούσδε τοὺς χρόνους ἤκουον καὶ συνεπυνθανόμην ὡς ὁ
δεῖνα καὶ ὁ δεῖνα γράφουσιν ἱστορίαν· οὓς ἐγὼ οὔτι νεμεσητὸν λέγω,
ἀλλὰ ἐπίσταμαί γε σαφῶς ἄνδρας ἀγερώχους τε καὶ σκιρτῶντας καὶ    10
ἀληθείας τοσοῦτον ἀφεστηκότας ὅσον ἐντὸς εἶναι ἀναγωγίας. καὶ
οὐκ ἐκείνοις μέμφομαι, τῆς δὲ ἀνθρωπίνης κρίσεως τὸ λίαν ἀκρατὲς
καὶ ὀλισθηρὸν καταμέμφομαι, ὅτι θελγόμενοι καὶ καταγοητευόμενοι
τὸ καθ᾿ ἕκαστον, ἂν ὀνόματος μνησθῇ τις περιττοῦ καὶ τοῖς πολλοῖς
γνωρίμου, καί τι τῶν περὶ τὴν αὐλὴν τὴν βασιλικὴν ἀκριβέστερον    15
ὑπορύξαντες ἐξενέγκωσιν εἰς τοὺς πολλούς, τόν τε κροτοθόρυβον
ἔχουσιν, ὡς ἀληθῆ λέγοντες καὶ πάντα εἰδότες, καὶ πολὺς περὶ αὐτοὺς
ὁ συνθέων ὅμιλος, μαρτυροῦντες ῥᾳδίως ὅτι ταῦτα οὕτως ἔχει, καὶ
τὴν ἀρετὴν τὴν τῆς συγγραφῆς εἰς τόδε συμβιασάμενοι καὶ κατα-
τείναντες, ὡς ἄρα τοῦτό ἐστιν αἰθέριον καὶ οὐρανόμηκες, ὅπερ αὐτοὶ    20
διὰ βίου τινὰ χλιδὴν ἴδωσι, καὶ ἁπλότητα χαυνότερον ἐπαινοῦντες ἐς
τὸ πιστευόμενον καὶ δημῶδες συνάγουσι καὶ καταβιάζονται. ἀλλ᾿
ὅμως εἰ καὶ ἀπίθανόν πως εἴρηται, πολλά τε αὐτοῦ τερατωδέστερα
καὶ μυθωδέστερα προτέθειται καὶ ἅπαντα ἦν τῆς ἡλιακῆς κινήσεως
ἀληθέστερα· μαρτυρεῖ δὲ αὐτοῖς ὁ ἥλιος τοῖς εἰρημένοις. καὶ ῥηθή-    25
σεταί γε ἴσως ἕτερα τούτων πολυπλανέστερα καὶ βαθυπλοκώτερα
πρὸς ἀπιστίαν· ἀλλὰ ἐξαγγέλλει γε αὐτὰ ἡ συγγραφὴ μετριώτερον,

21 ἰδόντες καὶ ⟨δι⟩ Kuiper

8. (*Exc. de Sent.* 62)

When the eunuch, a slave and a bedroom-attendant, had deprived a man of such importance, a consul and a soldier, of his way of life, he then formed an ambitious scheme beyond even the powers of men. Lest the fate of Abundantius, who had reached the consulship . . ..[143]


(Zosimus 5,8-10)


## 66

1. (*Exc. de Sent.* 63)

The written record is incredible. But if anyone else has the courage to write down these things, I salute him for his bravery and judge him a brave man for his endurance. It was proper that those who both made their accounts as accurate as they could, considering the times when and the persons about whom they were writing, and proposed to write in safety should incline their narrative to favour and disfavour. However, as I record these events, my path has led not in that direction, but to approach and stay as close as possible to the truth.[144] For during these times I heard and learned of various individuals who wrote history. But I also learned (to say nothing reprehensible about them) that they were clearly hasty and undisciplined, and as far from the truth as is the case with indiscipline. Them I do not blame, but I *do* blame the intemperate and unreliable judgement of mankind in that they are enchanted and bewitched every time if someone of considerable reputation and widely known is mentioned or if they ferret out some detail of the events at court and broadcast it to the public. These people are then applauded as if they were speaking the truth and were all-knowing, and a great crowd rushes to join them, readily testifying that it is as they say and perverting and forcing the objectivity of history to accommodate to this detail (as if it were some divinely important thing) which they observe in the midst of their life of luxury, and, heaping praise upon what is simplistic and vacuous, they twist and re-shape it into a believable version for the public.[145] Nevertheless, if something incredible is set down, details more marvellous and mythical than that are added, and all is more reliable than the course of the sun, the sun being witness to this account! Perhaps other 'facts' will be offered, even more remote from the truth than these and more tinged with falsehood. Even so, the history reports them in a temperate tone

καὶ ταῦτα ὑπὲρ τῶν λεγομένων καὶ ὅτι γε φίλος θεὸς καὶ φίλη ἀλήθεια. ἀλλ' οὐκ οἶδα ὅστις γίνομαι ταῦτα γράφων· πολὺ γὰρ τὸ
φροντίζειν ἀληθείας· ἀλλ' ὅ γε τοῖς γεγραμμένοις ἀκολουθῶν καὶ    30
πειθόμενος ἀκρίβειάν τε προσκυνήσει καὶ ἀλήθειαν.

2. (*Exc. de Sent.* 64)

    Ὅτι κατὰ τοὺς χρόνους Εὐτροπίου τοῦ εὐνούχου τῶν μὲν περὶ
τὴν ἑσπέραν οὐδὲν ἀκριβῶς γράφειν <ἦν> εἰς ἐξήγησιν. τό τε γὰρ
διάστημα τοῦ πλοῦ καὶ μῆκος μακρὰς ἐποίει τὰς ἀγγελίας καὶ διε-
φθαρμένας ὑπὸ χρόνου, καθάπερ ἐς χρόνιον καὶ παρέλκουσάν τινα
νόσον καταβεβλημένας· οἵ τε πραττόμενοι καὶ στρατευόμενοι εἰ μέν    5
τινες ἦσαν τῶν περὶ τὰ κοινὰ καὶ δυναμένων εἰδέναι, πρὸς χάριν καὶ
ἀπέχθειαν καὶ τὰ καθ' ἡδονὴν ἕκαστος κατὰ βούλησιν ἀπέφηνεν· εἰ
γοῦν τις αὐτῶν συνήγαγε τρεῖς ἢ τέσσαρας τἀναντία λέγοντας
ὥσπερ μάρτυρας, πολὺ τὸ παγκράτιον ἦν τῶν λόγων καὶ ὁ πόλεμος
ἐν χερσίν, ἀρχὰς λαβὼν ἀπὸ ῥηματίων καὶ ὑποθέρμων καὶ συγκε-    10
καυμένων. ταῦτα δὲ ἦν· "Σὺ πόθεν ταῦτα οἶδας;" "ποῦ δέ σε ὁ
Στελίχων εἶδε;" "σὺ δὲ τὸν εὐνοῦχον εἶδες ἄν;" ὥστε ἔργον ἦν
διαλύειν τὰς συμπλοκάς. τῶν δὲ ἐμπόρων οὐδὲν εἰς λόγον πλείονα
ψευδομένων ἢ ὅσοις κερδαίνειν βούλονται. ἀλλ' ὅσα τῷ σοφωτάτῳ
μάρτυρι κατὰ Πίνδαρον χρόνῳ τὴν ἀκριβεστέραν κατάληψιν ἐφευ-    15
ρήσει <γράφων>, ἐπὶ τὰς Ἀσιανὰς συμφορὰς στρέψω τὴν συγ-
γραφήν· τοιοῦτο γὰρ ὁ μακρὸς αἰὼν οὐδὲν ἤνεγκεν, οὐδέ τις περὶ τὸν
βίον τὸν ἀνθρώπινον ἐνεοχμώθη τοιαύτη φορὰ καὶ κίνησις. ἀλλ'
ὅμως οὕτως εἶχε, καὶ τὸ ἀληθὲς ἀσιώπητον, ὡς ἀδικοίη γε ἄν τις, εἰ
διὰ τὸ ἀπίθανον τἀληθῆ μὴ γράφοιτο. καὶ τοῦτό γε οὐδὲν διαφέρειν    20
δοκεῖ μοι τοῦ πιεῖν τι τῶν δριμέων καὶ πικρῶν ἐπὶ σωτηρίᾳ· ἀλλ'
ὥσπερ ἐκεῖνα κατακερασθέντα τοῖς σώμασιν ἀηδῶς τέλος ἔχει τὴν
ὑγείαν καὶ σωτηρίαν, οὕτω καὶ τὰ τερατευθέντα πρὸς τὸ παράλογον
οὐ τῆς γραφῆς ἐστιν ἀηδὲς ἁμάρτημα, ἀλλὰ γλυκύ τι καὶ πότιμον διὰ
τὴν ἀλήθειαν τοῖς ἀκριβῶς ἐξετάζειν βουλομένοις γίνεται.    25

2 ἦν add. Boissevain [ἐξῆν add. Niebuhr     5 πραττόμενοι Boissevain [πλατ-
τόμενοι cod. πλανώμενοι Niebuhr     7 ἀπέφηνεν Boissevain [ἀπέστειλεν Mai
ἐπέστελλεν Bekker     13 οὐδὲν εἰς λόγον scripsi [οὐδεὶς λόγος Boissevain
οὐδὲ εἷς λόγος Mai οὐδὲ καὶ λόγος ἦν Cobet     14 ὅσοις scripsi [ὅσα cod.
15-16 κατάληψιν ἐφευρήσει <γράφων>, ἐπὶ Boissevain [κατάληψιν. ὅτι ἐπὶ
edd., aut lac. post κατάληψιν indicant     24 ἐστιν [ἐστι <τὸ> Niebuhr

(Zosimus 5,11-12)

## 67

1. (*Exc. de Sent.* 65)

    Καὶ οὗτος μὲν ἐσώζετο καλῶς πονηρὸς ὤν· ὁμῶς δέ (τὸν

1 πονηρῶς ἔχων van Herwerden     ὁμῶς scripsi [ὅμως cod.

in deference to its avowed "love of God and love of the truth". But I do not know who I am to write these things, for to take thought for the truth is an onerous task. Nevertheless, he who heeds and obeys what I have written will do obeisance to accuracy and to truth.[146]

## 2. (*Exc. de Sent.* 64)

During the time of Eutropius the eunuch it was impossible to include in a history an accurate account of events in the West. For the length and duration of the sea-voyage made the reports late and useless because they were out of date, as if they had fallen into some chronic and long-drawn-out illness. If any officials or soldiers had access to information on political activity, they related it as they wished, biased by friendship or hostility or a desire to please someone. And if you brought together three or four of them with conflicting versions as witnesses, there would be a great argument which would proceed from passionate and heated interjections to a pitched battle. They would say, "Where did you get this from?" "Where did Stilicho see you?" "Would you have seen the eunuch?" so that it was quite a task to sort out the tangle. From the merchants there was no reasonable information, since they either told many lies or said what they wished to profit from. But when I have set down what will offer the closest sense of what happened in the light of the evidence of time, the wisest witness, as Pindar says,[147] I shall turn my narrative to the disasters of Asia.[148] Eternity has produced no single comparable phenomenon, and the life of mankind has suffered no similar disturbance and innovation. But thus it was, and the truth must not be suppressed, since one would act wrongly in failing to record the truth for fear of incredulity. It seems to me like the drinking of a bitter and pungent medicine for the sake of health. Just as those things, whose entrance into the body is unpleasant, bring health and recovery, so these remarkable tales which verge on the incredible are not unpleasantries to be blamed upon my History, but are, to those who want an accurate review of events, something pleasant and potable since they are true.[149]

(Zosimus 5,11-12)

## 67

## 1. (*Exc. de Sent.* 65)

He, though an evil man, was successfully saved. Likewise, suffering

σπλῆνα γὰρ ἐνόσει) διετέθη καλῶς ὑπὸ τῆς συνεχοῦς ἱππασίας,
κατεπράϋνέ τε καὶ τὸ λιθῶδες ὑπεμάλαξε. καὶ ὁ μὲν ἀπῄει τῷ τε
σφετέρῳ σώματι πολεμῶν ἢ πολεμήσων καὶ τοῖς περὶ τὴν αὐλὴν
ἐπαγγέλλων ἀληθέστερον πόλεμον.                                    5

2-3 ἱππασίας ἢ κατεπράϋνέ τε τὸ λιθῶδες καὶ van Herwerden    4 σώματι
[τάγματι Boissevain    5 ἐπαγγέλλων Dindorf [ἀπαγγέλλων cod.

2. (Exc. de Sent. 66)
    Ἡ δὲ Λυδία πλησιόχωρος οὖσα τὰ δεύτερα ἔμελλε τοῦ
ὀλέθρου φέρεσθαι.

3. (Exc. de Sent. 67)
    Πλὴν ὅσα γε τούτοις ἐν ἐλπίσιν ἦν τὸ σώζεσθαι· ἐλπὶς γὰρ ἐν
ἀπορρήτοις <τοῖς> ἔτι ζῶσι παραμύθιον.

2 τοῖς add. Boissevain [ἀπόροις τοῖς Bernhardy ἀπορωτάτοις Kuiper

4. (Exc. de Sent. 68)
    Ἐπὶ τά γε ἐν τοῖς ἔργοις ξίφη καὶ βάρβαροι . . . οὐ κατὰ τὴν
ἔννομον ἀπαίτησιν (καὶ γὰρ ἐκείνη τὸ διπλάσιον ὑπερέβαλεν) ἀλλὰ
κατὰ τὴν βαρβαρικὴν καὶ ἄμετρον πλεονεξίαν, ἀκινδύνως εἶχε πρὸς
ἕτερον . . ..

1 ἐπὶ cod. [ἐπεὶ Boissevain

[5. (Suda Λ 268)
    Λέων. οὗτος στρατηγὸς ἐπέμφθη παρὰ Εὐτροπίου τοῦ εὐ-
νούχου κατὰ τῶν βαρβάρων, εὔκολος ὢν καὶ διὰ μελέτην μέθης
εὐπαράγωγος· ἦν γὰρ αὐτῷ τὸ ἀνδρεῖον ἐπὶ τούτῳ συνηναγκασμένον,
πλείους ἔχειν παλλακίδας τῶν στρατιωτῶν, καὶ πλείονα πίνειν ἢ ὅσα
πάντες οἱ ἄνθρωποι πίνουσι.  (Cf. E 3636)]                          5

6. (Suda Α 3066)
    Εὐνάπιος· καὶ γὰρ οὐκ ἀπεστάτει τῆς τοῦ Λέοντος ἐπωνυμίας·
οὕτω γὰρ καὶ τὸ ζῷον ποιεῖν εἴωθεν.

7. (Suda Δ 1025)
    Εὐνάπιος· ὁ δὲ ἐπὶ τὰ λειπόμενα τῶν πραγμάτων διεξανιστά-
μενος, ἀνωρθοῦτο καὶ διηυχενίζετο πρὸς τὸν λεγόμενον Λέοντα,
ὅπως αὐτὸν φονεύσειεν.

[8. (Suda Σ 793)
    Σουβαρμάχιος. οὗτος τῶν δορυφόρων ἦν ἡγεμών, πιστότατος
τῷ εὐνούχῳ Εὐτροπίῳ, εἴπερ τις ἄλλος· ἔπωε δὲ οἶνον πλείονα ἢ
ὅσον ἠδύνατο χωρεῖν· ἀλλ' ὅμως τὰ περὶ γαστέρα διὰ συνήθειαν

as he did with his spleen, he was well served by the continual riding, which eased and softened his stones. He went away battling or intending to do battle with his body, while declaring a more genuine war upon the court officials.[150]

### 2. (*Exc. de Sent.* 66)

Lydia, being the closest province, was destined to suffer the second round of devastation.[151]

### 3. (*Exc. de Sent.* 67)

For them these things offered hope of safety; and in unspeakable circumstances hope is an encouragement for those still alive.

### 4. (*Exc. de Sent.* 68)

. . . against the swords used in these actions, and the barbarians . . . not according to the lawful level of requisition (and that was more than double) but according to the insatiable greed of barbarians. He was in no danger from the other . . ..[152]

### [5. (*Suda* Λ 268)

Leo. He was a general sent by the eunuch Eutropius against the barbarians, a placid man and easily led because of his addiction to drink. For him manly virtue consisted in having more whores than soldiers and drinking more than anybody.
(Cf. E 3636)]

### 6. (*Suda* A 3066)

He did not fail to live up to his name, Leo. For his behaviour was like that of the animal.

### 7. (*Suda* Δ 1025)

He applied himself to the rest of the business, pulled himself together and raised his head against the so-called Lion, seeking how he might slay him.[153]

### [8. (*Suda* Σ 793)

Subarmachius. He was count of the domestics and most loyal of all to Eutropius. Although he drank more than he could hold, because he did this habitually and because he took heavy and vigorous exercise

οὕτω καὶ γυμνασίαν ἰσχυρὰν καὶ νεανικὴν πάντα φέρειν ἐπὶ τὴν
φυσικὴν τῶν ὑγρῶν ἔκκρισιν. ἀεὶ γοῦν ἦν, πεπωκώς τε καὶ οὐ    5
πεπωκώς, μεθύων· τὴν δὲ μέθην παρεκάλυπτε σφαλερὸν διαβαίνων
τοῖς ποσί, καὶ πρὸς τὴν πτῶσιν πολεμῶν ὑφ' ἡλικίας καὶ [διὰ νεό-
τητα] συνιστάμενος. ἦν δὲ βασιλικοῦ μὲν γένους, Κόλχος ἀκριβὴς
τῶν ὑπὲρ Φᾶσιν καὶ Θερμώδοντα, τοξότης <δὲ> ἄριστος, εἴ γε μὴ
κατετόξευεν αὐτὸν τὸ περιττὸν τῆς τρυφῆς.]    10

6 οὐ ante σφαλερὸν add. edd.    7-8 διὰ νεότητα exp. Boissonade    9 δὲ add.
Bernhardy

## 9. (*Exc. de Sent.* 69)

Ὅτι <οὐχ οὕτω παρακεκινηκότες καὶ διεφθαρμένοι τὴν
γνώμην, ἀλλὰ> δι' ὑπεροχὴν κακῶν εἰς Ἰουλιανοῦ καιροὺς καὶ
χρόνους τὸν εὐνοῦχον ἀνέθεσάν τινες Εὐτρόπιον. ὥσπερ οὖν τῶν
ἰατρῶν ἐστιν ἀκούειν ὅτι τοῖς φιλοζώοις βέλτιόν ἐστι σπλῆνα νοσεῖν
ἢ κάμνειν ἧπαρ, καὶ ὅσον ὑπὲρ ἥπατος διὰ πνεύμονος ἐπὶ καρδίαν    5
συμπερατοῦται καὶ διέσφικται, οὕτω καὶ τότε συνέβαινεν, ὡς ἐν
αἱρέσει τῶν αἰσχίστων, εὐδοκιμεῖν εὐνοῦχον μανέντα πρὸς παρά-
θεσιν τῶν ἐπιλαβουσῶν συμφορῶν.    (Cf. *Suda* Π 363*)

1-2 verba in uncis addita e *Suda* Π 363

## 10. (*Exc. de Sent.* 70)

Ὅμως ὁ Γαϊνᾶς διαφθείρας τὸν πολέμιον (ἐπολέμει γὰρ
εὐνούχῳ μάλα ἐντεταμένως· οὕτω σφόδρα γενναῖός τις ἦν) ἐξ ὧν
ἐδόκει κατορθωκέναι, διὰ τούτων ἥττητο. ὑγρότερος γὰρ ὑπὸ τοῦ
κατορθώματος καὶ μαλακώτερος γενόμενος, ὡς ἂν ἤδη τὴν Ῥωμαϊκὴν ἀρχὴν συνηρηκὼς καὶ τοῖς ποσὶν ἐπεμβαίνων αὐτῆς, μαλακώ-    5
τερος ἦν ἀμφαφάασθαι· καὶ πρὸς τὸν Ἀργίβιλδον ἐπρεσβεύετο, ὡς
τὸ σπουδαζόμενον αὐτοῖς ἔχει τέλος.

6 Ἀργίβιλδον Boissevain [Ἀργίβολον Mai

## 11. (*Exc. de Sent.* 71)

Ὅτι Γαϊνᾶς καὶ Ἀργίβιλδος ἀπὸ ... ὁ μὲν ἡγούμενος ὁ δὲ
ἐφεπόμενος ... γινόμενα οὐδὲ αὐτὸς ἕτερον ἐπένθει· σφαγεὶς δὲ
ἔκειτο μηδὲ τὸν θάψοντα ἔχων καὶ κατορύξοντα.

1 Ἀργίβιλδος vel Ταργίβιλδος Boissevain [Ἀργίβολος Mai    post ἀπὸ lacunam
xvii litt. indicat Boissevain    2 post ἐφεπόμενος lac. fere xi vers. indicat
Boissevain in qua litterae et verba sparsa ac non intelligenda leguntur.

## 12. (*Suda* E 740)

Εὐνάπιος· οὕτως καὶ τότε ὁ μέγιστος Ἑλλανοδίκης Γαϊνᾶς
τὸν Ῥωμαϊκὸν ὄλεθρον ἠθλοθέτει.    (Cf. H 154)

his stomach was able to accept and pass all the liquid naturally. Whether he had been drinking or not, he was perpetually drunk, but he hid the fact because his walk was naturally unsteady and he was able, since he was a young man, to hold himself firm and avoid falling over. He was of royal blood, a pure Colchian from beyond Phasis and Thermodon, and would have been a first-rate archer had he not been shot down by his own dissipation.]

### 9. (*Exc. de Sent.* 69)

It was <not through disturbance or loss of wits but>[154] because of a surfeit of suffering that some compared the eunuch Eutropius to Julian's day and age. Just as the doctors tell us that for survival it is better to have a sick spleen than to suffer with the liver or with that part of the body which extends through the lungs close to the heart, so it happened that, when they were in the grip of the worst misfortunes, people esteemed the mad eunuch in comparison with the evils that were afflicting them.
(Cf. *Suda* II 363*)

### 10. (*Exc. de Sent.* 70)

But when Gainas had destroyed the enemy (for he waged an extremely vigorous campaign against the eunuch, so very noble a man was he), he was overcome by what he thought were his successes. For, as if he had already taken control of the Roman state, he softened and relaxed as a result of his success and thus became easier to deal with.[155] He sent a message to Argibild[156] declaring that they had achieved the goal for which they were working.

### 11. (*Exc. de Sent.* 71)

Gainas and Argibild . . .[157] the former leading, the latter following . . .[158] nor did he grieve another. But he lay there slaughtered, having no one to bury him or cover his body with earth.

### 12. (*Suda* E 740)

Then Gainas, the chief judge of the contest, presided over the destruction of the Romans in this manner.   (Cf. H 154)

[13. (*Suda* Π 1939)

Ὁ δὲ Γαυᾶς ἐξεχώρει τῆς πόλεως, καταλιπὼν αὐτὴν πολυ-
άνδριον καὶ πολυτελῆ τάφον, οὔπω τεθαμμένων τῶν ἐνῳκηκότων.]

(Zosimus 5,13,1 - 19,5)

## 68

(*Exc. de Sent.* 72)

Ὅτι Πέρσης ἦν ἐν Ῥώμῃ ἔπαρχος πρὸς χλευασίαν καὶ γέλωτα
τὴν Ῥωμαϊκὴν παραφέρων εὐτυχίαν· σανίδας δὴ πολλὰς μικρὰς πρὸς
ἥμισυ σταδίου συγκομισάμενος, καὶ εἰκόνα τινὰ τῶν ἔργων ὑπο-
γράψαι βουλόμενος, πάντα ἐνετίθει γελοῖα ταῖς γραφαῖς, καὶ ἀπορ-
ρήτως τὰ γραφόμενα κατεχλεύαζε διὰ τῆς εἰκόνος. ἀνδρείαν μὲν        5
γὰρ βασιλέως ἢ ῥώμην στρατιωτῶν ἢ πόλεμον ἐμφανῆ καὶ νόμιμον
οὐδαμοῦ τὰ γραφέντα παρεδήλου καὶ συνῃνίττετο· χειρὸς δέ τινος ὡς
ἂν ἐκ νεφῶν προτεινομένης ἐπίγραμμα ἦν τῇ χειρί· "θεοῦ χεὶρ ἐλαύ-
νουσα τοὺς βαρβάρους"· αἰσχρὸν τοῦτο καταγράφειν, ἀλλ' ἀναγκαῖον.
καὶ πάλιν ἑτέρωθι· "βάρβαροι τὸν θεὸν φεύγοντες", καὶ τούτων ἔτερα    10
παχύτερα καὶ ἀηδέστερα, κωθωνιζομένων γραφέων φλήναφος.

11  ἀηδέστερα Boissevain [δημωδέστερα Jordan

## 69

1. (*Exc. de Sent.* 73)

...οὗ καὶ πρότερον ἡ συγγραφὴ μέμνηται τῆς ἀκμαζούσης
ἀρετῆς, ἐνόσει τὸ σῶμα ὁ Φράβιθος τῆς ψυχῆς ὑγιαινούσης πλέον·
καὶ τό γε σῶμα διαλυόμενον ἤδη καὶ ἀποκολλώμενον εἰς τὴν λύσιν
συνεγόμφου καὶ διέπλεκεν εἰς πῆξίν τινα καὶ ἁρμονίαν, ὅπως ἂν
ἀρκέσειεν τῷ κάλῳ.                                                    5

In cod. legit Mai ἀκμαζούσης ἀρετῆς ... τὸ σῶμα ... τῆς ψυχῆς ... πλέον
κατὰ σῶμα διαλυόμενον ἤδη ... ἀπὸ ... Verba reliqua supplentur e *Suda* Φ
681

2. (*Suda* Φ 681)

Φράβιθος. οὗτος στρατηγὸς ἦν τῆς ἀνατολῆς, ὃς ἀκμάζων τὴν
ἀρετὴν ἐνόσει τὸ σῶμα, τῆς ψυχῆς ὑγιαινούσης πλέον· καὶ τό γε
σῶμα διαλυόμενον ἤδη καὶ ἀποκολλώμενον εἰς τὴν λύσιν συνεγόμφου
καὶ συνέπλεκεν εἰς πῆξίν τινα καὶ ἁρμονίαν, ὅπως ἂν ἀρκέσειε τῷ
καλῷ. ὃς τοὺς λῃστὰς ῥαδίως συνεῖλεν, ὥστε μικροῦ καὶ τὸ ὄνομα    5
τῆς λῃστείας ἐκ τῆς μνείας τῶν ἀνθρώπων ἐκπεσεῖν· ἦν δὲ Ἕλλην
τὴν θρησκείαν.

6  μνείας A [μνήμης GVM

[13. (*Suda* Π 1939)

Gainas departed from the city, which he left behind a populous and magnificent tomb, the occupants of which had not yet been buried.[159]]

(Zosimus 5,13,1 - 19,5)

## 68

(*Exc. de Sent.* 72)

There was a Persian, a prefect at Rome, who reduced the success of the Romans to mockery and laughter. Wishing to offer a representation of what had been done, he assembled many small panels in the middle of the Circus. But all the contents of his painting were laughable, and he unwittingly mocked his subject in his presentation. For nowhere did the painting show or allude to either the bravery of the Emperor, or the strength of the soldiers, or anything that was obviously a proper battle. But a hand extended as if from the clouds, and by the hand was inscribed, "The hand of God driving off the barbarians" (it is shameful, but necessary, to write this down), and on the other side, "The barbarians fleeing God", and other things even more stupid and odious than these, the nonsense of the drunken painters.

## 69

1. (*Exc. de Sent.* 73)

... whose outstanding virtue my narrative has remarked earlier. While Fravitta's body was sickly, his spirit was in greater health, and he glued and wove his body, which was already becoming unglued and falling to pieces, back into a solid framework, so as to be equal to his glorious task.[160]

2. (*Suda* Φ 681)

Fravitta. He was a general of the East, a man of outstanding virtue. While his body was sickly, his spirit was in greater health, and he glued and wove his body, which was already becoming unglued and falling to pieces, back into a solid framework, so as to be equal to his glorious task. He easily destroyed the brigands so that the word 'brigandage' almost disappeared from the lips of men. In his faith he was a Hellene.[161]

3. (*Suda* X 473 and E 1753 combined)

Εὐνάπιος· ὁ δὲ τὰς δυνάμεις ἤθροισε, τὸ χρῆμα τῆς διαβάσεως
ἐπισπέρχων ἤδη καὶ συμβιαζόμενος καὶ πλὴν ἀγαθῆς ψυχῆς σῶμα
οὐκ ἔχων, ὅμως ἔκαμε καὶ τὰς δυνάμεις ἐξῆσκει καὶ κατεκόσμει
πρὸς τὸ ἀνδρικώτερον.

4. (*Exc. de Sent.* 74)

Ὅτι Φράβιθος ὁ στρατηγὸς Ῥωμαίων νικήσας Γαΐνᾶν περὶ τὴν
Χερρόνησον διαμένοντα καὶ τοῦτον μὴ διώξας (ἀσφαλὴς γὰρ ἦν ἐπὶ
τῇ νίκῃ κερδαίνων τὸ ἔργον καὶ Λακωνικός τις ἦν ἐς τὸ τύχην
εἰδέναι καὶ μὴ πέραν τοῦ μετρίου ποιεῖσθαι τὴν δίωξιν). καὶ οὗτος
μὲν ἀσφαλέστερον βουλευόμενος ἡλίκον ἐστὶ τοῖς ἄλλοις τὸ καλῶς      5
στρατηγεῖν ἔδειξεν· οἱ δὲ πολλοὶ καὶ ὅσον ἠλίθιον καὶ πηλοῦ παχύ-
τερον, στρατηγικοί τινες εἶναι βουλόμενοι καὶ τὸ γεγονὸς ὑποσημαί-
νοντες διελήρουν καὶ παρεφλυάρουν, τὰς ὀφρῦς ἀνασπῶντες καὶ
διαφλεγόμενοι τῷ φθόνῳ πρὸς ἀπίθανόν τινα καὶ μυθώδη καταστροφήν, ἀπὸ μιᾶς γλώσσης καὶ πάθους ἑνός, ὁμόφωνοι κατὰ δόξαν      10
ὑπὸ δειλίας γεγονότες καὶ τῷ παραλόγῳ πληγέντες, τὸν Φράβιθον
ἐπεφήμιζον ‹νικᾶν› μὲν εἰδέναι, νίκῃ δὲ οὐκ εἰδέναι χρῆσθαι. ὁ γὰρ
… ἐπὶ τὴν Χερρόνησον· ἐγκατέλαβεν … αἰχμάλωτον ὀπίσω σωτηρίας … προσηκόντως τύχωσι· θέαμα τῆς νίκης ἄξιον. καὶ οὗτοι
μὲν ‹προδήλως ἐθρασύνοντο› καὶ ὑπέσπειρον εἰς τὰ βασίλεια τῷ      15
λόγῳ ποικίλλοντές τε καὶ περιγράφοντες, ὡς βάρβαρος βαρβάρῳ καὶ
μύστης μύστῃ παρέχοι διαφυγὴν καὶ σωτηρίαν· ὁ δὲ Φράβιθος μάλα
φαιδρῶς καὶ ‹λαμπρῶς ἐπανῄει› ἐπὶ τὴν Κωνσταντίνου πόλιν οὕτω
τῆς φήμης ‹κατ᾽ αὐτοῦ› τὸ ἀφανὲς καὶ σκοτεινὸν ὑφέρπον τῆς
προφερομένης ‹καταφρονήσας ὥστε› παρελθὼν εἰς τὰ βασίλεια      20
φαιδρὸς καὶ γεγηθὼς ‹ἁπάντων ἐκπεπληγ›μένων πρὸς τὸ παράλογον τῆς τύχης καὶ θεὸν ὁρᾶν ὑπολαμβανόντων μᾶλλον ἢ ἄνθρωπον (οὕτως τί ἐστι τὸ νικᾶν καὶ χεῖρα ἔχειν οὐκ ᾔδεσαν), πρὸς τὸν
βασιλέα μετὰ ἐλευθερίας ‹καὶ σφόδρα τὴν φωνὴν› διατεινάμενος

3 τὴν add. Boissevain ante τύχην    9-10 καταστροφήν Müller [καταστροφῆναι
Mai    10 κατὰ [παρὰ Bekker    12 ἐπεφήμιζον Dindorf [ἐπεψήφιζον cod.
νικᾶν add. Niebuhr    12-13 ὁ γὰρ … ἐπὶ τὴν Χερρόνησον· ἐγκατέλαβεν
Boissevain [ὁ γοῦν … τὴν Χ. ἐγκατέλιπεν Mai  ὁ γοῦν Φράβιθος διέπλευσεν
ἐπὶ τὴν Χ· ἐγκατέλαβεν van Herwerden    13-14 σωτηρίας Mai [σω …
Boissevain    14 προσηκόντως τύχωσι Mai [χειρούμενον καὶ ἐποίησεν van
Herwerden    15 προδήλως ἐθρασύνοντο Boissevain [πρ … εθρα cod.
πρᾶγμα ὀλέθρου … ἐστὶ van Herwerden    17 παρέχοι Boissevain [παρέχων
cod.    18 λαμπρῶς ἐπανῄει add. Boissevain    [… πρὸς … Mai  γελάδας πρὸς
… van Herwerden    19 ‹κατ᾽ αὐτοῦ›τὸ ἀφανὲς scripsi [‹κατ᾽ αὐτοῦ ψ εὖδος›
ἀφανὲς Boissevain  τὸ ἀφανὲς (sine lac.) van Herwerden    19-20 τῆς προφερομένης Mai [προσον … Boissevain    20 καταφρονήσας ὥστε add.
Boissevain    21 ἁπάντων ἐκπεπληγ- add. Bekker    23 τί Boissevain [ὅτι Mai
24 καὶ σφόδρα τὴν φωνὴν Boissevain

3. (*Suda* X 473 and E 1753 combined)

He gathered together his forces, even now attending to and organising the matter of the crossing, and, although he had no physical strength to go with his brave spirit, nevertheless he worked hard and equipped and trained his forces for bolder deeds.[162]

4. (*Exc. de Sent.* 74)

When Fravitta, the general of the Romans, had defeated Gainas, who was tarrying in the Chersonese, he did not pursue the latter, since, being secure in his victory, he was saving himself the trouble and in the Spartan manner he recognised his good fortune and did not carry pursuit beyond what was reasonable. In opting for the safer course he demonstrated to the rest the nature of good generalship. But the majority, who were silly people and thicker than mud, wishing to be generals and delivering their views on what had happened, prattled and chattered on. They arched their brows and, consumed by envy at the unbelievable and wonderful outcome, with one voice and one sentiment (they voiced their views in unison out of timidity, and they *were* stunned by the unexpected event) declared that Fravitta knew how to win a victory, but not how to use it. For he . . . to the Chersonese. He would have (?) taken . . . prisoner . . . a spectacle worthy of the victory.[163] Moreover, these people <apparently plucked up courage> and planted the allegation in the palace, sketching it out and embroidering it with their words, that a barbarian and initiate had allowed his fellow-barbarian and fellow-initiate to escape to safety. But Fravitta returned to Constantinople joyfully and gloriously and he so <scorned the obscure and> murky insinuations <that> he came joyfully and happily into the palace, and all the people, being amazed by his unexpected good fortune, thought that they were looking on a god rather than on a man (so unused were they to victory and physical prowess). Raising his voice he spoke loudly and openly to the Emperor . . .[164] hostile to the Roman state. Since as a very straightforward man he was

ἐξεβόησεν . . . τῶν καταφρυαττομένων φθόνων καὶ νηστείας καθάρ-     25
ματα . . . δεῖταί τε . . . πόσον ὁ θεὸς δύναται θεῷ μὲν ὅτε βού⟨λεται⟩
τὸ δυν⟨ατὸν⟩ ἐκείνου κακῶς . . . τηλικοῦτον ὄν . . . κατὰ πε . . . ειας
ἔργον οἶσθα, βασιλεῦ. τοῦτο δὲ τὸ ἔργον . . . ἀλλότριον τῆς Ῥωμαϊκῆς
ἀρχῆς. τοῦ δὲ μάλα ἐπινεύοντος πρόσωπον, διὰ γὰρ ἁπλότητα
πολλὴν συμπαθήσας πρὸς τὰ λεγόμενα . . . ὑπὸ τῶν εὐνούχων εἶπεν     30
ὅτι προσῆκόν ἐστιν ἐπινεύειν . . . τοῦ δὲ βασιλέως τοῦτο εἰπόντος ὡς
αἰτεῖν ἀνάγκη δωρεάν, ὁ Φράβιθος ᾔτησεν ἐπιτραπῆναι κατὰ τὸν
πάτριον νόμον θεραπεύειν θεόν. ὁ δὲ βασιλεὺς δι᾽ ὑπεροχὴν βασιλικῆς ἀρετῆς καὶ τὴν ὑπατείαν ἐπέτρεψεν· ὁ δ᾽ ἐδέξατο.

26-27 βού⟨λεται⟩ τὸ δυν⟨ατὸν⟩ Niebuhr     28 ἀλλότριον Mai [om. Boissevain
29 μάλα coni. Boissevain [μ.λ. cod.     32 ᾔτησεν Cobet ἔφησεν Mai

5. (*Exc. de Sent.* 75)
Ὅτι Φαμέας Ἰμίλκων ἐπικαλούμενος μυρία παρέχων κακὰ
Ῥωμαίοις, εἶτα Σκιπίωνος στρατηγοῦντος οὐ δυνάμενος, τὴν δὲ
αἰτίαν ἐρωτώμενος ἐξεῖπεν, τὰ μὲν πρόβατα εἶναι ταὐτά, τὸν δὲ ποι-
μένα σφοδρότερον καὶ τοῦ Ἄργου μᾶλλον πολυωπέστερον.

1 Ἰμίλκων Müller [ὁ Μίλκων cod.

(Zosimus 5,19,6 - 23,2)

70
(Zosimus 5,23,2 - 24,8; cf. Photius *Bibl. cod.* 77 = *Testimonium* 1)

71
[1. (*Suda* A 3752)
Ἀρβαζάκιος, Ἴσαυρος, ἐπὶ Ἀρκαδίου τοῦ βασιλέως, ὃν Ἁρπα-
ζάκιον ἐκάλουν διὰ τὸ πλεονεκτικόν. ἦν μὲν γὰρ ἐξ Ἀρμενίας, τοῖς
τρισὶν ἅμα συγκατειλημμένος πάθεσιν, ὥσπερ Ἡφαιστείοις δεσμοῖς
ἀρρήκτοις ἀλύτοις, καὶ ἔμενέ γε ἐν αὐτοῖς ἔμπεδον. ταῦτα δὲ ἦν ἐρωτο-
μανία καὶ μέθη καὶ πλεονεξία. οὕτω δὲ εἰς ἔσχατον ὅρον τὰς ἑαυτῷ     5
δοκούσας ἀρετὰς ἐπετήδευεν, ὥστε οὐκ ἄν τις ἐπίστευσε ⟨μὴ⟩
πειραθείς, ὅτι τὰς τρεῖς ἐκείνας οὕτως εἰς ἄκρον ἐξήσκησε. μουσουρ-
γοῖς μὲν γὰρ συνέζη τοσαύταις, ὅσας οὔτε ἐκεῖνος ἀριθμεῖν εἶχεν
οὔτε ἕτερός τις τῶν διακονουμένων. καὶ οἵγε προσήκοντες αὐτῷ
λογισταὶ τῶν στρατιωτικῶν ἔργων τὸν μὲν ἀριθμὸν τῶν στρατι-     10
ωτῶν ᾔδεσαν, τὸ δὲ πλῆθος τῶν ἑταιρῶν καὶ τὸν ἐκ τῶν χειρῶν
ἀριθμὸν αὐτοῦ διέφυγεν. ὥσπερ οὖν Ὀρόντην τὸν Πέρσην φασὶν
εἰπεῖν, ὅτι τῶν δακτύλων ὁ μικρότατος καὶ μύρια σημαίνει καὶ ἕνα

6 μὴ add. Portus

grimacing as he spoke, sympathising with what was being said . . . he declared through the eunuchs that it was proper to grimace . . .[165] and when the Emperor said that he must name a reward, Fravitta demanded that he be permitted to worship God in the ancestral manner.[166] The Emperor in an excess of kingly virtue granted him the consulship as well. And he accepted it.

5. (*Exc. de Sent.* 75)

Although Phameas, surnamed Himilco, had inflicted countless woes upon the Romans, he was unable to do so after Scipio became general. When asked the reason, he said that the sheep were the same but the shepherd was more energetic and had more eyes than Argus.[167]

(Zosimus 5,19,6 - 23,2)

## 70

(Zosimus 5,23,2 - 24,8; cf. Photius *Bibl. cod.* 77 = *Testimonium* 1)

## 71

[1. (*Suda* A 3752)

Arbazacius the Isaurian, during the reign of the Emperor Arcadius. They called him Harpazacius ['Grabber'] because of his greed. He was from Armenia and was a prisoner of three vices by which he remained bound fast as if by the unbreakable and unopenable fetters of Hephaestus. These were lust, drink and avarice. He had taken these virtues (as he thought them) to such an limit that no one who had not seen him would believe that he had polished them to such perfection. In his entourage was such a host of ladies devoted to the arts of entertainment that neither he nor any of his servants could count them; and while the military accountants under his command knew the number of his soldiers, the number of his mistresses defeated the combined efforts of all their fingers. Just as Orontes the Persian is said to have pointed out that the little finger stands for both one and ten thousand, so the

ἀριθμόν, οὕτω κἀκεῖνοι τὰς ἑταίρας κατὰ μονάδας καὶ μυριάδας
ἠρίθμουν. (Cf. H 657, M 1303, O 624)]    15

2. (*Exc. de Sent.* 76)

Ἱέραξ ἦν, ὄνομα δὲ τοῦτο ἀνθρώπου κύριον, ὃν εἶδεν ὁ συγγραφεὺς καὶ διελέχθη πρὸς αὐτόν, καὶ τὴν ψυχήν τε ἀνεμάξατο διὰ
τῶν λόγων· καὶ συνελόντι γε εἰπεῖν Ἀλεξανδρεὺς ἦν κορακώδης μὲν
κατὰ τὸ ἄπληστον ἐς τροφήν· προσῆν δὲ αὐτῷ καὶ τρυφή· πρὸς δὲ
ἡδονὰς ἀλεκτρυώδης, καὶ οἵος τις ἂν Ἀλεξανδρεὺς ἀσελγέστατος    5
γένοιτο καὶ εἴ γέ τι Ἀλεξανδρέως ἀσελγέστερον. ἀλλ' ὅμως ὁ
συγγραφεὺς αἰδεσθῆναι τὴν τοσαύτην ἀναίδειαν καὶ ἰταμότητα συμ-
πείσας ἐφ' οἷς ἦν λόγοις ᾤχετο ἀπιών, τεθηπότων τῶν παρόντων,
ὅτι ἄνθρωπος ἐξ Ἀλεξανδρείας γλῶσσάν τε ἐπέσχε καὶ φλυαρίαν
ἐπέστησε καὶ τὸ πρόσωπον κατέβαψεν ἐρυθήματι.    10

3 τῶν λόγων Bekker [τὸν λόγον cod.    5 ἀλεκτρυονώδης Meineke (e Phot.
*Bibl. Cod.* 77)    ἀσελγέστατος Niebuhr [ἀσελγέστερος cod.    8 λόγοις
Bekker [λόγος cod.    10 κατέβαψεν Dubner [κατέκρυψεν Niebuhr κατέ-
κοψεν Müller

3. (*Exc. de Sent.* 77)

Ὁ δὲ πρὸς τὸν Ἰωάννην ἐπιστρέψας τὸν λόγον, "ἀλλὰ σύγε"
εἶπε "πάντων εἶ τῶν κακῶν αἴτιος, τούς τε βασιλέας διατέμνων ἐκ
τῆς σφῶν αὐτῶν κολλήσεως καὶ τὸ θεοπρεπέστατον ἔργον καὶ
οὐρανόμηκες ὑπορύττων καὶ κατασείων ταῖς σαῖς μηχαναῖς ἐς διά-
λυσιν καὶ φθοράν. ἔστι δὲ πανόλβιόν τι χρῆμα καὶ τεῖχος ἄρρηκτον    5
καὶ ἀδαμάντινον τοὺς βασιλέας ἐν δύω σώμασι μίαν βασιλείαν
ἔχοντας φαίνεσθαι". καὶ οἱ παρόντες τούτων λεγομένων τὰς μὲν
κεφαλὰς ἀπέσειον ἡσυχῇ καὶ δεδοικότες· ἐδόκει γὰρ αὐτοῖς ἄριστα
λέγεσθαι, τὸν δὲ Ἰωάννην τρέμοντες καὶ πρὸς τὰ σφέτερα κέρδη
κεχηνότες (ἡ γὰρ διχοστασία καὶ τοῖς πονηροῖς, ἥπερ εἴρηται, τιμὴν    10
ἐχαρίζετο) τῆς κοινῆς σωτηρίας ἀμελήσαντες, καὶ προστησάμενοι
σφῶν αὐτῶν τὸν Ἰωάννην, τεχνικὸν δή τινα ἱερακοτρόφον, τὸν
Φράβιθον ἀφείλοντο τῆς ψυχῆς.

5 φθοράν Bekker [φοράν cod.    8 ἐπέσειον Dindorf

4. (*Exc. de Sent.* 78)

Παμφυλία γοῦν ὑπὸ τῶν Ἰσαυρικῶν πολέμων πορθουμένη
χρυσὸν ἐνόμισε τὰς Ἰσαυρικὰς συμφοράς· καὶ καθάπερ ἐν ταῖς
διοσημείαις ἀστραπῆς κεραυνὸς φοβερώτερος (ἡ μὲν γὰρ ἐφόβησε
μόνον, ὁ δὲ διέφθειρεν), οὕτω καὶ τοὺς Ἰσαυροὺς φρικωδεστάτους
ὄντας ἀκοῦσαί τε καὶ ἰδεῖν ἄνθος ἀπέδειξε καὶ τρυφερώτατόν τι καὶ    5
χλοερὸν ἔαρ ὁ βέλτιστος ἐξ Ἀλεξανδρείας Ἱέραξ, οὕτω πάντα διε-
ρευνησάμενος καὶ συναρπάσας ἀθρόως ἐπὶ τῷ Φραβίθου φόνῳ.

accountants calculated the number of his mistresses in the same way.[168] (Cf. H 657, M 1303, O 624)]

### 2. (*Exc. de Sent.* 76)

Hierax was the name of this man, whom the writer saw and argued with, and gained an impression of his soul from his speech. To put it in a word, he was an Alexandrian — like a crow in his insatiable gluttony, and in his debauchery (he was also lustful) like a rooster —, the lewdest kind of Alexandrian and worse, if that is possible. But the writer persuaded him with the arguments which he used to be abashed at his shamelessness and effrontery, and then walked out; and all present were astounded that a man from Alexandria held his tongue, stopped his prating and blushed crimson.[169]

### 3. (*Exc. de Sent.* 77)

He directed his words towards John, saying, "It is you who are the cause of all these troubles, destroying the unity of the Emperors, undermining with your schemes this most divine and wondrous arrangement, and laying it low in ruinous collapse. It is a remarkable thing, a most firm and unbroachable bulwark for us, that two separate Emperors rule an united Empire". As this was being said those present nodded disagreement silently and in fear.[170] For although they agreed wholeheartedly with these words, they were in fear of John and, eager for their own gain (for, as I have said, this period of dissension brought honours even to worthless men) and taking no account of the welfare of the state, they made John, the cunning patron of the hawk,[171] their leader and killed Fravitta.

### 4. (*Exc. de Sent.* 78)

While Pamphylia was being ravaged by the Isaurian war, the province thought that the misfortunes inflicted by the Isaurians were comparative heaven. Just as in thunderstorms a bolt is more to be feared than a flash of lightning (for the latter only frightens whereas the former kills), so, too, our noble Alexandrian Hierax, as he ferreted out everything after the murder of Fravitta and stole it all, showed that the Isaurians, who were most terrible to see and hear, were really just a dainty little flower of a green spring day. . . . and, receiving [a

116    Eunapius: Text

... καὶ παραλαβών, ὑπὸ μάλης ἐπειρᾶτο διαφεύγειν ἀετοῦ ῥύμην καὶ φοράν. ἀλλ᾽ οὐκ εἶχεν ἀλαοσκοπίην ὁ Λύκιος Ἑρεννιανὸς βικάριος ὤν· ἀετὸς δὲ γενόμενος αὐτὸν συνήρπασε τὸν Ἱέρακα, καὶ μόλις    10 ἀφῆκεν, εἰ μὴ τετρακισχιλίους ἐκείνως αὐτῷ χρυσοῦς ἀπέτισεν.

8 lacunam indicavi cum edd.    9 ἀλαοσκοπίην Bekker [ἄλλο σκοπεῖν cod.
10 αὐτὸς Boissevain

(Zosimus 5,25)

72
1. (Exc. de Sent. 79)

    Ὅτι ἐπὶ Πουλχερίας τῆς βασιλίσσης ἐξέκειτο δημοσίᾳ πιπρασ-
κόμενα τὰ ἔθνη τοῖς βουλομένοις ὠνεῖσθαι τὰς ἀρχάς· πᾶσι δὲ
ἐπιπράσκοντο μεγάλα τε καὶ μικρὰ φανερῶς ἐπὶ τῶν δημοσίων
τραπεζῶν, ὥσπερ ἄλλο τι τῶν ἐπ᾽ ἀγορᾶς ὠνίων. καὶ ὁ βουλόμενος
Ἑλλήσποντον ἀδικεῖν εἶχεν Ἑλλήσποντον πριάμενος, καὶ ἄλλος    5
Μακεδονίαν ἢ Θράκην, καὶ ὅπως ἕκαστος ἐνόσει πρὸς τὸ ἄδικον ἢ
ἐχθροὺς ἔχων. ἐξῆν δὲ καὶ καθ᾽ ἕκαστον ἔθνος τὴν μοχθηρίαν
ὠνεῖσθαι τὴν ἑαυτοῦ πρὸς τὸ βλάπτειν τοὺς ὑπηκόους καὶ πολλὰ
συλλαμβάνειν ἔθνη· τοῦτο γὰρ ὁ βικάριος ἐδύνατο καὶ ἡ ἀνθύπατος
ἀρχή. καὶ δέος ἦν οὐδὲν τῶν ἀθλίων γραμμάτων τοῖς νόμοις ἐντε-    10
θνηκότων ὡς δεῖ τὸν ἐπὶ χρήμασι δικάζοντα κολάζεσθαι· ἀλλ᾽ οἱ μὲν
νόμοι κατὰ τὸν Σκύθην Ἀνάχαρσιν οὐκ ἀραχνίων ἦσαν ἀσθενέστεροι
καὶ λεπτότεροι μόνον, ἀλλὰ καὶ κονιορτοῦ παντὸς πρὸς τὸ ῥεῖν εὐ-
κόλως καὶ διανεμοῦσθαι παραφορώτεροι. ὁ δὲ τὸ ἔθνος ἢ τὰ ἔθνη
παραλαβών, δύο τινὰς ἢ τρεῖς θεράποντας συνεφελκόμενος κατὰ    15
τὴν πλαγίαν εἰσιόντας θύραν, μὴ βουλόμενος λανθάνειν ὅτι τοῦτο
πράττουσιν, ἀλλ᾽ ἐπιδεικνύμενος ὅτι..., διὰ τούτων τῶν σιωπώντων
κηρύκων, εἰ δὴ κήρυγμα σιωπώμενον γίνεται, πρὸς πάντας περιήγγελλεν, ὥς φησιν Ὅμηρος· "κλήδην εἰς ἀγορὴν κικλήσκειν ἄνδρα
ἕκαστον μηδὲ βοᾶν, αὐτὸς δὲ μετὰ πρώτοισι πονεῖτο·" καὶ ὁ ἄρχων    20
διὰ τῶν ἀφθόγγων τούτων κηρύκων πρὸς τὸ οὖς ἑκάστῳ περιήγγελλεν ὡς πριάμενος εἴη τοὺς ὑπηκόους τόσου καὶ τόσου χρυσίου,
καὶ πᾶσά γε ἀνάγκη τοῦτο καταβάλλειν ἢ πράγματα ἔχοντας ἐπι-
τρέπεσθαι θανάτοις καὶ δημεύσεσιν. οἱ μὲν οὖν ἔχοντες καὶ συν-
τελεῖν ἐκ προϋπαρχούσης οὐσίας κατετίθεσαν οἰμώζοντες τὸ ἀρ-    25
γύριον· οἱ δὲ ἀποροῦντες δημοσίᾳ κατεδαπανῶντο ταῖς μάστιξι τὰ

1 Πουλχερίας iniuria pro Εὐδοξίας?    6 ἢ Θράκην Boissevain [Κυρήνην edd.
14 παραφορώτεροι van Herwerden [παραφοράμενοι Mai παραφερόμενοι Niebuhr    16 λανθάνειν Jordan [μανθάνειν cod.    17 ὅτι βίᾳ (sine lac.) van
Herwerden    18-19 πάντας περιήγγελλεν Niebuhr [πάντα περιήγγελλον cod.
23-24 ἐπιτρίβεσθαι Niebuhr

successor?], he covertly tried to escape the strength and speed of the eagle. But Lucius Herennianus, the vicar, kept no blind-man's watch and, becoming an eagle, seized the Hawk and finally let him go only on payment of 4,000 *solidi*.[172]

(Zosimus 5,25)

## 72

1. (*Exc. de Sent.* 79)

During the time of the Empress Pulcheria the provinces were up for public sale to whoever wished to buy their governorships. Large and small, they were openly offered to all in the public marts like any other piece of merchandise. Whoever wished to plunder Hellespontus could buy that province, likewise Macedonia or Thrace, wherever he craved to commit his crimes or had enemies. Wrongdoers could buy the right to oppress the population either of an individual province or of a collection of provinces, the latter being the prerogative of the vicar or proconsul. Moreover, no one had any fear of the harsh statutes which laid down penalties for judges in suits involving property, for they had become obsolete; and the laws themselves were not only, as the Scythian Anacharsis says, lighter and weaker than spiders' webs, but readier than any dust to swirl away and scatter.[173] The man who received one or a group of provinces took with himself two or three servants who entered his house by the side door. He did not wish it to go unnoticed that they were doing this, but he was showing that . . ., and through these silent messengers (if a message can be silent) he announced to all, in the words of Homer, "to summon each man to the assembly by name and not to shout, and he himself went to work with the foremost".[174] The governor, through these voiceless messengers, whispered into each man's ear that he had bought the provincials for so much gold and it was absolutely necessary that he either pay it up or hand over for death and confiscation persons who had some wealth. Those who had possessions agreed to pay up from their ready cash, lamenting the loss of their money, while those who had nothing paid with a public flogging. But there was another scheme afoot. One type

σώματα · πρόφασις δὲ ἦν ἑτέρα τις. εὑρέθη γὰρ γένος ἀνθρώπων δι'
ἀπορίαν καὶ ἀπόνοιαν ὀξυθάνατον καὶ φιλοκίνδυνον, οἳ τὰς ὕβρεις οὐκ
ἐνεγκόντες ἐπὶ κατηγορίᾳ τῆς λῃστείας ὥρμησαν ἐπὶ τὸν τῆς αὐλῆς
ἔπαρχον. κἀκεῖνος ἂν ἐπὶ τὸ πρᾶγμα διεσχηματισμένος πάλαι καὶ     30
αὐτὸς ἕτερα τοιαῦτα πάσχων τόν τε κατηγορηθέντα συνήρπασε καὶ
τοὺς κατηγορήσαντας ὡς παρρησίαν ἔχοντας ἐπήνεσεν ὅπωσ. . .οὖν
τοιαῦτα γένοιτο · καὶ πρὸς τὸν ἀγῶνα τῆς κρίσεως ἐλθούσης,
ἔφρασεν ἂν διὰ τοῦ πιστοτάτου τῶν εὐνούχων · "ἄπιτε, ὦ βέλτιστοι,
πάνυ θαυμάζοντες ὅτι μετὰ τῶν κεφαλῶν ἄπιτε · κατηγορεῖν γὰρ     35
ἀρχομένοις οὐκ ἔξεστιν". καὶ οἱ μὲν ἀπήεσαν ψηλαφῶντες τὰς
κεφαλὰς ἐπὶ τοῖς λόγοις καὶ ἀγαπῶντες, ὅτι ἔχουσι συνηρμοσμένας ·
ὁ δὲ νικήσας τὴν Καδμείαν μακρῷ πλέον ἦν ἀθλιώτερος καὶ τὴν
ἀρχὴν πριάμενος ὅλης τῆς ὑπαρχούσης οὐσίας καὶ τὸ κέρδος τῆς
ἀρχῆς προσκαταβαλὼν ταῖς τοσαύταις ἐνέδραις καὶ λόχοις. πᾶσαι     40
γοῦν οἰκίαι πρὸς τοῦτον ἐκενώθησαν ἂν τὸν δόλον · καὶ ῥᾶστα ἦν
ὁρᾶν τοὺς ἄρξαντας δεδημευμένους, ὥσπερ που καὶ ὁ κωμικός φησιν ·
"ἄρξαντος ἀνδρὸς δημόσια τὰ χρήματα". ὁ δὲ ἀγνοῶν τίς κωμικός,
οὐδὲ ἀναγιγνώσκειν ἄξιος τὴν συγγραφήν. οὕτω γοῦν καὶ ὁ Ἑρεννιανὸς τότε τὸν Ἱέρακα τῷ πολλὰ μὲν ὑφελέσθαι, τῷ πολλὰ κατα-     45
βαλεῖν συλλαβὼν ἀπέδειξε δικαίας ἀποτίνοντα τιμωρίας τοῦ κατὰ
Φράβιθον φόνου. ὁ δὲ Ἱέραξ καλούμενος ὑπὸ τοῦ πλείονα καταθέντος
ὥσπερ ἀετοῦ συνειλημμένος ἀηδὼν ἦν Ἡσιόδειος οὐ δυναμένη πρὸς
κρείττονα ἀντιφερίζειν. καὶ αὐτὸς δὲ ὁ ἀετὸς οὐδὲν διέφερεν ἀηδόνος,
πλὴν ὅσα καὶ εἰς τὸν τοῦ μύθου κολοιὸν ἐτέλει, τῶν ἰδίων πτερῶν     50
ὥσπερ ἀλλοτρίων ἐστερημένος.

30 πάλαι Niebuhr [πάλιν Mai    32 ὅπως. . .οὖν cod. [ὁποσακισοῦν Kuiper
ὁπωσποτοῦν van Herwerden ὁπωσοῦν Mai    36 ἀρχομένοις van Herwerden
[ἀρχομένους Mai    38 ἀθλιώτατος edd.    41 ἐκενώθησαν Boissevain [ἐκε-
νοῦντο Mai    ῥᾶστα Jordan [μάλιστα Mai    42 δεδημευμένους Bekker
[δεδηκεισμένους Mai    44 συγγραφήν Boissevain [γραφήν Mai    45 τῷ πολλὰ
Bekker [τὰ πλειόνα Mai et Boissevain

2. (*Exc. de Sent*. 80)

Ὅτι ἐπὶ τῆς αὐτῆς βασιλίδος οὐκ ἦν τινα παρὰ τὴν Κωνσταντίνου πόλιν μὴ τοῦτο ἀκοῦσαι · "τί δὲ σύ, πάντων ἀνδρῶν θαυμασιώτερε, πόλεων οὐκ ἄρχεις καὶ ἐθνῶν;" καὶ ὁ λόγος ἦν τοῦ κατὰ
<τὸν> μῦθον ἰοῦ τῶν διψάδων δυνατώτερος.

2-3 θαυμασιώτερε Mai [θαυμασιώτατε van Herwerden    4 τὸν add. Dindorf

3. (*Exc. de Sent*. 81)

Ὁ δὲ Στελίχων οὐκ ἐφόνευσε τοὺς ἀνθρώπους, ἀλλὰ ζῆν
αἰσχρῶς ἠνάγκαζε, πάντα ἀφαιρούμενος, καὶ πρὸς τὸ βαρύτατον, ὡς

of man was to be found whose destitution and desperation made him ready to risk danger and death. These men refused to endure the abuses and they laid charges of robbery before the praetorian prefect. He was well prepared to deal with this (since he had long been facing similar charges), and he used to arrest the accused and praise the accusers for their boldness of speech no matter how these things turned out. When the suit came to trial, he would declare through the most trusted of the eunuchs, "Go away, my friends, and be thankful that you leave with your heads. For subjects are not permitted to lay charges against their governor", and they went away feeling their heads and relieved to have them still on their shoulders. But the accused, having won his Cadmean victory, was far more wretched than his accusers. For he had spent all the wealth he had to obtain his governorship, and in addition had used up the profits of his term of office in evading these snares which had been laid for him. All the households were made destitute by this device, and it was very easy to observe former governors suffering confiscation — as the comedy-writer says, "The possessions of an ex-magistrate are public property".[175] (Whoever does not recognise the writer is unworthy to read this history.)

In this way, then, when Herennianus arrested Hierax, he made him pay more to escape than he had stolen and thus inflicted upon him a fitting penalty for the murder of Fravitta. The man called Hawk was seized, as if by an eagle, by the man who had paid more and he became like Hesiod's nightingale, unable to compete against the stronger. And the eagle himself differed in no way from the nightingale except that he was also like the jackdaw of the fable, since he was stripped of his own feathers as if they were another's.[176]

## 2. (*Exc. de Sent.* 80)

During the reign of the same Empress at Constantinople, one could not avoid being accosted with the words, "Most amazing of all men, why are you not governing cities and provinces?" This question was more powerful than the fabled poison of the *dipsas*.[177]

## 3. (*Exc. de Sent.* 81)

Stilicho did not kill the men but forced them to live in shame, taking away all their possessions and reducing and ... them to the

φησι Μένανδρος, τὴν πενίαν θηρίον καὶ . . . ων καὶ συστέλλων.

3 θηρίον cod. [φορτίον van Herwerden    καὶ . . . ων Boissevain [καὶ . . .
λέγων Mai

4. (*Exc. de Sent.* 82)

Ὅτι ὕπατον ὅμως διὰ φιλαρχίαν ἡροῦντο αὐτὸν συνάπαντες οἱ χρήματα ἔχοντες ζῆν μᾶλλον ἢ τοὺς . . . δεῶ πυρὶ καὶ φόνῳ καὶ σιδήρῳ πάντα δαπανήσασθαι . . . τησ . . . χης ἐν τῷ διαφαίνεσθαι ὅτι μόνος Στελίχων ὑπὲρ ἀνθρωπίνην ἐν . . . .

1 ὕπατον ὅμως van Herwerden [ὑπ . . .ως Mai    1-2 οἱ χρήματα van Herwerden [οἱ δὲ Mai

(Photius *Bibl. Cod.* 77 = *Testimonium* 1)

## Sedis Incertae

### 73
(*Suda* A 2447)

Ἀνεκρέμασε τοῖς θεοῖς. Εὐνάπιος.

### 74
(*Suda* A 2866)

Καὶ αὖθις Εὐνάπιος· πρὸς τὸ ἀφανὲς καὶ ἀόριστον τῆς χώρας ἐκπεσόντες, πρὸς τοὺς φόνους καὶ πρὸς τὴν λείαν ἀπαγορεύοντες.

### 75
(*Suda* A 3609)

Εὐνάπιος· καὶ οἱ μὲν αὐτοὺς διέφθειρον σχοινίοις ἀποτραχηλίζοντες.

### 76
(*Suda* A 4325)

Εὐνάπιος· γυναικῶν δὲ ὕβρις καὶ τὸ ἀτάσθαλον εἰς παῖδας εὖ γεγονότας συνεκυρώθη καὶ νόμος ἦν.

3 ἦν Boissonade [εἶναι codd.

### 77
(*Suda* B 67)

Εὐνάπιος· εἴτε φιλοχρήματος εἴη καὶ δοῦλος τῶν βαλαντίων· καὶ ταῦτα σαφῶς ἐκπυνθανόμενοι, πρὸς ταῦτα διεστρατήγουν τὸν πόλεμον.

most baneful beast of all, as Menander calls poverty.[178]


4. (*Exc. de Sent.* 82)

Nevertheless, all together out of lust for power those who had wealth destroyed the consul himself ... to live rather than ... everything ought to have been consumed by fire and slaughter and steel ... in the obvious fact that Stilicho above mankind ....[179]



(Photius *Bibl. Cod.* 77 = *Testimonium* 1)


## Unplaced Fragments[180]

### 73

(*Suda* A 2447)

He hung up for the gods.


### 74

(*Suda* A 2866)

Coming into the unknown and endless region and wearying of slaughter and rapine.


### 75

(*Suda* A 3609)

They killed them by strangling them with cords.


### 76

(*Suda* A 4325)

Abuse of women and depravity towards well-born children was sanctioned by law.[181]


### 77

(*Suda* B 67)

... if he were greedy for money and a slave to the purse. When they learned these things for certain, they made them the object of the war.

78

1. (*Suda* Δ 809)
Ὁ δὲ τὰ φρονήματα καὶ τοὺς θυμοὺς τῶν στρατιωτῶν ἀνηρέθιζε, καὶ διαυχενίζεσθαι πρὸς τὸ ἀγέρωχον ταῖς μελέταις ἐξεκάλει καὶ φιλοκίνδυνον. (Cf. A 2428*)

[2. (*Suda* Δ 1025)
Ἕτερα δὲ οὐ πολύ τι μείω ἀνωρθοῦτο καὶ διηυχενίζετο, ἀλλὰ τούτων βαρύτερα καὶ κεραυνῷ προσεμφερῆ . . .]

79

(*Suda* Δ 919)
Εὐνάπιος· κατὰ τούτους τοὺς χρόνους ὑπὸ τῆς ἀνδρώδους γυναικὸς ἔργον τι κατετολμήθη καὶ συνεπράχθη γενναῖον οὕτω καὶ ἀνδρῶδες, ὥστε ἄπιστον εἶναι διενεγκεῖν εἰς τὴν διήγησιν.

80

(*Suda* E 498)
Καὶ τἆλλα πάθη κατὰ τὴν ἐκμελῆ λύραν ἐθεραπεύετο, φησὶν Εὐνάπιος.

81

(*Suda* Z 33)
Εὐνάπιος· ἡ τοῦ ποταμοῦ διάβασις ἡ γέφυρα.

82

(*Suda* H 19)
Εὐνάπιος· οἱ δὲ παῖδες ἡβήσαντες καὶ γενόμενοι θυμοῦ καὶ χειρῶν κύριοι.

83

(*Suda* Θ 262)
Εὐνάπιος· τῶν δὲ Ῥωμαίων ἐπ᾽ αὐτὸ τοῦτο βιαζομένων ἄπορον αὐτοῖς ἀποδεῖξαι καὶ πλῆθος καὶ θέσιν καὶ βέλη καὶ μηχανὰς καὶ μεγέθη ποταμῶν, πρὸς τὸ μὴ πάντως ἡττᾶσθαι σφῶν καὶ ὁμολογεῖν εἶναι χείροσιν.

84

(*Suda* K 389)
Οἱ γὰρ Κᾶρες κύνα θύουσιν. Εὐνάπιος.

78

1. (*Suda* Δ 809)

He stirred the hearts and minds of the troops and, through the training he gave, he made them aspire to noble and dangerous deeds. (Cf. A 2428*)[182]

[2. (*Suda* Δ 1025)

In other matters almost as important he pulled himself together and held his head high, but more serious than these and like a thunderbolt . . .] [183]

79

(*Suda* Δ 919)

During these times a woman of manly virtue undertook and carried out a deed of such nobility and courage that if I set it in my narrative it will not be believed.

80

(*Suda* E 498)

And he treated the other passions as one would treat a lyre that was out of tune.

81

(*Suda* Z 33)

A river-crossing, a bridge.

82

(*Suda* H 19)

The boys reaching puberty and becoming masters of their mental and physical powers.

83

(*Suda* Θ 262)

It was the purpose of the Roman efforts to demonstrate to them that their numbers, location, missiles, machines and the size of their rivers would not save them from total defeat and confession of their inferiority.[184]

84

(*Suda* K 389)

For the Carians sacrifice a dog.[185]

## 85
[(*Suda* K 408)
Ὁ δὲ τὴν καρδίαν ταῖς τιμαῖς ἤδη κεκαρωμένος παρέδωκεν
ἑαυτὸν εἰς τὴν ὁδόν.]

## 86
(*Suda* K 570)
Ὁ δὲ τοξότης ἠφίει βέλος, εὔστοχος ὢν τοσούτους κατακαίνειν
ὅσα ἠφίει βέλη. Εὐνάπιός φησιν.

## 87
(*Suda* M 369)
Εὐνάπιος· οὔτε ἄλλως τὸ μεγαλοπρεπὲς κατὰ τὴν δίαιταν ἐν
ταῖς μάχαις ἐστὶ φιλοκίνδυνον.

## 88
(*Suda* M 474)
Καὶ Εὐνάπιος· τῶν αὐτῶν ἐθῶν γυναῖκά τινα στεῖλας ἐσθῆτι
λευκῇ καὶ στέμμασιν, ὡς δὴ μελεδωνὸν οὖσαν τῆς Συρίας οὕτω δὴ
καλουμένης θεοῦ.

1 ἐθῶν codd. [ἐτῶν Kuster

## 89
(*Suda* M 1274)
Εὐνάπιος· οὗτοι μὲν ὧδε μένοντες ὑπεμόσχευον τὸν πόλεμον.

## 90
(*Suda* M 1436)
Εὐνάπιος· ὁ βαρὺς ἐκεῖνος καὶ μυριέλικτος ὄφις [ὁ πολυέλικτος],
καθάπερ ὑπὸ τῆς Μηδείας ὑποψιθυριζόμενος καὶ βαρυνόμενος τὴν
ψυχήν, κεκαρωμένος παρέδωκεν ἑαυτόν.

1 βαρὺς [πολὺς G    ὁ πολυέλικτος del. H. Stephanus    2 βαρυνόμενος del. Toup

## 91
(*Suda* Π 857)
Εὐνάπιος· καὶ οἱ μὲν παιδιάν τινα ἐκ τῶν πολεμίων ἡγούμενοι,
τοσοῦτον ἐδυσχέραινον, ὅσον ἠναγκάζοντο βοᾶν καθ᾽ οὓς ἐμβάλοιεν.

## 85

[(*Suda* K 408)
His senses now dulled by the honours, he set out on the road.[186]]

## 86

(*Suda* K 570)
The archer shot an arrow, and his aim was so good that he killed a man with every arrow he shot.[187]

## 87

(*Suda* M 369)
Otherwise those who live magnificently are unwilling to risk themselves in war.

## 88

(*Suda* M 474)
They dress a woman who follows the same customs in a white garment and garlands as an attendant of the so-called Syrian goddess.

## 89

(*Suda* M 1274)
These men, remaining in this way, gradually propagated the war.

## 90

(*Suda* M 1436)
That noxious serpent with his countless coils, as if he were lulled and his senses stunned by the whispers of Medea, handed himself over.[188]

## 91

(*Suda* Π 857)
They thought it was some joke played by the enemy, and the more they were forced to shout, the more their anger grew against those whom they were attacking.

## 92
(*Suda* P 291)

'Ες τόξου ῥῦμα περιέπλεον τοῖς 'Ρωμαίοις οἱ βάρβαροι, πόλλ' ἅμα βέλη ἀφιέντες. Εὐνάπιος· πέτρα δέ τις ἀπεσπασμένη ἐς τόξου ῥῦμα.

## 93
(*Suda* Σ 1628)

Εὐνάπιος· τὸν πάντα βίον αὐτοῦ συντεκμηράμενος ἐκ τῶν ἐναργῶν περὶ αὐτὸν συμβόλων τε καὶ σημείων.

## 94
(*Suda* Οι 37)

Εὐνάπιος· τοσούτου δὲ οἰδοῦντος καὶ ὑποφυομένου κακοῦ.

## 95
(*Suda* Ψ 105)

Εὐνάπιος δὲ λέγει ψιλὸν δὲ οἷον κοῦφον.

## 92

(*Suda* P 291)

The barbarians sailed around the Romans at the distance of a bowshot, shooting many missiles at them .... A certain rock a bow-shot away.[189]

## 93

(*Suda* Σ 1628)

Deducing the whole of his life from the clear omens and signs about him.

## 94

(*Suda* Οι 37)

So great an evil swelling and growing secretly.

## 95

(*Suda* Ψ 105)

Eunapius uses *psilos* also in the sense of "light-armed".

# NOTES TO EUNAPIUS

**1.** The word appears in the more correct form ἀλεκτρυώδες at *Fr.* 71,2.

**2.** I take βιβλία to mean "collections of books" since in the following clause Photius seems to be saying that he has seen the two editions, in one collection on separate rolls in the case, in the other collection on the same roll. Goulet (1980 p.68) translates differently: "chaque édition étant disposée à part en deux tomes distincts". This is possible.

**3.** This conjecture of Photius' is probably wrong since the title of Zosimus' History, properly Ἱστορία νέα, seems to indicate not that it was a second edition, but that it was a 'Modern History' (cf. Cracco Ruggini 1973 pp.181-83; 1976 pp.34f.).

**4.** The meaning of this fragment is in places obscure. My translation is based upon the view, argued in *Byzantina* 1980, that the work of Dexippus which is being described was a chronicle and not a true history, as Jacoby suggested in *FGrH* II, C, p.305. For many of the details of interpretation the reader is referred to that paper, though in the present translation there are some differences.

**5.** Since this sentence appears to repeat and expand what has already been said, I have taken πρόθυρα to refer to the initial preface. But it could equally well indicate that each of the apparently twelve books (see *Byzantina* 1980 n.19) had a preface.

**6.** Since this follows after the mention of the preface, it might indicate that dating by the kings of Egypt was used for the chronology of the period before the Greek dating-system.

**7.** The MS reading τελεώτερα seems to jibe well with the principle of inclusion set out below (events of general importance or those connected with an especially distinguished person). The conjecture παλαιότερα does not help the sense at all.

**8.** This (with Jacoby, *loc.cit.* (n.4) ) I take to refer to a closing synoptic table listing Olympiads, archons and consuls, and divided into millennia.

**9.** Thuc. 4,122.

**10.** This and the following seem to be a declaration that other men of culture — pagan admirers of Julian — have contributed material to the History. This is confirmed by *Fr.* 15.

**11.** At this point the MS becomes illegible for a number of lines. In addition to the end of this fragment another excerpt from the first book has also been lost in this lacuna. With the closing sentiment cf. Ammianus 16,1,4.

**12.**    The second passage clearly summarises the first. The portrait of Carinus as a murderous debauchee appears also in the western sources (cf. *SHA* 'Carus' 16; *Epit. de Caes.* 38,7). The particular closeness of Eutropius 9,19 might indicate a common source, and his closing sentence, *ob quae omnibus hominibus invisus, non multo post poenas dedit*, suggests that the lacuna at the end of the second passage should be filled by a reference to Carinus' death. *Suda* Π 401 wrongly refers to the Emperor Macrinus.

**13.**    Usurper in Africa 309-311.

**14.**    Most of the period of Constantine's detention appears to have been spent in the East, but he does seem to have passed through Italy on his way to join his father in early 306 (Anon. Val. 2,2-4)

**15.**    The marriage was celebrated in 313. The Caesars were created on March 1, 317. Crispus was ten years old at the time.

**16.**    The *cursores*, the palatine messengers, were minor functionaries under the disposition of the master of the offices.

**17.**    The version of the deaths of Crispus and Fausta (in 326) is the same as that given by Zosimus (2,29,2). But while the latter says (2,39, 1) that Constantine died of disease, Philostorgius' version looks like a propagandistic justification of Constantius' execution of Constantine's brothers, and it would, therefore, not be Eunapian.

**18.**    The account errs in that Constans was the youngest not the eldest brother, and that Constantine was the aggressor; Bidez accepts emendations of the names to remove the errors. The account of Zosimus is even more erroneous (2,41 and Paschoud's note *ad loc.*).

**19.**    This passage is extremely close to Zosimus 2,42,2-3 and 5. The chronological information in the second part of the last sentence would probably not have been in Eunapius. Constans was killed in 350.

**20.**    This note is very like a short note in Zosimus 2,45,2, although the *Epitome* wrongly places it before the usurpation of Nepotian, who was proclaimed in 350, while Decentius was raised in 351.

**21.**    This mutilated sentence closes the lacuna in the *Exc. de Sent.* which began at the end of *Fr.* 1. On the interpretation see n.33 in vol. I p.158.

**22.**    This fragment, typically turgid and obscure, seems to be a prospective note on Julian's successes in Gaul and Constantius' reaction to them. It appears to have followed immediately upon the description of Julian's elevation to Caesar: βεβουλεῦσθαι καλῶς probably refers to the duplicitous motives for sending him to Gaul which Zosimus (3,1,3 - 2,1) attributes to Constantius. I have taken the reference to τῶν φύσει πολεμίων and what follows as an accusation that Constantius encouraged the German invaders against Julian. If this is so, it is far more direct than Libanius *Or.* 18,52, where a letter of Constantius is mentioned which ceded land west of the Rhine to the Germans. This is usually taken to refer to the Emperor's summoning of the Germans against Magnentius (cf. Zos. 2,53,3; Socr. 3,1), but the direct charge in Eunapius might suggest that Libanius implicitly accuses Constantius of working in this way against Julian. Zosimus (3,5,3 and 8,3) certainly implies that Constantius wished to weaken Julian in the face of the Germans.

**23.**   'Οστράκου μεταπεσόντος is a proverb quoted from Plato, *Phaedrus* 241B and it refers to the game of ὀστρακίνδα in which oyster shells or potsherds are tossed, the dark and light sides being regarded as our 'head' or 'tail'. The sentence probably comes from Eunapius' account of Julian's arrival in Gaul and the immediate improvement of Gallic fortunes (cf. the remark in Amm. 15,8,21, on the hopes which the people of Vienne placed in the Caesar).

**24.**   This refers to the early part of Julian's career in Gaul, of which Julian himself says that he had no real power (*Ep. ad Ath.* 277D-278A. Cf. Liban. *Or.* 18,42; Amm. 25,4,25). Zosimus (3,2,2) says that power was given to Salutius and Marcellus. The former was a civilian and a friend of Julian, and his omission here suggests that the passage from which this sentence was taken dealt solely with military affairs (cf. Socr. 3,1 and Soz. 5,2, who both say that power lay with the generals).

**25.**   Here Eunapius clearly refers only to a work on the battle of Strassburg. Since Libanius (*Or.* 13,25; *Epp.* 35 and 610) seems to speak of more expansive accounts of the Gallic campaigns in general, perhaps there were other pamphlets also. But, as Paschoud (*ad* Zos. 3,2,4) remarks, that is no evidence for the *Commentaries* which the Emperor is sometimes alleged to have written on his campaign. However, I cannot now agree with Paschoud (I p.liii), as I earlier did in vol. I n.36 on p.158, that Zosimus 3,2,4 is taken directly from the present passage. The words of Zosimus, which probably reflect an earlier passage of Eunapius, are a general statement on the sources (including Julian) for the whole of the reign and are, therefore, properly placed at the beginning of the account of the Gallic campaigns. The passage of Eunapius is prefatory only to the account of the battle of Strassburg.

**26.**   This fragment seems to describe a speech made by Julian to his troops after he had received the submission of the Salian Franks and was about to pass through their territory to attack the Chamavi. Its position corresponds to Zosimus 3,6,3 and perhaps to Ammianus 17,8,4.

**27.**   Though separate in the *Exc. de Sent.*, this phrase is clearly part of the line of thought of *Fr.* 18,1.

**28.**   The subject is the brigand Charietto, named in the next passage, who assisted Julian in his campaigns against the barbarians. The position of this fragment is indicated by the summary in Zosimus 3,7,1. The anecdotal interest which Eunapius and Zosimus give to the colourful activities of Charietto stands in contrast with the curt reference in

Ammianus 17,10,5 (in the context of a later campaign against the Alamanni) and the unnamed allusion in Libanius *Or.* 18,104 (who does,
however, add the important detail that Charietto and his fellows had
turned to brigandage after the failure of Magnentius, whom they had
supported).

**29.**  This corresponds closely with Zos. 3,7,3, on the growth of
Charietto's band (cf. esp. καθ᾽ ἕνα συνιόντες πλῆθος γεγόνασι). But,
typically, Zosimus has omitted the awkward simile of the Pythagorean
monad. The name Cercio, that of the Attic brigand killed by Theseus,
is here used as a trope of the first brigand to join Charietto.

**30.**  This would refer to Charietto's shaping his brigands into a
disciplined guerilla force before offering his services to Julian (cf. Zos.
3,7,3).

**31.**  Of the Meuse, or one of the branches of the Rhine. According
to Zosimus (3,6,2) these actions took place around the *Insula Bata-
vorum*, the land between these rivers and the sea. Ammianus (17,8,3)
includes Toxandria to the south-west as the sphere of operations.

**32.**  Ammianus (17,8,1; 9,2-3) mentions concern over food-supplies
in the context of these operations, and Zosimus (3,5,2), in a passage
which should be connected with the war with the Chamavi (the preceding sections 3-4 are intrusive), remarks the transportation of grain
from Britain. But only Julian himself (*Ep. ad Ath.* 280A-C) directly
mentions the blocking of the British grain-supplies as the reason for
the war.

**33.**  Petrus Patricius, *Fr.* 18, is a close summary of this fragment up
to this point. Petrus then closes with the words, τοῦτο δε τεκμήριον
εἶναι τοῦ σπονδὰς αὐτὸν μὴ ἐθέλειν ποιήσασθαι ("this [demanding the
dead as hostage] proves that he does not wish peace to be made"), a
charge not found in Eunapius.

**34.**  The tone of religious theatricality which is here imparted to
these (perhaps fictionalised) proceedings is peculiarly Eunapian. Zosimus suppresses it, and it does not appear in Ammianus.

**35.**  *PLRE* I 'Nebisgastes' identifies him as the king of the Chamavi.
He could equally well be the son.

**36.**  Eunapius is in error when he implies that this campaign ended
the war-year 358. In fact, it took place in the summer and was followed
by a crossing of the Rhine and an attack upon some of the Alamannic
tribes (Amm. 17,10; Liban. *Or.* 13,75; cf. Paschoud *ad* Zos. 3,6).
Eunapius presumably combined this later attack with Julian's invasion
of Alamannia in the next year, placing both in 359.

**37.**  This passage can be elucidated by comparison with Ammianus
18,2,8-19 (Zos. 3,4 is a garbled account of all the campaigns of that
year). It is from an account of a series of operations against various
Alamannic tribes in 359. According to Ammianus (*ibid.* 8-11), Julian
had crossed the Rhine somewhere south of Mainz, and Vadomar, in

common with other Alamannic kings, had come north from his territory opposite Augst to sue for peace (*ibid.* 16). Ammianus' version
(*ibid.* 18-19), which says that Julian marched south to ravage the
territory of other kings for whom Vadomar spoke, does not specifically
mention difficulties with Vadomar. But, like Eunapius, he does say that
the recovery of prisoners was the primary objective. If Eunapius'
number of 3,000 captives is correct (and lists seem to have been available
– cf. Zos. 3,4,7), only a small portion returned, since Julian forced the
return of prisoners by other tribes also, yet he himself (*Ep. ad Ath.*
280C) puts at 1,000 the total recovered as a result of the three invasions across the Rhine.

**38.**    Constantius had been Caesar since 324.

**39.**    Cf. Ammianus 17,11,1-4, also using historical *exempla*.

**40.**    This fragment, which Müller and Dindorf divide into two, I
have kept as one passage, following the punctuation of the *Exc. de
Sent.* The second part justifies and expands upon the opening statement
of the necessity of describing in order the actions at Constantius' court.
The corresponding passage of Zosimus (3,8,3-4) suggests that these
actions were the successive demands for troops from Julian, which are
alleged to have precipitated the Caesar's revolt (cf. Amm. 20,4,1-2).

**41.**    Julian took Oribasius with him to Gaul for his medical skills
(τέχνη) and as confidant. What the other virtues of Oribasius were is
left unclear, perhaps deliberately (cf. Baldwin 1975 p.90), although
skill in interpreting the dreams which confirmed Julian's determination
to revolt from Constantius was probably one (cf. Julian *Ep.* 4, ed.
Wright).

**42.**    The gist of this fragment seems to be that there was a conspiracy around Julian to revolt from Constantius and that the inner
circle numbered seven. Only Oribasius and Euhemerus are named,
though *Fr.* 21,1 above might implicate the hierophant, and Zosimus
(3,9,1) and Zonaras (13,10) suggest that some military tribunes were
involved.

**43.**    The subject is probably not the revolt of the soldiers which led
to Julian's acclamation in 360 (so Mai in Müller *ad loc.*), but the
desirability of Julian taking the initiative against Constantius in 361 (cf.
Zos. 3,9,5; Amm. 21,1,1-6). Julian's advance into Illyricum gained
surprise by its speed (cf. the image of a torrent in Liban. *Or.* 18,111).

**44.**    My reading of Δαρδάνων for the MS Ναρδινῶν has been
defended in *LCM* 6 (1981) pp.213f. The advance to Naissus in the
province of Dardania, evoking the Δάρδανοι/Trojans of Homer, leads
to the comparison of Julian with πολύτροπος Odysseus and by ex-
tension with the clever and literate Palamedes. This prefatory discussion
of Julian as a source for the Illyrian advance is comparable with *Fr.* 17
on Julian as a source for the battle of Strassburg (see n.25)

**45.**    This and the previous fragment are probably from a speech by
Julian before he set off on the Illyrian campaign. Libanius (*Or.* 18,111-

12) stresses the use of strategy and surprise; and with the sentiment of the first fragment cf. Ammianus 21,8,2-3, esp. *inter subita vehementer incertus [Julianus], id verebatur, ne contemptus ut comitantibus paucis, multitudinem offenderet repugnantem.*

**46.** On Julian's measures for the cities cf. Libanius *Or.* 18,146-48. Ammianus (22,6) mentions only the failure of an Egyptian delegation. The rhetor Eunapius is not, of course, the historian, who would have been only thirteen at this time.

**47.** Ammianus deals with Julian as judge at 22,9,8-11.

**48.** On Tuscianus see vol. I, p.23 and n.118.

**49.** The first speech in question is Julian *Or.* 7 'To the Cynic Heracleius'. Perhaps the second is *Or.* 6 addressed 'To the Uneducated Cynics'.

**50.** Although the *Suda* attributes this action to Salustius (properly Salutius – see *PLRE* I 'Secundus' 3), it is clear from ἡνίκα ἦν Καῖσαρ that the original source was speaking of Julian. There is no corroborative evidence of the claim that Julian honoured Marcellus. Ammianus (22,11,1) only notes the execution of the son.

**51.** The letter of Julian does not survive. The reference is to the Goths of the Lower Danube, who were raiding Pannonia and Thrace at the beginning of the reign of Valentinian I and Valens (Amm. 26,4,5; 6,11) and who supported the usurper Procopius in 365 (Amm. 24,10,3; Zos. 4,7,2), which led Valens to attack them in 367 (Amm. 27,5). Κωφῷ . . . κύματι imitates *Iliad* 14,16.

**52.** Cf. Ammianus 24,2,10. Οἰσυΐνας ἀσπίδας imitates Thucydides 4,9,1.

**53.** The saying of Epaminondas is in Plutarch, *Moralia* 193E.

**54.** Julian defeated the Persians before Ctesiphon and drove them back into the city (Amm. 24,6,8-16; Liban. *Or.* 18,253-55). In *Or.* 18, 249-50 Libanius speaks only of a pause for horse-races before the crossing of the Tigris and the battle before Ctesiphon (cf. Amm. 24,6, 3), but in *Or.* 1,133 he remarks horse-races and athletic contests held after the battle, which would be the ones noted here.

**55.** This refers probably not to the debate in council over whether to retreat from Ctesiphon or whether to press into the interior of Persia (Amm. 24,7,3), but to the somewhat later protests of the soldiers over the choice of the route home (Amm. 24,8,2). The proverb is based upon Homer, *Il.* 3,141 ff.

**56.** Perhaps from the account of the retreat from Ctesiphon, either the attack launched by the Persians between the villages of Danatē and Syncē (Zos. 3,27,4; Amm. 25,1,5) or the opening attack in the battle in which Julian was killed (Zos. 3,28,4; Amm. 25,3,4).

**57.** Nothing corresponding to this *post mortem* tribute to Julian as the philosopher king is found in Zosimus. Ammianus offers both a

Notes to p.43: Eunapius    135

speech of Julian in the form of a philosophical deathbed *consolatio*
(25,3,15-20) and a formal catalogue of his merits and defects (25,4).
The closest to the present passage is Libanius' dirge (*Or.* 18,276-95,
esp. 276-80) upon the loss of Julian to the state. The closing theme of
the fragment, Julian's care both for the people at large and for the
soldiers, draws upon Julian's own *Second Oration* (86D) for this
commonplace upon the ideal king (cf. Isocrates, *To Nicocles* 15). The
phrase φιλοστρατιώτης ... διαφερόντως is used again, of the general
Sebastian, at *Fr.* 44,3 (= *Suda* Σ 177). This fulsome praise of Julian
elicited an angry riposte from a Christian reader (possibly Arethas of
Patras), which is preserved in the *Exc. de Sent.* (24) under the title of
Στηλιτευτικὸς κατὰ Εὐναπίου ('Invective against Eunapius'):

Τί ταῦτα ληρεῖν ἀνέχῃ, ἐμβρόντητε τῷ ὄντι καὶ ἀνεπιγνώμων
τῶν πεφλυαρημένων; τίς γὰρ τῶν ἐγγενῶν Ἕλλησι δογμάτων
οὐρανίων μεμύηται μυστηρίων θεατὴν ὑπάρξαι τὸν ἀπαλλαττόμενον
τῆς ἐντεῦθεν βιοτῆς ἢ συνόμιλον ἀσωμάτων γενέσθαι; καὶ τίνες οἱ
ἀσώματοι οὗτοι, εἰ μή που Γαννυμήδης καὶ Ζεὺς ὁ Γαννυμήδους ἐκ   5
Τρώων ἐραστής, δι' οὗ καὶ Ἥρα παραγκωνίζεται ἡ ἀδελφὴ καὶ
γαμετὴ τῷ Φρυγὶ μειρακίῳ; ἀλλὰ τὰ μὲν κλέψας ἔχεις τῶν Χριστι-
ανικῶν ὀργίων, τὰς ἀσωμάτους φημὶ φρατρίας· ἐπεὶ τῶν γε σῶν
δογμάτων μὴ οὐχὶ καὶ ἐμπαθέστερον τῶν κατὰ τὸν φθαρτὸν τοῦτον
βίον ἀκρατεστάτων οἱ κατ' οὐρανόν σοι ἀλῶεν μάκαρες βιοῦντες; οἷς  10
Ἥβη μὲν οἰνοχοεῖ, <οἱ δὲ> πολλῷ τῷ νέκταρι μεθυσκόμενοι τὰ
ἀπαίσια διεξίασι Τρώων πόλιν εἰσορόωντες. πρὸς τίνα δὲ καὶ τῶν
καθ' Ἕλληνας ἑαυτὸν ἀναφέρων φιλοσόφων ἦρα βασιλείας; πρὸς
Ἀντισθένη; πρὸς Διογένη; ἀλλὰ τούτοις μὲν ἴσμεν οὕτως ἀπραγμο-
σύνης μέλον ὡς τὴν κυνῶν ἐζηλωκότας ζωὴν καὶ τῇ τούτων ἐγ-  15
καλλωπίζεσθαι κλήσει. οὔκουν ἐπανορθῶν τὸν ἀνθρώπινον βίον
εἵλετο βασιλεύειν, ὅτι μηδ' ἐπανώρθωσέ τι, εἰ μὴ πρῶτον μὲν φιλο-
δοξίας κακῷ λυσσήματι ἀχάριστος περὶ τὸν εὐεργέτην διαγινόμενος,
ἔπειτα καὶ ὅπως τοῖς ἄγουσιν αὐτὸν δαίμοσι τὸ ὀλέθριον ἀφοσιού-
μενος σέβας λάθοι πρὸς τῶν ὑπ' αὐτοῦ σπουδαζομένων δαιμόνων  20
τοιούτου καὶ τέλους κυρῆσαι, ἀξίου καὶ τῆς ἐκείνων ἀπάτης καὶ τῆς
ἑαυτοῦ ἐμπληξίας.

11 οἱ δὲ add. Bekker   17 ὅτι [ὅστις van Herwerden   21 κυρῆσαι [κυρήσας
Kuiper

"Why do you continue to babble on in this way? You really are a most
ignorant and stupid fool. For who has been so instructed in the native
doctrines of the Hellenes that, having escaped this life, he becomes a
watcher of the heavenly mysteries or a consort of incorporeal spirits?
Who are these incorporeal spirits, if not Ganymede and Zeus, the lover
of the Trojan Ganymede? As a result of this affair Hera, Zeus' sister and
wife, was thrown out for the Phrygian youth. But you have stolen these
things from the Christian mysteries — I mean, the bands of incorporeal
spirits. For according to *your* doctrines do not those who live blessed
lives in heaven take up those who have been the most passionate de-
bauchees in this mortal life? Hebe pours their wine, and, drunk on an
excess of nectar, they recount their unspeakable acts while looking at

the city of the Trojans. Again, to which of the philosophers of the Hellenes did he compare himself when he lusted after kingship? Antisthenes? Diogenes? But we know that they were so concerned to avoid politics that they lived the life of dogs and gloried in that name. He did not choose to rule in order to correct men's lives, for he set nothing aright. First, in his wicked and mad desire for glory he proved ungrateful towards his benefactor, and then, giving his fatal devotion to the demons who were leading him on, unwittingly at the hands of the demons whom he worshipped he met the end that he did, a fitting one for his treachery and stupidity."

**58.**    This and the following passages are from an anecdotal necrology on Julian, possibly similar to Ammianus 25,4. On Julian's readiness to submit to correction, cf. Ammianus 16,7,6 and 25,4,16.

**59.**    This and the preceding two passages are from the same section of the necrology. The story that Olympias rejected Alexander's claim to be the literal son of Zeus is from Plutarch *Vit. Alex.* 3,2. Julian, in contrast, is said by Eunapius to have conceived his relationship with Zeus (identified with Helios, as usual in late Neoplatonic thought – cf. Julian *Or.* 4, 'Hymn to King Helios') as that of an offspring of the father of all mankind (cf. esp. Julian *Or.* 4,131B-C), the particularity of the relationship lying in the excellence of his reign which mirrors that of the Sun. The quotation from Plato is *Phaedr.* 250B, while the reference to χρυσῆν σειράν is to the Platonic gloss (*Theaet.* 153C) on Homer, *Il.* 8,18ff., which explains the golden chain of Homer as that which binds our existence to that of the sun and the heavens.

**60.**    The theme of joy at release from the body is also found in the *consolatio* in Amm. 25,3,15.

**61.**    This first sentence is almost certainly not from Eunapius.

**62.**    Zosimus (3,33,1) mentions the fetching of supplies from Nisibis by the tribune Mauricius. John of Antioch, *Fr.* 181, which comes independently from the same source as the *Suda* article, adds after this sentence, νυκτὸς δὲ ὑπεχώρησε χαίρειν αὐτῇ πολλὰ φράσας, ὥσπερ ἐχθρῷ καὶ νεκρῷ σώματι μηδὲ δάκρυον ἐπισταλάξας, δι' ἣν αὐτός τε ἐσώθη καὶ τοὺς ὑπολειφθέντας ἐκ τῶν τοῦ πολέμου κινδύνων διέσωσεν ("Making many excuses, he refused at night to enjoy the facilities of the city and, as if it were the corpse of an enemy, he wept not a tear over it, although it was the means of salvation both for himself and for those who survived the dangers of the war"). Cf. Ammianus 25,8,17.

**63.**    John of Antioch has (probably inaccurately) τὴν Νισιβηνῶν πόλιν φεύγων.

**64.**    John of Antioch makes it clear that these were the people of Antioch and adds that they were angry, οὐχ ἥκιστα δὲ καὶ περὶ σφῶν αὐτῶν δεδιότες, μή ποτε καὶ αὐτοὺς πρόοιτο, ἀγαπήσας καὶ ἐν ὀλίγῳ μέρει τῆς Ῥωμαϊκῆς οἰκουμένης κρατεῖν ("and they were particularly concerned for themselves, lest he betray them, too, being content to rule in only a small part of the Roman world").

**65.** There must have been here a reference to the production of pamphlets, the omission resulting either from clumsy condensation or, as I have marked, a lacuna in the text.

**66.** Three references to Homer: *Il.* 3,428; 3,39 and 13,769; 2,261-63 (adapted).

**67.** For the proper form of the name see n.50.

**68.** Ammianus (25,10,4) confirms Jovian's eagerness to leave and the time of his leaving and offers a number of versions of his death (25, 10,13), but with only a hint (a comparison with Scipio Aemilianus) that he was murdered. John Chrysostom (*Homil. XV in Ep. ad Phil.* 5 [= *PG* 62 col. 295]) also says that he was poisoned. John of Antioch does not mention Jovian's death but says, καὶ Ἰοβιανὸς μὲν ἐν Δαδαστάνοις ἀφίκετο τὴν τοῦ Χριστοῦ δόξαν ἀνακηρύττων. If this is from Eunapius and was set close to the account of Jovian's death, the historian might here have been using a punishment-for-evil motif.

**69.** Goulet (1980 p.66 n.40) correctly points out that *PLRE* I 'Musonius' 2 is in error to associate this passage with Musonius' vicariate of Asia in 367/8. The *Suda* places this mission of Musonius during the reign of Jovian and makes it clear that his rank (whatever it was) was below that of the proconsul of Asia (who was perhaps Hesperius 6 in *PLRE* I). The mission itself, as Goulet suggests, appears to have been to arrange the collection of a superindiction probably for Constantinople in anticipation of Jovian's arrival with the army (thus τὴν θάλασσαν ἐπλήρωσε, indicating transportation by sea). Musonius stood in for the proconsul, while Eunapius administered the collection itself. (On Eunapius see *Fr.* 24 and n.46).

**70.** The quotation does not appear in the lexica.

**71.** Valentinian was acclaimed on Feb. 26th 364. This audience took place between then and Feb. 28th when he left for Nicomedia. The Emperor's reticence resulted from the intense lobbying during these days over whether to appoint a co-Emperor and, if so, whom (Amm. 26,2,3; 4,1); Valens was not acclaimed until March 28th. Eunapius, in drawing the implicit and rather unfair contrast between the terse Valentinian and the expansive Julian in the same situation (*Fr.* 24), reveals the cultivated easterner's distaste for the brusque Illyrian soldier.

**72.** This could refer, by contrast, to the fatal elation of Procopius at his initial successes against Valens in 365 (cf. Amm. 26,8,13; Zos. 4,7,1).

**73.** This probably refers to Procopius' justifying his usurpation by his distant relationship with Julian, although he did, in fact, more generally stress his relationship with the Constantinian dynasty (Blockley 1975 p.56).

**74.** Homer *Od.* 1,302; 3,200.

**75.** Both Zosimus (4,7,3) and Ammianus (26,9,4) remark the role of Arbitio in saving the day for Valens.

**76.** This and the previous three passages relate to the last phase of the war in 366. Valens, who had perhaps wintered in Ancyra, moved to Pessinus and then into Lydia where he defeated (or won over) Procopius' general Gomoar at Thyatira, in which battle, according to Zosimus (3,8,1), Hormizd almost tipped the scales for Procopius. Then Valens moved into Phrygia to finish off the usurper at Nacolia (cf. Paschoud, notes *ad* Zos. 4,8).

**77.** From a tirade against Valens' harsh punishment of the adherents of Procopius (cf. Zos. 4,8,4-5; Amm. 26,10,9-14).

**78.** Müller (*ad suum Fr.* 35) refers this *sententia* to Procopius' army after his death. But his army had disintegrated by then, and the comparison with Alexander does not seem very apt. Perhaps Eunapius was speaking of the Persian initiative in the East after the death of Julian, who would then be more suitably compared with Alexander. Zosimus (4,10,1), immediately after closing his account of the Procopian revolt, says Οὐάλης . . . ἀνεκόπτετο τῆς ἐπὶ Πέρσας ἐλάσεως . . . ("Valens . . . cut short his attack on Persia . . ."), which might be the remains of an Eunapian passage on Romano-Persian hostilities postponed by the Gothic war (cf. 4,11,4).

**79.** Aelianus is otherwise unknown. His city of origin was in Isauria.

**80.** The mistake lay in being awed by the large stature of the Germans.

**81.** The subject of this passage is the preliminaries to the Gothic campaigns of Valens from 367 to 369, described by Zosimus (4,10-11) and Ammianus (27,5). The Scythian (Gothic) king is almost certainly Athanaric. The levy in question appears not to be the same as the force which Ammianus remarks at 26,10,3, which appears to have arrived before the final crushing of the rebellion. Eunapius appears to see some merit in the position of the Goths, whereas Ammianus (27,5,2) dismisses their arguments as *excusationem vanissimam*. In vol. I pp.13f. I treated the last sentence of this passage as an example of Eunapius' clumsy use of hyperbole. I now wonder whether the whole last part, from τούτους ἀπῆτει τοὺς γενναίους, is not highly sarcastic, and thus the hyperbole more appropriate than I first thought.

**82.** I cannot identify this reference.

**83.** Since no other source says that military men were involved in this conspiracy, I have taken στρατεία as the equivalent of late-Latin *militia* = civil service (cf. Zos. 4,14,1, τῶν . . . στρατευομένων).

**84.** The conspiracy of Theodorus took place in 371. Ammianus (29,1) links this conspiracy with the investigation and punishment of many pagan philosophers which was conducted at about the same time or shortly thereafter, whereas Zosimus (4,13,3-4 and 14-15) keeps the two separate. Paschoud (*ad* Zos. 4,13,3-4) would follow Zosimus in this, but Ammianus may well have been right, since Zosimus (*loc. cit.*) certainly describes a pagan rite of divination connected with the conspiracy, a rite in which Ammianus says some of the philosophers, whose punishment Zosimus treats separately, participated.

**85.** Otherwise unknown. Could he be the same person as Euserius (also otherwise unknown) whom Ammianus (29,1,9, 10, 34, 35 and 38) mentions as one of the plotters against Valens and whose characterisation there fits well with that of Eueterius? Ammianus calls him (9) *virum praestabili scientia litterarum abundeque honoratum: Asiam quippe paulo ante rexerat pro praefectis*, and later (34) places him in the group of *honorati* at the heart of the conspiracy who thought only of themselves and tried to pass off the blame onto one another.

**86.** This and the two preceding passages (to which I have added E 3448) have been traditionally assigned to Eunapius and associated with the account of the plot of Theodorus on the ground that all three persons mentioned are named by Ammianus amongst the plotters (Zosimus names two). The difficulty (beyond the merely tentative attribution to Eunapius) is that the *Suda* places all three in the reign of Jovian. Goulet has suggested (1980 p.67) that this indicates that Eunapius mentioned Maximus' interpretation of the prophecy (*Vit. Soph.* 7,5,4-5; and see the following note) in his account of Jovian's reign. But why Eunapius should have placed it here is hard to see, for Maximus could not have been consulted until Valens' reign. In addition to the present four passages, only one other *Suda* article, M 1306 (also unattributed and also traditionally placed with Eunapius' fragments, = 29,2) dates its subject, the sophist and official Musonius, to Jovian's reign. One of two conclusions seems likely, either that the five passages in question are not from the History but from some pamphlet on philosophers who flourished under Jovian; or that the four (M 1306 being separate) are from the section on the conspiracy of Theodorus, in which Eunapius, while detailing the philosophers who suffered under Valens (note that Zos. 4,15,1 lists the philosophers together), made the point that, in contrast with Valens, the Christian Jovian allowed them to flourish (cf. *Vit. Soph.* 7,4,10, of the philosophers: ὅ τε Ἰοβιανὸς ἐβασίλευσε καὶ τιμῶν τοὺς ἄνδρας διετέλεσεν). This would have been the reference which the *Suda*'s source picked up, a reference that to Eunapius would have had value in that the tolerance of the Christian Jovian (evidence in Seeck 'Jovianus' 1, in *RE* IX 2 col. 2010) was in marked contrast not only with Valens' persecution, but equally importantly with the intolerance of Theodosius I.

**87.** The preceding passage of the *Vit. Soph.* tells how the philosopher Maximus was asked to interpret an oracle (probably the one of which Ammianus preserves three lines at 29,1,33) by some courtiers (οἱ ... περὶ τὰ βασίλεια, 7,6,3 = ὅσοι περὶ στρατείας of *Fr.* 39,1 above), whereat he predicted the death of Valens and the deaths of many others, including himself. This, too, suggests that Zosimus has misrepresented Eunapius in separating the conspiracy of Theodorus and the divinations of the philosophers (see n.84 above).

**88.** On Festus see *Vit. Soph.* 7,6,6-13, Zosimus 4,15,2-3 and Ammianus 29,2,22-28 (who gives his office of *mag. memoriae* at 22).

He was the author of an extant historical *Epitome* (*PLRE* I 'Festus' 3). Coeranus appears only here and in Ammianus 29,2,25, who calls him Coeranius.

**89.** From the final chapter of the account of the conspiracy, which would have picked up not only the greed of the conspirators (cf. 39,1, ἐπὶ τὰ κέρδη ... ἐπτοημένοι) but also the greed of the authorities in pressing the investigations (Zos. 4,14,4; Amm. 29,2,3).

**90.** The interpretation of this passage which is offered in the present translation differs sharply from the usual ones of, e.g., Chalmers (1953 pp.165-70), Vasiliev (in Maenchen-Helfen 1973 pp.8f.) and Goulet (1980 p.70). Eunapius, using the usual μέν ... δέ construction (which most scholars have chosen to ignore), simply says that he is incorporating two different versions of the origin and situation of the Huns, the old, inaccurate version of the written records (τὰ μὲν οὖν πρῶτα ... ἐκ τῶν παλαιῶν) and the new, accurate oral reports (τὰ δὲ ἐκ τῶν ἀπαγγελλομένων). The convoluted metaphors that follow this statement simply justify this procedure and make it clear that the old information will be set down first and the new subjoined to it, the order which Zosimus (4,20,3-4) preserves. Thus, Eunapius' concern here is to draw a distinction between two types of sources (a distinction already remarked at *Fr.* 30), and with the expression τὰ πρῶτα he is making no reference to a first edition or part of *his own* History. Furthermore, there is no indication here or in Zosimus that Eunapius is passing off 'a preposterous hodgepodge' (Maenchen-Helfen *loc. cit.*) on the Huns or even that he offered a full ethnographical digression comparable to that in Ammianus (31,2). He is well aware that the old records are inaccurate and states it firmly.

**91.** This whole passage is hardly legible in the MS. My own suggestion for the *locus desperatus* derives from the lack of the name of the Danube in the text and the fact that later in the passage Valens gives orders to admit the men.

**92.** The Mysians were proverbially feeble and could be plundered with impunity (cf. Demosth. *Or.* 18,72; Arist. *Rhet.* 1372ᵇ33). Eunapius, by developing the inappropriate image of the serpent's teeth in the context of the maturing of the young Goths, obscures the real reasons for their revolt, which were the mistreatment that they suffered at the hands of the Roman authorities, the failure to obtain adequate supplies, and, finally, an attempt upon the lives of their leaders, Alavivus and Fritigern. In contrast with Ammianus (31,5,1-8) the inferiority of Eunapius' information and the blindly 'patriotic' tone of his narrative are clear. Zosimus omits it all.

**93.** On the devastation cf. Ammianus 31,6,5-8, who, however, makes no remark upon the circumstances at the time of writing. Eunapius' comments seem to suggest that this passage was written soon after the insurrection and thus lend further support to Barnes' view (discussed in vol. I pp.3-5) that the History up to the battle of Adrianople was published around 380.

**94.** Zosimus (4,20,5 - 22,1) summarises this passage and keeps strictly to the order of events, although he seems to have added 21,2-3, on a portent that appeared to Valens, for which there is no room in the corresponding part of the Eunapian passage. Moreover, he has omitted all mention of the distribution of the non-combatants through the cities and their growth, which he mentions later (4,26,1-3) in the context of their massacre.

**95.** Although Boissevain divides this passage into two excerpts (40 and 41), the *Suda* M 208 confirms that the MS is correct in treating it as one. The first part (Μαρκιανός ... ἠκριβωμένος) is presumably the end of a longer sentence.

**96.** Emendation of συνηρῆσθαι is unnecessary: συναιρεῖν πόλεμον is a Plutarchan usage (*Marius* 45,1; *Lysander* 11,6-7). The identity of the war in question is uncertain. If it were the Isaurian raids on Lycia and Pamphylia in which Musonius was later killed (Amm. 27,9,6-7), Eunapius must here be remarking an end of the hostilities which turned out to be only temporary but at which Musonius set out from Sardis, his seat as vicar of Asia (Amm. *ibid.* 6), perhaps for the devastated areas, where the war flared up again and where he met his death. The identity of Theodorus is uncertain. Perhaps he is the former governor of a province of Asiana (= Theodorus 11 in *PLRE* I).

**97.** Eunapius seems to be explaining his insertion of the death of Musonius at the hands of the Isaurians, which occurred in 367/8, in an account of the Isaurian raids of 376/7, which are noted by Zosimus (4,20,1-2). The raids of 376/7 were described first and then the earlier fighting and Musonius' death, which, says Eunapius, found its sequel (what that was is not clear) at the later date. Thus, as Paschoud saw (note *ad* Zos. *loc. cit.*), Ammianus (*loc. cit.* at n.96 above) and Zosimus do not describe the same events. Both events were treated together by Eunapius, but Zosimus has omitted the raids of 367/8, while Ammianus does not touch upon those of 376/7.

**98.** Whereas Eunapius inserted his account of the Isaurian raids after the Hunnic assault on the Goths (and probably also after the crossing of the Danube and the first stage of the revolt), Zosimus has placed his account before all this other material.

**99.** This disquisition by Eunapius is reflected in the views of Sebastian noted by Zosimus (4,23,6).

**100.** This probably corresponds to Zosimus 4,22,4, on the corruption of Valens' officers.

**101.** The emendation ἐς τὸ εὐροπεῖν is suggested by πειθομένους μὲν ἐπαινῶν καὶ δωρεαῖς ἀμειβόμενοις of the parallel passage of Zosimus (4,23,3). The MS reading ἐς τὸ εἶναι apparently makes no sense, unless τὸ εἶναι is a colloquialism for 'wealth', 'possessions', which, my colleague Dr. A. Fotiou tells me, was an usage of Modern Greek before the twentieth century.

**102.** This part, on Sebastian's resignation of his western command

and migration to the East, is summarised by Zosimus at 4,22,4.

**103.** Zosimus summarises this at 4,23,2, incorporating some of the vocabulary.

**104.** The position of this fragment has been suggested by comparison with Zosimus 4,25,2, on a stratagem of the general Modares, which, however, differs in significant details from that described by Eunapius.

**105.** This passage is placed here by comparison with Zosimus 4,26, 6, where the count Julius is said to have communicated secretly (ἐν παραβύστῳ) with the senate of Constantinople over the massacre of the Gothic hostages. But the elaborate precautions described here (and not mentioned by Ammianus, 31,16,8) hardly seem necessary under the circumstances.

**106.** This and the two preceding *Suda* articles perhaps correspond with the diatribe against the corruption of Theodosius' governors in Zosimus 4,28,3 - 29,2. On the other hand, since the σιρομάστης is not only the term for the probe used by tax-collectors to search grain-pits but also the name of a weapon, Σ 478 could be from a note on weaponry.

**107.** Ammianus (31,11,2) indicates that the Goths were settled around Nicopolis and Beroea for a while in 378 before the battle of Adrianople. Since the present passage relates to 379 (or even 380) the Roman forces appear not to have regained control of parts of Thrace and Moesia II by that date. Thompson (*The Visigoths in the Time of Ulfila* Oxford [1966] p.103) takes Eunapius to mean that Nicopolis opened its gates to the Goths. This is not clear. Eunapius could simply be referring to their self-help, in the manner of Priscus' Asimuntines (*Fr.* 9,3).

**108.** Cf. Zosimus 4,32,2-3 on the harsh exactions laid by Theodosius upon the cities of Macedonia and Thessaly after the Gothic depredations.

**109.** Although it differs in a number of important details, the story is very similar to one in Lucian *Hist. Conscr.* 1 about the actor Archelaüs (also reciting Euripides' *Andromeda*) at Abdera in Thrace during the reign of Lysimachus (305-281 B.C.). In Eunapius the name of the city is missing, and editors have tried to restore it from τοιαύτην of the MS. However, that word is probably sound, since καὶ παρελθεῖς εἰς τοιαύτην ... and συναγείραί τε αὐτοὺς ... answer εἶτα πλανᾶσθαι ... and πρὸς ἀνθρώπους ἡμιβαρβάρους ἐπιδεικνύναι. In fact, τοιαύτην points back to the name of the city and suggests that it fell out from an earlier place, most probably after δόξαν αὐτῷ. Whether or not εἰς Ἄβδηραν should be restored there is hard to say. Certainly, ἡμιβαρβάρους would fit the Thracians, who had only recently been incorporated into the Empire in Nero's day. But just as other details of the story differ from those in Lucian, so might the name of the city.

**110.** The passage of Eunapius which preceded this long simile is probably that summarised at Zosimus 4,33,3-4, which details contemporary depravities, especially of the theatre. In the light of Zosimus' great concern with divine punishment for contemporary wickedness, it is noteworthy that, although he complains of attacks upon pagan believers and shrines, he has omitted the final remark of Eunapius that the Furies were in pursuit of mankind. (The passage of Zosimus is mutilated, but at a point where he is speaking of depravities of the theatre, not of dealings with the gods.)

111. For the proverb of trailing the fox-skin (i.e. laying a false scent) cf. Plato *Rep.* 365C.

112. Although I have followed Boissevain and the older editors in separating this fragment from the one before it in the *Exc. de Sent.*, perhaps the MS should be followed which makes them one continuous passage. In this case the behaviour of the barbarians would be an illustration of the Furies' pursuit of mankind (note especially that at the end of each fragment men of good sense are said to have been deceived). Eunapius' attack appears to be on both Emperors; and the Goths are characterised as true pagans following their ancestral rites, not, as Mai and others have thought, Christians (presumably Arians), an interpretation which makes nonsense of the passage.

113. The sense of this passage, whose theme of instability and divine interference is similar to the two preceding, is not wholly clear. The *sententia* of Philip (in Plutarch *Moralia* 178A and 790B) seems to suggest that 'asses' were meant literally, and thus there would be a reference to the cheapness of human life ($\tau\iota\mu\iota\dot{\omega}\tau\epsilon\rho\sigma\nu$ = "more valuable then men"). But the final sentence appears to suggest that the asses are the rulers of the Roman state.

114. Given that Eunapius likes to preface episodes in his narrative with methodological discussion (cf., e.g., *Frr.* 17; 30; 41,1), the present passage with its moralising interest probably introduced the account of the reasons for Gratian's loss of support, represented by Zosimus 4,35, 2-3.

115. On Tatianus, the praetorian prefect of the East replaced by Rufinus in 392, and Proculus see *PLRE* I 'Tatianus' 5, 'Proculus' 6. *Chron. Pasch. s.a.* 393 says that Tatianus was forced to watch his son's execution.

116. On Arbogast (misspelled in the *Suda*) see *PLRE* I 'Arbogastes'. He apparently on his own initiative took over Baudo's office (*magister militum*) on the death of the latter some time before 388, when Arbogast marched with Theodosius against Maximus. After the restoration of the young Valentinian II he remained in the West.

117. The first paragraph of this fragment, as is clear from the style and contents, is not from Eunapius. The condemnation of Valentinian's second marriage indicates that it came from a Christian writer (cf. the prayers at the defeat of Eugenius, remarked in the second part = *Fr.* 60,1). In fact, the whole of the fragment (which I have divided into two

parts following the ordering of Zosimus) probably came to John via an intermediary who used a Christian writer in addition to Eunapius. This writer (or the intermediary) wrote in a simpler, more colloquial style than that of Eunapius, inserted chronological computations and was less favourable to Arbogast (as comparison with Zosimus shows).

**118.** Müller (*ad loc.*), comparing Zosimus 4,53,1, which adds other qualities to Arbogast's warlike prowess, suggests that a lacuna should be marked after ῥώμην. But the text reflects the intermediary's summary.

**119.** Literally "with his nails".

**120.** John or his source is in error. Valentinian was killed at the Gallic city of Vienne (so Zosimus 4,54,3: ἐν Βιέννῃ Κελτικῇ πόλει).

**121.** The sentence as it stands in the MS is ungrammatical, probably as a result of clumsy excerpting; an easy correction is to read τοῦ ... ἔθνους .... ἐξελαυνομένου. This crossing (*pace* Paschoud *ad* Zos. 4,56) would have been subsequent to 378.

**122.** Homer, *Il.* 9,312-13.

**123.** This part has been clumsily excerpted by the compiler of the *Exc. de Legat.*, as the parallel passage of the *Exc. de Sent.* shows. The *Exc. de Sent.* (58) reads:

Συμποσίου δὲ προτεθέντος αὐτοῖς παρὰ τοῦ βασιλέως ἀδροτέρου καὶ πολυτελεστέρου, τὴν παροιμίαν ἀπέδειξαν ἀληθινὴν <τὴν> λέγουσαν· "οἶνος καὶ ἀλήθεια τοῦ Διονύσου". διὸ καὶ τὸν θεὸν εἰκότως Λυαῖον καλοῦσιν, ὡς οὐ μόνον διαλύοντα τὰς λύπας, ἀλλὰ καὶ τὸ στεγανὸν τῶν ἀπορρήτων διαχέοντα καὶ διακαλύπτοντα. 5 καὶ τότε ῥήξαντος αὐτοῖς παρὰ πότον τὴν βουλήν, διαλύεται τὸ συμπόσιον ἀτάκτως.

2 ἀληθῆ conj. Boissevain          τὴν add. Dindorf.

"At a very costly and grand banquet thrown for them by the Emperor they showed the truth of the proverb, 'The wine and the truth of Dionysus'. Therefore they properly call that god 'The Liberator', since he not only dissolves cares but also spills out and reveals closely guarded secrets. For on that occasion he with his wine brought into the open the plot, and the banquet broke up in confusion."

**124.** The statement that Serena was Theodosius' sister is an error (which also appears in the MS of Zosimus 4,57,2) and perhaps τῆς ... ἀδελφῆς should be corrected to τῆς ... ἀδελφοῦ θυγατρός, as Müller, *ad loc.*, suggested. On the other hand, the error might be that of John's source, since the whole sentence is clumsily condensed, as is shown by a comparison with Zosimus (*loc. cit.*), who states that Timasius was c.-in-c., Stilicho second-in-command, and that the others (with Bacurius) commanded the allies.

**125.** This is clarified by Zosimus (4,58,3) who says that at first Theodosius only committed the allies, who were slaughtered.

**126.** Most of Philostorgius' account is not from Eunapius, but

Eunapian influence on the attack on Theodosius is suggested both by the tone and by the phrase τρυφῆς ἀμετρίᾳ which Zosimus also uses of Theodosius at 4,33,1.

**127.** Two pages of the MS have been lost at this point.

**128.** The parallel part of John of Antioch (*Fr.* 188) ends here. He adds ῾Εκάτερός τε αὐτῶν τὴν βασιλείαν περιεσκόπει ("Each watched the Empire carefully"), which presumably refers to the activities of their agents rather than to any vigilance on behalf of the state.

**129.** The position of this passage is quite uncertain.

**130.** Marcellus was master of the offices from 394 to 395, having been appointed by Theodosius (*PLRE* I 'Marcellus' 7). If this article is from Eunapius, it perhaps comes from a note on Arcadius' high officials at the beginning of his reign.

**131.** I.e. of his daughter to Arcadius (see Zos. 5,3).

**132.** The phrase ἔπαυσε τῆς <κατὰ> τῶν ἐπιχωρίων ὁρμῆς is unclear, but it probably springs from poor condensation by John (or his intermediary) of Eunapius and represents the account in the original of the plundering of the provincials by Stilicho's troops after the retreat of Alaric and Stilicho's subsequent withdrawal to Italy (so Zos. 5,7,2-3).

**133.** Zosimus 5,8,2 suggests that "they" are Eutropius and his cronies.

**134.** The rest of *Fr.* 190 of John, although it shows some similarities with Eunapius (in Zosimus), is taken from Socrates (6,6).

**135.** This passage is obscure. For Barnes' interpretation, which I agree with, see vol. I pp.3f. The structure of the sentence is clumsy, and to remove the anacolouthon in the text Giangrande reads ὁ [τε] Ἀλλάριχος for ὅτε Ἀλλάριχος of the MS. I should prefer to read ὅ τε and assume that Eunapius has carelessly treated the genitive absolute clause (which is closely linked to the first main clause) as if it were another main clause. The word Θεσπιῶν is obelised by Giangrande, who conjectures ἐκ θεσπίσεων. Cumont's suggestion (1888 pp.179-81) Ἀγόριος Οὐέττιος (= Agorius Vettius Praetextatus = *PLRE* I 'Praetextatus' 1) is to be rejected, since it is almost never Eunapius' practice to give two names in this manner and Praetextatus may have been hierophant much earlier (cf. *PLRE*, *art. cit.*). The MS reading is best retained.

I have omitted the last part of the passage in which Eunapius accuses some monks of opening Thermopylae to Alaric. Zosimus (5,5, 2-8) gives a different version which probably reflects what Eunapius put in his History.

**136.** I have omitted the material in this passage on the deaths of various sophists, since Eunapius seems to make it clear that these were of concern only in the *Lives* and not in the History.

**137.** An error for Arcadius, which occurs elsewhere (cf. Cedrenus I p.587, where an Eutropius appears amongst a number of persons who dominated Theodosius II).

**138.** On the ugliness of Eutropius cf. Claudian *In Eutrop.* 1,110ff.

**139.** This fragment is separated by Boissevain from the next item (61). The MS marks a colon. Perhaps it should be joined (so Müller *ad suum Fr.* 71). For the subject might be a lucky opportunity, which could refer to the military command (so Zos. 5,10,1) which is mentioned in the next sentence as offering the chance for further plotting against benefactors (in this case Eutropius).

**140.** The Greek is unclear and probably badly condensed; the translation offers what seems to be the sense. Zosimus (5,10,1) only says that Eutropius anticipated treachery from Bargus and moved first.

**141.** For the position of this and the previous passage cf. Zosimus 5,10,4.

**142.** On this error see n.137 above.

**143.** Mai (approved by Müller, *ad suum Fr.* 72) takes the subject of the first part of this passage (sc. τοῦτον) to be Timasius, pointing out that he was not, however, killed, but exiled. Mai misinterprets ἐκβαλὼν τοῦ βίου which refers not to killing but to deprivation of lifestyle through confiscation. However, if τοῦτον is taken to be Timasius, the last part of the passage is awkward, since it reads as though Abundantius had already been discussed. It is better to take the whole passage as referring to Abundantius' exile and the confiscation of his property, remarked by Zosimus 5,10,5. The phrase μέγα δή τι ... ἐφρόνει then refers to Eutropius' next enterprise after Abundantius' ruin, the attack on Stilicho, which Zosimus (5,11,1) places after the fall of Abundantius, saying that Eutropius undertook this when he had no one left at Constantinople to worry about.

**144.** This sentence, like the whole of this passage, is obscure. The present interpretation is at variance with the older ones. I take Eunapius to be speaking first of writers who were publishing contemporaneously with events and who had to distort their narratives in order to avoid retribution. Then he speaks of himself (τῷ δὲ ταῦτα γράφοντι), who, presumably writing after the principals were dead or powerless, could be more single-minded in pursuit of the truth.

**145.** This long sentence is also obscure, but the tone seems to be sarcastic and objects of the attack appear to be both those who release unimportant tidbits of news about the doings in the palace and those who embroider these for the public. Although the structure of the sentence is awkward, with the punctuation I have adopted it does not need emendation.

**146.** This final sentence Boissevain and the other editors treat as part of what precedes, although the MS marks a break with a colon. The connection is rather awkward, but the sentence seems to be a formula of conclusion, and these are sometimes introduced rather awkwardly.

**147.** *Olymp.* 10,64.

**148.** The text and interpretation of this and the previous sentence are unsatisfactory, partly as a result of the illegibility of the MS at this point and probably also because of clumsy condensation. Müller and Dindorf, following Mai, both read ὅτι ἐπὶ τὰς Ἀσιανὰς and begin a new fragment, but Boissevain, rightly in my view, treats the whole as one continuous passage. Eunapius appears first to be discussing the deficiencies of a third source of information on the West (τῶν δὲ ἐμπόρων, as distinct from the officials and soldiers), then to be setting out his principle of selection, and finally to be announcing that after describing these events he will pass on to the misfortunes of Asia.

**149.** This and the previous fragment both come from a preface or a long discussion which describes the difficulties of collecting reliable evidence, first on the East (66,1) and then on the West (66,2, first part). The reason for treating the East and West together in this way is that the subject is the relations between Eutropius and Stilicho (cf. the corresponding part of Zosimus, 5,11-12, and especially the summary remark at 13,1: τῆς δὲ βασιλείας ἑκατέρωθεν οὔσης ἐν τούτοις). The juxtaposition of the two principals is reflected in the two questions, "Where did Stilicho see you?" and "Would you have seen the eunuch?" After his discussion of the sources for East-West relations at this period, Eunapius then says (66,2, last part) that he will pass on to the misfortunes of Asia, by which he means the final period of Eutropius' regime (the hyperbole of τοιοῦτο . . . κίνησις and τερατευθέντα suggests the eunuch-consul) and the revolt of Gainas.

**150.** The subject of the fragment is probably Gainas, but the reference is not to his leaving Constantinople on the pretext of illness (Zos. 5,19,1), which occurred later. Perhaps Eunapius remarks Gainas' hostility to Eutropius' regime at the beginning of the account of the insurrection (cf. Zos. 5,13,1).

**151.** This perhaps corresponds to Zosimus 5,13,3-4 where Tribigild first devastates Phrygia and is then expected to move on Lydia.

**152.** This fragment is unintelligible.

**153.** Perhaps of Gainas, giving support to Tribigild against Leo (cf. Zos. 5,17,1).

**154.** The addition to the text is from the *Suda* Π 363.

**155.** μαλακώτερος . . . ἀμφαφάασθαι is quoted from Homer, *Il.* 22, 373.

**156.** This seems to be the form of the name in the MS. He is usually called Tribigild.

**157.** Boissevain would fill this lacuna with τῆς Φρυγίας ἀνέστρεψαν based on Zosimus 5,18,4. This procedure is dangerous, in that Zosimus' language is rarely close to that of Eunapius.

**158.** After ἐφεπόμενος Boissevain's text has 10½ lines of scattered words and letters which yield no sense.

**159.** Probably of Gainas' departure from Constantinople and his plan to take over the city by treachery (cf. Zos. 5,19,1-3).

**160.** The text is fragmentary at this point. The restorations are the plausible ones of Boissevain's text drawn from the *Suda* Φ 681 (which is printed as the next fragment).

**161.** This passage is very close to Zosimus 5,20,1.

**162.** Zosimus 5,20,2 is a (rather longer) paraphrase of this passage (note esp. the shared ἐξήσκει). Fravitta is the subject of the passage, and the crossing is that which Gainas proposed to make of the Hellespont and which Fravitta sought to prevent.

**163.** The MS here is almost illegible. The text given is based upon the readings of Mai and Boissevain. I have placed in the apparatus other readings which the editors thought they could see. A conjectural version of the complete text is offered by Boissevain, but it is too damaged for reconstruction. The best that can be said is that the critics of Fravitta are still speaking and appear to be arguing that he should have crossed to the Chersonese and captured Gainas.

**164.** Here Boissevain's text marks seven lines of unintelligible phrases, words and letters. The parallel passage of Zosimus (5,21,5) is too condensed to allow any attempt at reconstructing Eunapius from it, but it does suggest that at this point Fravitta attributed his success to his religion.

**165.** This and the previous lacunae are brief. Eunapius seems to be describing how Fravitta inadvertently infringed court ceremonial.

**166.** Since Fravitta was romanised (cf. *Fr.* 59) and Eunapius is so sympathetic to him, τὸν πάτριον νόμον must refer to Greco-Roman, not German, paganism.

**167.** Probably Fravitta was compared with Scipio and Gainas with Phameas. Phameas was a Carthaginian cavalry officer in the Third Punic War, an admirer of Scipio Aemilianus, who defected to the Romans (Appian 8,16,107-09).

**168.** On the saying of Orontes see Aristides, *Or.* 46 (vol. II p.335, ed. Dindorf). On Arbazacius see *PLRE* II 'Arbazacius', where it is suggested that he was of Isaurian descent, but born in Armenia; alternatively his epithet 'Isaurian' could derive not from descent but from close association with that area. For the ordering of this and the following passages see my paper in *Antichthon* (1980) pp.170-76.

**169.** On Hierax see *PLRE* II 'Hierax', whose interpretation of the evidence on this person seems to be the same as mine (*art. cit.* at n.168 above). The parenthetical phrase in the first line is the excerptor's.

**170.** Although I know of no exact parallel for the meaning, I have kept the MS ἀπέσειον in preference to Dindorf's emendation ἐπέσειον (accepted by Boissevain) because it seems to me not only to make sense but also to be quite effective to have the audience disagreeing, but only reluctantly and out of fear of John. The isolation of the hero Fravitta is thus stressed, and his end becomes more pathetic.

**171.** I take ἱερακοτρόφον = ἱερακοβοσκόν (the meaning of the only other example in LSJ) since it makes more sense to have Hierax as the creature of John, the *comes sacrarum largitionum* in 404 and the alleged lover of the Empress Eudoxia (*PLRE* II 'Ioannes' 1).

**172.** The next passage (*Fr.* 72,1), which is a close continuation of the present one, picks up the imagery of birds of prey, which is suggested, of course, by the name Hierax ('Hawk'). Whether Hierax had bought his governorship (as in the cases remarked in *Fr.* 72,1) or had received it as a reward for the murder of Fravitta is unclear. But it is clear that Hierax was denounced for his robbery before the vicar, who milked him of his ill-gotten gains and more.

**173.** The saying of Anacharsis is from Plutarch, *Solon* 5,2. The sentence is awkward, although the general sense is clear. Perhaps ἐντεθειμένων should be read for ἐντεθνηκότων.

**174.** Homer, *Il.* 9,11-12.

**175.** The author of this is unknown.

**176.** The fable of the eagle and the nightingale is in Hesiod, *Erga* 202-12, that of the jackdaw that borrowed the peacock's feathers was in the collection of Aesop (cf. Lucian, *Apol.* 4). The point of their use by Eunapius is that Herennianus was just as corrupt as Hierax, and having bought a vicariate rather than a mere governorship, could milk a whole group of provinces. Nevertheless, in the end he, too, lost all, having been denounced before the praetorian prefect (almost certainly Fl. Eutychianus) and milked of both his plunder and his own wealth. If my interpretation of this fragment and *Fr.* 71,4 is correct, the structure of the original would have been as follows: murder of Fravitta; Hierax rewarded with Pamphylia, which he plundered; his replacement and attempt at flight; he is seized and milked by Herennianus; general complaint upon the sale of offices and plundering of provincials, the wealth flowing up to the praetorian prefect; summary on the fates of Hierax and Herennianus. It also follows, as I have argued in *art. cit.* (at n.168 above) p.175, that Πουλχερίας is to be regarded as an error for Εὐδοξίας, the wife of Arcadius.

**177.** A snake whose poison was said to cause intense thirst (cf. Aelian *N.A.* 6,51).

**178.** This is probably a misquotation of number 450 of the single-line sayings (γνῶμαι μονόστιχοι) of Menander in Meineke *Fr. Com. Gr.* IV p.352: πενίας βαρύτερον οὐδέν ἐστι φορτίον. The subject of the fragment might be Stilicho's treatment of his enemies in contrast with the murder of Fravitta by John and his partners.

**179.** The text is badly mutilated, but Eunapius appears to have returned to the murder of Fravitta and the preoccupation of his enemies with the overwhelming power of Stilicho. After this passage one leaf of the MS of the *Exc. de Sent.* is missing which contained almost entirely material excerpted from Eunapius.

**180.** The following are fragments from the *Suda* which are attributed to Eunapius by name or where affinities of language are clear, but which cannot be given a certain or reasonably certain location. Other anonymous articles or parts of articles which have been assigned to him are A 87, 3100, 3508, Aι 117, 156, Δ 326, E 239, 395, 566, 1011, 1055, 1994, K 539, 683, 745, 824, Λ 490, M 648, 1300, N 244 (cf. Υ 175), O 786, 806, Π 715, 1173, 1206, Σ 1191, T 865, 1155, Υ 321.

**181.** Müller (*ad suum Fr.* 89) suggests that this comes from the same place as *Suda* K 391 (= *Fr.* 5,1). But although the language is very similar, the import of the words differs slightly.

**182.** The language and sentiments are very like those of *Fr.* 69,3 on Fravitta.

**183.** For the Eunapian language cf. *Fr.* 67,7.

**184.** Although the language is awkward, the passage is probably not mutilated, as Müller (*ad suum Fr.* 92) thought. The subject appears to be diplomatic negotiations in which the Romans were arguing for the capitulation of a territory of some size and technological sophistication (Armenia or Persia?).

**185.** Doubt has been expressed that this fragment is from Eunapius (cf. Müller *ad suum Fr.* 4 who suggests that Εὐνάπιος refers to K 391 = *Fr.* 5,1).

**186.** Boissonade (in Müller *Fr.* 68) would refer this to Eutropius or Rufinus, but since the subject is one whose perceptions have been dimmed by honours heaped on him, it more probably refers to such as Timasius (cf. *Fr.* 65,3).

**187.** Boissonade (in Müller *Fr.* 3) would refer this to a skilled archer at the siege of Cremna during the reign of Probus, and certainly the language is similar to that of Zosimus 1,70,1. But it could also be from elsewhere.

**188.** Boissonade (in Müller *Fr.* 68) would refer this to Eutropius or Rufinus. The falling into a sense of security might be appropriate of Rufinus just before his murder, but there are other candidates too (e.g. Ablabius, Constantine's praetorian prefect).

**189.** This first quotation is possibly not from Eunapius. After the second quotation follows a third which has been attributed to Eunapius, but which Adler (*ad loc.*) more plausibly regards as from Arrian.

# OLYMPIODORUS

**Text and Translation**

# OLYMPIODORUS

## TESTIMONIUM

(Photius *Bibl. Cod.* 80, pp.166f.)

Ἀνεγνώσθη Ὀλυμπιοδώρου ἱστορικοὶ λόγοι κβ'. ἄρχεται ἀπὸ
τῆς Ὀνωρίου τοῦ βασιλέως Ῥώμης τῆς ὑπατείας τὸ ἔβδομον καὶ
Θεοδοσίου τὸ δεύτερον, κατέρχεται δὲ μέχρις ὅτου Βαλεντινιανὸς ὁ
Πλακιδίας καὶ Κωνσταντίνου παῖς εἰς τὴν βασίλειον τῆς Ῥώμης
ἀνερρήθη ἀρχήν.                                                                                              5

Οὗτος ὁ συγγραφεὺς Θηβαῖος μέν ἐστιν, ἐκ τῶν πρὸς Αἴγυπτον
Θηβῶν τὸ γένος ἔχων, ποιητής, ὡς αὐτός φησι, τὸ ἐπιτήδευμα,
Ἕλλην τὴν θρησκείαν, σαφὴς μὲν τὴν φράσιν, ἄτονος δὲ καὶ ἐκ-
λελυμένος καὶ πρὸς τὴν πεπατημένην κατενηνεγμένος χυδαιολογίαν,
ὥστε μήδ' ἄξιος εἰς συγγραφὴν ἀναγράφεσθαι ὁ λόγος. ὃ καὶ αὐτὸς      10
ἴσως συνιδὼν οὐ συγγραφὴν αὐτῷ ταῦτα κατασκευασθῆναι, ἀλλὰ
ὕλην συγγραφῆς ἐκπορισθῆναι διαβεβαιοῦται· οὕτως ἄμορφος καὶ
ἀνίδεος καὶ αὐτῷ τοῦ λόγου ὁ χαρακτὴρ κατεφαίνετο. καὶ γὰρ
οὐδεμίᾳ τῶν ἰδεῶν καλλωπίζεται, πλὴν εἴ τις ἔν τισι τῇ ἀφελείᾳ
πλησιάζειν ἐκβιάσοιτο· τῷ γὰρ λίαν ταπεινῷ καὶ ἐξηυτελισμένῳ καὶ      15
ταύτης ἐκπίπτων εἰς ἰδιωτισμὸν ὅλως ὑπενήνεκται. ὕλην δὲ αὐτὸς
ἱστορίας ταῦτα καλῶν, ὅμως καὶ λόγοις διαιρεῖ καὶ προοιμίοις
πειρᾶται κοσμεῖν, καὶ πρὸς Θεοδόσιον τὸν βασιλέα, ὃς ἀνεψιὸς
ἐχρημάτιζεν Ὀνωρίου καὶ Πλακιδίας, Ἀρκαδίου δὲ παῖς, πρὸς τοῦτον
τὴν ἱστορίαν ἀναφωνεῖ.                                                                                  20

## FRAGMENTA

### 1

1. (*Bibl. Cod.* 80, p.167)

Διαλαμβάνει τοίνυν περὶ Στελίχωνος, ὅσην τε περιεβέβλητο
δύναμιν, καταστὰς ἐπίτροπος τῶν παίδων Ἀρκαδίου καὶ Ὀνωρίου
ὑπ' αὐτοῦ τοῦ πατρὸς αὐτῶν Θεοδοσίου τοῦ μεγάλου, καὶ ὡς Σερῆναν
νόμῳ γάμου ἠγάγετο, Θεοδοσίου καὶ ταύτην αὐτῷ κατεγγυήσαντος.

# OLYMPIODORUS

## TESTIMONIUM

(Photius *Bibl. Cod.* 80, pp.166f.)

Read the twenty-two books of history by Olympiodorus. He begins from the seventh consulship of Honorius, the Emperor of Rome, and the second of Theodosius and continues to the time when Valentinian, the son of Placidia and Constantius, was proclaimed Emperor of Rome.

Originally from Thebes in Egypt, this historian was a poet by profession, as he himself says, and in religion a Hellene. His style is clear, but insipid, loosely organised and tending towards triteness and vulgarity, so that his work is hardly worthy to be classed as a history. Perhaps he realised this, since he maintains that what he is offering is not history but material for history[1] — so formless and inept did the style of the work appear even to him. For it displays no stylistic virtues, unless one were to insist that in some passages it comes close to simplicity; and the jejunity and low standards of his writing cause him to descend even from this into complete vulgarity. Although he calls this work 'material for history', he nevertheless divides it into books and tries to dress it up with prefaces. He dedicates the work to the Emperor Theodosius, the nephew of Honorius and Placidia and the son of Arcadius.

## FRAGMENTS

### 1

1. (*Bibl. Cod.* 80, p.167)

He writes about Stilicho, describing the great power which he acquired when Theodosius the Great appointed him guardian of his sons Arcadius and Honorius, and he tells of Stilicho's marriage to Serena, who was betrothed to him by Theodosius himself.

2. (Sozomen 9,4,2-4)

Οὗτος δὲ καὶ πρότερον ἔτι περιόντος Ἀρκαδίου καταστὰς εἰς
ἔχθραν τοῖς αὐτοῦ ἄρχουσιν ἐβεβούλευτο πρὸς ἑαυτὰ συγκροῦσαι τὰ
βασίλεια. καὶ στρατηγοῦ Ῥωμαίων ἀξίαν προξενήσας Ἀλαρίχῳ τῷ
ἡγουμένῳ τῶν Γότθων προὐτρέψατο καταλαβεῖν τοὺς Ἰλλυριούς.
καὶ ὕπαρχον αὐτῶν καταστάντα τὸν Ἰόβιον προπέμψας συνέθετο καὶ    5
αὐτὸς συνδραμεῖσθαι μετὰ τῶν Ῥωμαίων στρατιωτῶν, ὥστε καὶ
τοὺς τῇδε ὑπηκόους ὑπὸ τὴν Ὀνωρίου δῆθεν ἡγεμονίαν ποιῆσαι. καὶ
ὁ μὲν Ἀλάριχος ἐκ τῆς πρὸς τῇ Δαλματίᾳ καὶ Παννονίᾳ βαρβάρου
γῆς, οὗ διῆγεν, παραλαβὼν τοὺς ὑπ᾽ αὐτὸν ἧκεν εἰς τὰς Ἠπείρους·
καὶ συχνὸν ἐνταῦθα προσμείνας χρόνον ἄπρακτος ἐπανῆλθεν εἰς    10
Ἰταλίαν.

(Zosimus 5.26)

2
(Zosimus 5,27,1)

3
(*Bibl. Cod. loc. cit.*)

Ὅτι τε μετὰ ταῦτα Στελίχων εἰς τὴν ἑαυτοῦ θυγατέρα Θερ-
μαντίαν τὸν βασιλέα Ὀνώριον γαμβρὸν ἐποιήσατο, καὶ ὡς ἐπὶ
πλεῖστον ἔτι μᾶλλον ἤρθη δυνάμεως, καὶ πολλοὺς πολέμους ὑπὲρ
Ῥωμαίων πρὸς πολλὰ τῶν ἐθνῶν κατώρθωσε.

(Zosimus 5,27,2 - 28,3)

4
(Sozomen 1,6,5)

Οἱ γὰρ Ἀργοναῦται τὸν Αἰήτην φεύγοντες οὐ τὸν αὐτὸν πλοῦν
ἐν τῇ ἐπανόδῳ ἐποιήσαντο. περαιωθέντες δὲ τὴν ὑπὲρ Σκύθας
θάλασσαν διὰ τῶν τῇδε ποταμῶν ἀφίκοντο εἰς Ἰταλῶν ὅρια, καὶ
χειμάσαντες ἐνταῦθα πόλιν ἔκτισαν Ἤμωνα προσαγορευομένην. τοῦ
δὲ θέρους ἐπικαταλαβόντος, συμπραξάντων αὐτοῖς τῶν ἐπιχωρίων,    5
ἀμφὶ τοὺς τετρακοσίους σταδίους ὑπὸ μηχανῆς ἕλκοντες τὴν Ἀργὼ
διὰ γῆς ἐπὶ τὸν Ἄκυλιν ποταμὸν ἤγαγον, ὃς τῷ Ἠριδανῷ συμβάλλει·
Ἠριδανὸς δὲ εἰς τὴν κατὰ Ἰταλοὺς θάλασσαν τὰς ἐκβολὰς ἔχει.

(Zosimus 5,29)

2. (Sozomen 9,4,2-4)

Earlier, while Arcadius was still alive, he [Stilicho] became hostile to the ministers of that Emperor and planned to bring the two parts of the Empire to war. He recommended that Alaric, the leader of the Goths, be given a Roman generalship and urged him to seize Illyricum. He also sent ahead Jovius, who had been made praetorian prefect of that region, and promised that he would quickly join him with the Roman troops, in order to bring the population there under Honorius' rule. Alaric, collecting those under his command, quitted the barbarian lands by Dalmatia and Pannonia, where he was dwelling, and led his men to Epirus. There he waited for a long time and then retreated to Italy, having achieved nothing.[2]

(Zosimus 5,26)

## 2

(Zosimus 5,27,1)

## 3

(*Bibl. Cod. loc.cit.*)

Later Stilicho made the Emperor Honorius his son-in-law by marrying him to his daughter Thermantia[3] and accumulated even more power. He fought on behalf of the Romans many successful wars against many peoples.

(Zosimus 5,27,2 - 28,3)

## 4

(Sozomen 1,6,5)

For when the Argonauts were fleeing Aeëtes they did not sail the same way home, but, having crossed the Scythian Sea, they reached the land of Italy by way of the rivers of that region. There they wintered and founded the city called Emona. When summer came, with the help of the inhabitants of the area and by using machines, they dragged the Argo about 400 stades across land to the river Aquilis. This river joins the Eridanus, which in turn empties into the Italian Sea.

(Zosimus 5,29)

## 5

1. (Bibl. Cod. loc.cit.)

Καὶ ὅτι μιαιφόνῳ καὶ ἀπανθρώπῳ σπουδῇ Ὀλυμπίου, ὃν αὐτὸς
τῷ βασιλεῖ προσῳκείωσε, τὸν διὰ ξίφους ὑπέμεψε θάνατον.

2. (Sozomen 9,4,4-8)

Μέλλων γὰρ ἐκδημεῖν κατὰ τὰ συντεθειμένα Ὀνωρίου γράμμασιν ἐπεσχέθη. ἐπεὶ δὲ ἐτελεύτησεν Ἀρκάδιος, ὥρμησε μὲν Ὀνώριος φειδοῖ τῇ περὶ τὸν ἀδελφιδοῦν ἐλθεῖν εἰς Κωνσταντινούπολιν καὶ
πιστοὺς ἄρχοντας καὶ φύλακας καταστῆσαι τῆς αὐτοῦ σωτηρίας καὶ
βασιλείας, ἐν τάξει γὰρ υἱέος αὐτὸν ἔχων ἐδεδίει μή τι πάθοι διὰ τὸ    5
νέον ἕτοιμος ὢν πρὸς ἐπιβουλήν. ἤδη δὲ μέλλοντα ἔχεσθαι τῆς ὁδοῦ
πείθει Στελίχων ἐν τῇ Ἰταλίᾳ μένειν τὸν Ὀνώριον, ἀναγκαῖον εἶναι
τοῦτο εἰπών, καθότι Κωνσταντῖνός τις ἐτύγχανεν ἔναγχος ἐν Ἀρη-
λάτῳ τυραννήσας. θάτερον δὲ τῶν σκήπτρων, ὃ λάβωρον Ῥωμαῖοι
καλοῦσι, καὶ γράμματα βασιλέως λαβὼν ἐπιτρέποντα αὐτῷ τὴν εἰς    10
τὴν ἀνατολὴν ἄφιξιν, ἔμελλεν ἐκδημεῖν τέσσαρας ἀριθμοὺς στρατιωτῶν παραλαβών. ἐν τούτῳ δὲ φήμης διαδραμούσης, ὡς ἐπιβουλεύει
τῷ βασιλεῖ καὶ ἐπὶ τυραννίδα τοῦ υἱέος παρασκευάζεται συμπράττοντας ἔχων τοὺς ἐν δυνάμει, στασιάσαντες οἱ στρατιῶται κτείνουσι
τὸν Ἰταλίας ὕπαρχον καὶ τὸν τῶν Γαλατῶν καὶ τοὺς στρατηγοὺς καὶ    15
τοὺς ἄλλους τοὺς διέποντας τὰς ἐν τοῖς βασιλείοις ἀρχάς. ἀναιρεῖται
δὲ καὶ αὐτὸς παρὰ τῶν ἐν Ῥαβέννῃ στρατιωτῶν, ἀνὴρ εἴπερ τις
ἄλλος πώποτε ἐν πολλῇ δυνάμει γεγενημένος καὶ πάντας ὡς εἰπεῖν
βαρβάρους τε καὶ Ῥωμαίους πειθομένους ἔχων. Στελίχων μὲν οὖν
ὑπονοηθεὶς κακόνους εἶναι τοῖς βασιλείοις ὧδε ἀπώλετο· κτίννυται    20
δὲ καὶ Εὐχέριος ὁ αὐτοῦ παῖς.

3. (Philostorgius 12,1)

Ἄλλοι δὲ οὐκ Ὀλύμπιον, ἀλλ' Ὀλυμπιόδωρόν φασιν· οὐδ' ἐπα-
μῦναι τῷ βασιλεῖ, ἀλλ' ἐπιβουλεῦσαι τῷ εὐεργέτῃ Στελίχωνι καὶ εἰς
τυραννίδα συκοφαντῆσαι αὐτόν. καὶ οὐδὲ μάγιστρον τηνικαῦτα εἶναι,
ἀλλ' ὕστερον, μετὰ τὸν ἄδικον τοῦ Στελίχωνος φόνον, ἔπαθλον τὴν
ἀξίαν λαβεῖν. ἀλλ' οὐκ εἰς μακρὰν καὶ αὐτὸν ῥοπάλοις ἀναιρεθέντα    5
τῆς μιαιφονίας τὴν δίκην ἀποτῖσαι τῷ Στελίχωνι.

(Zosimus 5,30,1 - 35,4)

## 6

(Bibl. Cod. 80, pp.167f.)

Ὅτι Ἀλάριχος ὁ τῶν Γότθων φύλαρχος, ὃν Στελίχων μετε-
καλέσατο ἐπὶ τῷ φυλάξαι Ὀνωρίῳ τὸ Ἰλλυρικὸν (τῇ γὰρ αὐτοῦ ἦν

## 5

1. (*Bibl. Cod. loc.cit.*)

And [Stilicho] submitted to execution by the sword as the result of the murderous and inhuman plotting of Olympius, whom he himself had introduced to the Emperor.[4]

2. (Sozomen 9,4,4-8)

For although [Stilicho] was preparing to set out according to his promises [to Alaric], he was held back by letters from Honorius.[5] After the death of Arcadius, Honorius out of concern for his nephew was eager to visit Constantinople to appoint loyal ministers to ensure the safety of his nephew's person and throne. For Honorius regarded him as a son and was afraid that he might suffer harm, since he was young and liable to fall victim to plotting. When the Emperor was about to set out, Stilicho persuaded Honorius to remain in Italy by asserting that this was necessary since a certain Constantine had recently declared himself Emperor at Arles. Stilicho took one of the standards which the Romans call *labarum*, letters from the Emperor which appointed him to go to the East and four legions and prepared for his journey. Meanwhile a rumour was spreading that Stilicho was plotting against the Emperor and, in concert with the chief officials, was preparing to raise his son to the throne.[6] The troops broke out in revolt and slaughtered the prefects of Italy and the Gauls, the generals and other chief palatine ministers.[7] Stilicho himself was killed by the soldiery at Ravenna, a man who attained greater power than anyone and who controlled all men, so to speak, both barbarian and Roman. But he was suspected of plotting against the Emperors and perished in this manner; and his son, Eucherius, was also put to death.

3. (Philostorgius 12,1)

Others say that it was not Olympius but Olympiodorus [who caused Stilicho's death] and that he did not defend the Emperor but plotted against Stilicho, who had been his benefactor, and falsely accused him of aiming at usurpation. They also say that he was not master of the offices at that time, but received it later as his reward after the unjust murder of Stilicho, and that soon afterwards he was killed with clubs and so paid to Stilicho the penalty for his bloodthirstiness.[8]

(Zosimus 5,30,1 - 35,4)

## 6

(*Bibl. Cod.* 80, pp.167f.)

Alaric, the tribal leader of the Goths, whom Stilicho summoned to guard Illyricum for Honorius (since it had been attached to his part

παρὰ Θεοδοσίου τοῦ πατρὸς ἐκνενεμημένον βασιλείᾳ), οὗτος ὁ Ἀλάριχος διά τε τὸν φόνον Στελίχωνος, καὶ ὅτι ἃ συνέκειτο αὐτῷ οὐκ
ἐλάμβανε, πολιορκεῖ καὶ ἐκπορθεῖ τὴν Ῥώμην· ἐξ ἧς χρήματά τε    5
ἄπειρα ἐξεκόμισε, καὶ τὴν ἀδελφὴν Ὀνωρίου Πλακιδίαν ἐν Ῥώμῃ
διάγουσαν ἠχμαλώτισε, καὶ πρὸ τῆς ἁλώσεως δὲ ἕνα τινὰ τῶν κατὰ
τὴν Ῥώμην ἐπιδόξων (Ἄτταλος ἦν ὄνομα αὐτῷ) τὴν ἐπαρχότητα
τότε διέποντα εἰς βασιλέα ἀνηγόρευσεν. ἐπράχθη δὲ αὐτῷ ταῦτα διά
τε τὰς προειρημένας αἰτίας, καὶ ὅτι Σάρον, καὶ αὐτὸν Γότθον ὄντα,    10
καὶ πλήθους μὲν ὀλίγου ἐπάρχοντα (ἄχρι γὰρ σ' ἢ καὶ τ' αὐτῷ ὁ
λαὸς ἐξετείνετο) ἄλλως δὲ ἡρωϊκόν τινα καὶ ἐν μάχαις ἀκαταγώ-
νιστον, τοῦτον ὅτι Ῥωμαῖοι ἡταιρίσαντο δι' ἔχθρας Ἀλαρίχῳ ὄντα,
ἄσπονδον ἐχθρὸν Ἀλάριχον ἐποιήσαντο.

# 7

1. (Bibl. Cod. 80, p.168)
Ὅτι ἐν τῇ πολιορκίᾳ τῆς Ῥώμης ἀλληλοφαγία τῶν ἐνοικούντων ἐγίνετο.

2. (Bibl. Cod. loc.cit.)
Ὅτι Ἀλάριχος, ἔτι ζῶντος Στελίχωνος, μ' κεντηνάρια μισθὸν
ἔλαβε τῆς ἐκστρατείας.

3. (Bibl. Cod. loc.cit.)
Ὅτι μετὰ θάνατον Στελίχωνος ἀναιρεῖται ἐναποπνιγεῖσα καὶ
Σερῆνα ἡ τούτου γυνή, αἰτία νομισθεῖσα τῆς ἐπὶ Ῥώμην ἐφόδου
Ἀλαρίχου· ἀναιρεῖται δὲ πρότερον μετὰ τὴν ἀναίρεσιν Στελίχωνος
ὁ ταύτης κἀκείνου παῖς Εὐχέριος.

4. (Bibl. Cod. loc.cit.)
Ὅτι τὸ Βουκελλάριος ὄνομα ἐν ταῖς ἡμέραις Ὀνωρίου ἐφέρετο
κατὰ στρατιωτῶν οὐ μόνον Ῥωμαίων ἀλλὰ καὶ Γότθων τινῶν· ὡς
δ' αὕτως καὶ τὸ φοιδεράτων κατὰ διαφόρου καὶ συμμιγοῦς ἐφέρετο
πλήθους.

5. (Sozomen 9,6,1-5 and 7)
Τὰ δὲ πρὸς δύσιν ἐν ἀταξίαις ἦν πολλῶν ἐπανισταμένων
τυράννων· ἡνίκα δὴ μετὰ τὴν Στελίχωνος ἀναίρεσιν Ἀλάριχος ὁ
τῶν Γότθων ἡγούμενος πρεσβευσάμενος περὶ εἰρήνης πρὸς Ὀνώριον
ἀπέτυχε· καὶ καταλαβὼν τὴν Ῥώμην ἐπολιόρκει πολλοὺς βαρβάρους
ἐπιστήσας Θύβριδι τῷ ποταμῷ, ὥστε μὴ εἰσκομίζεσθαι τὰ ἐπιτήδεια    5
τοῖς ἐν τῇ πόλει ἀπὸ τοῦ Πόρτου (ὧδε γὰρ ὀνομάζουσι τὸ Ῥωμαίων
ἐπίνειον). χρονίας δὲ γενομένης τῆς πολιορκίας λιμοῦ τε καὶ λοιμοῦ

of the Empire by his father Theodosius), because of the execution of
Stilicho and because he had not received what had been promised to
him, besieged and sacked Rome. He carried from the city incalculable
wealth and made prisoner Honorius' sister Placidia, who was living in
Rome, and before the capture he proclaimed Emperor one of the
Roman notables named Attalus, who at the time was prefect of the
city. He did these things for the above-mentioned reasons and because
the Romans had made Sarus their ally on account of his hostility towards Alaric. Sarus was himself a Goth also and commanded a small
force of followers (about two or three hundred men) and, besides, he
was an heroic man and invincible in battle. Thus the Romans made
Alaric their relentless foe.[9]

# 7

### 1. (*Bibl. Cod.* 80, p.168)

During the siege of Rome the inhabitants turned to cannibalism.

### 2. (*Bibl. Cod. loc.cit.*)

While Stilicho was still alive Alaric received four thousand pounds
[of gold] to pay for his services.[10]

### 3. (*Bibl. Cod. loc.cit.*)

After the death of Stilicho his wife Serena was killed by strangu-
lation, since she was thought to be the reason for Alaric's march on
Rome. Earlier, after the death of Stilicho, their son Eucherius was also
put to death.[11]

### 4. (*Bibl. Cod. loc.cit.*)

In the time of Honorius the name *buccellarius* was given not only
to Roman soldiers but also to certain Goths. Similarly the name
*foederati* was given to a diverse and mixed body of men.

### 5. (Sozomen 9,6,1-5 and 7)

But the western parts of the Empire were in confusion, and many
usurpers arose. At that time after the death of Stilicho, Alaric, the
leader of the Goths, sent an embassy to Honorius to treat for peace, but
achieved nothing. Therefore, he made for Rome and besieged it, lining
the banks of the Tiber with many of his barbarians to prevent the con-
veyance of food to those in the city from Portus (that is the name of
the Roman sea-harbour). Since, after the siege had gone on for a long

τὴν πόλιν πιέζοντος δούλων τε πολλῶν καὶ μάλιστα βαρβάρων τῷ
γένει πρὸς τὸν Ἀλάριχον αὐτομολούντων, ἀναγκαῖον ἐδόκει τοῖς
ἑλληνίζουσι τῆς συγκλήτου θύειν ἐν τῷ Καπιτωλίῳ καὶ τοῖς ἄλλοις      10
ναοῖς. Θοῦσκοι γάρ τινες ἐπὶ τοῦτο μετακληθέντες παρὰ τοῦ ὑπάρχου
τῆς πόλεως ὑπισχνοῦντο σκηπτοῖς καὶ βρονταῖς ἀπελάσειν τοὺς
βαρβάρους· ηὔχουν δὲ τοιοῦτον αὐτοῖς εἰργάσθαι καὶ περὶ Ναρνίαν
πόλιν τῆς Θουσκίας, ἣν παριὼν Ἀλάριχος ἐπὶ τὴν Ῥώμην οὐχ εἷλεν.
ἀλλὰ τούτων μὲν οὐδὲν ὄφελος ἔσεσθαι τῇ πόλει ἡ ἀπόβασις ἔδειξεν.      15
... ἐν ᾧ δὲ ἐπολιόρκει, πλεῖστα δῶρα λαβὼν ἐπὶ χρόνον τινὰ τὴν
πολιορκίαν ἔλυσε, συνθεμένων Ῥωμαίων τὸν βασιλέα πείσειν εἰς
εἰρήνην αὐτὸν δέχεσθαι.

13 Ναρνίαν Valesius [Λαρνίαν codd.

[6. (Philostorgius 12,3)
    Ὅτι, Στελίχωνος ἀνῃρημένου, οἱ συνόντες βάρβαροι τὸν
ἐκείνου παῖδα λαβόντες τὴν ταχίστην ᾤχοντο. καὶ τῇ Ῥώμῃ πλησι-
άσαντες, τὸν μὲν ἐφεῖσαν εἴς τι τῶν ἀσύλων ἱερῶν καταφυγεῖν, οἱ δὲ
τὰ τῆς πόλεως πέριξ ἐπόρθουν, τὸ μὲν τῷ Στελίχωνι τιμωροῦντες,
τὸ δὲ λιμῷ πιεζόμενοι. ἐπεὶ δὲ παρὰ Ὀνωρίου γράμμα κρεῖττον τῆς      5
ἀσυλίας γενόμενον ἀναιρεῖ τὸν Εὐχέριον, διὰ ταῦτα συμμίξαντες οἱ
βάρβαροι Ἀλλαρίχῳ εἰς τὸν πρὸς Ῥωμαίους αὐτὸν ἐξορμῶσι
πόλεμον.]

3 ἱερῶν Bidez [ἱερὸν codd.

(Zosimus 5,35,5 - 42,3)

8

1. (Sozomen 9,7)
    Γενομένης δὲ περὶ τούτου πρεσβείας οἱ τὰ ἐναντία πράττοντες
Ἀλαρίχῳ ἐν τοῖς βασιλείοις ἐνεπόδιζον τῇ εἰρήνῃ. μετὰ δὲ ταῦτα
πρεσβευσαμένου Ἰννοκεντίου τοῦ Ῥωμαίων ἐπισκόπου μετακληθεὶς
Ἀλάριχος γράμμασι τοῦ βασιλέως ἧκεν εἰς Ἀρίμηνον πόλιν δέκα καὶ
διακοσίοις σταδίοις τῆς Ῥαβέννης ἀφεστῶσαν. ἐνταῦθα δὲ τὰς      5
σκηνὰς ἔχοντι πρὸ τῶν τειχῶν εἰς λόγους ἐλθὼν ὁ Ἰόβιος τῆς
Ἰταλίας ὕπαρχος ὢν δηλοῖ τῷ βασιλεῖ τὴν Ἀλαρίχου αἴτησιν καὶ ὡς
δέοι δέλτοις αὐτὸν τιμῆσαι στρατηγοῦ δυνάμεως ἑκατέρας. ὁ δὲ
βασιλεὺς χρημάτων μὲν καὶ σιτηρεσίων ὧν ᾔτει ὡς ὑπάρχῳ Ἰοβίῳ
τὴν ἐξουσίαν δέδωκεν, ἀξίας δὲ οὔποτε μεταδώσειν αὐτῷ ἀντεδή-      10
λωσεν. ἀβούλως δὲ Ἰόβιος ἐν τῇ Ἀλαρίχου σκηνῇ περιμείνας τὸν ἐκ
τῶν βασιλείων ἀπεσταλμένον ἀναγνώσκειν ἐκέλευσε παρόντων τῶν
βαρβάρων τὰ δόξαντα τῷ βασιλεῖ. ἐπὶ δὲ τῇ ἀρνήσει τοῦ ἀξιώματος

time, famine and pestilence were ravaging the city and many of the slaves, especially those of barbarian origin, were deserting to Alaric, those of the senate who were Hellenes thought it necessary to offer sacrifices on the Capitol and in the other temples. For certain Etruscans who had been summoned for this purpose by the prefect of the city promised to drive away the barbarians with thunder and lightning, and they boasted that they had done this at Narnia, a city of Etruria which Alaric had passed by on his way to Rome but had failed to take.[12] But, as events showed, these people would be of no help to the city. . . . While [Alaric] was besieging the city he received many gifts from the inhabitants, and for a while he lifted the siege since the Romans promised to persuade the Emperor to make peace with him.[13]

[6. (Philostorgius 12,3)

When Stilicho had been killed, the barbarians who were with him took his son and fled with all speed. When they came near to Rome, they allowed him to flee to the sanctuary of one of the churches while they ravaged the environs of the city, partly out of revenge for Stilicho and partly because they were suffering from hunger. When a letter from Honorius, outweighing the right of sanctuary, sealed Eucherius' fate, the barbarians as a result joined Alaric and urged him to make war on the Romans.[14]]

(Zosimus 5,35,5 - 42,3)

## 8

1. (Sozomen 9,7)

When an embassy was sent [from Rome] for this purpose [i.e. to make peace between Honorius and Alaric], those at court who were working against Alaric thwarted the attempt to make peace.[15] But when later Innocent, the bishop of Rome, went as an envoy, Alaric was summoned by letters from the Emperor and came to Ariminum, a city two hundred and ten stades from Ravenna. There, while he was encamped before the city walls, Jovius, the praetorian prefect of Italy, came to confer with him and sent Alaric's demands to the Emperor, including that the codicils of the generalship of both branches of the army be bestowed upon him. The Emperor gave to Jovius, as prefect, the power to give to Alaric as much money and grain as he demanded. But he replied that he would never grant him the military command. Jovius was awaiting the messenger from the palace in Alaric's tent, and he unwisely ordered him to read out before the barbarians the reply of the Emperor. Alaric, angered at the refusal of the command and regarding

ὀργισθεὶς Ἀλάριχος ὡς ὑβρισμένος αὐθωρὸν τῇ σάλπιγγι σημήνας
ἐπὶ τὴν Ῥώμην ἤλαυνε. δείσας δὲ Ἰόβιος, μὴ ὑπονοηθῇ παρὰ τῷ    15
βασιλεῖ Ἀλαρίχῳ σπουδάξειν, ἀβουλοτέρῳ ἢ πρότερον περιπεσών,
πρὸς τῆς σωτηρίας τοῦ βασιλέως αὐτός τε ὤμοσε καὶ τοὺς ἄλλους
ἄρχοντας παρεσκεύασε μήποτε εἰρήνην θέσθαι πρὸς Ἀλάριχον. οὐκ
εἰς μακρὰν δὲ μεταμεληθεὶς ὁ βάρβαρος ἐδήλωσε μηδὲν ἀξιωμάτων
δεῖσθαι, σύμμαχον δὲ παρέξειν ἑαυτὸν ἐπὶ μετρίᾳ σίτου δόσει καὶ    20
οἰκήσει τόπων οὐ πάνυ Ῥωμαίοις ἐσπουδασμένων.

2. (*Bibl. Cod. loc.cit.*)
    Ὅτι Ὀλύμπιος, ὁ ἐπιβουλεύσας Στελίχωνα, μάγιστρος τῶν
ὀφφικίων γέγονεν, εἶτα ἐξέπεσε τῆς ἀρχῆς, εἶτα πάλιν ἐπέβη ταύτης,
ἔπειτα ἐξέπεσεν, εἶτα ἐκπεσὼν ῥοπάλοις ὕστερον ὑπὸ Κωνσταντίου,
ὃς ἠγάγετο Πλακιδίαν, παιόμενος ἀναιρεῖται, τὰς ἀκοὰς πρότερον
ἐκκοπείς· καὶ ἡ δίκη τὸν ἀνοσιουργὸν εἰς τέλος οὐκ ἀφῆκεν ἀτιμώ-    5
ρητον.

(Zosimus 5,43-51)

## 9

(*Bibl. Cod. loc.cit.*)
    Ὅτι τῶν μετὰ Ῥοδογάϊσον Γότθων οἱ κεφαλαιῶται ὀπτίματοι
ἐκαλοῦντο, εἰς δώδεκα συντείνοντες χιλιάδας, οὓς καταπολεμήσας
Στελίχων Ῥοδογάϊσον προσηταιρίσατο.

## 10

1. (Sozomen 9,8)
    Ἐπεὶ δὲ δὶς ἀπέτυχε περὶ τούτου πρεσβευσάμενος διά τινων
ἐπισκόπων, ἐλθὼν εἰς Ῥώμην ἐπολιόρκει τὴν πόλιν· καὶ ἐξ ἑνὸς
μέρους τὸν Πόρτον ἑλὼν βιάζεται Ῥωμαίους βασιλέα ψηφίσασθαι
τὸν Ἄτταλον, ὕπαρχον ὄντα τότε τῆς πόλεως. Ῥωμαίων δὲ προ-
βληθέντων ἐπὶ τὰς ἄλλας ἀρχὰς χειροτονεῖται Ἀλάριχος στρατηγὸς    5
ἑκατέρας δυνάμεως, Ἀδαοῦλφος δὲ ὁ τῆς αὐτοῦ γαμετῆς ἀδελφὸς
ἡγεμὼν τῶν ἱππέων δομεστίκων καλουμένων. συγκαλέσας δὲ τὴν
γερουσίαν Ἄτταλος λόγον διῆλθε μακρὸν καὶ λαμπρῶς μάλα πε-
πονημένον, ὑπισχνούμενος τὰ πάτρια τῇ συγκλήτῳ φυλάξειν καὶ τὴν
Αἴγυπτον καὶ πᾶσαν τὴν πρὸς ἕω ἀρχομένην ὑπήκοον Ἰταλοῖς    10
ποιήσειν. καὶ ὁ μὲν ὧδε ἀλαζονευσάμενος οὐδὲ εἰς ἐνιαυτὸν ὁλό-
κληρον ἤμελλε βασιλεὺς καλεῖσθαι· μάντεσι δέ τισιν ὑπαχθεὶς
ὑπισχνουμένοις ἀμαχητὶ τὴν Ἀφρικὴν καθέξειν, οὔτε Ἀλαρίχῳ
ἐπείσθη μετρίαν δύναμιν εἰσηγησαμένῳ πέμψαι εἰς Καρχηδόνα ἐπὶ

it as a slight, immediately ordered the trumpet to give the signal and marched on Rome. Jovius, fearing that the Emperor would suspect him of favouring Alaric, committed an error even more foolish than his earlier one and swore upon the safety of the Emperor that peace should never be made with Alaric, persuading the other officials to do the same. Shortly afterwards Alaric repented his haste and declared that the commands were not necessary: he would make an alliance upon payment of a moderate amount of grain and permission to live in some territory which was of little importance to the Romans.[16]

## 2. (*Bibl. Cod. loc.cit.*)

Olympius, the man who had plotted against Stilicho, became master of the offices, then lost the position, then regained it and finally lost it again. After the second loss he was later killed by Placidia's husband, Constantius, who first cut off his ears and then had him beaten with clubs. And so at the end justice did not allow that impious man to escape unpunished.[17]

(Zosimus 5,43-51)

## 9

(*Bibl. Cod. loc.cit.*)

The chiefs of the Goths who were with Rodogaisus were called 'optimates', and they were twelve thousand in number. When he had defeated Rodogaisus, Stilicho made them his allies.[18]

## 10

1. (Sozomen 9,8)

When he had twice sent certain bishops as envoys on this matter [i.e. the reduced peace terms] and had twice achieved nothing, [Alaric] came to Rome and besieged the city. On one side he occupied Portus and compelled the Romans to choose Attalus, who was then prefect of the city, as their Emperor. While Romans were advanced to other offices, Alaric was appointed master of both branches of the soldiery and Ataulf, his brother-in-law, count of the so-called domestic cavalry.[19] Convening the senate, Attalus delivered a long and most brilliantly worked speech in which he promised to protect the senate's traditional rights and to make Egypt and all the eastern Empire subject to the people of Italy — thus boasted a man who was destined to be called Emperor for less than a full year.[20] He was deluded by certain seers who promised that he would take Africa without a fight, and he followed the advice neither of Alaric, who urged him to send a moderate force to Carthage in order

ἀναιρέσει τῶν Ὀνωρίου ἀρχόντων, εἰ ἀντιπαρατάξοιεν αὐτῷ, οὔτε    15
Ἰωάννῃ, ὃν προεστήσατο τῶν ἀμφ' αὐτὸν βασιλικῶν τάξεων, φάσ-
κοντι χρῆναι Κώνσταντα τὸν ἐκδημεῖν εἰς Λιβύην παρ' αὐτοῦ τεταγμένον, ὡς παρὰ Ὀνωρίου ἀπεσταλμένον, γράμματι συνήθει, ὃ
διάταγμα καλοῦσι, παῦσαι τῆς ἀρχῆς Ἡρακλειανὸν τὸν τηνικάδε τῶν
ἐν Ἀφρικῇ στρατιῶν ἐπιτετραμμένον τὴν ἡγεμονίαν. ἴσως δὲ ἂν καὶ    20
τοῦτο προὐχώρησεν· οὔπω γὰρ δῆλα ἐγεγόνει τοῖς ἐν Λιβύῃ τὰ κατὰ
Ἄτταλον. ἐπεὶ δὲ Κώνστας, τοῦτο τοῖς μάντεσι δόξαν, ἔπλευσεν εἰς
Καρχηδόνα, Ἄτταλος δὲ ἐπὶ τοσοῦτον ἐβλάβη τὸν νοῦν, ὡς μηδὲ
ἀμφιβάλλειν ἀξιοῦν, ἀλλὰ πεπεῖσθαι τοὺς Ἄφρους ὑπηκόους ἔχειν
κατὰ τὴν πρόρρησιν τῶν μάντεων, ἐπιστρατεύει τῇ Ῥαβέννῃ. ἅμα δὲ    25
ἠγγέλθη εἰς Ἀρίμηνον ἀφῖχθαι μετὰ τῆς Ῥωμαίων καὶ βαρβάρων
στρατιᾶς, γράφει αὐτῷ Ὀνώριος ὡς βασιλεῖ καὶ πρεσβεύεται διὰ
τῶν ἀμφ' αὐτὸν τὰς μεγίστας ἀρχὰς λαχόντων, κοινωνὸν ἀγαπῶν
ἔχειν τῆς βασιλείας. Ἄτταλος δὲ τὴν μὲν κοινωνίαν τοῦ κράτους
ἀπαρνεῖται· δηλοῖ δὲ Ὀνωρίῳ νῆσον ἢ τόπον ἑλέσθαι ὃν βούλεται    30
καὶ καθ' ἑαυτὸν διάγειν πάσης βασιλικῆς θεραπείας ἀξιούμενον. εἰς
τοῦτο δὲ περιστάντων τῶν πραγμάτων, ὡς εὐτρεπεῖς αὐτὸν ἔχειν
ναῦς, ἵν' εἰ δεήσειεν ἀποπλεύσῃ πρὸς τὸν ἀδελφιδοῦν, ἀδοκήτως ἐν ἓξ
ἀριθμοῖς ἀμφὶ τετρακισχίλιοι στρατιῶται νύκτωρ τῇ Ῥαβέννῃ προσ-
έπλευσαν ἐκ τῆς ἀνατολῆς· οἷς τὴν φυλακὴν τῶν τειχῶν ἐπέτρεψε    35
δεδιὼς τῶν ἐπιχωρίων στρατιωτῶν τὸ ἕτοιμον εἰς προδοσίαν. ἐν
τούτῳ δὲ Ἡρακλειανὸς ἀνελὼν τὸν Κώνσταντα φύλακας ἐπέστησεν
ἐν τοῖς λιμέσι καὶ ταῖς ἀκταῖς τῆς Ἀφρικῆς καὶ τὰ πλοῖα τῶν ἐμπόρων ἐκώλυσεν εἰς Ῥώμην ἀνάγεσθαι. λιμοῦ δὲ ἐντεῦθεν κατα-
λαβόντος τοὺς Ῥωμαίους πρεσβεύονται περὶ τούτου πρὸς Ἄτταλον.    40
ὁ δὲ πρὸς τὸ πρακτέον ἀμηχανῶν ἐπανῆλθεν εἰς Ῥώμην ὡς μετὰ
τῆς συγκλήτου συμβουλευσόμενος. ἐπικρατήσαντος δὲ τοῦ λιμοῦ ἐπὶ
τοσοῦτον ὡς καστάνοις ἀντὶ σίτου κεχρῆσθαι τὸν δῆμον, ὑπονοηθῆναι
δέ τινας καὶ ἀνθρωπείων ἀπογεύσασθαι κρεῶν, Ἀλάριχος μὲν
συνεβούλευεν πεντακοσίους βαρβάρους κατὰ Ἡρακλειανοῦ πέμψαι,    45
τῇ δὲ συγκλήτῳ καὶ τῷ Ἀττάλῳ ἐδόκει μὴ δεῖν πιστευθῆναι βαρβάροις τὴν Ἀφρικήν. ἐπεὶ δὲ δῆλον ἦν τὸν θεὸν ἀντιπράττειν τῇ
Ἀττάλου βασιλείᾳ, συνιδὼν Ἀλάριχος μάτην πονεῖν ἐπὶ πράγματι
οὐκ ἐν αὐτῷ κειμένῳ, συντίθεται περὶ καταλύσεως τῆς αὐτοῦ ἀρχῆς
πρὸς Ὀνώριον, ὑποσχέσεις λαβὼν περὶ εἰρήνης. πάντων τοίνυν    50
συνελθόντων πρὸ τῆς πόλεως, ἀποτίθεται Ἄτταλος τὰ σύμβολα τοῦ
βασιλέως· συναποτίθενται δὲ τὰς ζώνας καὶ οἱ αὐτοῦ ἄρχοντες, καὶ
συγγνώμην ἐπὶ τοῖς συμβεβηκόσι νέμει πᾶσιν Ὀνώριος, μετ' οὐ πολὺ

20 στρατιῶν codd. [στρατιωτῶν Stephanus (cf. Zos. 6,7,6)

to destroy Honorius' officials if they should oppose him, nor of John, his own master of the offices, who said that Constans, whom Attalus had appointed to go to Libya, must, as if he had been sent by Honorius, be furnished with the customary letter (which the Romans call an 'edict') relieving Heraclian of the command which he currently held over the forces in Africa. Perhaps this device would have succeeded; for those in Libya did not yet know of Attalus' activities. But Constans sailed off to Carthage as the seers advised, and Attalus was so deluded that, entertaining no doubts, he remained convinced that, as the seers had foretold, the Africans would fall under his sway. He himself marched against Ravenna, and when it was reported that he had reached Ariminum with an army composed of Romans and barbarians, Honorius wrote to him as if to a fellow Emperor and sent an embassy made up of his highest ministers, declaring his willingness to share his Empire. Attalus rejected this proposal to share power and told Honorius to retire to an island or any other place of his choosing, where he would retain the trappings of his sovereignty. Honorius' situation was now so desperate that he was keeping ships ready in order to sail off to his nephew if necessary, when, unexpectedly, six divisions, a total of about four thousand men, sailed at night into Ravenna from the East.[21] To these he entrusted the guarding of the city wall, since he feared that the Italian troops were ready to betray him.

Meanwhile Heraclian had killed Constans and stationed guards in the ports and along the coast of Africa. He also stopped the sailing of merchantmen to Rome. As a result the Romans began to suffer from famine and sent a delegation to Attalus about this. He, not knowing what measures to take, returned to Rome to consult with the senate. The famine became so bad that chestnuts were used in place of grain and some people were suspected of cannibalism. Alaric advised that five hundred barbarians should be sent against Heraclian, but the senate and Attalus declined to entrust Africa to barbarians.[22] Since it was clear that God was working against the regime of Attalus, Alaric, realising that his efforts in a cause over which he had no control were futile, came to an agreement with Honorius to depose him, having first received assurances that peace would be made. Then all gathered before the city.[23] Attalus laid aside the symbols of the Emperor, and at the same time his ministers laid aside their belts of office. Honorius pardoned them all for what they had done and shortly afterwards restored

νομοθετήσας ἕκαστον ἔχεω τὴν τιμὴν καὶ τὴν ἀξίαν ἧς πρὸ τοῦ μετε-
λάγχανεν. Ἄτταλος δὲ ἅμα τῷ παιδὶ Ἀλαρίχῳ συνῆν οὐκ ἀσφαλὲς 55
τέως ἡγούμενος ἐν Ῥωμαίοις διάγεω.

55 οὐκ codd. [ὡς ἂν οὐκ Bidez

[2. (Philostorgius 12,3)
῾Ο δὲ θᾶττον καταλαμβάνει τὸν Πόρτον. μέγιστον δὴ οὗτος
νεώριον Ῥώμης, λιμέσι τρισὶ περιγραφόμενον καὶ εἰς πόλεως μικρᾶς
παρατεωόμενον μέγεθος· ἐν τούτῳ δὲ καὶ ὁ δημόσιος ἅπας σῖτος
κατὰ παλαιὸν ἔθος ἐταμιεύετο. ἐλὼν δὲ ῥᾷον τὸν Πόρτον, καὶ τῇ
σιτοδείᾳ ἢ ταῖς ἄλλαις μηχαναῖς πολιορκήσας τὴν Ῥώμην κατὰ 5
κράτος αἱρεῖ· καὶ ψηφισαμένων τῶν Ῥωμαίων (τοῦτο γὰρ αὐτοῖς
Ἀλλάριχος ἐνεδίδου), Ἄτταλον αὐτοῖς ἀναγορεύει βασιλέα. οὗτος δὲ
Ἴων μὲν ἦν τὸ γένος, Ἕλλην δὲ τὴν δόξαν, τῆς αὐτῆς δὲ πόλεως
ἔπαρχος. οὗτος δὲ λοιπὸν μετὰ τὴν ἀναγόρευσω τὸ λείψανον τῶν
Ῥωμαίων, ὅπερ ὁ λιμὸς αὐτὸς καὶ ἡ ἀλληλοφαγία ὑπελείπετο, τροφὴν 10
αὐτοῖς κομίζεω ἀπὸ τοῦ Πόρτου ἐφίησω. εἶτα τὸν Ἄτταλον λαβὼν καὶ
στρατηγοῦ σχῆμα πληρῶν αὐτῷ, ἐπὶ τὴν Ῥάβενναν κατὰ Ὀνωρίου
στρατεύει. καὶ κελεύει Ἄτταλος τὸν Ὀνώριον τὸν ἰδιώτην ἀνθελέσθαι βίον, καὶ τῶν τοῦ σώματος ἀκρωτηριῶν τῇ περιτομῇ τὴν τοῦ
ὅλου σωτηρίαν ὠνήσασθαι. Σάρος δέ, ὃς μετὰ Στελίχωνα τὴν 15
στρατηγικὴν ἀρχὴν Ὀνωρίου δεδωκότος εἶχεν, συμβαλὼν Ἀλλαρίχῳ, κρατεῖ τῇ μάχῃ καὶ τῆς Ῥαβέννης ἀποδιώκει. ὁ δὲ τὸν
Πόρτον καταλαβών, ἀποδύει μὲν τῆς βασιλείας τὸν Ἄτταλον, οἱ μέν
φασω μὴ εὔνουν εἶναι διαβληθέντα, οἱ δὲ διότι σπονδὰς διενοεῖτο πρὸς
Ὀνώριον θέσθαι, καὶ τὸ δοκοῦν ἐμποδὼν ἑστάναι δέον ἡγεῖτο προ- 20
αποσκευάσασθαι.]

6 αἱρεῖ Gothofredus [αἵρει codd.

[3. (Procopius Wars 3,2,28-30)
᾽Επειδὴ δὲ Ἀλάριχος ἐκ Ῥώμης ἐξανίστασθαι ἔμελλεν,
Ἄτταλον τῶν τινα εὐπατριδῶν βασιλέα Ῥωμαίων ἀνεῖπε, περι-
θέμενος αὐτῷ τό τε διάδημα καὶ τὴν ἁλουργίδα καὶ εἴ τι ἄλλο ἐς
βασιλικὸν ἀξίωμα ἥκει. ἔπρασσε δὲ ταῦτα ὡς παραλύσων μὲν τῆς
βασιλείας Ὀνώριον, παραδώσων δὲ ἅπαν Ἀττάλῳ τὸ ἑσπέριον 5
κράτος. τοιαύτη μὲν γνώμη Ἄτταλός τε καὶ Ἀλάριχος ἐπὶ Ῥάβενναν
στρατῷ πολλῷ ἤεσαν. ἦν δὲ ὁ Ἄτταλος οὗτος οὔτε αὐτός τι νοεῖν
ἱκανὸς οὔτε τῷ εὖ εἰπόντι πεισθῆναι. Ἀλαρίχου γοῦν ἥκιστα ἐπαι-
νοῦντος ἐς Λιβύην στρατιᾶς χωρὶς ἄρχοντας ἔπεμψε. ταῦτα μὲν οὖν
ἐπράσσετο τῇδε.] 10

(Zosimus 6,6-12)

each to the rank and honours which he had held before.[24] Attalus, thinking that it was unsafe to live among the Romans for a while, remained together with his son with Alaric.


[2. (Philostorgius 12,3)

[Alaric] quickly occupied Portus, which is the largest dockyard of Rome, consisting of three harbours and comparable in size to a small city. In it, too, all the public grain supplies are stored according to the old custom. When he had easily taken Portus, he besieged Rome and captured it through famine rather than through other means. With Alaric's permission the Romans held a vote and chose Attalus as their Emperor. He was an Ionian by origin, a Hellene by religion and prefect of Rome. After the acclamation Alaric allowed the remnant of the people of Rome, such as had survived starvation and cannibalism, to fetch supplies from Portus. Then, taking with him Attalus, to whom he acted as master of the soldiers, he marched against Honorius at Ravenna. Attalus told Honorius to retire voluntarily to private life[25] and to purchase his survival by cutting off his extremities.[26] But Sarus, whom Honorius had appointed general after Stilicho, met Alaric in battle, defeated him and drove him from Ravenna.[27] Alaric then occupied Portus and deprived Attalus of his sovereignty, according to some because he was accused of being ill-disposed towards Alaric, while others say it was because Alaric himself was contemplating a treaty with Honorius and thought that he should first remove what appeared to be an obstacle.]


[3. (Procopius *Wars* 3,2,28-30)

When Alaric was about to leave Rome, he declared Attalus, one of the nobles, Emperor of the Romans and dressed him in the diadem and the purple and whatever else was appropriate to the office of Emperor. He did this intending to depose Honorius and hand the sole sovereignty in the West to Attalus. With this intention Attalus and Alaric moved against Ravenna with a large army. But Attalus was incapable either of planning wisely or of accepting good advice. Thus, although Alaric disapproved of it, he sent generals to Libya without an army. These things, then, were being done in this way.]


(Zosimus 6,6-12)

11

1. (Sozomen 9,9,2-5)

Οὐ πολλῷ δὲ ὕστερον Ἀλάριχος καταλαβὼν τὰς Ἄλπεις (χωρίον δὲ τοῦτο ἀμφὶ τὰ ἑξήκοντα στάδια διεστὼς τῆς Ῥαβέννης) εἰς λόγους ἦλθε τῷ βασιλεῖ περὶ τῆς εἰρήνης. Σάρος δέ τις βάρβαρος τὸ γένος, εἰς ἄκρον δὲ τὰ πολέμια ἠσκημένος, ἀμφὶ τριακοσίους μόνους περὶ αὐτὸν ἔχων πάντας εὔνους καὶ ἀρίστους, ὕποπτος ὢν     5
Ἀλαρίχῳ διὰ προτέραν ἔχθραν, ἐλογίσατο μὴ συνοίσειν αὐτῷ τὰς μεταξὺ Ῥωμαίων καὶ Γότθων σπονδάς, καὶ ἐξαπίνης μετὰ τῶν ἰδίων ἐπελθὼν ἀναιρεῖ τινας τῶν βαρβάρων. ἐκ τούτου δὲ εἰς ὀργὴν καὶ δέος καταστὰς Ἀλάριχος τὴν αὐτὴν ὁδὸν ἀναστρέφει· καὶ περι-
καθεσθεὶς τὴν Ῥώμην εἷλε προδοσίᾳ, καὶ τοῖς αὐτοῦ πλήθεσιν     10
ἐπέτρεψε ἑκάστῳ, ὡς ἂν δύναιτο, τὸν Ῥωμαίων πλοῦτον διαρπάζειν καὶ πάντας τοὺς οἴκους ληΐζεσθαι, ἄσυλον εἶναι προστάξας αἰδοῖ τῇ πρὸς τὸν ἀπόστολον Πέτρον τὴν περὶ τὴν αὐτοῦ σορὸν ἐκκλησίαν, μεγάλην τε καὶ πολὺν χῶρον περιέχουσαν. τουτὶ δὲ γέγονεν αἴτιον τοῦ μὴ ἄρδην ἀπολέσθαι τὴν Ῥώμην· οἱ γὰρ ἐνθάδε διασωθέντες     15
(πολλοὶ δὲ ἦσαν) πάλιν τὴν πόλιν ᾤκισαν.

1 τὰς Ἄλπεις codd. [Κλάσσην Cluverius

[2. (Philostorgius 12,3-4)

Μετὰ τοῦτο πρὸς Ῥάβενναν ὁ Ἀλλάριχος ἐπανελθὼν καὶ σπονδὰς προτέων, ὑπὸ τοῦ προειρημένου διεκρούσθη Σάρου, φαμένου τὸν δίκας ὀφείλοντα τῶν τολμηθέντων μὴ ἂν ἄξιον εἶναι φίλοις συντάττεσθαι. ἐκεῖθεν Ἀλλάριχος ὀργισθεὶς μετὰ ἐνιαυτὸν τῆς προτέρας ἐπὶ τὸν Πόρτον ἐφόδου ὡς πολέμιος ἐπελαύνει τῇ     5
Ῥώμῃ. καὶ τὸ ἐντεῦθεν τῆς τοσαύτης δόξης τὸ μέγεθος καὶ τὸ τῆς δυνάμεως περιώνυμον ἀλλόφυλον πῦρ καὶ ξίφος πολέμιον καὶ αἰχμαλωσία κατεμερίζετο βάρβαρος. ἐν ἐρειπίοις δὲ τῆς πόλεως κειμένης, Ἀλλάριχος τὰ κατὰ Καμπανίαν ἐληΐζετο, κἀκεῖ νόσῳ φθείρεται. ὁ δὲ τῆς αὐτοῦ γυναικὸς ἀδελφὸς ....]     10

10 post ἀδελφός lac. in codd.

[3. (Procopius Wars 3,2,27)

Τινὲς δὲ οὐχ οὕτω Ῥώμην Ἀλαρίχῳ ἁλῶναί φασιν, ἀλλὰ Πρόβην γυναῖκα, πλούτῳ τε καὶ δόξῃ ἔν γε τῇ Ῥωμαίων βουλῇ ἐπιφανεστάτην μάλιστα οὖσαν οἰκτεῖραι μὲν λιμῷ τε καὶ τῇ ἄλλῃ κακοπαθείᾳ διαφθειρομένους Ῥωμαίους, οἵ γε καὶ ἀλλήλων ἤδη ἐγεύοντο· ὁρῶσαν δὲ ὡς πᾶσα αὐτοὺς ἐλπὶς ἀγαθὴ ἐπιλελοίπει, τοῦ     5
τε ποταμοῦ καὶ τοῦ λιμένος ἐχομένου πρὸς τῶν πολεμίων, τοῖς οἰκέταις ἐγκελεύσασθαι νύκτωρ ἀνοιγνύναι τὰς πύλας.]

## 11

1. (Sozomen 9,9,2-5)

Soon afterwards Alaric occupied the Alps (which is a place about sixty stades from Ravenna)[28] and met the Emperor in a peace conference. A certain Sarus, a barbarian by birth and a highly skilled commander whose followers, though numbering only about three hundred, were all loyal and first-rate soldiers, was suspected by Alaric because of an old enmity.[29] He, thinking that it would not be to his advantage if the Romans and Goths made a treaty, suddenly launched an attack with his own men and killed some of the barbarians. Alaric, angered and shaken by this, retreated whence he had come and, blockading Rome, captured it by treachery. All of his followers he allowed to seize the wealth of the Romans as they were able and to plunder all the houses. But out of reverence for the apostle Peter he ordered that the great and spacious church over his tomb be treated as a sanctuary; and as a result of this Rome escaped utter annihilation. For those who survived there – and they were many – rebuilt the city.[30]

[2. (Philostorgius 12,3-4)

After this [i.e. the deposition of Attalus] Alaric returned to Ravenna and offered to make a treaty [with Honorius], but he was driven off by the above-mentioned Sarus, who said that one who should have paid the penalty for his audacity was unworthy to be counted amongst the friends of the Emperor. From there Alaric in anger marched as an enemy against Rome one year after his previous attack upon Portus. The great glory of her erstwhile renown and her far-famed power were then rent asunder by alien fire and enemy sword and captivity at the hands of the barbarian. And while the city lay in ruins, Alaric ravaged Campania and there died of disease. His brother-in-law . . . .[31]]

[3. (Procopius *Wars* 3,2,27)

Some say that Rome was not captured by Alaric in this way. Rather, Proba, a woman of the highest repute amongst the Roman senatorial class for her wealth and fame, felt pity for the Romans who were being killed off by starvation and who were already turning to cannibalism. Seeing that all hope of successful resistance had gone, since the river and the harbour were blockaded by the enemy, she ordered her servants at night to open the gates.[32]]

170     Olympiodorus: Text

4. (*Bibl. Cod.* 80, pp.168f.)
Ὅτι Ἀλαρίχου νόσῳ τελευτήσαντος, διάδοχος αὐτοῦ Ἀδαούλφος καθίσταται, ὁ τῆς γυναικὸς ἀδελφός.

(Zosimus 6,13)

12

(*Bibl. Cod.* 80, p.169)
Ὅτι τὸν ξηρὸν ἄρτον βουκελλάτον ὁ συγγραφεὺς καλεῖσθαί φησι, καὶ χλευάζει τὴν τῶν στρατιωτῶν ἐπωνυμίαν, ὡς ἐκ τούτου βουκελλαρίων ἐπικληθέντων.

13

1. (*Bibl. Cod.* 80, pp.169f.)
Ὅτι Κωνσταντῖνος εἰς τυραννίδα ἀρθεὶς πρεσβεύεται πρὸς Ὀνώριον, ἄκων μὲν καὶ ὑπὸ τῶν στρατιωτῶν βιασθεὶς ἀπολογούμενος ἄρξαι, συγγνώμην δὲ αἰτῶν καὶ τὴν τῆς βασιλείας ἀξιῶν κοινωνίαν· καὶ βασιλεὺς διὰ τὰ ἐνεστηκότα δυσχερῆ τέως καταδέχεται τὴν τῆς βασιλείας κοινωνίαν. κατὰ τὰς Βρεττανίας δὲ ὁ     5
Κωνσταντῖνος ἐτύγχανεν ἀνηγορευμένος, στάσει τῶν ἐκεῖσε στρατιωτῶν εἰς ταύτην ἀνηγμένος τὴν ἀρχήν. καὶ γὰρ ἐν ταύταις ταῖς
Βρεττανίαις, πρὶν ἢ Ὀνώριον τὸ ἕβδομον ὑπατεῦσαι, εἰς στάσιν
ὁρμῆσαν τὸ ἐν αὐταῖς στρατιωτικὸν Μάρκον τινὰ ἀνεῖπον αὐτοκράτορα· τοῦ δὲ ὑπ' αὐτῶν ἀναιρεθέντος, Γρατιανὸς αὐτοῖς ἀντι     10
καθίσταται· ἐπεὶ δὲ καὶ οὗτος εἰς τετράμηνον αὐτοῖς προσκοπῆς
γεγονὼς ἀπεσφάγη, Κωνσταντῖνος τότε εἰς τὸ τοῦ αὐτοκράτορος
ἀναβιβάζεται ὄνομα. οὗτος Ἰουστῖνον καὶ Νεοβιγάστην στρατηγοὺς
προβαλόμενος, καὶ τὰς Βρεττανίας ἐάσας, περαιοῦται ἅμα τῶν αὐτοῦ
ἐπὶ Βονωνίαν πόλιν οὕτω καλουμένην, παραθαλασσίαν καὶ πρώτην     15
ἐν τοῖς τῶν Γαλλιῶν ὁρίοις κειμένην. ἔνθα διατρίψας, καὶ ὅλον τὸν
Γάλλον καὶ Ἀκύτανον στρατιώτην ἰδιοποιησάμενος, κρατεῖ πάντων
τῶν μερῶν τῆς Γαλατίας μέχρι τῶν Ἄλπεων τῶν μεταξὺ Ἰταλίας
τε καὶ Γαλατίας. οὗτος δύο παῖδας ἔσχε, Κώνσταντα καὶ Ἰουλιανόν,
ὧν τὸν μὲν Κώνσταντα Καίσαρα χειροτονεῖ, εἶτα ὕστερον κατὰ τὰς     20
αὐτὰς ἡμέρας καὶ τὸν Ἰουλιανὸν νωβελίσσιμον.

16 Γαλλιῶν ὁρίοις A [Γαλατῶν ὅροις M     18, 19 Γαλατίας A [Γαλλίας M

2. (Sozomen 9,11,2 - 12,3)
Πρῶτον μὲν γὰρ οἱ ἐν Βρεττανίᾳ στρατιῶται στασιάσαντες
ἀναγορεύουσι Μάρκον τύραννον, μετὰ δὲ τοῦτον Γρατιανόν, ἀνελόντες
Μάρκον· ἐπεὶ δὲ καὶ οὗτος οὐ πλέον τεσσάρων μηνῶν διελθόντων

4. (*Bibl. Cod.* 80, pp.168f.)

When Alaric died of disease, his brother-in-law, Ataulf, succeeded him.

(Zosimus 6,13)

## 12

(*Bibl. Cod.* 80, p.169)

The historian says that dry bread is called *buccellatum* and uses it as the scornful nickname for the soldiers, who are called from it *buccellarii*.

## 13

1. (*Bibl. Cod.* 80, pp.169f.)

When Constantine had been raised to imperial power, he sent an embassy to Honorius claiming that he was Emperor unwillingly and under compulsion by the soldiers, asking pardon and proposing that he be accepted as co-ruler. Honorius, because of his current difficulties, temporarily accepted him as co-ruler. Constantine had been proclaimed Emperor in Britain as the result of a mutiny by troops there. Even before Honorius' seventh consulship [A.D. 407] the military of those provinces had revolted and proclaimed a certain Marcus Emperor. Then they killed him and raised Gratian in his stead. After about four months they grew tired of him, put him to death and proclaimed Constantine Emperor. He appointed Justinus and Neobigastes[33] generals and, leaving Britain, crossed with his forces to the port named Boulogne, which is the nearest on the coast of Gaul. There he waited and, having won the troops of Gaul and Aquitaine to his side, became master of the whole of Gaul up to the Alps which separate Italy from Gaul. Constantine had two sons, Constans and Julian, the former of whom he named Caesar; and later, during the same period, he proclaimed Julian *nobilissimus*.

2. (Sozomen 9,11,2 - 12,3)

First, the soldiers in Britain rose in revolt and named Marcus Emperor and, having killed Marcus, proclaimed Gratian. After no more than four months they killed him and raised Constantine in turn,

ἐφονεύθη παρ' αὐτῶν, πάλιν Κωνσταντῖνον χειροτονοῦσιν, οἰηθέντες,
καθότι ταύτην εἶχε προσηγορίαν, καὶ βεβαίως αὐτὸν κρατήσειν τῆς         5
βασιλείας. ἐκ τοιαύτης γὰρ αἰτίας φαίνονται καὶ τοὺς ἄλλους εἰς
τυραννίδα ἐπιλεξάμενοι. περαιωθεὶς δὲ Κωνσταντῖνος ἐκ τῆς
Βρεττανίας ἐπὶ Βονωνίαν πόλιν τῆς Γαλατίας παρὰ θάλασσαν
κειμένην προσηγάγετο τοὺς παρὰ Γαλάταις καὶ Ἀκοιτανοῖς στρατι-
ώτας· καὶ τοὺς τῇδε ὑπηκόους περιεποίησεν ἑαυτῷ μέχρι τῶν μεταξὺ   10
Ἰταλίας καὶ Γαλατίας ὅρων, ἃς Κοττίας Ἄλπεις Ῥωμαῖοι καλοῦσι.
Κώνσταντα δὲ τὸν πρεσβύτερον τῶν αὐτοῦ υἱέων, ὃν ὕστερον βασιλέως σχῆμα ἐνέδυσε, Καίσαρα τότε ἀναγορεύσας πέπομφε εἰς
Σπανίαν· ὁ δὲ τὸ ἔθνος καταλαβὼν ἄρχοντας ἰδίους κατέστησε. καὶ
δεσμίους ἀχθῆναι αὐτῷ προσέταξεν Δίδυμον καὶ Βερενιανὸν τοὺς   15
Ὀνωρίου συγγενεῖς· οἳ τὰ πρῶτα διαφερόμενοι πρὸς ἑαυτούς, εἰς
κίνδυνον καταστάντες ὡμονόησαν· καὶ πλῆθος ἀγροίκων καὶ
οἰκετῶν συλλέξαντες κοινῇ κατὰ τὴν Λυσιτανίαν παρετάξαντο καὶ
πολλοὺς ἀνεῖλον τῶν εἰς σύλληψιν αὐτῶν ἀποσταλέντων παρὰ τοῦ
τυράννου στρατιωτῶν.                                                  20
    Μετὰ δὲ ταῦτα συμμαχίας προστεθείσης τοῖς ἐναντίοις ἐζω-
γρήθησαν καὶ ἅμα ταῖς αὐτῶν γαμεταῖς ἀπήχθησαν καὶ ὕστερον
ἀνῃρέθησαν. ἐν ἑτέραις δὲ ἐπαρχίαις διατρίβοντες Θεοδοσίωλος καὶ
Λαγώδιος οἱ αὐτῶν ἀδελφοὶ φεύγουσι τὴν πατρίδα· καὶ διασῴζονται
Θεοδοσίωλος μὲν εἰς Ἰταλίαν πρὸς Ὀνώριον τὸν βασιλέα, Λαγώδιος   25
δὲ πρὸς Θεοδόσιον εἰς τὴν ἀνατολήν. καὶ ὁ μὲν Κώνστας ταῦτα
διαπραξάμενος ἐπανῆλθε πρὸς τὸν πατέρα φρουρὰν καταστήσας ἀπὸ
τῶν στρατιωτῶν τῆς ἐπὶ τὰς Σπανίας παρόδου· ἣν δεομένοις
Ἰσπανοῖς κατὰ τὸ ἀρχαῖον ἔθος φυλάττειν οὐκ ἐπέτρεψεν. ὃ καὶ
αἴτιον ἐγένετο μετὰ ταῦτα τῆς ἀπωλείας τῶν τῇδε· καταπεσούσης   30
γὰρ τῆς Κωνσταντίνου δυνάμεως ἀναλαβόντες ἑαυτοὺς Οὐάνδαλοί τε
καὶ Σούηβοι καὶ Ἀλανοί, ἔθνη βάρβαρα, τῆς παρόδου ἐκράτησαν καὶ
πολλὰ φρούρια καὶ πόλεις τῶν Ἰσπανῶν καὶ Γαλατῶν εἷλον καὶ
τοὺς ἄρχοντας τοῦ τυράννου.

(Zosimus 6,1-5)

## 14

(Bibl. Cod. 80, p.170)

    Ὅτι Ἄτταλος βασιλεύσας κατὰ Ὀνωρίου ἐπὶ Ῥάβενναν ἐκ-
στρατεύεται, καὶ πέμπεται πρὸς αὐτόν, ὡς ἐκ βασιλέως Ὀνωρίου
πρὸς βασιλέα, Ἰοβιανὸς ἔπαρχος καὶ πατρίκιος, καὶ Οὐάλης στρατηγὸς ἑκατέρας δυνάμεως, καὶ Ποτάμιος ὁ κυαίστωρ, καὶ Ἰουλιανὸς

3 Ἰοβιανὸς Α [Ἰώβιος Μ

thinking that with such a name he would certainly conquer the whole
Empire. (Others, too, seem to have been named Emperor for such a
reason.) Constantine left Britain and crossed to Boulogne, a city on the
coast of Gaul, and, having won over the soldiers in Gaul and Aquitaine,
he attached to his side the inhabitants of those regions right up to the
boundaries which divide Italy from Gaul and which the Romans call the
Cottian Alps. At that time he proclaimed Constans, his elder son,
Caesar (he later advanced him to Augustus) and sent him to Spain,
which he occupied, setting up his own officials.[34] He ordered that
Didymus and Verenianus, relatives of Honorius, be brought to him in
chains. They had initially been on bad terms, but they settled their
differences in the face of danger and, putting together an army from
amongst their peasants and servants, offered battle in Lusitania and
killed many of the soldiers whom the usurper had sent to arrest them.

Afterwards, when their enemies had received reinforcements,
Didymus and Verenianus were taken alive, carried off with their wives
and later put to death. Their brothers Theodosiolus and Lagodius, who
were living in different provinces, fled their homeland. Theodosiolus
sought safety in Italy with the Emperor Honorius, Lagodius with
Theodosius in the East. When Constans had achieved this, he returned
to his father and left some of his own soldiers to garrison the pass into
Spain, refusing to entrust this duty to the Spaniards, as was the old
custom, although they begged him to do so. Later this was the cause of
the destruction of the Spanish provinces. For when Constantine's
power had collapsed, the barbarian peoples (Vandals, Sueves and Alans)
regrouped themselves,[35] seized the pass and captured many forts and
cities of Spain and Gaul together with the officials of the usurper.

(Zosimus 6,1-5)


## 14

(*Bibl. Cod.* 80, p.170)

When Attalus became Emperor he marched against Honorius at
Ravenna. There came to him, as if from the Emperor Honorius to a
fellow Emperor, Jovian,[36] the prefect and patrician, Valens, the master
of both branches of the soldiery, Potamius, the quaestor, and Julian,

πριμικήριος τῶν νοταρίων· οἳ ἐδήλουν Ἀττάλῳ ἐπὶ κοινωνίᾳ τῆς    5
βασιλείας ἀπεστάλθαι παρὰ Ὀνωρίου. ὁ δὲ ἀπένευσεν, ἀλλὰ νῆσον
οἰκεῖν ἢ ἕτερόν τινα τόπον, ὃν ἂν βούλοιτο, συγχωρεῖν Ὀνώριον
κακῶν ἀπαθῆ. ἀποκρίνεται δὲ Ἰοβιανὸς ἡσθείς, ἐπαγγελλόμενος καὶ
σῶσαι καθ᾽ ἑνὸς μέλους τὸν βασιλέα Ὀνώριον. ἐφ᾽ ᾧ ἐπετίμησεν
Ἄτταλος Ἰοβιανῷ, ὡς οὐθενὸς ἔθους ὄντος σῶοῦσθαι βασιλέα    10
ἑκοντὶ τὴν βασιλείαν ἀποτιθέμενον. ἀλλὰ Ἰοβιανὸς μὲν πολλάκις
πρεσβεύσας καὶ μηδὲν ἀνύσας καταμένει πρὸς Ἄτταλον, πατρίκιος
Ἀττάλου ὀνομασθείς, μετέρχεται δὲ κατὰ τὴν Ῥάβενναν ἐπὶ τὸν
πραιπόσιτον Εὐσέβιον ἡ δυναστεία, ὃς μετὰ ἱκανὸν χρόνον Ἀλλοβίχου
ἐπηρείᾳ καὶ ὑποθήκῃ δημοσίᾳ καὶ ἐπ᾽ ὄψεσι τοῦ βασιλέως ῥάβδοις    15
ἀναιρεῖται.

Χρόνος ἔρρευσεν ἱκανός, καὶ μὴ πειθόμενος Ἄτταλος Ἀλαρίχῳ, σπουδῇ δὲ μάλιστα Ἰοβιανοῦ, ὃς ἦν τὴν Ὀνωρίου πρεσβείαν
προδεδωκώς, καθαιρεῖται τῆς βασιλείας, καὶ μένει τὸν ἰδιώτην παρὰ
Ἀλαρίχῳ βίον ἀνθηρημένος. ἔπειτα, μετὰ χρόνον τινὰ βασιλεύει,    20
εἶτα καθαιρεῖται. καὶ μετὰ ταῦτα ὕστερον ἐπὶ Ῥάβενναν παρα-
γεγονὼς καὶ τοὺς τῆς δεξιᾶς χειρὸς δακτύλους ἀκρωτηριασθεὶς
ἐξορίᾳ παραπέμπεται.

10 Ἰοβιανῷ A³₁ [Ἰοβίῳ A Ἰωβίῳ M    11 Ἰοβιανὸς A¹ [Ἰούβιος A Ἰώβιος M
18 Ἰοβιανοῦ A¹ [Ἰουβίου A Ἰωβίου M

15

1. (*Bibl. Cod.* 80, pp.170f.)

Ὅτι Ἀλλόβιχος μετὰ βραχὺ τὴν ἐφ᾽ ᾧ τὸν πραιπόσιτον Εὐσέβιον ἀνεῖλε δίκην τιννύς, γνώμῃ τοῦ βασιλέως κατὰ πρόσωπον
αὐτοῦ ἀναιρεῖται· καὶ Κωνσταντῖνος ὁ τύραννος τὸν Ἀλλοβίχου
θάνατον μαθών, ἐπειγόμενος πρὸς Ῥάβενναν ὥστε σπείσασθαι
Ὀνωρίῳ, φοβηθεὶς ὑποστρέφει.    5

(Sozomen 9,12,4-6)

Κωνσταντῖνος δὲ τέως κατὰ γνώμην πράττειν δοκῶν, Κώνσταντα τὸν υἱὸν ἀντὶ Καίσαρος βασιλέα καταστήσας, ἐβουλεύετο τὴν
Ἰταλίαν καταλαβεῖν· καὶ παραμείψας τὰς Κοττίας Ἄλπεις ἧκεν εἰς
Λιβερῶνα πόλιν τῆς Λιγουρίας. μέλλων δὲ περαιοῦσθαι τὸν Ἠρι-
δανὸν τὴν αὐτὴν ὁδὸν ἀνέστρεψε, μαθὼν τὸν Ἀλαβίχου θάνατον· ὃν    5
δὴ στρατηγὸν Ὀνωρίου ὄντα καὶ ὕποπτον ὡς Κωνσταντίνῳ πραγμα-
τευόμενον πᾶσαν τὴν πρὸς τὴν δύσιν ἡγεμονίαν, ἀναιρεθῆναι συνέβη
τότε, προηγούμενον, ὡς ἔθος, ἐπανιόντος ἐκ προόδου τινὸς τοῦ

4 Λιβερῶνα codd. [Βέρωνα Valesius, Bidez

the chief of the notaries. They told Attalus that they had been sent by Honorius to discuss sharing the sovereignty. This Attalus rejected, but he offered to allow Honorius, without suffering any harm, to retire to an island or any other place of his own choosing. This pleased Jovian, who added that Honorius should be mutilated in one limb. Attalus censured Jovian for this suggestion, saying that it was not customary to mutilate an Emperor who had willingly resigned his office. Jovian, having shuttled between the two Emperors often and to no avail, remained with Attalus and was given the title of Attalus' patrician. At Ravenna power then passed to the chamberlain Eusebius. However, after a time, as a result of the manoeuvrings of Allobich, by public decree he was beaten to death with rods before the eyes of the Emperor.

After a while Attalus, who refused to take orders from Alaric, was deposed at the urging of Jovian (the betrayer of his mission for Honorius) and chose to remain with Alaric as a private individual. Then, some time later he became Emperor again and was again deposed. Later still he came to Ravenna where the fingers of his right hand were cut off and he was sentenced to exile.

## 15

1. (*Bibl. Cod.* 80, pp.170f.)

Shortly afterwards Allobich was put to death with the consent of the Emperor and before his eyes, and thus paid the penalty for his destruction of the chamberlain Eusebius. The usurper Constantine, who was marching to Ravenna to treat with Honorius, became afraid and turned back when he learned of the death of Allobich.

2. (Sozomen 9,12,4-6)

While things seemed to be proceeding as Constantine planned, he promoted his son Constans from Caesar to Augustus and laid plans to take Italy. Skirting the Cottian Alps, he came to Libarna,[37] a city of Liguria, and was about to cross the Po when he heard of Allobich's death, at which he retraced his steps. Allobich was one of Honorius' generals who was suspected of plotting to hand over the sovereignty of all the West to Constantine. It happened that he was killed as he was marching ahead of the Emperor, as was customary, when the latter was returning from

κρατοῦντος· ἡνίκα δὴ καὶ ὁ βασιλεὺς αὐτίκα τοῦ ἵππου ἀποβὰς δημοσίᾳ εὐχαριστήρια τῷ θεῷ ηὔξατο ὡς προφανοῦς ἐπιβούλου ἀπαλ-   10
λαγείς. Κωνσταντῖνος δὲ φεύγων τὴν Ἀρήλατον κατέλαβε, κατὰ
ταὐτὸν δὲ καὶ Κώνστας ὁ αὐτοῦ παῖς φεύγων ἐκ τῆς Ἰσπανίας. καταπεσούσης γὰρ τῆς Κωνσταντίνου δυνάμεως ἀναλαβόντες ἑαυτοὺς
Οὐάνδαλοί τε καὶ Σουῆβοι καὶ Ἀλανοὶ σπουδῇ τὸ Πυρηναῖον ὄρος
κατέλαβον, εὐδαίμονα καὶ πλουσιωτάτην τὴν χώραν ἀκούοντες.   15
παρημεληκότων τε τῶν ἐπιτραπέντων παρὰ Κώνσταντος τὴν
φρουρὰν τῆς παρόδου παρῆλθον εἰς Ἰσπανίαν.

## 16
(*Bibl. Cod.* 80, p.171)

Ὅτι τὸ Ῥήγιον μητρόπολίς ἐστι τῆς Βρεττίας, ἐξ οὗ φησὶν ὁ
ἱστορικὸς Ἀλάριχον ἐπὶ Σικελίαν βουλόμενον περαιωθῆναι ἐπισχε-
θῆναι· ἄγαλμα γάρ, φησί, τετελεσμένον ἱστάμενον ἐκώλυσε τὴν
περαίωσιν. τετέλεστο δέ, ὡς μυθολογεῖ, παρὰ τῶν ἀρχαίων ἀπο-
τρόπαιόν τε τοῦ ἀπὸ τῆς Αἴτνης πυρὸς καὶ πρὸς κώλυσιν παρόδου διὰ   5
θαλάσσης βαρβάρων· ἐν γὰρ τῷ ἑνὶ ποδὶ πῦρ ἀκοίμητον ἐτύγχανε,
καὶ ἐν τῷ ἑτέρῳ ὕδωρ ἀδιάφθορον. οὗ καταλυθέντος, ὕστερον ἔκ τε
τοῦ Αἰτναίου πυρὸς καὶ ἐκ τῶν βαρβάρων βλάβας ἡ Σικελία ἐδέξατο.
κατέστρεψε δὲ τὸ ἄγαλμα Ἀσκληπιὸς ὁ τῶν ἐν Σικελίᾳ κτημάτων
Κωνσταντίου καὶ Πλακιδίας διοικητὴς καταστάς.   10

## 17
1. (*Bibl. Cod.* 80, pp.171f.)

Ὅτι Κωνσταντίνου τοῦ τυράννου καὶ Κώνσταντος τοῦ παιδός,
ὃς πρότερον μὲν Καῖσαρ ἔπειτα δὲ καὶ βασιλεὺς ἐκεχειροτόνητο,
τούτων ἡττηθέντων καὶ πεφευγότων, Γερόντιος ὁ στρατηγός, τὴν
πρὸς τοὺς βαρβάρους ἀσμενίσας εἰρήνην, Μάξιμον τὸν ἑαυτοῦ παῖδα,
εἰς τὴν τῶν δομεστίκων τάξιν τελοῦντα, βασιλέα ἀναγορεύει· εἶτα   5
ἐπιδιώξας Κώνσταντα κατεπράξατο ἀναιρεθῆναι, καὶ κατὰ πόδας
εἵπετο διώκων καὶ τὸν πατέρα Κωνσταντῖνον. ἐν ᾧ δὲ ταῦτα ἐγίνετο,
Κωνστάντιος καὶ Οὐλφιλᾶς ἀποστέλλονται παρὰ Ὀνωρίου κατὰ
Κωσταντίνου, καὶ καταλαβόντες τὴν Ἀρήλατον, ἔνθα τὰς διατριβὰς
ἐποιεῖτο Κωνσταντῖνος σὺν Ἰουλιανῷ τῷ παιδί, ταύτην πολιορκοῦσι.   10
καὶ Κωνσταντῖνος καταφυγὼν εἰς εὐκτήριον πρεσβύτερος τότε χειροτονεῖται, ὅρκων αὐτῷ ὑπὲρ σωτηρίας δοθέντων· καὶ τοῖς πολιορ-
κοῦσιν αἱ πύλαι τῆς πόλεως ἀναπετάννυνται. καὶ πέμπεται σὺν τῷ
υἱῷ Κωνσταντῖνος πρὸς Ὀνώριον· ὁ δὲ μνησικακῶν αὐτοῖς ὑπὲρ τῶν
ἀνεψιῶν αὐτοῦ, οὓς ἐτύγχανε Κωνσταντῖνος ἀνελών, πρὸ τριάκοντα   15

15 αὐτοῦ Bekker [αὐτοῦ codd.

some procession. On that occasion the Emperor dismounted and pub-
licly gave thanks to God for his deliverance from a manifest plotter.[38]
Constantine in retreat reached Arles at the same time as his son Constans, who was in flight from Spain. For when Constantine's power
collapsed, the Vandals, Sueves and Alans regrouped themselves,
speedily seized the Pyrenees mountains, hearing that the land there was
fertile and very rich, and entered Spain. For those to whom Constans
had entrusted the guarding of the pass neglected their duty.[39]

## 16

(*Bibl. Cod.* 80, p.171)
   Rhegium is the metropolis of Bruttium. According to the historian, Alaric wished to cross from there to Sicily, but was prevented.
The reason, he says, was that a statue, endowed with magic powers, was
standing there and it thwarted the crossing. The story is that this statue
was consecrated by the ancients to ward off the fires of Etna and to
prevent the barbarians from crossing by sea. In one foot there was a
perpetual flame, in the other a never-ending spring. When it was destroyed, Sicily later suffered harm from both Etna's fires and the
barbarians. It was Asclepius, who had been appointed steward of the
Sicilian estates of Constantius and Placidia, who overthrew the statue.

## 17

1. (*Bibl. Cod.* 80, pp.171f.)
   When Constantine the usurper and his son Constans, whom he
had first named Caesar and then Augustus, had been beaten and put to
flight, the general Gerontius eagerly made peace with the barbarians
and proclaimed Emperor his own son[40] Maximus, who was enrolled in
the corps of the *domestici*. Then he pursued Constans and brought
about his death and dogged the steps of his father Constantine also.
While these things were happening, Constantius and Ulfilas, who had
been sent by Honorius against Constantine, reached Arles, where
Constantine was staying with his son Julian, and besieged the city.
Constantine fled to an oratory where he was ordained priest after oaths
had been given to him for his safety. Then the gates of the city were
opened to the besiegers. Constantine and his son were sent to Honorius,
who held a grudge against them because of his cousins whom Constantine had killed and ordered them to be executed thirty miles from

τῆς Ραβέννης μιλίων παρὰ τοὺς ὅρκους προστάττει τούτους ἀναιρε-
θῆναι· Γερόντιος δὲ παραγενομένων Οὐλφιλᾶ καὶ Κωνσταντίνου
φεύγει, καὶ καταληφθείς, ὅτι ἐγκρατῶς ἦρχε τοῦ οἰκείου στρατοῦ, ὑπ'
αὐτῶν ἐκείνων ἐπιβουλεύεται· πῦρ γὰρ κατὰ τῆς οἰκίας αὐτοῦ
ἀνῆψαν. ὁ δὲ πρὸς τοὺς ἐπαναστάντας κρατερῶς ἐμάχετο, ἕνα συν-          20
αγωνιστὴν ἔχων Ἀλανὸν τὸ γένος, εἰς δούλους αὐτοῦ ἀριθμούμενον.
τέλος τόν τε Ἀλανὸν καὶ τὴν γυναῖκα, τοῦτο προθυμουμένους, ἀναιρεῖ,
ἐπικατασφάζει δὲ καὶ ἑαυτόν. Μάξιμος δὲ ὁ παῖς ταῦτα μαθὼν πρὸς
τοὺς ὑποσπόνδους φεύγει βαρβάρους.

2. (Sozomen 9,13,1 - 15,3)

Ἐν τούτῳ δὲ Γερόντιος ὁ τῶν Κωνσταντίνου στρατηγῶν
ἄριστος δυσμενὴς αὐτῷ γέγονεν· ἐπιτήδειόν τε εἰς τυραννίδα
Μάξιμον τὸν αὐτοῦ οἰκεῖον νομίσας βασιλικὴν ἐνέδυσεν ἐσθῆτα καὶ ἐν
Ταρακόνῃ διάγειν εἴασεν. αὐτὸς δὲ Κωνσταντίνῳ ἐπεστράτευσεν, ἐν
παρόδῳ Κώνσταντα τὸν υἱὸν αὐτοῦ ἐν Βιέννῃ ὄντα ἀναιρεθῆναι            5
παρασκευάσας. ἐπεὶ δὲ ἔμαθε Κωνσταντῖνος τὰ κατὰ Μάξιμον, Ἐδόβιχον μὲν τὸν αὐτοῦ στρατηγὸν πέραν τοῦ Ῥήνου πέπομφε Φράγκων
τε καὶ Ἀλαμανῶν συμμαχίαν προτρεψόμενον, Κώνσταντι δὲ τῷ
αὐτοῦ παιδὶ Βιέννης καὶ τῶν τῇδε πόλεων τὴν φυλακὴν ἐπέτρεψε.
καὶ Γερόντιος μὲν ἐπὶ τὴν Ἀρήλατον ἐλάσας ἐπολιόρκει τὴν πόλιν,        10
μετ' οὐ πολὺ δὲ στρατιᾶς Ὀνωρίου κατὰ τοῦ τυράννου παραγενο-
μένης, ἧς ἡγεῖτο Κωνστάντιος ὁ τοῦ Οὐαλεντινιανοῦ τοῦ βασιλέως
πατήρ, φεύγει παραχρῆμα μετ' ὀλίγων στρατιωτῶν· οἱ γὰρ πλείους
τοῖς ἀμφὶ τὸν Κωνστάντιον προσεχώρησαν. οἱ δὲ ἐν Ἱσπανίᾳ στρατιῶται εὐκαταφρόνητον ἀπὸ τῆς φυγῆς δόξαντα τὸν Γερόντιον ἐβουλεύ-       15
σαντο ἀνελεῖν· καὶ φραξάμενοι νύκτωρ αὐτοῦ τὴν οἰκίαν κατέδραμον.
ὁ δὲ μεθ' ἑνὸς Ἀλανοῦ ἐπιτηδείου καὶ ὀλίγων οἰκετῶν ἄνωθεν
τοξεύων ὑπὲρ τοὺς τριακοσίους ἀναιρεῖ στρατιώτας. ἐπιλειψάντων
δὲ τῶν βελῶν φεύγουσιν οἱ οἰκέται καθέντες ἑαυτοὺς λάθρα ἀπὸ τοῦ
οἰκήματος. Γερόντιος δὲ τὸν ἴσον τρόπον διασωθῆναι δυνάμενος οὐχ      20
εἵλετο, κατασχεθεὶς ἔρωτι Νοννιχίας τῆς αὐτοῦ γαμετῆς. περὶ δὲ
τὴν ἕω πῦρ ἐμβαλόντων τῇ οἰκίᾳ τῶν στρατιωτῶν οὐκ ἔχων λοιπὸν
σωτηρίας ἐλπίδα ἑκόντος τοῦ συνόντος αὐτῷ Ἀλανοῦ ἀποτέμνει τὴν
κεφαλήν. μετὰ δὲ ταῦτα καὶ τῆς ἰδίας γαμετῆς, ὀλοφυρομένης καὶ
μετὰ δακρύων προσωθούσης ἑαυτὴν τῷ ξίφει καὶ πρὶν ὑφ' ἑτέροις        25
γενέσθαι παρὰ τοῦ ἀνδρὸς ἀποθανεῖν αἰτούσης καὶ τοῦτο δῶρον
ὕστατον παρ' αὐτοῦ λαβεῖν ἀντιβολούσης. καὶ ἡ μὲν ἀνδρεία γυνὴ τῆς
θρησκείας ἐπαξίως (ἦν γὰρ Χριστιανή) ὧδε τέθνηκε, κρείττονα

21 Νοννιχίας codd. [Νουνεχίας Valesius          28 φανεῖσα post ἐπαξίως add.
aliqui codd.

Ravenna contrary to the oaths. Gerontius, who had fled at the arrival of Constantius and Ulfilas, because he had been a firm commander fell victim to a conspiracy of his own troops, who ambushed him, setting fire to his house. With the help of one of his slaves, an Alan by race, he fought stoutly against his assailants, but finally killed the Alan and his own wife at their request and then ran himself through. When this news reached his son Maximus, he fled to the barbarian allies.

2. (Sozomen 9,13,1 - 15,3)

Meanwhile Gerontius, the best of Constantine's generals, became hostile to him and, thinking that his own dependent Maximus was well qualified to be Emperor, clothed him in the imperial raiment and allowed him to reside in Tarraco. He himself marched against Constantine and on the way killed his son Constans at Vienne.[41] When Constantine learned that Maximus had been made Emperor, he sent his general Edobich across the Rhine to obtain reinforcements from the Franks and the Alamanni and entrusted to his own son Constans the defence of Vienne and the other cities of the region. Gerontius attacked Arles and besieged the city, but when shortly afterwards an army arrived which Honorius had sent against the usurper and which was led by Constantius, the father of the Emperor Valentinian, Gerontius fled in haste with a few of his troops, since the majority joined Constantius' forces. The Spanish soldiery, thinking that Gerontius seemed an object of scorn as a result of his flight, plotted to destroy him and, surrounding his house during the night, attacked it.[42] But he, with one Alan friend and a few dependents, poured arrows down upon the soldiers and killed over three hundred of them. When the arrows had run out the dependents escaped by letting themselves down secretly from the building. Gerontius could have done likewise, but love for his wife Nonnichia detained him. Around daybreak the soldiers set fire to the house and, since all hope of safety had gone, Gerontius, at the request of the Alan, who had stayed with him, cut off his head. Thereupon Gerontius' wife, with tears and lamentations, threw herself upon the sword, demanding to die by her husband's hand before she came into the power of others and beseeching him to grant her this last gift. In this way the brave woman died a death worthy of her religion (for she was a Christian) and handed down to posterity an immortal memory

λήϑης τὴν περὶ αὐτῆς μνήμην τῷ χρόνῳ παραδοῦσα· Γερόντιος δὲ
τρίτον ἑαυτὸν τῷ ξίφει παίσας, ὡς οὐ καιρίαν λαβὼν ᾔσϑετο, σπασά-    30
μενος τὸ παρὰ τὸν μηρὸν ξιφίδιον κατὰ τῆς καρδίας ἤλασε.
Κωνσταντῖνος δὲ περικαϑημένης τῆς Ὀνωρίου στρατιᾶς ἔτι
πρὸς τὴν πολιορκίαν ἀντεῖχεν, ἀγγελϑέντος Ἐδοβίχου μετὰ πλείστης
συμμαχίας ἥξειν. τοῦτο δὲ καὶ τοὺς Ὀνωρίου στρατηγοὺς οὐ μετρίως
ἐφόβει· βουλευσαμένων τε αὐτῶν ἀναστρέφειν εἰς Ἰταλίαν κἀκεῖ    35
πειραϑῆναι τοῦ πολέμου καί, ἐπειδὴ τοῦτο συνεδόκει, πλησίον ἀγγελϑέντος Ἐδοβίχου περῶσι Ῥοδανὸν τὸν ποταμόν. καὶ Κωνστάντιος
μὲν ἔχων τοὺς πεζοὺς ἐπιόντας περιμένει τοὺς πολεμίους, Οὐλφίλας
δὲ ὁ Κωνσταντίου συστράτηγος οὐ πόρρωϑεν ἀποκρυβεὶς μετὰ τῶν
ἱππέων ἐλάνϑανεν. ἐπεὶ δὲ τὸν λόχον παραμείψαντες ἡ Ἐδοβίχου    40
στρατιὰ ἔμελλον εἰς χεῖρας ἰέναι τῶν ἀμφὶ τὸν Κωνστάντιον, σημείου
δοϑέντος ἐξαπίνης ἀναφανεὶς Οὐλφίλας κατὰ νώτου τῶν πολεμίων
ἤλαυνεν· αὐτίκα τε τροπῆς γενομένης οἱ μὲν φεύγουσιν, οἱ δὲ ἀναι-
ροῦνται· οἱ δὲ πλείους τὰ ὅπλα ἀποϑέμενοι συγγνώμην ᾔτησαν καὶ
φειδοῦς ἠξιώϑησαν. Ἐδόβιχος δὲ ἵππου ἐπιβὰς ἔφυγεν εἰς ἀγρόν τινα    45
πρὸς Ἐκδίκιον τὸν κεκτημένον, πλεῖστα παρ' αὐτοῦ Ἐδοβίχου
πρότερον εὐηργετημένον καὶ φίλον νομιζόμενον. ὁ δὲ τὴν αὐτοῦ
κεφαλὴν ἀποτεμὼν προσφέρει τοῖς Ὀνωρίου στρατηγοῖς ἐπ' ἐλπίδι
μεγάλων δώρων καὶ τιμῆς. Κωνστάντιος δὲ τὴν μὲν κεφαλὴν
δεχϑῆναι προσέταξε, χάριν ἔχειν Ἐκδικίῳ τὸ δημόσιον εἰπὼν τῆς    50
ἀφίλου πράξεως· συνεῖναι δὲ σπουδάζοντα αὐτὸν ἀναχωρῆσαι
ἐκέλευσεν, οὐκ ἀγαϑὴν ἡγησάμενος κακοῦ ξενοδόχου τὴν συνουσίαν
ἔσεσϑαι αὐτῷ ἢ τῇ στρατιᾷ. καὶ ὁ μὲν φίλου ἀνδρὸς καὶ ξένου ἐν
δυσπραγίᾳ διακειμένου ἀνοσιώτατον φόνον τολμήσας κατὰ κενῆς,
τοῦτο δὴ τὸ τοῦ λόγου, χανὼν ἀπῆλϑε.    55

Μετὰ δὲ τὴν νίκην ἀντιπεραιωϑείσης αὖϑις πρὸς τὴν πόλιν τῆς
Ὀνωρίου στρατιᾶς, μαϑὼν Κωνσταντῖνος ἀνηρῆσϑαι τὸν Ἐδόβιχον
αὐτὸς ἑαυτῷ τὴν ἁλουργίδα καὶ τὰ τῆς βασιλείας σύμβολα ἀπέϑετο·
καὶ καταλαβὼν τὴν ἐκκλησίαν χειροτονεῖται πρεσβύτερος. ὅρκους
τε πρότερον λαβόντες οἱ ἔσω τειχῶν ἀνοίγουσι τὰς πύλας καὶ    60
φειδοῦς ἀξιοῦνται πάντες. καὶ τὸ ἐξ ἐκείνου πάλιν τὸ τῇδε ὑπήκοον εἰς
τὴν Ὀνωρίου ἡγεμονίαν ἐπανῆλϑε καὶ τοῖς ὑπ' αὐτὸν ἄρχουσιν
ἐπείϑετο. Κωνσταντῖνος δὲ ἅμα Ἰουλιανῷ τῷ παιδὶ παραπεμφϑεὶς
εἰς Ἰταλίαν, πρὶν φϑάσαι κατὰ τὴν ὁδὸν κτίννυται.

---

40-41 ἡ Ἐδοβίχου στρατιὰ alt. οἱ πολέμιοι τοῦ Οὐλφίλα τῇ στρατιᾷ    51 ἀφίλου
alt. Οὐλφίλα

of herself. Thirdly, Gerontius struck himself with his sword and, when he realised that the blow was not fatal, drew the dagger which he carried by his thigh and plunged it into his heart.

Although Honorius' army was still pressing the siege of Arles, Constantine refused to yield since he had been informed that Edobich was on his way with a very large army of reinforcements. This news greatly alarmed Honorius' generals, who decided to fall back to Italy and prosecute the war there. When they had agreed upon this course of action, it was reported that Edobich was close at hand. They crossed the Rhone, and Constantius with the infantry awaited the enemy's attack, while Ulfilas, his co-commander, remained in ambush with the cavalry. When Edobich's army had passed by the ambush and began to engage with Constantius' force, at a given signal Ulfilas suddenly charged and took the enemy from the rear. The rout was immediate: some fled, some were killed, but most threw down their weapons, called for quarter and received it. Edobich mounted a horse and fled to the lands possessed[43] by one Ecdicius, for whom in the past he had performed many favours and whom he thought to be his friend. But Ecdicius cut off his head and took it to Honorius' generals hoping to receive great gifts and high honour as a reward. Constantius ordered the head to be accepted and declared that the state thanked Ecdicius for his unfriendly action.[44] But when Ecdicius sought to stay with him Constantius ordered him to depart, thinking that the presence of one who had been such a poor host would be a bad thing both for himself and for the army. Thus, having committed the sin of murdering a friend and a guest in dire straits, Ecdicius went away, his mouth agape to no avail, as the saying goes.[45]

After the victory, the army of Honorius re-crossed the river and recommenced the siege of the city. When Constantine learned that Edobich had been destroyed, he himself put off the purple and the symbols of sovereignty and, entering a church, was ordained priest. Those within the walls, having first received oaths of safety, opened the gates and all were spared. Thenceforth the population of that area again came under Honorius' sovereignty and obeyed his governors. Constantine and Julian his son were sent to Italy, but they were killed before they arrived.

## 18

(*Bibl. Cod.* 80, pp.172f.)

Ὅτι Ἰοβῖνος ἐν Μουνδιακῷ τῆς ἑτέρας Γερμανίας κατὰ σπουδὴν Γώαρ τοῦ Ἀλανοῦ καὶ Γυντιαρίου, ὃς φύλαρχος ἐχρημάτιζε τῶν Βουργουντιόνων, τύραννος ἀνηγορεύθη. πρὸς ὃν παραγενέσθαι Ἄτταλος Ἀδαοῦλφον παραινεῖ· καὶ παραγίνεται ἅμα τοῦ πλήθους. καὶ Ἰοβῖνος ἀνιᾶται ἐπὶ τῇ Ἀδαούλφου παρουσίᾳ καὶ μέμφεται δι᾽    5
αἰνιγμάτων τῷ παραινέσαντι Ἀττάλῳ τὴν ἄφιξιν. καὶ Σάρος δὲ ἔμελλε πρὸς Ἰοβῖνον παραγενέσθαι· ἀλλ᾽ Ἀδαοῦλφος τοῦτο μαθὼν προϋπαντιάζει χιλιάδας δέκα συνεπαγόμενος στρατιώτην, ἔχοντι ἄνδρας περὶ αὐτὸν Σάρῳ ὀκτωκαίδεκα ἢ καὶ εἴκοσιν. ὃν ἔργα ἡρωϊκὰ καὶ θαυμάσαι ἄξια ἐπιδειξάμενον μόλις σόκκοις ἐζώγρησαν, καὶ    10
ὕστερον ἀναιροῦσι. Σάρος δ᾽ ἦν ἀποστὰς Ὀνωρίου ὅτι Βελλερίδου, ὃς ἦν αὐτῷ δομέστικος, ἀναιρεθέντος οὐδεὶς λόγος τῷ βασιλεῖ τῆς ἀναιρέσεως οὐδὲ τοῦ φόνου γίνεται εἴσπραξις.
(Cf. Sozomen 9,15,3 = *Fr.* 20,2; Philostorgius 12,6 = *Fr.* 20,3)

3 ὃν M [οὓς A²    4 τοῦ πλήθους A [τῷ πληθῷ M    9 Σάρῳ edd. [Ἀσάρῳ
codd., Henry    10 σόκκοις A [σάκκοις M

## 19

(*Bibl. Cod.* 80, p.173)

Ὅτι διαλαμβάνει περὶ Δονάτου καὶ περὶ τῶν Οὔννων, καὶ περὶ τῶν ῥηγῶν αὐτῶν τῆς εὐφυεστάτης τοξείας, καὶ ὡς πρὸς αὐτοὺς καὶ Δόνατον ὁ ἱστορικὸς ἐπρέσβευσε. καὶ τὴν διὰ θαλάσσης αὐτοῦ πλάνην ἐκτραγῳδεῖ καὶ τὸν κίνδυνον. καὶ ὅπως ὅρκῳ Δόνατος ἀπατηθεὶς ἐκθέσμως ἀποσφάζεται, καὶ ὅπως Χαράτων, ὁ τῶν    5
ῥηγῶν πρῶτος, ἐπὶ τῷ φόνῳ εἰς θυμὸν ἀνάπτεται, ὅπως τε πάλιν βασιλικοῖς δώροις διαπραΰνεται καὶ ἡσυχάζει· ἐν οἷς καὶ ἡ πρώτη τῆς ἱστορίας δεκάλογος.

3 αὐτοῦ Bekker [αὑτοῦ codd.

## 20

1. (*Bibl. Cod. loc.cit.*)

Ἄρχεται δὲ ἡ δευτέρα ὧδε, ὅτι Ἰοβῖνος, παρὰ γνώμην Ἀδα-ούλφου τὸν ἴδιον ἀδελφὸν Σεβαστιανὸν βασιλέα χειροτονήσας, εἰς ἔχθραν Ἀδαούλφῳ κατέστη· καὶ πέμπει Ἀδαοῦλφος πρὸς Ὀνώριον πρέσβεις ὑποσχόμενος τάς τε τῶν τυράννων κεφαλὰς καὶ εἰρήνην ἄγειν. ὧν ὑποστρεψάντων καὶ ὅρκων μεσιτευσάντων Σεβαστιανοῦ    5
μὲν πέμπεται τῷ βασιλεῖ ἡ κεφαλή, Ἰοβῖνος δὲ ὑπὸ Ἀδαούλφου πολιορκούμενος ἑαυτὸν ἐκδίδωσι. καὶ πέμπεται κἀκεῖνος τῷ βασιλεῖ,

**18**

(*Bibl. Cod.* 80, pp.172f.)

At Mundiacum[46] in Second Germany Jovinus was proclaimed Emperor with the support of Goar the Alan and Guntiarius, whose title was tribal chief of the Burgundians. Attalus advised Ataulf to join Jovinus, which he did together with his army. Jovinus was distressed by the presence of Ataulf and in oblique terms[47] blamed Attalus, who had advised him to come. Sarus, too, was on his way to join Jovinus, but Ataulf, when he learned this, went out to meet him with an army of ten thousand men. Although Sarus had with him only eighteen or twenty men, he performed heroic deeds remarkable to recount, and was only with difficulty captured alive with lassoes[48] and later put to death. Sarus had left Honorius because when Belleridus his attendant had been killed, the Emperor neither explained the death nor punished the murder.

(Cf. Sozomen 9,15,3 = *Fr.* 20,2; Philostorgius 12,6 = *Fr.* 20,3)

**19**

(*Bibl. Cod.* 80, p.173)

[Olympiodorus] discusses Donatus and the Huns and the natural talent of their kings for archery. The historian describes the embassy on which he went to them and to Donatus and he waxes tragical on his wanderings over the sea and the danger he faced. He tells how Donatus was deceived by an oath and wickedly killed, how Charaton, the first of the kings, flared up with rage at the murder and how he was calmed down and pacified with regal gifts. This marks the end of the first group of ten books.[49]

**20**

1. (*Bibl. Cod. loc.cit.*)

The second part of the History begins as follows. Against the wish of Ataulf Jovinus named his own brother, Sebastian, Emperor and incurred Ataulf's enmity. The latter sent an embassy to Honorius promising him both the heads of the usurpers and a peace treaty. The embassy returned, oaths were exchanged and the head of Sebastian was sent to the Emperor. Jovinus was besieged by Ataulf and surrendered. He was sent to the Emperor, but the prefect Dardanus, when he had

## 184   Olympiodorus: Text

ὃν αὐθεντήσας Δάρδανος ὁ ἔπαρχος ἀναιρεῖ· καὶ ἀποτίθενται ἄμφω
αἱ κεφαλαὶ Καρθαγένης ἔξωθεν, ἔνθα καὶ ἡ Κωνσταντίνου καὶ ἡ
Ἰουλιανοῦ ἀπετμήθησαν πρότερον, ἥ τε Μαξιμίνου καὶ ἡ Εὐγενίου, οἳ   10
ἐπὶ Θεοδοσίου τοῦ μεγάλου τυραννίδι ἐπιθέμενοι, εἰς τοῦτο τέλους
κατέστρεψαν.

9 Καρθαγένης codd. [᾿Ραβέννης Schottus       10 Μαξιμίνου codd. [Μαξίμου
Labbaeus.

2. (Sozomen 9,15,3)
    Οὐ πολλῷ δὲ ὕστερον ἀδοκήτως ἀναιροῦνται Ἰοβιανός τε καὶ
Μάξιμος οἱ προειρημένοι τύραννοι καὶ Σάρος καὶ ἄλλοι πλεῖστοι ἐπὶ
τούτοις ἐπιβουλεύσαντες τῇ Ὀνωρίου βασιλείᾳ.

[3. (Philostorgius 12,6)
    Κατὰ δὲ τοὺς αὐτοὺς χρόνους Ἰωβιανός τε ἐπανέστη <τῷ
βασιλεῖ, καὶ ταχὺ> εἰς φθορὰν ἀπέσβη, καὶ Σεβαστιανὸς ὁ ἀδελφὸς
αὐτοῦ τοῖς ἴσοις ἐποφθαλμήσας τὴν ἴσην ἔδωκε δίκην.]

1-2 τῷ βασιλεῖ, καὶ ταχὺ add. Bochart in lac. xiii litterarum

[21]
[(Philostorgius 12,6)
    <Ὁ δ᾿ Ἡρακλειανὸς> μιμησάμενος τούτους καὶ πλέον τῷ τῆς
τύχης γέλῳ ἐπιβάς, εὐκλεεστέραν ἔσχεν τὴν καταστροφήν....]

1 Ὁ δ᾿ Ἡρακλειανὸς add. Gothofredus in lac. xii litterarum

22
1. (Bibl. Cod. 80, pp.173f.)
    Ἀδαοῦλφος δὲ Πλακιδίαν ἀπῃτεῖτο κατὰ σπουδὴν μάλιστα
Κωνσταντίου, ὃς ὕστερον αὐτῇ καὶ εἰς γάμον ἔζευξεν. ἀλλὰ τῶν
πρὸς Ἀδαοῦλφον ὑποσχέσεων μὴ περαιουμένων, καὶ μάλιστα τῆς
σιτοπομπίας, οὔτε ταύτην ἀπεδίδου καὶ εἰς μάχην ἐμελετᾶτο τὰ τῆς
εἰρήνης διαλύεσθαι.

2. (Bibl. Cod. 80, p.174)
    Ὅτι Ἀδαοῦλφος ἀπαιτούμενος Πλακιδίαν ἀνταπῄτει τὸν ὁρισ-
θέντα σῖτον. ἀπόρων δ᾿ ὄντων τῶν ὑποσχομένων εἰς τὸ δοῦναι, οὐδὲν
δὲ ἧττον ὁμολογούντων, εἰ λάβοιεν Πλακιδίαν παρασχεῖν, καὶ ὁ βάρβαρος τὰ ὅμοια ὑπεκρίνετο, καὶ πρὸς Μασσαλίαν, πόλιν οὕτω καλουμένην, παραγενόμενος δόλῳ ταύτην λαβεῖν ἤλπιζεν. ἔνθα πληγεὶς   5
Βονηφατίου τοῦ γενναιοτάτου βαλόντος, καὶ μόλις τὸν θάνατον
διαφυγών, εἰς τὰς οἰκείας ὑπεχώρησε σκηνάς, τὴν πόλιν ἐν εὐθυμίᾳ

him in his power, slew him. Both of the heads were exposed outside
Carthage, in the same place where the heads of Constantine and Julian
had been cut off earlier and where those of Maximinus and Eugenius,
who had tried usurpation during the reign of Theodosius the Great, had
met the same end.[50]

2. (Sozomen 9,15,3)
    Shortly afterwards Jovianus and Maximus, the aforementioned
usurpers, were unexpectedly killed and Sarus and many others who
plotted against the Emperor Honorius during these times.[51]

[3. (Philostorgius 12,6)
    During the same period Jovianus revolted <from the Emperor
and quickly> came to destruction, and his brother Sebastian, who had
similar ambitions, paid the same penalty.]

# [21]

[(Philostorgius 12,6)
    <Heraclian> followed their example [i.e. of Jovinus and Se-
bastian] and, having for the amusement of fortune enjoyed greater
success, he suffered a more disgraceful downfall . . . .][52]

## 22

1. (*Bibl. Cod.* 80, pp.173f.)
    Ataulf was asked to return Placidia at the urging especially of
Constantius, who later married her. But when the promises to Ataulf,
especially that to supply grain, were not met, he did not hand over
Placidia and prepared to break the peace and make war.

2. (*Bibl. Cod.* 80, p.174)
    When Ataulf was asked to return Placidia, he demanded the grain
which had been promised. Although they could not fulfil their promises, they nevertheless swore to deliver it, if they received Placidia.
The barbarian pretended to agree and advanced to the city named
Marseilles, which he hoped to capture by treachery. There he was
wounded by a blow from the most noble Boniface and, barely escaping
death, he retired to his own tent, leaving the city rejoicing and full

λιπὼν καὶ δι' ἐπαίνων καὶ εὐφημίας ποιουμένην Βονηφάτιον.

3. (*Bibl. Cod. loc.cit.*)

'Ότι Ἀδαούλφος τὸν γάμον μελετῶν Πλακιδίας, Κωνσταντίου
ταύτην ἀπαιτοῦντος βαρυτέρας προὔτεινεν αἰτήσεις, ἵνα διὰ τὴν
ἀποτυχίαν τῶν αἰτήσεων εὔλογον δόξῃ τὴν κατάσχεσιν αὐτῆς
πεποιηκέναι.

## 23

(*Bibl. Cod.* 80, pp.174f.)

'Ότι Κωνστάντιος δισίγνατος πάλαι γεγονὼς ὕπατος κατὰ τὴν
Ῥάβενναν προέρχεται, μεθ' οὗ κατὰ τὴν Κωνσταντινούπολιν ὑπατεύει
Κώνστας· καὶ χρυσίον μὲν σύμμετρον καὶ ἱκανὸν πρὸς τὸ τῆς ὑπατείας ἀνάλωμα εὕρηται ἐκ τῶν τοῦ Ἡρακλειανοῦ ὃς τυραννίδα
μελετῶν ἀνῄρητο, οὐ μήν γε τοσοῦτον εὑρέθη ὅσον καὶ ἠλπίζετο·    5
χρυσίον μὲν γὰρ οὐδὲ μέχρι κεντηναρίων κ' εὕρηται, ἡ δὲ ἀκίνητος
αὐτοῦ οὐσία καὶ αὐτὴ εἰς δισχιλίας λίτρας συνέτεινε. καὶ ταύτην
ἅπασαν τὴν ὑπόστασιν Κωνστάντιος ἐκ μιᾶς αἰτήσεως παρὰ
Ὀνωρίου εἰλήφει.

Ἦν δὲ Κωνστάντιος ἐν μὲν ταῖς προόδοις κατηφὴς καὶ σκυθ-    10
ρωπός, μεγαλόφθαλμός τε καὶ μεγαλαύχην καὶ πλατυκέφαλος,
νεύων διόλου ἐπὶ τὸν τράχηλον τοῦ φέροντος αὐτὸν ἵππου, καὶ οὕτω
τῇδε κἀκεῖσε λοξὸν ἐκπέμπων τὸ ὄμμα, ὡς (τὸ τοῦ λόγου) πᾶσι
φαίνεσθαι εἶδος ἄξιον τυραννίδος. ἐν δὲ δείπνοις καὶ συμποσίοις
τερπνὸς καὶ πολιτικός, ὡς καὶ ἐρίζειν τοῖς μίμοις πολλάκις παίζουσι    15
πρὸ τῆς τραπέζης.

12 οὕτω Bekker [οὕπω codd.

## 24

(*Bibl. Cod.* 80, p.175)

'Ότι Ἀδαούλφῳ σπουδῇ καὶ ὑποθήκῃ Κανδιδιανοῦ ὁ πρὸς
Πλακιδίαν συντελεῖται γάμος· μὴν ὁ Ἰαννουάριος ἐνειστήκει, ἐπὶ δὲ
τῆς πόλεως Νάρβωνος, ἐν οἰκίᾳ Ἰγγενίου τινὸς πρώτου τῶν ἐν τῇ
πόλει· ἔνθα προκαθεσθείσης Πλακιδίας ἐν παστάδι τε Ῥωμαϊκῶς
ἐσκευασμένῃ καὶ σχήματι βασιλικῷ, συγκαθέζεται αὐτῇ καὶ Ἀδα-    5
ούλφος ἐνδεδυμένος χλανίδα καὶ τὴν ἄλλην Ῥωμαίων ἐσθῆτα. ἐν
οἷς μετὰ τῶν ἄλλων γαμικῶν δώρων δωρεῖται Ἀδαούλφος καὶ ν'
εὐειδεῖς νεανίας σηρικὴν ἐνδεδυμένους ἐσθῆτα, φέροντος ἑκάστου
ταῖς χεροῖν ἀνὰ δύο μεγίστων δίσκων, ὧν ὁ μὲν χρυσίου πλήρης, ὁ
δὲ τιμίων λίθων, μᾶλλον δὲ ἀτιμήτων ἐτύγχανεν· ἃ τῆς Ῥώμης    10

6 Ῥωμαίων M [Ῥωμαίαν A

of praise and acclaim for Boniface.

3. (*Bibl. Cod. loc.cit.*)

Ataulf was preparing to marry Placidia and, since Constantius was demanding her return, he increased his demands so that, when those were not met, he might seem to have acted reasonably in detaining her.

## 23

(*Bibl. Cod.* 80, pp.174f.)

Constantius, having been earlier named consul designate, entered his consulship at Ravenna, with Constans his fellow consul at Constantinople. Enough gold to cover the costs of the consulship was found amongst the estate of Heraclian (who had been killed while attempting usurpation), although not as much was found as expected. For a little less than two thousand pounds of gold were found, and his land and buildings came to two thousand *litrai*. All of this estate Constantius received from Honorius in response to a single request.

In public processions Constantius was downcast and sullen, a man with bulging eyes, a long neck and a broad head, who always slumped over the neck of the horse he was riding, darting glances here and there out of the corners of his eyes, so that all saw in him "a mien worthy of a tyrant", as the saying goes. But at banquets and parties he was so cheerful and affable that he even competed with the clowns who often played before his table.

## 24

(*Bibl. Cod.* 80, p.175)

With the advice and encouragement of Candidianus, Ataulf married Placidia at the beginning of the month of January in the city of Narbo at the house of Ingenuus, one of the leading citizens of the place. There Placidia, dressed in royal raiment, sat in a hall[53] decorated in the Roman manner, and by her side sat Ataulf, wearing a Roman general's cloak and other Roman clothing. Amidst the celebrations, along with other wedding gifts Ataulf gave Placidia fifty handsome young men dressed in silk clothes, each bearing aloft two very large dishes, one full of gold, the other full of precious – or rather, priceless – stones,

188    Olympiodorus: Text

ὑπῆρχε κατὰ τὴν ἅλωσιν τοῖς Γότθοις ἀποσυληθέντα. εἶτα λέγονται
καὶ ἐπιθαλάμιοι, Ἀττάλου πρῶτον εἰπόντος, εἶτα Ῥουστικίου καὶ Φοι-
βαδίου· καὶ συντελεῖται ὁ γάμος παιζόντων καὶ χαιρόντων ὁμοῦ τῶν
τε βαρβάρων καὶ τῶν ἐν αὐτοῖς Ῥωμαίων. (Cf. Philostorgius 12.4)

25

(*Bibl. Cod. loc.cit.*)

Ὅτι μετὰ τὴν ὑπὸ Γότθων ἅλωσιν τῆς Ῥώμης Ἀλβῖνος ὁ τῆς
Ῥώμης ἔπαρχος, ἤδη ταύτης πάλιν ἀποκαθισταμένης, ἔγραψε μὴ
ἐξαρκεῖν τὸ χορηγούμενον μέρος τῷ δήμῳ εἰς πλῆθος ἤδη τῆς
πόλεως ἐπιδιδούσης· ἔγραψε γὰρ καὶ ἐν μιᾷ ἡμέρᾳ τετάχθαι
ἀριθμὸν χιλιάδων δεκατεσσάρων.                                      5

4 τετάχθαι M [τετέχθαι A δεδέχθαι Stein.

26

1. (*Bibl. Cod.* 80, p.176)

Ὅτι Ἀδάουλφος τεχθέντος αὐτῷ ἐκ τῆς Πλακιδίας παιδός, ᾧ
ἐπέθετο κλῆσιν Θεοδόσιον, πλέον ἠσπάζετο τὴν πρὸς Ῥωμαίους
φιλίαν· Κωνσταντίου δὲ καὶ τῶν περὶ Κωνστάντιον ἀντιπραττόντων
ἔμενεν ἄπρακτος ἡ τούτου καὶ Πλακιδίας ὁρμή. τελευτήσαντος δὲ τοῦ
παιδός, πένθος μέγα ποιοῦσιν ἐπ᾽ αὐτῷ καὶ θάπτουσιν ἐν λάρνακι     5
καταθέντες ἀργυρᾷ πρὸ τῆς Βαρκέλλωνος ἔν τινι εὐκτηρίῳ. εἶτα
ἀναιρεῖται καὶ Ἀδάουλφος, εἰς ἐπιτήρησιν τῶν οἰκείων ἵππων, ὡς
εἴθιστο αὐτῷ, διατρίβων ἐν τῷ ἱππῶνι. ἀναιρεῖ δὲ αὐτὸν εἷς τῶν
οἰκείων Γότθων Δούβιος τοὔνομα, ἔχθραν παλαιὰν καιροφυλακήσας·
πάλαι γὰρ ἦν ὁ τούτου δεσπότης, μοίρας Γοτθικῆς ῥήξ, ὑπὸ Ἀδα-   10
ούλφου ἀνῃρημένος, ἐξ οὗ καὶ τὸν Δούβιον λαβὼν Ἀδάουλφος ᾠκει-
ώσατο· ὁ δὲ τῷ πρώτῳ δεσπότῃ ἀμύνων τὸν δεύτερον διεχρήσατο.

Τελευτῶν δὲ Ἀδάουλφος προσέταττε τῷ ἰδίῳ ἀδελφῷ ἀποδοθῆναι τὴν Πλακιδίαν, καί, εἴ τι δύναιτο, τὴν Ῥωμαίων φιλίαν
ἑαυτοῖς περιποιήσασθαι. διάδοχος δὲ ὁ τοῦ Σάρου ἀδελφὸς Σιγ-   15
γέριχος σπουδῇ μᾶλλον καὶ δυναστείᾳ ἢ ἀκολουθίᾳ καὶ νόμῳ γίνεται·
ὃς τά τε παιδία, ἃ ἐκ τῆς προτέρας γυναικὸς ἐτύγχανεν Ἀδαούλφῳ
γεγενημένα, ἀνεῖλε βίᾳ τῶν τοῦ ἐπισκόπου Σιγησάρου κόλπων ἀπο-
σπάσας, καὶ τὴν βασιλίδα Πλακιδίαν εἰς ὕβριν Ἀδαούλφου ἐκ ποδὸς
προηγήσασθαι τοῦ ἵππου ἅμα λοιπῶν αἰχμαλώτων ἐπέταξε· καὶ τὸ   20
διάστημα ἦν τῆς προπομπῆς ἐκ τῆς πόλεως μέχρι δωδεκάτου
σημείου. ἑπτὰ δὲ ἡμέρας ἄρξας ἀναιρεῖται, ἡγεμὼν δὲ τῶν Γότθων
Οὐαλίας καθίσταται.

20 λοιπῶν αἰχμαλώτων A [λοιποῖς αἰχμαλώτοις M

which had been carried off by the Goths at the sack of Rome. Then nuptial hymns were sung, first by Attalus, then by Rusticius and Phoebadius. Then the ceremonies were completed amidst rejoicings and celebrations by both the barbarians and the Romans amongst them.[54] (Cf. Philostorgius 12,4)[55]

## 25

*(Bibl. Cod. loc.cit.)*

After the Gothic capture of Rome, the city was already re-covering to such an extent that Albinus, the city prefect, wrote that the supplies allotted to the inhabitants were insufficient for the increased population of the city. For he wrote that in one day fourteen thousand persons had been entered on the rolls.[56]

## 26

1. *(Bibl. Cod.* 80, p.176)

When Placidia had borne him a son, whom he named Theodosius, Ataulf became even more friendly towards the Romans. But his and Placidia's desires remained unfulfilled in the face of the opposition by Constantius and his supporters. When the child died, his parents grieved for him greatly and buried him in a silver coffin in a chapel outside Barcelona. Then Ataulf himself was killed while, as was his custom, he was spending some time in the stable inspecting his horses. His slayer was one of his own dependents, Dubius by name, who had been waiting the chance to avenge an old grudge. For long ago his master, a king of part of the Goths, had been slain by Ataulf,[57] who afterwards took Dubius into his own service. So, in killing his second master Dubius avenged the first.

On his deathbed Ataulf told his brother to hand back Placidia and, if they could, ensure Roman friendship towards themselves. But Singeric, the brother of Sarus, by conspiracy and coup rather than by the Gothic law of succession, became his successor and he killed Ataulf's children by his first wife, tearing them by force from the arms of the bishop Sigesarus. To spite Ataulf he ordered his queen, Placidia, to walk before his horse with the rest of the prisoners for a distance of twelve miles from the city. After a reign of seven days Singeric was killed and Wallia was declared leader of the Goths.

[2. (Philostorgius 12,4-5)

... ἐλπίδας τρέφων, ὡς αὐτὸς καταπολεμήσας Ἀδαοῦλφον τὴν
Πλακιδίαν νυμφεύσαιτο. οὐ πολὺ δὲ τὸ μέσον καὶ πολλὰ δραματουρ-
γήσας, ἐξ ὀργῆς Ἀδαοῦλφος ὑπό τινος τῶν οἰκείων ἀποσφάττεται. ἐκ
τούτου τὸ βάρβαρον πρὸς Ὀνώριον σπένδεται· καὶ τὴν οἰκείαν
ἀδελφὴν καὶ τὸν Ἄτταλον τῷ βασιλεῖ παρατίθενται, αὐτοὶ σιτήσεσί    5
τε δεξιωθέντες καὶ μοῖράν τινα τῆς τῶν Γαλατῶν χώρας εἰς
γεωργίαν ἀποκληρωσάμενοι.
   Μετὰ ταῦτα δὲ καὶ ἡ Ῥώμη τῶν πολλῶν κακῶν ἀνασχοῦσα
συνοικίζεται· καὶ ὁ βασιλεὺς αὐτῇ παραγεγονώς, χειρὶ καὶ γλώττῃ
τὸν συνοικισμὸν ἐπεκρότει. ὑπὲρ δὲ βήματος ἀναβάς, ὃ τὴν πρώτην    10
αὐτῷ βαθμίδα τὸν Ἄτταλον διαβαίνειν ἐπετίθει ... δεξιᾶς χειρὸς
ἀπέτεμεν τοὺς β΄ δακτύλους, ὧν ὁ μὲν <ἀντίχειρ> ὁ δὲ λιχανὸς ἔχει
τὴν κλῆσιν· καὶ εἰς Λίπαρα τὴν νῆσον τοῦτον φυγαδεύει, μηδενὸς
ἄλλου κακοῦ πρὸς πεῖραν καταστήσας, ἀλλὰ καὶ τὰς εἰς τὸν βίον
χρείας παρασχόμενος ....]    15

1 ante ἐλπίδας lacuna circa clxxx litterarum    καταπολεμήσας Bochart
κατὰ πολεμίας codd.    11 αὐτῷ codd. [αὐτοῦ Valesius    ἐπετίθει codd.
[ὑποτίθει Holstein, Valesius    post ἐπετίθει lacuna circa lxxv litterarum
12 ἀντίχειρ Holstein in lacuna xii litterarum    13 τοῦτον Holstein [τούτους
codd.    15 post παρασχόμενος lacuna circa xiv litterarum

27
(Bibl. Cod. 80, p.177)
   Ὅτι ὁ ἱστορικός φησι παρὰ Οὐαλερίου τινὸς τῶν ἐπισήμων
ἀκοῦσαι περὶ ἀνδριάντων ἀργυρῶν τετελεσμένων εἰς βαρβάρων
ἀποκώλυσιν. ἐν γὰρ ταῖς ἡμέραις, φησί, Κωνσταντίου τοῦ βασιλέως,
ἐν τῇ Θράκῃ Οὐαλερίου ἄρχοντος, μήνυσις γέγονεν ὡς θησαυρὸς
εὑρεθείη. Οὐαλέριος δὲ παρὰ τὸν τόπον παραγενόμενος μανθάνει    5
παρὰ τῶν ἐπιχωρίων ἱερὸν εἶναι τὸν τόπον, καὶ ἐξ ἀρχαίας τελετῆς
ἀνδριάντας ἐν αὐτῷ ἀφιερῶσθαι. εἶτα ἀναφέρει ταῦτα τῷ βασιλεῖ,
καὶ δέχεται γράμμα ἐπιτρέπον αὐτῷ ἀναλαβεῖν τὰ μηνυθέντα. ἀνο-
ρυχθέντος τοίνυν τοῦ τόπου εὑρίσκονται τρεῖς ἀνδριάντες δι᾽ ὅλου ἐξ
ἀργύρου πεποιημένοι, ἐν σχήματι βαρβαρικῷ κατακείμενοι καὶ    10
ἐξηγκωνισμένοι κατ᾽ ἀμφοῖν ταῖν χεροῖν, ἐνδεδυμένοι δὲ βάρβαρον
πεποικιλμένην ἐσθῆτα, καὶ κομῶντες τὰς κεφαλάς, νεύοντες ἐπὶ τὸ
ἀρκτῷον μέρος, τουτέστι κατὰ τοῦ βαρβαρικοῦ χώρου. ὧν ἀνδριάντων ἀναληφθέντων πάραυτα καὶ μετ᾽ ὀλίγας ἡμέρας πρῶτον μὲν
τὸ Γότθων ἔθνος πᾶσαν ἐπιτρέχει τὴν Θράκην, ἔμελλε δὲ μικρὸν    15
ὕστερον καὶ τὸ τῶν Οὔννων καὶ τὸ τῶν Σαρματῶν καταδραμεῖσθαι
τό τε Ἰλλυρικὸν καὶ αὐτὴν τὴν Θράκην· ἐν μέσῳ γὰρ αὐτῆς τε

[2. (Philostorgius 12,4-5)

... <Constantius>, cherishing the hope that if he conquered Ataulf in war, he would marry Placidia. Shortly afterwards, having committed many crimes, Ataulf was slain in anger by one of his dependents. After this the barbarians made a treaty with Honorius. They handed over to the Emperor his sister and Attalus,[58] having themselves received supplies of grain and a part of Gaul to cultivate.

After these events the city of Rome also began to recover from its many disasters and was re-populated. The Emperor himself visited the city and by gesture and word indicated his approval of the revival. Ascending the tribunal, Honorius ordered Attalus to ascend the first step of the tribunal ... he cut off two of the fingers of his right hand, namely the <thumb> and the forefinger, and he exiled him[59] to Lipara, inflicting no other punishment upon him and even supplying him with the necessities of life . . ..]

## 27

(*Bibl. Cod.* 80, p.177)

The historian says that he heard from a certain Valerius, a man of high rank, about silver statues which had been consecrated to ward off barbarians. He says that during the reign of Constantius the Emperor, when Valerius was governor of Thrace, it was reported that a treasure had been found. Valerius visited the site and learned from the locals that it was sacred and that statues had been consecrated there according to an ancient rite. This he then reported to the Emperor and received a rescript empowering him to take possession of the objects reported. When the spot was excavated, three solid silver statues were found deposited there, of barbarous style, with hands bound, dressed in the embroidered clothing of the barbarians, with long hair and inclining towards the North, that is towards the land of the barbarians. As soon as the statues were removed, a few days later the whole Gothic nation poured over Thrace and shortly afterwards the Huns and the Sarmatians were to invade Illyricum and Thrace also. For the site of the

192    Olympiodorus: Text

Θράκης καὶ τοῦ Ἰλλυρικοῦ κατέκειτο τὰ τῆς τελετῆς, καὶ ἐῴκει τῶν
τριῶν ἀνδριάντων ὁ ἀριθμὸς κατὰ παντὸς τετελέσθαι βαρβάρου.

19 post παντὸς M ἔθνους add.

28

(Bibl. Cod. 80, pp.177f.)
    Ὅτι ὁ ἱστορικὸς περὶ τοῦ οἰκείου διαλαμβάνων διάπλου πολλὰ
παθεῖν καὶ δυστυχῆσαί φησι. λέγει δὲ καὶ εἰς τὰς Ἀθήνας κατᾶραι,
καὶ τῇ αὐτοῦ σπουδῇ καὶ ἐπιμελείᾳ εἰς τὸν σοφιστικὸν θρόνον ἀναχ-
θῆναι Λεόντιον οὔπω ἐθέλοντα. λέγει δὲ καὶ περὶ τοῦ τρίβωνος, ὡς
οὐκ ἐξῆν κατὰ τὰς Ἀθήνας περιβαλέσθαι αὐτόν τινα, καὶ μάλιστα      5
ξένον, ᾧ μὴ τῶν σοφιστῶν ἡ γνώμη ἐπέτρεπε καὶ αἱ κατὰ τοὺς
σοφιστικοὺς νόμους τελεταὶ ἐβεβαίουν τὸ ἀξίωμα. ἦν δὲ τὰ τελούμενα
τοιαῦτα· πρῶτον μὲν κατήγοντο ἐπὶ τὸ δημόσιον βαλανεῖον ὅσοι
νεήλυδες, ἄν τε μικροὶ ἄν τε μεγάλοι. ἐξ ὧν καὶ οἱ πρὸς τὸν τρίβωνα
ἐπιτήδειοι, ἡλικίας ἤδη καιροῦ γεγονότες, οὓς εἰς μέσον ἔβαλλον οἱ     10
κατάγοντες σχολαστικοί. εἶτα τῶν μὲν ἔμπροσθεν τρεχόντων καὶ
κωλυόντων, τῶν δὲ ὠθούντων καὶ ἐπεχόντων, πάντων δὲ τῶν
κωλυόντων ταῦτα βοώντων· "στᾶ, στᾶ, οὐ λούει", κατακρατεῖν
δῆθεν τοῦ ἀγῶνος ἐδόκουν οἱ ἀντωθοῦντες εἰς τιμὴν τοῦ κατα-
γομένου σχολαστικοῦ· ὅστις μετὰ πολλὴν ὥραν, στάσεως πολλῆς ἐπὶ     15
τοῖς προαχθεῖσιν ἐθίμοις ῥήμασι προγενομένης, εἰσάγεται εἰς τὸν
θερμὸν οἶκον καὶ ἀπολούεται, εἶτα ἐνδυσάμενος ἐδέχετο τὴν τοῦ
τρίβωνος ἐξουσίαν, καὶ αὐτόθεν μετὰ τοῦ τρίβωνος ἐκ τοῦ βαλανείου
ἐντίμῳ καὶ περιδόξῳ δορυφορούμενος πομπῇ ἀπῄει, δαπάνας ἐπιγνοὺς φανερὰς εἰς τοὺς τῶν διατριβῶν προστάτας τοὺς λεγομένους    20
Ἀκρωμίτας.

29

1. (Bibl. Cod. 80, p.178)
    Ὅτι οἱ Οὐάνδαλοι τοὺς Γότθους Τρούλους καλοῦσι διὰ τὸ λιμῷ
πιεζομένους αὐτοὺς τροῦλαν σίτου παρὰ τῶν Οὐανδάλων ἀγοράζειν
ἑνὸς χρυσίου· ἡ δὲ τροῦλα οὐδὲ τρίτον ξέστου χωρεῖ.

2. (Bibl. Cod. 80, pp.178f.)
    Ὅτι κατὰ τὰς Ἰσπανίας τῶν Οὐανδάλων καταδραμόντων, καὶ
τῶν Ῥωμαίων εἰς τὰς τετειχισμένας πόλεις καταφυγόντων, τοσοῦ-
τος αὐτῶν λιμὸς κατεκράτησεν ὡς εἰς ἀλληλοφαγίαν ἐκβιασθῆναι·
καὶ γυνὴ τέσσαρα τέκνα ἔχουσα πάντα κατέφαγε, πρόφασιν ἐφ'
ἑκάστου ποιουμένη τὴν τῶν ὑπολοίπων τροφὴν καὶ σωτηρίαν, ἕως ἂν    5
πάντα καταφαγοῦσα λίθοις ὑπὸ τοῦ δήμου ἀνῃρέθη.

consecration lay between Thrace and Illyricum and to judge from the
number of the statues, they had been consecrated against the whole of
barbary.

### 28
(*Bibl. Cod.* 80, pp.177f.)

When the historian describes his voyage by sea, he says that he
encountered many sufferings and misfortunes. He says that he put in at
Athens,[60] and as a result of his zealous support Leontius was appointed
to his sophistic chair, although he did not yet desire it. He speaks of
the sophistic cloak, saying that at Athens no one (and especially a
foreigner) was allowed to wear it who had not been granted permission
by a decision of the sophists and the honour confirmed by the performance of the rites laid down by the sophistic laws. These rites were
as follows. First, all the novices, junior and senior, were conducted to
the public bath. Those of them who, being of the right age, were
ready for the philosopher's cloak were pushed to the front by the
scholars who were conducting them. Then, while some ran before them
and blocked their way, others pushed them and directed them towards
the bath; and while all of those blocking their way shouted, "Stop,
stop, don't take the bath", those who were pushing in the opposite
direction were determined, of course, to win the struggle in order to
bring honour to the scholars who were conducting the novices. After a
long time and a long struggle carried out in ritual terms, those who were
led into the bath house and washed were then dressed and received the
right to wear the philosopher's cloak. Thereafter, having agreed to pay
certain sums of money to the heads of the schools (who are called
*Acromitai*),[61] they left the bath in their cloaks escorted by a procession
of high-ranking and reputable men.

### 29
1. (*Bibl. Cod.* 80, p.178)

The Vandals call the Goths *Truli* because when they were oppressed by hunger they bought grain from the Vandals at one *solidus*
per *trula*. A *trula* is less than one-third of a *sextarius*.[62]

2. (*Bibl. Cod.* 80, pp.178f.)

When the Vandals overran Spain and the Romans fled to their
walled cities, such a famine afflicted them that they were reduced to
cannibalism. A woman who had four children ate them all, in each case
giving as her excuse the nourishment and survival of those remaining.
Finally, when she had eaten them all, the people stoned her to death.

## 30

(*Bibl. Cod.* 80, p.179)

Ὅτι Εὐπλούτιος ὁ μαγιστριανὸς πρὸς Οὐάλιον, ὃς τῶν Γότθων ἐχρημάτιζε φύλαρχος, ἀποστέλλεται ἐφ᾽ ᾧ σπονδάς τε θέσθαι εἰρηνικὰς καὶ ἀπολαβεῖν τὴν Πλακιδίαν· ὁ δὲ ἑτοίμως δέχεται καὶ ἀποσταλέντος αὐτῷ σίτου ἐν μυριάσιν ἑξήκοντα, ἀπολύεται Πλακιδία παραδοθεῖσα Εὐπλουτίῳ πρὸς Ὀνώριον τὸν οἰκεῖον αὐτῆς ἀδελφόν.    5

## 31

(*Bibl. Cod. loc.cit.*)

Ὅτι ζητήματος ἐν ταῖς Ἀθήναις ἀνακύψαντος περὶ τῶν κεκωλισμένων βιβλίων μωθεῶ τοῖς ἐπιζητοῦσι τὸ μέτρον τοῦ κώλου, Φιλτάτιος ὁ τοῦ ἱστορικοῦ ἑταῖρος εὐφυῶς περὶ γραμματικὴν ἔχων, τοῦτο ἐπέδειξε καὶ εὐδοκιμήσας τυγχάνει παρὰ τῶν πολιτῶν εἰκόνος.

1-2 κεκωλισμένων Dindorf [κεκολλημένων (aut κεκωλλημένων) codd., Henry
2 κώλου A, Dindorf [κόλλου M, Henry

## 32

(*Bibl. Cod.* 80, pp.179f.)

Ὅτι περὶ τῆς Ὀάσεως ὁ συγγραφεὺς πολλὰ παραδοξολογεῖ, περί τε τῆς εὐκρασίας αὐτῆς καὶ ὅτι οἱ τὴν ἱερὰν νόσον ἔχοντες οὐ μόνον ἐκεῖσε οὐ γίνονται, ἀλλὰ καὶ ἀλλαχόθεν παραγινόμενοι ἀπαλλάττονται διὰ τὴν τοῦ ἀέρος εὐκρασίαν τοῦ νοσήματος. καὶ περὶ τῆς ψάμμου τῆς πολλῆς ἐκείνης καὶ τῶν ὀρυσσομένων φρεάτων, ὡς εἰς    5
διακοσίους καὶ τριακοσίους, ἔσθ᾽ ὅτε δὲ καὶ εἰς πεντακοσίους πήχεις ὀρυσσόμενα ἀναβλύζουσι τὸ ῥεῖθρον αὐτοῦ τοῦ στομίου προχεόμενον· ἐξ οὗ κατὰ διαδοχὴν ἀρυόμενοι, ὅσοις κοινὸν γέγονε τὸ ἔργον, τὰς οἰκείας ἀρούρας ποτίζουσιν οἱ γεωργοί. καὶ ὅτι αἱ ὀπῶραι ἀεὶ τοῖς δένδρεσι φέρονται, καὶ ὅτι ὁ σῖτος παντὸς κρείττων σίτου καὶ χιόνος    10
λευκότερος, καὶ ὅτι ἔσθ᾽ ὅτε δὶς τοῦ ἔτους σπείρεται ἡ κριθή, τρὶς δὲ ἀεὶ ἡ κέγχρος. ἀρδεύουσι δὲ τὰ γήδια αὐτῶν ἐν θέρει μὲν διὰ τρίτης ἡμέρας, ἐν χειμῶνι δὲ διὰ ἕκτης, ἐξ οὗ καὶ ἡ εὐφορία γίνεται. καὶ ὅτι οὐδέποτε συννεφία γίνεται. καὶ περὶ τῶν ποιουμένων αὐτοῖς ὡρολογίων.    15

Λέγει δὲ ὅτι νῆσος τὸ παλαιὸν ἦν καὶ ἀπεχερσώθη, καὶ ὅτι ταύτην καλεῖ Ἡρόδοτος μακάρων νήσους· Ἡρόδωρος δέ, ὁ τὴν Ὀρφέως καὶ Μουσαίου συγγράψας ἱστορίαν, Φαιακίδα ταύτην καλεῖ. τεκμηριοῖ δὲ νῆσον αὐτὴν γεγονέναι ἔκ τε τοῦ ὀστρακα θαλάσσια καὶ

12  αὐτῶν Bekker [αὑτῶν codd.

## 30

(*Bibl. Cod.* 80, p.179)

Euplutius the *agens in rebus* was sent to Wallia, who had been
proclaimed tribal leader of the Goths, to negotiate a peace treaty and
the return of Placidia. He was readily received, and when 600,000
measures of grain had been sent, Placidia was freed and handed over to
Euplutius for Honorius, her brother.[63]

## 31

(*Bibl. Cod. loc.cit.*)

An inquiry was instituted at Athens concerning the transcription
of books by *cola*, the object being to ascertain the length of a *colon*.
Philtatius, the historian's companion, being very adept at textual work,
settled the matter and won such a reputation that the Athenians
erected a statue to him.[64]

## 32

(*Bibl. Cod.* 80, pp.179f.)

Concerning the Oasis the historian tells many wonderful tales.
He says that the climate there is good, and not only are there no epi-
leptics but those who arrive from elsewhere are cured of the disease
because of the quality of the air. He tells of the vast amount of sand
there and says that the wells, which are dug to a depth of two, three
and sometimes five hundred cubits, actually pour water out from their
openings. From here the farmers who have shared the labour of digging
the well draw water in turn and irrigate their fields. The trees are
always in fruit, the wheat is of the highest quality and whiter than
snow, and sometimes the barley is sown twice a year, the millet always
thrice. The farmers irrigate their plots every three days in the summer
and every six in winter, hence their fertility. He says that there are
never any clouds and he describes the sundials made by the inhabitants.[65]

He says that once it was an island separated from the land mass
and called by Herodotus the Isles of the Blessed. Herodorus, who wrote
a history of Orpheus and Musaeus, calls it Phaeacia. He proves that it
was an island from two observations, the first that sea shells and oyster

ὀστρέα λίθοις τοῦ ὄρους προσπεπλασμένα εὑρίσκεσθαι τοῦ ἐπὶ τὴν    20
Ὄασιν ἀπὸ τῆς Θηβαίδος φέροντος, δεύτερον ὅτι ψάμαθος πολλὴ
ἐπεκχεῖται ἀεὶ καὶ τὰς τρεῖς ἀναπληροῖ Ὀάσεις. τρεῖς γάρ φησιν
Ὀάσεις καὶ αὐτὸς εἶναι, δύο μεγάλας, τὴν μὲν ἐξωτέρω, τὴν δὲ
ἐσωτέρω, καταντικρὺ κειμένας ἀλλήλαις, συντείνοντος εἰς ἑκατὸν
σημεῖα τοῦ μεταξὺ διαστήματος. ἔστι δὲ καὶ ἄλλη τρίτη μικρά,    25
πολλῷ διαστήματι τῶν δύο κεχωρισμένη. λέγει δὲ εἰς πίστιν τοῦ
νῆσον γενέσθαι ὅτι καὶ ὑπὸ ὀρνέων ὁρᾶσθαι συμβαίνει πολλάκις
ἰχθῦς φερομένους καὶ ἰχθύων ἄλλοτε λείψανα, ὡς ἐντεῦθεν εἰκά-
ζεσθαι μὴ πολὺ πόρρω εἶναι τὴν θάλασσαν. φησὶ δὲ καὶ Ὅμηρον
ἐκ τῆς πρὸς ταύτῃ Θηβαΐδος ἕλκειν τὸ γένος.    30

## 33

1. (Bibl. Cod. 80, pp.180f.)

Ὅτι ὕπατος ὁ βασιλεὺς Ὀνώριος προελθὼν τὸ ἑνδέκατον,
καὶ σὺν αὐτῷ Κωνστάντιος τὸ δεύτερον, τὸν Πλακιδίας γάμον ἐπι-
τελοῦσιν· ἐφ' ᾧ πολλὰ μὲν αὐτὴ ἀνανεύουσα Κωνστάντιον παρεσκεύασε κατὰ τῶν αὐτῆς ὀργίζεσθαι θεραπόντων. τέλος ἐν τῇ τῆς
ὑπατείας ἡμέρᾳ ἀπὸ χειρὸς ταύτην ὁ βασιλεὺς καὶ ἀδελφὸς Ὀνώριος    5
ἄκουσαν λαβὼν ἐγχειρίζει παραδιδοὺς Κωνσταντίῳ, καὶ ἐπιτελεῖται
εἰς τὸ λαμπρότατον ὁ γάμος. εἶτα καὶ παῖς αὐτοῖς τίκτεται, ἣν ὀνομά-
ζουσιν Ὀνωρίαν, καὶ ἕτερος πάλιν, ᾧ κλῆσιν ἔθεντο Οὐαλεντινιανόν·
ὃς ζῶντος μὲν Ὀνωρίου νοβελίσσιμος γίνεται βιασαμένης τῆς
Πλακιδίας τὸν ἀδελφόν, μετὰ δὲ τὸν θάνατον τοῦ βασιλέως, καὶ ἔτι    10
μετὰ τὴν κατάλυσιν τοῦ τυραννήσαντος Ἰωάννου, καὶ Ῥώμης
βασιλεὺς ἀποδείκνυται.
Ὁ δὲ Κωνστάντιος συμβασιλεύει τῷ Ὀνωρίῳ, αὐτοῦ μὲν
χειροτονοῦντος, ἀλλὰ σχεδόν τι ἄκοντος. χειροτονεῖται δὲ καὶ ἡ Πλακιδία Αὐγούστα, τοῦ τε ἰδίου ἀδελφοῦ καὶ τοῦ ἰδίου ἀνδρὸς χειροτονη-    15
σάντων· εἶτα πέμπεται πρὸς Θεοδόσιον, ὃς ἀδελφιδοῦς ὢν Ὀνωρίου
τῶν πρὸς ἕω μερῶν ἐβασίλευεν, ἡ ἀνάρρησις μηνυομένη τῆς τοῦ
Κωνσταντίου βασιλείας, καὶ μένει ἀπαράδεκτος. ἐφίσταται νόσος
Κωνσταντίῳ, καὶ μετέμελεν αὐτῷ ἡ βασιλεία, ὅτι οὐκέτι ἦν αὐτῷ ἐπ'
ἀδείας ὥσπερ πρότερον ἐξιέναι τε καὶ ἀπιέναι ὅπῃ καὶ ὅπως βούλοιτο,    20
καὶ ὅτι οὐκ ἐξῆν χρῆσθαι βασιλεύοντι οἷς ἔθος εἶχε χρῆσθαι παιγνίοις.
τέλος ἑπτὰ βασιλεύσας μῆνας, ὥσπερ αὐτῷ καὶ ὁ ὄνειρος εἶπεν "ἓξ
ἤδη πεπλήρωνται καὶ ἄρχονται ἑπτά", πλευριτικῇ νόσῳ τελευτᾷ,
συντελευτησάσης αὐτῷ καὶ τῆς κατὰ τὴν ἀνατολὴν ὀργῆς καὶ ὁρμῆς
ἣν ὤδινεν, ὅτι τὴν ἀναγόρευσιν αὐτοῦ τῆς βασιλείας οὐ προσήκαντο.    25

8 Οὐαλεντινιανόν Bekker [Οὐαλεντινιανός codd., edd.

shells are found embedded in the rocks of the desert that stretches between the Oasis and the Thebaid, the second that a great quantity of sand is continually pouring forth and filling up the three Oases. (He himself says that there are three Oases, two great ones, an outer and an inner, lying opposite and separated by a distance of about one hundred miles. There is also a third small one, a great distance from the other two.) To clinch his case that it was an island he says that birds are often seen carrying fish and the remains of fish are also seen, so that the sea is conjectured to be not far away. He says that Homer derived his origin from the part of the Thebaid near to this place.[66]

## 33

1. (*Bibl. Cod.* 80, pp.180f.)

When Honorius was celebrating his eleventh consulship and Constantius his second, they solemnised Placidia's marriage. Her frequent rejections of Constantius had made him angry at her attendants. Finally, the Emperor Honorius, her brother, on the day on which he entered his consulship, took her by the hand and, despite her protests, gave her over to Constantius, and the marriage was solemnised in the most dazzling fashion.[67] Later a child was born to them, whom they named Honoria, and then a boy, whom they named Valentinian. While Honorius was still alive he became *nobilissimus* at Placidia's insistence, and after his death and the overthrow of the usurper John he was proclaimed Emperor of Rome.

Constantius became co-Emperor with Honorius, who appointed him, but rather unwillingly. Placidia was proclaimed Augusta jointly by her brother and husband. The proclamation announcing the elevation of Constantius was then sent to Theodosius, Honorius' nephew and the ruler of the eastern Empire, but it was not accepted. Constantius fell ill and regretted his elevation, that he no longer had the freedom to leave and go off wherever and in whatever manner he wished and could not, because he was Emperor, enjoy the pastimes which he had been accustomed to enjoy. Finally, having reigned for seven months, as the dream foretold to him – "six have already been completed, and the seventh begins" –, he died of pleurisy. With him died the hostility towards the East and the expedition which he had been preparing because they did not approve his proclamation as Emperor.

[2. (Philostorgius 12,12)

Ὅτι Ὀνώριος ὁ βασιλεὺς Κωνστάντιον τὸν στρατηγὸν κατὰ τιμὴν τοῦ κήδους εἰς τὸ τῆς βασιλείας προσλαμβάνεται σκῆπτρον, ἤδη καὶ παῖδα Οὐαλεντινιανὸν τῆς Πλακιδίας αὐτῷ γεναμένης· ᾧ καὶ τὴν τοῦ ἐπιφανεστάτου περιῆψεν ὁ Ὀνώριος ἀξίαν. αἱ δὲ τοῦ Κωνσταντίου εἰκόνες, ὡς ἔθος ἦν τοῖς ἄρτι παρελθοῦσιν εἰς βασιλείαν 5 πράττειν, ἀναπέμπονται πρὸς τὴν Ἑῴαν· ἀλλ᾽ ὅ γε Θεοδόσιος, οὐκ ἀρεσκόμενος τῇ ἀναρρήσει, οὐ προσίετο ταύτας. καὶ δὴ Κωνσταντίῳ, παρασκευαζομένῳ διὰ τὴν ὕβρω ἐπὶ πόλεμον, καὶ τῆς ζωῆς καὶ τῶν φροντίδων ἐπιστὰς ὁ θάνατος τὴν ἀπαλλαγὴν παρέχει, βασιλεύσαντι μῆνας ἕξ.]    10

## 34

(*Bibl. Cod.* 80, p.181)

Ὅτι Οὐαλίου τοῦ φυλάρχου τελευτήσαντος, Θευδέριχος τὴν ἀρχὴν διαδέχεται.

## 35

1. (*Bibl. Cod.* 80, pp.181f.)

Ὅτι κατὰ θάλασσαν πολλὰ παθὼν ὁ συγγραφεὺς μόλις διασῴζεται. ἐν ᾧ καὶ περὶ ἀστέρος τινὸς τερατολογεῖ ἐπιβρίσαντος τῷ ἱστίῳ τοῦ πλοίου μέλλειν αὐτοὺς βυθίζεσθαι. Οὐρανίαν δὲ τὸ φανὲν παρὰ τῶν ναυτῶν καλεῖσθαι. λέγει δὲ περὶ ψιττακοῦ, ᾧ εἴκοσιν ἔτεσι συνδιῆγεν, ὡς σχεδόν τι οὐδὲν τῶν ἀνθρώπῳ πραττομένων 5 ἀμίμητον κατελίμπανεν· ὠρχεῖτό τε γὰρ καὶ ᾖδε καὶ ἐκάλει ἐξ ὀνόματος καὶ τἆλλα ἔπραττεν.

3 μέλλειν codd. [μέλλον Niebuhr

2. (*Bibl. Cod.* 80, p.182)

Ὅτι ὁ ἱστορικός φησι διάγοντος αὐτοῦ κατὰ τὰς Θήβας καὶ τὴν Σοήνην ἱστορίας ἕνεκα, ἐν ἐπιθυμίᾳ γενέσθαι τοὺς φυλάρχους καὶ προφήτας τῶν κατὰ τὴν Τάλμιν βαρβάρων, ἤτοι τῶν Βλεμμύων, τῆς ἐντυχίας αὐτοῦ· ἐκίνει γὰρ αὐτοὺς ἐπὶ τοῦτο ἡ φήμη. καὶ ἔλαβόν με, φησί, μέχρι αὐτῆς τῆς Τάλμεως, ὥστε κἀκείνους τοὺς χώρους ἱστορῆσαι διέχοντας ἀπὸ τῶν Φιλῶν διάστημα ἡμερῶν πέντε, μέχρι πόλεως τῆς λεγομένης Πρῖμα, ἥτις τὸ παλαιὸν πρώτη πόλις τῆς Θηβαΐδος ἀπὸ τοῦ βαρβαρικοῦ ἐτύγχανε· διὸ παρὰ τῶν Ῥωμαίων ῥωμαίᾳ φωνῇ Πρῖμα ἤτοι πρώτη ὠνομάσθη, καὶ νῦν οὕτω καλεῖται καίτοι ἐκ πολλοῦ οἰκειωθεῖσα τοῖς βαρβάροις μεθ᾽ ἑτέρων τεσσάρων 10 πόλεων, Φοινικῶνος, Χίριδος, Θάπιδος, Τάλμιδος.

[2. (Philostorgius 12,12)

The Emperor Honorius, out of respect for his familial relationship, elevated his general Constantius to the imperial throne at a time when Placidia had already borne him a son, Valentinian. Honorius conferred upon Valentinian the title of *nobilissimus*. As was the custom in the case of newly proclaimed Emperors, Constantius' images were sent to the East. But Theodosius was displeased at the proclamation and refused to admit them. Because of this insult Constantius was preparing for war when death came upon him and freed him from his life and his cares. He had reigned for six months.]

## 34

(*Bibl. Cod.* 80, p.181)

When Wallia, the tribal leader of the Goths, died, Theoderic succeeded him in office.

## 35

1. (*Bibl. Cod.* 80, pp.181f.)

At sea the historian suffered much and hardly survived. In his account he tells a marvellous story about a star which fell down upon the mast of the ship and they were in danger of sinking.[68] The sailors call this phenomenon Urania.[69] He also speaks of a parrot which he had for twenty years. He says that there was hardly any human action which it could not imitate. It could dance, sing, call out names and do other things.[70]

2. (*Bibl. Cod.* 80, p.182)

The historian says that when he was spending time in the area of Thebes and Syene for the purposes of research, the tribal leaders and prophets of the barbarians near to Talmis (that is, the Blemmyes) were eager to meet him because of his reputation. "They took me", he says, "to Talmis itself, so that I could investigate those regions which lie five days distant from Philae as far as the city called Prima, which was in olden times the first city of the Thebaid that one reached when travelling from the land of the barbarians. Hence the Romans called it Prima in Latin, that is "First", and even now it is so called although it, along with four other cities – Phoenico, Chiris, Thapis and Talmis –, has long been inhabited by the barbarians."[71]

200     Olympiodorus: Text

Παρὰ τούτους τοὺς χώρους φησὶ καὶ σμαράγδου μέταλλα εἶναι
μαθεῖν, ἐξ ὧν τοῖς Αἰγυπτίων βασιλεῦσιν ἡ σμάραγδος ἐπλεόναζε.
καὶ ταῦτα, φησίν, οἱ προφῆται τῶν βαρβάρων προὔτρεπόν με θεά-
σασθαι· ἀλλ᾽ οὐκ ἦν τοῦτο δυνατὸν γενέσθαι χωρὶς βασιλικῆς    15
προστάξεως.

36
(Bibl. Cod. 80, pp.182f.)

Ὅτι Λιβάνιόν τινα τερατολογεῖ, Ἀσιανὸν τὸ γένος, κατὰ τὴν
βασιλείαν Ὀνωρίου καὶ Κωνσταντίου ἐπὶ Ῥάβενναν παραγενέσθαι.
ἄκρον δὲ τοῦτον εἶναι τελεστικόν. καὶ δύνασθαι δέ, φησί, καὶ
ὑπισχνεῖσθαι αὐτὸν χωρὶς ὁπλιτῶν καὶ κατὰ βαρβάρων ἐνεργεῖν.
εἶτα πεῖραν δούς, φησώ, οὗτος τῆς ὑποσχέσεως καὶ τῆς φήμης    5
δραμούσης ὥστε καὶ Πλακιδίαν τὴν βασιλίδα μαθεῖν, ἀναιρεῖται ὁ
τελεστής· ἠπείλει γάρ, φησίν, ἡ Πλακιδία Κωνσταντίῳ χωρισμὸν
τοῦ γάμου εἰ τοῖς ζῶσι Λιβάνιος περιλείποιτο, ἀνὴρ γόης καὶ ἄπιστος.

4 χωρὶς ὁπλιτῶν καὶ κατὰ codd. [καὶ χωρὶς ὁπλιτῶν κατὰ Niebuhr

37
(Bibl. Cod. 80, p.183)

Ὅτι Κωστάντιος Ἰλλυριὸς ἦν τὸ γένος, ἀπὸ Ναΐσσου πόλεως
τῆς Δακίας, καὶ πολλὰς στρατείας ἀπὸ τῶν Θεοδοσίου χρόνων τοῦ
μεγάλου διελθών, ὕστερον καὶ τὴν βασίλειον ἀρχήν, ὡς ἐρρήθη,
ὑπέδυ. ἦν δὲ τἆλλα μὲν ἐπαινετός, καὶ χρημάτων δὲ κρείττων πρὶν
ἢ συναφθῆναι Πλακιδίᾳ· ἐπεὶ δὲ αὐτῇ συνέζευκτο, εἰς φιλοχρηματίαν    5
ἐξώκειλε. μετὰ μέντοι τὸν αὐτοῦ θάνατον δεήσεις κατ᾽ αὐτοῦ τῶν εἰς
χρήματα ἀδικηθέντων ἐπὶ Ῥάβενναν πανταχόθεν συνέρρεον· ἀλλ᾽ ἡ
τοῦ Ὀνωρίου, φησί, κουφότης καὶ ἡ τῆς Πλακιδίας πρὸς αὐτὸν
οἰκειότης ἀπράκτους αὐτῶν τὰς αἰτήσεις καὶ τὴν ἰσχὺν τοῦ δικαίου
ἀπέφηνεν.    10

1 Ναΐσσου Labbaeus [Παναΐσσου codd.    2 Δακίας Labbaeus [Καδίας codd.

38
(Bibl. Cod. 80, pp.183f.)

Ὅτι τοσαύτη διάθεσις Ὀνωρίῳ πρὸς τὴν οἰκείαν ἀδελφήν, ἐξ
οὗπερ ὁ ταύτης ἀνὴρ Κωνστάντιος ἀπεβίω παρεμπεφύκει, ὡς τὴν
ἄμετρον ἀγάπην αὐτῶν καὶ τὰ συνεχῆ κατὰ στόμα φιλήματα εἰς
ὑπόληψιν αἰσχρὰν αὐτῶν τοῖς πολλοὺς ἐμβαλεῖν. ἀλλὰ τοσαύτη

3 φιλήματα M [φίλημα A    4 αὐτῶν τοὺς πολλοὺς A [αὐτοὺς τοῖς πολλοῖς M

He says he learned that in those regions there were emerald mines from which emeralds were supplied in large quantities to the kings of Egypt. He says, "The prophets of the barbarians invited me to visit these. But this could not be done without the authorisation of the king."[72]

## 36

(*Bibl. Cod.* 80, pp.182f.)

He tells a marvellous story about a certain Libanius, an Asian by race, who came to Ravenna during the reign of Honorius and Constantius. According to the historian, he was a consummate magician, able to achieve results even against barbarians without resort to weapons, and this he promised to do. He was given permission to make the attempt, but when his promise and his high repute came to the ears of the Empress Placidia, the magician was put to death. For Placidia threatened Constantius that she would break up their marriage if Libanius, a wizard and an unbeliever, remained amongst the living.[73]

## 37

(*Bibl. Cod.* 80, p.183)

Constantius was an Illyrian by birth, from Naissus, a city of Dacia. From the time of Theodosius the Great he had taken part in many campaigns and, as has been told, was later elevated to the rank of Emperor. In addition to his other virtues he was free from greed until he married Placidia. But when he was joined to her, he fell into lust for money. After his death Ravenna was inundated from all sides with suits over his misappropriation of possessions. But Honorius' unresponsiveness and the close relationship of Placidia to him rendered both the complaints and the power of justice ineffectual.

## 38

(*Bibl. Cod.* 80, pp.183f.)

The affection of Honorius towards his sister grew so great after the death of her husband Constantius that their immoderate pleasure in each other and their constant kissing on the mouth caused many people to entertain shameful suspicions about them. But as a result of

πάλιν αὐτοῖς ἐναπετέχϑη ἔχϑρα σπουδῇ Σπαδούσης καὶ Ἐλπιδίας 5
(τροφὸς δ᾽ ἦν αὕτη Πλακιδίας), αἷς καὶ τὰ πολλὰ προσεῖχε, συμ-
πράττοντος αὐταῖς καὶ Λεοντέως τοῦ ταύτης κουράτωρος, ὥστε
στάσεις μὲν πολλάκις ἐν τῇ Ῥαβέννῃ συστῆναι (περιῆν γὰρ κἀκείνη
πλῆϑος βαρβάρων ἐκ τῆς πρὸς Ἀδαοῦλφον συναφείας καὶ ἐκ τῆς
πρὸς Κωνστάντιον συζυγίας) καὶ πληγὰς δὲ προελϑεῖν ἐξ ἑκατέρου 10
μέρους. τέλος ἐκ τῆς ἀναφϑείσης ἐκείνης ἔχϑρας καὶ τοῦ ἀντιρρόπου
τῆς πρὶν φιλίας μίσους εἰς Βυζάντιον Πλακιδία, τοῦ ἀδελφοῦ ὑπερ-
ισχύσαντος, σὺν τοῖς οἰκείοις παισὶν ἐξορίζεται. καὶ μόνος αὐτῇ Βονηφάτιος τὰ πιστὰ φυλάττων ἀπὸ τῆς Ἀφρικῆς, ἧς ἦρχε, καὶ χρήματα
ὡς ἐδύνατο ἔπεμπε καὶ πρὸς τὴν ἄλλην αὐτὸς ἔσπευδε ϑεραπείαν, 15
ὕστερον δὲ καὶ εἰς τὴν τῆς βασιλείας ἀνάληψιν ἅπαντα συνεβάλετο.

## 39

1. (*Bibl. Cod.* 80, p.184)

Ὅτι Ὀνώριος ὑδερικῷ νοσήματι ἁλοὺς πρὸ ἓξ καλανδῶν
Σεπτεμβρίων τελευτᾷ· καὶ πέμπονται γράμματα πρὸς τὴν ἀνατολὴν
τὸν βασιλέως ϑάνατον μηνύοντα. ἐν ᾧ δὲ ταῦτα ἐπέμποντο,
Ἰωάννης τις αὐϑεντήσας τυραννεῖ. ἐφ᾽ οὗ καὶ τῆς ἀναρρήσεως γινο-
μένης ἐρρήϑη ὥσπερ ἀπό τινος προρρήσεως προαχϑέν· "πίπτει, οὐ 5
στήκει", καὶ τὸ πλῆϑος ὥσπερ ἀναλύοντες ἐπὶ τὸ ῥηϑὲν ἀνα-
φωνοῦσι· "στήκει, οὐ πίπτει".

[2. (Philostorgius 12,13)

Ὅτι ἐν ὑπατείᾳ τοῦ βασιλέως Θεοδοσίου τὸ δέκατον καὶ
Ὀνωρίου τὸ τρισκαιδέκατον αὐτὸς Ὀνώριος ὑδέρῳ τελευτᾷ καὶ
Ἰωάννης τυραννίδι ἐπιϑέμενος διαπρεσβεύεται πρὸς Θεοδόσιον.
ἀπράκτου δὲ τῆς πρεσβείας γεγενημένης, καὶ οἱ πρέσβεις ὑβρισ-
ϑέντες ἄλλος ἀλλαχῇ κατὰ τὴν Προποντίδα φυγῇ προσετιμήϑησαν.] 5

5 προσετιμήϑησαν Bidez [προετιμήϑησαν codd.

## 40

(*Bibl. Cod.* 80, pp.184f.)

Ὅτι Βονηφάτιος ἀνὴρ ἦν ἡρωϊκός, καὶ κατὰ πολλῶν πολλάκις
βαρβάρων ἠρίστευσεν, ἄλλοτε μὲν σὺν ὀλίγοις ἐπερχόμενος, ἄλλοτε
δὲ καὶ σὺν πλείοσιν, ἐνίοτε δὲ καὶ μονομαχῶν. καὶ ἁπλῶς εἰπεῖν,
παντὶ τρόπῳ πολλῶν βαρβάρων καὶ διαφόρων ἐϑνῶν ἀπήλλαξε τὴν
Ἀφρικήν. ἦν δὲ καὶ δικαιοσύνης ἐραστὴς καὶ χρημάτων κρείττων. 5
ἐπράχϑη δὲ αὐτῷ καί τι τοιοῦτον. ἀνήρ τις ἄγροικος ἔχων ἀνϑοῦσαν
γυναῖκα τὴν ὥραν, ὑπό τινος τῶν συμμάχων βαρβάρων ἐμοιχεύετο.

7 ἐμοιχεύετο A [ἔγνω αὐτὴν μοιχευομένην M

the efforts of Spadusa[74] and of Placidia's nurse, Elpidia, (to both of whom she paid great attention) and through the co-operation of Leontius, her steward, this affection was replaced by such a degree of hatred, that fighting often broke out in Ravenna and blows were delivered on both sides. For Placidia was surrounded by a host of barbarians because of her marriages to Ataulf and Constantius. Finally, as a result of this flare-up of enmity and the hatred as strong as their previous love, when Honorius proved the stronger, Placidia was exiled to Byzantium with her children. Only Boniface continued loyal to her and from Africa, which he governed, sent whatever money he could and promised other kinds of assistance. Later, he contributed all his resources towards her restoration as Empress.

### 39

1. (*Bibl. Cod.* 80, p.184)
Honorius was attacked by dropsy and died on August 27th [A.D. 423]. Letters were sent to the East reporting the Emperor's death. While these were being sent, a certain John seized power and ruled illegally. When his proclamation was taking place a cry rang out as if from some oracle, "He falls, he does not stand", and the crowd responded to the cry as if to undo it, "He stands, he does not fall".[75]

[2. (Philostorgius 12,13)
In the tenth consulship of Theodosius and the thirteenth of Honorius the latter died of dropsy, and John seized the throne and sent an embassy to Theodosius. The embassy failed, and the envoys were treated harshly and exiled to various places along the Propontis.]

### 40

(*Bibl. Cod.* 80, pp.184f.)
Boniface was an heroic[76] man who was frequently victorious against hordes of barbarians, sometimes attacking them with a few men, sometimes with many, and occasionally fighting in single combat. In a word, he used every means to free Africa from many barbarians and various tribes. He was also a lover of justice and free from avarice. The following is one of his acts. A certain peasant had a young and pretty wife who was having an affair with one of the barbarian allies.

δεῖται τοιγαροῦν Βονηφατίου τὴν ὕβριν ὀλοφυρόμενος. ὁ δὲ Βονηφάτιος μαθὼν τὸ διάστημα τοῦ τόπου καὶ τὸ ὄνομα τοῦ ἀγροῦ ἐν ᾧ τὰ
τῆς μοιχείας ἐπράττετο, τὸν μὲν ἱκέτην τέως ἀπέπεμπε, προστάξας    10
πάλιν τῇ ἑξῆς αὐτῷ προσελθεῖν, ὀψίας δέ, λαθὼν ἅπαντας, καὶ ἐπὶ
τὸν ἀγρὸν ἐλάσας ἑβδομήκοντα διϊστάμενον σταδίοις, καὶ εὑρὼν τὸν
βάρβαρον τῇ μοιχευομένῃ συγκαθεύδοντα, τέμνει τε αὐτοῦ τὴν
κεφαλὴν καὶ δι᾽ αὐτῆς ὑποστρέφει νυκτός. προσελθόντι δὲ κατὰ τὸ
πρόσταγμα εἰς τὴν αὔριον τῷ ἀνδρὶ ἐπιδίδωσι τοῦ βαρβάρου τὴν    15
κεφαλὴν διαπυνθανόμενος εἰ ἐπιγνώσκοι αὐτήν. ὁ δὲ τοῖς παροῦσιν
ἅμα καταπλαγεὶς καὶ ἀμηχανήσας, ἔπειτα ἐπιγνοὺς καὶ πολλὰ τῆς
δικαιοσύνης εὐχαριστήσας, σὺν χαρᾷ ἀπῄει.

## 41

1. (Bibl. Cod. 80, p.185)

Ὅτι ἕκαστος τῶν μεγάλων οἴκων τῆς Ῥώμης, ὥς φησιν,
ἅπαντα εἶχεν ἐν ἑαυτῷ ὁπόσα πόλις σύμμετρος ἠδύνατο ἔχειν, ἱππόδρομον καὶ φόρους καὶ ναοὺς καὶ πηγὰς καὶ λουτρὰ διάφορα. διὸ καὶ ὁ
συγγραφεὺς ἀπεφθέγξατο·
　　Εἷς δόμος ἄστυ πέλει· πόλις ἄστεα μυρία κεύθει.    5
ἦσαν δὲ καὶ λουτρὰ δημόσια παμμεγέθη. αἱ δὲ Ἀντωνιαναὶ οὕτω
καλούμεναι εἰς χρείαν τῶν λουομένων καθέδρας εἶχον παρακειμένας
χιλίας ἑξακοσίας, ἐκ μαρμάρου κατεσκευασμένας ξεστοῦ. αἱ δὲ
Διοκλητιαναὶ ἐγγὺς διπλασίους. τό τε τεῖχος τῆς Ῥώμης μετρηθὲν
παρὰ Ἄμμωνος τοῦ γεωμέτρου, καθ᾽ ὃν καιρὸν Γότθοι τὴν    10
προτέραν κατ᾽ αὐτῆς ἐπιδρομὴν ἐποιήσαντο, εἴκοσι καὶ ἑνὸς μιλίου
διάστημα ἔχον ἀπεδείχθη.

11 ἐπιδρομὴν A [καταδρομὴν M

2. (Bibl. Cod. 80, pp.185f.)

Ὅτι πολλοὶ οἶκοι Ῥωμαίων προσόδους κατ᾽ ἐνιαυτὸν ἐδέχοντο
ἀπὸ τῶν κτημάτων αὐτῶν ἀνὰ μ᾽ χρυσοῦ κεντηνάρια, χωρὶς τοῦ
σίτου καὶ τοῦ οἴνου καὶ τῶν ἄλλων ἁπάντων εἰδῶν, ἃ εἰς τρίτον
συνέτεψεν, εἰ ἐπιπράσκετο, τοῦ εἰσφερομένου χρυσίου. τῶν δὲ μετὰ
τοὺς πρώτους δευτέρων οἴκων τῆς Ῥώμης πεντεκαίδεκα καὶ δέκα    5
κεντηναρίων ἡ πρόσοδος ἦν. καὶ ὅτι Πρόβος ὁ παῖς Ὀλυβρίου
τελέσας τὴν οἰκείαν πραιτοῦραν κατὰ τὸν καιρὸν τῆς Ἰωάννου τυραννίδος, δώδεκα κεντηνάρια χρυσίου ἀνήλωσε. Σύμμαχος δὲ ὁ λογογράφος, συγκλητικὸς ὢν τῶν μετρίων, πρὶν ἢ τὴν Ῥώμην ἁλῶναι,
τοῦ παιδὸς Συμμάχου πραιτοῦραν τελοῦντος κ᾽ κεντηνάρια ἐδαπά-    10
νησε· Μάξιμος δέ, εἷς τῶν εὐπόρων, εἰς τὴν τοῦ υἱοῦ πραιτοῦραν

6 Ὀλυβρίου Reinesius, Niebuhr [Ὀλυμπίου A Ἀλυπίου M

Complaining of the injury, he sought Boniface's help. Boniface asked the distance to the place and the name of the field in which they committed their adultery and sent the petitioner away for the meanwhile, telling him to return on the next day. That evening he slipped away completely unnoticed and went to the field which was seventy stades away. Discovering the barbarian lying with his adulteress, he cut off his head and returned the same night. When the husband returned on the next day as he was bidden, Boniface gave him the barbarian's head and asked if he recognised it. The husband was struck dumb by the sight and was at loss for words, but when he realised what had happened he was full of thanks for the justice done him and went away happily.

## 41

1. (*Bibl. Cod.* 80, p.185)

Each of the great houses of Rome contained within itself, as he says, everything which a medium-sized city could hold, a hippodrome, fora, temples, fountains and different kinds of baths. At this the historian emotes:

One house is a town; the city hides ten thousand towns.[77]

There were also enormous public baths. Those called the Antonine Baths had 1600 seats made of polished marble for the use of the bathers, while the Baths of Diocletian had nearly twice as many. The wall of Rome was shown by the geometrician Ammon, who measured it at the time when the Goths made their first invasion, to have a circuit of twenty-one miles.[78]

2. (*Bibl. Cod.* 80, pp.185f.)

Many of the Roman households received an income of four thousand pounds of gold per year from their properties, not including grain, wine and other produce which, if sold, would have amounted to one-third of the income in gold. The income of the households at Rome of the second class was one thousand or fifteen hundred pounds of gold. When Probus, the son of Olybrius,[79] celebrated his praetorship during the reign of the usurper John, he spent twelve hundred pounds of gold. Before the capture of Rome, Symmachus the orator,[80] a senator of middling wealth, spent two thousand pounds when his son, Symmachus, celebrated his praetorship. Maximus, one of the wealthy

μ' κατεβάλετο κεντηνάρια. ἑπτὰ δὲ ἡμέρας οἱ πραίτωρες τὰς πανηγύρεις ἐτέλουν.

## 42

(*Bibl. Cod.* 80, p.186)

''Ὅτι ὁ συγγραφεὺς τῷ Ὀδυσσεῖ τὴν πλάνην οὐ κατὰ Σικελίαν φησὶ γεγενῆσθαι, ἀλλὰ κατὰ τὰ πέρατα τῆς Ἰταλίας· καὶ τὴν εἰς Ἅιδου κάθοδον παρὰ τὸν Ὠκεανὸν γεγενῆσθαι, ἐν ᾧ καὶ ἡ πολλὴ πλάνη. ἀγωνίζεται δὲ διὰ πολλῶν τοῦτο παραστῆσαι. ἡμεῖς δὲ καὶ ἄλλους διαφόρους ἀνέγνωμεν ἐν τούτοις αὐτῷ συμφωνοῦντας.    5

## 43

1. (*Bibl. Cod.* 80, pp.186f.)

''Ὅτι ἀποστέλλεται ἀπὸ Κωνσταντινουπόλεως παρὰ Θεοδοσίου Πλακιδία ἅμα παισὶ κατὰ τοῦ τυράννου καὶ ἐπαναλαμβάνει αὐτὴ μὲν τὸ τῆς Αὐγούστης, ὁ δὲ Οὐαλεντινιανὸς τὸ τοῦ νωβελισσίμου ἀξίωμα· συνεκπέμπεται δὲ αὐτοῖς καὶ στρατὸς καὶ στρατοπεδάρχης ἑκατέρας δυνάμεως Ἀρδαβούριος ἅμα τῷ παιδὶ Ἄσπαρι, καὶ τρίτος Κανδιδιανός. κατὰ δὲ τὴν Θεσσαλονίκην Ἡλίων ὁ τῶν ὀφφικίων μάγιστρος    5
παρὰ Θεοδοσίου ἀποσταλεὶς ἐνδύει Βαλεντινιανὸν ἐπ' αὐτῆς Θεσσαλονίκης τὴν τοῦ Καίσαρος ἐσθῆτα, πέμπτον ἔτος ἄγοντα τῆς ἡλικίας. κατιόντων δὲ αὐτῶν, Ἀρδαβούριος μὲν ἁλίσκεται παρὰ τῶν τοῦ τυράννου καὶ ἀναπέμπεται πρὸς αὐτόν, καὶ φιλιάζει αὐτῷ. ὁ δὲ τούτου   10
παῖς ἅμα Πλακιδίᾳ ἐν ἀθυμίᾳ καὶ λύπῃ ἦσαν· Κανδιδιανὸς δὲ πολλὰς πόλεις αἱρῶν καὶ εὐδοκιμῶν λαμπρῶς τὸ λυποῦν διεσκέδαζε καὶ ἐψυχαγώγει. εἶτα σφάζεται ὁ τύραννος Ἰωάννης, καὶ Πλακιδία ἅμα Καίσαρι τῷ παιδὶ εἰσέρχεται εἰς τὴν Ῥάβενναν. Ἡλίων δὲ ὁ μάγιστρος καὶ πατρίκιος καταλαβὼν τὴν Ῥώμην, καὶ πάντων ἐκεῖσε   15
συνδραμόντων, τὴν βασιλικὴν ἐσθῆτα ἑπταετηρὸν ὄντα ἐνδύει Βαλεντινιανόν. ἐν οἷς καὶ τὰ τῆς ἱστορίας.

[2. (Philostorgius 12,13-14)

Τὴν μέντοι Πλακιδίαν καὶ τὸν τρίτον Οὐαλεντινιανὸν (μετὰ γὰρ Κωνσταντίου θάνατον πρὸς τὸ Βυζάντιον ἀνεκομίσθησαν) ἀποστέλλει πρὸς τὴν Θεσσαλονίκην Θεοδόσιος, κἀκεῖ τὴν τοῦ Καίσαρος ἀξίαν τῷ ἀνεψιῷ παρατίθησιν, Ἀρδαβουρίῳ τῷ στρατηγῷ καὶ τῷ τούτου υἱῷ Ἄσπαρι τὴν κατὰ τοῦ τυράννου στρατηγίαν ἐγχειρίσας.   5
οἳ δὴ καὶ συνεπαγόμενοι Πλακιδίαν τε καὶ Οὐαλεντινιανὸν καὶ τούς τε Παίονας καὶ τοὺς Ἰλλυριοὺς διελάσαντες, τὰς Σάλωνας, πόλιν τῆς

4 παρατίθησιν codd. [περιτίθησιν Valesius

men, spent four thousand pounds on his son's praetorship. The praetors celebrated their festivals for seven days.[81]

## 42

(*Bibl. Cod.* 80, p.186)

The historian says that Odysseus' wanderings did not take place around Sicily but along the coast of Italy, and that the descent to Hades took place by the Ocean upon which the long wanderings happened. He uses many arguments to establish this thesis. I have read various other authors who agree with him on these matters.

## 43

1. (*Bibl. Cod.* 80, pp.186f.)

Theodosius sent Placidia and her children from Constantinople against the usurper. She received back the title of Augusta, and Valentinian the rank of *nobilissimus*. With them was dispatched an army and Ardabur, the master of both branches of the soldiery, with his son Aspar and a third commander, Candidianus. Helion, the master of the offices, was sent by Theodosius to Thessalonika and in that city he placed the robes of a Caesar on Valentinian, who was in his fifth year.[82] As they were moving down into Italy Ardabur was captured by the usurper's men, was sent to him and struck up a friendship with him. His son and Placidia were sunk in despair and distress. But Candidianus, by capturing many cities and winning high renown, dispelled their distress and raised up their spirits. Then the usurper John was killed and Placidia and her son the Caesar entered Ravenna. Helion, the master of the offices and patrician, went to Rome and, when all had assembled there, he placed the robe of Emperor upon Valentinian, who was in his seventh year.[83] At this point the History ends.

[2. (Philostorgius 12,13-14)

Theodosius sent Placidia and Valentinian III, who had been dispatched to Byzantium after the death of Constantius, to Thessalonika. There he conferred the dignity of Caesar upon his cousin and entrusted the expedition against the usurper to the general Ardabur and his son Aspar. Accompanied by Placidia and Valentinian they crossed Pannonia and Illyricum and stormed Salonae, a city of Dalmatia. From

Δαλματίας, ἀναιροῦσι κατὰ κράτος. ἐντεῦθεν ὁ μὲν Ἀρδαβούριος
νηΐτῃ στόλῳ κατὰ τοῦ τυράννου χωρεῖ. ὁ δὲ Ἄσπαρ τὴν ἱππικὴν
δύναμιν συναναλαβὼν καὶ τῷ τάχει τῆς ἐφόδου κλέψας τὰς αἰσ-    10
θήσεις, τῆς Ἀκυληΐας μεγάλης πόλεως ἐγκρατὴς γίνεται, συνόντων
αὐτῷ Οὐαλεντινιανοῦ τε καὶ Πλακιδίας.
    Ἀλλ' ὁ μὲν οὕτω τὴν μεγάλην ἀταλαιπώρως παρεστήσατο
<πόλιν>, τὸν δὲ Ἀρδαβούριον βίαιον ἀπολαβὸν πνεῦμα σὺν δυσὶν
ἑτέραις τριήρεσιν εἰς χεῖρας ἄγει τοῦ τυράννου. ὁ δὲ πρὸς σπονδὰς    15
ἀφορῶν φιλανθρώπως ἐκέχρητο τῷ Ἀρδαβουρίῳ. καὶ πολλῆς οὗτος
ἀπολαύων τῆς ἀδείας, τοὺς ἀποστρατήγους τοῦ τυράννου <ὑπαγό-
μενος>, ἤδη καὶ αὐτοὺς ὑποκεκνημένους, τὴν ἐπιβουλὴν κρατύνει τὴν
κατὰ τοῦ τυράννου· καὶ σημαίνει Ἄσπαρι τῷ παιδὶ παραγενέσθαι,
ὡς ἐφ' ἑτοίμῳ τῷ κατορθώματι. τοῦ δὲ θᾶττον σὺν τῷ ἱππότῃ    20
στρατῷ παραγεγονότος καὶ μάχης τινὸς συρραγείσης, συλλαμ-
βάνεται ὁ Ἰωάννης τῇ τῶν ἀμφ' αὐτὸν προδοσίᾳ καὶ πρὸς Πλακιδίαν
καὶ Οὐαλεντινιανὸν εἰς Ἀκυληΐαν ἐκπέμπεται· κἀκεῖ τὴν χεῖρα
προδιατμηθείς, εἶτα καὶ τῆς κεφαλῆς ἀποτέμνεται, ἕνα τυραννήσας
ἐπὶ τῷ ἡμίσει ἐνιαυτόν. τότε καὶ βασιλέα ὁ Θεοδόσιος τὸν Οὐαλεν-    25
τινιανὸν ἀποστείλας ἀναγορεύει.
    Ὅτι Ἀέτιος ὁ ὑποστράτηγος Ἰωάννου τοῦ τυράννου μετὰ τρεῖς
ἡμέρας τῆς ἐκείνου τελευτῆς βαρβάρους ἄγων μισθωτοὺς εἰς ξ'
χιλιάδας παραγίνεται· καὶ συμπλοκῆς αὐτοῦ τε καὶ τῶν περὶ τὸν
Ἄσπαρα γεγενημένης, φόνος ἑκατέρωθεν ἐρρύη πολύς. ἔπειτα    30
σπονδὰς ὁ Ἀέτιος τίθεται πρὸς Πλακιδίαν καὶ Οὐαλεντινιανὸν καὶ
τὴν τοῦ κόμητος ἀξίαν λαμβάνει· καὶ οἱ βάρβαροι χρυσίῳ καταθέμενοι τὴν ὀργὴν καὶ τὰ ὅπλα, ὁμήρους τε δόντες καὶ τὰ πιστὰ
λαβόντες, εἰς τὰ οἰκεῖα ἤθη ἀπεχώρησαν.]

---

14 πόλιν add. Bidez    17 ἀποστρατήγους codd. [ὑποστρατήγους Valesius
17-18 ὑπαγόμενος post ἀποστρατήγους add. Bidez

there Ardabur sailed with a force against the usurper, while Aspar took over command of the cavalry. The latter, still accompanied by Placidia and Valentinian, outstripped the enemy's intelligence by the swiftness of his advance and gained control of Aquileia, a large city.

While Aspar had without difficulty taken control of this very important place, Ardabur was driven off course by a gale and swept, with two of his triremes, into the hands of the usurper. He, with a view to making a treaty, dealt with Ardabur in a kindly manner. Ardabur, enjoying complete freedom of movement, suborned the generals who had been retired from their commands[84] and who were already disaffected, organised a plot against the usurper and sent a message to his son Aspar to come, since success was in their grasp. Aspar came quickly with the cavalry, and after a short struggle John was captured through the treachery of his own officials and sent to Aquileia to Placidia and Valentinian. There his hand was first cut off as a punishment, and then he was decapitated, having usurped power for a year and a half. Then Theodosius sent Valentinian [to Rome] and proclaimed him Emperor.

Aetius, one of John's subordinate commanders, arrived three days after his death leading barbarian mercenaries to the number of sixty thousand. His and Aspar's forces engaged, and there was a heavy slaughter on both sides. Then Aetius made an agreement with Placidia and Valentinian and he received the rank of count. The barbarians in exchange for gold laid aside their anger and their weapons, gave hostages and exchanged oaths, and returned to their homelands.]

# NOTES TO OLYMPIODORUS

1.     Baldwin (*Ant. Class.* 1980, p.221) cites Quintilian (10,13,7), Suetonius (*De Vir. Ill.* 10) and Gellius (*N.A. praef.* 5-6) on ὕλη or *silva* as "a compilation of heterogenous information in bulk", with a "secondary connotation of hasty composition". Cf. *OLD s.v. silva* 5b.

2.     The tone of this passage, hostile to Stilicho, is hardly likely to have come from Olympiodorus. But the details parallel Zosimus 5,26 (cf. 27,2), except that the latter says that Stilicho acted because he realised the hostility of Arcadius' ministers to him and that Alaric was already in Epirus when the agreement with Stilicho was made.

3.     Thermantia was married in 408 to Honorius, who had been married to Maria, the elder daughter of Stilicho and Serena, since 398. Zosimus (5,28,1) says that Stilicho objected to the marriage, and, since his account mentions manoeuvres between Stilicho and Serena over it, Photius here seems to have oversimplified Olympiodorus to the point of inaccuracy.

4.     With the words τὸν διὰ ξίφους ὑπέμεινε θάνατον cf. τὸν τράχηλον αὐτὸς ὑπέσχε τῷ ξίφει (Zos. 5,34,5), a detail which Sozomen and Philostorgius omit.

5.     This sentence, like other parts of this passage, is poorly condensed, and the subject of μέλλων is missing. It must, however, be Stilicho, not Alaric (the subject of the previous sentence). Some editors supply ὁ Στελίχων.

6.     Stilicho was accused of plotting to replace Theodosius II with Eucherius according to Zosimus 5,32,1.

7.     The list of the slain in Zosimus 5,32,4-7 is: Longinianus, praetorian prefect of Italy; Limenius, p.p. of Gaul; Chariobaudes, master of the soldiers in Gaul; Vincentius, master of the cavalry; Salvius, count of the domestics; Nemorius, master of the offices; Patroinus, count of the sacred largesses; the count of the privy purse, whose name is missing; and Salvius, quaestor of the sacred palace.

8.     This version agrees with the longer account in Zosimus 5,32,1 - 34,7, whereas the first version given is pro-Olympius and says that he personally cut down Stilicho, who was plotting against the Emperor. The naming of Olympiodorus not as the source for the second version, but as an alternative name for Olympius, is clearly an error, probably of Philostorgius (so Bidez in his edition of the latter, p.140), rather than of Photius (so Mendelssohn in his edition of Zosimus, p.xlvii n.1); cf. most recently Baldwin, *art.cit.* (at n.1 above) pp.228-31, who argues the use of Olympiodorus by Philostorgius. In the present passage of

Philostorgius verbal parallels with Olympiodorus appear: with ἐπι-βουλεῦσαι ... ῥοπάλοις ἀναιρεθέντα cf. Olymp. *Fr.* 8,2, ἐπιβουλεύσας ... ῥοπάλοις ... ἀναιρεῖται; with μιαιφονίας cf. μιαιφόνῳ (*Fr.* 5,1); and both Philostorgius and Olympiodorus (*Fr.* 8,2) speak of δίκη being satisfied by Olympius' death.

**9.** Here Zosimus differs from Olympiodorus since he says (5,36,1) that Alaric first tried to make peace with Honorius and (*ibid.* 2-3) that Honorius did not ally himself with Sarus. Thus, it is likely that the passage of Olympiodorus refers to a later breakdown of negotiations in which Sarus was directly involved (cf. Philostorgius 12,3 = *Fr.* 10,2).

**10.** Zosimus says that the payment was for the march into Epirus (5,28,7) and that it was in gold (*ibid.* 9).

**11.** Zosimus (5,38,1) says that the charge against Serena was unfounded. Eucherius, after finding sanctuary in a church (Zos. 5,35,4), was later executed by order of Honorius (Zos. 5,37,4).

**12.** The same account, in rather more detail, is given by Zosimus (5,41,1-3), who names the prefect as Pompeianus and says that Innocent, the bishop of Rome, consented to the invocation of thunder and lightning providing the ceremonies were carried out in secret. In the MSS of Sozomen the name of the Etrurian town is given as Larnia, which is nowhere attested; Narnia, an easy correction based on the readings of Zosimus' MS, was in fact in Umbria, but close to the Etruscan border. The juxtaposition of λιμός and λοιμός, which is also found in Zosimus 5,39,2, suggests that here Olympiodorus was imitating Thucydides on the Athenian plague (noted by Baldwin, *Ant. Class.* 1980, p.227). This passage is followed by a Christian exposition of the futility of pagan hopes, since the siege was a punishment from God for the immorality and cruelty of the people of Rome.

**13.** The gifts, or rather the price of a truce, are set out by Zosimus 5,41,4: 5,000 lbs. of gold, 30,000 lbs. of silver, 4,000 silk tunics, 3,000 scarlet-dyed skins, 3,000 lbs. of pepper.

**14.** This passage is compatible with Zosimus' account, and in some details the two are complementary. While Philostorgius fails to note that Stilicho's barbarian troops revolted after the massacre of their families (Zos. 5,35,5-6) and wholly omits the first siege of Rome, he is the sole source for the details that they ravaged the city environs before the first siege and that they renewed their offer of help to Alaric after the murder of Eucherius (Zosimus, *loc.cit.*, puts the offer of help before the murder).

**15.** Zosimus (5,44,1) names Olympius as the culprit.

**16.** This passage exactly parallels the much more detailed account in Zosimus 5,44,1 - 51,2 (except that the latter plays down the role of Innocent). Certain of the details in Zosimus clarify Jovius' actions: he had been an old friend of Alaric's; he had made the suggestion that Alaric be given the military command; and, as the result of his oath, he blocked the implementation of Alaric's second, more reasonable, set of demands. The "territory of little importance to the Romans" was the two Noricums. Previously he had demanded land in Dalmatia and the two Venetias also (Zos. 5,48,3).

**17.** Olympius' second spell as master of the offices is attested nowhere else. Constantius did not marry Placidia until 417, but Olympius was probably killed long before that date. Philostorgius 12,1 (= *Fr.* 5,3) says that he was killed soon after holding the post of master of the offices.

**18.** The reference is to Radagaisus' invasion of Italy in 405-06. Zosimus, too, (5,26,5) says that Stilicho incorporated some of the survivors (probably Ostrogoths) into his auxiliary forces. This note could come from a discussion of the followers of Stilicho who joined Alaric (cf. Zos. 5,35,5-6).

**19.** Other names in Olympiodorus *Fr.* 14. Zosimus (6,7,2) records Lampadius, praetorian prefect of Italy; Marcianus, urban prefect; Valens, master of the cavalry (so Zos. 6,10,1). Tertullus was named consul (Zos. 6,7,4). On the splitting of the domestics into cavalry and infantry see Jones 1964, II p.636.

**20.** Zosimus (6,7,1) is equally scornful of Attalus' pretensions. Valesius took πάτρια to refer to a promise to restore the ancestral pagan rites. More probably it reflects the traditional promise of new Emperors to respect the general rights of the Roman senate (= *iura patria*). Attalus' speech was thoroughly anachronistic.

**21.** According to Zosimus (6,8,2) these were expected while Stilicho was still alive.

**22.** According to Zosimus (6,12,1) most of the senate now agreed with Alaric's advice.

**23.** Zosimus (6,12,2) says that Attalus was deposed before Ariminum. He also seems to suggest that the deposition did not follow an agreement with Honorius but was rather designed to facilitate one.

**24.** The Greek is ambiguous here. I take Sozomen to be saying that Honorius restored Attalus' officials to the rank and honours which they had held before his usurpation, not before his deposition.

**25.** With τὴν ἰδιώτην ἀνθελέσθαι βίον cf. Olymp. *Fr.* 14: τὸν ἰδιώτην . . . βίον ἀνθῃρημένος, but used of Attalus.

**26.** Olymp. *Fr.* 14 ascribes this demand to Jovianus (Jovius). Zosimus (6,8,1) is ambiguous, reporting that Jovius put it forward as a demand of Attalus.

**27.** This is probably an error. Sarus had perhaps been master of the soldiers in Gaul in 407, but Zosimus (5,36,2) is explicit that Honorius passed over Sarus after Stilicho's death. Sarus' defeat of Alaric is a doublet of his attack which aborted the peace-conference after the deposition of Attalus and precipitated the sack of Rome (Sozomen 9,9,2-5 = *Fr.* 11,1); at this time he was in Picenum siding with neither party (Zos. 6,13,2). Similarly, the second occupation of Portus was probably a part of the third siege of Rome rather than a prelude to Attalus' deposition.

**28.**  The reading τὰς Ἄλπεις is clearly wrong and probably hides the name of a place now unknown. Cluverius (in Valesius *ad loc.*) suggested Κλάσσην, the port of Ravenna, which is only twenty-three stades distant. But this has not found acceptance.

**29.**  Zosimus (6,13,2) says that the enmity was with Ataulf.

**30.**  The final part of this passage is clearly a Christian version. But it is not impossible that Olympiodorus mentioned sanctuary in St. Peter's (cf. Zos. 5,35,4 on Eucherius' sanctuary in a Roman church).

**31.**  The rest of the passage of Philostorgius is broken by two lacunae of 2 and 2 ²/₅ lines (so Bidez). In it the historian speaks of someone of Sarmatian origin (who, it has been conjectured, was a first wife of Ataulf) and then refers forward to Ataulf's marriage to Placidia, which is interpreted as a fulfilment of the prophecy of *Daniel* 2: 31-45 (the image seen by Nebuchodonosor with the feet partly of iron and partly of clay).

**32.**  Although in vol. I p.163 n.11 I dismissed this passage, I have included it as possibly from Olympiodorus for the following (I confess, rather weak) reasons: Socrates 9,9,4 (= *Fr.* 11,1) says that the city fell by treachery; Olympiodorus seems to have liked to remark cannibalism; if Zosimus 6,7,4 is good evidence, Olympiodorus seems to have been hostile to the Anicii, and it would have been a nice touch to record the treachery (however well-meant) of one of the leading females of that family.

**33.**  Zosimus (6,2,2) calls them Justinianus and Nebigastios (emended to Nebiogastes by the editors). The accounts of Photius, Zosimus and Sozomen are here very close, even to verbal parallels.

**34.**  At this point, if a mutilated passage of Zosimus (6,4,2) is any guide, the original listed the officials given to Constans as Caesar.

**35.**  I translate ἀναλαβόντες ἑαυτοὺς thus on the basis of Zosimus 6,3,2, who says that earlier Constantine had routed these tribes (for the sense of ἀναλαμβάνω cf. Thuc. 6,26,2).

**36.**  Called Jovius by Zosimus and Sozomen. The error is probably Photius's.

**37.**  The MSS read Λιβερῶνα, which I have retained. Bidez, following Valesius, reads Βέρωνα, which is impossible if Constantine started from Arles, as he seems to have done. Ortelius (cited by Valesius in *PG* LXVII col. 1619) identified the town as Libarna in Liguria, which in my view is correct. (Another suggestion is a Libero, identified with modern Viverone, near to Vercellae, which, however, like Verona, is not in Liguria.) If Libarna is meant, then Constantine would have marched from Arles via the coast road (thus παραμείψας is absolutely correct) and turned north through Libarna intending to cross the Po and secure his rear by taking the northern cities before the advance upon Ravenna. This passage, indeed, is a good example of the attention to geographical detail which was remarked in vol. I p.38.

**38.** This sentence, so baldly Christian, would not be from Olympiodorus.

**39.** The words from καταπεσούσης to Ἀλανοί repeat almost verbatim those of 12,3 (= *Fr.* 13,2). Sozomen has omitted to inform us that Constans had been sent back to Spain (Zosimus 6,5,2 puts the return, probably wrongly, before his elevation to Augustus) to supersede Gerontius (so Bury 1958 I p.192), who had failed to keep the barbarians out of Spain. This precipitated Gerontius' revolt.

**40.** In this passage Maximus is twice called the son of Gerontius, whereas Sozomen (9,13,1 = *Fr.* 17,2) calls him οἰκεῖος and Gregory of Tours (*Hist. Franc.* 2,9) *cliens.* Usually the latter are followed, and Maximus is called a dependent (e.g. *PLRE* II 'Maximus' 4). However, Photius is quite specific, and it is perhaps easier to see how οἰκεῖος (with its secondary Byzantine usage as a possessive) developed out of the statement that he was one of the δομέστικοι (= the imperial bodyguards) than how he was transformed from a dependent to a son. Valesius (in *PG* LXVII col. 1622) is wrong to cite Prosper Tiro, *Chron. s.a.* 412, as evidence of Maximus' low birth and status as a dependent. Prosper's words, *modestia humilitasque hominis*, refer to his character, not station in life.

**41.** In the next sentence Constans is sent out to Vienne. This ordering of material may reflect Olympiodorus' own confused narrative or it may indicate that this first sentence is from a source (an epitome?) other than Olympiodorus. Sozomen does have a second, Christian, source, as is clear from the later praise of Nonnichia.

**42.** This explanation is compatible with the apparently different one offered by Photius' summary; they are, in fact, complementary. The flight of Gerontius from Arles and the loss of most of his (non-Spanish) troops meant that the Spanish soldiery, who presumably resented not only the firm hand of the regime but also a foreign general with a foreign garrison allied with the barbarians, could now attempt a coup since he was badly weakened. Thus, οἰκείου στρατοῦ of Photius does not mean Gerontius' private army (as Gordon 1960, p.37) but his troops as opposed to those of the other generals and usurpers, and εὐκαταφρόνητον of Sozomen does not impute personal cowardice to Gerontius (as it is usually taken) but means that he could now be taken lightly because of the crumbling of his power.

**43.** Κεκτημένον appears to render the Latin legal term *possessor.*

**44.** Τῆς ἀφίλου πράξεως is the reading of Bidez, the sense of which is clear. The older editors read τῆς Οὐλφίλα πράξεως, which Valesius takes as a jest: the state thanked Ecdicius for what Ulfilas had already achieved by defeating Edobich. Nicephorus Callistus, in his transcription of this passage (*HE* 14,6 = *PG* CXLVI col. 1073), has simply τῆς πράξεως.

**45.** The proverb of the wolf gaping unsuccessfully for food is common in comedy: cf. Euphron in Athenaeus *Deipn.* 9,380B, χανεῖν λύκον διὰ κενῆς. Nicephorus Callistus, in his transcription of this passage (*loc.cit.*), adds λύκος.

**46.** The identity of this place has caused much dispute; see Bijvank 1938 p.381 and Vannerus 1936 pp.5-22 (with older bibliography). Mayence (Mogontiacum) is the obvious candidate, but that requires both the emendation of the name of the town and the changing of ἑτέρας to πρώτης (i.e. Germania Prima). The best guess is probably that of H. Gregoire, supported hesitantly by Vannerus, Montzen in Belgium. The place is obscure, but Olympiodorus seems to have liked such details.

**47.** The phrase δι' αἰνιγμάτων is unclear. Perhaps Olympiodorus had Jovinus, a presumably well-educated Gallo-Roman, use his learning to launch an oblique attack, in a speech or a *bon mot*, upon Attalus' interference, which escaped the notice of the uneducated barbarians.

**48.** The MSS vary between σάκκοις ("with sacks") and σόκκοις (rare = "with lassoes"). With Gordon (1960 p.198 n.9) I prefer the latter on the ground that it makes sense. Henry (*ad* Phot. *loc.cit.*) prints the latter, but translates "en lui jetant un sac sur la tête," which conjures up a rather bathetic image.

**49.** As Maenchen-Helfen pointed out (1973 p.73), Photius does not say that Donatus was a Hunnic king; in fact, the name is Roman, and he could have been a renegade (cf. *ibid.* p.432). On the other hand, his prominence in the fragment suggests that he was some kind of leader amongst the Huns. There is no basis at all for the view of Cameron (1965 p.497, accepted by Matthews 1970 pp.79f.) that Olympiodorus' mission on this embassy was to have Donatus killed.

**50.** 'Maximinus' is clearly an error for (Magnus) 'Maximus'; Μαξίμου would certainly have been in Olympiodorus. The identity of 'Carthage' is unclear. It is generally taken to be African Carthage, but Bury (1958 I p.195 n.2) thinks that while the heads of Jovinus and Sebastian were sent to Africa in view of Heraclian's revolt, those of Constantine and Julian were sent to Carthagena in Spain. Since Photius says not that the heads of Constantine and Julian were exposed but that they were cut off at Carthage, and since they were killed near to Ravenna, perhaps Schottus' proposal to read 'Ραβέννης should be accepted. In fact, the *Annals of Ravenna* (cited in *PLRE* II 'Iovinus' 2) state that the heads of Jovinus and Sebastian were brought there on August 30th 412 (cf. Theophanes *Chron. a.m.* 5904, who says that they were taken to Rome).

**51.** Jovinus seems to be the correct form, not Jovianus (as also Philostorgius). *PLRE* II 'Maximus' 4 takes this Maximus to be Gerontius' Emperor who earlier fled to the barbarians, and it suggests that the report of his execution is wrong (alternatively, that he is the same as a later usurper in Spain = 'Maximus' 7). However, perhaps this report is an error arising out of Olympiodorus' mention at this point of the exposure of the head of Magnus Maximus (see previous note). Does ἀδοκήτως suggest that Olympiodorus had written up his account of Jovinus' usurpation as one that had high hopes of success, but that was ruined by a sudden reversal, the unwise estrangement of Ataulf?

**52.** What follows is a Christian disquisition upon God's hatred of usurpers, which corresponds (though the sentiments differ) to Sozomen 9,16.

**53.** Παστάς is usually translated "bridal chamber", but it was not the Roman custom to hold the marriage celebrations there. Here, therefore, it must just mean "hall" as in, e.g., Apollonius Rhodius 1,789.

**54.** The juxtaposition of this wedding description with the consular procession of Constantius, which was remarked in vol. I p.46, is pointed up by its dating to the beginning of January, the time of the consular procession, and Ataulf's wearing a Roman military cloak (χλανίς = χλαμύς = *paludamentum*).

**55.** On the passage of Philostorgius cf. n.31.

**56.** In vol. I p.140 n.70 I wrongly accepted Thompson's (1944 p.49 and n.1) interpretation of this passage. Matthews (1973 p.355 and n.4), citing A. Chastagnol, *La Préfecture urbaine à Rome sous le bas-empire* (Paris, 1960) p.292 takes the number 14,000 to be the total increase since the last assessment ("conducted, perhaps, shortly after the sack of Rome") of the inhabitants eligible for the dole. Such an increase between 410 and 414 (the date of Albinus' prefecture) seems rather too small to be an indicator of significant recovery. What I now take Albinus to be saying is that the number of eligible recipients has increased enormously. As an example of the scale of the increase he points out that on one day of the assessment − but not the only day − 14,000 were registered. In this case 14,000 would not be the total increase, but the most spectacular result of a day's registration (presumably the first) and an indication of a much larger overall growth. If Philostorgius 12,5 (= *Fr.* 26,2) is to be trusted, the increase was comparatively recent.

**57.** Dubius is called Everulf by Jordanes (*Get.* 31,163), who seems to offer a different motive (Ataulf's mockery of his short stature) for the murder. But since it is likely that his first master was Sarus (cf. Oost 1968 pp.134f.), he was probably part of the plot to replace Ataulf by Singeric.

**58.** This seems to be an error. Attalus had earlier been abandoned by the Goths and had been captured while trying to flee (Oost 1968 pp.132f.).

**59.** The MSS here read τούτους, and it is just possible that other names have been lost in the preceding lacuna. But Nicephorus Callistus (*HE* 13,35 = *PG* CXLVI col. 1044), who places his account of Attalus' punishment after the first deposition (perhaps reflecting ultimately

Olympiodoran repetition), speaks only of Attalus' punishment. So the emendation τοῦτον is probably correct.

**60.**    This phrase imitates κατῆρας εἰς τὰς Ἀθήνας of Plato, *Hipp. Mai.* 281A, which is used by Socrates to introduce Hippias of Elis, a much-travelled polymath who, like Olympiodorus, was used to conduct state business.

**61.**    Hesychius, *s.v.* Ἀκρωμεῖται, glosses this with οἱ μείζονες.

**62.**    The word τροῦλα is, of course, the Latin *trulla* ("scoop"). Thus the Goths paid one *solidus* for a scoop of grain holding under one-third of one-sixteenth of a *modius*, that is the enormous price of 48 *solidi* per *modius*. This compares with the standard rate of 40 *modii* per *solidus* for Numidia and Mauretania set by Valentinian III in 445 (*Nov. Val.* 13,4) and a price of 10 *modii* per *solidus* in a time of scarcity in Liguria given by Cassiodorus (*Var.* 10,27; 12,27-28). It reflects not only the utter dependency of the Visigoths upon the grain supplied (and currently withheld) by the Romans, but perhaps Vandal willingness to relieve them of the treasures accumulated at the sack of Rome. The Vandals in question would be the Silings who had settled in Baetica and whom the Goths later annihilated.

**63.**    The measures are probably *modii* (each = approx. ¼ bushel). Photius omits to record that Wallia also agreed to fight for the Empire against the Vandals, Sueves and Alans in Spain.

**64.**    In reading κεκωλισμένων and κώλου I follow Frantz (1966 pp.377-80). The alternative readings, κεκολλημένων and κόλλου, would have the investigation concerned with the glueing of books, a menial task and hardly worth a statue. The object of the inquiry seems to have been to ascertain the standard length of a line of writing, either for the calculation of the rate of pay for the copyists (so Frantz) or simply as an academic question in its own right. Recently R.J. Penella (1980 pp.245f.) has pointed out that it is not wholly clear from Photius' summary that the statue was a reward for solving the problem of the κῶλα since καί need not be explanatory; it may have marked some other achievement.

**65.**    Given the proximity to the remark about the lack of clouds, it is a reasonable assumption that the writer is speaking of sundials rather than water clocks (as Gordon 1960 p.17).

**66.**    The Herodotean reference is 3,26,1, where it is said that Oasis is seven days from Thebes across the sand (ψάμμου). Herodorus is otherwise only known as a writer on the Argonauts ('Herodorus' 5 in *RE* VII col.988). Photius does not make it clear whether the proofs that Oasis was an island were Olympiodorus' own or quoted from Herodorus. I have assumed the former, since this passage is part of what was probably a longer dissertation on Olympiodorus' own homeland. The 'proofs' presumably have the sand blowing in from the West and assume that the sea is only a short distance to the West. The great Oasis would be El Kharga, the other large one probably Dakhla, somewhat under 100 miles to the West (thus both ἐξωτέρω and καταντικρύ are apposite), the smaller one Farafra, about 200 miles north-west of El Kharga. (For the translation of ὄρος = "desert", an Egyptian usage, see the examples in L. & S.)

67.   Despite the hesitation of Oost (1968 p.142), Olympiodorus seems to indicate clearly that the wedding took place on the same day as the consular procession (Jan. 1, 417).

68.   The ungrammatical English reflects Photius' Greek. Niebuhr's correction, μέλλον, is tidy, but not necessary.

69.   Haupt (1866 p.30) explained the phenomenon as St. Elmo's Fire.

70.   This bird would probably have been a parrakeet. The Alexandrine parrakeet (*Psittacula eupatria*) and the plumhead parrakeet (*Psittacula cyanocephala*), both introduced by Alexander from the East (cf. Ctesias in Photius *Bibl. Cod.* 72, I p.134 ed. Henry), were popular in antiquity.

71.   The Blemmyes inhabited the region between the Nile and the Red Sea, roughly south of the First Cataract. After a series of raids by the Blemmyes, Diocletian moved the border northward to the area of Philae, abandoning Prima and the four other towns named by Olympiodorus.

72.   The translation of σμάραγδος is never certain, since it might refer to a number of green stones. But in this case the reference is probably to the emerald mines to the north of Berenice on the Red Sea coast.

73.   This Libanius is otherwise unknown. Henry's translation indicates that he was successful in his demonstration, but the Greek does not say that, although Olympiodorus seems to have felt confident in his powers (cf. δύνασθαι). As in the case of the refusal to use the Etruscan diviners during the siege of Rome (Sozomen 9,6,5 = *Fr.* 7,5), Olympiodorus probably presented this as a missed opportunity.

74.   Sometimes identified with Padusia, the wife of Felix, who was the first master of the soldiers of Valentinian III and a rival of Aetius (*PLRE* II 'Spadusa').

75.   John was proclaimed at Rome and accepted by the western military authorities, including the master of the soldiers, Castinus (Matthews 1975 pp.379f.).

76.   Baldwin (*Ant. Class.* 1980 p.222) points out that ἡρωϊκός is also used of Sarus (*Fr.* 6). The portraits of both Boniface and Sarus lay stress upon personal courage and prowess in single combats or small-group skirmishes. The vocabulary might be heroic in the Greek tradition (cf. ἠρίστευεν of Boniface in the present passage), but it describes prowess which, in the fifth century A.D., was Germanic rather than Greek or Roman.

**77.** This seems to be Olympiodorus' own composition. Baldwin (*art. cit.* p.216) takes it as sardonic. I doubt that (see below n.81).

**78.** This measurement would have been carried out in connection with the repairing of the walls of Rome by Honorius and Stilicho on the eve of Alaric's invasion of Italy in 402-03 (not 408-10, as Gordon 1960 p.23). The figure is far too high. The circuit of the Aurelian Wall was about twelve miles.

**79.** The best MS of Photius reads Ὀλυμπίου, and Gordon (1960 p.197 n.26) suggested that this Olympius might have been identical with Stilicho's enemy. But his career (*PLRE* II 'Olympius' 2) is not that of a leading Roman aristocrat, and it is unlikely that the wealth here envisaged would have survived his fall. Olympius is not a name common amongst the high Roman aristocrats of the period, and the emendation Ὀλυβρίου has often been accepted, the identification being made with the Olybrius who was consul in 395 and who died before 410 (*PLRE* I 'Olybrius' 2). This fits well with the passage of Olympiodorus, who indicates that when Probus celebrated his praetorship, in 423-25, he gave the games himself (and therefore his father was presumably dead). Moreover, if he were about seventeen when he gave the games (which was about the usual age for the praetorship at the time), he would have been born *ca* 406-08. (For the corruption cf. *P.Oxy.* 1133, cited in *PLRE* I *art.cit.*, where Olybrius' name is rendered Olymbrius.) An alternative would be to read Ἀλυπίου with Photius' MS. M, who could be Alypius 13 in *PLRE* I. At any rate, it is quite likely that Probus was a member of the Anician *gens*, which made much use of both the names Olybrius and Alypius.

**80.** Baldwin (*Ant. Class.* 1980 p.216 n.15) suggests that the term λογογράφος might be mocking. More likely it is admiringly archaic.

**81.** The suggestion of Thompson that in this passage Olympiodorus is condemning the unequal distribution of wealth was rejected in vol. I n.97 on p.142. Even the hesitant suggestion of Matthews (1970 p.95) that at least the contrast with imperial bankruptcy is implicitly recognised, must be rejected. This and the previous passage are wholly panegyrical and preparatory to the climactic coronation of Valentinian III.

**82.** He was five years and three months old, having been born on July 2nd (or 3rd), 419. The ceremony took place at Thessalonika on October 23rd, 424.

**83.** The coronation took place on October 23rd, 425, so that Valentinian was six years and three months old.

**84.** Valesius' emendation ὑποστρατήγους ("junior officers") is often accepted, but if John, coming from Rome to Ravenna, had compulsorily retired some of the senior officers loyal to Honorius, that would have been a good reason for the disaffection.

# PRISCUS

**Text and Translation**

# PRISCUS

## TESTIMONIA

### 1

(*Suda* Π 2301)

Πρίσκος, Πανίτης, σοφιστής, γεγονὼς ἐπὶ τῶν χρόνων Θεοδοσίου τοῦ μικροῦ· ἔγραψεν Ἱστορίαν Βυζαντιακὴν καὶ τὰ κατὰ Ἀττήλαν ἐν βιβλίοις ὀκτώ, Μελέτας τε Ῥητορικὰς καὶ Ἐπιστολάς.

3 Ἀττήλαν edd. [Ἄτταλον codd.

### 2

(Evagrius *HE* 1,17)

Ἐν τούτοις τοῖς χρόνοις ὁ πολὺς τῷ λόγῳ πόλεμος ἐκεκίνητο Ἀττίλα τοῦ τῶν Σκυθῶν βασιλέως· ὃν περιέργως καὶ ἐς τὰ μάλιστα λογίως Πρίσκος ὁ ῥήτωρ γράφει, μετὰ πολλῆς τῆς κομψείας διηγούμενος ὅπως τε κατὰ τῶν ἑῴων καὶ ἑσπερίων ἐπεστράτευσε μερῶν, οἵας τε καὶ ὅσας πόλεις ἑλὼν κατήγαγε, καὶ ὅσα πεπραχὼς τῶν ἐντεῦθεν μετέστη.    5

## FRAGMENTA

### 1

(Jordanes, *Get.* 24,123-26)

Quorum natio saeva, ut Priscus istoricus refert, Meotida palude ulteriore ripa insidens, venationi tantum nec alio labore experta, nisi quod, postquam crevisset in populis, fraudibus et rapinis vicinarum gentium quiete conturbans. huius ergo gentis, ut adsolet, venatores, dum in interioris Meotidae ripam venationes inquirent, animadvertunt, quomodo ex inproviso cerva se illis optulit ingressaque    5
paludem nunc progrediens nunc subsistens index viae se tribuit. quam secuti venatores paludem Meotidam, quem inpervium ut pelagus aestimant, pedibus transierunt. mox quoque Scythica terra

7 indicem viae se praebuit XY    9 affirmabant XYZ

# PRISCUS

## TESTIMONIA

### 1.

(*Suda* Π 2301)

Priscus of Panium, sophist, lived during the time of Theodosius the Younger. He wrote a History of Byzantium and of Attila in eight books, Exercises in Rhetoric, and Letters.

### 2

(Evagrius *HE* 1,17)

At this time was fought the very famous war with Attila, the king of the Scythians, of which Priscus the rhetor wrote a detailed and very erudite History. With great elegance he describes how Attila campaigned against both the eastern and western parts of the Empire, the nature and size of the cities which he captured and destroyed, and the great damage which he wreaked before he withdrew.

## FRAGMENTS

### 1

(Jordanes, *Get.* 24,123-26)

According to the historian Priscus, this savage tribe [i.e. the Huns] lived on the further shore of the Maeotic marsh, practising only hunting and no other form of labour except that when they increased in numbers, they harassed the neighbouring peoples with treachery and rapine. Hunters from this tribe, who, as was their custom, were seeking game along their shore of Maeotis, noticed a hind which suddenly appeared to them, entered the marsh and, now moving ahead and now waiting for them, led them along a path. This the hunters followed and crossed on foot the Maeotic marsh which they thought to be as impassable as a sea. Soon the land of Scythia, which was unknown to

ignotis apparuit, cerva disparuit. quod, credo, spiritus illi, unde pro-    10
geniem trahunt, ad Scytharum invidia id egerunt.

Illi vero, qui praeter Meotidam alium mundum esse paenitus
ignorabant, admiratione ducti terrae Scythicae et, ut sunt sollertes,
iter illud nullae ante aetati notissimum divinitus sibi ostensum rati,
ad suos redeunt, rei gestum edocent, Scythiam laudant persuasaque    15
gente sua via, qua cerva indice dedicerant, ad Scythiam properant, et
quantoscumque prius in ingressu Scytharum habuerunt, litavere
victoriae, reliquos perdomitos subegerunt. nam mox ingentem illam
paludem transierunt, ilico Alpidzuros, Alcildzuros, Itimaros, Tun-
carsos et Boiscos, qui ripae istius Scythiae insedebant, quasi    20
quaedam turbo gentium rapuerunt.
(Cf. Procopius, *Wars* 8,5,4 and 7-12)

2

(*Exc. de Leg. Rom.* 1)

    Ὅτι Ῥοῦα βασιλεύοντος Οὔννων, Ἀμιλζούροις καὶ Ἰτιμάροις
καὶ Τούνσουρσι καὶ Βοΐσκοις καὶ ἑτέροις ἔθνεσι προσοικοῦσι τὸν
Ἴστρον καὶ ἐς τὴν Ῥωμαίων ὁμαιχμίαν καταφυγγάνουσιν ἐς μάχην
ἐλθεῖν προῃρημένος ἐκπέμπει Ἤσλαν εἰωθότα ἐπὶ τοῖς διαφόροις
αὐτῷ τε καὶ Ῥωμαίοις διακονεῖσθαι, λύεω τὴν προϋπάρχουσαν    5
εἰρήνην ἀπειλῶν, εἰ μή γε πάντας τοὺς παρὰ σφᾶς καταφυγόντας
ἐκδοῖεν. βουλευομένων δὲ Ῥωμαίων στεῖλαι πρεσβείαν παρὰ τοὺς
Οὔννους, πρεσβεύεω μὲν ἤθελον Πλίνθας καὶ Διονύσιος, Πλίνθας
μὲν τοῦ Σκυθικοῦ, Διονύσιος δὲ τοῦ Θρακίου γένους, ἀμφότεροι δὲ
στρατοπέδων ἡγούμενοι καὶ ἄρξαντες τὴν ὕπατον παρὰ Ῥωμαίοις    10
ἀρχήν. ἐπειδὴ δὲ ἐδόκει Ἤσλαν παρὰ τὸν Ῥοῦαν ἀφικνεῖσθαι πρότερον τῆς ἐκπεμφθησομένης πρεσβείας, συνεκπέμπει Πλίνθας
Σηγγίλαχον, ἄνδρα τῶν ἐπιτηδείων, πεῖσαι τὸν Ῥοῦαν αὐτῷ καὶ μὴ
ἑτέροις Ῥωμαίων ἐς λόγους ἐλθεῖν.

    Τελευτήσαντος δὲ Ῥοῦα, καὶ περιστάσης τῆς Οὔννων βασι-    15
λείας ἐς Ἀττήλαν καὶ Βλήδαν, ἐδόκει τῇ Ῥωμαίων βουλῇ Πλίνθαν
πρεσβεύεσθαι παρ' αὐτούς. καὶ κυρωθείσης ἐπ' αὐτῷ παρὰ βασιλέως ψήφου, ἐβούλετο καὶ Ἐπιγένην ὁ Πλίνθας συμπρεσβεύεω
αὐτῷ ὡς μεγίστην ἐπὶ σοφίᾳ δόξαν ἐπιφερόμενον καὶ τὴν ἀρχὴν
ἔχοντα τοῦ κοιαίστορος. χειροτονίας δὲ καὶ ἐπ' αὐτῷ γενομένης,    20
ἄμφω ἐπὶ τὴν πρεσβείαν ἐξώρμησαν καὶ παραγίνονται ἐς Μάργον
(ἡ δὲ πόλις τῶν ἐν Ἰλλυρίᾳ Μυσῶν πρὸς τῷ Ἴστρῳ κεμμένη ποταμῷ
ἀντικρὺ Κωνσταντίας φρουρίου κατὰ τὴν ἑτέραν ὄχθην διακειμένου),

1 Ἀλπιζούροις Maenchen-Helfen (1973 p.402)

them, came into view, and the hind disappeared. I believe that those spirits, of whom the Huns were engendered, did this out of hatred for the Scythians.[1]

The hunters, who were completely unaware that there was another world beyond Maeotis, were seized with wonder at the land of Scythia and, concluding that the way which was utterly unknown to any age before theirs had been revealed to them by a divine power (since they were knowledgeable of such things), returned to their own people. They related what they had done, praised Scythia and, having won over their tribe, led them to Scythia by the route which the hind had revealed to them. Whomsoever they came upon immediately after their entrance into Scythia they annihilated, the others they utterly defeated and made their subjects. For as soon as they had crossed the great marsh, they fell like some human whirlwind upon the Alpizuri, the Alcilzuri, the Itimari, the Tuncarsi and the Boisci, who inhabited that area of Scythia.[2]     (Cf. Procopius, *Wars* 8,5,4 and 7-12)

## 2

(*Exc. de Leg. Rom.* 1)

When Rua was king of the Huns, the Amilzuri, Itimari, Tounsoures, Boisci and other tribes who were living near to the Danube were fleeing to fight on the side of the Romans.[3] Rua decided to go to war with these tribes and sent Eslas, a man who usually handled negotiations over differences between himself and the Romans, threatening to break the present peace if they did not hand over all who had fled to them. The Romans wished to send an embassy to the Huns, and both Plinthas and Dionysius wished to go. Plinthas was a Scythian, Dionysius a Thracian; both were generals and had held the Roman consulship. Since it seemed that Eslas would reach Rua before the embassy was despatched, Plinthas sent along with him Sengilach, one of his own retainers, to persuade Rua to negotiate with none of the Romans but himself.

When Rua died, the kingship of the Huns devolved upon Attila and Bleda, and the Roman senate recommended that Plinthas be sent as ambassador to them. When this vote had been ratified for him by the Emperor, Plinthas wanted Epigenes as his fellow ambassador, since he had a great reputation for wisdom and held the office of quaestor.[4] When this had been agreed upon, they both set out on this embassy and came to Margus, where the Scythian kings, too, were assembled. (Margus is a city of Moesia in Illyria lying on the river Danube, and opposite it on the far bank is the fortress of Constantia.) They held a meeting

εἰς ἣν καὶ οἱ βασίλειοι συνῆεσαν Σκύθαι. καὶ τὴν σύνοδον ἔξω τῆς
πόλεως ἐποιοῦντο ἐπιβεβηκότες ἵππων· οὐ γὰρ ἐδόκει τοῖς βαρβάροις     25
ἀποβᾶσι λογοποιεῖσθαι, ὥστε καὶ τοὺς Ῥωμαίων πρέσβεις τῆς σφῶν
αὐτῶν ἀξίας προνοουμένους ἀπὸ τῆς αὐτῆς προαιρέσεως ἐς ταὐτὸν
τοῖς Σκύθαις ἐλθεῖν, πρὸς τὸ μὴ τοὺς μὲν ἀφ' ἵππων, τοὺς δὲ πεζοὺς
διαλέγεσθαι . . . τοὺς ἀπὸ τῆς Σκυθικῆς καταφεύγοντας, ἀλλὰ καὶ
τοὺς ἤδη πεφευγότας σὺν καὶ τοῖς αἰχμαλώτοις Ῥωμαίοις τοῖς ἄνευ     30
λύτρων ἐς τὰ σφέτερα ἀφιγμένοις ἐκδίδοσθαι, εἰ μή γε ὑπὲρ ἑκάστου
πεφευγότος τοῖς κατὰ πόλεμον κτησαμένοις ὀκτὼ δοθεῖεν χρυσοῖ·
ἔθνει δὲ βαρβάρῳ μὴ συμμαχεῖν Ῥωμαίους πρὸς Οὔννους αἱρουμένους πόλεμον· εἶναι δὲ καὶ τὰς πανηγύρεις ἰσονόμους καὶ ἀκιν-
δύνους Ῥωμαίοις τε καὶ Οὔννοις· φυλάττεσθαι δὲ καὶ διαμένειν τὰς     35
συνθήκας ἑπτακοσίων λιτρῶν χρυσίου ἔτους ἑκάστου τελουμένων
παρὰ Ῥωμαίων τοῖς βασιλείοις Σκύθαις· πρότερον δὲ πεντήκοντα
καὶ τριακόσιαι αἱ τοῦ τέλους ἐτύγχανον οὖσαι. ἐπὶ τούτοις ἐσπένδοντο
Ῥωμαῖοί τε καὶ Οὗννοι καὶ πάτριον ὅρκον ὀμόσαντες ἐς τὰ ἀμφότερα
ἐπανῆεσαν. οἱ δὲ παρὰ Ῥωμαίους καταφυγόντες ἐξεδόθησαν βαρ-     40
βάροις, ἐν οἷς καὶ παῖδες Μάμα καὶ Ἀτακὰμ τοῦ βασιλείου γένους,
οὓς ἐν Καρσῷ φρουρίῳ Θρακίῳ οἱ παρειληφότες ἐσταύρωσαν δίκας
αὐτοὺς πραττόμενοι τῆς φυγῆς.
    Οἱ δὲ περὶ Ἀττήλαν καὶ Βλήδαν τὴν εἰρήνην πρὸς Ῥωμαίους
θέμενοι διεξῄεσαν τὰ ἐν τῇ Σκυθικῇ ἔθνη χειρούμενοι καὶ πόλεμον     45
πρὸς Σορόσγους συνεστήσαντο.

24 συνῆεσαν Σκύθαι Niebuhr [συνῆσαν Σκύθαις codd.    29 Ῥωμαίους οὐ
μόνον εἰς τὸ μέλλον μὴ δέχεσθαι suppl. Niebuhr in lac.    33-34 αἱρουμένους
de Boor [αἱρουμένους codd. αἱρομένους edd. αἱρομένῳ Niebuhr in app. crit.
39 σφέτερα ante ἀμφότερα add. Bekker

[3]
[1. (John of Antioch Fr. 194 = Exc. de Virt. et Vit. 72)
    Ὅτι Θεοδόσιος τὴν ἀρχὴν παρὰ Ἀρκαδίου τοῦ πατρὸς <δια->
δεξάμενος ἀπόλεμος ἦν καὶ δειλίᾳ συνέζη καὶ τὴν εἰρήνην χρήμασι
καὶ οὐχ ὅπλοις ἐκτήσατο. καὶ ὑπὸ τοῖς εὐνούχοις πάντα ἔπραττεν. καὶ
ἐς τοσοῦτον τὰ πράγματα ἀτοπίας φέρεσθαι οἱ εὐνοῦχοι παρεσκεύα-
σαν, ὡς συνελόντι εἰπεῖν ἀποβουκολοῦντες τὸν Θεοδόσιον, ὥσπερ     5
τοὺς παῖδας ἀθύρμασιν, οὐδὲν ὅ τι καὶ ἄξιον μνήμης διαπράξασθαι
συνεχώρησαν, καίτοι ἀγαθῆς ὑπάρχοντα φύσεως· ἀλλ' ἐς ν' ἐνι-
αυτοὺς συνελάσαντα βαναύσοις τέ τισι τέχναις καὶ θήραις προσκαρτερεῖν παρέπεισαν, ὥστε αὐτούς τε καὶ τὸν Χρυσάφιον ἔχειν τὸ

1 δια- add. Valesius    2-3 συζῶν . . . κτησάμενος Suda    7 συνεχώρησαν
[παρεσκεύασαν Suda    8-9 συνελάσαντα . . . καὶ [ἐληλυθὼς διετέλεσε βαναύ-
σους τέ τινας μετιὼν τέχνας καὶ θήρα προσκαρτερῶν, ὥστε τοὺς εὐνούχους
καὶ Suda

outside the city mounted on horseback. For the barbarians do not think it proper to confer dismounted, so that the Romans, mindful of their own dignity, chose to meet the Scythians in the same fashion, lest one side speak from horseback, the other on foot . . . <it was agreed> not only that for the future the Romans not receive those who fled from Scythia, but also that those who had already fled should be handed back together with the Roman prisoners-of-war who had made their way back to their own country without ransom, unless for each one who escaped eight *solidi* were given to those who had captured him in war; that the Romans should make no alliance with a barbarian people against the Huns when the latter were preparing for war against them;[5] that there should be safe markets with equal rights for Romans and Huns; that the treaty should be maintained and last as long as the Romans paid seven hundred pounds of gold each year to the Scythian kings (previously the payments had been three hundred and fifty pounds of gold). On these terms the Romans and the Huns made a treaty and, having sworn their native oaths, they returned each to their own country. The fugitives amongst the Romans were handed back to the barbarians, amongst whom were Mama and Atakam, children of the royal house. Those who received them exacted the penalty for their flight by impaling them near to Carsum, a fortress in Thrace.

When they had made peace with the Romans, Attila, Bleda and their forces marched through Scythia subduing the tribes there and also made war on the Sorosgi.[6]

## [3]

[1. (John of Antioch *Fr.* 194 = *Exc. de Virt. et Vit.* 72)

Theodosius, who succeeded his father Arcadius as Emperor, was unwarlike and lived a life of cowardice. He obtained peace by money, not by fighting for it. Everything he did was under the influence of eunuchs, and they brought affairs to such a level of absurdity that, to put it briefly, they distracted Theodosius, as children are distracted with toys, and allowed him to do nothing at all worthy of record, although he had a good character. Even when he had reached fifty years of age they persuaded him to persist in certain low-class pursuits and in wild-beast hunting, so that they, and Chrysaphius in particular,

τῆς βασιλείας κράτος, ὅνπερ ἡ Πουλχερία μετῆλθε, τοῦ ἀδελφοῦ    10
τελευτήσαντος.
(Cf. Suda Θ 145)]

[2. (Suda Θ 145)
Θεοδόσιος, βασιλεὺς Ῥωμαίων, ὁ μικρός. οὗτος διαδεξάμενος
παρὰ πατρὸς τὴν ἀρχήν, ἀπόλεμος ὢν καὶ δειλίᾳ συζῶν καὶ τὴν
εἰρήνην χρήμασιν οὐχ ὅπλοις κτησάμενος, πολλὰ προεξένησε κακὰ
τῇ Ῥωμαίων πολιτείᾳ. ὑπὸ γὰρ τοῖς εὐνούχοις τραφεὶς πρὸς πᾶν
σφίσιν ἐπίταγμα εὐπειθὴς ἦν· ὥστε καὶ τοὺς λογάδας τῆς ἐκείνων    5
δεῖσθαι ἐπικουρίας καὶ πολλὰ νεοχμεῖσθαι ἐν τοῖς πολιτικοῖς καὶ
στρατιωτικοῖς τάγμασι, μὴ παριόντων ἐς τὰς ἀρχὰς ἀνδρῶν τῶν
διέπειν ταύτας δυναμένων ἀλλὰ τῶν χορηγούντων χρυσίον διὰ τὴν
τῶν εὐνούχων πλεονεξίαν.]

8 δὲ post διὰ add. A


[4]
[ (Suda Θ 145)
...καὶ τῶν Σεβαστιανοῦ δορυφόρων πειρατικὸν συστὰν τόν
τε Ἑλλήσποντον καὶ τὴν Προποντίδα διαταράξαι.]


5
(Fr. 1a Dindorf, Müller V p.24)
Οὐάλιψ ὁ πάλαι τοὺς Ῥούβους τοῖς Ῥωμαίοις ἐπαναστήσας
τοῖς ἑῴοις, καταλαβὼν Νοβίδουνον πόλιν πρὸς τῇ ὄχθῃ κειμένην τοῦ
ποταμοῦ, τινάς τε τῶν πολιτῶν διεχειρίσατο καὶ σύμπαντα τὰ ἐν τῷ
ἄστει ἀθροίσας χρήματα κατατρέχειν τὴν Θρακῶν καὶ Ἰλλυριῶν
παρεσκευάζετο μετὰ τῶν νεωτερίζειν σὺν αὐτῷ ἑλομένων. τῆς δὲ    5
παραστησομένης αὐτὸν πεμφθείσης ἐκ βασιλέως δυνάμεως τειχήρης
γενόμενος τοὺς πολιορκοῦντας ἐκ τῶν περιβόλων ἡμύνετο, ἐφ᾽ ὅσον
αὐτῷ τε καὶ τοῖς ἀμφ᾽ αὐτὸν οἷά τε ἦν καρτερεῖν. ἡνίκα γὰρ ἀπη-
γόρευον τῷ πόνῳ διὰ τὸ ἐκ διαδοχῆς τὸ Ῥωμαϊκὸν μάχεσθαι πλῆθος,
ἐς τὰς ἐπάλξεις τοὺς παῖδας τῶν αἰχμαλώτων ἱστῶντες τὴν τῶν    10
ἐναντίων βελῶν ἐπεῖχον φοράν. φίλοι γὰρ τῶν Ῥωμαϊκῶν παίδων οἱ
στρατιῶται οὔτε ἔβαλλον ἐς τοὺς ἐπὶ τοῦ τείχους οὔτε ἠκόντιζον. καὶ
οὕτως αὐτῷ τριβομένου τοῦ χρόνου ἐπὶ συνθήκαις ἡ πολιορκία
ἐλύετο.    (Cf. Suda A 3145, T 458)

1 Ῥούγους Müller    6 αὐτὸν Müller aut αὐτὴν [αὐτῶν cod.    6-7 τειχήρης γενόμενος Suda T 458 [τειχρης [sic] γενομένη̣ς̣ cod.    9 πρός τὸ ʽΡ. μ. πλῆθος
aut τῷ ʽΡωμαϊκῷ μ. πλήθει Müller    11 ὄντες post γὰρ add. Müller

wielded the royal power. After her brother's death Chrysaphius was the object of Pulcheria's vengeance.
(Cf. *Suda* Θ 145)

[2. (*Suda* Θ 145)
Theodosius the Younger, Emperor of the Romans. He became Emperor after his father and because he was unwarlike and lived in cowardice and obtained peace by money, not by fighting, he was the cause of many subsequent evils for the Roman state. Since he had been brought up under the thumbs of eunuchs, he was open to their every demand. The result was that even the senior officials needed their support, and there were many innovations in the civil and military administrations, since positions were not filled by people who could administer them but by people who paid gold for them because of the greed of the eunuchs.]

## [4]

[ (*Suda* Θ 145)
Moreover, piracy broke out amongst Sebastian's retainers and harassed the Hellespont and the Propontis.] [7]

## 5

(*Fr.* 1a Dindorf; Müller V p.24)
Valips, who had earlier roused the Rubi against the eastern Romans, seized Novidunum, a city which lies on the river, slew some of its citizens and, having collected all the wealth in the city, prepared, together with those who had chosen to revolt with him, to overrun Thrace and Illyria.[8] When a force sent by the Emperor was upon him and he was besieged within the city, he kept the besiegers away from the circuit wall for as long as he and those with him could hold out. But when they were worn out by the toil of continually fighting the great number of Romans, they checked the clouds of enemy missiles by placing the children of their prisoners on the ramparts. For the soldiers loved the Roman children and hurled neither missiles nor javelins against those on the wall. In this way Valips gained a breathing space, and the siege was ended on terms.
(Cf. *Suda* A 3145, T 458)

# 6

1. (*Exc. de Leg. Gent.* 1)

Ὅτι τῶν Σκυθῶν κατὰ τὸν τῆς πανηγύρεως καιρὸν καταστρατηγησάντων Ῥωμαίους καὶ πολλοὺς ἀνελόντων, οἱ Ῥωμαῖοι ἐπέστελλον πρὸς τοὺς Σκύθας ἐν αἰτίᾳ σφᾶς ποιούμενοι τῆς τοῦ φρουρίου αἱρέσεως ἔνεκεν καὶ τῆς τῶν σπονδῶν ὀλιγωρίας. οἱ δὲ ἀπεκρίναντο ὡς οὐκ ἀρξάμενοι ἀλλ᾽ ἀμυνόμενοι ταῦτα δράσειαν· τὸν      5
γὰρ τῆς Μάργου ἐπίσκοπον εἰς τὴν αὐτῶν διαβεβηκότα γῆν καὶ διερευνησάμενον τὰς παρὰ σφίσι βασιλείους θήκας σεσυληκέναι τοὺς ἀποκειμένους θησαυρούς· καὶ εἰ μὴ τοῦτον ἐκδοῖεν, ἐκδοῖεν δὲ καὶ τοὺς φυγάδας κατὰ τὰ ὑποκείμενα (εἶναι γὰρ παρὰ Ῥωμαίοις πλείστους) τὸν πόλεμον ἐπάξειν. Ῥωμαίων δὲ τὴν αἰτίαν οὐκ ἀληθῆ      10
φαμένων εἶναι, ἐν τοῖς σφετέροις λόγοις τὸ πιστὸν οἱ βάρβαροι θέμενοι κρίσεως μὲν τῶν ἀμφιβόλων κατωλιγώρουν, πρὸς πόλεμον δὲ ἐτράπησαν, καὶ περαιωθέντες τὸν Ἴστρον πόλεις καὶ φρούρια πλεῖστα ἐπὶ τῷ ποταμῷ ἐκάκωσαν. ἐν οἷς καὶ τὸ Βιμινάκιον εἷλον· πόλις δὲ αὕτη τῶν ἐν Ἰλλυριοῖς Μυσῶν. ὧν γινομένων, καί τινων      15
λογοποιούντων ὡς ὁ τῆς Μάργου ἐπίσκοπος ἐκδοθείη, ὥστε μὴ ἑνὸς ἀνδρὸς περὶ τῷ παντὶ Ῥωμαίων τὸν ἐκ τοῦ πολέμου ἐπαχθῆναι κίνδυνον, ὑποτοπήσας ὁ ἄνθρωπος ἐκδοθήσεσθαι, λαθὼν τοὺς ἐν τῷ ἄστει πρὸς τοὺς πολεμίους παραγίνεται καὶ αὐτοῖς παραδώσειν ὑπισχνεῖται τὴν πόλιν, εἴ γε ἐπιεικές τι οἱ τῶν Σκυθῶν βουλεύσαιντο      20
βασιλεῖς. οἱ δὲ ἔφασαν πάντα ποιήσειν τὰ ἀγαθά, εἰ τὴν αὐτοῦ ἄγοι ἐς ἔργον ὑπόσχεσιν· δεξιῶν τε καὶ ὅρκων ἐπὶ τοῖς εἰρημένοις δοθέντων, μετὰ βαρβαρικῆς πολυπληθίας ἐς τὴν Ῥωμαϊκὴν ἐπάνεισι γῆν καὶ ταύτην προλοχίσας ἀντικρὺ τῆς ὄχθης νυκτὸς διανίστησιν ἐκ συνθήματος καὶ ὑπὸ τοῖς ἀντιπάλοις τὴν πόλιν ποιεῖ. δῃωθείσης δὲ τῆς      25
Μάργου τὸν τρόπον τοῦτον, ἐπὶ μεῖζον ηὐξήθη τὰ τῶν βαρβάρων πράγματα.

2. (*Fr.* 1b Dindorf, Müller V pp.25f.)

Ἐπολιόρκουν οἱ Σκύθαι τὴν Ναϊσσόν· πόλις δὲ αὕτη τῶν Ἰλλυριῶν ἐπὶ †Δανουβα κειμένη ποταμῷ. Κωνσταντῖνον αὐτῆς εἶναι οἰκιστήν φασιν, ὃς καὶ τὴν ὁμώνυμον ἑαυτῷ πόλιν ἐπὶ τῷ Βυζαντίῳ ἐδείματο. οἷα δὴ οὖν πολυάνθρωπόν τε πόλιν αἱρήσειν οἱ βάρβαροι μέλλοντες καὶ ἄλλως ἐρυμνὴν διὰ πάσης ἐχώρουν πείρας. τῶν δὲ      5
ἀπὸ τοῦ ἄστεως οὐ θαρρούντων ἐπεξιέναι πρὸς μάχην, τὸν ποταμὸν ὥστε ῥᾳδίαν εἶναι πλήθει τὴν διάβασιν ἐγεφύρωσαν κατὰ τὸ μεσημβρινὸν μέρος, καθ᾽ ὃ καὶ τὴν πόλιν παρρεῖ, καὶ μηχανὰς τῷ

---

2 Δανουβα cod. [τῷ Ναϊσσῷ ποταμῷ Müller τῷ Νούβᾳ ποταμῷ Dindorf
7 τῷ ante πλήθει add. Müller

# 6

1. (*Exc. de Leg. Gent.* 1)

When the Scythians at the time of the market overcame the Romans by a trick and killed many of them, the Romans sent to the Scythians, blaming them for the capture of the fort and their contempt for the treaty. They replied that they had done these things not to initiate the trouble but as a riposte.[9] For they claimed that the bishop of Margus had crossed over to their land and, searching out their royal tombs,[10] had stolen the valuables stored there. Furthermore, they said that if they did not hand him over and also hand over the fugitives as had been agreed (and there were very many amongst the Romans), they would prosecute the war. When the Romans replied that this claim was untrue, the barbarians, confident in the truth of their own allegations, rejected arbitration of the disputed matters and turned to war. They crossed the Danube and ravaged very many cities and forts along the river, amongst which they took Viminacium, a city of Moesia in Illyria. While these things were happening, some were arguing that the bishop of Margus should be handed over, so that the whole Roman people should not be endangered by the war for the sake of one man. He, suspecting that he would be surrendered, slipped away from those in the city, crossed over to the enemy and promised that he would betray the city to them if the Scythian kings made him any reasonable offer. They said that if he fulfilled his promise, they would treat him well in every way, and hands were shaken and oaths given for what had been promised. He re-crossed to Roman territory with a large force of barbarians, which he concealed right by the river bank, and, rousing it during the night, he handed the city over to the enemy. When Margus had been laid waste in this way, the position of the barbarians was greatly improved.

2. (*Fr.* 1b Dindorf, Müller V pp.25f.)

The Scythians were besieging Naissus, a city of the Illyrians on the river Danuba.[11] They say that it was founded by Constantine,[12] who also built the city at Byzantium named after himself. Since the barbarians were destined to take this populous and also well-fortified city, they made progress with every attempt. Since the citizens did not dare to come out to battle, the Scythians, to make crossing easy for their forces, bridged the river from the southern side at the point where it flowed past the city and brought their machines up to the circuit wall.[13]

περιβόλῳ προσῆγον, πρῶτον μὲν δοκοὺς ἐπὶ τροχῶν κειμένας διὰ τὸ
πρόχειρον αὐτῶν εἶναι [ὡς] τὴν προσαγωγήν· αἷς ἐφεστῶτες      10
ἄνθρωποι ἐς τοὺς ἀπὸ τῶν ἐπάλξεων ἀμυνομένους ἐτόξευον, τῶν ἐξ
ἑκατέρας κεραίας ἑστώτων ἀνδρῶν ὠθούντων τοῖς ποσὶ τοὺς
τροχοὺς καὶ προσαγόντων ὅπη καὶ δέοι τὰς μηχανάς, ὡς ἂν εἴη
βάλλειν ἐπίσκοπα διὰ τῶν ἐν ταῖς ἐφεστρίσι πεποιημένων θυρίδων.
ὥστε γὰρ [ἐν] τοῖς ἐπὶ τῆς δοκοῦ ἀνδράσιν ἀκίνδυνον εἶναι τὴν μάχην,   15
λύγοις διαπλόκοις ἐκαλύπτοντο δέρρεις καὶ διφθέρας ἐχούσαις, κώλυμα τῶν τε ἄλλων βελῶν καὶ ὅσα ἐπὶ σφᾶς πυρφόρα ἐκπέμποιτο.
πολλῶν δὲ τῷ τρόπῳ τούτῳ ἐπιτειχισθέντων ὀργάνων τῇ πόλει,
ὥστε διὰ πλῆθος βελῶν ἐνδοῦναι καὶ ὑποχωρῆσαι τοὺς ἐπὶ τῶν
ἐπάλξεων, προσήγοντο καὶ οἱ καλούμενοι κριοί. μεγίστη δὲ ἄρα καὶ   20
ἥδε ἡ μηχανή· δοκὸς ἐκ ξύλων πρὸς ἄλληλα νευόντων χαλαραῖς
ἀπῃωρημένη ἀλύσεσιν, ἐπιδορατίδα καὶ προκαλύμματα ὃν εἴρηται
τρόπον ἔχουσα, ἀσφαλείας ἕνεκα τῶν ἐργαζομένων. καλῳδίοις γὰρ
ἐκ τῆς ὄπισθεν κεραίας εἷλκον βιαίως ἄνδρες αὐτὴν ἐς τὸ ἐναντίον
τοῦ δεξομένου τὴν πληγήν, καὶ μετὰ ταῦτα ἠφίεσαν, ὥστε τῇ ῥύμῃ   25
πᾶν τὸ ἐμπῖπτον τοῦ τείχους ἀφανίζεσθαι μέρος. οἱ δὲ ἀπὸ τῶν
τειχῶν ἀμυνόμενοι ἁμαξιαίους λίθους πρὸς τοῦτο ἤδη παρεσκευασ-
μένους, ἡνίκα τῷ περιβόλῳ προσαχθείη τὰ ὄργανα, ἐνέβαλλον, καί
τινα μὲν αὐτοῖς ἀνδράσι συνέτριψαν, πρὸς δὲ τὸ πλῆθος οὐκ ἀντήρ-
κουν τῶν μηχανῶν. καὶ γὰρ δὴ προσῆγον καὶ κλίμακας, ὥστε πῇ μὲν   30
ἐκ τῶν κριῶν λυθέντος τοῦ τείχους, πῇ δὲ τῶν ἐν ταῖς ἐπάλξεσι
βιαζομένων ὑπὸ τοῦ πλήθους τῶν μηχανῶν, ἁλῶναι τὴν πόλιν, τῶν
βαρβάρων ἐσφρησάντων κατὰ τὸ ῥαγὲν τοῦ περιβόλου μέρος ἐκ τῆς
τοῦ κριοῦ πληγῆς. τοῦτο δὲ καὶ διὰ τῶν κλιμάκων, αἳ τῷ μήπω
πεσόντι τοῦ τείχους προσήγοντο.      35

10 ὡς secl. Müller [αὐτῶν εἶ)(αι οὗ)ως τὴν Thompson 1947    15 ἐν secl.
Müller    16 λύγοις Müller [αὐτοῖς cod.    19 ἐνδοῦναι Müller [δοῦναι cod.
25 ῥύμῃ Müller [τυμη cod.

[7]

[(Malalas, *Chron.* 14 p.361)

Ὁ δὲ αὐτὸς Θεοδόσιος βασιλεὺς ἐποίησε κακῶς Ἀντιόχῳ τῷ
πραιποσίτῳ καὶ πατρικίῳ, δυναμένῳ ἐν τῷ παλατίῳ καὶ κρατήσαντι
τῶν πραγμάτων. ἦν γὰρ καὶ ἀναθρεψάμενος τὸν αὐτὸν Θεοδόσιον ἐν
τῇ ζωῇ τοῦ αὐτοῦ πατρός, ὡς κουβικουλάριος καὶ διοικῶν ἀπὸ τοῦ
αὐτοῦ πατρὸς Ἀρκαδίου τὴν πολιτείαν Ῥωμαίων. καὶ ἔμεινε μετὰ τὸ   5
πληρῶσαι αὐτόν, ὡς πατρίκιος κατευθεντῶν τοῦ αὐτοῦ Θεοδοσίου.
καὶ ἀγανακτήσας κατ' αὐτοῦ ἐδήμευσεν αὐτὸν καὶ κουρεύσας ἐποίησε
παπᾶν τῆς μεγάλης ἐκκλησίας Κωνσταντινουπόλεως, ποιήσας

First, because their access was easy,[14] they brought up beams mounted on wheels, upon which men stood who shot across at the defenders on the ramparts. At the other end of the beams stood men who pushed the wheels with their feet and propelled the machines wherever they were needed, so that one could shoot successfully through the openings made in the screens. In order that the men on the beam should fight in safety, they were sheltered by screens woven from willow covered with rawhide and leather to protect them against other missiles and whatever fire darts might be shot at them.[15] When in this manner a large number of machines had been brought up to the wall with the result that the defenders on the battlements gave in because of the clouds of missiles and evacuated their positions, the so-called 'rams' were brought up also. This is a very large machine. A beam is suspended by slack chains from timbers which incline together, and it is provided with a sharp metal point and, for the safety of those working it, screens like those described. With short ropes attached to the rear men vigorously swing the beam away from the target of the blow and then release it, so that by its force all the part of the wall facing it is smashed away. From the walls the defenders tumbled down wagon-sized boulders which they had prepared for this purpose when the machines were brought up to the circuit. Some they crushed together with the men working them, but they could not hold out against the great number of machines. Then the enemy brought up scaling ladders, so that in some places the wall was breached by the rams and elsewhere those on the battlements were overcome by the number of machines. The barbarians entered through the part of the circuit wall broken by the blows of the rams and also over the scaling ladders which were set against that part which was not crumbling, and the city was taken.

## [7]

[(Malalas, *Chron.* 14 p.361)

The Emperor Theodosius did harm to the head chamberlain and patrician Antiochus who was powerful in the palace and determined state policy. He, as a chamberlain, had been responsible for Theodosius' education while his father, Arcadius, was alive, and after the latter's death ran the Roman state. Even after Theodosius had grown up, Antiochus, as patrician, retained power over him. The Emperor, becoming angry at him, confiscated his property, had him tonsured and made him a priest of the great church at Constantinople. He also issued

διάταξιν μὴ εἰσέρχεσθαι εἰς ἀξίας συγκλητικῶν ἢ πατρικίων τοὺς
εὐνούχους κουβικουλαρίους μετὰ τὸ πλήρωμα τῆς αὐτῶν στρατείας,      10
τοῦτ᾽ ἐστὶ τοὺς ἀπὸ πραιποσίτων παλατίου. καὶ ἐτελεύτα ὁ αὐτὸς
Ἀντίοχος, ὢν πρεσβύτερος. (Cf. Theophanes *Chron, a.m.* 5936;
*Suda* A 2694, E 3604, Θ 145, Π 793, Υ 169)]

**[8]**

[(Malalas *Chron.* 14 pp.361f.)

Ὁ δὲ αὐτὸς βασιλεὺς προεβάλετο ἔπαρχον πραιτωρίων καὶ
ἔπαρχον πόλεως τὸν πατρίκιον Κῦρον, τὸν φιλόσοφον, ἄνδρα σοφώ-
τατον ἐν πᾶσι. καὶ ἦρξεν ἔχων τὰς δύο ἀρχὰς ἔτη τέσσαρα, προϊὼν
εἰς τὴν καροῦχαν τοῦ ἐπάρχου τῆς πόλεως καὶ φροντίζων τῶν
κτισμάτων καὶ ἀνανεώσας πᾶσαν Κωνσταντινούπολιν· ἦν γὰρ      5
καθαριώτατος. περὶ οὗ ἔκραξαν οἱ Βυζάντιοι εἰς τὸ ἱππικὸν πᾶσαν
τὴν ἡμέραν θεωροῦντος Θεοδοσίου ταῦτα, "Κωνσταντῖνος ἔκτισε,
Κῦρος ἀνενέωσεν· αὐτὸν ἐπὶ τόπον, Αὔγουστε". Κῦρος δὲ ἐκπλαγεὶς
ἀπεφθέγξατο, "οὐκ ἀρέσκει μοι τύχη πολλὰ γελῶσα". καὶ ἐχόλεσεν
ὁ βασιλεύς, ὅτι ἔκραξαν περὶ Κύρου καὶ μετὰ Κωνσταντίνου αὐτὸν      10
ἔκραξαν, ὡς ἀνανεώσαντα τὴν πόλιν· καὶ κατεσκευάσθη λοιπὸν καὶ
ἐπλάκη ὡς Ἕλλην ὁ αὐτὸς Κῦρος, καὶ ἐδημεύθη παυθεὶς τῆς ἀρχῆς.
καὶ προσφυγὼν ἐγένετο καὶ αὐτὸς παπᾶς, καὶ ἐπέμφθη εἰς τὴν
Φρυγίαν, ἐπίσκοπος γενάμενος εἰς τὸ λεγόμενον Κοτυάειον.
(Cf. *Chron. Pasch.* p.588; Theophanes *Chron. a.m.* 5937; *Suda* Θ
145, Κ 2776; Nicephorus Callistus *HE* 14,57)]

**9**

1. (*Exc. de Leg. Gent.* 2)

Ὅτι ἐπὶ Θεοδοσίου τοῦ μικροῦ βασιλέως Ἀττήλας ὁ τῶν
Οὔννων βασιλεὺς τὸν οἰκεῖον στρατὸν ἀγείρας γράμματα στέλλει
παρὰ τὸν βασιλέα τῶν τε φυγάδων καὶ τῶν φόρων πέρι, ὅσοι προφάσει τοῦδε τοῦ πολέμου οὐκ ἐδέδοντο, τὴν ταχίστην οἱ ἐκπέμπεσθαι
παρακελευόμενος· συντάξεως δὲ ἕνεκα <τοῦ> μέλλοντος φόρου παρ᾽      5
αὐτὸν πρέσβεις τοὺς διαλεξομένους ἀφικνεῖσθαι, ὡς, εἰ μελλήσειαν ἢ
πρὸς πόλεμον ὁρμήσειαν, οὐδὲ αὐτὸν ἔτι ἐθέλοντα τὸ Σκυθικὸν
ἐφέξειν πλῆθος. ταῦτα ἀναγνόντες οἱ ἀμφὶ τὰ βασίλεια οὐδαμῶς τοὺς
παρὰ σφᾶς καταφυγόντας ἐκδώσειν ἔφασαν, ἀλλὰ σὺν ἐκείνοις τὸν
πόλεμον ὑποστήσεσθαι, πέμψειν δὲ πρέσβεις τοὺς τὰ διάφορα λύ-      10
σοντας. ὡς δὲ τῷ Ἀττήλᾳ τὰ δεδογμένα Ῥωμαίοις ἠγγέλλετο, ἐν
ὀργῇ τὸ πρᾶγμα ποιούμενος τὴν Ῥωμαϊκὴν ἐδῄου γῆν, καὶ φρούριά
τινα καθελὼν τῇ Ῥατιαρίᾳ προσέβαλε μεγίστῃ καὶ πολυανθρώπῳ.

5 τοῦ add. Maltese (1977)

a decree that no eunuch chamberlain, after he had completed his official career (that is, those who had served as head chamberlain of the palace), might advance to the rank of senator or patrician. Antiochus died a presbyter.[16]    (Cf. Theophanes *Chron a.m.* 5936; *Suda* A 2694, E 3604, Θ 145, Π 793, Υ 169)]

## [8]

[(Malalas *Chron.* 14 pp.361f.)

The Emperor made the patrician Cyrus, a philosopher and the wisest man of all, praetorian prefect and prefect of the city. He held these combined offices for four years. He used to go forth in the carriage of prefect of the city and he cared for the buildings and renovated the whole of Constantinople, for he was completely incorruptible. While Theodosius was watching at the Hippodrome, the populace of Byzantium hailed Cyrus for a whole day, "Constantine founded, Cyrus restored. That is his place, Augustus".[17] Cyrus was stunned and said, "I don't like Fortune when she laughs a lot". The Emperor was angry that they had hailed Cyrus and named him with Constantine as the restorer of the city. Then a plot was laid and a charge contrived to the effect that Cyrus was a Hellene, and he was stripped of his office and his property was confiscated. He sought asylum, and was ordained a cleric and sent to Phrygia where he became bishop of the place called Cotyaeum.[18] (Cf. *Chron. Pasch.* p.588; Theophanes *Chron. a.m.* 5937; *Suda* Θ 145, K 2776; Nicephorus Callistus *HE* 14,57)]

## 9

1. (*Exc. de Leg. Gent.* 2)

During the reign of Theodosius the Younger, Attila, the king of the Huns, collected his army and sent letters to the Emperor concerning the fugitives and the payments of tribute, commanding that all that had not been handed over under the pretext of the present state of war should be sent to him with all speed. Moreover, concerning the future tribute ambassadors should come to him for discussions, for, if they prevaricated or prepared for war, he would not willingly restrain his Scythian forces. When those at court read these demands, they said that they would by no means hand over the fugitives amongst them and that, along with these, they would submit to war; but they would send ambassadors to settle the disputes. When the views of the Romans were reported to him, Attila reacted in anger and ravaged Roman territory, destroying some forts and attacking Ratiaria, a very large and populous city.

2. (Exc. de Leg. Rom. 2)
Ὅτι Θεοδόσιος ἔπεμπε Σηνάτορα ἄνδρα ὑπατικὸν παρὰ τὸν
Ἀττήλαν πρεσβευσόμενον. ὃς οὐδὲ τὸ τοῦ πρεσβευτοῦ ἔχων ὄνομα
ἐθάρρησε πεζὸς παρὰ τοὺς Οὔννους ἀφικέσθαι, ἀλλ᾽ ἐπὶ τὸν Πόντον
καὶ τὴν Ὀδυσσηνῶν ἔπλευσε πόλιν, ἐν ᾗ καὶ Θεόδουλος στρατηγὸς
ἐκπεμφθεὶς διέτριβεν.                                                                5

4 Ὀδυσσηνῶν Niebuhr ['Ὀδυσσὸς cod.

3. (Exc. de Leg. Gent. 3)
Ὅτι μετὰ τὴν ἐν Χερρονήσῳ μάχην Ῥωμαίων πρὸς Οὔννους
ἐγίνοντο καὶ αἱ συμβάσεις, Ἀνατολίου πρεσβευσαμένου. καὶ ἐπὶ
τοῖσδε ἐσπένδοντο, ὅπως ἐκδοθεῖεν μὲν τοῖς Οὔννοις οἱ φυγάδες, καὶ
ἓξ χιλιάδες χρυσίου λιτρῶν ὑπὲρ τῶν πάλαι συντάξεων δοθεῖεν
αὐτοῖς· φόρον δὲ ἔτους ἑκάστου δισχιλίας καὶ ἑκατὸν λίτρας χρυσοῦ    5
σφίσι τεταγμένον εἶναι· ὑπὲρ δὲ αἰχμαλώτου Ῥωμαίου φεύγοντος καὶ
ἐς τὴν σφετέραν γῆν ἄνευ λύτρων διαβαίνοντος δώδεκα χρυσοῦς
εἶναι ἀποτίμησιν, μὴ καταβάλλοντας δὲ τοὺς ὑποδεχομένους ἐκδιδόναι
τὸν φεύγοντα· μηδένα δὲ βάρβαρον Ῥωμαίους κατὰ σφᾶς φεύγοντα
δέχεσθαι.                                                                             10
Ταύτας προσεποιοῦντο μὲν ἐθελονταὶ Ῥωμαῖοι τὰς συνθήκας
τίθεσθαι· ἀνάγκη δὲ ὑπερβάλλοντι δέει, ὅπερ κατεῖχε τοὺς σφῶν
ἄρχοντας, πᾶν ἐπίταγμα καίπερ ὂν χαλεπὸν τυχεῖν τῆς εἰρήνης
ἐσπουδακότες ἠσμένιζον, καὶ τὴν τῶν φόρων σύνταξιν βαρυτάτην
οὖσαν προσίεντο, τῶν χρημάτων αὐτοῖς καὶ τῶν βασιλικῶν θησαυ-     15
ρῶν οὐκ εἰς δέον ἐκδεδαπανημένων, ἀλλὰ περὶ θέας ἀτόπους καὶ
φιλοτιμίας οὐκ εὐλόγους καὶ ἡδονὰς καὶ δαπάνας ἀνειμένας, ἃς οὐδεὶς
τῶν εὖ φρονούντων οὐδὲ ἐν εὐπραγίαις ὑποσταίη, μήτι γε δὴ οἱ τῶν
ὅπλων ὀλιγωρήσαντες, ὥστε μὴ μόνον Σκύθαις, ἀλλὰ γὰρ καὶ τοῖς
λοιποῖς βαρβάροις τοῖς παροικοῦσι τὴν Ῥωμαίων ὑπακούειν ἐς φόρου   20
ἀπαγωγήν.
Τούτων τῶν συντάξεων καὶ τῶν χρημάτων πέρι, ἅπερ ἔδει
τοῖς Οὔννοις ἐκπέμπεσθαι, συνεισφέρειν πάντας ἠνάγκασαν δασμὸν
εἰσπραττομένους καὶ τοὺς κατὰ χρόνον τινὰ τὴν βαρυτάτην κουφισ-
θέντας τῆς γῆς ἀποτίμησιν εἴτε δικαστῶν κρίσει εἴτε βασιλέων φιλο-   25
τιμίαις. συνεισέφερον δὲ ῥητὸν χρυσίον καὶ οἱ ἐν τῇ γερουσίᾳ ἀνα-
γεγραμμένοι ὑπὲρ τῆς σφῶν αὐτῶν ἀξίας. καὶ ἦν πολλοῖς ἡ λαμπρὰ
τύχη βίου μεταβολή· ἐσεπράττοντο γὰρ μετὰ αἰκισμῶν ἅπερ ἕκαστον
ἀπεγράψαντο οἱ παρὰ βασιλέως τοῦτο ποιεῖν ἐπιτεταγμένοι, ὥστε
τὸν κόσμον τῶν γυναικῶν καὶ τὰ ἔπιπλα τοὺς πάλαι εὐδαίμονας προ-   30
τιθέναι ἐν ἀγορᾷ. τοῦτο μὲν μετὰ τὸν πόλεμον τὸ κακὸν Ῥωμαίους

18 ἂν post εὐπραγίαις add. Dindorf    23 †ἠνάγκασε edd.

2. (*Exc. de Leg. Rom.* 2)

Theodosius sent Senator, a man of consular rank, as ambassador to Attila. Although he had the title of ambassador, he was not confident of reaching the Huns by land and so he sailed to the Black Sea to the city of Odessus, where Theodulus, who had been sent out as a general, was stationed.

3. (*Exc. de Leg. Gent.* 3)

After the battle between the Romans and the Huns in the Chersonese, a treaty was negotiated by Anatolius. The terms were as follows: that the fugitives should be handed over to the Huns, and six thousand pounds of gold be paid to complete the oustanding instalments of tribute; that the tribute henceforth be set at 2,100 pounds of gold per year; that for each Roman prisoner of war who escaped and reached his home territory without ransom, twelve *solidi* were to be the payment, and if those who received him did not pay, they were to hand over the fugitive; and that the Romans were to receive no barbarian who fled to them.

The Romans pretended that they had made these agreements voluntarily, but because of the overwhelming fear which gripped their commanders[19] they were compelled to accept gladly every injunction, however harsh, in their eagerness for peace. They paid over the instalments of the tribute, heavy as they were, although both their own wealth and that of the imperial treasuries had been squandered not on necessities but upon disgusting spectacles, unreasonable displays of generosity, pleasures and dissolute banquets, such as no right-minded person would participate in, even in times when things were going well, even if military matters were of no concern to him. The result of this was that they submitted to pay tribute not only to the Scythians but also to the other barbarian neighbours of the Roman Empire.

To these payments of tribute and the other monies which had to be sent to the Huns they forced all taxpayers to contribute, even those who for a period of time had been relieved of the heaviest category of land tax through a judicial decision or through imperial liberality. Even members of the Senate contributed a fixed amount of gold according to their rank. To many their high station brought a change of lifestyle. For they paid only with difficulty what they had each been assigned by those whom the Emperor appointed to the task, so that formerly wealthy men were selling on the market their wives' jewellery and their furniture. This was the calamity that befell the Romans after the war,

ἐδέξατο, ὥστε πολλοὺς ἢ ἀποκαρτερήσαντας ἢ βρόχον ἀψαμένους
τὸν βίον ἀπολιπεῖν. τότε δὲ ἐκ τοῦ παραχρῆμα τῶν θησαυρῶν
ἐξαντληθέντων, τό τε χρυσίον καὶ οἱ φυγάδες ἐπέμποντο, Σκόττα ἐπὶ
ταύτην τὴν πρᾶξιν ἀφιγμένου· ὧν πλείστους Ῥωμαῖοι ἀπέκτειναν    35
ἀπειθοῦντας πρὸς τὴν ἔκδοσιν, ἐν οἷς καὶ τῶν βασιλικῶν ὑπῆρχον
Σκυθῶν, οἱ ὑπὸ Ἀττήλᾳ τάττεσθαι ἀνηνάμενοι παρὰ Ῥωμαίους
ἀφίκοντο.

Τοῖς δὲ αὐτοῦ ὁ Ἀττήλας προστιθεὶς ἐπιτάγμασι καὶ Ἀσημουντίους ἐκέλευσεν ἐκδιδόναι ὅσους αἰχμαλώτους ὑπῆρχον ἔχοντες εἴτε    40
Ῥωμαίους εἴτε βαρβάρους. Ἀσημοῦς δέ ἐστι φρούριον καρτερόν, οὐ
πολὺ μὲν ἀπέχον τῆς Ἰλλυρίδος, τῷ δὲ Θρακίῳ προσκείμενον μέρει·
ὅπερ οἱ ἐνοικοῦντες ἄνδρες πολλὰ δεινὰ τοὺς ἐχθροὺς εἰργάσαντο,
οὐκ ἀπὸ τειχῶν ἀμυνόμενοι, ἀλλ᾽ ἔξω τῆς τάφρου μάχας ὑφιστάμενοι
πρός τε ἄπειρον πλῆθος καὶ στρατηγοὺς μέγιστον παρὰ Σκύθαις    45
ἔχοντας κλέος, ὥστε τοὺς μὲν Οὔννους ἀπορρεύσαντας τοῦ φρουρίου
ὑπαναχωρῆσαι, τοὺς δὲ ἐπεκτρέχοντας καὶ περαιτέρω τῶν οἰκείων
γινομένους ἡνίκα ἀπήγγελλον αὐτοῖς οἱ σκοποὶ διιέναι τοὺς πολεμίους
λείαν Ῥωμαϊκὴν ἀπάγοντας, ἀδοκήτοις τε ἐμπίπτειν καὶ σφέτερα τὰ
ἐκείνων ποιεῖσθαι λάφυρα, πλήθει μὲν λειπομένους τῶν ἀντιπολε-    50
μούντων, ἀρετῇ δὲ καὶ ῥώμῃ διαφέροντας. πλείστους τοίνυν οἱ
Ἀσημούντιοι ἐν τῷδε τῷ πολέμῳ Σκύθας μὲν ἀπέκτειναν, Ῥωμαίους
δὲ ἠλευθέρωσαν, τοὺς δὲ καὶ ἀποδράσαντας τῶν ἐναντίων ἐδέξαντο.

Οὐκ ἀπάγειν οὖν ἔφη ὁ Ἀττήλας τὸν στρατὸν οὐδὲ ἐπικυροῦν
τὰς τῆς εἰρήνης συνθήκας, εἰ μὴ ἐκδοθεῖεν οἱ παρ᾽ ἐκείνους κατα-    55
φυγόντες Ῥωμαῖοι ἢ καὶ ὑπὲρ αὐτῶν δοθεῖεν ἀποτιμήσεις, ἀφε-
θείησαν δὲ καὶ οἱ παρὰ Ἀσημουντίων ἀπαχθέντες αἰχμάλωτοι βάρβαροι. ἀντιλέγειν δὲ αὐτῷ ὡς οὐκ οἷός τε ἦν οὔτε Ἀνατόλιος πρεσ-
βευόμενος οὔτε Θεόδουλος ὁ τῶν στρατιωτικῶν κατὰ τὸ Θράκιον
ταγμάτων ἡγούμενος, (οὔτε γὰρ ἔπειθον οὔτε τὰ εὔλογα προ-    60
τείνοντες, τοῦ μὲν βαρβάρου τεθαρρηκότος καὶ προχείρως ἐς τὰ
ὅπλα ὁρμῶντος, αὐτῶν δὲ κατεπτηχότων διὰ τὰ προϋπάρξαντα)
γράμματα παρὰ τοὺς Ἀσημουντίους ἔστελλον ἢ ἐκδιδόναι τοὺς παρ᾽
αὐτοὺς καταφυγόντας αἰχμαλώτους Ῥωμαίους, ἢ ὑπὲρ ἑκάστου
δώδεκα τιθέναι χρυσοῦς, διαφεθῆναι δὲ καὶ τοὺς αἰχμαλώτους    65
Οὔννους. οἱ δὲ τὰ αὐτοῖς ἐπεσταλμένα ἀναγνόντες ἔφασαν τοὺς μὲν
παρ᾽ αὐτοὺς καταφυγόντας Ῥωμαίους ἀφεῖναι ἐπ᾽ ἐλευθερίᾳ, Σκύθας
δὲ ὅσους αἰχμαλώτους ἔλαβον ἀνῃρηκέναι, δύο δὲ συλλαβόντας ἔχειν
διὰ τὸ καὶ τοὺς πολεμίους μετὰ τὴν γενομένην ἐπὶ χρόνον πολιορκίαν
ἐξ ἐνέδρας ἐπιθεμένους τῶν πρὸ τοῦ φρουρίου νεμόντων παίδων    70

59 στρατιωτικῶν Niebuhr [στρατιωτῶν τῶν A        61 γὰρ post μὲν exp.
Niebuhr    67 αὐτοὺς Niebuhr [αὐτοῖς A

and the outcome was that many killed themselves either by starvation or by the noose. On that occasion the treasuries were suddenly emptied, and the gold and fugitives sent off when Scottas arrived to collect them. The majority of the fugitives, who refused to be handed over, were killed by the Romans, amongst whom were some of the Scythian royalty who were unwilling to take orders from Attila and had come across to the Romans.

Attila added to these orders of his and demanded that the people of Asemus hand over the prisoners in their hands, both Roman and barbarian. Asemus is a strong fortress close both to Illyria and the border of Thrace. The garrison of this place inflicted much damage upon the enemy, for they did not merely fight from their walls, but gave battle outside the ditch against an overwhelming force and generals of the greatest repute amongst the Scythians, so that the Huns, their numbers melting away, slowly withdrew from the fortress. Since their spies reported to the Asimuntians that the enemy were retreating, taking with them Roman booty, they set out to attack them a good distance from their homes and, falling upon the enemy unawares, they made the Hunnic spoils their own, since, though outnumbered by their adversaries, they were their superiors in courage and strength. Thus, in this war the Asimuntians killed many Scythians, freed many Romans and gave refuge to those who had fled from the enemy.

Attila said that he would neither withdraw his army nor ratify the terms of the peace unless the Romans who had fled to the Asimuntians were either handed over or a ransom paid for them and the barbarian prisoners whom they had taken were set free. Neither Anatolius the ambassador nor Theodulus the commander of the forces in Thrace was able to dispute Attila's claim. Indeed, even when they put forward strong arguments they could not persuade him, since he was confident and ready to resort to arms, whereas they were cowed by what had happened. Therefore, they sent letters to the people of Asemus telling them either to hand over the escaped Roman prisoners who were amongst them or pay twelve *solidi* for each and to set the Hunnic prisoners free. When they received these messages the Asimuntians declared that the Roman fugitives amongst them had departed to freedom and the Scythians who had been taken prisoner had been put to death except for two whom they had kept because, after the siege had been underway for a while, the enemy had sprung an ambush and seized some of the children as they were pasturing flocks before the

ἁρπάσαι τινάς, οὓς εἰ μὴ ἀπολάβοιεν, οὐδὲ σφᾶς τοὺς νόμῳ πολέμου
κτηθέντας ἀποδώσειν. ταῦτα ἀπαγγειλάντων τῶν παρὰ τοὺς Ἀσημουντίους ἀφιγμένων, τῷ τε Σκυθῶν βασιλεῖ καὶ τοῖς Ῥωμαίοις
ἄρχουσιν ἐδόκει μὲν ἀναζητεῖσθαι οὓς οἱ Ἀσημούντιοι ἔφασαν
ἡρπάσθαι παῖδας, οὐδενὸς δὲ φανέντος, οἱ παρὰ τοῖς Ἀσημουντίοις    75
βάρβαροι ἀπεδόθησαν, πίστεις τῶν Σκυθῶν δόντων ὡς παρ' αὐτοῖς
οἱ παῖδες οὐκ εἴησαν. ἐπωμνύοντο δὲ καὶ οἱ Ἀσημούντιοι, ὡς οἱ παρὰ
σφᾶς καταφυγόντες Ῥωμαῖοι ἐπ' ἐλευθερίᾳ ἀφείθησαν. ὤμνυον δέ,
καίπερ παρὰ σφίσιν ὄντων Ῥωμαίων· οὐ γὰρ ἐπίορκον ᾤοντο ὅρκον
ὀμνύναι ἐπὶ σωτηρίᾳ τῶν ἐκ τοῦ σφετέρου γένους ἀνδρῶν.    80

[4. (Theophanes *Chron. a.m.* 5942)
    Τοῦ δὲ στόλου, ὡς προέφημεν, ἐν Σικελίᾳ ἐκδεχομένου τὴν τῶν
πρεσβευτῶν Γιζερίχου ἄφιξιν καὶ τὴν τοῦ βασιλέως κέλευσιν, ἐν τῷ
μεταξὺ Ἀττίλας, ὁ Μουνδίου παῖς, Σκύθης, γενόμενος ἀνδρεῖος καὶ
ὑπερήφανος, ἀποβαλὼν Βδελλάν, τὸν πρεσβύτερον ἀδελφόν, καὶ
μόνος ἄρχων τὸ τῶν Σκυθῶν βασίλειον, οὓς καὶ Οὔννους καλοῦσιν,    5
κατατρέχει τὴν Θράκην. δι' ὃν μάλιστα Θεοδόσιος σπένδεται <πρὸς>
Γιζέριχον καὶ ἐπανάγει τὸν στόλον ἐκ Σικελίας. ἀποστέλλει δὲ τὸν
Ἄσπαρα σὺν τῇ ὑπ' αὐτὸν δυνάμει καὶ Ἀρεόβινδον καὶ Ἀργαγίσκλον
ἐπὶ τὸν Ἀττίλαν Ῥατιαρίαν ἤδη καὶ Νάϊσον καὶ Φιλιππούπολιν καὶ
Ἀρκαδιούπολιν καὶ Κωνσταντίαν καὶ ἕτερα πλεῖστα πολίσματα    10
καταστρεψάμενον καὶ σὺν αἰχμαλώτοις πολλοῖς ὑπέρογκον συμ-
φορήσαντα λείαν. τῶν οὖν στρατηγῶν ἐλαττωθέντων σφόδρα ταῖς
μάχαις, προῆλθεν Ἀττίλας καὶ μέχρι θαλάσσης ἑκατέρας, τῆς τε τοῦ
Πόντου καὶ τῆς πρὸς Καλλιπόλει καὶ Σηστῷ κεχυμένης, πᾶσαν πόλιν
καὶ φρούρια δουλούμενος πλὴν Ἀδριανουπόλεως καὶ Ἡρακλείας, τῆς    15
ποτε Πειρίνθου κληθείσης, ὥστε καὶ εἰς τὸν Ἀθύραν αὐτὸν φρούριον
ἐλθεῖν. ἀναγκάζεται οὖν Θεοδόσιος πρεσβεύσασθαι πρὸς Ἀττίλαν
καὶ ἑξακισχιλίας χρυσίου λίτρας ὑπὲρ τῆς ἀναχωρήσεως παρασχεῖν,
χιλίων δὲ χρυσίου λιτρῶν ἐτήσιον φόρον αὐτῷ ἠρεμοῦντι προσομο-
λογῆσαι τελεῖν.    (Cf. Nicephorus Callistus *HE* 14,57)]    20

1 στόλου b [λαοῦ xyz    6 πρὸς add. de Boor    12 τῶν οὖν στρατηγῶν b
[τῶν συστρατηγῶν xz    13 προσῆλθεν y    19-20 προσωμολόγησε cg

10

(*Exc. de Leg. Gent.* 4)
    Ὅτι γενομένων τῶν σπονδῶν Ἀττήλας αὖθις παρὰ τοὺς
ἑῴους ἔπεμψε πρέσβεις φυγάδας αἰτῶν. οἱ δὲ τοὺς πρεσβευομένους
δεξάμενοι καὶ πλείστοις δώροις θεραπεύσαντες ἀπέπεμψαν φυγάδας
μὴ ἔχειν φήσαντες. ὁ δὲ πάλιν ἑτέρους ἔπεμψεν. χρηματισαμένων δὲ

fortress. Unless these were returned, they would not hand over their prisoners whom they had captured under the rules of war. When the messengers to the Asimuntians brought back this reply, the Scythian king and the Roman commanders agreed that a search should be made for the children whom the Asimuntians claimed had been seized, and, when none were found, the Scythians swore that they did not have the children, and the barbarians in Asimuntian hands were given back. The Asimuntians also swore that the Romans who had escaped to them had departed to freedom, and they swore this although there were Romans amongst them. For they did not consider that they had sworn a false oath, since they had done it for the safety of men of their own race.

[4. (Theophanes *Chron. a.m.* 5942)

While the fleet was, as we have described,[20] in Sicily receiving the envoys of Gaiseric and awaiting the commands of the Emperor, Attila, the son of Mundius, a Scythian and a brave and haughty man, killed his elder brother Bleda, became sole ruler of the kingdom of the Scythians (whom they also call 'Huns') and devastated Thrace. Particularly be-cause of him Theodosius made a treaty with Gaiseric and withdrew the fleet from Sicily. Against Attila, who had already sacked Ratiaria, Naissus, Philippopolis, Arcadiopolis, Constantia and very many other cities and had collected an enormous plunder and many prisoners, he sent Aspar with the force under his command and Areobindus and Argagisclus.[21] The generals were badly beaten in the battles they fought, and Attila advanced to both seas, the Black Sea and that which washes Callipolis and Sestus. He captured every city and fortress except for Adrianople and Heracleia (which was once called Perinthus), so that he reached the fortress of Athyras itself. Theodosius was forced, there-fore, to send an embassy to Attila, to buy his withdrawal for six thousand pounds of gold and to promise to pay him a yearly tribute of one thousand pounds of gold if he kept the peace.
(Cf. Nicephorus Callistus *HE* 14,57)][22]

## 10

(*Exc. de Leg. Gent.* 4)

When the treaty was in force, Attila again sent envoys to the eastern Romans demanding the fugitives. They received the envoys, honoured them with many gifts and sent them away saying that they had no fugitives. Again, he sent others, and, when they had been enriched,

καὶ αὐτῶν, τρίτη παρεγένετο πρεσβεία, καὶ τετάρτη μετ᾽ αὐτήν. ὁ    5
γὰρ βάρβαρος ἐς τὴν Ῥωμαίων ἀφορῶν φιλοτιμίαν, ἢν ἐποιοῦντο
εὐλαβείᾳ τοῦ μὴ παραβαθῆναι τὰς σπονδάς, ὅσους τῶν ἐπιτηδείων
εὖ ποιεῖν ἐβούλετο ἔπεμπε παρ᾽ αὐτούς, αἰτίας τε ἀναπλάττων καὶ
προφάσεις ἐφευρίσκων κενάς. οἱ δὲ παντὶ ὑπήκουον ἐπιτάγματι καὶ
δεσπότου ἡγοῦντο τὸ πρόσταγμα, ὅπερ ἂν ἐκεῖνος παρεκελεύσατο. οὐ    10
γὰρ μόνον τὸν πρὸς αὐτὸν ἀνελέσθαι πόλεμον εὐλαβοῦντο, ἀλλὰ καὶ
Παρθυαίους ἐν παρασκευῇ τυγχάνοντας ἐδεδίεσαν καὶ Βανδίλους τὰ
κατὰ θάλασσαν ταράττοντας καὶ Ἰσαύρους πρὸς τὴν λῃστείαν δια-
νισταμένους καὶ Σαρακηνοὺς τῆς αὐτῶν ἐπικρατείας τὴν ἕω κατατρέ-
χοντας καὶ τὰ Αἰθιοπικὰ ἔθνη συνιστάμενα. διὸ δὴ τεταπεινωμένοι    15
τὸν μὲν Ἀττήλαν ἐθεράπευον, πρὸς δὲ τὰ λοιπὰ ἔθνη ἐπειρῶντο παρα-
τάττεσθαι δυνάμεις τε ἀθροίζοντες καὶ στρατηγοὺς χειροτονοῦντες.

# 11

1. (Exc. de Leg. Gent. 5)

Ὅτι καὶ αὖθις Ἐδέκων ἧκε πρέσβις, ἀνὴρ Σκύθης μέγιστα
κατὰ πόλεμον ἔργα διαπραξάμενος, σὺν Ὀρέστῃ, ὃς τοῦ Ῥωμαϊκοῦ
γένους ὢν ᾤκει τὴν πρὸς τῷ Σάῳ ποταμῷ Παιόνων χώραν τῷ
βαρβάρῳ κατὰ τὰς Ἀετίου στρατηγοῦ τῶν ἑσπερίων Ῥωμαίων συνθήκας ὑπακούουσαν. οὗτος ὁ Ἐδέκων ἐς τὰ βασίλεια παρελθὼν    5
ἀπεδίδου τὰ παρὰ Ἀττήλα γράμματα, ἐν οἷς ἐποιεῖτο τοὺς Ῥωμαίους
ἐν αἰτίᾳ τῶν φυγάδων πέρι· ἀνθ᾽ ὧν ἠπείλει ἐπὶ τὰ ὅπλα χωρεῖν, εἰ
μὴ ἀποδοθεῖεν αὐτῷ καὶ ἀφέξονται Ῥωμαῖοι τὴν δοριάλωτον
ἀροῦντες. εἶναι δὲ μῆκος μὲν αὐτῆς κατὰ τὸ ῥεῦμα τοῦ Ἴστρου ἀπὸ
τῆς Παιόνων ἄχρι Νοβῶν τῶν Θρακίων, τὸ δὲ βάθος πέντε ἡμερῶν    10
ὁδόν· καὶ τὴν ἀγορὰν τὴν ἐν Ἰλλυριοῖς μὴ πρὸς τῇ ὄχθῃ τοῦ Ἴστρου
ποταμοῦ γίνεσθαι, ὥσπερ καὶ πάλαι, ἀλλ᾽ ἐν Ναϊσσῷ, ἣν ὅριον ὡς
ὑπ᾽ αὐτοῦ δῃωθεῖσαν τῆς Σκυθῶν καὶ Ῥωμαίων ἐτίθετο γῆς, πέντε
ἡμερῶν ὁδὸν εὐζώνῳ ἀνδρὶ τοῦ Ἴστρου ἀπέχουσαν ποταμοῦ. πρέσβεις δὲ ἐκέλευσε πρὸς αὐτὸν ἀφικνεῖσθαι τοὺς περὶ τῶν ἀμφιβόλων    15
διαλεξομένους, οὐ τῶν ἐπιτυχόντων, ἀλλὰ τῶν ὑπατικῶν ἀνδρῶν
τοὺς μεγίστους· οὓς εἰ ἐκπέμπειν εὐλαβηθεῖεν, αὐτὸν δεξόμενον σφᾶς
ἐς τὴν Σερδικὴν διαβήσεσθαι.

Τούτων ἀναγνωσθέντων βασιλεῖ τῶν γραμμάτων, ὡς ὑπεξ-
ῆλθεν ὁ Ἐδέκων σὺν τῷ Βιγίλᾳ ἑρμηνεύσαντι ὅσαπερ ὁ βάρβαρος    20
ἀπὸ στόματος ἔφρασε τῶν Ἀττήλα δεδογμένων, καὶ ἐς ἑτέρους
οἴκους παρεγένετο, ὥστε αὐτὸν Χρυσαφίῳ τῷ βασιλέως ὑπασπιστῇ
οἷα δὴ τὰ μέγιστα δυναμένῳ ἐς ὄψιν ἐλθεῖν, ἀπεθαύμασε τὴν τῶν

13 ὑπ᾽ Papabasileios (1896) [ἐπ᾽ codd.

he sent a third embassy and a fourth after it. For the barbarian, mindful of the Romans' liberality, which they showed out of caution lest the treaty be broken, sent to them those of his retinue whom he wished to benefit, inventing new reasons and discovering new pretexts. The Romans heeded his every bidding and obeyed whatever order their master issued. They were not only wary of starting a war with Attila, but they were afraid also of the Parthians who were preparing for hostilities, the Vandals who were harrying the coastal regions, the Isaurians whose banditry was reviving, the Saracens who were ravaging the eastern parts of their dominions, and the Ethiopian tribes who were in the process of uniting. Therefore, having been humbled by Attila, they paid him court while they tried to organise themselves to face the other peoples by collecting their forces and appointing generals.[23]

## 11

1. (*Exc. de Leg. Gent.* 5)

Edeco, a Scythian who had performed outstanding deeds in war, came again as ambassador together with Orestes, a Roman by origin who lived in the part of Pannonia close to the river Save which became subject to the barbarian by the treaty made with Aetius, the general of the western Romans. This Edeco came to the court and handed over the letters from Attila, in which he blamed the Romans in respect of the fugitives. In retaliation he threatened to resort to arms if the Romans did not surrender them and if they did not cease cultivating the land which he had won in the war. This, he asserted, was a strip five days' journey wide and extending along the Danube from Pannonia to Novae in Thrace. Furthermore, he said that the market in Illyria was not on the bank of the Danube, as it had been before, but at Naissus, which he had laid waste and established as the border point between the Scythian and the Roman territory, it being five days' journey from the Danube for an unladen man. He ordered that ambassadors come to him and not just ordinary men but the highest ranking of the consulars; if the Romans were wary of sending them, he would cross to Serdica to receive them.

When the letters had been read out to the Emperor, Edeco departed with Vigilas, who had interpreted all of Attila's views which the barbarian had communicated, and went to another suite to meet Chrysaphius, the Emperor's chamberlain and the most powerful of his ministers. The barbarian expressed wonder at the magnificence of the

βασιλείων οἴκων περιφάνειαν. Βιγίλας δέ, ὡς τῷ Χρυσαφίῳ ἐς
λόγους ἦλθεν ὁ βάρβαρος, ἔλεγεν ἑρμηνεύων, ὡς ἐπαινοίη ὁ    25
Ἐδέκων τὰ βασίλεια καὶ τὸν παρὰ σφίσι μακαρίζοι πλοῦτον. ὁ δὲ
Χρυσάφιος ἔφασκεν ἔσεσθαι καὶ αὐτὸν οἴκων τε χρυσοστέγων καὶ
πλούτου κύριον, εἴ γε περιίδοι μὲν τὰ παρὰ Σκύθαις, ἔλοιτο δὲ τὰ
Ῥωμαίων. τοῦ δὲ ἀποκριναμένου ὡς τὸν ἑτέρου δεσπότου θερά-
ποντα ἄνευ τοῦ κυρίου οὐ θέμις τοῦτο ποιεῖν, ἐπυνθάνετο ὁ εὐνοῦχος    30
εἴ γε ἀκώλυτος αὐτῷ ἡ παρὰ τὸν Ἀττήλαν εἴη εἴσοδος καὶ δύναμιν
παρὰ Σκύθαις ἔχει τινά. τοῦ δὲ ἀποκριναμένου ὡς καὶ ἐπιτήδειος εἴη
τῷ Ἀττήλᾳ καὶ τὴν αὐτοῦ ἅμα τοῖς εἰς τοῦτο ἀποκεκριμένοις λογάσιν
ἐμπιστεύεται φυλακήν, (ἐκ διαδοχῆς γὰρ κατὰ ῥητὰς ἡμέρας ἕκαστον
αὐτῶν ἔλεγε μεθ᾿ ὅπλων φυλάττειν τὸν Ἀττήλαν) ἔφασκεν ὁ εὐ-    35
νοῦχος, εἴπερ πίστεις δέξοιτο, μέγιστα αὐτῷ ἐρεῖν ἀγαθά· δεῖσθαι δὲ
σχολῆς· ταύτην δὲ αὐτῷ ὑπάρχειν, εἴ γε παρ᾿ αὐτὸν ἐπὶ δεῖπνον ἔλθοι
χωρὶς Ὀρέστου καὶ τῶν ἄλλων συμπρεσβευτῶν. ὑποσχόμενος δὲ
τοῦτο ποιεῖν, καὶ ἐπὶ τὴν ἑστίασιν πρὸς τὸν εὐνοῦχον παραγενόμενος,
ὑπὸ τῷ Βιγίλᾳ ἑρμηνεῖ δεξιὰς καὶ ὅρκους ἔδοσαν, ὁ μὲν εὐνοῦχος ὡς    40
οὐκ ἐπὶ κακῷ τῷ Ἐδέκωνι, ἀλλ᾿ ἐπὶ μεγίστοις ἀγαθοῖς τοὺς λόγους
ποιήσοιτο, ὁ δὲ ὡς οὐκ ἐξείποι τὰ αὐτῷ ῥηθησόμενα, εἰ καὶ μὴ
πέρατος κυρήσοι. τότε δὴ ὁ εὐνοῦχος ἔλεγε τῷ Ἐδέκωνι, εἰ διεβὰς ἐς
τὴν Σκυθικὴν ἀνέλοι τὸν Ἀττήλαν καὶ παρὰ Ῥωμαίους ἥξει, ἔσεσθαι
αὐτῷ βίον εὐδαίμονα καὶ πλοῦτον μέγιστον. τοῦ δὲ ὑποσχομένου καὶ    45
φήσαντος ἐπὶ τῇ πράξει δεῖσθαι χρημάτων, οὐ πολλῶν δέ, ἀλλὰ
πεντήκοντα λιτρῶν χρυσίου δοθησομένων τῷ ὑπ᾿ αὐτὸν τελοῦντι
πλήθει, ὥστε αὐτῷ τελείως συνεργῆσαι πρὸς τὴν ἐπίθεσιν, καὶ τοῦ
εὐνούχου τὸ χρυσίον παραχρῆμα δώσειν ὑποσχομένου, ἔλεγεν ὁ
βάρβαρος ἀποπέμπεσθαι μὲν αὐτὸν ἀπαγγελοῦντα τῷ Ἀττήλᾳ περὶ    50
τῆς πρεσβείας, συμπέμπεσθαι δ᾿ αὐτῷ Βιγίλαν τὴν παρὰ τοῦ Ἀττήλα
ἐπὶ τοῖς φυγάσιν ἀπόκρισιν δεξόμενον. δι᾿ αὐτοῦ γὰρ περὶ τοῦ αὐτοῦ
χρυσίου μηνύσειν, καὶ ὃν τρόπον τοῦτο ἐκπεμφθήσεται. ἀπεληλυθότα
γάρ, ὥσπερ καὶ τοὺς ἄλλους, πολυπραγμονήσειν τὸν Ἀττήλαν, τίς τε
αὐτῷ δωρεὰ καὶ ὁπόσα παρὰ Ῥωμαίων δέδοται χρήματα· μὴ οἶόν τε    55
δὲ ταῦτα ἀποκρύπτειν διὰ τοὺς συμπορευομένους.

Ἔδοξε δὴ τῷ εὐνούχῳ εὖ λέγειν, καὶ τῆς γνώμης τὸν βάρβαρον ἀποδεξάμενος ἀποπέμπει μετὰ τὸ δεῖπνον καὶ ἐπὶ βασιλέα φέρει
τὴν βουλήν. ὃς Μαρτιάλιον τὴν τοῦ μαγίστρου διέποντα ἀρχὴν προσ-
μεταπεμψάμενος ἔλεγε τὰς πρὸς τὸν βάρβαρον συνθήκας. ἀνάγκη δὲ    60
ἐθάρρει τὸ τῆς ἀρχῆς· πασῶν γὰρ τῶν βασιλέως βουλῶν ὁ μά-
γιστρός ἐστι κοινωνός, οἷα δὴ τῶν τε ἀγγελιαφόρων καὶ ἑρμηνέων

32 ἔχει de Boor [ἔχοι E, Niebuhr ἔχειν A    39-40 καὶ ante ὑπὸ in codd.
trans. ante ἐπὶ de Boor    44 Ῥωμαίους Hoeschel [Ῥωμαίοις A

palace rooms, and when he came to speak to Chrysaphius, Vigilas, while translating, said that Edeco was praising the palace and congratulating the Romans on their wealth. Chrysaphius said that he, too, would become the owner of wealth and of rooms with golden ceilings if he were to disregard Scythian interests and work for those of the Romans. When Edeco replied that it was not right for the servant of another master to do this without his lord's permission, the eunuch asked if he had unrestricted access to Attila and any authority amongst the Scythians. When Edeco replied that he was one of Attila's intimates and that he, together with others selected from amongst the leading men, was entrusted with guarding Attila (he explained that on fixed days each of them in turn guarded Attila under arms), the eunuch said that if he would receive oaths, he would speak greatly to his advantage; there was, however, need of leisure for this, and they would have it if Edeco came to dinner with him without Orestes and his other fellow ambassadors. Edeco promised to do this and came to dinner at the eunuch's residence. With Vigilas interpreting, they clasped right hands and exchanged oaths, the eunuch that he would speak not to Edeco's harm but to his great advantage, Edeco that he would not reveal what would be said to him even if he did not work towards its achievement. Then the eunuch said that if Edeco should cross to Scythia, slay Attila and return to the Romans, he would enjoy a life of happiness and very great wealth. Edeco promised to do this and said that for its accomplishment he required money – not much, only fifty pounds of gold to be given to the force acting under his orders, to ensure that they co-operated fully with him in the attack. When the eunuch replied that he would give the money immediately, the barbarian said that he should be sent off to report to Attila upon the embassy and that Vigilas should be sent with him to receive Attila's reply on the subject of the fugitives. Through Vigilas he would send instructions as to how the gold was to be dispatched. Since he had been away, he, like the others, would be closely questioned by Attila as to who amongst the Romans had given him gifts and how much money he had received, and because of his companions he could not hide the fifty pounds of gold.

Edeco's words seemed sensible to the eunuch, and, accepting the barbarian's advice, he dismissed him after dinner and took the plan to the Emperor. The Emperor summoned Martialis, the master of the offices, and told him of the agreements with the barbarian. (Of necessity he confided in this official, since the master of the offices, being

καὶ στρατιωτῶν τῶν ἀμφὶ τὴν βασιλέως φυλακὴν ὑπ' αὐτὸν ταττο-
μένων. ἐδόκει δὲ αὐτοῖς βουλευομένοις τῶν προκειμένων πέρι μὴ
μόνον Βιγίλαν, ἀλλὰ γὰρ καὶ Μαξιμῖνον ἐκπέμπειν πρεσβευόμενον    65
παρὰ τὸν Ἀττήλαν.

2. (*Exc. de Leg. Rom.* 3)

Ὅτι τοῦ Χρυσαφίου τοῦ εὐνούχου παραινέσαντος Ἐδέκωνι
ἀνελεῖν τὸν Ἀττήλαν, ἐδόκει τῷ βασιλεῖ Θεοδοσίῳ καὶ τῷ μαγίστρῳ
Μαρτιαλίῳ βουλευομένοις τῶν προκειμένων πέρι μὴ μόνον Βιγίλαν
ἀλλὰ καὶ Μαξιμῖνον ἐκπέμπειν πρεσβευόμενον παρὰ τὸν Ἀττήλαν, καὶ
Βιγίλαν μὲν τῷ φαινομένῳ τὴν τοῦ ἑρμηνέως ἐπέχοντα τάξιν    5
πράττειν ἅπερ Ἐδέκωνι δοκεῖ, τὸν δὲ Μαξιμῖνον μηδὲν τῶν αὐτοῖς
βουλευθέντων ἐπιστάμενον τὰ βασιλέως ἀποδιδόναι γράμματα.
ἀντεγέγραπτο δὲ τῶν πρεσβευομένων ἀνδρῶν ἕνεκα ὡς ὁ μὲν
Βιγίλας ἑρμηνεύς, ὁ δὲ Μαξιμῖνος μείζονος ἤπερ ὁ Βιγίλας ἀξίας
γένους τε περιφανοῦς καὶ ἐπιτήδειος ἐς τὰ μάλιστα βασιλεῖ, ἔπειτα    10
ὡς οὐ δεῖ παρασαλεύοντα τὰς σπονδὰς τῇ Ῥωμαίων ἐμβατεύειν γῇ,
φυγάδας δὲ μετὰ τοὺς ἤδη ἐκδοθέντας ἑπτακαίδεκα ἀπέσταλκά σοι,
ὡς ἑτέρων οὐκ ὄντων. καὶ ταῦτα μὲν ἦν ἐν τοῖς γράμμασιν. φράζειν
δὲ τὸν Μαξιμῖνον ἀπὸ στόματος τῷ Ἀττήλᾳ μὴ χρῆναι αἰτεῖν πρέσβεις
μεγίστης ἀξίας παρ' αὐτὸν διαβῆναι· τοῦτο γὰρ οὐδὲ ἐπὶ τῶν αὐτοῦ    15
προγόνων οὐδὲ ἐπὶ ἑτέρων τῶν ἀρξάντων τῆς Σκυθικῆς γενέσθαι,
ἀλλὰ πρεσβεύσασθαι τόν τε ἐπιτυχόντα στρατιώτην καὶ ἀγγελια-
φόρον. εἰς δὲ τὸ διευκρινῆσαι τὰ ἀμφιβαλλόμενα ἐδόκει πέμπειν
Ὀνηγήσιον παρὰ Ῥωμαίους· μὴ οἷόν τε γὰρ αὐτὸν Σερδικῆς
δῃωθείσης σὺν ὑπατικῷ ἀνδρὶ ἐς αὐτὴν προϊέναι.    20
Ἐπὶ ταύτην τὴν πρεσβείαν ἐκλιπαρήσας πείθει με Μαξιμῖνος
αὐτῷ συναπᾶραι. καὶ δῆτα ἅμα τοῖς βαρβάροις ἐχόμενοι τῆς ὁδοῦ ἐς
Σερδικὴν ἀφικνούμεθα τρισκαίδεκα ὁδὸν ἀνδρὶ εὐζώνῳ τῆς Κωνσταντίνου ἀπέχουσαν· ἐν ᾗ καταλύσαντες καλῶς ἔχειν ἡγησάμεθα
ἐπὶ ἑστίαν Ἐδέκωνα καὶ τοὺς μετ' αὐτοῦ βαρβάρους καλεῖν. πρόβατα    25
οὖν καὶ βόας ἀποδομένων τῶν ἐπιχωρίων ἡμῖν, κατασφάξαντες
ἠριστοποιούμεθα. καὶ παρὰ τὸν τοῦ συμποσίου καιρὸν τῶν μὲν βαρβάρων τὸν Ἀττήλαν, ἡμῶν δὲ τὸν βασιλέα θαυμαζόντων, ὁ Βιγίλας
ἔφη ὡς οὐκ εἴη θεὸν καὶ ἄνθρωπον δίκαια συγκρίνειν, ἄνθρωπον
μὲν τὸν Ἀττήλαν, θεὸν δὲ τὸν Θεοδόσιον λέγων. ἤσχαλλον οὖν οἱ    30
Οὖννοι καὶ κατὰ μικρὸν ὑποθερμαινόμενοι ἐχαλέπαινον. ἡμῶν δὲ ἐς
ἕτερα τρεψάντων τὸν λόγον καὶ φιλοφροσύνῃ τὸν σφῶν αὐτῶν
καταπραϋνάντων θυμόν, μετὰ τὸ δεῖπνον ὡς διανέστημεν, δώροις ὁ

8 ἐνεγέγραπτο Bekker    12 ἀπέσταλκά σοι Niebuhr [ἀπέσταλκέ σοι codd.
ἀπέσταλκέν οἱ Valesius    25 ἑστίασιν Papabasileios (1896)    33 κατα-
πραϋνόντων B, edd.

in charge of the messengers, interpreters and imperial bodyguard, is informed of all the Emperor's plans.) They discussed the proposal and decided to send as envoys to Attila not only Vigilas but also Maximinus.

2. (*Exc. de Leg. Rom.* 3)

When Chrysaphius had proposed to Edeco that he kill Attila, the Emperor Theodosius and the master of the offices Martialis discussed the proposal and decided to send as envoys to Attila not only Vigilas but also Maximinus. They told Vigilas, while apparently serving as interpreter, to take his orders from Edeco, and Maximinus, who knew nothing of what they had planned, to deliver the Emperor's letters. In reply to Attila it was written on behalf of the ambassadors that Vigilas was the interpreter and that Maximinus was a man of higher rank than Vigilas, of illustrious lineage and a confidant of the Emperor in matters of the highest importance. Then it was written, "It is not proper that one who is undermining the treaty should enter Roman territory", and, "In addition to those already handed over I have sent you seventeen fugitives, since there are no more".[24] These were the words in the letters. Maximinus was ordered to speak personally to Attila in order that he need not demand that envoys of the highest rank come to him; for this had not been the case with his ancestors or other rulers of Scythia, but ordinary soldiers and messengers had acted as ambassadors. To settle the matters in dispute it seemed best to send Onegesius to the Romans, for, since Serdica had been sacked, Attila could not proceed there with a man of consular rank.

Maximinus by his pleadings persuaded me to accompany him on this embassy. So, we set out together with the barbarians and reached Serdica, which is thirteen days from Constantinople for an unladen traveller. There we broke our journey and thought it proper to offer hospitality to Edeco and the barbarians with him. The inhabitants supplied us with sheep and cattle which we slaughtered, and we prepared a meal. While we were drinking, the barbarians toasted Attila and we Theodosius. But Vigilas said that it was not proper to compare a god and a man, meaning Attila by a man and Theodosius by a god. This annoyed the Huns, and gradually they grew heated and angry. But we turned the conversation to other things and by our friendly manner calmed their anger, and when we were leaving after dinner, Maximinus

Μαξιμῖνος Ἐδέκωνα καὶ Ὀρέστην ἐθεράπευσε σηρικοῖς ἐσθήμασι
καὶ λίθοις Ἰνδικοῖς.                                                    35
    Ἀναμείνας δὲ τὴν Ἐδέκωνος Ὀρέστης ἀναχώρησιν πρὸς τὸν
Μαξιμῖνον φράζει, ὡς σοφός τε εἴη καὶ ἄριστος μὴ ὅμοια σὺν τοῖς
ἀμφὶ τὰ βασίλεια πλημμελήσας· χωρὶς γὰρ αὐτοῦ ἐπὶ δεῖπνον τὸν
Ἐδέκωνα καλοῦντες δώροις ἐτίμων. ἀπόρου δὲ τοῦ λόγου ὡς μηδὲν
ἐπισταμένοις φανέντος, καὶ ἀνερωτήσασιν ὅπως καὶ κατὰ ποῖον    40
καιρὸν περιῶπται μὲν αὐτός, τετίμηται δὲ ὁ Ἐδέκων, οὐδὲν ἀποκρινάμενος ἐξῆλθεν· τῇ δὲ ὑστεραίᾳ ὡς ἐβαδίζομεν, φέρομεν ἐπὶ
Βιγίλαν ἅπερ ἡμῖν Ὀρέστης εἰρήκει. ὃς δὲ ἐκεῖνον ἔλεγεν μὴ δεῖν
χαλεπαίνειν ὡς τῶν αὐτῶν Ἐδέκωνι μὴ τυγχάνοντα· αὐτὸν μὲν γὰρ
ὀπάονά τε καὶ ὑπογραφέα εἶναι Ἀττήλᾳ, Ἐδέκωνα δὲ τὰ κατὰ    45
πόλεμον ἄριστον καὶ τοῦ Οὔννου γένους ἀναβεβηκέναι τὸν Ὀρέστην
πολύ. ταῦτα εἰπὼν καὶ τῷ Ἐδέκωνι ἰδιολογησάμενος ἔφασκεν
ὕστερον πρὸς ἡμᾶς, εἴτε ἀληθιζόμενος εἴτε ὑποκρινόμενος, ὡς εἴποι
μὲν αὐτῷ τὰ εἰρημένα, μόγις δὲ αὐτὸν καταπραΰναι τραπέντα ἐπὶ
τοῖς λεχθεῖσιν εἰς ὀργήν.                                              50
    Ἀφικόμενοι δὲ ἐς Ναϊσσὸν ἔρημον μὲν εὕρομεν ἀνθρώπων τὴν
πόλιν ὡς ὑπὸ τῶν πολεμίων ἀνατραπεῖσαν, ἐν δὲ τοῖς ἱεροῖς κατα-
λύμασι τῶν ὑπὸ νόσων κατεχομένων τινὲς ἐτύγχανον ὄντες. μικρὸν
δὲ ἄνω τοῦ ποταμοῦ ἐν καθαρῷ καταλύσαντες (σύμπαντα γὰρ τὰ ἐπὶ
τὴν ὄχθην ὀστέων ἦν πλέα τῶν ἐν πολέμῳ ἀναιρεθέντων) τῇ ἐπαύ-    55
ριον πρὸς Ἀγίνθεον τὸν ἐν Ἰλλυριοῖς ταγμάτων ἡγούμενον ἀφικόμεθα οὐ πόρρω ὄντα τῆς Ναϊσσοῦ, ἐφ' ᾧ τὰ παρὰ βασιλέως ἀγγεῖλαι
καὶ τοὺς φυγάδας παραλαβεῖν· τοὺς γὰρ ε' τῶν ιζ', περὶ ὧν Ἀττήλα
ἐγέγραπτο, αὐτὸν ἔδει παραδιδόναι. ἤλθομεν οὖν ἐς λόγους καὶ τοὺς
ε' φυγάδας παραδοῦναι αὐτὸν τοῖς Οὔννοις παρεσκευάσαμεν· οὓς    60
φιλοφρονησάμενος σὺν ἡμῖν ἀπέπεμψεν.
    Διανυκτερεύσαντες δὲ καὶ ἀπὸ τῶν ὁρίων τῆς Ναϊσσοῦ τὴν
πορείαν ποιησάμενοι ἐπὶ τὸν Ἴστρον ποταμὸν ἔς τι χωρίον ἐσβάλ-
λομεν συνηρεφές, καμπὰς δὲ καὶ ἐλιγμοὺς καὶ περιαγωγὰς πολλὰς
ἔχον. ἐν ᾧπερ τῆς ἡμέρας διαφανούσης, οἰομένοις ἐπὶ δυσμὰς πορεύ-    65
εσθαι <ἡ> τοῦ ἡλίου ἀνατολὴ κατεναντίον ὤφθη, ὥστε τοὺς ἀ-
πείρως ἔχοντας τῆς τοῦ χωρίου θέσεως ἀναβοῆσαι, οἷα δὴ τοῦ ἡλίου
τὴν ἐναντίαν ποιουμένου πορείαν καὶ ἕτερα παρὰ τὰ καθεστῶτα
σημαίνοντος· ὑπὸ δὲ τῆς τοῦ τόπου ἀνωμαλίας ἐπὶ ἀνατολὰς ἐκεῖνο
τὸ μέρος ἔβλεπε τῆς ὁδοῦ. μετὰ δὲ τὴν δυσχωρίαν ἐν πεδίῳ καὶ αὐτῷ    70
ὑλώδει παρεγενόμεθα. ἐντεῦθεν βάρβαροι πορθμεῖς ἐν σκάφεσι

55 τῇ ὄχθῃ coni. de Boor    65 διαφανοῦσης Niebuhr διαφανούσης de Boor
66 ἡ add. Bekker    71 παρεγενόμεθα Dindorf [παραγενόμεθα codd. παραγινόμεθα Niebuhr

won over Edeco and Orestes with gifts of silk garments and pearls.[25]

While Orestes was awaiting Edeco's departure he said to Maximinus that he was a wise and very good man not to have committed the same offence as those at court, for they had invited Edeco to dinner without himself and had honoured him with gifts. This remark was meaningless to us since we were in ignorance of what had been done, and we asked him how and on what occasion he had been slighted and Edeco honoured. But he made no reply and went away. On the following day as we were travelling along, we told Vigilas what Orestes had said to us. Vigilas said that he should not be angry at being treated differently from Edeco, since Orestes was a servant and secretary of Attila, whereas Edeco, as one of the leading warriors and of the Hunnic race,[26] was by far his superior. Having said this and having spoken privately with Edeco, he later told us (either truthfully or otherwise) that he had reported to Edeco what had been said and had only with difficulty calmed him down since he had become very angry at the report.

When we arrived at Naissus, we found the city empty of people since it had been laid waste by the enemy. In the Christian hostels there were some persons suffering from disease. A short distance away from the river we halted in a clean place[27] (for all towards the river bank was full of the bones of men killed in the fighting) and on the following day we came to Agintheus, the general of the forces in Illyricum, who was not far from Naissus, to convey to him the Emperor's orders and to receive the fugitives. He was to hand over five of the seventeen about whom it had been written to Attila.[28] We spoke to him and caused him to hand over the five fugitives to the Huns. He treated them kindly and sent them off with us.

Having spent the night we set out on our journey from the border at Naissus to the river Danube.[29] We came upon a thickly-shaded place where the path took many twists and turns and detours. While we were here the day dawned, and, thinking that we were journeying westwards, we saw the sun rise[30] right in front of us. As a result those who were unfamiliar with the lie of the land cried out that the sun was travelling in the opposite direction and portended unusual events. But because of the irregularity of the terrain that part of the path turned to the East. After this difficult ground we came to a plain which was also wooded.[31] Here barbarian ferrymen received us and conveyed us across

μονοξύλοις, ἅπερ αὐτοὶ δένδρα ἐκτέμνοντες καὶ διαγλύφοντες κατασκευάζουσιν, ἐδέχοντο ἡμᾶς καὶ διεπόρθμευον τὸν ποταμόν, οὐχ ἡμῶν
ἕνεκα παρασκευασάμενοι, ἀλλὰ διαπορθμεύσαντες πλῆθος βαρ-
βαρικόν, ὅπερ ἡμῖν κατὰ τὴν ὁδὸν ἀπηντήκει, οἷα δὴ βουλομένου ὡς      75
ἐπὶ θήραν Ἀττήλα διαβαίνειν ἐς τὴν Ῥωμαίων γῆν. τοῦτο δὲ ἦν
πολέμου παρασκευὴν ποιουμένῳ τῷ βασιλείῳ Σκύθῃ, προφάσει τοῦ
μὴ πάντας αὐτῷ τοὺς φυγάδας δεδόσθαι.

Περαιωθέντες δὲ τὸν Ἴστρον καὶ σὺν τοῖς βαρβάροις ὡς ο'
πορευθέντες σταδίους ἐν πεδίῳ τινὶ ἐπιμένειν ἠναγκάσθημεν, ὥστε      80
τοὺς ἀμφὶ τὸν Ἐδέκωνα τῷ Ἀττήλᾳ γενέσθαι τῆς ἡμετέρας ἀφίξεως
μηνυτάς. καταμεινάντων δὲ σὺν ἡμῖν καὶ τῶν ξεναγησάντων ἡμᾶς
βαρβάρων, ἀμφὶ δείλην ὀψίαν δεῖπνον ἡμῶν αἱρουμένων, κρότος
ἵππων ὡς ἡμᾶς ἐρχομένων ἠκούετο, καὶ δὴ ἄνδρες β' Σκύθαι παρε-
γίνοντο ὡς τὸν Ἀττήλαν ἡμᾶς ἀπιέναι παρακελευόμενοι. ἡμῶν δὲ      85
πρότερον ἐπὶ τὸ δεῖπνον αὐτοὺς ἐλθεῖν αἰτησάντων, ἀποβάντες τῶν
ἵππων εὐωχήθησαν καὶ ἡμῖν τῆς ὁδοῦ τῇ ὑστεραίᾳ ἡγήσαντο. παραγενομένων δὲ ἐς τὰς Ἀττήλα σκηνὰς ἀμφὶ θ' τῆς ἡμέρας ὥρᾳ
(πολλαὶ δὲ αὖται ἐτύγχανον οὖσαι) ἐπί τε λόφου τινὸς σκηνοποιῆσαι
βουληθέντων, οἱ ἐπιτυχόντες διεκώλυσαν βάρβαροι, ὡς τῆς Ἀττήλα      90
ἐν χθαμαλῷ ὑπαρχούσης σκηνῆς.

Καταλυσάντων δὲ ὅπου τοῖς Σκύθαις ἐδόκει, Ἐδέκων καὶ
Ὀρέστης καὶ Σκόττας καὶ ἕτεροι τῶν ἐν αὐτοῖς λογάδων ἧκον
ἀνερωτῶντες τίνων τυχεῖν ἐσπουδακότες τὴν πρεσβείαν ποιούμεθα.
ἡμῶν δὲ τὴν ἄλογον ἀποθαυμαζόντων ἐρώτησιν καὶ ἐς ἀλλήλους      95
ὁρώντων, διετέλουν πρὸς ὄχλου τῆς ἀποκρίσεως ἕνεκα γινόμενοι.
εἰπόντων δὲ Ἀττήλᾳ καὶ οὐχ ἑτέροις λέγειν βασιλέα παρακελεύσασθαι, χαλεπήνας ὁ Σκόττας ἀπεκρίνατο τοῦ σφῶν αὐτῶν ἡγουμένου ἐπίταγμα εἶναι· οὐ γὰρ ἂν πολυπραγμοσύνῃ σφετέρᾳ παρ'
ἡμᾶς ἐληλυθέναι. φησάντων δὲ μὴ τοῦτον ἐπὶ τοῖς πρέσβεσι κεῖσθαι      100
τὸν νόμον, ὥστε μὴ ἐντυγχάνοντας μηδὲ ἐς ὄψιν ἐρχομένους παρ' οὓς
ἐστάλησαν δι' ἑτέρων ἀνακρίνεσθαι ὧν ἕνεκα πρεσβεύοιντο, καὶ
τοῦτο μηδὲ αὐτοὺς ἀγνοεῖν Σκύθας θαμινὰ παρὰ βασιλέα πρεσβευο-
μένους· χρῆναι δὲ τῶν ἴσων κυρεῖν· μὴ γὰρ ἄλλως τὰ τῆς πρεσβείας ἐρεῖν· ὡς τὸν Ἀττήλαν ἀνέζευξαν· καὶ αὖθις ἐπανῆκον Ἐδέ-      105
κωνος χωρὶς καὶ ἅπαντα, περὶ ὧν ἐπρεσβευόμεθα, ἔλεγον προσ-
τάττοντες τὴν ταχίστην ἀπιέναι, εἰ μὴ ἕτερα φράζειν ἔχοιμεν. ἐπὶ δὲ
τοῖς λεχθεῖσι πλέον ἐπαποροῦντες (οὐ γὰρ ἦν ἐφικτὸν γινώσκειν,
ὅπως ἔκδηλα ἐγεγόνει τὰ ἐν παραβύστῳ δεδογμένα βασιλεῖ) συμφέρειν ἡγούμεθα μηδὲν περὶ τῆς πρεσβείας ἀποκρίνεσθαι, εἰ μὴ τῆς      110

77 παρασκευὴ ποιουμένη Bekker    88 τὰς Bekker [τοῦ codd.    109 ἐν παραβύστῳ Niebuhr [ἐν παραβύστα Ε   θὺ παραβύστα Χ   θεῶν παραβύστα edd.

the river in boats which they had made from single trunks, themselves cutting and hollowing out the trees. They had not made these boats for our sake, but had already ferried across a force of barbarians, which had met us on the road, since Attila wished to cross over to Roman territory as if to hunt. But the royal Scythian was really doing this in preparation for war, on the pretext that all the fugitives had not been given up.[32]

When we had crossed the Danube and travelled about seventy stades with the barbarians, we were compelled to wait on some flat ground while Edeco's attendants went to Attila to announce our arrival. Our barbarian guides remained with us, and in the late afternoon we were taking our dinner when we heard the clatter of horses coming towards us and two Scythians arrived and told us to come to Attila.[33] We bade them first join us for dinner, and they dismounted and were well entertained. On the next day they led us on the road, and we arrived at Attila's tents (of which there were many) at about the ninth hour of the day. When we wanted to pitch our tents on a hill, the barbarians who had come to meet us prevented us because Attila's tent was on low ground.

When we had encamped where the Scythians thought best, Edeco, Orestes, Scottas and others of the leading men amongst the Huns came and asked what we hoped to achieve in making the embassy. We were shocked by this unreasonable question and looked at each other, but they persisted, becoming troublesome in their demands for a reply. When we said that the Emperor had ordered us to speak to Attila and no others, Scottas became angry and replied that this was the command of their leader; for they would not have come to us meddling on their own. We said that it was not the rule for ambassadors that they should wrangle through others over the purpose of their mission without meeting or coming into the presence of those to whom they had been sent. The Scythians, moreover, were not ignorant of this since they had sent frequent embassies to the Emperor: we deserved equal treatment, and if we did not receive it we would not tell the purpose of the embassy. They went off to Attila and came back again without Edeco and told us everything for which we had come on the embassy, ordering us to leave with all speed if we had nothing further to say. At these words we were even more puzzled, since we could not see how things which the Emperor had decided in secret had come to their knowledge. We considered that it was of no advantage to our

παρὰ τὸν Ἀττήλαν εἰσόδου τύχοιμεν. διὸ ἐφάσκομεν, εἴτε τὰ εἰρημένα
τοῖς Σκύθαις εἴτε καὶ ἕτερα ἥκομεν πρεσβευόμενοι, τοῦ σφῶν αὐτῶν
ἡγουμένου τὴν πεῦσιν εἶναι, καὶ μηδαμῶς ἄλλοις τούτου χάριν δια-
λεχθήσεσθαι· οἱ δὲ ἡμᾶς παραχρῆμα ἀναχωρεῖν προσέταττον.

Ἐν παρασκευῇ δὲ τῆς ὁδοῦ γενομένους τῆς ἀποκρίσεως ἡμᾶς    115
ὁ Βιγίλας κατεμέμφετο, ἐπὶ ψεύδει ἁλῶναι ἄμεινον λέγων ἢ
ἀπράκτους ἀναχωρεῖν. εἰ γὰρ ἐς λόγους τῷ Ἀττήλᾳ ἔτυχον, φησίν,
ἐληλυθώς, ἐπεπείκειν ῥᾳδίως ἂν αὐτὸν τῆς πρὸς Ῥωμαίους ἀποστῆναι διαφορᾶς, οἷα δὴ ἐπιτήδειος αὐτῷ ἐν τῇ κατὰ Ἀνατόλιον
πρεσβείᾳ γενόμενος. <πρὸς> ταῦτα εὔνουν αὐτῷ τὸν Ἐδέκωνα    120
ὑπάρχειν ἔφασκεν, ὥστε λόγῳ τῆς πρεσβείας καὶ τῶν ὁπωσοῦν εἴτε
ἀληθῶς εἴτε ψευδῶς ῥηθησομένων προφάσεως τυχεῖν ἐπὶ τῷ
βουλεύσασθαι περὶ τῶν αὐτοῖς κατὰ Ἀττήλα δεδογμένων, καὶ ὅπως
τὸ χρυσίον, οὗπερ ἔφασκε δεῖσθαι ὁ Ἐδέκων, κομίσαι τὸ διανεμηθη-
σόμενον <τοῖς ὑπ' αὐτὸν> ταττομένοις ἀνδράσι. προδεδομένος δὲ    125
ἐλελήθει. ὁ γὰρ Ἐδέκων, εἴτε δόλῳ ὑποσχόμενος εἴτε καὶ τὸν
Ὀρέστην εὐλαβηθείς, μὴ ἐς τὸν Ἀττήλαν ἀγάγοι ἅπερ ἡμῖν ἐν τῇ
Σερδικῇ μετὰ τὴν ἑστίασιν εἰρήκει, ἐν αἰτίᾳ ποιούμενος τὸ χωρὶς
αὐτοῦ βασιλεῖ καὶ τῷ εὐνούχῳ ἐς λόγους αὐτὸν ἐληλυθέναι, κατεμη-
νύει τὴν μελετηθεῖσαν αὐτῷ ἐπιβουλὴν καὶ τὸ ποσὸν τοῦ ἐκπεμφθη-    130
σομένου χρυσίου, ἐκλέγει δὲ καὶ ἐφ' οἷς τὴν πρεσβείαν ἐποιούμεθα.

Τῶν δὲ φορτίων ἤδη τοῖς ὑποζυγίοις ἐπιτεθέντων, καὶ ἀνάγκη
τὴν πορείαν κατὰ τὸν τῆς νυκτὸς καιρὸν ποιεῖσθαι πειρώμενοι,
μετεξέτεροι τῶν βαρβάρων παραγενόμενοι ἐπιμεῖναι ἡμᾶς τοῦ
καιροῦ χάριν παρακελεύσασθαι τὸν Ἀττήλαν ἔλεγον. ἐν αὐτῷ οὖν    135
τῷ χωρίῳ, ὅθεν καὶ διανέστημεν, ἧκον ἡμῖν βοῦν ἄγοντές τινες καὶ
ποταμίους ἰχθύας παρὰ τοῦ Ἀττήλα διαπεμφθέντας. δειπνήσαντες
οὖν ἐς ὕπνον ἐτράπημεν.

Ἡμέρας δὲ γενομένης ᾠόμεθα μὲν ἥμερόν τι καὶ πρᾶον παρὰ
τοῦ βαρβάρου μηνυθήσεσθαι· ὁ δὲ πάλιν τοὺς αὐτοὺς ἔπεμπε παρα-    140
κελευόμενος ἀπιέναι, εἰ μὴ ἔχοιμέν τι παρὰ τὰ αὐτοῖς ἐγνωσμένα
λέγειν. οὐδὲν οὖν ἀποκρινάμενοι πρὸς τὴν ὁδὸν παρασκευαζόμεθα,
καίπερ τοῦ Βιγίλα διαφιλονεικοῦντος λέγειν εἶναι καὶ ἕτερα ἡμῖν
ῥηθησόμενα. ἐν πολλῇ δὲ κατηφείᾳ τὸν Μαξιμῖνον ἰδών, παραλαβὼν
Ῥουστίκιον ἐξεπιστάμενον τὴν βαρβάρων φωνήν (ὃς σὺν ἡμῖν ἐπὶ τὴν    145
Σκυθικὴν ἐληλύθει οὐ τῆς πρεσβείας ἕνεκα, ἀλλὰ κατὰ πρᾶξίν τινα
πρὸς Κωνστάντιον, ὃν Ἰταλιώτην ὄντα ὑπογραφέα Ἀττήλᾳ ἀπεστάλκει Ἀέτιος ὁ τῶν ἑσπερίων Ῥωμαίων στρατηγός) παρὰ τὸν
Σκότταν ἀφικνούμενος (οὐ γὰρ Ὀνηγήσιος τηνικαῦτα παρῆν) καὶ

---

120 ταῦτα κ.τ.λ. corrupta indicant edd., πρὸς scripsi [διὰ ταῦτα ... [ἔφασκεν]
Hoeschel ταῦτα δ' ἔλεγεν ἐλπίζων Bekker    125 τοῖς ὑπ' αὐτὸν add. Bekker

embassy to give a reply unless we were granted access to Attila. We, therefore, said that their leader was asking whether we had come as envoys on the matters mentioned by the Scythians or on other business and that we would by no means discuss this with others than himself. They ordered us to depart immediately.

While we were preparing for our journey Vigilas criticised us for our answer, saying that it was better to be caught in a lie than to leave without achieving anything. "If", he said, "I had been able to speak with Attila, I should easily have persuaded him to set aside his differences with the Romans, since I became friendly with him on the embassy with Anatolius".[34] He claimed that Edeco supported him in this,[35] in order that by arguing for continuing the embassy and for saying anything, whether true or false, he might have an excuse to consult over what they had decided against Attila and as to how the gold, which Edeco said he needed for distribution amongst those under his orders, might be brought. But he did not know that he had been betrayed. For Edeco had either made his promise falsely or he was afraid of Orestes, lest he say to Attila what he had said to us at Serdica after the banquet, blaming Edeco for having spoken with the Emperor and the eunuch without himself. Therefore, he reported to Attila the plot that had been hatched against him and the amount of gold that was to be sent, and he revealed the purpose of the embassy.

Our baggage had already been loaded upon the animals, and out of necessity we were attempting to start out on our journey at night, when some barbarians came to us and said that Attila bade us wait because of the hour. At that very spot from which we had set out men came bringing us an ox and fish from the river, which Attila had sent us. Therefore, we ate dinner and turned to sleep.

When day came we thought that there would be some mild and conciliatory indication from the barbarian. But he again sent the same men, ordering us to leave if we had nothing to say beyond what was already known to them. We said nothing and prepared for our journey, although Vigilas argued persistently that we should claim that we had other things to say. Seeing that Maximinus was very dejected, I took with me Rusticius,[36] who knew the language of the barbarians (he had come with us to Scythia not on the embassy but on business with Constantius, who was an Italian and secretary of Attila, sent to him by Aetius, the general of the western Romans),[37] and approached Scottas, for Onegesius was not there at the time. With Rusticius as interpreter,

αὐτὸν προσειπὼν ὑπὸ ἑρμηνεῖ τῷ Ῥουστικίῳ ἔλεγον δῶρα πλεῖστα    150
παρὰ τοῦ Μαξιμίνου λήψεσθαι, εἴπερ αὐτὸν τῆς παρὰ τὸν Ἀττήλαν
εἰσόδου παρασκευάσοι τυχεῖν. τὴν γὰρ αὐτοῦ πρεσβείαν οὐ μόνον
Ῥωμαίοις καὶ Οὔννοις συνοίσειν, ἀλλὰ καὶ Ὀνηγησίῳ, ὃν παρ' αὐτὸν
βασιλεὺς ἰέναι βούλεται καὶ τὰ τοῖς ἔθνεσι διευκρινῆσαι ἀμφίβολα·
ἀφικόμενον δὲ μεγίστων τεύξεσθαι δωρεῶν. χρῆναι οὖν μὴ παρόντος    155
Ὀνηγησίου ἡμῖν, μᾶλλον δὲ τἀδελφῷ, ἐπὶ τῇ ἀγαθῇ συναγωνίζεσθαι
πράξει. πείθεσθαι δὲ καὶ αὐτῷ τὸν Ἀττήλαν μεμαθηκέναι ἔλεγον·
οὐκ ἐν ἀκοῇ δὲ ἔσεσθαι βεβαίως τὰ κατ' αὐτόν, εἰ μή γε πείρᾳ τὴν
αὐτοῦ γνοίημεν δύναμιν. ὃς δὲ ὑπολαβὼν μηκέτι ἀμφιβόλους εἶναι ἔφη
τοῦ καὶ αὐτὸν ἴσα τῷ ἀδελφῷ παρὰ Ἀττήλᾳ λέγειν τε καὶ πράττειν·    160
καὶ παραχρῆμα τὸν ἵππον ἀναβὰς ἐπὶ τὴν Ἀττήλα διήλασε σκηνήν.

Πρὸς δὲ τὸν Μαξιμῖνον ἐπανελθὼν ἀλύοντα ἅμα τῷ Βιγίλᾳ καὶ
διαπορούμενον ἐπὶ τοῖς καθεστῶσιν ἔλεγον ἅ τε τῷ Σκόττᾳ διεί-
λεγμαι καὶ ἅπερ παρ' αὐτοῦ ἠκηκόειν, καὶ ὡς δεῖ τὰ τῷ βαρβάρῳ
δοθησόμενα παρασκευάζειν δῶρα καὶ τὰ αὐτῷ παρ' ἡμῶν ῥηθησό-    165
μενα ἀναλογίζεσθαι. ἀμφότεροι οὖν ἀναπηδήσαντες (ἐπὶ γὰρ τοῦ
ἐδάφους καὶ τῆς πόας κεῖσθαι σφᾶς συνέβαινεν) ἐπῄνεσάν τε τὴν
πρᾶξιν καὶ τοὺς ἤδη μετὰ τῶν ὑποζυγίων ἐξορμήσαντας ἀνεκάλουν
καὶ διεσκέψαντο, ὅπως τε προσείποιεν τὸν Ἀττήλαν καὶ ὅπως αὐτῷ
τά τε βασιλέως δῶρα δοῖεν καὶ ἅπερ αὐτῷ ὁ Μαξιμῖνος ἐκόμιζεν.    170

Ἀμφὶ δὲ ταῦτα πονουμένους διὰ τοῦ Σκόττα ὁ Ἀττήλας μετεπέμψατο, καὶ δῆτα ἐς τὴν ἐκείνου <σκηνὴν> παραγινόμεθα ὑπὸ
βαρβαρικοῦ κύκλῳ φρουρουμένην πλήθους. ὡς δὲ εἰσόδου ἐτύχομεν,
εὕρομεν ἐπὶ ξυλίνου δίφρου τὸν Ἀττήλαν καθήμενον. στάντων δὲ
ἡμῶν μικρὸν ἀπωτέρω τοῦ θρόνου, προσελθὼν ὁ Μαξιμῖνος ἠσπά-    175
σατο τὸν βάρβαρον, τά τε παρὰ βασιλέως γράμματα δοὺς ἔλεγεν ὡς
σῶν εἶναι αὐτὸν καὶ τοὺς ἀμφ' αὐτὸν εὔχεται βασιλεύς. ὁ δὲ ἀπεκρίνατο ἔσεσθαι Ῥωμαίοις ἅπερ αὐτῷ βούλοιντο. καὶ ἐπὶ τὸν Βιγίλαν
εὐθὺς τρέπει τὸν λόγον θηρίον ἀναιδὲς ἀποκαλῶν, ὅτου χάριν παρ'
αὐτὸν ἐλθεῖν ἠθέλησεν ἐπιστάμενος τά τε αὐτῷ καὶ Ἀνατολίῳ ἐπὶ    180
τῇ εἰρήνῃ δόξαντα, ὡς εἴρητο μὴ πρότερον πρέσβεις παρ' αὐτὸν
ἐλθεῖν πρὶν ἢ πάντες οἱ φυγάδες ἐκδοθεῖεν βαρβάροις. τοῦ δὲ
φήσαντος ὡς ἐκ τοῦ Σκυθικοῦ γένους παρὰ Ῥωμαίοις οὐκ εἴη φυγάς,
τοὺς γὰρ ὄντας ἐκδεδόσθαι, χαλεπήνας μᾶλλον καὶ αὐτῷ πλεῖστα
λοιδορησάμενος μετὰ βοῆς ἔλεγεν ὡς αὐτὸν ἀνασκολοπίσας πρὸς    185
βορὰν οἰωνοῖς ἐδεδώκει ἄν, εἰ μή γε τῷ τῆς πρεσβείας θεσμῷ
λυμαίνεσθαι ἐδόκει. καὶ ταύτην αὐτῷ ἐπὶ τῇ ἀναιδείᾳ καὶ τῇ τῶν

168 ἀνεκαλοῦντο Thompson (1947)        172 σκηνὴν add. de Boor
173 φρουρουμένην de Boor [ἐφρουρουμένην codd. πεφρουρουμένην Hoeschel
186 ἐδεδώκει Hoeschel [ἐδεδώρει codd. ἐδεδώρητ' de Boor

I spoke to Scottas and said that he would receive many gifts from Maximinus if he obtained him an interview with Attila. For his embassy would benefit not only the Romans and the Huns, but also Onegesius whom the Emperor wished to come to him to settle the disputes between the two peoples and who, if he came, would receive very great gifts. Since Onegesius was absent he must help us – or, rather, his brother – in this laudable enterprise. I said that we had heard that he, too, had influence with Attila, but that the reports about him would not seem well-founded unless we had an example of his power. He rose to the challenge and said that we should no longer doubt that he spoke and acted before Attila on an equality with his brother. Then he immediately mounted his horse and galloped off to Attila's tent.

I returned to Maximinus, who, like Vigilas, was in despair and at a loss in the present situation, and I told him what I had said to Scottas and what he had replied. I said that they should prepare the gifts to give the barbarian and work out what they would say to him. Both of them leaped up (for they had been lying on the grass) and applauded what I had done. They called back those who had already set out with the pack animals and fell to considering how they should address Attila and how to present to him the gifts from the Emperor and those which Maximinus had brought for him.

While we were busy with these matters, Attila summoned us through Scottas, and we came to his tent, which was surrounded by a ring of barbarian guards. When we were granted entrance, we saw Attila seated on a wooden chair. We halted a little before the throne, and Maximinus advanced, greeted the barbarian, gave him the letters from the Emperor and said that the Emperor prayed that he and his followers were safe and well. He replied that the Romans would have what they wished for him. Then he immediately directed his words towards Vigilas, calling him a shameless beast and asking why he had wished to come to him when he knew the peace terms agreed between himself and Anatolius, which specified that no ambassadors should come to him before all the fugitives had been surrendered to the barbarians. When Vigilas replied that there was not one fugitive of the Scythian race amongst the Romans, for all who were there had been surrendered, Attila became even more angry and abused him violently, shouting that he would have impaled him and left him as food for the birds if he had not thought that it infringed the rights of ambassadors to punish him in this way for the shamelessness and effrontery of his

λόγων ἰταμότητι ἐπιθεῖναι δίκην· φυγάδας γὰρ τοῦ σφετέρου ἔθνους
παρὰ Ῥωμαίοις εἶναι πολλούς, ὧν ἐκέλευε τὰ ὀνόματα ἐγγεγραμμένα χάρτῃ τοὺς ὑπογραφέας ἀναγινώσκειν. ὡς δὲ διεξῆλθον      190
ἅπαντας, προσέτατte μηδὲν μελλήσαντα ἀπιέναι· συμπέμψειν δὲ
αὐτῷ καὶ Ἤσλαν Ῥωμαίοις λέξοντα πάντας τοὺς παρὰ σφίσι καταφυγόντας βαρβάρους ἀπὸ τῶν Καρπιλέονος χρόνων, ὃς ὡμήρευσε
παρ' αὐτῷ παῖς ὢν Ἀετίου τοῦ ἐν τῇ ἑσπέρα Ῥωμαίων στρατηγοῦ,
ἐκπέμψαι παρ' αὐτόν. μὴ γὰρ συγχωρήσειν τοὺς σφετέρους θερά-     195
ποντας ἀντίον αὐτοῦ ἐς μάχην ἰέναι, καίπερ μὴ δυναμένους ὠφελεῖν
τοὺς τὴν φυλακὴν αὐτοῖς τῆς οἰκείας ἐπιτρέψαντας γῆς. τίνα γὰρ
πόλιν ἢ ποῖον φρούριον σεσῶσθαι, ἔλεγεν, ὑπ' ἐκείνων, οὗπερ αὐτὸς
ποιῆσαι τὴν αἵρεσιν ὥρμησεν; ἀπαγγείλαντας δὲ τὰ αὐτῷ περὶ τῶν
φυγάδων δεδογμένα αὖθις ἐπανήκειν μηνύοντας, πότερον αὐτοὺς     200
ἐκδιδόναι βούλονται ἢ τὸν ὑπὲρ αὐτῶν ἀναδέχονται πόλεμον. παρακελευσάμενος δὲ πρότερον καὶ τὸν Μαξιμῖνον ἐπιμένειν, ὡς δι' αὐτοῦ
περὶ τῶν γεγραμμένων ἀποκρινούμενος βασιλεῖ, ἐπέτρεπε τὰ δῶρα
δόντας, ἅπερ ὁ Μαξιμῖνος ἔφερεν, ὑπεξιέναι.

Δόντες τοίνυν καὶ ἐπανιόντες ἐς τὴν σκηνὴν ἑκάστου τῶν     205
λεχθέντων περὶ ἰδιολογούμεθα. καὶ Βιγίλα θαυμάζοντος, ὅπως
πάλαι αὐτῷ πρεσβευομένῳ ἤπιός τε καὶ πρᾶος νομισθεὶς τότε
χαλεπῶς ἐλοιδορήσατο, ἔλεγον, μήποτέ τινες τῶν βαρβάρων τῶν ἐν
Σερδικῇ ἐστιαθέντων σὺν ἡμῖν δυσμενῆ αὐτῷ τὸν Ἀττήλαν παρε-
σκεύασαν ἀπαγγείλαντες, ὡς θεὸν μὲν τὸν Ῥωμαίων ἐκάλει βασιλέα,     210
ἄνθρωπον δὲ τὸν Ἀττήλαν. τοῦτον τὸν λόγον ὁ Μαξιμῖνος ὡς
πιθανὸν ἐδέχετο οἷα δὴ ἀμέτοχος ὢν τῆς συνωμοσίας, ἣν κατὰ τοῦ
βαρβάρου ὁ εὐνοῦχος ἐποιήσατο. ὁ δὲ Βιγίλας ἀμφίβολός τε ἦν καὶ
ἐμοὶ ἐδόκει προφάσεως ἀπορεῖν, δι' ἣν αὐτῷ ὁ Ἀττήλας ἐλοιδορή-
σατο· οὔτε γὰρ τὰ ἐν Σερδικῇ, ὡς ὕστερον ἡμῖν διηγεῖτο, οὔτε τὰ τῆς     215
ἐπιβουλῆς εἰρῆσθαι τῷ Ἀττήλᾳ ἐνόμιζεν, μηδενὸς μὲν ἑτέρου τῶν ἐκ
τοῦ πλήθους διὰ τὸν ἐπικρατοῦντα κατὰ πάντων φόβον ἐς λόγους
αὐτῷ θαρροῦντος ἐλθεῖν, Ἐδέκωνος δὲ πάντως ἐχεμυθήσοντος διά
τε τοὺς ὅρκους καὶ τὴν ἀδηλίαν τοῦ πράγματος, μήποτε καὶ αὐτός, ὡς
τοιούτων μέτοχος λόγων, ἐπιτήδειος νομισθεὶς θάνατον ὑφέξει     220
ζημίαν.

Ἐν τοιαύτῃ οὖν ἀμφιβολίᾳ τυγχάνουσιν ἐπιστὰς Ἐδέκων καὶ
τὸν Βιγίλαν ἔξω τῆς ἡμετέρας ἀπαγαγὼν συνόδου ὑποκρινάμενός τε
ἀληθίζεσθαι τῶν αὐτοῖς βεβουλευμένων ἕνεκα καὶ τὸ χρυσίον
κομισθῆναι παρακελευσάμενος τὸ δοθησόμενον τοῖς ἅμα αὐτῷ περὶ     225
τὴν πρᾶξιν ἐλευσομένοις ἀνεχώρει. πολυπραγμονοῦντας δὲ τίνες οἱ

195 μὴ γὰρ codd. [καὶ γὰρ Hoeschel καὶ γὰρ οὐ Niebuhr     204 δόντας . . .
ὑπεξιέναι om. X et edd.     212 ἀμέτοχος Valesius [μέτοχος codd.

words. He continued that there were many fugitives of his own race amongst the Romans and he ordered the secretaries to read out their names, which were written on papyrus. When the secretaries had read out all the names, Attila told Vigilas to depart immediately and he said that he would send with him Eslas to tell the Romans to return to him all the barbarians who had fled to them from the time of Carpilio (the son of Aetius, the general of the Romans in the West), who had been a hostage at his court.[38] He would not allow his own servants to go to war against himself, even though they were unable to help those who entrusted to them the guarding of their own land. For, asked Attila, what city or fortress had been saved by them after he had set out to capture it? When they had announced his views on the fugitives, they were to return and report whether the Romans were willing to give them up or would go to war on their behalf. Maximinus he first ordered to remain with the court so that through him he might reply to the Emperor's written messages, and then he told us to hand over the gifts which Maximinus was bringing and to withdraw.[39]

We handed over the gifts and, returning to our tent, discussed amongst ourselves each of the things which had been said. Vigilas expressed amazement that while Attila had seemed calm and mild towards him on the previous embassy, on the present occasion he abused him violently. I said that perhaps some of the barbarians who had dined with us at Serdica had made Attila angry by telling him that Vigilas had called the Roman Emperor a god and Attila a man. Maximinus, since he had no part in the plot which the eunuch had devised against the barbarian, accepted this explanation as likely. But Vigilas was at a loss and appeared to me to have no explanation of why Attila had railed at him. For he did not think, as he told us later, that either the business at Serdica or the details of the plot had been reported to Attila, since no one else from the group, because of the fear which constrained all of them, would dare to go to speak with him, and Edeco would keep entirely quiet both because of his oaths and because of the uncertainty in the matter, in case he should be judged to have forwarded the plot, since he took part in the talks, and be killed as a punishment.

While we were in this state of uncertainty, Edeco arrived. He drew Vigilas aside from our group and, pretending to be serious about what they had planned, said that the gold should be brought to be given to those who would co-operate with him in the attempt. Then he left.

τοῦ Ἐδέκωνος πρὸς αὐτὸν λόγοι ἀπατᾶν ἔσπευδεν ἠπατήμενος αὐτός,
καὶ τὴν ἀληθῆ αἰτίαν ἀποκρυψάμενος ἔφασκε παρ' αὐτοῦ Ἐδέκωνος
εἰρῆσθαι ὡς καὶ αὐτῷ ὁ Ἀττήλας περὶ τῶν φυγάδων χαλεπαίνοι·
ἔδει γὰρ ἢ πάντας ἀπολαβεῖν ἢ πρέσβεις ἐκ τῆς μεγίστης ἐξουσίας          230
ἀφικέσθαι πρὸς αὐτόν.

Ταῦτα διαλεγομένοις παραγενόμενοί τινες τοῦ Ἀττήλα ἔλεγον
μήτε Βιγίλαν μήτε ἡμᾶς Ῥωμαῖον αἰχμάλωτον ἢ βάρβαρον ἀνδρά-
ποδον ἢ ἵππους ἢ ἕτερόν τι πλὴν τῶν εἰς τροφὴν ὠνεῖσθαι, ἄχρις
ὅτου τὰ μεταξὺ Ῥωμαίων καὶ Οὔννων ἀμφίβολα διακριθείη. σεσοφισ-      235
μένως δὲ ταῦτα καὶ κατὰ τέχνην ἐγένετο τῷ βαρβάρῳ, ὥστε τὸν μὲν
Βιγίλαν ῥᾳδίως ἐπὶ τῇ κατ' αὐτοῦ ἁλῶναι πράξει ἀποροῦντα αἰτίας,
ἐφ' ᾗπερ τὸ χρυσίον κομίζοι, ἡμᾶς δὲ προφάσει ἀποκρίσεως ἐπὶ τῇ
πρεσβείᾳ δοθησομένης Ὀνηγήσιον ἀπεκδέξασθαι τὰ δῶρα κομιού-
μενον, ἅπερ ἡμεῖς τε διδόναι ἐβουλόμεθα καὶ βασιλεὺς ἀπεστάλκει.      240

Συνέβαινε γὰρ αὐτὸν σὺν τῷ πρεσβυτέρῳ τῶν Ἀττήλα παίδων
ἐς τὸ τῶν Ἀκατζίρων ἔθνος ἐστάλθαι, ὅ ἐστι Σκυθικὸν ἔθνος,
παρέστη δὲ τῷ Ἀττήλᾳ ἐξ αἰτίας τοιᾶσδε. πολλῶν κατὰ φῦλα καὶ
γένη ἀρχόντων τοῦ ἔθνους, Θεοδόσιος ὁ βασιλεὺς ἐκπέμπει δῶρα,
ὥστε ὁμονοίᾳ σφετέρᾳ ἀπαγορεῦσαι μὲν τῇ τοῦ Ἀττήλα συμμαχίᾳ,     245
τὴν δὲ πρὸς Ῥωμαίους εἰρήνην ἀσπάζεσθαι. ὁ δὲ τὰ δῶρα ἀπο-
κομίζων οὐ κατὰ τάξιν ἑκάστῳ τῶν βασιλέων τοῦ ἔθνους δίδωσιν,
ὥστε τὸν Κουρίδαχον πρεσβύτερον ὄντα τῇ ἀρχῇ τὰ δῶρα δεξάμενον
δεύτερον, οἷα δὴ περιοφθέντα καὶ τῶν σφετέρων στερηθέντα γερῶν,
ἐπικαλέσασθαι τὸν Ἀττήλαν κατὰ τῶν συμβασιλευόντων, τὸν δὲ μὴ    250
μελλήσαντα πολλὴν ἐκπέμψαι δύναμιν, καὶ τοὺς μὲν ἀνελόντα, τοὺς
δὲ παραστησάμενον καλεῖν τὸν Κουρίδαχον τῶν νικητηρίων
μεθέξοντα. τὸν δὲ ἐπιβουλὴν ὑποτοπήσαντα εἰπεῖν ὡς χαλεπὸν
ἀνθρώπῳ ἐλθεῖν ἐς ὄψιν θεοῦ· εἰ γὰρ οὐδὲ τὸν τοῦ ἡλίου δίσκον
ἀτενῶς ἔστιν ἰδεῖν, πῶς τὸν μέγιστον τῶν θεῶν ἀπαθῶς τις ὄψοιτο;   255
οὕτω μὲν οὖν ὁ Κουρίδαχος ἔμεινεν ἐπὶ τοῖς σφετέροις καὶ διεφύλαξε
τὴν ἀρχήν, τοῦ λοιποῦ παντὸς τοῦ Ἀκατζίρων ἔθνους τῷ Ἀττήλᾳ
παραστάντος· οὗπερ ἔθνους βασιλέα τὸν πρεσβύτερον τῶν παίδων
καταστῆσαι βουλόμενος Ὀνηγήσιον ἐπὶ ταύτην ἐκπέμπει τὴν πρᾶξιν.
διὸ δὴ καὶ ἡμᾶς, ὡς εἴρηται, ἐπιμεῖναι παρακελευσάμενος τὸν          260
Βιγίλαν διαφῆκεν ἅμα Ἤσλᾳ προφάσει μὲν τῶν φυγάδων ἐς τὴν
Ῥωμαίων διαβησόμενον, τῇ δὲ ἀληθείᾳ τῷ Ἐδέκωνι τὸ χρυσίον
κομιοῦντα.

Τοῦ δὲ Βιγίλα ἐξορμήσαντος, μίαν μετὰ τὴν ἐκείνου ἀναχώρησιν ἡμέραν ἐπιμείναντες τῇ ὑστεραίᾳ ἐπὶ τὰ ἀρκτικώτερα τῆς     265

242 Ἀκατζίρων ΒΕ [Ἀκατίρων Müller     257 Ἀκατζίρων scripsi [Κατζίρων
codd. Ἀκατίρων Müller

When we asked what Edeco had said to him, Vigilas, being himself deceived, tried to deceive us. Hiding the true reason, he said that Edeco had told him that Attila was angry with him over the fugitives, since it was necessary either that he receive them all or that ambassadors of the highest rank come to him.

While we were discussing these things, some of Attila's men came and said that neither Vigilas nor ourselves were to buy any Roman prisoner, or barbarian slave, or horses, or anything else except for food until the disputes between the Romans and the Huns had been settled. This was cunningly contrived and part of the barbarian's plan that Vigilas should be easily trapped in the plot against himself without a reason for bringing the gold, and that, on the excuse of a reply to be given to the embassy, we should await Onegesius, who would thus receive the gifts which the Emperor had sent and which we wished to deliver.

It happened that Onegesius had been sent together with Attila's eldest son[40] to the Akatziri, a Scythian people that had submitted to Attila for the following reason.[41] This people had many rulers according to their tribes and clans, and the Emperor Theodosius sent gifts to them to the end that they might unanimously renounce their alliance with Attila and seek peace with the Romans. The envoy who conveyed the gifts did not deliver them to each of the kings by rank, with the result that Kouridachus, the senior in office, received his gifts second and, being thus overlooked and deprived of his proper honours, called in Attila against his fellow kings. Attila without delay sent a large force, destroyed some and forced the rest to submit. He then summoned Kouridachus to share in the prizes of victory. But he, suspecting a plot, declared that it was hard for a man to come into the sight of a god: "For if it is not possible to look directly at the sun's disc, how could one look at the greatest of the gods without harm?" In this way Kouridachus remained amongst his own folk and saved his realm, while all the rest of the Akatzirian people submitted to Attila. He, wishing to make his eldest son king of this people, sent Onegesius for this purpose. Therefore, as I have said, he ordered us to remain with him and sent off Vigilas with Eslas to cross to Roman territory on the pretext of the fugitives, but in reality so that Vigilas might bring the gold to Edeco.

When Vigilas had left, we waited for one day after his departure and on the next set out with Attila for the more northerly parts of the

χώρας σὺν Ἀττήλᾳ ἐπορεύθημεν, καὶ ἄχρι τινὸς τῷ βαρβάρῳ συμ-
προελθόντες ἑτέραν ὁδὸν ἐτράπημεν, τῶν ξεναγούντων ἡμᾶς Σκυθῶν τοῦτο ποιεῖν παρακελευσαμένων, ὡς τοῦ Ἀττήλα ἐς κώμην τινὰ
παρεσομένου, ἐν ᾗ γαμεῖν θυγατέρα Ἐσκὰμ ἐβούλετο, πλείστας μὲν
ἔχων γαμετάς, ἀγόμενος δὲ καὶ ταύτην κατὰ νόμον τὸν Σκυθικόν.    270
ἐνθένδε ἐπορευόμεθα ὁδὸν ὁμαλὴν ἐν πεδίῳ κειμένην ναυσιπόροις τε
προσεβάλομεν ποταμοῖς, ὧν οἱ μέγιστοι μετὰ τὸν Ἴστρον ὅ τε Δρή-
κων λεγόμενος καὶ ὁ Τίγας καὶ ὁ Τιφήσας ἦν. καὶ τούτους μὲν
ἐπεραιώθημεν τοῖς μονοξύλοις πλοίοις, οἷς οἱ προσοικοῦντες τοὺς
ποταμοὺς κέχρηνται, τοὺς δὲ λοιποὺς ταῖς σχεδίαις διεπλεύσαμεν, ἃς    275
ἐπὶ τῶν ἁμαξῶν οἱ βάρβαροι διὰ τοὺς λιμνάζοντας φέρουσι τόπους.
ἐχορηγοῦντο δὲ ἡμῖν κατὰ κώμας τροφαί, ἀντὶ μὲν σίτου κέγχρος,
ἀντὶ δὲ οἴνου ὁ μέδος ἐπιχωρίως καλούμενος. ἐκομίζοντο δὲ καὶ οἱ
ἑπόμενοι ἡμῖν ὑπηρέται κέγχρον καὶ τὸ ἐκ κριθῶν χορηγούμενον
πόμα · κάμον οἱ βάρβαροι καλοῦσιν αὐτό.    280
      Μακρὰν δὲ ἀνύσαντες ὁδὸν περὶ δείλην ὀψίαν κατεσκηνώσαμεν
πρὸς λίμνῃ τινὶ πότιμον ὕδωρ ἐχούσῃ, ὅπερ οἱ τῆς πλησίον ὑδρεύοντο
κώμης. πνεῦμα δὲ καὶ θύελλα ἐξαπίνης διαναστᾶσα μετὰ βροντῶν
καὶ συχνῶν ἀστραπῶν καὶ ὄμβρου πολλοῦ οὐ μόνον ἡμῶν ἀνέτρεψε
τὴν σκηνήν, ἀλλὰ καὶ τὴν κατασκευὴν σύμπασαν ἐς τὸ ὕδωρ ἐκύλισε    285
τῆς λίμνης. ὑπὸ δὲ τῆς κρατούσης τὸν ἀέρα ταραχῆς καὶ τοῦ συμβάντος δεματωθέντες τὸ χωρίον ἀπελείπομεν καὶ ἀλλήλων χωριζό-
μεθα, ὡς ἐν σκότῳ καὶ ὑετῷ, τραπέντες ὁδόν, ἣν αὐτῷ ῥᾳδίαν
ἕκαστος ἔσεσθαι ᾤετο. ἐς δὲ τὰς καλύβας τῆς κώμης παραγενόμενοι
(τὴν αὐτὴν δὲ πάντες διαφόρως ἐτράπημεν) ἐς ταὐτὸν συνῇειμεν καὶ    290
τῶν ἀπολειπομένων σὺν βοῇ τὴν ζήτησιν ἐποιούμεθα. ἐκπηδήσαντες
δὲ οἱ Σκύθαι διὰ τὸν θόρυβον τοὺς καλάμους, οἷς πρὸς τῷ πυρὶ
κέχρηνται, ἀνέκαιον φῶς ἐργαζόμενοι, καὶ ἀνηρώτων ὅ τι βουλόμενοι κεκράγαμεν. τῶν δὲ σὺν ἡμῖν βαρβάρων ἀποκριναμένων ὡς διὰ
τὸν χειμῶνα ταραττόμεθα, πρὸς σφᾶς τε αὐτοὺς καλοῦντες ὑπε-    295
δέχοντο καὶ ἀλέαν παρεῖχον καλάμους πλείστους ἐναύοντες.
      Τῆς δὲ ἐν τῇ κώμῃ ἀρχούσης γυναικὸς (μία δὲ αὕτη τῶν Βλήδα
γυναικῶν ἐγεγόνει) τροφὰς ἡμῖν διαπεμψαμένης καὶ ἐπὶ συνουσίᾳ
γυναῖκας εὐπρεπεῖς (Σκυθικὴ δὲ αὕτη τιμή) τὰς μὲν γυναῖκας ἐκ τῶν
προκειμένων ἐδωδίμων φιλοφρονησάμενοι, τῇ πρὸς αὐτὰς ὁμιλίᾳ    300
ἀπαγορεύσαντες, ἐγκαταμείναντες δὲ ταῖς καλύβαις ἅμα ἡμέρᾳ ἐς
τὴν τῶν σκευῶν ἐτράπημεν ἀναζήτησιν, καὶ σύμπαντα εὑρηκότες, τὰ
μὲν ἐν τῷ χωρίῳ, ἐν ᾧπερ τῇ προτεραίᾳ καταλύσαντες ἐτύχομεν,
τὰ δὲ καὶ πρὸς τῇ ὄχθῃ τῆς λίμνης, τὰ δὲ καὶ ἐν αὐτῷ τῷ ὕδατι,

country. For a while we travelled with him and then turned off onto a different road at the command of our Scythian guides, since Attila was to go to a certain village where he wished to marry a daughter of Escam.[42] (Although he had many wives, he was marrying her according to Scythian custom.) From there we travelled along a level road over a plain and crossed navigable rivers, of which the greatest, after the Danube, were the ones named the Drecon, the Tigas and the Tiphesas.[43] These we crossed in boats made of single tree trunks, which those living near the rivers used; the others we negotiated on the rafts which the barbarians carry on their wagons because of the marshy areas. At the villages we were abundantly supplied with foodstuffs, millet instead of wheat and instead of wine what is called by the natives *medos*. The attendants in our train also carried millet and the drink made from barley which the barbarians call *kamon*.[44]

Having completed a long journey, in the late afternoon we encamped near to a pool containing drinkable water which supplied the inhabitants of the nearby village. Suddenly a wind and a storm arose with thunder and a great deal of lightning and rain, and it not only collapsed our tent but blew all our baggage into the pool. Terrified by the tumult that was raging in the air and by what had already happened, we fled the place and scattered, each of us in the darkness and the downpour taking the path which we thought would be the easiest.[45] Arriving at the huts of the village (which we all reached by our different routes), we gathered together and began to shout for the things we needed. At the uproar the Scythians rushed out, kindling the reeds which they used for fire and making light, and asked us what we wanted with our shouting. When the barbarians who were with us replied that we were panicked by the storm, they called to us and took us into their own homes and, burning a great quantity of reeds, gave us warmth.

The woman who ruled the village (she had been one of Bleda's wives) sent us food and attractive women for intercourse, which is a mark of honour amongst the Scythians. We plied the women generously from the foods placed before us, but refused intercourse with them. We remained in the huts and at about daybreak we went to search for our baggage and found it all, some in the spot in which we had happened to halt on the previous day, some at the edge of the pool, and some actually in the water. We gathered it up and spent the day in

ἀνελάβομεν καὶ ἐκείνην τὴν ἡμέραν ἐν τῇ κώμῃ διετρίψαμεν ἄπαντα    305
διατερσαίνοντες· ὅ τε γὰρ χειμὼν ἐπέπαυτο καὶ λαμπρὸς ἥλιος ἦν.
ἐπιμεληθέντες δὲ καὶ τῶν ἵππων καὶ τῶν λοιπῶν ὑποζυγίων παρὰ
τὴν βασιλίδα ἀφικόμεθα, καὶ αὐτὴν ἀσπασάμενοι καὶ δώροις ἀμειψά-
μενοι, τρισί τε ἀργυραῖς φιάλαις καὶ ἐρυθροῖς δέρμασι καὶ τῷ ἐξ
Ἰνδίας πεπέρει καὶ τῷ καρπῷ τῶν φοινίκων καὶ ἑτέροις τραγήμασι    310
διὰ τὸ μὴ ἐπιχωριάζειν τοῖς βαρβάροις οὖσι τιμίοις, ὑπέξιμεν εὐξά-
μενοι αὐτῇ ἀγαθὰ τῆς ξενίας πέρι.

Ἡμερῶν δὲ ϛ' ὁδὸν ἀνύσαντες ἐν κώμῃ τινὶ ἐπεμείναμεν, τῶν
ξεναγούντων παρακελευσαμένων Σκυθῶν, οἷα δὴ τοῦ Ἀττήλα ἐς
αὐτὴν ἐμβαλοῦντος τὴν ὁδὸν καὶ ἡμῶν κατόπιν αὐτοῦ πορεύεσθαι    315
ὀφειλόντων. ἔνθα δὴ ⟨ἐνε⟩τυγχάνομεν ἀνδράσι τῶν ἑσπερίων
Ῥωμαίων καὶ αὐτοῖς παρὰ τὸν Ἀττήλαν πρεσβευομένοις· ὧν Ῥωμύλος ἦν, ἀνὴρ τῇ τοῦ κόμητος ἀξίᾳ τετιμημένος, καὶ Προμοῦτος τῆς
Νωρικῶν ἄρχων χώρας καὶ Ῥωμανὸς στρατιωτικοῦ τάγματος
ἡγεμών. συνῆν δὲ αὐτοῖς Κωνστάντιος, ὃν ἀπεστάλκει Ἀέτιος παρὰ    320
τὸν Ἀττήλαν ὑπογραφέως χάριν, καὶ Τατοῦλος ὁ Ὀρέστου πατὴρ
τοῦ μετὰ Ἐδέκωνος, οὐ τῆς πρεσβείας ἕνεκα, ἀλλὰ οἰκειότητος χάριν
ἅμα σφίσιν αὐτοῖς τὴν πορείαν ποιούμενοι, Κωνστάντιος μὲν διὰ ⟨τὴν
ἐν⟩ ταῖς Ἰταλίαις προϋπάρξασαν πρὸς τοὺς ἄνδρας γνῶσιν, Τατοῦλος δὲ διὰ συγγένειαν· ὁ γὰρ αὐτοῦ παῖς Ὀρέστης Ῥωμύλου    325
θυγατέρα ἐγεγαμήκει. . . . ἀπὸ Παταβίωνος τῆς ἐν Νωρικῷ πόλεως
ἐπρεσβεύοντο ἐκμειλιττόμενοι τὸν Ἀττήλαν ἐκδοθῆναι αὐτῷ βουλόμενον Σιλβανόν, ἀσήμου τραπέζης κατὰ τὴν Ῥώμην προεστῶτα,
ὡς φιάλας χρυσᾶς παρὰ Κωνσταντίου δεξάμενον, ὃς ἐκ Γαλατῶν
μὲν τῶν ἐν τῇ ἑσπέρᾳ ὡρμᾶτο, ἀπέσταλτο δὲ καὶ αὐτὸς παρὰ Ἀττή-    330
λαν τε καὶ Βλήδαν, ὥσπερ ὁ μετ' αὐτὸν Κωνστάντιος, ὑπογραφέως
χάριν. κατὰ δὲ τὸν χρόνον, ἐν ᾧ ὑπὸ Σκυθῶν ἐν τῇ Παιόνων ἐπο-
λιορκεῖτο τὸ Σίρμιον, τὰς φιάλας παρὰ τοῦ τῆς πόλεως ἐπισκόπου
ἐδέξατο ἐφ' ᾧ αὐτὸν λύσασθαι, εἴ γε περιόντος αὐτοῦ ἁλῶναι τὴν
πόλιν συμβαίη, ἢ ἀναιρεθέντος ὠνήσασθαι τοὺς αἰχμαλώτους    335
ἀπαγομένους τῶν ἀστῶν. ὁ δὲ Κωνστάντιος μετὰ τὸν τῆς πόλεως
ἀνδραποδισμὸν ὀλιγωρήσας τῶν Σκυθικῶν ἐς τὴν Ῥώμην κατὰ
πρᾶξίν τινα παραγίνεται καὶ κομίζεται παρὰ τοῦ Σιλβανοῦ χρυσίον
τὰς φιάλας δούς, ὥστε ῥητοῦ χρόνου ἐντὸς ἢ ἀποδόντα τὸ ἐκδα-
νεισθὲν χρυσίον ἀναλαβεῖν τὰ ἐνέχυρα, ἢ αὐτοῖς τὸν Σιλβανὸν ἐς ὃ    340

316 ἐνε- add. Hoeschel    323-24 τὴν ἐν add. Niebuhr    326 lac. post ἐγεγαμήκει ponit de Boor, post πόλεως edd.    328 ἀσήμου Bury [ἀρμίου X (aut
ἀσμίου E) ἀργυρίου Valesius    336 τὸν post πόλεως ponunt MP, omittunt BE
337 Σκυθικῶν codd. praeter M (συνθικῶν) [συνθηκῶν Niebuhr    339-40
ἐκδαπανησθὲν P

the village drying it all out, for the storm had ceased and the sun was shining brightly. When we had taken care of the horses and the rest of the baggage animals, we visited the queen, thanked her, and repaid her with three silver bowls, red skins, Indian pepper, dates and other dried fruits which the barbarians value because they are not native to their own country. Then we called blessings upon her for her hospitality and departed.

When we had completed a journey of seven days, on the orders of our Scythian guides we halted at a village, since Attila was to take the same road and we had to follow behind him. There we met some western Romans who were also on an embassy to Attila. Amongst them were Romulus, who had the rank of count, Promotus, the governor of Noricum, and the general Romanus.[46] With them were Constantius, whom Aetius had sent to Attila as his secretary, and Tatulus, the father of Orestes who was with Edeco. They were not members of the embassy but were travelling with the envoys out of personal friendship, Constantius because of his earlier acquaintance with them in Italy, Tatulus out of kinship, since his son Orestes had married a daughter of Romulus. ... They were making this embassy from Patavio, a city in Noricum,[47] in order to pacify Attila, who wanted Silvanus, the manager of the bank dealing in bullion at Rome,[48] to be handed over to him on the ground that he had received some golden bowls from Constantius. This Constantius came from the Gauls of the West[49] and he too, like the later Constantius, had been sent by Aetius to Attila and Bleda as secretary. At the time when Sirmium, a city of Pannonia, was being besieged by the Scythians,[50] Constantius was given the bowls by the bishop of the city for the purpose of ransoming him if the city were captured and he survived, or, if he were killed, of buying the freedom of those citizens who were being led off as prisoners. However, after the capture of the city, Constantius ignored the rights of the Scythians[51] and, coming to Rome on business, handed over the bowls to Silvanus and received from him gold on condition that either within a stated period of time he repay the gold with interest and recover the sureties or Silvanus do with them as he wished. But Attila and Bleda

τι βούλοιτο χρήσασθαι. τοῦτον δὴ τὸν Κωνστάντιον ἐν ὑποψίᾳ
προδοσίας ποιησάμενοι Ἀττήλας τε καὶ Βλήδας ἀνεσταύρωσαν·
μετὰ δὲ χρόνον τῷ Ἀττήλᾳ ὡς τὰ περὶ τῶν φιαλῶν ἐμηνύθη, ἐκδοθῆναι αὐτῷ τὸν Σιλβανὸν οἷα δὴ φῶρα τῶν αὐτοῦ γενόμενον
ἐβούλετο. πρέσβεις τοίνυν παρὰ Ἀετίου καὶ τοῦ βασιλεύοντος τῶν      345
ἑσπερίων Ῥωμαίων ἐστάλησαν ἐροῦντες ὡς χρήστης Σιλβανὸς
Κωνσταντίου γενόμενος τὰς φιάλας ἐνέχυρα καὶ οὐ φώρια λαβὼν
ἔχοι, καὶ ὡς ταύτας ἀργυρίου χάριν ἱερεῦσι καὶ <οὐ> τοῖς ἐπι-
τυχοῦσιν ἀπέδοτο· οὔτε γὰρ θέμις ἀνθρώποις εἰς σφετέραν διακονίαν
κεχρῆσθαι ἐκπώμασιν ἀνατεθεῖσι θεῷ. εἰ οὖν μὴ <μετὰ> τῆς      350
εὐλόγου προφάσεως καὶ εὐλαβείᾳ τοῦ θείου ἀποσταίη τοῦ τὰς φιάλας
αἰτεῖν, ἐκπέμπειν τὸ ὑπὲρ αὐτῶν χρυσίον τὸν Σιλβανὸν παραιτου-
μένους· οὐ γὰρ ἐκδώσειν ἄνθρωπον ἀδικοῦντα οὐδέν. καὶ αὕτη μὲν
αἰτία τῆς τῶν ἀνδρῶν πρεσβείας, καὶ παρείποντο ὅ τι καὶ ἀποκρινάμενος ἀποπέμψοι σφᾶς ὁ βάρβαρος.                                    355
    Ἐπὶ τῆς αὐτῆς οὖν ὁδοῦ γενόμενοι, προπορευθῆναι αὐτὸν ἀνα-
μείναντες σὺν τῷ παντὶ ἐπηκολουθήσαμεν πλήθει. καὶ ποταμούς
τινας διαβάντες ἐν μεγίστῃ παρεγινόμεθα κώμῃ, ἐν ᾗ τὰ τοῦ Ἀττήλα
οἰκήματα περιφανέστερα τῶν ἁπανταχοῦ εἶναι ἐλέγετο ξύλοις τε καὶ
σανίσιν εὐξέστοις ἡρμοσμένα καὶ περιβόλῳ ξυλίνῳ κυκλούμενα οὐ      360
πρὸς ἀσφάλειαν, ἀλλὰ πρὸς εὐπρέπειαν συλλαμβάνοντι. μετὰ δὲ τὰ
τοῦ βασιλέως ἦν τὰ τοῦ Ὀνηγησίου διαπρεπῆ καὶ περίβολον μὲν ἐκ
ξύλων καὶ αὐτὰ ἔχοντα, οὐχ ὁμοίως δὲ ὥσπερ ὁ Ἀττήλα πύργοις
ἐκοσμεῖτο. βαλανεῖον δὲ ἦν οὐ πόρρω τοῦ περιβόλου, ὅπερ Ὀνηγήσιος μετὰ τὸν Ἀττήλαν παρὰ Σκύθαις ἰσχύων μέγα ᾠκοδόμει λίθους      365
ἐκ τῆς Παιόνων διακομίσας γῆς· οὐδὲ γὰρ οὐδὲ λίθος οὐ δένδρον
παρὰ τοῖς ἐκεῖνο τὸ μέρος οἰκοῦσι βαρβάροις ἐστίν, ἀλλὰ ἐπεισάκτῳ
τῇ ὕλῃ κέχρηνται ταύτῃ. ὁ δὲ ἀρχιτέκτων τοῦ βαλανείου ἀπὸ τοῦ
Σιρμίου αἰχμάλωτος ἀχθείς, μισθὸν τοῦ εὑρέματος ἐλευθερίαν
λήψεσθαι προσδοκῶν ἔλαθε μείζονι πόνῳ περιπεσὼν τῆς παρὰ      370
Σκύθαις δουλείας· βαλανέα γὰρ αὐτὸν Ὀνηγήσιος κατέστησεν, καὶ
λουομένῳ αὐτῷ τε καὶ τοῖς ἀμφ' αὐτὸν διηκονεῖτο.
    Ἐν ταύτῃ τῇ κώμῃ εἰσιόντα τὸν Ἀττήλαν ἀπήντων κόραι
στοιχηδὸν προπορευόμεναι ὑπὸ ὀθόναις λεπταῖς τε καὶ λευκαῖς
ἐπὶ πολὺ ἐς μῆκος παρατεινούσαις, ὥστε ὑπὸ μιᾷ ἑκάστῃ ὀθόνῃ      375
ἀνεχομένῃ ταῖς χερσὶ τῶν παρ' ἑκάτερα γυναικῶν κόρας ζ' ἢ καὶ
πλείους βαδιζούσας (ἦσαν δὲ πολλαὶ τοιαῦται τῶν γυναικῶν ὑπὸ ταῖς
ὀθόναις τάξεις) ᾄδειν ᾄσματα Σκυθικά. πλησίον δὲ τῶν Ὀνηγησίου

---

348 οὐ add. Bekker [καὶ exp. Müller    350 μετὰ post μὴ inserui, quod Niebuhr
pro μὴ scripsit    351 εὐλόγῳ προφάσει Bornmann (1974)    353 ἐκδωσεις X
366 οὐδὲν γὰρ MP  οὐδὲ post γὰρ exp. Hoeschel

came to suspect Constantius of treachery and crucified him, and, after a time, Attila, being informed of the matter of the bowls, wished Silvanus to be handed over to him as a thief of his own possessions. Therefore, envoys had been sent by Aetius and the Emperor of the western Romans to say that, as Constantius' creditor, Silvanus had received the bowls as sureties and not as stolen property and that he had sold them for silver to priests and not to common citizens; for it was not right that men should use for their own purposes vessels dedicated to God. Accordingly, if, after[52] this reasonable explanation and out of respect for divinity, Attila would not drop his demand for the bowls, they would send gold for them but would not surrender Silvanus, since they would not hand over a man who had done no wrong. This was the reason for their embassy, and they were attending him so that the barbarian might give his reply and dismiss them.

Since we were on the same journey, we waited for Attila to go ahead and followed with our whole party. Having crossed some rivers, we came to a very large village[53] in which Attila's palace was said to be more spectacular than those elsewhere. It was constructed of timbers and smoothly planed boards[54] and was surrounded by a wooden wall which was built with an eye not to security but to elegance. The buildings of Onegesius were second only to those of the king in magnificence, and they too had a circuit wall made of timbers but not embellished with towers, as was Attila's. Not far from this wall was a bath which Onegesius, whose power amongst the Scythians was second only to that of Attila, had built, fetching stones from Pannonia. For there is neither stone nor timber amongst the barbarians who inhabit this area, but the wood that they use is imported. The builder of the bath had been taken prisoner at Sirmium, and he hoped to gain his freedom as a reward for his inventive work. But he was disappointed and fell into greater distress than slavery amongst the Scythians. For Onegesius made him bath attendant, and he waited upon him and his followers when they bathed.

In this village, as Attila was entering, young girls came to meet him and went before him in rows under narrow cloths of white linen, which were held up by the hands of women on either side. These cloths were stretched out to such a length that under each one seven or more girls walked. There were many such rows of women under the cloths, and they sang Scythian songs. When Attila came near to Onegesius'

οἰκημάτων γενόμενον (δι᾽ αὐτῶν γὰρ ἡ ἐπὶ τὰ βασίλεια ἦγεν ὁδός)
ὑπεξελθοῦσα ἡ τοῦ Ὀνηγησίου γαμετὴ μετὰ πλήθους θεραπόντων,        380
τῶν μὲν ὄψα, τῶν δὲ καὶ οἶνον φερόντων (μεγίστη δὲ αὕτη παρὰ
Σκύθαις ἐστὶ τιμή) ἠσπάζετό τε καὶ ἠξίου μεταλαβεῖν ὧν αὐτῷ φιλο-
φρονουμένη ἐκόμισεν. ὃς δὲ ἐπιτηδείου ἀνδρὸς χαριζόμενος γαμετῇ
ἤσθιεν ἐπὶ τοῦ ἵππου ἥμενος, τῶν παρεπομένων τὸν πίνακα (ἀργύ-
ρεος δὲ ἦν οὗτος) ἐς ὕψος ἀράντων βαρβάρων. ἀπογευσάμενος δὲ        385
καὶ τῆς προσενεχθείσης αὐτῷ κύλικος ἐς τὰ βασίλεια ἐχώρει ὄντα
τῶν ἄλλων ὑπέρτερα καὶ ἐν ὑψηλῷ διακείμενα χωρίῳ.
    Ἡμεῖς δὲ ἐν τοῖς Ὀνηγησίου, ἐκείνου παρακελευσαμένου, ἐγ-
κατεμείναμεν· ἐπανεληλύθει γὰρ σὺν τῷ Ἀττήλα παιδί. ἠριστο-
ποιησάμεθα <δέ>, δεξιωσαμένης ἡμᾶς τῆς τε γαμετῆς καὶ τῶν        390
κατὰ γένος αὐτῷ διαφερόντων· αὐτὸς γὰρ τῷ Ἀττήλα μετὰ τὴν
ἐπάνοδον τότε πρῶτον ἐς ὄψιν ἐλθὼν καὶ αὐτῷ τὰ ἐπὶ τῇ πράξει,
ἐφ᾽ ἣν ἔσταλτο, ἀπαγγέλλων καὶ τὸ πάθος τὸ τῷ Ἀττήλα παιδὶ
συνενεχθέν (τὴν γὰρ δεξιὰν χεῖρα ἐξολισθήσας κατέαξεν) συνευ-
ωχεῖσθαι ἡμῖν οὐκ ἦγε σχολήν. μετὰ δὲ τὸ δεῖπνον ἀπολιπόντες τὰ        395
τοῦ Ὀνηγησίου οἰκήματα πλησίον τῶν Ἀττήλα κατεσκηνώσαμεν
ἐπιτραπέντες, ὥστε καιροῦ καλοῦντος ἢ παρὰ τὸν Ἀττήλαν ἐσιέναι
τὸν Μαξιμῖνον ἤγουν καὶ τοῖς ἄλλοις τοῖς ἀμφ᾽ αὐτὸν ἐς λόγους ἰέναι
ὀφείλοντα μὴ πολλῷ κεχωρίσθαι διαστήματι. διαγαγόντων δὲ ἡμῶν
ἐκείνην τὴν νύκτα ἐν ᾧπερ κατελύσαμεν χωρίῳ, ὑποφαινούσης        400
ἡμέρας ὁ Μαξιμῖνος στέλλει με παρὰ τὸν Ὀνηγήσιον τὰ δῶρα
δώσοντα, ἅ τε αὐτὸς ἐδίδου, ἅ τε βασιλεὺς ἀπεστάλκει, καὶ ὅπως
γνοίη οἷ βούλεται αὐτῷ καὶ ὁπότε ἐς λόγους ἐλθεῖν. παραγενόμενος
δὲ ἅμα τοῖς κομίζουσιν αὐτῷ ὑπηρέταις προσεκαρτέρουν, ἔτι τῶν
θυρῶν κεκλεισμένων, ἄχρις ὅτου τις ὑπεξελθὼν τὴν ἡμετέραν        405
μηνύσειεν ἄφιξιν.
    Διατρίβοντι δέ μοι καὶ περιπάτους ποιουμένῳ πρὸ τοῦ περι-
βόλου τῶν οἰκημάτων προσελθών τις, ὃν βάρβαρον ἐκ τῆς Σκυθικῆς
ᾠήθην εἶναι στολῆς, Ἑλληνικῇ ἀσπάζεταί με φωνῇ, χαῖρε προσει-
πών, ὥστε με θαυμάζειν ὅτι γε δὴ ἑλληνίζει Σκύθης ἀνήρ. ξύγκλυδες        410
γὰρ ὄντες πρὸς τῇ σφετέρᾳ βαρβάρῳ γλώσσῃ ζηλοῦσιν ἢ τὴν
Οὔννων ἢ τὴν Γότθων ἢ καὶ τὴν Αὐσονίων, ὅσοις αὐτῶν πρὸς Ῥωμαίους ἐπιμιξία· καὶ οὐ ῥαδίως τις σφῶν ἑλληνίζει τῇ φωνῇ, πλὴν
ὧν ἀπήγαγον αἰχμαλώτων ἀπὸ τῆς Θρᾳκίας καὶ Ἰλλυρίδος παρά-
λου. ἀλλ᾽ ἐκεῖνοι μὲν γνώριμοι τοῖς ἐντυγχάνουσιν ἐτύγχανον ἔκ τε        415
τῶν διερρωγότων ἐνδυμάτων καὶ τοῦ αὐχμοῦ τῆς κεφαλῆς ὡς ἐς

390 δέ add. de Boor    397 ἐπιτραπέντες … καλοῦντος om. X et edd.    399
διαγαγόντων Bekker [διαγόντων codd.    400 ὑπερφανούσης M ex quo ὑπερ-
φαυούσης Dindorf    403 οἷ Dindorf [οἱ codd. εἱ Bekker

compound, through which the road to the palace passed,[55] Onegesius' wife came out to meet him with a crowd of servants, some carrying food and others wine (this is a very great honour amongst the Scythians), welcomed him and asked him to partake of what she had brought out of friendship. In order to please the wife of a close friend, he ate while sitting on his horse, the barbarians who were accompanying him having raised aloft the platter which was of silver. When he had also drunk from the cup of wine which was offered to him, he proceeded to the palace, which was higher than the other structures and built on a rise.

We waited at the compound of Onegesius as he had ordered, for he had returned with Attila's son. His wife and the most important members of his clan received us, and there we dined. Onegesius did not have time to dine with us, since immediately upon his return he had gone to speak with Attila to report to him upon the business for which he had been sent and upon the accident suffered by Attila's son, who had fallen and broken his right arm. After the meal we left Onegesius' compound, moved closer to Attila's palace and camped there, so that when the time came for Maximinus to have an audience with Attila or else to speak with others of his retinue, he should not be far away. We spent the night where we had encamped, and at daybreak Maximinus sent me to Onegesius to give him the gifts, both those which he was giving and those which the Emperor had sent, and to learn where and when he wished to speak with him. I arrived with the servants who were carrying the gifts for him and, since the doors were still shut, I waited until someone should come out and report our arrival.

As I was waiting and walking about before the circuit wall of the palace, someone, whom I took to be a barbarian from his Scythian dress, approached me and greeted me in Greek, saying, *"khaire"* ("Hello"). I was amazed that a Scythian was speaking Greek. Being a mixture of peoples, in addition to their own languages they cultivate Hunnic or Gothic or (in the case of those who have dealings with the Romans) Latin. But none of them can easily speak Greek, except for those whom they have taken prisoner from the sea coasts of Thrace and Illyria;[56] and whoever met them could easily recognise them from their tattered clothes and filthy hair as persons who had fallen into

τὴν χείρονα μεταπεσόντες τύχην· οὗτος δὲ τρυφῶντι ἐῴκει Σκύθῃ
εὐείμων τε ὢν καὶ ἀποκειράμενος τὴν κεφαλὴν περιτρόχαλα.
Ἀντασπασάμενος δὲ ἀνηρώτων τίς ὢν καὶ πόθεν ἐς τὴν βάρ-
βαρον παρῆλθε γῆν καὶ βίον ἀναιρεῖται Σκυθικόν. ὁ δὲ ἀπεκρίνατο ὅ      420
τι βουλόμενος ταῦτα γνῶναι ἐσπούδακα. ἐγὼ δὲ ἔφην αἰτίαν πολυ-
πραγμοσύνης εἶναί μοι τὴν Ἑλλήνων φωνήν. τότε δὴ γελάσας ἔλεγε
Γραικὸς μὲν εἶναι τὸ γένος, κατ᾽ ἐμπορίαν δὲ εἰς τὸ Βιμινάκιον
ἐληλυθέναι τὴν πρὸς τῷ Ἴστρῳ ποταμῷ Μυσῶν πόλιν. πλεῖστον δὲ
ἐν αὐτῇ διατρῖψαι χρόνον καὶ γυναῖκα γῆμασθαι ζάπλουτον. τὴν δὲ      425
ἐντεῦθεν εὐπραγίαν ἐκδύσασθαι ὑπὸ τοῖς βαρβάροις τῆς πόλεως
γενομένης, καὶ διὰ τὸν ὑπάρξαντα πλοῦτον αὐτῷ Ὀνηγησίῳ ἐν τῇ
τῶν λαφύρων προκριθῆναι διανομῇ· τοὺς γὰρ ἁλόντας ἀπὸ τῶν
εὐπόρων μετὰ τὸν Ἀττήλαν ἐκκρίτους εἶχον οἱ τῶν Σκυθῶν λογάδες
διὰ τὸ ἐπὶ πλείστοις διατίθεσθαι. ἀριστεύσαντα δὲ ἐν ταῖς ὕστερον      430
πρὸς Ῥωμαίους μάχαις καὶ τὸ τῶν Ἀκατίρων ἔθνος, δόντα τῷ
βαρβάρῳ δεσπότῃ κατὰ τὸν παρὰ Σκύθαις νόμον τὰ κατὰ τὸν
πόλεμον αὐτῷ κτηθέντα, ἐλευθερίας τυχεῖν. γυναῖκα δὲ γῆμασθαι
βάρβαρον, εἶναί τε αὐτῷ παῖδας· καὶ Ὀνηγησίῳ τραπέζης κοινω-
νοῦντα ἀμείνονα τοῦ προτέρου τὸν παρόντα βίον ἡγεῖσθαι.      435
Τοὺς μὲν γὰρ παρὰ Σκύθαις μετὰ τὸν πόλεμον ἐν ἀπραγ-
μοσύνῃ διατελεῖν, ἑκάστου τῶν παρόντων ἀπολαύοντος καὶ οὐδαμῶς
ἢ ὀλίγα ἐνοχλοῦντος ἢ ἐνοχλουμένου, τοὺς μέντοι παρὰ Ῥωμαίοις ἐν
μὲν πολέμῳ ῥᾳδίως ἀναλίσκεσθαι εἰς ἑτέρους τὰς τῆς σωτηρίας
ἐλπίδας ἔχοντας, ὡς πάντων διὰ τοὺς τυράννους μὴ χρωμένων      440
ὅπλοις· καὶ τοῖς χρωμένοις δὲ σφαλερωτέρα ἡ τῶν στρατηγῶν
κακία μὴ ὑφισταμένων τὸν πόλεμον. ἐν δὲ τῇ εἰρήνῃ ὀδυνηρότερα
ὑπάρχειν τὰ συμβαίνοντα τῶν ἐν τοῖς πολέμοις κακῶν διά τε τὴν
βαρυτάτην εἴσπραξιν τῶν δασμῶν καὶ τὰς ἐκ τῶν πονηρῶν βλάβας,
τῶν νόμων οὐ κατὰ πάντων κειμένων, ἀλλὰ εἰ μὲν ὁ παραβαίνων τὸν      445
θεσμὸν τῶν πλουτούντων εἴη, ἔστι τῆς ἀδικίας αὐτὸν μὴ διδόναι
δίκας· εἰ δὲ πένης εἴη, οὐκ ἐπιστάμενος χρῆσθαι πράγμασιν ὑπομένει
τὴν ἀπὸ τοῦ νόμου ζημίαν, εἴπερ μὴ πρὸ τῆς κρίσεως ἀπολείποι τὸν
βίον, μακροῦ ἐπὶ ταῖς δίκαις παρατεινομένου χρόνου καὶ πλείστων
ἐκδαπανωμένων χρημάτων· ὅπερ τῶν πάντων ἀνιαρότατον εἴη, ἐπὶ      450
μισθῷ τῶν ἀπὸ τοῦ νόμου τυγχάνειν. οὐδὲ γὰρ τῷ ἀδικουμένῳ τις
δικαστήριον παραδώσει, εἰ μή τι ἀργύριον τῷ τε δικαστῇ καὶ τοῖς
ἐκείνῳ διακονουμένοις κατάθοιτο.

421 ἔφη X et edd.    431 Ἀκατίρων Müller [Ἀκατήρων codd.    441 τοῖς
χρωμένοις Maltese (1977) [τῶν χρωμένων codd.    441-42 ἡ τύχη τῇ τῶν
στρατηγῶν κακία de Boor    442 μηδὲ M et Dindorf    446 ἔστι Bekker [ἐπὶ
codd.    451 τις Niebuhr [εἰς codd.    452 τῷ τε Hoeschel [τότε codd.

adversity. This one, however, was like a well-cared-for Scythian with good clothing and his hair clipped all around.[57]

I returned his greeting and asked who he was and where he came from to the land of the barbarians and took up a Scythian way of life. In reply he asked why I was so eager to know this. I said that his Greek speech was the reason for my curiosity. He laughed and said that he was a Greek and for purposes of trade he had gone to Viminacium, the city in Moesia on the river Danube. He had lived there for a very long time and married a very rich woman. When the city was captured by the barbarians,[58] he was deprived of his prosperity and, because of his great wealth, was assigned to Onegesius himself in the division of the spoils; for after Attila the leading men of the Scythians, because they were in command of very many men,[59] chose their captives from amongst the well-to-do. Having proven his valour in later battles against the Romans and the nation of the Akatiri and having, according to Scythian law, given his booty to his master, he had won his freedom. He had married a barbarian wife and had children, and, as a sharer at the table of Onegesius, he now enjoyed a better life than he had previously.

He continued, saying that after a war men amongst the Scythians live at ease, each enjoying his own possessions and troubling others or being troubled not at all or very little. But amongst the Romans, since on account of their tyrants[60] not all men carry weapons, they place their hope of safety in others and are thus easily destroyed in war. Moreover, those who do use arms are endangered still more by the cowardice of their generals, who are unable to sustain a war. In peace misfortunes await one even more painful than the evils of war because of the imposition of heavy taxes and injuries done by criminals. For the laws are not applied to all. If the wrongdoer is rich, the result is that he does not pay the penalty for his crime, whereas if he is poor and does not know how to handle the matter, he suffers the prescribed punishment — if he does not die before judgement is given (since lawsuits are much protracted and much money is spent on them). And this may be the most painful thing, to have to pay for justice. For no one will grant a hearing to a wronged man unless he hands over money for the judge and his assessors.

Τοιαῦτα καὶ πλεῖστα ἕτερα προτιθέντος, ὑπολαβὼν ἔφασκον
πράως αὐτὸν καὶ τὰ ἐξ ἐμοῦ ἀκούειν. καὶ δὴ ἔλεγον ὡς οἱ τῆς Ῥω-     455
μαίων πολιτείας εὑρεταὶ σοφοί τε καὶ ἀγαθοὶ ἄνδρες, ὥστε τὰ
πράγματα τηνάλλως μὴ φέρεσθαι, τοὺς μὲν τῶν νόμων εἶναι φύλακας, τοὺς δὲ ποιεῖσθαι τῶν ὅπλων ἐπιμέλειαν ἔταξαν καὶ τὰς
πολεμικὰς μελέτας ἀσκεῖν, πρὸς μηδὲν ἕτερον ἐπαγομένους ἢ ὥστε
εἶναι πρὸς μάχην ἑτοίμους καὶ ὡς ἐπὶ τὴν συνήθη γυμνασίαν θαρ-     460
ροῦντας ἐπὶ τὸν πόλεμον ἰέναι, προαναλωθέντος αὐτοῖς διὰ τῆς
μελέτης τοῦ φόβου· τοὺς δὲ προσκειμένους τῇ γεωργίᾳ καὶ τῇ ἐπιμελείᾳ τῆς γῆς ἑαυτούς τε καὶ τοὺς ὑπὲρ σφῶν αὐτῶν ἀγωνιζομένους
τρέφειν ἔταξαν [δὲ καὶ τοὺς] τὸ στρατιωτικὸν εἰσπραττομένους
σιτηρέσιον· ἄλλους δὲ τῶν ἀδικουμένων προνοεῖν, καὶ τοὺς μὲν τοῦ     465
δικαίου προΐστασθαι ὑπὲρ τῶν δι᾽ ἀσθένειαν φύσεως μὴ οἵων τε
ὄντων τὰ σφέτερα προΐσχεσθαι δίκαια, τοὺς δὲ δικάζοντας φυλάττειν
ἅπερ ὁ νόμος βούλεται· μὴ ἐστερῆσθαι δὲ φροντίδος μηδὲ τῶν παρα-
στάντων τοῖς δικασταῖς, ἀλλὰ κἀκείνων εἶναι τοὺς πρόνοιαν ποιησο-
μένους, ὅπως τοῦ τε δικαίου τεύξοιτο ὁ τῆς τῶν δικαστῶν τυχῶν     470
κρίσεως καὶ ὁ ἀδικεῖν νομισθεὶς μὴ εἰσπραχθείη πλέον ἤπερ ἡ
δικαστικὴ βούλεται ψῆφος. εἰ γὰρ μὴ ὑπῆρχον οἱ ταῦτα ἐν φροντίδι
ποιούμενοι, ἐκ τῆς αὐτῆς αἰτίας ἑτέρας δίκης ἐγίνετο ἂν πρόφασις, ἢ
τοῦ νενικηκότος χαλεπώτερον ἐπεξιόντος, ἢ τοῦ τὴν χείρονα ἀπ-
ενεγκαμένου τῇ ἀδίκῳ ἐπιμένοντος γνώμῃ.     475

Εἶναι δὲ καὶ τούτοις τεταγμένον ἀργύριον παρὰ τῶν τὰς δίκας
ἀγωνιζομένων, ὡς παρὰ τῶν γεωργῶν τοῖς ὁπλίταις. ἢ οὐκ ὅσιον
τὸν ἐπικουροῦντα τρέφειν καὶ τῆς εὐνοίας ἀμείβεσθαι; ὥσπερ ἀγαθὸν
ἱππεῖ μὲν ἡ τοῦ ἵππου κομιδή, ἀγαθὸν δὲ βουκόλῳ ἡ τῶν βοῶν καὶ
θηρατῇ ἡ τῶν κυνῶν ἐπιμέλεια, καὶ τῶν ἄλλων ὧν πρὸς σφετέραν     480
φυλακήν τε καὶ ὠφέλειαν ἔχουσιν ἄνθρωποι, ὁπότε τὴν δαπάνην τὴν
ἐπὶ τῇ δίκῃ γενομένην ἀλόντες ἐκτίνουσιν, ἀνατιθέντες ἀδικίᾳ
σφετέρᾳ καὶ οὐχ ἑτέρῳ τὴν βλάβην.

Τὸν δὲ ἐπὶ ταῖς δίκαις μακρότερον, ἂν οὕτω τύχοι, χρόνον τῆς
τοῦ δικαίου προνοίας γίνεσθαι χάριν, ὥστε μὴ σχεδιάζοντας τοὺς     485
δικαστὰς τῆς ἀκριβείας διαμαρτεῖν, λογιζομένους ἄμεινον εἶναι ὀψὲ
πέρας ἐπιτεθῆναι δίκῃ ἢ ἐσπουδακότας μὴ μόνον ἄνθρωπον ἀδικεῖν,
ἀλλὰ εἰς <τὸν> τοῦ δικαίου εὑρετὴν θεὸν πλημμελεῖν. κεῖσθαι δὲ
τοὺς νόμους κατὰ πάντων, ὥστε αὐτοῖς καὶ βασιλέα πείθεσθαι, καὶ
οὐχ, ὃ τῇ αὐτοῦ ἔνεστι κατηγορίᾳ, ὅτι γε δὴ οἱ εὔποροι τοὺς πένητας     490

---

464 δὲ καὶ τοὺς exp. Bekker  [ἔταξαν, ἔταξαν δὲ καὶ τὸ σ. εἰσπράττεσθαι
Thompson (1947)     474 τοῦ τὴν χείρονα [sc. ψῆφον] de Boor [τοῦ τὴν
χείρονος E  τῇ τοῦ χείρονος X  τοῦ τὸ χεῖρον Niebuhr     482 ἀντιτιθέντων
Valesius  488 τὸν add. Niebuhr  490 ὃ Bekker [ὃς codd. ὡς Valesius

While he was putting these and many other complaints, I said gently in reply that he should also hear my point of view. "Those who founded the Roman polity were," I said, "wise and good men. So that things should not be done haphazardly, they ordained that some should be guardians of the laws and that others should attend to weaponry and undergo military training, with their sole object that they be ready for battle and go out confidently to war as if to some familiar exercise, their fear having been already eradicated by their training. Our founders also ordained that those whose care was farming and the cultivation of the land should support both themselves and those fighting on their behalf by contributing the military grain-tax. Still others they appointed to take thought for those who had suffered wrongs, some to have charge of the cases of those who, through their own natural incapability, were unable to plead for themselves, and others to sit in judgement and uphold the intent of the law. Furthermore, they took thought for those who came before the courts, that there should be persons to ensure that the one who obtained the judgement should receive his award and that the one adjudged guilty should not pay more than the judge decided. If there did not exist persons to take thought for these matters, a reason for a second case would arise out of the cause of the first, because either the victor would proceed too harshly or the one who had obtained the adverse decision would persist in his injustice.[61]

"There is also a set sum of money laid down for these men to be paid by the litigants, just as the farmers pay a set sum to the soldiers. Is it not right to support one who comes to your aid and to reward his good will (in the same way as the feeding of a horse benefits the horseman and the care of cattle, dogs and other animals benefits herdsmen, hunters and others who keep the animals for their own safety and profit) and to blame one's own illegal act rather than another person whenever the court costs have to be paid even though the case has been lost?

"The excessive time taken over the cases, if that happens, is the result of a concern for justice, lest the judges deal with them carelessly and err in their decisions. For they think it is better to conclude a case late than by hurrying to wrong a man and offend against God, the founder of justice. The laws apply to all, and even the Emperor obeys them. It is not a fact" — as was part of his charge — "that the rich do

272    Priscus: Text

ἀκινδύνως βιάζοιντο, εἰ μή γε διαλαθών τις φύγοι τὴν δίκην. ὅπερ
οὐκ ἐπὶ τῶν πλουσίων, ἀλλὰ καὶ πενήτων εὕροι τις ἄν· πλημμε-
λοῦντες γὰρ οὐδὲ αὐτοὶ ἀπορίᾳ ἐλέγχων δοῖεν δίκας. καὶ τοῦτο παρὰ
πᾶσι καὶ οὐ παρὰ Ῥωμαίοις μόνον συμβαῖνόν ἐστιν.

Χάρω δὲ ὁμολογεῖν τῇ τύχῃ ἐπὶ τῇ αὐτῷ ὑπαρξάσῃ ἐλευθερίᾳ,     495
καὶ μὴ τῷ ἐπὶ πόλεμον ἐξάγοντι δεσπότῃ, ὥστε αὐτὸν δι' ἀπειρίαν ἢ
ὑπὸ τῶν πολεμίων ἀναιρεθῆναι ἢ φεύγοντα ὑπὸ τοῦ κτησαμένου
κολάζεσθαι. ἄμεινον δὲ καὶ τοῖς οἰκέταις διατελοῦσι Ῥωμαῖοι χρώ-
μενοι. πατέρων γὰρ ἢ διδασκάλων ἐς αὐτοὺς ἔργα ἐπιδείκνυνται,
ἐφ' ᾧ τῶν φαύλων ἀπεχομένους μετιέναι ἅπερ αὐτοῖς καλὰ νενό-     500
μισται, <καὶ> σωφρονίζουσι σφᾶς ἐπὶ τοῖς ἁμαρτήμασιν ὥσπερ τοὺς
οἰκείους παῖδας· οὐδὲ γὰρ οὐδὲ αὐτοῖς θάνατον, ὥσπερ Σκύθαις,
ἐπάγειν θέμις.

Ἐλευθερίας δὲ τρόποι παρ' αὐτοῖς πλεῖστοι, ἣν οὐ μόνον
περιόντες ἀλλὰ καὶ τελευτῶντες χαρίζονται διατάττοντες κατὰ τῆς     505
περιουσίας ὃν βούλονται τρόπον, καὶ νόμος ἐστὶν ὅπερ ἕκαστος
τελευτῶν περὶ τῶν προσηκόντων βουλεύσοιτο.

Καὶ ὃς δακρύσας ἔφη ὡς οἱ μὲν νόμοι καλοὶ καὶ ἡ πολιτεία
Ῥωμαίων ἀγαθή, οἱ δὲ ἄρχοντες οὐχ ὅμοια τοῖς πάλαι φρονοῦντες
αὐτὴν διαλυμαίνονται.     510

Ταῦτα διαλεγομένων ἡμῶν, προσελθών τις τῶν ἔνδοθεν
ἀνοίγει τὰς θύρας τοῦ περιβόλου. ἐγὼ δὲ προσδραμὼν ἐπυθόμην ὅ τι
πράττων Ὀνηγήσιος τυγχάνοι· ἀπαγγεῖλαι γὰρ αὐτῷ με βούλεσθαί
τι τοῦ παρὰ Ῥωμαίων ἥκοντος πρεσβευτοῦ. ὃς δὲ ἀπεκρίνατο αὐτῷ
με ἐντεύξεσθαι μικρὸν ἀναμείναντα· μέλλειν γὰρ αὐτὸν ὑπεξιέναι.     515
καὶ δὴ οὐ πολλοῦ διαγενομένου χρόνου, ὡς προϊόντα εἶδον, προσελθὼν ἔλεγον ὡς ὁ Ῥωμαίων αὐτὸν ἀσπάζεται πρεσβυτής, καὶ
δῶρα ἐξ αὐτοῦ ἥκω φέρων σὺν καὶ τῷ παρὰ βασιλέως πεμφθέντι
χρυσίῳ· ἐσπουδακότι δὲ ἐς λόγους ἐλθεῖν οἳ καὶ πότε βούλεται
διαλέγεσθαι. ὃς δὲ τό τε χρυσίον τά τε δῶρα ἐκέλευσε τοὺς προσή-     520
κοντας δέξασθαι, ἐμὲ δὲ ἀπαγγέλλειν Μαξιμίνῳ ὡς ἥξοι αὐτίκα παρ'
αὐτόν. ἐμήνυον τοίνυν ἐπανελθὼν τὸν Ὀνηγήσιον παραγίνεσθαι· καὶ
εὐθὺς ἧκεν ἐς τὴν σκηνήν.

Προσειπὼν δὲ τὸν Μαξιμῖνον ἔφασκε χάριν ὁμολογεῖν ὑπὲρ τῶν
δώρων αὐτῷ τε καὶ βασιλεῖ καὶ ἀνηρώτα ὅ τι λέγειν βουλόμενος αὐτὸν     525
μετεπέμψατο. ὁ δὲ ἔφασκεν ἥκειν καιρὸν ὥστε Ὀνηγήσιον μεῖζον ἐν
ἀνθρώποις ἕξειν κλέος, εἴπερ παρὰ βασιλέα ἐλθὼν διευκρινήσει τὰ

499 ἐπιδεικνύντες Classen    501 καὶ add. Thompson (1947)    514 τοῦ παρὰ
Bekker παρὰ τοῦ codd. παρὰ τοῦ παρὰ Bekker παρὰ τοῦ ʽΡωμαίων ἥκοντα de
Boor    515 με . . . ἀναμείναντα de Boor [μοι . . . ἀναμείψαντα codd. μοι . . .
ἀναμείναντι Hoeschel    519 οἱ Valesius [ᾧ codd. ποῦ Bekker

violence to the poor with impunity, unless one escapes justice through escaping detection; and this is a recourse for the poor as well as for the rich. These offenders would go unpunished because of lack of evidence, something which happens not only amongst the Romans but amongst all peoples.

"For your freedom you should give thanks to fortune rather than to your master. He led you out to war, where, through inexperience, you might have been killed by the enemy or, fleeing the battle, have been punished by your owner. The Romans are wont to treat even their household slaves better. They act as fathers or teachers towards them and punish them, like their own children, if they do wrong, so that they are restrained from improper behaviour and pursue what is thought right for them. Unlike amongst the Scythians, it is forbidden to punish them with death.

"Amongst the Romans there are many ways of giving freedom. Not only the living but also the dead bestow it lavishly, arranging their estates as they wish; and whatever a man has willed for his possessions at his death is legally binding."

My acquaintance wept and said that the laws were fair and the Roman polity was good, but that the authorities were ruining it by not taking the same thought for it as those of old.

While we were discussing these things, one of those inside came out and opened the gates of the wall. I ran forward and asked what Onegesius was doing, saying that I wished to pass him a message from the ambassador of the Romans. He replied that if I waited a little I should meet him, since he was about to go out. Shortly afterwards I saw him coming out and I went forward and said that the ambassador of the Romans sent him greetings and that I had come bearing gifts from him and gold sent by the Emperor. I also asked where and when he was willing to speak with the ambassador, who was eager to confer with him. He ordered his attendants to take the gold and the gifts and told me to report to Maximinus that he would come to him straightaway. I returned to Maximinus and reported that Onegesius was on his way; and he came to the tent immediately.

Onegesius addressed Maximinus, thanking both him and the Emperor for the gifts and asking what he wished to say in sending for him. Maximinus said that the time had come when Onegesius would win greater fame amongst men if he went to the Emperor and, by his

ἀμφίβολα τῇ σφετέρᾳ συνέσει καὶ ὁμόνοιαν Ῥωμαίοις καὶ Οὔννοις
καταστήσεται. γενήσεται γὰρ ἐνθένδε οὐ μόνον τοῖς ἔθνεσιν ἀμφοτέροις συμφέρον, ἀλλὰ καὶ τῷ σφετέρῳ οἴκῳ ἀγαθὰ παρέξει πολλά,                530
ἐπιτήδειος ἐς ἀεὶ αὐτός τε καὶ οἱ αὐτοῦ παῖδες βασιλεῖ τε καὶ τῷ
ἐκείνου ἐσόμενοι γένει. ὁ δὲ Ὀνηγήσιος ἔφη· καὶ τί ποιῶν ἔσται
κεχαρισμένος βασιλεῖ ἢ ὅπως παρ' αὐτοῦ τὰ ἀμφίβολα λυθείη; ἀποκριναμένου δὲ ὡς διαβὰς μὲν εἰς τὴν Ῥωμαίων βασιλεῖ τὴν χάριν
καταθήσει, διευκρινήσει δὲ τὰ ἀμφίβολα τὰς αἰτίας διερευνῶν καὶ                535
ταύτας κατὰ <τὸν> τῆς εἰρήνης λύων θεσμόν, ἔφασκεν ἐκεῖνα ἐρεῖν
βασιλεῖ τε καὶ τοῖς ἀμφ' αὐτόν, ἅπερ Ἀττήλας βούλεται. ἢ οἴεσθαι
ἔφη Ῥωμαίους τοσοῦτον ἐκλιπαρήσειν αὐτὸν ὥστε καταπροδοῦναι
δεσπότην καὶ ἀνατροφῆς τῆς παρὰ Σκύθαις καὶ γαμετῶν καὶ παίδων
κατολιγωρῆσαι, μὴ μείζονα δὲ ἡγεῖσθαι τὴν παρὰ Ἀττήλᾳ δουλείαν                540
τοῦ παρὰ Ῥωμαίοις πλούτου; συνοίσειν δὲ ἐπιμένοντα τῇ οἰκείᾳ τὸν
[γὰρ] τοῦ δεσπότου καταπραΰνειν θυμόν, ἐφ' οἷς αὐτὸν ὀργίζεσθαι
κατὰ Ῥωμαίων συμβαίνει, ἢ παρὰ σφᾶς ἐλθόντα αἰτίᾳ ὑπάγεσθαι
ἕτερα ἤπερ ἐκείνῳ δοκεῖ διαπραξάμενον. ταῦτα εἰρηκὼς κἀμὲ
ποιεῖσθαι τὴν πρὸς αὐτὸν εἰσηγησάμενος ἔντευξιν περὶ ὧν πυνθά-                545
νεσθαι αὐτοῦ βουλόμεθα, (οὐ γὰρ τῷ Μαξιμίνῳ ὡς ἐν ἀξίᾳ τελοῦντι
ἡ συνεχὴς πρόσοδος ἦν εὐπρεπής) ἀνεχώρει. ἐγὼ δὲ τῇ ὑστεραίᾳ ἐς
τὸν Ἀττήλα περίβολον ἀφικνοῦμαι δῶρα τῇ αὐτοῦ κομίζων γαμετῇ,
(Ἡρέκαν δὲ ὄνομα αὐτῇ) ἐξ ἧς αὐτῷ παῖδες ἐγεγόνεισαν τρεῖς, ὧν ὁ
πρεσβύτερος ἦρχε τῶν Ἀκατίρων καὶ τῶν λοιπῶν ἐθνῶν τῶν                        550
νεμομένων τὴν πρὸς τῷ Πόντῳ Σκυθικήν. ἔνδον δὲ τοῦ περιβόλου
πλεῖστα ἐτύγχανεν οἰκήματα, τὰ μὲν ἐκ σανίδων ἐγγλύφων καὶ
ἡρμοσμένων εἰς εὐπρέπειαν, τὰ δὲ ἐκ λίθων κεκαθαρμένων καὶ πρὸς
εὐθύτητα ἐπεξεσμένων, ἐμβεβλημένων δὲ ξύλοις <κύκλους> ἀπο-
τελοῦσιν· οἱ δὲ κύκλοι ἐν τοῦ ἐδάφους ἀρχόμενοι ἐς ὕψος ἀνέβαινον                555
μετρίως. ἐνταῦθα τῆς Ἀττήλα ἐνδιαιτωμένης γαμετῆς, διὰ τῶν
πρὸς τῇ θύρᾳ βαρβάρων ἔτυχον εἰσόδου καὶ αὐτὴν ἐπὶ στρώματος
μαλακοῦ κεμένην κατέλαβον, τοῖς ἐκ τῆς ἐρέας πιλωτοῖς τοῦ
ἐδάφους σκεπομένου, ὥστε ἐπ' αὐτῶν βαδίζειν. περιεῖπε δὲ αὐτὴν
θεραπόντων πλῆθος κύκλῳ· καὶ θεράπαιναι ἐπὶ τοῦ ἐδάφους ἀντικρὺ                560
αὐτῆς καθήμεναι ὀθόνας τινὰς χρώμασι διεποίκιλλον ἐπιβληθησο-
μένας πρὸς κόσμον ἐσθημάτων βαρβαρικῶν. προσελθὼν τοίνυν καὶ

532-33 ποιῶν ἔσται κεχαρισμένος de Boor [ποιῶντες καιχαρισμένος codd.
ποιοῦντες κεχαρισμένως Hoeschel    536 τὸν add. Müller    540 κατολιγωρῆσαι de Boor [κατολιγωρηθεὶς Ε   κατολιγωρήσεω Hoeschel    542 γὰρ exp.
Müller    545 ἡγησάμενος Χ et edd.    549 Ἡρέκαν scripsi (cf. n.62) [Κρέκα
codd.    ἐγεγόνησαν Β ἐγεγόνεσαν edd.    550 Ἀκατίρων Müller [Ἀκατήρων
codd.    551 πρὸς τῷ Πόντῳ de Boor [πρὸς τὸ Πόν codd.    πρὸς τὸν Πόντον
edd.    553 λίθων Hoeschel [λόγων codd.    λύγων de Boor    δοκῶν Cantoclar.
554 κύκλους add. Bekker

own sagacity, settled the disputes and established harmony between the Romans and the Huns. From this not only would advantage come for both nations, but also he would derive many benefits for his own household, since he and his children would be forever friends of the Emperor and his family. Onegesius asked what he was to do to win the Emperor's friendship and how the disputes were to be settled. When Maximinus replied that if he crossed over to Roman territory, he would earn the Emperor's gratitude and he would settle the disputes by investigating the causes and removing them in accordance with the terms of the peace, Onegesius said that he would simply tell the Emperor and his officials what Attila wished. "Or do the Romans think," he retorted, "that they will bring so much persuasion to bear on me that I shall betray my master, turn my back upon my upbringing amongst the Scythians, my wives and my children and think that slavery to Attila is not preferable to wealth amongst the Romans?" He concluded that it would be better for him to remain in his own country and to calm his master's rage on those matters over which he was angry at the Romans rather than to go to them and incur the charge that he had acted other than seemed best to Attila. Having said this and having instructed that I should confer with him on questions we wished to ask of him (for continual visiting was not proper for Maximinus, a man in an official position), he went away.

On the following day I approached Attila's wall bearing gifts for Attila's wife, whose name was Hereka[62] and who had borne him three sons, the eldest of whom ruled the Akatiri and the other tribes dwelling by the Black Sea in Scythia.[63] Inside the wall there was a large cluster of buildings, some made of planks carved and fitted together for ornamental effect, others from timbers which had been debarked and planed straight. They were set on circular piles made of stones, which began from the ground and rose to a moderate height.[64] Here lived Attila's wife. I entered through the barbarians at her door and found her reclining on a soft couch. The floor was covered with woollen-felt rugs for walking upon. A group of servants stood around her in attendance, and servant girls sat facing her working coloured embroidery on fine linens to be worn as ornaments over the barbarian clothing. I went forward, greeted her, presented the gifts and withdrew.

τὰ δῶρα μετὰ τὸν ἀσπασμὸν δοὺς ὑπεξήεω καὶ ἐπὶ τὰ ἕτερα ἐβάδιζον
οἰκήματα, ἐν οἷς διατρίβεω τὸν Ἀττήλαν ἐτύγχανεν, ἀπεκδεχόμενος
ὁπότε ὑπεξέλθοι Ὀνηγήσιος· ἤδη γὰρ ἀπὸ τῶν αὐτοῦ οἰκημάτων    565
ἐξεληλύθει καὶ ἔνδον ἦν. μεταξὺ δὲ τοῦ παντὸς ἱστάμενος πλήθους
(γνώριμός τε γὰρ ὢν τοῖς Ἀττήλα φρουροῖς καὶ τοῖς παρεπομένοις
αὐτῷ βαρβάροις ὑπ᾽ οὐδενὸς διεκωλυόμην) εἶδον πλῆθος πορευόμενον
καὶ θροῦν καὶ θόρυβον περὶ τὸν τόπον γενόμενον, ὡς τοῦ Ἀττήλα
ὑπεξιόντος. προῄει δὲ τοῦ οἰκήματος βαδίζων σοβαρῶς τῇδε κἀκεῖ    570
περιβλεπόμενος. ὡς δὲ ὑπεξελθὼν σὺν τῷ Ὀνηγησίῳ ἔστη πρὸ τοῦ
οἰκήματος, πολλοὶ δὲ τῶν ἀμφισβητήσεις πρὸς ἀλλήλους ἐχόντων
προσῄεσαν καὶ τὴν αὐτοῦ κρίσιω ἐδέχοντο. εἶτα ἐπανῄει ὡς τὸ οἴκημα
καὶ πρέσβεις παρ᾽ αὐτὸν ἥκοντας βαρβάρους ἐδέχετο.

Ἐμοὶ δὲ ἀπεκδεχομένῳ τὸν Ὀνηγήσιον Ῥωμύλος καὶ Προμοῦ-    575
τος καὶ Ῥωμανὸς οἱ ἐξ Ἰταλίας ἐλθόντες παρὰ τὸν Ἀττήλαν πρέσβεις τῶν φιαλῶν ἕνεκα τῶν χρυσῶν, συμπαρόντος αὐτοῖς καὶ Ῥουστικίου τοῦ κατὰ Κωνστάντιον, καὶ Κωνσταντιόλου, ἀνδρὸς ἐκ τῆς
Παιόνων χώρας τῆς ὑπὸ Ἀττήλα ταττομένης, ἐς λόγους ἦλθον καὶ
ἀνηρώτων, πότερον διηφείθημεν ἢ ἐπιμένεω ἀναγκαζόμεθα. καὶ    580
ἐμοῦ φήσαντος, ὡς τούτου χάριν πευσόμενος τοῦ Ὀνηγησίου τοῖς
περιβόλοις προσκαρτερῶ, καὶ ἀντερωτήσαντος, <εἰ> αὐτοῖς ὁ
Ἀττήλας ἥμερόν τι καὶ πρᾶον περὶ τῆς πρεσβείας ἀπεκρίνατο,
ἔλεγον μηδαμῶς μετατρέπεσθαι τῆς γνώμης, ἀλλὰ πόλεμον καταγ-
γέλλεω, εἰ μή γε αὐτῷ Σιλβανὸς ἢ τὰ ἐκπώματα πεμφθείη.    585

Ἀποθαυμαζόντων δὲ ἡμῶν τῆς ἀπονοίας τὸν βάρβαρον, ὑπολαβὼν ὁ Ῥωμύλος, πρεσβευτὴς ἀνὴρ καὶ πολλῶν πραγμάτων
ἔμπειρος, ἔλεγε τὴν αὐτοῦ μεγίστην τύχην καὶ τὴν ἐκ τῆς τύχης
δύναμιν ἐξαίρεω αὐτόν, ὥστε μὴ ἀνέχεσθαι δικαίων λόγων, εἰ μὴ
πρὸς αὐτοῦ νομίσῃ ὑπάρχεω αὐτούς. οὔπω γὰρ <τῷ> τῶν πώποτε    590
τῆς Σκυθικῆς ἢ καὶ ἑτέρας ἀρξάντων γῆς τοσαῦτα ἐν ὀλίγῳ κατε-
πράχθη, ὥστε καὶ τῶν ἐν τῷ Ὠκεανῷ νήσων ἄρχεω καὶ πρὸς πάσῃ
τῇ Σκυθικῇ καὶ Ῥωμαίους ἔχεω ἐς φόρου ἀπαγωγήν. ἐφιέμενον δὲ
πρὸς τοῖς παροῦσι πλειόνων καὶ ἐπὶ μεῖζον αὔξοντα τὴν ἀρχὴν καὶ
ἐς Πέρσας ἐπιέναι βούλεσθαι.    595

Τῶν δὲ ἐν ἡμῖν τινος πυθομένου, ποίαν ὁδὸν τραπεὶς ἐς Πέρσας
ἐλθεῖν δυνήσεται, ἔλεγεν ὁ Ῥωμύλος μὴ πολλῷ διαστήματι τὴν
Μήδων ἀφεστάναι τῆς Σκυθικῆς· οὐδὲ γὰρ Οὔννους ἀπείρους τῆς
ὁδοῦ ταύτης εἶναι, ἀλλὰ πάλαι ἐς αὐτὴν ἐμβεβληκέναι, λιμοῦ τε τὴν
χώραν κρατήσαντος, καὶ Ῥωμαίων διὰ τὸν τότε συνιστάμενον    600

565 ὑπεξέλθοι van Herwerden [ἐπεξέλθοι codd.       582 εἰ add. Bekker
583 τι Niebuhr [τε codd.       590 τῷ add. de Boor [οὐδενὶ pro οὔπω coni.
Niebuhr    591-92 καταπεπράχθαι Bekker    595 ἀπιέναι X et edd.

Then I walked to the other group of buildings, where Attila was living, and waited for Onegesius to come out, since he had already left his own dwellings and was within. As I was standing in the midst of the whole throng (for I was known to Attila's guards and followers, and no one hindered me), I saw a group of persons advancing and heard murmuring and shouts around the place, since Attila was coming out. He came out of the house swaggering and casting his eyes around. When he had come out, he stood with Onegesius in front of the building, and many persons who had disputes with one another stepped forward and received his judgement. Then he re-entered the house and received the barbarian envoys who had come to him.

While I was waiting for Onegesius, Romulus, Promotus and Romanus, who had come from Italy as envoys to Attila over the golden bowls, came to speak to me. With them were Rusticius, the subordinate of Constantius,[65] and Constantiolus, a man from the part of Pannonia subject to Attila. They asked whether we had been dismissed or whether we were being forced to remain. I said that I was waiting by the enclosures to learn this from Onegesius. When I, in my turn, asked whether Attila had given them a mild and gentle reply on the matter of their embassy, they said that he had changed his mind not at all and was threatening war unless either Silvanus or the bowls were sent to him.

When we expressed amazement at the unreasonableness of the barbarian, Romulus, an ambassador of long experience, replied that his very great good fortune and the power which it had given him had made him so arrogant that he would not entertain just proposals unless he thought that they were to his advantage. No previous ruler of Scythia or of any other land had ever achieved so much in so short a time. He ruled the islands of the Ocean and, in addition to the whole of Scythia, forced the Romans to pay tribute. He was aiming at more than his present achievements and, in order to increase his empire further, he wanted to attack the Persians.

When one of those amongst us asked what road Attila could take to reach Persia, Romulus replied that the land of the Medes was not a great distance from Scythia, and the Huns were not ignorant of the route. They came upon it long ago when famine was sweeping their land and the Romans did not oppose them on account of the war in

278     Priscus: Text

πόλεμον μὴ συμβαλλόντων. παρεληλυθέναι δὲ ἐς τὴν Μήδων τόν τε
Βασὶχ καὶ Κουρσὶχ τοὺς ὕστερον ἐς τὴν Ῥώμην ἐληλυθότας εἰς
ὁμαιχμίαν, ἄνδρας τῶν βασιλείων Σκυθῶν καὶ πολλοῦ πλήθους
ἄρχοντας. καὶ τοὺς διαβεβηκότας λέγειν ὡς ἔρημον ἐπελθόντες
χώραν καὶ λίμνην τινὰ περαιωθέντες, ἣν ὁ Ῥωμύλος τὴν Μαιῶτιν   605
εἶναι ᾤετο, πεντεκαίδεκα διαγενομένων ἡμερῶν ὄρη τινὰ ὑπερ-
βάντες ἐς τὴν Μηδικὴν ἐσέβαλον. ληιζομένοις δὲ καὶ τὴν γῆν κατα-
τρέχουσι πλῆθος Περσικὸν ἐπελθὸν τὸν σφῶν ὑπερκείμενον ἀέρα
πλῆσαι βελῶν, ὥστε σφᾶς δέει τοῦ κατασχόντος κινδύνου ἀναχωρῆσαι εἰς τοὐπίσω καὶ τὰ ὄρη ὑπεξελθεῖν ὀλίγην ἄγοντας λείαν· ἡ   610
γὰρ πλείστη ὑπὸ τῶν Μήδων ἀφήρητο. εὐλαβουμένους δὲ τὴν των
πολεμίων δίωξιν ἑτέραν τραπῆναι ὁδόν, καὶ μετὰ τὴν ἐκ τῆς ὑφάλου
πέτρας ἀναπεμπομένην φλόγα ἐκεῖθεν πορευθέντας ἡμερῶν ὀλίγων
ὁδὸν εἰς τὰ οἰκεῖα ἀφικέσθαι καὶ γνῶναι οὐ πολλῷ διαστήματι τῶν
Μήδων ἀφεστάναι τὴν Σκυθικήν. τὸν οὖν Ἀττήλαν ἐπ' αὐτὴν ἰέναι   615
βουλόμενον οὐ πονήσειν πολλὰ οὔτε μακρὰν ἀνύσειν ὁδόν, ὥστε καὶ
Μήδους καὶ Πάρθους καὶ Πέρσας παραστήσεσθαι καὶ ἀναγκάσειν
ἐλθεῖν ἐς φόρου ἀπαγωγήν· παρεῖναι γὰρ αὐτῷ μάχιμον δύναμιν,
ἣν οὐδὲν ἔθνος ὑποστήσεται.

Ἡμῶν δὲ κατὰ Περσῶν ἐλθεῖν αὐτὸν ἐπευξαμένων καὶ ἐπ'   620
ἐκείνους τρέψαι τὸν πόλεμον, ὁ Κωνσταντίολος ἔλεγε δεδιέναι
μήποτε καὶ Πέρσας ῥᾳδίως παραστησάμενος ἀντὶ φίλου δεσπότης
ἐπανήξει. νῦν μὲν γὰρ τὸ χρυσίον κομίζεσθαι παρ' αὐτῶν τῆς ἀξίας
ἕνεκα· εἰ δὲ καὶ Πάρθους καὶ Μήδους καὶ Πέρσας παραστήσοιτο,
οὐκ ἔτι Ῥωμαίων ἀνέξεσθαι τὴν αὐτοῦ νοσφιζομένων ἀρχήν, ἀλλὰ   625
θεράποντας περιφανῶς ἡγησάμενον χαλεπώτερα ἐπιτάξειν καὶ οὐκ
ἀνεκτὰ ἐκείνοις ἐπιτάγματα. ἦν δ' <ἡ> ἀξία, ἧς ὁ Κωνσταντίολος
ἐπεμνήσθη, στρατηγοῦ Ῥωμαίων, ἧς χάριν ὁ Ἀττήλας παρὰ βασιλέως ἐδέδεκτο τὸ τοῦ φόρου ἐπικαλύπτοντος ὄνομα, ὥστε αὐτῷ
σιτηρεσίου προφάσει τοῦ τοῖς στρατηγοῖς χορηγουμένου τὰς συν-   630
τάξεις ἐκπέμπεσθαι. ἔλεγεν οὖν μετὰ Μήδους καὶ Πάρθους καὶ
Πέρσας τοῦτο τὸ ὄνομα, ὅπερ αὐτὸν βούλονται Ῥωμαῖοι καλεῖν, καὶ
τὴν ἀξίαν, ᾗ αὐτὸν τετιμηκέναι νομίζουσιν, ἀποσεισάμενον ἀναγκάσειν σφᾶς ἀντὶ στρατηγοῦ βασιλέα προσαγορεύειν. ἤδη γὰρ καὶ
χαλεπαίνοντα εἰπεῖν ὡς ἐκείνῳ μὲν οἱ αὐτοῦ θεράποντές εἰσι   635
στρατηγοί, αὐτῷ δὲ οἱ τοῖς βασιλεύουσι Ῥωμαίων ὁμότιμοι.

613 ἀναπεμπομένην codd. praeter B [ἀναφλεγομένην Hoeschel cum B ἀναφε-
ρομένην Niebuhr   ὀλίγων om. X et edd.   615 αὐτοὺς coni. Niebuhr
623 αὐτῷ codd.   627 ἦ add. Dindorf   633-4 ἀναγκάσειν Niebuhr [ἀν-
αγκάσας codd. praeter B (ἀναγκάσαι)   636 οἱ Bekker [οὐ codd.

which they were then involved.[66] Basich and Kursich, members of the Scythian royalty and commanders of a large force (who later came to Rome to make an alliance), reached the land of the Medes. Those Huns who have gone over to the Romans[67] say that, having come into a desert land and having crossed a lake (which Romulus thought was Maeotis), after fifteen days they passed over some mountains and entered Media. As they were overrunning and plundering the land, a Persian army confronted them and filled the air above them with missiles, so that they had to retreat from their immediate danger and retire across the mountains. They gained little plunder, since the Medes took most of it from them. As a precaution against enemy pursuit they took a different route and, after a journey of a few days from the flame that issues from the rock beneath the sea,[68] they reached their own land. Thus they know that Scythia is not far from Media and, if Attila wished to go there, he would neither have much toil nor a long journey. And so, since he has a military force which no nation can withstand, he would subdue the Medes, the Parthians, and the Persians and force them to pay tribute.

When we prayed that he would go against the Persians and direct the war against them, Constantiolus said that he feared that when he had easily subdued the Persians, he would return as a master rather than as a friend. At present, gold is brought to him because of his rank. However, if he were to subdue the Parthians, Medes and the Persians, he would not continue to endure a Roman state independent of himself and, holding them to be obviously his servants, would lay upon them very harsh and intolerable injunctions. (The rank which Constantiolus mentioned was that of a Roman general,[69] which the Emperor had granted to Attila, thus concealing the word tribute. As a result, the payments were sent to him disguised as provisions issued to the generals.) Constantiolus said that after the Medes, Parthians and Persians, Attila would reject the title by which the Romans wished to call him and the rank with which they thought they had honoured him and would force them to address him as king instead of general. Already when angry he would say that his own subjects were generals of [Theodosius][70] and that his own generals were of equal worth to the Emperors of the Romans.

3. (Jordanes *Get.* 34,178-80 and 182)

Ad quem in legatione se missum a Theodosio iuniore Priscus
istoricus tali voce inter alia refert: ingentia si quidem flumina, id est
Tisia Tibisiaque et Dricca transientes venimus in loco illo, ubi dudum
Vidigoia Gothorum fortissimus Sarmatum dolo occubuit; indeque
non longe ad vicum, in quo rex Attila morabatur, accessimus, vicum       5
inquam ad instar civitatis amplissimae, in quo lignea moenia ex
tabulis nitentibus fabricata repperimus, quarum compago ita solidum
mentiebatur, ut vix ab intentu possit iunctura tabularum conprae-
hendi. videres triclinia ambitu prolixiore distenta porticusque in
omni decore dispositas. area vero curtis ingenti ambitu cingebatur, ut   10
amplitudo ipsa regiam aulam ostenderet. hae sedes erant Attilae regis
barbariae tota tenenti; haec captis civitatibus habitacula prae-
ponebat.

Is namque Attila patre genitus Mundzuco, cuius fuere germani
Octar et Roas, qui ante Attilam regnum tenuisse narrantur, quamvis   15
non omnino cunctorum quorum ipse . . . . vir in concussione gentium
natus in mundo, terrarum omnium metus, qui, nescio qua sorte,
terrebat cuncta formidabili de se opinione vulgata. erat namque
superbus incessu, huc atque illuc circumferens oculos, ut elati
potentia ipso quoque motu corporis appareret; bellorum quidem        20
amator, sed ipse manu temperans, consilio validissimus, sup-
plicantium exorabilis, propitius autem in fide semel susceptis;
forma brevis, lato pectore, capite grandiore, minutis oculis, rarus
barba, canis aspersus, semo nasu, teter colore, origenis suae signa
restituens.                                                          25

7 nitentibus [ingentibus XYZ    8 metiebatur O    15 Hunnorum *post* regnum
*add.* B    16 confusionem XYZ    22 autem *om.* SOB [enim XYZ    receptis
ASOB acceptis XYZ

## 12

1. (*Exc. de Leg. Rom.* 3)

Ἔσεσθαι δὲ οὐκ εἰς μακρὰν τῆς παρούσης αὐτῷ δυνάμεως
αὔξησιν· σημαίνειν καὶ τοῦτο τὸν θεὸν τὸ τοῦ Ἄρεος ἀναφήναντα
ξίφος, ὅπερ ὂν ἱερὸν καὶ παρὰ τῶν Σκυθικῶν βασιλέων τιμώμενον,
οἷα δὴ τῷ ἐφόρῳ τῶν πολέμων ἀνακείμενον, ἐν τοῖς πάλαι ἀφανισθῆναι χρόνοις, εἶτα διὰ βοὸς εὑρεθῆναι.                               5

2. (Jordanes *Get.* 35,183)

Qui quamvis huius esset naturae, ut semper magna confideret,
addebat ei tamen confidentia gladius Martis inventus, sacer apud

2 ei [et BXY

3. (Jordanes *Get.* 34,178-80 and 182)

The historian Priscus says that he was sent on an embassy to him [Attila] by the younger Theodosius. Amongst other things, he reports as follows: When we had crossed some great rivers, namely the Tisia, Tibisia and Dricca,[71] we came to that place where long ago Vidigoia, the bravest of the Goths, was killed through the treachery of the Sarmatians.[72] Not far from this place we reached a village in which Attila was staying, a village actually like a very large city, in which we found wooden walls made of smoothed planks. These were joined together to suggest solidity in such a way that even by looking hard one could scarcely see the joints.[73] You might see dining rooms of great dimensions and colonnades laid out with every form of decoration.[74] The area of the courtyard was enclosed by a circuit wall of high extent so that its size might show that this was a royal palace. This was the seat of Attila, the king who ruled the whole barbarian world; this was the dwelling he preferred to the cities which he had captured.

Attila's father was Mundzuc, whose own brothers were Octar and Ruas, who are said to have held the kingship before Attila, though by no means over all the peoples whom he ruled . . . .[75] [Attila] was a man born in the world for the shattering of nations, the terror of all the lands who, through some chance, made all quake as his fearsome reputation spread abroad. His gait was haughty, and he cast his eyes hither and thither, so that the power of his pride was reflected in the movements of his body. Though a lover of war, he was not prone to violence. He was a very wise counsellor, merciful to those who sought it and loyal to those whom he had accepted as friends. He was short, with a broad chest and large head; his eyes were small, his beard sparse and flecked with grey, his nose flat and his complexion dark, which showed the signs of his origin.

## 12

1. (*Exc. de Leg. Rom.* 3)

[Constantiolus said that] in a short time there would be an increase in his [Attila's] present power. God had indicated this by revealing the sword of Ares, which is a sacred object honoured by the Scythian kings, since it was dedicated to the guardian of wars. In ancient times it had disappeared and then it was found through the agency of an ox.[76]

2. (Jordanes *Get.* 35,183)

Although he [Attila] was by nature always self-assured, his confidence was increased by the finding of the sword of Mars, which is held

Scytharum reges semper habitus, quem Priscus istoricus tali refert
occasione detectum.

cum pastor, inquiens, quidam gregis unam bo-
culam conspiceret claudicantem nec causam tanti vulneris inveniret,       5
sollicitus vestigia cruoris insequitur tandemque venit ad gladium,
quem depascens herbas incauta calcaverat, effossumque protinus ad
Attilam defert. quo ille munere gratulatus, ut erat magnanimis,
arbitratur se mundi totius principem constitutum et per Martis
gladium potestatem sibi concessam esse bellorum.                          10

7 incaute LSOB

## 13

1. (*Exc. de Leg. Rom.* 3)

Καὶ ἑκάστου λέγειν τι περὶ τῶν καθεστώτων βουλομένου,
Ὀνηγησίου ὑπεξελθόντος, παρ᾽ αὐτὸν ἤλθομεν καὶ ἐπειρώμεθα περὶ
τῶν ἐσπουδασμένων μανθάνειν. ὁ δέ τισι πρότερον βαρβάροις διαλεχθεὶς πυθέσθαι με παρὰ Μαξιμίνου ἐπέτρεπε, τίνα Ῥωμαῖοι ἄνδρα
τῶν ὑπατικῶν παρὰ τὸν Ἀττήλαν πρεσβευόμενον στέλλουσιν. ὡς δὲ       5
παρελθὼν εἰς τὴν σκηνὴν ἔφραζον ἅπερ εἴρητό μοι, καὶ ὅ τι δεῖ
λέγειν ὧν χάριν ὁ βάρβαρος ἡμῶν ἐπύθετο ἅμα τῷ Μαξιμίνῳ
βουλευσάμενος ἐπανῆλθον ὡς τὸν Ὀνηγήσιον, λέγων ὡς ἐθέλουσι
μὲν Ῥωμαῖοι αὐτὸν παρὰ σφᾶς ἐλθόντα τῶν ἀμφιβόλων ἕνεκα διαλέγεσθαι, εἰ δὲ τούτου διαμάρτοιεν, ἐκπέμψειν βασιλέα ὃν βούλεται    10
πρεσβευσόμενον. καὶ εὐθὺς μετιέναι με τὸν Μαξιμῖνον παρεκελεύσατο, καὶ ἥκοντα αὐτὸν ἦγε παρὰ τὸν Ἀττήλαν. καὶ μικρὸν ὕστερον
ὑπεξελθὼν ὁ Μαξιμῖνος ἔλεγεν ἐθέλειν τὸν βάρβαρον Νόμον ἢ Ἀνατόλιον ἢ Σενάτορα πρεσβεύεσθαι· μὴ γὰρ ἂν ἄλλον παρὰ τοὺς εἰρη-
μένους δέξεσθαι. καὶ ὡς αὐτοῦ ἀποκριναμένου μὴ χρῆναι ἐπὶ τὴν     15
πρεσβείαν τοὺς ἄνδρας καλοῦντα ὑπόπτους καθιστᾶν βασιλεῖ, εἰρηκέναι τὸν Ἀττήλαν, εἰ μὴ ἕλοιντο ποιεῖν ἃ βούλεται, ὅπλοις τὰ ἀμφίβολα διακριθήσεσθαι.

Ἐπανελθόντων δὲ ἡμῶν ἐς τὴν σκηνήν, Τατοῦλος ὁ τοῦ
Ὀρέστου πατὴρ ἧκε λέγων ὡς ἀμφοτέρους ὑμᾶς Ἀττήλας ἐπὶ τὸ       20
συμπόσιον παρακαλεῖ· γενήσεσθαι δὲ αὐτὸ περὶ θ᾽ τῆς ἡμέρας. ὡς
δὲ τὸν καιρὸν ἐφυλάξαμεν καὶ ἐπὶ τὸ δεῖπνον κληθέντες παρεγενόμεθα ἡμεῖς τε καὶ οἱ ἀπὸ τῶν ἑσπερίων Ῥωμαίων πρέσβεις, ἔστημεν
ἐπὶ τοῦ οὐδοῦ ἀντία Ἀττήλα. καὶ κύλικα οἱ οἰνοχόοι κατὰ τὸ ἐπι-
χώριον ἐπέδοσαν ἔθος, ὡς καὶ ἡμᾶς πρὸ τῆς ἕδρας ἐπεύξασθαι· οὗ   25
δὴ γενομένου, τῆς κύλικος ἀπογευσάμενοι ἐπὶ τοὺς θρόνους ἤλθομεν,

9 αὐτὸν Niebuhr [τὸν codd.    15 δεξέσθαι Niebuhr [δεξάσθαι codd.    21 ὥραν
post ἡμέρας coni. de Boor    24 κύλικα Hoeschel [ἐπόλικα codd.    de Boor
suspicitur versum archetypi intercidisse inter ἐπό- et -λικα

sacred amongst the Scythian kings. The historian Priscus says it was found under the following circumstances. When a herdsman noticed one of his heifers limping and could find no reason for such a wound, he was troubled and followed the trail of blood. At length he came to a sword which the animal had carelessly trodden on while grazing. He dug it up and took it straight to Attila. He was pleased by this gift and, since he was a high-spirited man, he concluded that he had been appointed ruler of the whole world and that through the sword of Mars he had been granted invincibility in war.

## 13

1. (*Exc. de Leg. Rom.* 3)

As each of us was wanting to say something about the present situation, Onegesius came out and we went over to him and attempted to obtain information upon our own business. When he had first spoken to some barbarians, he sent me to Maximinus to ask which man of consular rank the Romans were sending as ambassador to Attila. When I came to the tent, I reported what had been said to me and discussed with Maximinus what I should reply to the question which the barbarian had asked of us. I returned to Onegesius and said that the Romans wished him to go to them to discuss the disputes, but if this were denied them, the Emperor would send whomever he desired. He immediately told me to bring Maximinus, and when he arrived, took him to Attila. Shortly afterwards Maximinus came out and said that the barbarian wanted Nomus, Anatolius or Senator as ambassador and that he would receive no other than those named. When Maximinus had replied that he ought not render these men suspect to the Emperor by naming them for an embassy, Attila said that if the Romans were unwilling to follow his wishes, the disputes would be settled by arms.

When we returned to our tent, Tatulus, the father of Orestes, came to us and announced, "Attila invites you both to his banquet. It will begin at about the ninth hour of the day." We waited for the time, and those of us who had been invited and the envoys of the western Romans presented ourselves. We stood at the threshold facing Attila, and, as was the custom of the land, the wine waiters gave us a cup[77] so that we might make a prayer before taking our seats. When we had

οὐ ἔδει καθεσθέντας δειπνεῖν.

Πρὸς δὲ τοῖς τοίχοις τοῦ οἰκήματος πάντες ὑπῆρχον οἱ δίφροι ἐξ
ἑκατέρας πλευρᾶς. ἐν μεσωτάτῳ δὲ ἧστο ἐπὶ κλίνης ὁ Ἀττήλας,
ἑτέρας ἐξόπισθεν κλίνης ὑπαρχούσης αὐτῷ, μεθ' ἣν βαθμοί τινες ἐπὶ     30
τὴν αὐτοῦ ἀνῆγον εὐνὴν καλυπτομένην ὀθόναις καὶ ποικίλοις παρα-
πετάσμασι κόσμου χάριν, καθάπερ ἐπὶ τῶν γαμούντων Ἕλληνές τε
καὶ Ῥωμαῖοι κατασκευάζουσιν. καὶ πρώτην μὲν ἐνόμιζον τῶν δειπ-
νούντων τάξιν τὴν ἐν δεξιᾷ τοῦ Ἀττήλα, δευτέραν δὲ τὴν εὐώνυμον,
ἐν ᾗ ἐτυγχάνομεν ὄντες, προκαθεσθέντος ἡμῶν Βερίχου παρὰ         35
Σκύθαις εὖ γεγονότος ἀνδρός· ὁ γὰρ Ὀνηγήσιος ἐπὶ δίφρου ἧστο ἐν
δεξιᾷ τῆς τοῦ βασιλέως κλίνης. ἀντικρὺ δὲ τοῦ Ὀνηγησίου ἐπὶ δίφρου
ἐκαθέζοντο δύο τῶν Ἀττήλα παίδων· ὁ γὰρ πρεσβύτερος ἐπὶ τῆς
ἐκείνου ἧστο κλίνης, οὐκ ἐγγύς, ἀλλ' ἐπ' ἄκρου, αἰδοῖ τοῦ πατρὸς
βλέπων ἐς γῆν.                                                         40

Πάντων δὲ ἐν κόσμῳ καθεστώτων, παρελθὼν οἰνοχόος τῷ
Ἀττήλα οἴνου κισσύβιον ἐπιδίδωσιν· δεξάμενος δὲ τὸν τῇ τάξει
πρῶτον ἠσπάζετο. ὁ δὲ τῷ ἀσπασμῷ τιμηθεὶς διανίστατο· καὶ οὐ
πρότερον ἱζῆσαι θέμις ἦν, πρὶν ἢ τῷ οἰνοχόῳ ἀπογευσάμενος ἢ καὶ
ἐκπιὼν ἀπέδωκε τὸ κισσύβιον. καθεσθέντα δὲ αὐτὸν τῷ <αὐτῷ>      45
τρόπῳ οἱ παρόντες ἐτίμων δεχόμενοι τὰς κύλικας καὶ μετὰ τὸν
ἀσπασμὸν ἀπογευόμενοι. ἑκάστῳ δὲ εἷς οἰνοχόος παρῆν, ὃν ἔδει
κατὰ στοῖχον εἰσιέναι, τοῦ Ἀττήλα οἰνοχόου ὑπεξιόντος. τιμηθέντος
δὲ καὶ τοῦ δευτέρου καὶ τῶν ἑξῆς, καὶ ἡμᾶς τοῖς ἴσοις ὁ Ἀττήλας
ἐδεξιώσατο κατὰ τὴν τῶν θάκων τάξιν. ᾧ δὴ ἀσπασμῷ πάντων     50
τιμηθέντων, ὑπεξῄεσαν μὲν οἱ οἰνοχόοι, τράπεζαι δὲ μετὰ τὴν τοῦ
Ἀττήλα παρετίθεντο κατὰ τρεῖς καὶ τέτταρας ἄνδρας ἢ καὶ πλείους·
ὅθεν ἕκαστος οἷός τε ἦν τῶν τῇ μαγίδι ἐπιτιθεμένων μεταλαβεῖν μὴ
ὑπεξιὼν τῆς τῶν θρόνων τάξεως. καὶ πρῶτος εἰσῄει ὁ τοῦ Ἀττήλα
ὑπηρέτης κρεῶν πλήρη πίνακα φέρων, καὶ οἱ πᾶσι διακονούμενοι μετ'  55
αὐτὸν σῖτον καὶ ὄψα ταῖς τραπέζαις ἐπέθεσαν. ἀλλὰ τοῖς μὲν ἄλλοις
βαρβάροις καὶ ἡμῖν πολυτελῆ δεῖπνα κατεσκεύαστο κύκλοις ἐπι-
κείμενα ἀργυροῖς, τῷ δὲ Ἀττήλα ἐπὶ τοῦ ξυλίνου πίνακος ἦν οὐδὲν
πλέον κρεῶν. μέτριον δὲ ἑαυτὸν καὶ ἐν τοῖς ἄλλοις ἅπασιν ἐδείκνυ.
τοῖς γὰρ τῆς εὐωχίας ἀνδράσι κύλικες χρυσαῖ τε καὶ ἀργυραῖ ἐπε-   60
δίδοντο, τὸ δὲ αὐτοῦ ἔκπωμα ξύλινον ἦν. λιτὴ δὲ αὐτῷ καὶ ἡ ἐσθὴς
ἐτύγχανεν οὖσα μηδὲν τῶν ἄλλων πλὴν τοῦ καθαρὰ εἶναι διαφυλάτ-
τουσα· καὶ οὔτε τὸ παρηωρημένον αὐτῷ ξίφος οὔτε οἱ τῶν βαρβαρικῶν ὑποδημάτων δεσμοὶ οὔτε τοῦ ἵππου ὁ χαλινός, ὥσπερ τῶν
ἄλλων Σκυθῶν, χρυσῷ ἢ λίθοις ἤ τινι τῶν τιμίων ἐκοσμεῖτο.        65

45  τὸ Hoeschel [τὸν codd.    αὐτῷ add. Bekker

done this and had tasted from the cup, we went to the seats where we were to sit for dinner.

All the seats were arranged around the walls of the building on both sides. In the very middle of the room Attila sat upon a couch. Behind him was another couch, and behind that steps led up to Attila's bed, which was screened by fine linens and multicoloured ornamental hangings like those which the Greeks and Romans prepare for weddings. The position of those dining on the right of Attila was considered the most honourable, that on the left, where we were, less so. Ahead of us sat Berichus, a Scythian noble, for Onegesius sat on a chair to the right of Attila. Opposite Onegesius two of Attila's sons sat on a chair; the eldest one sat upon Attila's couch, not close to him but right at the end, gazing at the ground out of respect for his father.[78]

When all were seated in order, a wine waiter came up to Attila and offered him a wooden cup of wine. He took the cup and greeted the first in the order. The one who was honoured with the greeting stood up, and it was the custom that he not sit down until he had either tasted the wine or drunk it all and had returned the wooden cup to the waiter. When he had sat down, all present honoured him in the same manner, taking our cups and tasting them after the greeting. Each guest had a wine waiter in attendance, who had to step forward in line after Attila's waiter retired. When the second had been honoured and the rest in order, Attila greeted us with the same ceremony according to the order of the seats.[79] When all had been honoured with this greeting, the wine waiters withdrew and, beginning from Attila,[80] tables were set up for three or four or more persons, from which each could partake of what was placed on the platter without leaving the line of chairs. Attila's servant entered first bearing a plate full of meat, and after him those who were serving us placed bread and cooked foods on the tables. While for the other barbarians and for us there were lavishly prepared dishes served on silver platters, for Attila there was only meat on a wooden plate. He showed himself temperate in other ways also. For golden and silver goblets were handed to the men at the feast, whereas his cup was of wood. His clothing was plain and differed not at all from that of the rest, except that it was clean. Neither the sword that hung at his side nor the fastenings of his barbarian boots nor his horse's bridle was adorned, like those of the other Scythians, with gold or precious stones or anything else of value.

Τῶν δὲ ὄψων τῶν ἐν τοῖς πρώτοις πίναξιν ἐπιτεθέντων ἀνα-
λωθέντων, πάντες διανέστημεν, καὶ οὐ πρότερον ἐπὶ τὸν δίφρον
ἀναστὰς ἦλθεν, πρὶν ἢ κατὰ τὴν προτέραν τάξιν ἕκαστος τὴν ἐπι-
διδομένην αὐτῷ οἴνου πλήρη ἐξέπιε κύλικα τὸν Ἀττήλαν σῶν εἶναι
ἐπευξάμενος. καὶ τοῦτον τιμηθέντος αὐτοῦ τὸν τρόπον ἐκαθέσθημεν,    70
καὶ δεύτερος ἑκάστῃ τραπέζῃ ἐπετίθετο πίναξ ἕτερα ἔχων ἐδώδιμα.
ὡς δὲ καὶ αὐτοῦ οἱ πάντες μετέλαβον, καὶ τῷ αὐτῷ ἐξαναστάντες
τρόπῳ αὖθις ἐκπιόντες ἐκαθέσθημεν, ἐπιγενομένης ἑσπέρας δᾷδες
ἀνήφθησαν, δύο δὲ ἀντικρὺ τοῦ Ἀττήλα παρελθόντες βάρβαροι
ᾄσματα πεποιημένα ἔλεγον νίκας αὐτοῦ καὶ τὰς κατὰ πόλεμον    75
ᾄδοντες ἀρετάς. ἐς οὓς οἱ τῆς εὐωχίας ἀπέβλεπον, καὶ οἱ μὲν ἥδοντο
τοῖς ποιήμασιν, οἱ δὲ τῶν πολέμων ἀναμιμνησκόμενοι διηγείροντο
τοῖς φρονήμασιν, ἄλλοι δὲ ἐχώρουν ἐς δάκρυα, ὧν ὑπὸ τοῦ χρόνου
ἠσθένει τὸ σῶμα καὶ ἡσυχάζειν ὁ θυμὸς ἠναγκάζετο.
Μετὰ δὲ τὰ ᾄσματα Σκύθης τις παρελθὼν φρενοβλαβὴς    80
ἀλλόκοτα καὶ παράσημα καὶ οὐδὲν ὑγιὲς φθεγγόμενος ἐς γέλωτα
πάντας παρεσκεύασε παρελθεῖν. μεθ' ὃν ὑπεισῆλθε Ζέρκων ὁ
Μαυρούσιος.

2. (Suda Z 29)
Ζέρκων, Σκύθης οὕτω καλούμενος, Μαυρούσιος τὸ γένος. διὰ
δὲ κακοφυΐαν σώματος καὶ τὸ γέλωτα ἐκ τῆς τραυλότητος τῆς
φωνῆς καὶ ὄψεως παρέχειν (βραχὺς γάρ τις ἦν, κυρτός, διάστροφος
τοῖς ποσί, τὴν ῥῖνα τοῖς μυκτῆρσι παραφαίνων διὰ σιμότητος ὑπερ-
βολήν), Ἄσπαρι τῷ Ἀρδαβουρίῳ ἐδεδώρητο, καθ' ὃν ἐν Λιβύῃ    5
διέτριβε χρόνον. ἥλω δὲ τῶν βαρβάρων ἐς τὴν Θρακῶν ἐμβαλόντων
καὶ παρὰ τοὺς βασιλείους ἤχθη Σκύθας. καὶ Ἀττήλας μὲν οὐδὲ τὴν
αὐτοῦ ἤνεγκεν ὄψιν· ὁ δὲ Βλήδας ἥσθη τε λίαν αὐτῷ φθεγγομένῳ οὐ
μόνον γέλωτος ἄξια, εἰ μή γε καὶ βαδίζοντι καὶ περιττῶς κινοῦντι τὸ
σῶμα. συνῆν δὲ αὐτῷ εὐωχουμένῳ καὶ ἐκστρατεύοντι, πεποιημένην    10
πρὸς τὸ γελοιότερον ἀναλαμβάνων ἐν ταῖς ἐξόδοις πανοπλίαν. διὸ δὴ
περισπούδαστον αὐτὸν ὁ Βλήδας ποιούμενος μετὰ αἰχμαλώτων ἀπο-
δράντα Ῥωμαίων, τῶν μὲν ἄλλων κατωλιγώρησεν, αὐτὸν δὲ μετὰ
πάσης φροντίδος ἀναζητεῖσθαι προσέταξεν. καὶ ἁλόντα καὶ παρ'
αὐτὸν ἀχθέντα ἐν δεσμοῖς ἰδὼν ἐγέλασεν. καὶ καθυφεὶς τῆς ὀργῆς    15
ἐπυνθάνετο τὴν αἰτίαν τῆς φυγῆς, καὶ ὅτου χάριν νομίζοι τὰ Ῥωμαίων τῶν παρὰ σφίσιν ἀμείνονα. ὁ δὲ ἀπεκρίνατο, ἁμάρτημα μὲν
τὴν φυγὴν εἶναι, ἔχειν δὲ τοῦ ἁμαρτήματος λόγον, τὸ μὴ γαμετὴν
αὐτῷ δεδόσθαι. τῷ δὲ γέλωτι μᾶλλον ὁ Βλήδας ὑπαχθεὶς δίδωσιν
αὐτῷ γυναῖκα τῶν μὲν εὖ γεγονότων καὶ τῇ βασιλίδι διακονησα-    20
μένων, ἀτόπου δέ τινος πράξεως ἕνεκα οὐκέτι παρ' ἐκείνην φοιτῶσαν.

When we had finished the food on the first platters, we all stood up, and no one resumed his seat until, in the order as before, we had each drained the cup full of wine which was given to us and prayed for Attila's health. When he had been honoured in this way we resumed our seats, and a second platter, containing different dishes, was placed on each table. When all had partaken of this, again we stood up in the same manner, drank a cup of wine and sat down. Since it was now evening, pine torches were lit. Two barbarians came and stood before Attila and chanted songs which they had composed, telling of his victories and his deeds of courage in war. The guests fixed their eyes on the singers: some took pleasure in the verses, others recalling the wars became excited, while others, whose bodies were enfeebled by age and whose spirits were compelled to rest, were reduced to tears.

After the songs a Scythian whose mind was deranged came forward and, by uttering outlandish, unintelligible and altogether crazy words, caused all to burst into laughter. After him Zercon the Moor entered.

## 2. (*Suda* Z 29)

Zercon: a Scythian so-called,[81] but a Moor by origin. Because of his physical deformity and the laughter which his stammering and his general appearance caused (for he was rather short, hunchbacked, with distorted feet and a nose that, because of its excessive flatness, was indicated only by the nostrils) he was presented to Aspar, the son of Ardabur, when he was in Libya. When the barbarians attacked Thrace, he was captured and taken to the Scythian kings. Attila could not stand the sight of him, but Bleda was most pleased by him, not only when he was saying amusing things but even when he was not, because of the strange movements of his body as he walked. He accompanied Bleda both at feasts and on campaigns, and on these expeditions he wore a suit of armour made for amusing effect. Bleda thought so highly of him that when he ran off with some Roman prisoners, he ignored the rest but ordered him to be sought for with all diligence. When Zercon was recaptured and brought back in chains, Bleda, at the sight of him, burst into laughter, abated his anger and asked the reason for his flight and why he thought life amongst the Romans was better than that amongst themselves. He answered that his flight had been a crime, but he had a reason for the crime, that he had not been given a wife. Bleda laughed even more and gave him a wife from one of the well-born attendants upon the queen, who was no longer in her service because of some

καὶ οὕτω διετέλει ἅπαντα τὸν χρόνον τῷ Βλήδᾳ συνών. μετὰ δὲ τὴν
αὐτοῦ τελευτὴν Ἀττήλας Ἀετίῳ τῷ στρατηγῷ τῶν Ἑσπερίων
Ῥωμαίων δῶρον τὸν Ζέρκωνα δίδωσιν, ὃς αὐτὸν παρὰ τὸν Ἄσπαρα
ἀπέπεμψεν.                                                                    25

### 3. (Exc. de Leg. Rom. 3)

Ὁ γὰρ Ἐδέκων αὐτὸν παρὰ τὸν Ἀττήλαν ἐλθεῖν παρέπεισεν
ὡς τῇ ἐκείνου σπουδῇ τὴν γαμετὴν ἀποληψόμενον, ἣν κατὰ τὴν τῶν
βαρβάρων εἰλήφει χώραν τῷ Βλήδᾳ περισπούδαστος ὤν, ἀπολε-
λοίπει δὲ αὐτὴν ἐν τῇ Σκυθικῇ παρὰ τοῦ Ἀττήλα δῶρον Ἀετίῳ
πεμφθείς. ἀλλὰ τῆς μὲν τοιαύτης διήμαρτεν ἐλπίδος, τοῦ Ἀττήλα      5
χαλεπήναντος, ὅτι γε δὴ ἐς τὴν αὐτοῦ ἐπανῆλθεν· τότε δὲ διὰ τὸν τῆς
εὐωχίας καιρὸν παρελθὼν τῷ τε εἴδει καὶ τοῖς ἐσθήμασι καὶ τῇ
φωνῇ καὶ τοῖς συγκεχυμένως παρ' αὐτοῦ προφερομένοις ῥήμασι (τῇ
γὰρ Αὐσονίων τὴν τῶν Οὔννων καὶ τὴν τῶν Γότθων παραμιγνὺς
γλῶτταν) πάντας διέχεε καὶ ἐς ἄσβεστον ὁρμῆσαι γέλωτα παρε-     10
σκεύασε πλὴν Ἀττήλα· αὐτὸς γὰρ ἔμενεν ἀστεμφὴς καὶ τὸ εἶδος
ἀμετάτρεπτος καὶ οὐδὲν οὔτε λέγων οὔτε ποιῶν γέλωτος ἐχόμενον
ἐφαίνετο, πλὴν ὅτι τὸν νεώτατον τῶν παίδων (Ἡρνᾶς δὲ ὄνομα
τούτῳ) εἰσιόντα καὶ παρεστῶτα εἷλκε τῆς παρειᾶς γαληνοῖς ἀπο-
βλέπων ὄμμασι πρὸς αὐτόν. ἐμοῦ δὲ θαυμάζοντος, ὅπως τῶν μὲν     15
ἄλλων παίδων ὀλιγωροίη, πρὸς δὲ ἐκεῖνον ἔχοι τὸν νοῦν, ὁ παρα-
καθήμενος βάρβαρος συνιεὶς τῆς Αὐσονίων φωνῆς καὶ τῶν παρ'
αὐτοῦ μοι ῥηθησομένων μηδὲν ἐκλέγειν προειπὼν ἔφασκε τοὺς
μάντεις τῷ Ἀττήλα προηγορευκέναι τὸ μὲν αὐτοῦ πεσεῖσθαι γένος,
ὑπὸ δὲ τοῦ παιδὸς ἀναστήσεσθαι τούτου. ὡς δὲ ἐν τῷ συμποσίῳ     20
εἴλκον τὴν νύκτα, ὑπεξήλθομεν ἐπὶ πολὺ μὴ βουληθέντες τῷ πότῳ
προσκαρτερεῖν.

9 παρεμίγνυ Papabasileios (1896) [παραμίγνυσι aut παραμιγνὺς ἦν de Boor
11 αὐτὸς [οὗτος Dindorf   16 ἔχοι Niebuhr [ἔχει codd.

### 14
### (Exc. de Leg. Rom. 3)

Ἡμέρας δὲ γενομένης ἐπὶ τὸν Ὀνηγήσιον ἤλθομεν χρῆναι
ἡμᾶς διαφεθῆναι λέγοντες καὶ μὴ τηνάλλως τρίβειν τὸν χρόνον. καὶ
ὃς ἔφη ἐθέλειν καὶ τὸν Ἀττήλαν ἀποπέμπειν ἡμᾶς. καὶ μικρὸν δια-
λιπὼν ἅμα τοῖς λογάσιν ἐβουλεύετο περὶ τῶν Ἀττήλᾳ δεδογμένων
καὶ τὰ βασιλεῖ ἀποδοθησόμενα συνέταττε γράμματα, ὑπογραφέων    5
αὐτῷ παρόντων καὶ Ῥουστικίου, ἀνδρὸς ὁρμωμένου μὲν ἐκ τῆς ἄνω
Μυσίας, ἁλόντος δὲ ἐν τῷ πολέμῳ καὶ διὰ λόγων ἀρετὴν τῷ βαρβάρῳ ἐπὶ τῇ τῶν γραμμάτων διαπονουμένου συντάξει.

misdemeanour. Thus he passed all his time with Bleda. After his death Attila gave Zercon as a gift to Aetius, the general of the western Romans, who sent him back to Aspar.

3. (*Exc. de Leg. Rom.* 3)

Edeco had persuaded him [Zercon] to come to Attila in order to recover his wife, whom he had been given in the country of the barbarians as a result of his great favour with Bleda, but whom he had left behind in Scythia when Attila had sent him as a gift to Aetius. But he was disappointed in his hopes, since Attila was angry that he had returned to his country. Now, during the banquet he came forward and by his appearance, his clothing, his voice and the words which he spoke all jumbled together (for he mixed Latin, Hunnic and Gothic) he put all in a good humour and caused all to burst into uncontrollable laughter,[82] except Attila. He remained unmoved with no change of expression and neither said nor did anything that hinted at laughter, except when his youngest son, whose name was Ernach,[83] came up and stood by him. Then he drew him closer by the cheek and gazed at him with gentle eyes. When I expressed amazement that he paid attention to this son while ignoring the others, the barbarian who sat next to me and who knew Latin, warning me to repeat nothing of what he would tell me, said that the prophets had foretold to Attila that his race would fall, but would be restored by this boy. Since they were spending the night over the banquet, we departed, not wishing to continue drinking for a long time.

## 14

(*Exc. de Leg. Rom.* 3)

When day came we went to Onegesius and said that we ought to be dismissed without any pointless delay. He said that Attila was willing to send us away. After a short time he deliberated with the leading men upon Attila's views and had the letters drawn up to be delivered to the Emperor. Present at this transaction were his own secretaries and Rusticius, a man from Upper Moesia who had been captured in war and who, because of his literary skills, was employed by the barbarian in drawing up letters.

290     Priscus: Text

Ὡς δὲ ἐκ τῆς συνόδου διανέστη, ἐδεήθημεν αὐτοῦ περὶ λύσεως
τῆς Σύλλου γαμετῆς καὶ τῶν ἐκείνης παίδων ἐν τῇ Ῥατιαρίας       10
ἀνδραποδισθέντων ἁλώσει. καὶ πρὸς μὲν τὴν αὐτῶν οὐκ ἀπηγό-
ρευσε λύσιν, ἐπὶ πολλοῖς δὲ σφᾶς ἐβούλετο χρήμασιν ἀπεμπολᾶν.
ἡμῶν δὲ ἐλεεῖν αὐτοὺς τῆς τύχης ἱκετευσάντων τὴν προτέραν εὐδαιμονίαν λογιζόμενον, διέβη τε πρὸς τὸν Ἀττήλαν, καὶ τὴν μὲν
γυναῖκα ἐπὶ πεντακοσίοις διαφῆκε χρυσοῖς, τοὺς δὲ παῖδας δῶρον   15
ἔπεμπε βασιλεῖ.
    Ἐν τούτῳ δὲ καὶ Ἡρέκαν ἡ τοῦ Ἀττήλα γαμετὴ παρὰ Ἀδάμει
τῶν αὐτῆς πραγμάτων τὴν ἐπιτροπὴν ἔχοντι δειπνεῖν ἡμᾶς παρεκάλει. καὶ παρ' αὐτὸν ἐλθόντες ἅμα τισὶ ἐκ τοῦ ἔθνους λογάδων
φιλοφροσύνης ἐτύχομεν· ἐδεξιοῦτο γὰρ ἡμᾶς μειλιχίοις τε λόγοις καὶ  20
τῇ τῶν ἐδωδίμων παρασκευῇ. καὶ ἕκαστος τῶν παρόντων Σκυθικῇ
φιλοτιμίᾳ κύλικα ἡμῖν πλήρη διανιστάμενος ἐδίδου καὶ τὸν ἐκπιόντα
περιβαλὼν καὶ φιλήσας ταύτην ἐδέχετο. μετὰ δὲ τὸ δεῖπνον ἐπὶ τὴν
σκηνὴν ἐλθόντες ἐς ὕπνον ἐτράπημεν.
    Τῇ δὲ ὑστεραίᾳ ἐπὶ συμπόσιον αὖθις ἡμᾶς Ἀττήλας ἐκάλει, καὶ  25
τῷ προτέρῳ τρόπῳ παρά τε αὐτὸν εἰσήλθομεν καὶ ἐς τὴν εὐωχίαν
ἐτράπημεν. συνέβαινε δὲ ἐπὶ τῆς κλίνης ἅμα αὐτῷ μὴ τὸν πρεσβύτερον τῶν παίδων ἧσθαι, ἀλλὰ γὰρ Ὠηβάρσιον θεῖον αὐτῷ τυγχά-
νοντα πρὸς πατρός. παρὰ πᾶν δὲ τὸ συμπόσιον λόγοις φιλοφρονού-
μενος φράζειν ἡμᾶς βασιλεῖ παρεκελεύετο τῷ Κωνσταντίῳ, ὃς αὐτῷ  30
παρὰ Ἀετίου ἀπέσταλτο ὑπογραφέως χάριν, διδόναι ἣν αὐτῷ γυναῖκα
καὶ ὑπέσχετο. παρὰ γὰρ τὸν βασιλέα Θεοδόσιον ἅμα τοῖς σταλεῖσι
παρὰ τοῦ Ἀττήλα πρέσβεσιν ἀφικόμενος ὁ Κωνστάντιος τὴν εἰρήνην
Ῥωμαίοις καὶ Σκύθαις ἔφησεν ἐπὶ μακρὸν φυλάττεσθαι χρόνον
παρασκευάσειν, ἂν αὐτῷ γυναῖκα εὔπορον δοίη. καὶ πρὸς τοῦτο   35
ἐπένευσε βασιλεὺς καὶ Σατορνίλου περιουσίᾳ καὶ γένει κοσμουμένου
θυγατέρα εἰρήκει δώσειν. τὸν δὲ Σατορνῖλον ἀνῃρήκει Ἀθηναΐς ἡ
καὶ Εὐδοκία· ἀμφοτέροις γὰρ ἐκαλεῖτο τοῖς ὀνόμασιν. ἐς ἔργον δὲ τὴν
αὐτοῦ οὐ συνεχώρησεν ἀχθῆναι ὑπόσχεσιν Ζήνων ὑπατικὸς ἀνὴρ καὶ
πολλὴν ἀμφ' αὐτὸν ἔχων Ἰσαύρων δύναμιν, μεθ' ἧς καὶ τὴν Κων-  40
σταντίνου κατὰ τὸν τοῦ πολέμου καιρὸν φυλάττειν ἐπετέτραπτο. τότε
δὴ τῶν ἐν τῇ ἕῳ στρατιωτικῶν ἄρχων ταγμάτων ὑπεξάγει τοῦ
φρουρίου τὴν κόρην καὶ Ῥούφῳ τινὶ ἑνὶ τῶν ἐπιτηδείων κατεγγυᾷ.
ταύτης δὲ ἀφῃρημένης, ὁ Κωνστάντιος ἐδεῖτο τοῦ βαρβάρου ἐνυβρισ-
μένον αὐτὸν μὴ περιορᾶσθαι, ἀλλὰ ἢ τὴν ἀφαιρεθεῖσαν ἢ καὶ ἄλλην  45
αὐτῷ δίδοσθαι γαμετὴν τοσαύτην φερνὴν εἰσοίσουσαν. παρὰ τὸν
τοῦ δείπνου τοίνυν καιρὸν ὁ βάρβαρος λέγειν τῷ βασιλεύοντι τὸν

17 Ἡρέκαν ΒΕ [Ἡρέκα ΜΡ Κρέκα Niebuhr et Müller (qui ἡ Ρέκαν in textu
habet)   20 γὰρ Ε [δὲ Χ   32 καὶ exp. Dindorf

When he came out of the meeting, we asked him to free the wife of Syllus and her children, who had been taken prisoner at the capture of Ratiaria. He did not object to their freedom, but wished to sell them for a high price. When we begged him to think of their previous happiness and have pity for their current misfortune, he went to Attila and dismissed the wife for five hundred *solidi* and sent the children to the Emperor as a gift.

Meanwhile Hereka,[84] Attila's wife, invited us to dine at the house of Adamis, the manager of her affairs. We went there together with some of the leading men of the nation and were generously received. He welcomed us with gracious words and an array of foods. With Scythian hospitality each of those present stood up, handed us a cup full of wine, after we had drunk, embraced and kissed us, and took back the cup. After the dinner we returned to our tent and turned to sleep.

On the next day Attila again invited us to a banquet, and in the same manner as before we presented ourselves and took part in the feast. On this occasion it was not the eldest of his sons who was seated next to him on the couch, but Oebarsius, his paternal uncle. Throughout the banquet Attila addressed friendly words to us and he bade us tell the Emperor to give to Constantius, who had been sent to him as secretary from Aetius, the wife whom he had also[85] promised to him. When Constantius had come to the Emperor in the company of the envoys sent from Attila, he said that if Theodosius gave him a wealthy wife, he would ensure that the peace between the Romans and the Scythians would be preserved for a long time. The Emperor agreed to this proposal and said that he would give him the daughter of Saturnilus, a man of considerable wealth and family connections, who had been destroyed by Athenais (or Eudocia — she was called by both names).[86] But the fulfilment of this promise was prevented by Zeno,[87] a man of consular rank who commanded a large force of Isaurians with which he had been assigned the guarding of Constantinople during the war. Then, being master of the soldiers in the East, he carried off the girl from the fortress[88] and betrothed her to Rufus, one of his associates.[89] When the girl was taken away from him, Constantius asked the barbarian not to overlook the insult to him, but that either the girl who had been taken away or another with a comparable dowry be given to him as his wife. During the banquet, therefore, the barbarian

292    Priscus: Text

Μαξιμῖνον ἐκέλευε μὴ χρῆναι τῆς ἐξ αὐτοῦ τὸν Κωνστάντιον ἐλπίδος
διαμαρτεῖν· οὔτε γὰρ βασιλέως τὸ ψεύδεσθαι. ταῦτα δὲ ὁ Ἀττήλας
ἐνετέλλετο, ὑποσχομένου Κωνσταντίου χρήματα δώσειν, εἰ τῶν     50
ζαπλούτων αὐτῷ παρὰ Ῥωμαίοις κατεγγυηθείη γυνή.
    Τοῦ δὲ συμποσίου ὑπεξελθόντες μετὰ τὴν νύκτα ἡμερῶν δια-
γενομένων τριῶν διηρείθημεν δώροις τοῖς προσήκουσι τιμηθέντες.
ἔπεμπε δὲ ὁ Ἀττήλας καὶ Βέριχον τὸν ἡμῶν ἐν τῷ συμποσίῳ προκαθ-
εσθέντα ἄνδρα τῶν λογάδων καὶ πολλῶν ἐν τῇ Σκυθικῇ κωμῶν     55
ἄρχοντα παρὰ βασιλέα πρεσβευσόμενον, ἄλλως τε καὶ αὐτόν, οἷα δὴ
πρέσβυ, <δῶρα> παρὰ Ῥωμαίων δέξασθαι.
    Ποιουμένων δὲ ἡμῶν τὴν πορείαν καὶ πρὸς κώμῃ κατα-
λυσάντων τινί, ἥλω Σκύθης ἀνὴρ κατασκοπῆς ἕνεκα ἐκ τῆς Ῥωμαίων ἐς τὴν βάρβαρον διαβεβηκὼς χώραν· καὶ αὐτὸν Ἀττήλας     60
ἀνασκολοπισθῆναι παρεκελεύσατο. τῇ δὲ ἐπιούσῃ δι᾽ ἑτέρων κωμῶν
πορευομένων ἡμῶν, ἄνδρες β᾽ τῶν παρὰ Σκύθαις δουλευόντων
ἤγοντο ὀπίσω τὼ χεῖρε δεδεμένω ὡς τοὺς κατὰ πόλεμον ἀνελόντες
δεσπότας· καὶ ἐπὶ ξύλων β᾽ κεραίας ἐχόντων ἀμφοῖν τὰς κεφαλὰς
ἐμβαλόντες ἀνεσταύρωσαν.     65
    Ἐφ᾽ ὅσον δὲ τὴν Σκυθικὴν διεξῄειμεν, ὁ Βέριχος ἐκοινώνει τε
ἡμῖν τῆς ὁδοῦ καὶ ἥσυχός τις καὶ ἐπιτήδειος ἐνομίζετο. ὡς δὲ τὸν
Ἴστρον ἐπεραιώθημεν, ἐν ἐχθροῦ ἡμῖν ἐγένετο μοίρᾳ διά τινας
ἑώλους προφάσεις ἐκ τῶν θεραπόντων συνενεχθείσας. καὶ πρότερον μὲν τὸν ἵππον ἀφείλετο, ᾧ τὸν Μαξιμῖνον δωρησάμενος ἦν. ὁ     70
γὰρ Ἀττήλας πάντας τοὺς ἀμφ᾽ αὐτὸν λογάδας παρεκελεύσατο
δώροις τὸν Μαξιμῖνον φιλοφρονήσασθαι, καὶ ἕκαστος ἐπεπόμφει
ἵππον αὐτῷ, μεθ᾽ ὧν καὶ ὁ Βέριχος. ὀλίγους δὲ λαβὼν τοὺς ἄλλους
ἀπέπεμπε τὸ σῶφρον δηλῶσαι ἐκ τῆς μετριότητος ἐσπουδακώς.
τοῦτον οὖν ἀφείλετο τὸν ἵππον καὶ οὔτε συνοδοιπορεῖν οὔτε συνεστι-     75
ᾶσθαι ἠνέσχετο· ὥστε ἡμῖν ἐν τῇ βαρβάρων χώρᾳ γενόμενον σύμ-
βουλον ἐς τοῦτο προελθεῖν.
    Καὶ ἐντεῦθεν διὰ τῆς Φιλίππου ἐπὶ τὴν Ἀδριανούπολιν τὴν
πορείαν ἐποιησάμεθα. ἐν ᾗ διαναπαυσάμενοι ἐς λόγους ἤλθομεν τῷ
Βερίχῳ καὶ αὐτὸν τῆς πρὸς ἡμᾶς σιωπῆς κατεμεμψάμεθα, ὅτι γε     80
δὴ ὀργίζεται οὐκ ἀδικοῦσιν οὐδέν. θεραπεύσαντες οὖν αὐτὸν καὶ ἐπὶ
ἑστίασιν καλέσαντες ἐξωρμήσαμεν. καὶ τῷ Βιγίλᾳ ἐν τῇ ὁδῷ ἀπαν-
τήσαντες ἐπὶ τὴν Σκυθικὴν ἐπαναζευγνύντι καὶ τὰ παρὰ Ἀττήλα

---

49 βασιλέως scripsi [βασιλεῖ codd. βασιλικόν βασιλέα ψεύδεσθαι (sc. χρῆναι)
Gordon (1960 p.203 n.60)  πρέπειν post ψεύδεσθαι add. Niebuhr   57 δῶρα
scripsi [de Boor corruptelam indicat δῶρα παρὰ ᾽Ρ. δέξασθαι βουλόμενος
Müller  70 ᾧ Niebuhr [ὡς codd. 76-77 γενόμενον σύμβολον de Boor [γενο-
μένου συμβόλου edd.

commanded Maximinus to tell the Emperor that Constantius should not be disappointed in his hopes of him, for it was not the mark of a king to lie. Attila gave these orders since Constantius had promised to give him money if a woman from one of the very rich Roman families were betrothed to him.

After nightfall we left the banquet and three days later we were dismissed, having been honoured with appropriate gifts. Attila also sent along on an embassy to the Emperor Berichus, one of the leading men and the ruler of many villages in Scythia, who had sat before us at the banquet. There were various reasons, but the particular purpose was that he should receive <gifts> from the Romans.[90]

When we were on our journey and had halted near to a certain village, a Scythian, who had crossed from Roman to barbarian territory in order to spy, was captured. Attila ordered him impaled. On the following day, while we were travelling through other villages, two men who were in slavery amongst the Scythians were brought in, their hands tied behind them, because they had killed their masters in battle. They gibbetted them by affixing their heads to two lengths of wood with v-shaped clefts at the top.[91]

While we were journeying through Scythia, Berichus rode with us, and we thought him gentle and friendly. But when we had crossed the Danube, as a result of some old issues which had arisen out of the servants, he adopted the attitude of an enemy towards us. First, he took back the horse which he had given as a gift to Maximinus. (For Attila had ordered each of his leading men to show friendship to Maximinus with gifts, and each of them, including Berichus, had sent him a horse. Maximinus had kept a few of these, but had sent back the rest, since he was eager to show his restraint by his temperate behaviour.) Berichus, then, took back this horse and refused to ride or to eat with us. And so, the pact which existed towards us in the land of the barbarians now came to this.

From here we made our journey through Philippopolis to Adrianople. Here we halted and approached Berichus, complaining to him of his silence towards us and saying that he was angry at men who did him no wrong. When we had tried to win him over and had invited him to dinner, we set out. On the road we met Vigilas, who was returning to Scythia. We told him what reply Attila had made to our embassy and

ἡμῖν τῆς ἐπὶ τῇ πρεσβείᾳ ἀποκρίσεως εἰρημένα ἀφηγησάμενοι τῆς
ἐπανόδου εἰχόμεθα. ὡς δὲ ἐς τὴν Κωνσταντίνου παρεγενόμεθα,    85
μεταβεβλῆσθαι μὲν ᾠόμεθα τὸν Βέριχον τῆς ὀργῆς· ὃς δὲ τῆς
ἀγρίας οὐκ ἐπελέληστο φύσεως, ἀλλ' ἐς διαφορὰς ἐχώρει καὶ ἐν
κατηγορίᾳ ἐποιεῖτο τὸν Μαξιμῖνον, ὡς ἔφησεν εἰς τὴν Σκυθικὴν
διαβὰς τὸν Ἀρεόβινδον καὶ τὸν Ἄσπαρα ἄνδρας στρατηγοὺς μηδε-
μίαν παρὰ βασιλεῖ ἔχειν μοῖραν, καὶ ὡς ἐν ὀλιγωρίᾳ τὰ κατ' αὐτοὺς    90
ἐποιήσατο τὴν βαρβαρικὴν ἐλέγξας κουφότητα.

## Liber IV
## 15

1. (*Exc. de Leg. Rom. 3*)

Ἀναξεύξαντα δὲ τὸν Βιγίλαν εἰς τὴν Σκυθικὴν καὶ ἐν οἷς τὸν
Ἀττήλαν τόποις διατρίβειν συνέβαινεν ἀφικόμενον περιστάντες εἶχον
οἱ πρὸς τοῦτο παρεσκευασμένοι βάρβαροι καὶ τὰ χρήματα, ἅπερ τῷ
Ἐδέκωνι ἐκόμιζεν, ἀφείλοντο. ὡς δὲ καὶ αὐτὸν παρὰ τὸν Ἀττήλαν
ἦγον, καὶ ἀνηρωτᾶτο, ὅτου χάριν τοσοῦτον φέροι χρυσίον, ἔφη οἰκείας    5
τε καὶ τῶν παρεπομένων προνοίας ἕνεκα, ὥστε μὴ ἐνδείᾳ τροφῶν ἢ
ἵππων σπάνει ἢ καὶ τῶν φορτηγῶν ὑποζυγίων ὑπὸ τῆς μακρᾶς ἐκ-
δαπανηθέντων ὁδοῦ διαμαρτεῖν τῆς περὶ τῆς πρεσβείας σπουδῆς·
παρεσκευάσθαι δὲ αὐτῷ καὶ ἐς αἰχμαλώτων ὠνήν, πολλῶν κατὰ
τὴν Ῥωμαίων δεηθέντων αὐτοῦ τοὺς σφίσι προσήκοντας λύσασθαι.    10
καὶ ὁ Ἀττήλας· ἀλλ' οὔτι, ἔφη, σὺ πονηρὸν θηρίον, τὸν Βιγίλαν
λέγων, τὴν δίκην σοφιζόμενος λήσεις, οὐδὲ ἔσται σοι πρόφασις ἱκανὴ
εἰς τὸ τὴν κόλασιν διαφυγεῖν, μείζονος μὲν τῆς σῆς δαπάνης παρασκευῆς σοι χρημάτων ὑπαρχούσης, καὶ τῶν ὑπὸ σοῦ ἵππων καὶ ὑποζυγίων ὠνηθησομένων, καὶ τῆς τῶν αἰχμαλώτων λύσεως, ἣν σὺν    15
Μαξιμίνῳ παρ' ἐμὲ ἀφικομένῳ ποιεῖν ἀπηγόρευσα.

Ταῦτα εἰπὼν τὸν υἱόν (ἦν δὲ καὶ τῷ Βιγίλα τότε πρῶτον εἰς
τὴν βαρβάρων ἠκολουθηκὼς χώραν) ξίφει καταβληθῆναι παρεκελεύσατο, εἰ μὴ φθάσας εἴποι, ὅτῳ τὰ χρήματα καὶ δι' ἣν αἰτίαν
κομίζει. ὁ δὲ ὡς ἐθεάσατο τὸν παῖδα ἐπὶ θάνατον στείχοντα, ἐς    20
δάκρυά τε καὶ ὀλοφυρμοὺς ἐτράπη καὶ ἀνεβόα τὴν δίκην ἐπ' αὐτὸν
φέρειν τὸ ξίφος, οὐκ ἐπὶ τὸν νέον τὸν ἀδικοῦντα οὐδέν. καὶ μηδὲν
μελλήσας τά τε αὐτῷ καὶ Ἐδέκωνι καὶ τῷ εὐνούχῳ καὶ τῷ βασιλεῖ
μελετηθέντα ἔλεγεν, συνεχῶς δὲ εἰς ἱκεσίας τρεπόμενος, ὥστε αὐτὸν
μὲν ἀναιρεθῆναι, διαφεθῆναι δὲ τὸν παῖδα. γνοὺς δὲ ὁ Ἀττήλας ἀπὸ    25
τῶν Ἐδέκωνι εἰρημένων μηδὲν διεψεῦσθαι τὸν Βιγίλαν ἐν δεσμοῖς
εἶναι προσέταττεν, οὐ πρότερον λύσειν ἀπειλήσας, πρὶν ἢ τὸν παῖδα

2 εἶχον [συνεῖχον Niebuhr

then continued our return journey. When we reached Constantinople, we thought Berichus had put off his anger, but he had not shed his savage nature. He came into dispute with us and accused Maximinus of saying, when he crossed into Scythia, that the generals Areobindus and Aspar carried no weight with the Emperor and of pouring contempt upon their achievements by arguing that they were unreliable barbarians.[92]

## Book IV
## 15

1. (*Exc. de Leg. Rom.* 3)

When Vigilas had returned to Scythia and reached the district where Attila was staying, barbarians who had been readied for this purpose surrounded and detained him and took away the money which he was bringing for Edeco. When they brought him before Attila and he was asked for what reason he was carrying so much gold, he replied that it was for the purposes of himself and those with him, so that they would not fail to achieve the object of the embassy through lack of supplies or inadequacy of the horses and baggage animals which had been exhausted by the long journey. Moreover, money had been supplied to him to purchase captives, since many in Roman territory had begged him to ransom their relatives. Then Attila, calling Vigilas a "worthless beast", said, "You will escape justice no longer with your tricks. Your excuses will not be enough for you to avoid punishment. Your supply of money is more than you need to buy provisions for yourself, and horses, and baggage animals, and to ransom the captives, which I forbade you to do when you came to me with Maximinus."

Saying this he ordered that Vigilas' son, who on that occasion had accompanied his father to the land of the barbarians for the first time, be struck down with a sword unless Vigilas first told why and for what purpose he was bringing the money. When Vigilas saw his son facing death, he burst into tears and lamentations and called upon justice to use the sword on him, not upon an innocent youth. Without hesitation he described what had been planned by himself, Edeco, the eunuch and the Emperor, all the time begging that he be put to death and his son be sent away. When Attila knew from what Edeco had told him that Vigilas was not lying, he ordered him to be put in chains and promised that he would not free him until he sent his son back and

ἐκπέμψας ἑτέρας αὐτῷ ν΄ χρυσίου λίτρας ὑπὲρ τῶν σφετέρων
κομίσοι λύτρων. καὶ ὁ μὲν ἐδέδετο, ὁ δὲ ἐς τὴν Ῥωμαίων ἐπανῄει. ἔ-
πεμπε δὲ καὶ Ὀρέστην καὶ Ἤσλαν ὁ Ἀττήλας ἐς τὴν Κωνσταντίνου.    30

2. (*Exc. de Leg. Gent.* 6)

Ὅτι φωραθέντα τὸν Βιγίλαν ἐπιβουλευόμενον τῷ Ἀττήλᾳ, καὶ
τοῦ χρυσίου τὰς ἑκατὸν λίτρας τὰς παρὰ τοῦ Χρυσαφίου τοῦ εὐνούχου
σταλείσας ἀφελόμενος, παρευθὺ ἔπεμπεν Ὀρέστην καὶ Ἤσλαν ὁ
Ἀττήλας ἐς τὴν Κωνσταντίνου ἐντειλάμενος τὸν μὲν Ὀρέστην τὸ
βαλλάντιον, ἐν ᾧπερ ἐμβεβλήκει Βιγίλας τὸ χρυσίον Ἐδέκωνι    5
δοθησόμενον, τῷ σφετέρῳ περιθέντα τραχήλῳ ἐλθεῖν τε παρὰ
βασιλέα καὶ αὐτῷ ἐπιδείξαντα καὶ τῷ εὐνούχῳ ἀνερωτᾶν, εἴ γε αὐτὸ
ἐπιγιγνώσκοιεν, τὸν δὲ Ἤσλαν λέγειν ἀπὸ στόματος εὖ μὲν γεγονότος
εἶναι πατρὸς τὸν Θεοδόσιον παῖδα, εὖ δὲ καὶ αὐτὸν φύντα καὶ τὸν
πατέρα Μουνδίουχον διαδεξάμενον διαφυλάξαι τὴν εὐγένειαν· ταύτης    10
δε τὸν Θεοδόσιον ἐκπεπτωκότα δουλεύειν αὐτῷ τὴν τοῦ φόρου ἀπαγωγὴν ὑφιστάμενον. οὐ δίκαιον οὖν ποιεῖ τῷ βελτίονι καὶ ὃν αὐτῷ
ἡ τύχη δεσπότην ἀνέδειξεν ὡς πονηρὸς οἰκέτης λαθριδίως ἐπιτιθέ-
μενος. οὐ λύσειν οὖν τὴν αἰτίαν ἔφη τῶν ἐς αὐτὸν ἡμαρτημένων, εἰ
μή γε τὸν εὐνοῦχον ἐκπέμψοι πρὸς κόλασιν.    15
Καὶ οὗτοι μὲν ἐπὶ τοῖσδε ἐς τὴν Κωνσταντίνου παρεγένοντο·
συνηνέχθη δὲ τὸν Χρυσάφιον ἐξαιτεῖσθαι καὶ παρὰ Ζήνωνος. Μαξιμίνου γὰρ εἰρηκέναι τὸν Ἀττήλαν ἀπαγγείλαντος χρῆναι βασιλέα
πληροῦν τὴν ὑπόσχεσιν καὶ τῷ Κωνσταντίῳ τὴν γυναῖκα διδόναι, ἣν
οὐδαμῶς παρὰ τὴν ἐκείνου βουλὴν ἑτέρῳ κατεγγυηθῆναι οἷόν τε ἦν    20
(ἢ γὰρ ἂν ὁ τολμήσας ἐκδεδώκει δίκας, ἢ τοιαῦτα τὰ βασιλέως ἐστίν,
ὥστε μηδὲ τῶν σφετέρων κρατεῖν οἰκετῶν, καθ᾿ ὧν συμμαχίαν, εἴ
γε βούλοιτο, ἕτοιμον εἶναι παρασχεῖν), ἐδήχθη τε ὁ Θεοδόσιος τὸν
θυμὸν καὶ δημοσίαν τὴν τῆς κόρης οὐσίαν ποιεῖ.

3 ἀφελόμενος Classen [ἀφελομένου codd.    5 τὸ post χρυσίον add. Dindorf

3. (*Exc. de Leg. Rom.* 4)

Ὅτι ὑπ᾿ ἀμφοτέρων Ἀττήλα τε καὶ Ζήνωνος αἰτούμενος ὁ
Χρυσάφιος ἐν ἀγωνίᾳ καθεστήκει. πάντων δὲ αὐτῷ εὔνοιάν τε καὶ
σπουδὴν συνεισφερόντων, ἐδόκει παρὰ τὸν Ἀττήλαν πρεσβεύεσθαι
Ἀνατόλιον καὶ Νόμον, τὸν μὲν Ἀνατόλιον τῶν ἀμφὶ βασιλέα ἄρχοντα
τελῶν καὶ τὰς συνθήκας τῆς ἐκείνου εἰρήνης προθέμενον, τὸν δὲ    5
Νόμον τὴν τοῦ μαγίστρου ἀρχὴν ἄρξαντα καὶ ἐν τοῖς πατρικίοις σὺν
ἐκείνῳ καταλεγόμενον, οἳ δὴ τὰς ἀρχὰς ἀναβεβήκασι πάσας. συν-
επέμπετο δὲ Ἀνατολίῳ Νόμος οὐ διὰ μέγεθος τῆς τύχης μόνον, ἀλλὰ

6 ἀρχὴν EMP [τιμὴν B (ἀρχὴν in mg.) et edd.

brought another fifty pounds of gold to pay for his own ransom. Vigilas was bound, and the son returned to Roman territory, and Attila also sent Orestes and Eslas to Constantinople.

## 2. (*Exc. de Leg. Gent.* 6)

When Attila had seized Vigilas, who was discovered plotting against him, and the hundred pounds of gold which had been sent by Chrysaphius the eunuch,[93] he immediately sent Orestes and Eslas to Constantinople. He ordered Orestes to go before the Emperor wearing around his neck the bag in which Vigilas had placed the gold to be given to Edeco. He was to show him and the eunuch the bag and to ask if they recognised it. Eslas was then to say directly that Theodosius was the son of a nobly-born father, and Attila, too, was of noble descent, having succeeded his father, Mundiuch.[94] But whereas he had preserved his noble lineage, Theodosius had fallen from his and was Attila's slave, bound to the payment of tribute. Therefore, in attacking him covertly like a worthless slave, he was acting unjustly towards his better, whom fortune had made his master. As a result, Attila declared, he would not absolve Theodosius from blame for the crime against himself unless he handed over the eunuch for punishment.

These men, then, came to Constantinople for this purpose; and it also happened that Zeno was seeking Chrysaphius. For Maximinus had reported Attila's declaration that the Emperor ought to fulfil his promise and give Constantius his wife, who could not have been betrothed to another without the Emperor's consent: either the man who had dared to do this would have already paid the penalty, or the Emperor's affairs were in such a state that he could not control his own servants, against whom, should he wish it, Attila was ready to make an alliance. Mortified by this, Theodosius confiscated the girl's property.[95]

## 3. (*Exc. de Leg. Rom.* 4)

Being sought by both Attila and Zeno, Chrysaphius was in dire straits. Since all unanimously gave him their goodwill and support,[96] it was decided that Anatolius and Nomus should go as ambassadors to Attila. Anatolius, who had fixed the terms of peace with Attila, was master of the soldiers in the presence, and Nomus had been master of the offices and was, like Anatolius, one of the patricians (who are senior to all other ranks).[97] Nomus was sent with Anatolius not only because of his high rank, but also because he was friendly towards

ὡς καὶ τῷ Χρυσαφίῳ εὔνους ὢν καὶ φιλοτιμίᾳ τοῦ βαρβάρου περι-
εσόμενος· ὅτι γὰρ μάλιστα προσῆν αὐτῷ τὸ μὴ φείδεσθαι χρημάτων    10
τὸ παρὸν διαθεῖναι ἐσπουδακότι. καὶ οὗτοι μὲν ἐστέλλοντο τὸν Ἀττήλαν ἀπάξοντες τῆς ὀργῆς καὶ τὴν εἰρήνην ἐπὶ ταῖς συντάξεσι δια-
φυλάττειν πείσοντες, λέξοντες δὲ καὶ ὡς τῷ Κωνσταντίῳ κατεγγυη-
θήσεται γυνὴ οὐ μείων τῆς Σατορνίλου γένει τε καὶ περιουσίᾳ·
ἐκείνην γὰρ μὴ βεβουλῆσθαι, ἀλλ' ἑτέρῳ κατὰ νόμον γήμασθαι· οὐ    15
γὰρ θέμις παρὰ Ῥωμαίοις ἄκουσαν γυναῖκα κατεγγυᾶσθαι ἀνδρί.
ἔπεμπε δὲ καὶ ὁ εὐνοῦχος τῷ βαρβάρῳ χρυσίον ὥστε αὐτὸν μειλιχ-
θέντα ἀπαχθῆναι τοῦ θυμοῦ.

4. (*Exc. de Leg. Rom.* 5)

Ὅτι οἱ ἀμφὶ τὸν Ἀνατόλιον καὶ Νόμον τὸν Ἴστρον περαιωθέντες ἄχρις τοῦ Δρέγκωνος λεγομένου ποταμοῦ ἐς τὴν Σκυθικὴν
διέβησαν. αἰδοῖ γὰρ τῶν ἀνδρῶν ὁ Ἀττήλας ὥστε μὴ τῷ τῆς ὁδοῦ
ἐπιτρίβεσθαι διαστήματι ἐν ἐκείνῳ τῷ χωρίῳ τὴν πρὸς αὐτοὺς
ἐποιήσατο ἔντευξιν. καὶ πρῶτον μὲν ὑπερηφάνως διαλεχθεὶς ὑπήχθη    5
τῷ πλήθει τῶν δώρων, καὶ λόγοις προσηνέσι μαλαχθεὶς φυλάττειν
τὴν εἰρήνην ἐπὶ ταῖς αὐταῖς ἐπώμνυτο συνθήκαις, ἀναχωρεῖν δὲ καὶ
τῆς τῷ Ἴστρῳ ὁριζομένης Ῥωμαίων γῆς καὶ τοῦ πράγματα ἔτι
παρέχειν περὶ φυγάδων βασιλεῖ, εἰ μή γε Ῥωμαῖοι αὖθις ἑτέρους
καταφεύγοντας παρ' αὐτοῦ δέξοιντο. ἠφίει δὲ καὶ Βιγίλαν τὰς ν' τοῦ    10
χρυσοῦ λίτρας δεξάμενος· ταύτας γὰρ αὐτῷ ἐκεκομίκει ὁ παῖς σὺν
τοῖς πρέσβεσιν ἐς τὴν Σκυθικὴν διαβάς· καὶ αἰχμαλώτους ἄνευ
λύτρων ἀφῆκε πλείστους Ἀνατολίῳ καὶ Νόμῳ χαριζόμενος. δωρησάμενος δὲ καὶ ἵππους αὐτοῖς καὶ θηρίων δοράς, αἷς οἱ βασίλειοι κοσ-
μοῦνται Σκύθαι, ἀπέπεμπε συμπέμψας καὶ τὸν Κωνστάντιον ὥστε    15
αὐτῷ βασιλέα ἐς ἔργον ἀγαγεῖν τὴν ὑπόσχεσιν. ὡς δὲ ἐπανῆλθον οἱ
πρέσβεις καὶ ἅπαντα τά τε παρ' αὐτῶν τά τε παρὰ τοῦ βαρβάρου
διεξῆλθον, κατεγγυᾶται τῷ Κωνσταντίῳ γυνὴ γαμετὴ Ἀρματίου
γενομένη παιδὸς Πλίνθου τοῦ παρὰ Ῥωμαίοις στρατηγήσαντος καὶ
τὴν ὕπατον ἀρχὴν ἄρξαντος. συνεβεβήκει δὲ τὸν Ἀρμάτον ἐς τὴν    20
Λιβύων διαβάντα ἐπὶ τῇ πρὸς Αὐσοριανοὺς μάχῃ εὐημερῆσαι μὲν ἐν
τῷ πρὸς ἐκείνους πολέμῳ, νοσήσαντα δὲ τελευτῆσαι τὸν βίον.
οὗ δὴ τὴν γαμετὴν καὶ γένει καὶ περιουσίᾳ διαπρέπουσαν ἔπεισεν ὁ
βασιλεὺς τῷ Κωνσταντίῳ γήμασθαι. οὕτω καὶ τῶν πρὸς Ἀττήλαν
λυθέντων διαφόρων, ὁ Θεοδόσιος ἐδεδίει μήποτε καὶ Ζήνων τυ-    25
ραννίδι ἐπιθήσεται.

(Cf. *Suda* A 2107)

18 Ἀρματίου P    20 Ἄρματον EP

Chrysaphius and would prevail over the barbarian with his generosity, for when he was keen to settle a matter he was unsparing with his money. These men were sent to turn Attila from his anger and persuade him to keep the peace on the terms agreed, and to tell him that a wife would be betrothed to Constantius not at all inferior to the daughter of Saturnilus in background or wealth. Saturnilus' daughter had been unwilling and had been married to another according to the law, since amongst the Romans it was not right to betroth a woman to a man against her will. The eunuch, too, sent gold to the barbarian to mollify him and turn him from his anger.

4. (*Exc. de Leg. Rom.* 5)

Anatolius and Nomus and their party crossed the Danube and travelled into Scythia as far as the river called the Drecon. Out of regard for these men Attila came to meet them at that place in order that they not be worn out by the length of the journey. At first Attila negotiated arrogantly, but he was overwhelmed by the number of their gifts and mollified by their words of appeasement. He swore that he would keep the peace on the same terms, that he would withdraw from the Roman territory bordering the Danube and that he would cease to press the matter of the fugitives with the Emperor providing the Romans did not again receive other fugitives who fled from him. He also freed Vigilas, having received the fifty pounds of gold which his son, who had crossed to Scythia with the ambassadors, had brought. Furthermore, he freed a large number of prisoners without ransom, gratifying Anatolius and Nomus. Having given them gifts of horses and skins of wild animals, with which the Scythian kings adorn themselves, he dismissed them and sent along with them Constantius in order that the Emperor might fulfil his promise to him. When the ambassadors had returned and had reported everything discussed by themselves and by the barbarian, to Constantius a woman was betrothed who had been the wife of Armatus, the son of Plinthas who had been a Roman general and had held the consulship.[98] Armatus had been serving in Libya during the fighting with the Ausoriani[99] and had distinguished himself in that war, but had fallen ill and died. The Emperor persuaded his wife, who was distinguished by both birth and wealth, to marry Constantius. When he had settled the differences with Attila in this manner, Theodosius feared that Zeno would at some time attempt usurpation. (Cf. *Suda* A 2107)

300    Priscus: Text

5. (John of Antioch *Fr.* 198 = *Exc. de Ins.* 83)

Ὅτι ἐπὶ Θεοδοσίου τοῦ νέου Χρυσάφιος διώκει τὰ πάντα, τὰ
πάντων ἁρπάζων καὶ ὑπὸ πάντων μισούμενος. τότε μὲν οὖν Ἀττήλας
πρόφασιν τὴν Κωνσταντίου προβαλλόμενος αἴτησιν, ἣν αὐτὸν περὶ
τοῦ γάμου τῆς Σατορνίλου θυγατρὸς ἥτει, ἐπανίσταται τῇ Ῥωμαίων
ἀρχῇ καὶ τὸν εὐνοῦχον Χρυσάφιον ἐκδοθῆναι οἱ παρεκελεύετο, ὡς    5
φωραθέντα τῆς κατ᾽ αὐτοῦ ἐπιβουλῆς. ἐντεῦθεν πάλιν Ἀνατόλιος καὶ
Νόμος πρὸς τὸν Ἀττήλαν παραγίνονται, καὶ πείθουσιν αὐτὸν δώροις
ἀποσχέσθαι τῆς κατὰ τοῦ εὐνούχου ὀργῆς.

## 16

(John of Antioch *Fr.* 199,1 = *Exc. de Ins.* 84)

Ὅτι Θεοδόσιος ὁ νέος πρὸς τὸν Ζήνωνα ἐχαλέπαινεν. ἐδεδίει
γὰρ μήποτε καὶ τυραννίδι ἐπίθηται, ἀκινδύνου αὐτῷ γενομένης τῆς
ἁρπαγῆς. ὅπερ ἔτι μάλιστα ἐξετάραττεν αὐτόν. καὶ πᾶσι τοῖς ἁμαρ-
τήμασι ῥᾳδίως νέμων συγγνώμην, χαλεπός τε καὶ ἀμετάτρεπτος
ἦν οὐ μόνον κατὰ τῶν τυραννίδα μελετησάντων, ἀλλὰ καὶ τῶν    5
βασιλείας ἀξίων νομισθέντων, καί σφας ἐκποδῶν ποιεῖν διὰ παντὸς
ἐχώρει τρόπου. καὶ πρὸς τοῖς εἰρημένοις προσώποις καὶ Βαύδωνα
καὶ Δανίηλον ὡς τυραννίδι ἐπιθεμένους ἐξέβαλεν. ἀπὸ τῆς αὐτῆς
τοίνυν προαιρέσεως καὶ τὸν Ζήνωνα ἀμύνασθαι ἐσπουδακὼς τῆς
προτέρας εἴχετο βουλῆς, ὥστε διαβῆναι μὲν τὸν Μαξιμῖνον εἰς τὴν    10
Ἰσαυρόπολιν καὶ τὰ ἐκεῖ χωρία προκαταλαβεῖν, στεῖλαι δὲ διὰ
θαλάσσης ἐπὶ τὴν ἕω δύναμιν τὴν τὸν Ζήνωνα παραστησομένην·
καὶ τῶν αὐτῷ δεδογμένων οὐκ ἀφίστατο· μείζονος δὲ αὐτὸν ἐκ-
ταράξαντος φόβου, τὴν παρασκευὴν ἀνεβάλετο.

2 γενομένης scripsi [γενέσθαι codd. γενέσθαι μελλούσης Müller   7 Βαύδωνα
Müller [Βάνδωνα codd.

## 17

(John of Antioch *Fr.* 199,2 = *Exc. de Ins.* 84)

Ἧκε γάρ τις ἀγγέλλων τὸν Ἀττήλαν τοῖς κατὰ τὴν Ῥώμην
ἐπιθέσθαι βασιλείοις, Ὁνωρίας τῆς Βαλεντινιανοῦ ἀδελφῆς ἐς ἐπι-
κουρίαν ἐπικαλεσαμένης αὐτόν. ἡ γὰρ Ὁνωρία τῶν βασιλικῶν καὶ
αὐτὴ ἐχομένη σκήπτρων Εὐγενίῳ τινὶ τὴν ἐπιμέλειαν τῶν αὐτῆς
ἔχοντι πραγμάτων ἥλω ἐς λαθραῖον ἐρχομένη λέχος, καὶ ἐπὶ τῷ    5
ἁμαρτήματι ἀνῃρέθη μὲν ἐκεῖνος, ἡ δὲ τῶν βασιλείων ἐλαθεῖσα
Ἑρκουλάνῳ κατεγγυᾶται, ἀνδρὶ ὑπατικῷ καὶ τρόπων εὖ ἔχοντι,
ὡς μήτε πρὸς βασιλείαν μήτε πρὸς νεωτερισμὸν ὑποτοπεῖσθαι. ἐν

4 αὕτη P

5. (John of Antioch *Fr.* 198 = *Exc. de Ins.* 83)

During the reign of Theodosius Chrysaphius controlled everything, seizing the possessions of all and being hated by all. Then Attila, using as his excuse the demand which Constantius had made of him concerning the daughter of Saturnilus, began again to be hostile to the Roman state and demanded that the eunuch Chrysaphius be handed over to him on the ground that he had been discovered in a plot against him.[100] Thereupon Anatolius and Nomus again came to him and by gifts persuaded him to lay aside his anger against the eunuch.

## 16

(John of Antioch *Fr.* 199,1 = *Exc. de Ins.* 84)

The younger Theodosius was angry with Zeno. For he feared that on some occasion he would attempt usurpation, when the attack brought no danger to himself. This disturbed Theodosius very greatly. Although he readily gave forgiveness to all other misdemeanours, he was harsh and unappeasable not only towards those who attempted usurpation but even to those who were held worthy to be Emperor, and he moved by every means to eliminate them. In addition to the persons mentioned he banished Baudo and Daniel on the ground that they were aiming at usurpation. For the same reason in his eagerness to forestall Zeno he kept to his earlier plan. Therefore, Maximinus crossed to Isauropolis and seized the districts there beforehand, and Theodosius also sent a force to the East to subdue Zeno. He did not abandon his designs, but he postponed his preparations when a greater fear distracted him.[101]

## 17

(John of Antioch *Fr.* 199,2 = *Exc. de Ins.* 84)

For a messenger arrived [at Constantinople] with the news that Attila was preparing hostilities against the rulers of Rome, since Honoria, Valentinian's sister, had summoned him to her assistance. Honoria, who herself had the symbols of royal authority, was caught in a clandestine affair with a certain Eugenius, who was in charge of her affairs. He was executed for the crime, and she was deprived of her royal authority and betrothed to Herculanus, a man of consular rank and of such good character that he was suspected of designs neither on kingship nor on revolution. She brought the business to an

συμφορᾷ δὲ καὶ ἀνίᾳ δεινῇ τὸ πρᾶγμα ποιουμένη παρὰ τὸν Ἀττήλαν
Ὑάκινθον εὐνοῦχον ἐκπέμπει τινά, ὥστε ἐπὶ χρήμασιν αὐτῇ τιμω-    10
ρῆσαι τῷ γάμῳ· ἐπὶ δὲ τούτοις καὶ δακτύλιον ἔπεμψε πιστουμένη τὸν
βάρβαρον. καὶ ὁ μὲν παρεσκεύαζεν ἑαυτὸν χωρεῖν κατὰ τῆς τῶν
ἑσπερίων βασιλείας, ἐβουλεύετο δὲ ὅπως τὸν Ἀέτιον προκαταλάβοι·
μὴ γὰρ ἄλλως τεύξεσθαι τῆς ἐλπίδος, εἰ μή γε ἐκεῖνον ποιήσοιτο
ἐκποδῶν.    15
    Ταῦτα τοίνυν Θεοδόσιος μεμαθηκὼς ἐπιστέλλει τῷ Βαλεν-
τιανῷ τὴν Ὀνωρίαν ἐκπέμπειν τῷ Ἀττήλᾳ. καὶ ὁ μὲν συλλαβὼν τὸν
Ὑάκινθον ἅπαντα διηρεύνησε καὶ μετὰ πολλοὺς τοῦ σώματος
αἰκισμοὺς τῆς κεφαλῆς ἀποτμηθῆναι ἐκέλευσεν, Ὀνωρίαν δὲ τὴν
ἀδελφὴν Βαλεντινιανὸς τῇ μητρὶ δῶρον ἔδωκε πολλὰ αἰτησαμένη    20
αὐτήν. οὕτως μὲν οὖν Ὀνωρία τότε τῆς . . . ἀπελύετο.
(Cf. *Suda* O 404; Jordanes *Get.* 42,223-24 = *Fr.* 22,1; *Rom.* 328;
Theophanes *Chron. a.m.* 5943 = *Fr.* 21,3)

13 ἐβουλεύετο Müller [ἐβούλετο codd.    21 lac. indicavit Cramer

## Liber V

## 18

(Evagrius *HE* 2,1)

    Μαρκιανὸς τοίνυν, ὡς ἄλλοις τε πολλοῖς καὶ μὴν καὶ Πρίσκῳ
ἱστόρηται τῷ ῥήτορι, ἦν μὲν Θρᾷξ γένος, ἀνδρὸς στρατιωτικοῦ παῖς·
ὅς γε τῆς τοῦ πατρὸς βιοτῆς μεταλαχεῖν ἐπειγόμενος πρὸς τὴν
Φιλιππούπολιν τὰς ὁρμὰς ἔσχεν, ἔνθα καὶ στρατιωτικοῖς ἐδύνατο
συντετάχθαι τάγμασιν. ἀνὰ δὲ τὴν ὁδὸν τεθέαται νεοσφαγὲς σῶμα    5
ἐπὶ γῆς ἐρριμμένον· ᾧ παρεστώς, ἦν γὰρ τά τε ἄλλα πανάριστος καὶ
ἐς τὰ μάλιστα φιλανθρωπότατος, ᾤκτειρε τὸ γεγονός, καὶ ἐπὶ πολὺ
τὴν πορείαν ἐπεῖχε τῶν εἰκότων μεταδοῦναι βουλόμενος. ἐπειδὴ δέ
τινες τοῦτο τεθέανται, ταῖς ἐν τῇ Φιλιππουπόλει προσήγγελλον
ἀρχαῖς· αἳ τὸν Μαρκιανὸν παραλαβοῦσαι τὰ περὶ τῆς μιαιφονίας    10
ἀνηρώτων. καὶ δὴ τῶν στοχασμῶν καὶ τῶν εἰκότων πλέον τῆς
ἀληθείας καὶ τῆς γλώσσης ἐσχηκότων, τὸν φόνον τε τἀνδρὸς ἀναιρο-
μένου καὶ μιαιφόνου γε ποινὰς μέλλοντος ἀποτίσειν, θεία τις ἐξαπίνης
ῥοπὴ τὸν μιαιφόνον παραδίδωσιν· ὃς τὴν κεφαλὴν ἀποθέμενος ποινὴν
τοῦ δράματος τὴν κεφαλὴν τῷ Μαρκιανῷ χαρίζεται. οὕτω παρα-    15
δόξως σωθεὶς ἔν τινι τῶν αὐτόθι στρατιωτικῶν τελῶν ἀφικνεῖται,
ἐν αὐτῷ παραγγέλλειν βουλόμενος. οἳ τὸν ἄνδρα θαυμάσαντες
μέγαν τε ἔσεσθαι καὶ ἀξιολογώτατον εἰκότως τεκμηράμενοι ἥδιστα

2 τὸ ante γένος add. V    7 ἐπὶ πολὺ [μικρόν τι Nicephorus    9 προήγγελλον Β

unfortunate and disastrous state by sending the eunuch Hyacinthus to Attila offering him money to avenge her marriage. In addition to this she also sent her ring as her pledge to the barbarian. He was preparing himself to go against the western Empire and was planning how he might first capture Aetius, since he thought that he would not achieve his object unless he eliminated him.

When Theodosius learned this, he sent to Valentinian to hand Honoria over to Attila. But Valentinian arrested Hyacinthus and carried out a thorough investigation of the matter. After inflicting many tortures upon him, he ordered him decapitated. He gave Honoria, his sister, as a gift to her mother, after the latter had made many requests for her. In this manner at the time Honoria escaped . . . .[102]
(Cf. *Suda* O 404; Jordanes *Get.* 42,223-24 = *Fr.* 22,1; *Rom.* 328; Theophanes *Chron. a.m.* 5943 = *Fr.* 21,3)

## Book V

## 18

(Evagrius *HE* 2,1)

Marcian, as many writers, and especially the rhetor Priscus, report, was a Thracian and the son of a military man. He was eager to follow the same career and was making his way to Philippopolis, where he could enrol in the forces. On his way he saw a corpse which had been recently slain and thrown onto the ground. Since he was an altogether good man and especially kindly, when he came to the body, he grieved at what had happened and, wishing to give it the proper rites, made a considerable[103] break in his journey to do so. Some persons saw this and reported it to the authorities in Philippopolis. They arrested Marcian and were interrogating him about the murder. Inference from the rites that he had performed carried more weight than his true account, and, despite his denials of the murder, he was about to pay the penalty for the killing when suddenly divine intervention revealed the murderer. He was executed as punishment for his action and so saved Marcian's neck. Having been thus unexpectedly saved, Marcian approached one of the regiments there, wishing to be enrolled in it. They were impressed by the man and, judging that he would probably be a strong and most estimable soldier, gladly accepted him and enrolled

προσδέχονται, καὶ σφίσιν αὐτοῖς ἐγκαταλέγουσιν, οὔτι ἔσχατον, ὡς ὁ
στρατιωτικὸς ἐθέλει νόμος, ἐς δέ τινα βαθμὸν ἄρτι τετελευτηκότος    20
ἀνδρός (Αὔγουστος ὄνομα τούτῳ), Μαρκιανὸν τὸν καὶ Αὔγουστον ἐς
τὴν παραγγελίαν ἐγγράψαντες, ὡς φθάσαι τοὔνομα τὴν προσηγορίαν τῶν ἡμετέρων βασιλέων, τὸ καλεῖσθαι Αὔγουστοι μετὰ τῆς
ἁλουργίδος περιβαλλομένων· ὥσπερ οὐκ ἀνασχομένου τοῦ ὀνόματος
ἐπ᾿ αὐτῷ χωρὶς τῆς ἀξίας μεῖναι, μηδ᾿ αὖ πάλιν τῆς ἀξίας ἕτερον    25
ὄνομα ζητησάσης εἰς σεμνολόγημα, ὥστε κύριον καὶ προσηγορικὸν
τὸ αὐτὸ καθεστάναι, διὰ μιᾶς κλήσεως τῆς τε ἀξιώσεως τῆς τε
προσηγορίας σημαινομένων.    (Cf. Nicephorus Callistus HE 15,1)

21 τὸν καὶ [ὡς Bidez

[19]
[(Suda A 3803)
Ἀρδαβούριος, υἱὸς Ἄσπαρος, γενναῖος τὸν θυμὸν καὶ τοὺς τὴν
Θρᾴκην πολλάκις καταδραμόντας βαρβάρους εὐρώστως ἀποκρουσά-
μενος. τούτῳ οὖν γέρα ἀριστείων ὁ βασιλεὺς Μαρκιανὸς παρέσχετο
τὴν ἕω στρατοπεδαρχίαν. καταλαβὼν δὲ ἐν εἰρήνῃ ταύτην ὁ στρατηγὸς πρὸς ἄνεσιν ἐτράπη καὶ ῥαστώνην θηλυδριῶτιν. ἔχαιρε γὰρ    5
μίμοις καὶ θαυματοποιοῖς καὶ πᾶσι σκηνικοῖς ἀθύρμασι, καὶ τοῖς
τοιούτοις διημερεύων αἰσχροῖς ἠλόγει πάμπαν τῶν πρὸς εὔκλειαν
τεινόντων. Μαρκιανοῦ δὲ τοῦ βασιλέως χρηστοῦ μὲν γεγονότος,
θᾶττον δὲ ἐκβεβιωκότος, αὐτοκελεύστῳ γνώμῃ Ἄσπαρ Λέοντα διά-
δοχον αὐτοῦ γενέσθαι παρεσκεύασεν.]    10

6 σκηνῶν V

20

1. (Exc. de Leg. Gent. 7)
Ὅτι ὡς ἠγγέλθη τῷ Ἀττήλᾳ τὸν Μαρκιανὸν ἐς τὰ κατὰ τὴν
ἕω Ῥωμαϊκὰ παρεληλυθέναι βασίλεια μετὰ τὴν Θεοδοσίου τελευτήν,
ἠγγέλθη δὲ αὐτῷ καὶ τὰ τῆς Ὀνωρίας πέρι γεγενημένα, πρὸς μὲν
τὸν κρατοῦντα τῶν ἑσπερίων Ῥωμαίων ἔστελλε τοὺς διαλεξομένους
μηδὲν Ὀνωρίαν πλημμελεῖσθαι, ἣν ἑαυτῷ πρὸς γάμον κατενεγύησε·    5
τιμωρήσειν γὰρ αὐτῇ, εἰ μὴ καὶ τὰ τῆς βασιλείας ἀπολάβῃ σκῆπτρα.
ἔπεμπε δὲ καὶ πρὸς τοὺς ἑῴους Ῥωμαίους τῶν ταχθέντων φόρων
ἕνεκα. ἀπράκτων δὲ ἐξ ἀμφοτέρων τῶν αὐτοῦ ἐπανελθόντων
πρέσβεων· οἱ μὲν γὰρ τῆς ἑσπέρας ἀπεκρίναντο Ὀνωρίαν αὐτῷ ἐς
γάμον ἐλθεῖν μήτε δύνασθαι ἐκδεδομένην ἀνδρί· σκῆπτρον δὲ αὐτῇ    10
μὴ ὀφείλεσθαι· οὐ γὰρ θηλειῶν, ἀλλὰ ἀρρένων ἡ τῆς Ῥωμαϊκῆς

him not at the bottom of the scale, as military regulations require, but in the place of a soldier recently dead, whose name was Augustus. They entered Marcian also as Augustus on the roll, and thus his name anticipated the title of our Emperors, who are hailed as Augustus while they are being clothed in the purple. For it is not acceptable that the Emperor bear the title without the rank, nor again does the rank require any other title to confer dignity upon it. As a result, the power and the title are conferred together, and the rank and the title are comprehended by this one word.[104]

(Cf. Nicephorus Callistus *HE* 15,1)

## [19]

[(*Suda* A 3803)

Ardabur, the son of Aspar, a man of noble spirit who stoutly beat off the barbarians who frequently overran Thrace. As a reward for his prowess the Emperor Marcian made him general of the East. Since he received this office in time of peace, the general turned to self-indulgence and effeminate leisure. He amused himself with mimes and conjurors and stage spectacles, and, spending his days in such shameful pursuits, he took no thought at all for things that would bring him glory. Marcian, having proven himself a good Emperor, quickly passed away, and Aspar on his own initiative made Leo his successor.] [105]

## 20

1. (*Exc. de Leg. Gent.* 7)

When it was announced to Attila that Marcian had become Roman Emperor of the East after the death of Theodosius, what had happened in the case of Honoria was also reported to him. To the ruler of the western Romans he sent envoys to declare that Honoria, whom he had engaged to himself, should not be wronged at all and that, if she did not receive the sceptre of sovereignty, he would avenge her. He also sent to the eastern Romans over the appointed tribute. From both his envoys returned without achieving anything. The western Romans replied that Honoria could not come to him in marriage since she had been given to another and that she had no right to the sceptre since the rule of the Roman state belonged not to females but to males.

βασιλείας ἀρχή. οἱ δὲ τῆς ἔω ἔφασαν οὐχ ὑποστήσεσθαι τὴν τοῦ
φόρου ἀπαγωγήν, ἣν ὁ Θεοδόσιος ἔταξεν· καὶ ἡσυχάζοντι μὲν δῶρα
δώσειν, πόλεμον δὲ ἀπειλοῦντι ὅπλα καὶ ἄνδρας ἐπάξειν τῆς αὐτοῦ μὴ
λειπομένους δυνάμεως. ἐμερίζετο οὖν τὴν γνώμην καὶ διηπόρει        15
ποίοις πρότερον ἐπιθήσεται, καὶ ἔχεω αὐτῷ ἐδόκει καλῶς τέως ἐπὶ
τὸν μείζονα τρέπεσθαι πόλεμον καὶ ἐς τὴν ἑσπέραν στρατεύεσθαι,
τῆς μάχης αὐτῷ μὴ μόνον πρὸς Ἰταλιώτας, ἀλλὰ καὶ πρὸς Γότθους
καὶ Φράγγους ἐσομένης, πρὸς μὲν Ἰταλιώτας ὥστε τὴν Ὀνωρίαν
μετὰ τῶν χρημάτων λαβεῖν, πρὸς δὲ Γότθους χάριν Γεζερίχῳ        20
κατατιθέμενον.

15 τῇ γνώμῃ de Boor

## 2. (Jordanes *Get.* 36,184)

Huius ergo mentem ad vastationem orbis paratam comperiens
Gyzericus, rex Vandalorum, quem paulo ante memoravimus, multis
muneribus ad Vesegotharum bella precipitat, metuens, ne Theo-
doridus Vesegotharum rex filiae suae ulcisceretur iniuriam, quae
Hunerico Gyzerici filio iuncta prius quidem tanto coniugio laeta-        5
retur, sed postea, ut erat ille et in sua pignora truculentus, ob sus-
picionem tantummodo veneni ab ea parati, naribus abscisam
truncatamque auribus, spolians decore naturali, patri suo ad Gallias
remiserat, ut turpe funus miseranda semper offerret et crudelitas,
qua etiam moverentur externi, vindictam patris efficacius impetraret.        10

1 urbis XYZ    10 imperaret B

## 3. (*Exc. de Leg. Gent.* 8)

Ὅτι τῷ Ἀττήλᾳ ἦν τοῦ πρὸς Φράγγους πολέμου πρόφασις ἡ
τοῦ σφῶν βασιλέως τελευτὴ καὶ ἡ τῆς ἀρχῆς τῶν ἐκείνου παίδων
διαφορά, τοῦ πρεσβυτέρου μὲν Ἀττήλαν, τοῦ δὲ νεωτέρου Ἀέτιον ἐπὶ
συμμαχίᾳ ἐπάγεσθαι ἐγνωκότος· ὃν κατὰ τὴν Ῥώμην εἴδομεν πρεσβευόμενον μήπω ἰούλου ἀρχόμενον, ξανθὸν τὴν κόμην τοῖς αὐτοῦ        5
περικεχυμένην διὰ μέγεθος ὤμοις. θετὸν δὲ αὐτὸν ὁ Ἀέτιος ποιησάμενος παῖδα καὶ πλεῖστα δῶρα δοὺς ἅμα τῷ βασιλεύοντι ἐπὶ φιλίᾳ
τε καὶ ὁμαιχμίᾳ ἀπέπεμψεν. τούτων ἕνεκα ὁ Ἀττήλας τὴν ἐκστρατείαν ποιούμενος αὖθις τῶν ἀμφ' αὐτὸν ἄνδρας ἐς τὴν Ἰταλίαν
ἔπεμπεν ὥστε τὴν Ὀνωρίαν ἐκδιδόναι· εἶναι γὰρ αὐτῷ ἡρμοσμένην        10
πρὸς γάμον, τεκμήριον ποιούμενος τὸν παρ' αὐτῆς πεμφθέντα
δακτύλιον, ὃν καὶ ἐπιδειχθησόμενον ἐστάλκει· παραχωρεῖν δὲ αὐτῷ
τὸν Βαλεντινιανὸν καὶ τοῦ ἡμίσεως τῆς βασιλείας μέρους, ὡς καὶ τῆς

4-5 πρεσβευόμενοι Niebuhr    6 περικεχυμένον Bekker

The eastern Romans said that they would not consent to pay the tribute agreed by Theodosius and that if he kept the peace they would give him gifts, but if he threatened war they would bring against him men and weaponry equal to his own forces. Attila was undecided and at a loss as to whom he should attack first, but it seemed best for him first to undertake the greater war and march against the West. For there he would be fighting against not only the Italians, but also the Goths and the Franks — against the Italians to secure Honoria and her wealth and against the Goths in order to please Gaiseric.

2. (Jordanes *Get.* 36,184)

When Gaiseric, the king of the Vandals whom I have mentioned shortly before, learned that Attila's mind was set upon laying waste the world, with many gifts he urged him on to war against the Visigoths, since he feared lest Theodorid, the king of the Visigoths, would avenge the injury to his daughter. She had been married to Huneric, Gaiseric's son, and was at first happy in such a marriage. But because he was hostile towards his family, on the mere suspicion of preparing poison for him he had her ears and nose cut off and sent her back to her father in Gaul, her natural beauty ruined. Thus the wretched woman continually offered a terrible sight, and the act of cruelty, which moved even strangers, strongly urged her father to avenge her.[106]

3. (*Exc. de Leg. Gent.* 8)

Attila's excuse for war against the Franks was the death of their king and dissension between his sons over the sovereignty.[107] The elder decided to bring in Attila as his ally, the younger Aetius. The latter we saw when he was on an embassy to Rome. His first beard had not yet begun to grow, and his yellow hair was so long that it poured over his shoulders. Aetius had made him his adopted son and, along with the Emperor, had given him many gifts and sent him away as a friend and an ally.[108]

Attila, who was making his expedition for these reasons, again sent men of his court to Italy that Honoria might be handed over. He claimed that she had been betrothed to him and as proof sent the ring which she had despatched to him in order that it might be shown. He said also that Valentinian should resign to him half of his empire,

Ὀνωρίας διαδεξαμένης μὲν παρὰ πατρὸς τὴν ἀρχήν, ταύτης δὲ τῇ
τοῦ ἀδελφοῦ ἀφαιρεθεῖσαν πλεονεξίᾳ. ὡς δὲ οἱ ἑσπέριοι Ῥωμαῖοι τῆς    15
προτέρας ἐχόμενοι γνώμης πρὸς οὐδὲν τῶν αὐτῷ δεδογμένων
ὑπήκουον, εἴχετο μᾶλλον τῆς τοῦ πολέμου παρασκευῆς πᾶν τὸ τῶν
μαχίμων ἀγείρων πλῆθος.

## 21

1. (*Chron. Pasch.* pp.587f.)

Ἐπὶ τῆς βασιλείας Θεοδοσίου καὶ Οὐαλεντινιανοῦ Αὐγούστων
ἐπεστράτευσεν κατὰ Ῥώμης καὶ Κωνσταντινουπόλεως Ἀττίλας ὁ ἐκ
τοῦ γένους τῶν Γηπέδων Οὔννων, ἔχων πλῆθος μυριάδων πολλῶν.
καὶ ἐδήλωσεν διὰ Γότθου ἑνὸς πρεσβευτοῦ Οὐαλεντινιανῷ βασιλεῖ
Ῥώμης, Ἐκέλευσέ σοι δι᾿ ἐμοῦ ὁ δεσπότης μου καὶ δεσπότης σου    5
Ἀττίλας ἵνα εὐτρεπίσῃς αὐτῷ παλάτιον. ὁμοίως δὲ καὶ Θεοδοσίῳ
βασιλεῖ τὰ αὐτὰ ἐν Κωνσταντινουπόλει ἐδήλωσεν δι᾿ ἑνὸς Γότθου
πρεσβευτοῦ. καὶ ἀκηκοὼς Ἀέτιος ὁ πρῶτος συγκλητικὸς Ῥώμης τὴν
ὑπερβάλλουσαν τόλμαν τῆς ἀπονενοημένης ἀποκρίσεως Ἀττίλα,
ἀπῆλθε πρὸς Ἀλλάριχον εἰς τὰς Γαλλίας, ὄντα ἐχθρὸν Ῥώμης διὰ    10
Ὀνώριον, καὶ προετρέψατο αὐτὸν ἅμα αὐτῷ κατὰ Ἀττίλα, ἐπειδὴ
ἀπώλεσεν πόλεις πολλὰς τῆς Ῥώμης. καὶ ἐξαίφνης ἐπιρρίψαντες
αὐτῷ, ὡς ἔστιν ἠπληκευμένος πλησίον τοῦ Δανουβίου ποταμοῦ,
ἔκοψαν αὐτοῦ χιλιάδας πολλάς· εἰς δὲ τὴν συμβολὴν ὁ Ἀλλάριχος
πληγὴν λαβὼν ἀπὸ σαγίττας τελευτᾷ. ὡσαύτως δὲ καὶ ὁ Ἀττίλας    15
τελευτᾷ καταφορᾷ αἵματος διὰ τῶν ῥινῶν ἐνεχθεὶς νυκτὸς μετὰ
Οὔννας παλλακίδος αὐτοῦ καθεύδων, ἥτις κόρη καὶ ὑπενοήθη ὅτι
αὐτὴ ἀνεῖλεν αὐτόν· περὶ οὗ πολέμου συνεγράψατο ὁ σοφώτατος
Πρίσκος ὁ Θρᾷξ.
(Cf. Malalas *Chron.* pp.358f.)

6 παλάτιον P    παλάτην V

[2. (Theophanes *Chron. a.m.* 5943)

Ὁ δὲ Ἀττίλας ἐπανίσταται τοῖς βασιλεῦσι ... <τῷ βασιλεῖ>
Ῥώμης Οὐαλεντινιανῷ, διότι οὐκ ἔδωκεν αὐτῷ εἰς γυναῖκα τὴν
οἰκείαν ἀδελφὴν Ὀνωρίαν· καὶ ἐλθὼν μέχρι πόλεως Αὐρηλίας,
συμπλακεὶς Ἀετίῳ, τῷ στρατηγῷ Ῥωμαίων καὶ ἡττηθείς, πλείστους ἀποβαλὼν τῆς δυνάμεως παρὰ Λίγυν ποταμὸν ὑπέστρεψε    5
κατῃσχυμμένος.]

1 τῷ βασιλεῖ addidi    3 οἰκείαν b [ἰδίαν xyz    4 καὶ ante συμπλακεὶς habent
xyz

since Honoria had received the sovereignty of it from her father and had been deprived of it by her brother's greed. When the Romans maintained their earlier position and rejected all of his proposals, Attila pressed on more eagerly with his preparations for war and mustered all of his fighting force.

## 21

1. (*Chron. Pasch.* pp.587f.)

During the reigns of the Emperors Theodosius and Valentinian, Attila, of the race of the Gepid Huns, marched against Rome and Constantinople, having an army of many tens of thousands. Through a Gothic envoy he declared to the Emperor Valentinian, "Through me Attila, my lord and yours, has ordered you to make ready the palace for him". Likewise, through a Gothic envoy he sent the same message to the Emperor Theodosius at Constantinople. When Aetius, the leader of the Roman senate, heard the overbearing insolence of the reply[109] which Attila had made, he went off to Gaul to Alaric,[110] who was an enemy of Rome on account of Honorius, and made him his ally against Attila, since the latter had destroyed many cities of the Roman Empire. They suddenly fell upon him while he was encamped near to the river Danube and slaughtered many thousands of his men. In the fighting Alaric was struck by an arrow and killed. Similarly, Attila too was carried off by a haemorrhage from the nose as he was sleeping with his Hunnic concubine, as a result of which the girl was suspected of his murder. The most wise Priscus the Thracian wrote about this war.[111]

(Cf. Malalas *Chron.* pp.358f.)


[2. (Theophanes *Chron. a.m.* 5943)

Attila attacked the Emperors ... Valentinian, ⟨the Emperor⟩ of Rome, because he had not given him his sister Honoria in marriage. He advanced as far as the city of Orleans where he met Aetius, the general of the Romans. Having been defeated with the loss of a large part of his force by the river Ligus, he beat a dishonourable retreat.]

## 22

1. (Jordanes *Get.* 42,219-24)

Attila vero nancta occasione de secessu Vesegotharum, et,
quod saepe optaverat, cernens hostium solutione per partes, mox
iam securus ad oppressionem Romanorum movit procinctum,
primaque adgressione Aquileiensem obsidet civitatem, quae est
metropolis Venetiarum, in mucrone vel lingua Atriatici posita sinus,        5
cuius ab oriente murus Natissa amnis fluens a monte Piccis elambit.
ibique cum diu multumque obsidens nihil paenitus praevaleret,
fortissimis intrinsecus Romanorum militibus resistentibus, exercitu
iam murmurante et discedere cupiente, Attila deambulans circa
muros, dum, utrum solveret castra an adhuc remoraretur, deliberat,       10
animadvertit candidas aves, id est ciconias, qui in fastigia domorum
nidificant, de civitate foetos suos trahere atque contra morem per
rura forinsecus conportare. et ut erat sagacissimus inquisitor, pre-
sensit et ad suos: "respicite", inquid, "aves futurarum rerum providas
perituram relinquere civitatem casurasque arces periculo imminente       15
deserere. non hoc vacuum, non hoc credatur incertum; rebus presciis
consuetudinem mutat ventura formido." quid plura? animos suorum
rursus ad oppugnandam Aquileiam inflammat. qui machinis con-
structis omniaque genera tormentorum adhibita, nec mora et in-
vadunt civitatem, spoliant, dividunt vastantque crudeliter, ita ut vix       20
eius vestigia ut appareat reliquerunt. exhinc iam audaciores et
necdum Romanorum sanguine satiati per reliquas Venetum civitates
Hunni bacchantur. Mediolanum quoque Liguriae metropolim et
quondam regiam urbem pari tenore devastant nec non et Ticinum
aequali sorte deiciunt vicinaque loca saevientes allidunt demoliunt-       25
que pene totam Italiam.

Cumque ad Romam animus fuisset eius adtentus accedere, sui
eum, ut Priscus istoricus refert, removerunt, non urbi, cui inimici
erant, consulentes, sed Alarici quondam Vesegotharum regis ob-
icientes exemplo, veriti regis sui fortunam, quia ille post fractam       30
Romam non diu supervixerit, sed protinus rebus humanis excessit.
igitur dum eius animus ancipiti negotio inter ire et non ire fluctu-
aret secumque deliberans tardaret, placida ei legatio a Roma advenit.
nam Leo papa per se ad eum accedens in agro Venetum Ambuleio,

1 recessu SOB ˌdiscessu XYZ    2 dissolutionem XYZ    4 urbem A    10
moraretur SOBᵇ    11 qui HPVLSO [quae ABXY    12 aedificantur SO
13 ut erat [hoc sicut erat B    13-14 persensit SB    19 tormentorum [arma-
mentorum S    21 et hinc SXYZ    24 timore O    30 quia [quod XYZ
33 pervenit XYZ

## 22

1. (Jordanes *Get.* 42,219-24)

But Attila seized his opportunity upon the withdrawal of the Visigoths and, observing what he had often hoped for, that his enemies were divided, he thereupon confidently moved his army to attack the Romans. At the beginning of his attack he besieged the city of Aquileia, the metropolis of Venetia, which lies on a point or a tongue of the Adriatic Gulf. To the East its walls are washed by the river Natissa, which flows from Mount Piccis. Although he pressed the siege there long and hard, he made no progress at all, since from within the bravest of the Roman soldiers opposed him. The army was already muttering and wishing to leave when Attila, as he was walking around the walls deliberating whether he should break camp or remain longer, noticed some white birds which make their nests on rooftops (that is to say, storks) taking their young away from the city and, contrary to their custom, conveying them out into the country. Since he was very skilled at interpreting events, he drew his conclusions and said to his men, "Look at the birds, which can foresee the future, leaving the city because it will perish and deserting their strongholds which will fall to the danger threatening them. Do not think that this is without meaning or certainty, for they foresee events and change their behaviour out of fear of what is to come." What more did he have to say? He aroused their spirits to renew their attack on Aquileia; they built machines and brought up all kinds of artillery and quickly entered the city, which they despoiled, smashed asunder and devastated so savagely that they left hardly a trace of it to be seen. Then, growing bolder and still not sated in their thirst for Roman blood, the Huns raged through the other cities of Venetia. Milan, the metropolis of Liguria and once an imperial city, they destroyed in the same manner and condemned Ticinum to a similar fate. Then in their rampage they devastated the neighbouring districts and wrecked almost the whole of Italy.

Although Attila's mind was set upon going to Rome, his followers, as the historian Priscus tells us, deterred him, not out of consideration for the city, to which they were hostile, but confronting him with the example of Alaric, who was once the king of the Visigoths. For they feared for the fortune of their king because after the sack of Rome Alaric did not long survive but straightaway died. Therefore, while his mind was in doubt and vacillating between going and not going and he was proceeding slowly as he deliberated, a peace mission came to him from Rome. For Pope Leo in person came to him in the district of Ambuleium in Venetia, at the place where a busy ford crosses the river

ubi Mincius amnis commeantium frequentatione transitur. qui mox    35
deposuit exercitatu furore et rediens, quo venerat, iter ultra Da-
nubium promissa pace discessit, illud pre omnibus denuntians atque
interminando decernens, graviora se in Italia inlaturum, nisi ad se
Honoriam Valentiniani principis germanam, filiam Placidiae Augustae, cum portione sibi regalium opum debita mitterent. ferebatur    40
enim, quia haec Honoria, dum propter aulae decus ad castitatem
teneretur nutu fratris inclusa, clam eunucho misso Attilam invitasse,
ut contra fratris potentiam eius patrociniis uteretur: prorsus in-
dignum facinus, ut licentiam libidinis malo publico conpararet.

42 motu O    clam [clandestino O²BXY

2. (Procopius *Wars* 3,4,29-35)

Ἀετίου γοῦν τελευτήσαντος Ἀττίλας, οὐδενός οἱ ἀντιπάλου
ὄντος, Εὐρώπην τε ξύμπασαν πόνῳ οὐδενὶ ἐληΐζετο καὶ βασιλείαν
ἑκατέραν ἐπακούουσαν ἐς φόρου ἀπαγωγὴν ἔσχε. δασμοὶ γὰρ αὐτῷ
πρὸς τῶν βασιλέων ἐπέμποντο ἀνὰ πᾶν ἔτος. τότε τῷ Ἀττίλᾳ πόλιν
Ἀκυληΐαν πολιορκοῦντι μεγάλην τε καὶ ἀτεχνῶς πολυάνθρωπον,    5
παραλίαν μέν, ἐκτὸς δὲ κόλπου τοῦ Ἰονίου οὖσαν, τοιόνδε φασὶν
εὐτύχημα ξυνενεχθῆναι. λέγουσι γὰρ αὐτόν, ἐπειδὴ οὔτε βίᾳ οὔτε τῷ
ἄλλῳ τρόπῳ οἷός τε ἦν τὸ χωρίον ἑλεῖν, πρός τε τὴν προσεδρείαν
ἀπειπεῖν, ἤδη ἐπὶ μακρότατον γεγενημένην, καὶ ἅπαν κελεῦσαι τὸ
στράτευμα τὰ ἐς τὴν ἀναχώρησιν ἐν παρασκευῇ αὐτίκα δὴ μάλα    10
ποιήσασθαι, ὅπως δὴ τῇ ὑστεραίᾳ ἐνθένδε ἅπαντες ἐξανιστῶνται
ἅμα ἡλίῳ ἀνίσχοντι. ἡμέρᾳ δὲ τῇ ἐπιγινομένῃ ἀμφὶ ἡλίου ἀνατολὰς
λύσαντας μὲν τὴν προσεδρείαν τοὺς βαρβάρους τῆς ἀφόδου ἔχεσθαι
ἤδη, ἕνα δὲ πελαργὸν ἐπὶ πύργου τινὸς τοῦ τῆς πόλεως περιβόλου
καλιάν τε ἔχοντα καὶ νεοττοὺς τρέφοντα ἐνθένδε ἐκ τοῦ αἰφνιδίου    15
ξὺν τοῖς τέκνοις ἐξαναστῆναι. καὶ τὸν μὲν πατέρα πελαργὸν
ἵπτασθαι, τοὺς δὲ πελαργιδεῖς, ἅτε οὔπω ἐκπετησίμους παντάπασιν
ὄντας, τὰ μὲν αὐτῷ μετέχειν τῆς πτήσεως, τὰ δὲ ἐπὶ τοῦ νώτου τοῦ
πατρὸς φέρεσθαι, οὕτω τε ἀποπτάντας τῆς πόλεως ἑκαστάτω
γενέσθαι. ὃ δὴ Ἀττίλαν κατιδόντα (ἦν γὰρ δεινότατος ξυνεῖναί τε    20
καὶ ξυμβαλεῖν ἅπαντα) κελεῦσαι τὸν στρατὸν αὖθις ἐν χώρῳ τῷ
αὐτῷ μένειν, ἐπειπόντα οὐκ ἄν ποτε εἰκῇ ἐνθένδε ἀποπτάντα ξὺν τοῖς
νεοττοῖς τὸν ὄρνιν οἴχεσθαι, εἰ μή τι ἐμαντεύετο φλαῦρον οὐκ εἰς
μακρὰν τῷ χωρίῳ ξυμβήσεσθαι. οὕτω μὲν τὸ τῶν βαρβάρων
στρατόπεδον αὖθις ἐς τὴν πολιορκίαν καταστῆναί φασι, τοῦ δὲ περι-    25
βόλου μοῖράν τινα οὐ πολλῷ ὕστερον ἐκείνην, ᾗ τὴν τοῦ ὄρνιθος

13 ἐφόδου V    15 τρέφοντα [φέροντα V    20 ξυνεῖναί [ξυνιδεῖν V

Mincius.[112] Attila soon abandoned his usual fury and, with a promise of peace, retreated beyond the Danube by the way by which he had come. But before all he declared, emphasising it with threats, that he would cause even heavier damage to Italy unless they sent to him Honoria, the sister of the Emperor Valentinian and the daughter of Placidia Augusta, together with that part of the royal wealth which was her due. For it was said that this Honoria, while she was confined at the behest of her brother and compelled to remain chaste in keeping with the dignity of the court, secretly sent an eunuch and summoned Attila, in order that she might make use of his protection against the power of her brother — a shameful act, indeed, to obtain freedom for one's lust at the cost of harm to the state.

2. (Procopius *Wars* 3,4,29-35)

After the death of Aetius,[113] Attila, since no one stood in his way, ravaged the whole of Europe without difficulty, compelled both parts of the Empire to obey his commands and forced them to pay tribute. For payments were sent to him every year by the Emperors. At that time they say that while Attila was besieging Aquileia, a large and very populous city on the coast beyond the Ionic gulf, the following stroke of good fortune befell him. They say that since neither by force nor by any other means was he able to take the place, he had abandoned the siege, which had already lasted for a very long time, and had ordered the whole of his army immediately to prepare everything for the retreat, so that at sunrise on the following day they might all quit the place. On the following day about sunrise, when the barbarians had raised the siege and were already departing, a single male stork, which had its nest on one of the towers of the city's circuit wall and was raising its young there, suddenly left the place together with its fledgelings. The father stork was flying, and the young storks, which were not fully fledged, sometimes flew with him and at others were carried on his back; and thus they flew very far away from the city. When Attila saw this (for he was very skilled at understanding and interpreting everything), he ordered his army to remain still in the same place, saying that the bird would never have gone flying off from there with its young and with no particular destination, unless it was fore-telling that some disaster would strike the place within a very short time. Thus, they say, the barbarian army again settled down to the siege, and shortly afterwards the very part of the circuit wall which held

τούτου καλιὰν εἶχεν, ἀπ᾽ οὐδεμιᾶς αἰτίας ἐξαπιναίως καταπεσεῖν καὶ
τοῖς πολεμίοις ταύτῃ ἐσιτητὰ ἐς τὴν πόλιν γενέσθαι, οὕτω τε τὴν
Ἀκυληίαν κατὰ κράτος ἁλῶναι. τὰ μὲν οὖν ἀμφὶ τῇ Ἀκυληίᾳ ταύτῃ
πῃ ἔσχεν.                                                               30

[3. (*Suda* M 405)
    Μεδιολάνον ... πολυάνθρωπος πόλις, ἣν καταλαβὼν Ἀττήλας
ἠνδραποδίσατο. ὡς δὲ εἶδεν ἐν γραφῇ τοὺς μὲν Ῥωμαίων βασιλεῖς
ἐπὶ χρυσῶν θρόνων καθημένους, Σκύθας δὲ ἀνῃρημένους καὶ πρὸ
τῶν σφῶν ποδῶν κειμένους, ζητήσας ζωγράφον ἐκέλευσεν αὐτὸν μὲν
γράφειν ἐπὶ θάκου, τοὺς δὲ Ῥωμαίων βασιλεῖς κωρύκους φέρειν ἐπὶ      5
τῶν ὤμων καὶ χρυσὸν πρὸ τῶν αὐτοῦ χέειν ποδῶν.  (Cf. K 2123)]

4 σφῶν ποδῶν A [ποδῶν αὐτῶν GVM

## 23

1. (*Exc. de Leg. Gent.* 9)
    Ὅτι ὁ Ἀττήλας μετὰ τὸ τὴν Ἰταλίαν ἀνδραποδίσασθαι ἐπὶ τὰ
σφέτερα ἀναζεύξας τοῖς κρατοῦσι τῶν ἑῴων Ῥωμαίων πόλεμον
καὶ ἀνδραποδισμὸν τῆς χώρας κατήγγελλεν, ὡς μὴ ἐκπεμφθέντος
τοῦ παρὰ Θεοδοσίου τεταγμένου φόρου.

[2. (Jordanes *Get.* 43,225)
    Reversus itaque Attila in sedes suas et quasi otii penitens
graviterque ferens a bello cessare, ad Orientis principem Marcianum
legatos dirigit, provinciarum testans vastationem, quod sibi pro-
missum a Theodosio quondam imperatore minime persolveretur, et
inhumanior solito suis hostibus appareret.]                             5

1 itaque [namque A   suas [proprias X propria Y    4 minime [munus A
persolveretur [solveretur A

3. (*Exc. de Leg. Rom.* 6)
    Ὅτι τοῦ Ἀττήλα <τὸν> παρὰ Θεοδοσίου τεταγμένον φόρον
ζητοῦντος ἢ πόλεμον ἀπειλοῦντος, τῶν Ῥωμαίων στέλλειν παρ᾽
αὐτὸν πρέσβεις ἀποκριναμένων, Ἀπολλώνιος ἐπέμπετο, οὗπερ ὁ
ἀδελφὸς τὴν Σατορνίλου γεγαμήκει θυγατέρα, ἣν ὁ Θεοδόσιος
ἐβούλετο Κωνσταντίῳ κατεγγυᾶν, Ζήνων δὲ Ῥούφῳ ἐδεδώκει πρὸς   5
γάμον· τότε δὲ ἐξ ἀνθρώπων ἐγεγόνει. τοῦ Ζήνωνος οὖν τῶν ἐπιτηδείων ὁ Ἀπολλώνιος γεγονὼς καὶ τὴν στρατηγίδα λαχὼν ἀρχὴν
παρὰ τὸν Ἀττήλαν ἐπέμπετο πρεσβευσόμενος, καὶ τὸν μὲν Ἴστρον
ἐπεραιοῦτο, οὐκ ἔτυχε δὲ τῆς πρὸς τὸν βάρβαρον προσόδου. ἐν ὀργῇ

1 τὸν add. Bekker   9 προσόδου Hoeschel [πρόοδου codd.

that bird's nest suddenly collapsed for no reason. At that point the enemy gained access to the city, and so Aquileia was taken by storm. This is what befell Aquileia.

[3. (*Suda* M 405)

Milan, a very populous city which Attila captured and enslaved. When he saw in a painting the Roman Emperors sitting upon golden thrones and Scythians lying dead before their feet, he sought out a painter and ordered him to paint Attila upon a throne and the Roman Emperors heaving sacks upon their shoulders and pouring out gold before his feet. (Cf. K 2123)]

## 23

1. (*Exc. de Leg. Gent.* 9)

After enslaving Italy Attila returned to his own territories and threatened the rulers of the eastern Romans with war and the enslavement of their land because the tribute agreed by Theodosius had not been sent.

[2. (Jordanes *Get.* 43,225)

Attila returned, therefore, to his own lands and, as if he regretted the peace and were angry that he was not at war, sent envoys to Marcian, the Emperor of the East, threatening to devastate his provinces because what the previous Emperor, Theodosius, had promised had not been sent and in order that he might appear still more cruel to his enemies.]

3. (*Exc. de Leg. Rom.* 6)

When Attila demanded the tribute agreed by Theodosius and threatened war, the Romans replied that they were sending envoys to him, and they sent Apollonius. His brother had married Saturnilus' daughter, whom Theodosius had wished to betroth to Constantius, but whom Zeno had given in marriage to Rufus; then he had died.[114] Therefore, Apollonius, one of Zeno's associates who held the rank of general, was sent to Attila as ambassador. He crossed the Danube but was not given admittance to the barbarian. For Attila was angry that

γὰρ ἐκεῖνος ποιούμενος τὸ μὴ κεκομίσθαι τοὺς φόρους, οὓς ἔλεγεν   10
αὐτῷ παρὰ τῶν βελτιόνων καὶ βασιλικωτέρων τετάχθαι, οὐδὲ τὸν
πρεσβευσάμενον ἐδέχετο τοῦ πέμψαντος κατολιγωρῶν. ὁ δὲ Ἀπολλώνιος ἀνδρὸς ἔργον κατὰ τοῦτον τὸν καιρὸν φαίνεται διαπραξάμενος. τοῦ γὰρ Ἀττήλα μὴ προσιεμένου τὴν αὐτοῦ πρεσβείαν μηδὲ ἐς
λόγους αὐτῷ ἐλθεῖν βουλομένου, παρακελευομένου δὲ πέμπειν ἅπερ   15
αὐτῷ ἐκ βασιλέως δῶρα ἐκόμιζεν, καὶ θάνατον ἀπειλοῦντος, εἰ μὴ
δοίη, ἔφησεν· οὐκ αἰτεῖν προσῆκε Σκύθαις ἅπερ αὐτοῖς ἔξεστιν ἢ
δῶρα ἢ σκῦλα λαβεῖν, παραδηλῶν δῶρα μὲν αὐτοῖς δοθήσεσθαι, εἰ
αὐτὸν προσδέξοιντο πρεσβευόμενον, σκῦλα δέ, εἰ ἀνελόντες ἀφέ-
λοιντο. οὕτω μὲν οὖν ἄπρακτος ἐπανῄει.   20

## 24

1. (Jordanes *Get.* 49,254-55; [256-58])

Qui, ut Priscus istoricus refert, exitus sui tempore puellam
Ildico nomine decoram valde sibi in matrimonio post innumerabiles
uxores, ut mos erat gentis illius, socians eiusque in nuptiis hilaritate
nimia resolutus, vino somnoque gravatus resupinus iaceret, re-
dundans sanguis, qui ei solite de naribus effluebat, dum consuetis   5
meatibus impeditur, itinere ferali faucïbus illapsus extinxit. ita
glorioso per bella regi temulentia pudendos exitos dedit. sequenti
vero luce cum magna pars diei fuisset exempta, ministri regii triste
aliquid suspicantes post clamores maximos fores effringunt in-
veniuntque Attilae sine ullo vulnere necem sanguinis effusione   10
peractam puellamque demisso vultu sub velamine lacrimantem. tunc,
ut gentis illius mos est, crinium parte truncata informes facies cavis
turpavere vulneribus, ut proeliator eximius non femineis lamen-
tationibus et lacrimis, sed sanguine lugeretur virile. de quo id accessit
mirabile, ut Marciano principi Orientis de tam feroci hoste sollicito   15
in somnis divinitas adsistens arcum Attilae in eadem nocte fractum
ostenderet, quasi quod gens ipsa eo telo multum praesumat. hoc
Priscus istoricus vera se dicit adtestatione probare. nam in tantum
magnis imperiis Attila terribilis habitus est, ut eius mortem in locum
muneris superna regnantibus indicarent.   20

[Cuius manes quibus a sua gente honoratae sunt, pauca de
multis dicere non omittamus. in mediis si quidem campis et intra
tenturia sirica cadavere conlocato spectaculum admirandum et
sollemniter exhibetur. nam de tota gente Hunnorum lectissimi

1 exitii HPA extinctionis OB   5 affluebat HB   6 elapsus HPVLA   8 regni
O   13 turbavere HVLA   21 modis *post* quibus *habet* B   24 sollemne
B^bXYZ   electissimi B

the tribute, which he said was agreed with him by better and more kingly men, had not been brought, and he would not receive the ambassador since he scorned the one who had sent him. On that occasion Apollonius performed what was clearly the act of a brave man. For when Attila would not receive his embassy and refused to speak with him, but ordered him to send whatever gifts he had brought from the Emperor, threatening to kill him if he did not hand them over, Apollonius replied, "It is not right for the Scythians to demand what they can take either as gifts or as spoils". He meant that they would be given as gifts to them if they received him as ambassador and would be spoils if they killed him and took them away. Thus he left having accomplished nothing.

## 24

1. (Jordanes *Get.* 49,254-55; [256-58])

At the time of his death, as the historian Priscus relates, [Attila], after countless other wives, took in marriage according to the custom of his race a very beautiful girl named Ildico. At his wedding he gave himself up to excessive celebration and he lay down on his back sodden with wine and sleep. He suffered a haemorrhage, and the blood, which would ordinarily have drained through his nose, was unable to pass through the usual passages and flowed in its deadly course down his throat, killing him. Thus drunkenness brought a shameful end to a king who had won glory in war. On the morrow, when most of the day had passed, the king's attendants, suspecting something was amiss, first shouted loudly and then broke open the doors. They found Attila unwounded but dead from a haemorrhage and the girl weeping with downcast face beneath her veil. Then, after the custom of their race, they cut off part of their hair and disfigured their already hideous faces with deep wounds to mourn the famous warrior not with womanly tears and wailings, but with the blood of men. In connection with his death the following marvel occurred. Marcian, the Emperor of the East, was troubled over such a fierce enemy, and in his sleep a divine figure stood by him and showed him the bow of Attila broken that very night – for the Huns place much store by that weapon. This story the historian Priscus says he accepts upon reliable evidence.[115] For so terrible was Attila held to be to great empires, that the powers above revealed his death to their rulers as a boon.

[We shall not omit to describe a few of the many ways in which his spirit was honoured by his race. In the middle of a plain his body was laid out in a silken tent, and a remarkable spectacle was solemnly performed. For in the place where he had been laid out the best horsemen

equites in eo loco, quo erat positus, in modum circensium cursibus     25
ambientes, facta eius cantu funereo tali ordine referebant.

"Praecipuus Hunnorum rex Attila, patre genitus Mundzuco,
fortissimarum gentium dominus, qui inaudita ante se potentia solus
Scythica et Germanica regna possedit nec non utraque Romani urbis
imperia captis civitatibus terruit et, ne praedae reliqua subderentur,     30
placatus praecibus annuum vectigal accepit: cumque haec omnia
proventu felicitatis egerit, non vulnere hostium, non fraude suorum,
sed gente incolume inter gaudia laetus sine sensu doloris occubuit.
quis ergo hunc exitum putet, quem nullus aestimat vindicandum?"

Postquam talibus lamentis est defletus, stravam super tumulum     35
eius quam appellant ipsi ingenti commessatione concelebrant, et
contraria invicem sibi copulantes luctu funereo mixto gaudio
explicabant, noctuque secreto cadaver terra reconditum coopercula
primum auro, secundum argento, tertium ferri rigore communiunt,
significantes tali argumento potentissimo regi omnia convenisse:     40
ferrum, quod gentes edomuit, aurum et argentum, quod ornatum rei
publicae utriusque acceperit. addunt arma hostium caedibus ad-
quisita, faleras vario gemmarum fulgore praetiosas et diversi generis
insignia, quibus colitur aulicum decus. et, ut tantis divitiis humana
curiositas arceretur, operi deputatos detestabili mercede trucidarunt,     45
emersitque momentanea mos sepelientibus cum sepulto.]

34 dicat exitum OB     36 celebrant B     38 explicabant OBXY [celebrabant
AHPVL     44 aulicum [aliquod OB

2. (Theophanes *Chron. a.m.* 5946)

Ὁ δὲ Ἀττίλας εὐτρεπίζετο πολεμῆσαι Μαρκιανῷ μὴ ἀνεχο-
μένῳ τὸν φόρον αὐτῷ παρασχέσθαι τὸν ὑπὸ Θεοδοσίου ταχθέντα.
μεταξὺ δὲ κόρης εὐπρεποῦς τινος ἐρασθεὶς καὶ τὸν πρὸς αὐτὴν γάμον
ἐπιτελῶν οἰνωθείς τε σφόδρα καὶ ὕπνῳ βαρηθείς, αἵματος ἀθρόον
διὰ ῥινῶν τε καὶ τοῦ στόματος ἐνεχθέντος, τελευτᾷ τὸν βίον. τὴν δὲ     5
τοσαύτην αὐτοῦ δυναστείαν οἱ παῖδες τούτου διαδεξάμενοι καὶ στασιάσαντες πρὸς ἀλλήλους διαφθείρονται.

(Cf. Malalas *Chron.* 14 p.359; *Chron. Pasch.* p.558 = *Fr.* 21,1)

3 αὐτὴν [αὐτῇ f αὐτῆς m     4 ἀθρόου c     5 ῥινός y

[25]

[(Jordanes *Get.* 50,259-63)

Talibus peractis, ut solent animi iuvenum ambitu potentiae
concitari, inter successores Attilae de regno orta contentio est, et

2 contio HPV

of the whole Hunnic race rode around in a circle, as if at the circus games, and recited his deeds in a funeral chant as follows.

"Chief king of the Huns, Attila, son of Mundzuc, lord of the bravest peoples, who possessed alone the sovereignty of Scythia and Germany with power unheard of before him and who terrorised both empires of the city of Rome by capturing their cities and, placated by their prayers, accepted a yearly tribute lest he plunder the rest. When he had achieved all these things through his good fortune, he died not by an enemy's wound or through treachery of his followers, but painlessly while his people was safe and happy amidst his pleasures. Who, then, shall call this a death, which no one thinks needs be avenged?"

When they had bewailed him with such lamentations, over his tomb they celebrated with great revelry what they call a *strava* and abandoned themselves to a mixture of joy and funereal grief, displaying both extremes of emotion. They committed his body to the earth in the secrecy of night and bound his coffins, the first with gold, the second with silver and the third with the strength of iron, demonstrating by this means that all three metals were appropriate for the most powerful king of all: iron because he had subdued nations, gold and silver because he had taken the valuables of both Empires. They added the arms of enemies won in combat, trappings gleaming with various precious stones and ornaments of various types, the marks of royal glory. Moreover, in order that such great riches be kept safe from human curiosity, those to whom the task was delegated they rewarded abominably by killing them. Thus, sudden death engulfed both the one who was buried and those who buried him.] [116]

2. (Theophanes *Chron. a.m.* 5946)
     Attila prepared to make war upon Marcian, who refused to pay the tribute which Theodosius had agreed. Meanwhile he fell in love with a beautiful girl. In the midst of his marriage celebrations, when he was drunk and heavy with sleep, a haemorrhage through his nostrils and mouth killed him. His sons inherited his great empire, came to war with one another and were destroyed. [117]
(Cf. Malalas *Chron.* 14 p.359; *Chron. Pasch.* p.558 = *Fr.* 21,1)

## [25]
[(Jordanes *Get.* 50,259-63)
     When these [funeral rites] had been completed, Attila's successors began to fight over his kingdom (for the minds of the young are usually

dum inconsulti imperare cupiunt cuncti, omnes simul imperium
perdiderunt. sic frequenter regna gravat copia quam inopia suc-
cessorum. nam fili Attilae, quorum per licentiam libidinis pene      5
populus fuit, gentes sibi dividi aequa sorte poscebant, ut ad instar
familiae bellicosi reges cum populis mitterentur in sortem. quod ut
Gepidarum rex conperit Ardarichus, indignatus de tot gentibus velut
vilissimorum mancipiorum condicione tractari, contra filios Attilae
primus insurgit inlatumque serviendi pudore secuta felicitate de-    10
tersit, nec solum suam gentem, sed et ceteras qui pariter prae-
mebantur sua discessione absolvit, quia facile omnes adpetunt, quod
pro cunctorum utilitate temptatur. in mutuum igitur armantur
exitium bellumque committitur in Pannonia iuxta flumen, cui
nomen est Nedao. illic concursus factus est gentium variarum, quas  15
Attila in sua tenuerat dicione. dividuntur regna cum populis,
fiuntque ex uno corpore membra diversa, nec quae unius passioni
conpaterentur, sed quae exciso capite in invicem insanirent; quae
numquam contra se pares invenerant, nisi ipsi mutuis se vulneribus
sauciantes se ipsos discerperent fortissimae nationes. nam ibi ad-   20
mirandum reor fuisse spectaculum, ubi cernere erat contis pugnan-
tem Gothum, ense furentem Gepida, in vulnere suo Rugum tela
frangentem, Suavum pede, Hunnum sagitta praesumere, Alanum
gravi, Herulum levi armatura aciem strui. post multos ergo gravesque
conflictos favit Gepidis inopinata victoria. nam xxx fere milia tam   25
Hunnorum quam aliarum gentium, quae Hunnis ferebant auxilium,
Ardarici gladius conspiratioque peremit. in quo proelio filius Attilae
maior natu nomine Ellac occiditur, quem tantum parens super
citeros amasse perhibebatur, ut eum cunctis diversisque liberis suis
in regno preferret; sed non fuit vota patris fortuna consentiens. nam  30
post multas hostium cedes sic viriliter eum constat peremptum, ut
tam gloriosum superstis pater optasset interitum. reliqui vero germani eius eo occiso fugantur iuxta litus Pontici maris, ubi prius
Gothos sedisse descripsimus.

   Cesserunt itaque Hunni, quibus cedere putabatur universitas.   35
adeo discidium perniciosa res est, ut divisi corruerent, qui adunatis
viribus territabant. haec causa Ardarici regis Gepidarum felix affuit
diversis nationibus, qui Hunnorum regimini inviti famulabantur,
eorumque diu maestissimos animos ad helaritatem libertatis votivam

4 plus *ante* copia B    6 etiam *pro* aequa XYZ    7 quod ut [quod dum B
(quodum O)    12 quia [quam OB    quod [quae A    17 compassioni A
22 suo Rugum [suorum cuncta B    24 instrui O (instruere B)    28 parens
[pater OB    29 liberis [filiis OB

fired with ambition for power), and while they all were mindlessly eager to rule, they together destroyed his empire.[118] For the sons of Attila, who because of his lust themselves amounted almost to a people, sought to divide the tribes equally amongst themselves and to allot war-like kings and peoples like household servants. When Ardaric, the king of the Gepids, learned this, he became enraged that so many peoples were being treated like the lowest of slaves and began the revolt against the sons of Attila. Success attended him, and he erased the stain of servitude that was upon him. Moreover, through his revolt he freed not only his own people but also the others who were equally oppressed; for all readily strive for what is undertaken for the common good. They took up arms against the destruction that faced them all and met in battle in Pannonia near to the river named Nedao. There the various peoples over whom Attila held sway clashed. The kingdoms and the peoples were split asunder, and a united body became various limbs which did not act together under one impulse but raged independently now that the head was removed. Whenever the bravest of nations found their equals ranged against them they wounded each other and tore themselves to pieces. There, I think, a remarkable spectacle took place, where the Goth fought with his pike, the Gepid raged with his sword, the Rugian broke the weapons in his own wound, the Suavian was on foot, the Hun fought with his arrows, the Alan formed his heavy-armed battle line, the Herul his light-armed one. After much heavy fighting, victory unexpectedly went to the Gepids. For the sword and the alliance of Ardaric destroyed almost thirty thousand of the Huns and those who were assisting them. In this battle was killed Attila's eldest son, Ellac, whom his father is said to have loved so much more than the rest that he preferred him to all his various children in his kingdom. But fortune did not consent to the father's wish. It is known that after killing many of the enemy, he died fighting so bravely that, had his father been alive, he would have wished for an end so glorious. When he was killed the rest of his brothers fled near to the coast of the Black Sea, where, as we have said, the Goths earlier had their homes.

Thus ended the Huns, before whom it was thought the whole world would fall. So ruinous a thing is dissension, that those who terrified the world when united in their strength, perished when divided. The cause of Ardaric, the king of the Gepids, was fortunate for those who chafed at their subjection to the rule of the Huns, and it raised their spirits, long most downcast, to the joyous hope of freedom.

erexit; venientesque multi per legatos suos ad solum Romanum et a    40
principe tunc Marciano gratissime suscepti distributas sedes, quas
incolerent, acceperunt.]

## 26

(*Exc. de Leg. Gent.* 10)

Ὅτι Ἀρδαβούριος ὁ τοῦ Ἄσπαρος Σαρακηνοῖς ἐπολέμει κατὰ
τὴν Δαμασκόν· καὶ ἐκεῖσε παραγενομένου Μαξιμίνου τοῦ στρατηγοῦ
καὶ Πρίσκου τοῦ συγγραφέως, εὗρον αὐτὸν τοῖς Σαρακηνῶν πρέσβεσι
περὶ εἰρήνης διαλεγόμενον.

## 27

1. (*Exc. de Leg. Gent.* 11)

Ὅτι Βλέμμυες καὶ Νουβάδες ἡττηθέντες ὑπὸ Ῥωμαίων πρέσβεις παρὰ τὸν Μαξιμῖνον ἔπεμπον ἐξ ἀμφοτέρων τῶν ἐθνῶν εἰρήνης
πέρι, βουλόμενοι σπένδεσθαι, καὶ ταύτην διατηρήσειν ἔφασαν, ἐφ'
ὅσον ὁ Μαξιμῖνος τῇ Θηβαίων ἐγκαταμένοι χώρᾳ. τοῦ δὲ μὴ προσ-
δεξαμένου ἐπὶ χρόνῳ σπένδεσθαι τοσούτῳ, ἔλεγον ἄχρι τῆς αὐτοῦ    5
ζωῆς μὴ κινήσειν ὅπλα. ὡς δὲ οὐδὲ τοὺς δευτέρους τῆς πρεσβείας
προσίετο λόγους, ἑκατοντούτεις ἔθεντο σπονδάς· ἐν αἷς ἐδόκει
Ῥωμαῖον μὲν αἰχμάλωτον ἄνευ λύτρων ἀφεῖσθαι, εἴτε κατὰ ἐκείνην
εἴτε κατὰ ἑτέραν ἔφοδον ἥλω, τὰ δὲ τότε ἀπαχθέντα ἀποδοθῆναι
βοσκήματα, καὶ τῶν δαπανηθέντων κατατίθεσθαι τὴν ἀποτίμησιν,    10
ὁμήρους δὲ τοὺς εὖ γεγονότας παρὰ σφίσι δίδοσθαι πίστεων ἕνεκα
τῶν σπονδῶν. εἶναι δὲ αὐτοῖς κατὰ τὸν παλαιὸν νόμον ἀκώλυτον τὴν
εἰς τὸ ἱερὸν τῆς Ἴσιδος διάβασιν, τοῦ ποταμίου σκάφους Αἰγυπτίων
ἐχόντων τὴν ἐπιμέλειαν, ἐν ᾧπερ τὸ ἄγαλμα τῆς θεοῦ ἐντιθέμενον
διαπορθμεύεται. ἐν ῥητῷ γὰρ οἱ βάρβαροι χρόνῳ ἐς τὴν οἰκείαν δια-    15
κομίζοντες τὸ ξόανον πάλιν αὐτῷ χρηστηριασάμενοι ἐς τὴν νῆσον
ἀποσῴζουσιν.

Ἐμπεδωθῆναι τοίνυν ἐν τῷ <ἐν> Φίλαις ἱερῷ τὰς συνθήκας
ἐδόκει τῷ Μαξιμίνῳ ἐπιτήδειον ὄν. ἐπέμποντο μετεξέτεροι· παρε-
γίνοντο δὲ καὶ τῶν Βλεμμύων καὶ Νουβάδων οἱ τὰς σπονδὰς ἐν τῇ    20
νήσῳ τιθέμενοι. ἐγγραφέντων δὲ τῶν συνδοξάντων καὶ τῶν ὁμή-
ρων παραδοθέντων· ἦσαν δὲ τῶν τε τυραννησάντων καὶ ὑπὸ
τυράννων γεγονότων παῖδες, ὅπερ οὐδεπώποτε ἐν τῷδε τῷ πολέμῳ
ἐγένετο· οὔποτε γὰρ Νουβάδων καὶ Βλεμμύων παρὰ Ῥωμαίοις

3 διατηρήσειν scripsi [διατηρῆσαι codd.    4 τῇ... χώρᾳ Dindorf [τὴν ...
χώραν Α    8-9 Ῥωμαῖον μὲν αἰχμάλωτον ... ἥλω de Boor [Ῥωμαίων μὲν
αἰχμαλώτων ... ἥλω Α    Ῥωμαίων μὲν αἰχμαλώτους ... ἥλωσαν Niebuhr
11 τοὺς [τριακοσίους Niebuhr    πίστεων Classen [ὥστε ὧν Α    πίστεως Dindorf    18 ἐν add. Valesius

Many approached the Roman Empire through legates and were very gladly admitted by Marcian, who was then Emperor, and they received homelands which were given them to dwell in.] [119]

## 26

*(Exc. de Leg. Gent.* 10)

Ardabur, the son of Aspar, was fighting the Saracens around Damascus. When the general Maximinus and the historian Priscus arrived there, they found him in peace negotiations with the envoys of the Saracens.

## 27

1. *(Exc. de Leg. Gent.* 11)

The Blemmyes and the Nubades were defeated by the Romans and sent envoys from both their races to Maximinus to discuss peace. They wished to make a treaty and said that they would keep it as long as Maximinus remained in the area of Thebes. When he refused to accept a treaty for this length of time, they said that they would not take up arms during his lifetime. When he rejected this second proposal by the embassy, they suggested a hundred-year treaty. They agreed that the Roman prisoners, whether they had been taken in the present attack or another one, should be released without ransom; that the cattle which had been driven off should be returned; that compensation should be paid for those which had been eaten; and that they should hand over nobly-born hostages as security for the treaty. In accordance with the ancient custom they were to have the right to cross un-hindered to the temple of Isis, while the Egyptians had the care of the river boat in which the statue of the goddess was placed and ferried across the river. At a fixed time the barbarians take the statue across to their own land and, when they have taken oracles from it, return it safely to the island.[120]

It seemed to Maximinus that the treaty should be ratified in the temple at Philae. Certain men were sent there, and those of the Blem-myes and Nubades who had negotiated the treaty arrived. When the terms agreed had been written down and the hostages handed over (these were children of the rulers and of the sons of the rulers, a thing which had never happened before in this war, for children of the Nubades and Blemmyes had never been hostages amongst the Romans),

324    Priscus: Text

ὠμήρευσαν παῖδες. συνηνέχϑη δὲ τὸν Μαξιμῖνον ἀνωμάλως δια-   25
τεϑῆναι τὸ σῶμα καὶ ἀποϑανεῖν. τὴν δὲ τοῦ Μαξιμίνου τελευτὴν
μαϑόντες οἱ βάρβαροι τούς τε ὁμήρους ἀφείλοντο βιασάμενοι καὶ τὴν
χώραν κατέδραμον.

[2. (Jordanes *Rom.* 333)
... Novades Blemmesque Ethiopia prolapsos per Florum
Alexandrinae urbis procuratorem sedavit et pepulit a finibus Ro-
manorum ....]

## 28

1. (Evagrius *HE* 2,5)
Ἐπὶ τούτοις Διόσκορος μὲν τὴν τῶν Γαγγρηνῶν τῶν Παφλα-
γόνων οἰκεῖν κατακρίνεται, Προτέριος δὲ τὴν ἐπισκοπὴν ψήφῳ κοινῇ
τῆς συνόδου τῆς Ἀλεξανδρέων κληροῦται. ὃς ἐπειδὴ τὸν οἰκεῖον
κατειλήφει θρόνον, μέγιστος καὶ ἀνύποιστος τάραχος τῷ δήμῳ
ἀνέστη πρὸς διαφόρους κυμαινομένῳ γνώμας. οἱ μὲν γὰρ Διόσκορον   5
ἐπεζήτουν, οἷά περ εἰκὸς ἐν τοῖς τοιούτοις γίγνεσθαι, οἱ δὲ Προτερίου
μάλα γεννικῶς ἀντείχοντο, ὡς καὶ πολλὰ καὶ ἀνήκεστα προελθεῖν.
ἱστορεῖ δ᾽ οὖν Πρίσκος ὁ ῥήτωρ φθῆναι τηνικαῦτα <ἐς> τὴν Ἀλεξάνδρου <ἐκ> τῆς Θηβαίων ἐπαρχίας ἰδεῖν τε τὸν δῆμον ὁμόσε κατὰ
τῶν ἀρχόντων χωροῦντα, τῆς τε στρατιωτικῆς δυνάμεως τὴν   10
στάσιν διακωλύειν βουλομένης, λίθων βολαῖς αὐτοὺς χρήσασθαι,
τρέψασθαί τε τούτους καὶ ἀνὰ τὸ ἱερὸν τὸ πάλαι Σαράπιδος ἀνα-
δραμόντας ἐκπολιορκῆσαι, καὶ πυρὶ ζῶντας παραδοῦναι. ταῦτά τε τὸν
βασιλέα μαθόντα δισχιλίους νεολέκτους ἐκπέμψαι, καὶ οὕτω πνεύ-
ματος ἐπιτυχόντας οὐριοδρομῆσαι ὡς ἀνὰ τὴν ἕκτην τῶν ἡμερῶν τῇ   15
μεγάλῃ τῶν Ἀλεξανδρέων προσσχεῖν πόλει. κἀντεῦθεν τῶν στρατιωτῶν παροινούντων ἔς τε τὰς γαμετὰς καὶ θυγατέρας τῶν Ἀλεξανδρέων, τῶν προτέρων πολλῷ δεινότερα προελθεῖν. ὕστερόν τε
δεηθῆναι τὸν δῆμον τοῦ Φλώρου, τῶν στρατιωτικῶν ταγμάτων
ἡγουμένου ὁμοῦ τε καὶ τὴν πολιτικὴν διέποντος ἀρχήν, ἀνὰ τὴν ἱππο-   20
δρομίαν ἁλισθέντα, ὥστε καταπράξασθαι αὐτοῖς τὴν τοῦ σιτηρεσίου
χορηγίαν, ἥνπερ παρ᾽ αὐτῶν ἀφῄρητο, τά τε βαλανεῖα καὶ τὴν θέαν
καὶ ὅσα διὰ τὴν γενομένην παρ᾽ αὐτῶν ἀταξίαν ἀπεκόπησαν. καὶ
οὕτω τὸν Φλῶρον, εἰσηγήσει τῇ αὐτοῦ, φανέντα τῷ δήμῳ ὑπο-
σχέσθαι ταῦτα, καὶ τὴν στάσιν πρὸς βραχὺ διαλῦσαι.   25
(Cf. Nicephorus Callistus *HE* 15,8)

5 διανέστη zv    8 δ᾽οὖν codd. [γοῦν Müller    8-9 ἐς et ἐκ add. Valesius
23 παρ᾽ exp. Müller    25 ταῦτα [ταὐτῷ Bv τε αὐτῷ Müller

Maximinus' health failed, and he died. When the barbarians learned of the death of Maximinus, they recovered the hostages by force and overran the land.

[2. (Jordanes *Rom.* 333)

... and through Florus, the procurator of Alexandria, [Marcian] subdued the Novades and Blemmyes, who had invaded from Ethiopia, and drove them out of Roman territory . . ..] [121]

## 28

1. (Evagrius *HE* 2,5)

Moreover, Dioscorus was exiled to the city of Gangra in Paphlagonia, and Proterius was appointed bishop by the unanimous vote of the synod of Alexandria. When he took over his throne, the populace, who seethed with different opinions, broke out into a very great and uncontrollable disorder. Some, as was natural under the circumstances, supported Dioscorus, while others opposed them most vigorously on behalf of Proterius. As a result much damage was done.[122] Priscus the rhetor writes that at the time he had already arrived at Alexandria from the province of Thebes and he observed the populace gathering to attack the authorities. When a force of soldiers tried to stop the riot, the rioters threw rocks, put the troops to flight and, when they took refuge in the former temple of Isis, laid siege to them and burned them alive. When the Emperor learned of this, he sent two thousand newly-enrolled troops, and the wind happened to be so favourable that they arrived at the great city of Alexandria on the sixth day.[123] Then, as the soldiers maltreated[124] the wives and daughters of the Alexandrians, things far worse than before happened. Later the populace assembled in the Hippodrome and asked Florus,[125] who was both commander of the troops and head of the civil administration, to restore the grain ration, which he had taken from them, and the baths, shows and everything else which they had stopped because of the disorders which the populace had caused. Florus, therefore, at his[126] advice went before the populace and promised to do these things, and the rioting quickly ceased.

(Cf. Nicephorus Callistus *HE* 15,8)

[2. (Nicephorus Callistus *HE* 15,8)

Σέραπις δ᾽ ἐστὶν ὁ Ζεύς, ἢ ὁ Νεῖλος, ἢ Ἆπις τις ἀνὴρ ἐν
Μέμφιδι πόλει, ὃς λιμοῦ γενομένου ἐκ τῶν ἰδίων Ἀλεξανδρεῦσιν
ἐπήρκεσεν· ᾧ τελευτήσαντι νεὼν καὶ στήλην ἱδρύσαντο, ὅπου δὴ καὶ
βοῦς ἐπίσημά τινα ἔχων διετρέφετο, εἰς σύμβολον, ὡς εἰκάσαι, τῆς
γεωργίας, ὃν καὶ αὐτὸν Ἆπιν ὁμωνύμως τῷ δεσπότῃ ἐκάλουν. τὴν        5
δὲ σορὸν τοῦ Ἄπιδος ἐκείνου τοῦ ἀνθρώπου μεταγαγόντος εἰς τὸν
ναόν, Σόραπιν ἐκάλουν αὐτοῦ τὴν στήλην, ἢ καὶ Σέραπιν μεταθέσει
τῶν στοιχείων. οὗ νεὼς πάγκαλος καὶ ἄγαλμα μέγιστόν τε καὶ
φοβερώτατον ἐκ διαφόρου ὕλης ἐσκευασμένον, ὡς ἑκατέρᾳ χειρὶ
ἑκατέρου τοίχου ἐφάπτεσθαι. ἐν δὲ μέσῳ τοῦ ἀγάλματος νεὼς          10
ἕτερος πλάνης ἦν, ᾧ καὶ ξόανον ἕτερον χαλκοῦν, οὐ μέγα δὲ ἀπη-
ώρητο, οὗ τῇ κεφαλῇ ἐνείραντες σίδηρον, καὶ τοῖς τῆς στέγης
φατνώμασι μαγνῆτιν λίθον κατὰ κάθετον θέμενοι, εἰς ἀέρα τοῦτο
μεθῆκαν μετέωρον, καὶ οὔτε γῆς οὔτε στέγης αὐτῆς ἐφαπτόμενον.]

[29]
[(Jordanes *Rom.* 333)
... obitumque Attilae et Zenonis Isauri interitum, antequam
moriretur, felix conperit infelicium ....]

[30]
[1. (John of Antioch *Fr.* 201 = *Exc. de Ins.* 85)

Ὅτι τὰ τῶν ἑσπερίων Ῥωμαίων ἐν ταραχῇ ἦν. Μάξιμός τις
ἀνὴρ εὐγενὴς καὶ δυνατὸς καὶ δεύτερον ὑπατεύσας Ἀετίῳ τῷ
στρατηγῷ τῶν κατὰ τὴν Ἰταλίαν ταγμάτων δυσμενὴς ὤν, ὡς ἔγνω
καὶ τὸν Ἡράκλειον (εὐνοῦχος δὲ οὗτος καὶ τὴν μεγίστην παρὰ τῷ
βασιλεύοντι ἔχων ῥοπήν), τῆς αὐτῆς τῷ Ἀετίῳ ἔχθιστον ὄντα προ-           5
αιρέσεως (ἄμφω γὰρ τῆς ἐκείνου τὴν σφετέραν ἐπειρῶντο ἀντεισ-
άγειν δύναμιν), ἐς συνωμοσίαν ἔρχεται· καὶ πείθουσι τὸν βασιλέα
ὡς, εἰ μὴ φθάσοι τὸν Ἀέτιον ἀνελεῖν ταχέως, ὑπ᾽ αὐτοῦ φθαρήσεται.

Ὁ δὲ Βαλεντινιανός, ἐπειδὴ αὐτῷ ἐχρῆν γενέσθαι κακῶς τὸ
τεῖχος τῆς ἑαυτοῦ ἀρχῆς καταλύοντι, προσίετό τε τοὺς λόγους Μαξί-         10
μου τε καὶ Ἡρακλείου καὶ διαρτύει τῷ ἀνδρὶ τὸν θάνατον, ὅτε δὴ ὁ
Ἀέτιος ἐν τοῖς βασιλείοις ἐγίνετο κοινωνεῖν τῷ κρατοῦντι μέλλων
ἐπὶ τοῖς βουλεύμασιν καὶ προνοίας χρυσίον εἰσάγειν πειρώμενος. ὡς
δὲ τὰ περὶ τῶν πόρων Ἀέτιος προύθηκε καὶ ἀναλογισμὸν ἐποιεῖτο
τῶν ἐκ τῆς εἰσφορᾶς ἀθροισθέντων χρημάτων, ἀθρόον ὁ Βαλεν-          15
τινιανὸς ἀνακραγὼν ἀνέθορέ τε τοῦ θάκου καὶ οὐκέτι ἔφη οἴσειν

13 χρυσίον Müller [χρυσίου codd.      15 χρημάτων, ἀθρόον ὁ codd. [χρη-
μάτιον ἀθρόων, ὁ edd.

[2. (Nicephorus Callistus *HE* 15,8)

Serapis is Zeus, or Nilus, or Apis, a man of the city of Memphis. In a time of famine he supported the Alexandrians out of his own resources, and when he died they erected a temple and a statue to him. There a bull was kept which had certain marks, a symbol, it seems, of agriculture, and they called it Apis after the lord of the temple. They transferred the sarcophagus of Apis the man to the temple and they called his statue Sorapis (or Serapis, by the change of a letter). His temple was very beautiful and his statue, which was made of various materials, was so very large and terrifying that both of its hands touched the walls. Inside the statue was a second, trick shrine, in which another statue, small and of bronze, floated in the air. They had set some iron in its head and a magnet in the ceiling panels directly above, and had let the statue hover in mid-air, touching neither the floor nor the ceiling.] [127]

## [29]

[(Jordanes *Rom.* 333)

... before [Marcian] died his fortune overwhelmed that of Attila and Zeno the Isaurian, for he learned of their deaths ....]

## [30]

[1. (John of Antioch *Fr.* 201 = *Exc. de Ins.* 85)

The affairs of the western Romans were in turmoil. Maximus, a powerful noble who had been twice consul, was hostile to Aetius, the general of the forces in Italy. Since he knew that Heracleius, an eunuch who carried very great weight with the Emperor, was extremely hostile to Aetius for the same reason (since they both wished to replace his sway with their own), he made an agreement with him, and they persuaded the Emperor that if he did not act first and kill Aetius, Aetius would kill him.

Since Valentinian was doomed to come to ruin by destroying the bulwark of his own sovereignty, he approved the suggestions of Maximus and Heracleius and prepared to kill Aetius in the palace when he was about to hold a planning meeting with the Emperor and was evaluating proposals to raise money. As Aetius was explaining the finances and calculating the tax revenues, with a shout Valentinian suddenly leaped up from his throne and cried out that he would no

τοσαύταις ἐμπαροινούμενος μοχθηρίαις· ἐπ᾽ αὐτὸν γὰρ φέροντα τὴν
κακῶν αἰτίαν παρελέσθαι αὐτόν, ὥσπερ τῆς ἑῴας βασιλείας, καὶ τοῦ
τῆς ἑσπέρας βούλεσθαι κράτους, παραδηλῶν ὡς δι᾽ ἐκεῖνον οὐκ ᾔει
τὸν Μαρκιανὸν ἐκβαλῶν τῆς ἀρχῆς. τὸ δὲ παράδοξον τῆς ὀργῆς ὡς    20
ἀπεθαύμαζεν ὁ Ἀέτιος καὶ ἐπειρᾶτο τῆς ἀλόγου κωήσεως ἀπαγαγεῖν
αὐτόν, σπασάμενος ὁ Βαλεντινιανὸς τοῦ κολεοῦ τὸ ξίφος σὺν τῷ
Ἡρακλείῳ ὥρμησεν, ἤδη καὶ αὐτοῦ τὴν κοπίδα εὐτρεπῆ ὑπὸ τὴν
χλαμύδα φέροντος· πριμικήριος γὰρ τῶν κοιτώνων ἦν. καὶ ἄμφω
κατὰ τῆς Ἀετίου κεφαλῆς συνεχεῖς ἐπενεγκόντες πληγὰς ἀνεῖλον    25
αὐτόν, πολλὰ ἀνδρὸς ἔργα διαπραξάμενον πρός τε ἐμφυλίους καὶ
ὀθνείους πολέμους. τὴν μὲν γὰρ Πλακιδίαν, ἥτις τοῦ Βαλεντινιανοῦ
μήτηρ ἦν, καὶ τὸν παῖδα νέον ὄντα ἐπετρόπευσε διὰ τῆς τῶν βαρβάρων συμμαχίας, τὸν δὲ Βονιφάτιον σὺν πολλῇ διαβάντα χειρὶ ἀπὸ
τῆς Λιβύης κατεστρατήγησεν, ὥστε ἐκεῖνον μὲν ὑπὸ φροντίδων νόσῳ    30
τελευτῆσαι, αὐτὸν δὲ τῆς αὐτοῦ γαμετῆς καὶ τῆς περιουσίας κύριον
γενέσθαι. ἀνεῖλε δὲ καὶ Φήλικα δόλῳ τὴν στρατηγικὴν σὺν αὐτῷ
λαχόντα ἀρχήν, ὡς ἔγνω ὑποθήκῃ τῆς Πλακιδίας ἐς τὴν αὐτοῦ
ἀναίρεσιν παρασκευαζόμενον. κατηγωνίσατο δὲ καὶ Γότθους τοὺς ἐν
Γαλατίᾳ τῇ πρὸς ἑσπέραν τῶν Ῥωμαίων ἐμβατεύσαντας χωρίοις.    35
παρεστήσατο καὶ Αἰμοριχιανοὺς ἀφηνιάσαντας Ῥωμαίων. ὡς δὲ
συνελόντα εἰπεῖν, μεγίστην κατεστήσατο δύναμιν, ὥστε μὴ μόνον
βασιλεῖς, ἀλλὰ καὶ παροικοῦντα ἔθνη τοῖς ἐκείνου ἥκειν ἐπιτάγμασιν.
    Μετὰ δὲ τὸν Ἀετίου φόνον καὶ Βοήθιον ὁ Βαλεντινιανός, ὕπ-
αρχον ὄντα, ἀνεῖλεν, ἐκείνῳ ἐς τὰ μάλιστα κεχαρισμένον. ὡς δὲ    40
ἀτάφους αὐτοὺς ἐπὶ τὴν ἀγορὰν προύθηκεν, εὐθέως τὴν γερουσίαν
μετακαλεσάμενος πολλὰς τῶν ἀνδρῶν ἐποιεῖτο κατηγορίας, εὐλα-
βούμενος μή πως διὰ τὸν Ἀέτιον ἐπανάστασιν ὑπομείνοι. ὁ δὲ Μάξιμος
μετὰ τὴν Ἀετίου ἀναίρεσιν παρὰ τὸν Βαλεντινιανὸν ἐφοίτα, ὡς ἂν
ἐπὶ τὴν ὕπατον ἀρχὴν προαχθείη· ταύτης δὲ διαμαρτὼν τῆς πατρι-    45
κιότητος τυχεῖν ἐβούλετο. ἀλλ᾽ οὐδὲ ταύτης αὐτὸν ὁ Ἡράκλειος τῆς
ἐξουσίας <τυχεῖν> συνεχώρει· ἐκ τῆς αὐτῆς γὰρ ὁρμώμενος προαιρέσεως καὶ βουλόμενος μὴ ἔχειν ἀντίρροπον δύναμιν τὰς τοῦ
Μαξίμου ἀνέκοπτεν ὁρμάς, παραπείθων τὸν Βαλεντινιανόν, ἀπηλλαγ-
μένον τῆς Ἀετίου βαρύτητος μὴ χρῆναι τὴν ἐκείνου πάλιν εἰς ἑτέρους    50
μεταφέρειν δύναμιν. ἐντεῦθέν τε ὁ Μάξιμος ἀμφοτέρων διαμαρτὼν
ἐχαλέπαινεν, καὶ τὸν Ὀπτήλαν καὶ Θραυστήλαν μεταπεμψάμενος,

19 οὐκ ᾔει de Boor [οἰκείει aut οἰκίει S    20 [ἐκβαλῶν S [ἐκβαλὼν de Boor
25 τῆς de Boor [τοῦ codd.    26 διαπραξάμενον Müller [διαπραξάμενος codd.
28 ἐπετρόπευσε P (ex corr.) [ἐπετρόπευε S    32 Φήλικα Müller [Φίλικα codd.
38 ἥκειν codd. [εἴκειν de Boor    47 τυχεῖν addidi [κρατεῖν post συνεχώρει
add. de Boor    50 ἑτέρους S [ἐκείνους P ἐκεῖνον Müller

longer endure to be abused[128] by such treacheries. He alleged that, by
blaming him for the troubles, Aetius wished to deprive him of power in
the West, as he had done in the East, insinuating that only because of
Aetius did he not go to remove Marcian from his throne.[129] While
Aetius was stunned by this unexpected rage and was attempting to calm
his irrational outburst, Valentinian drew his sword from his scabbard
and, together with Heracleius, who was carrying a cleaver[130] ready
under his cloak (for he was a head chamberlain), fell upon him. They
both rained blows on his head and killed him, a man who had performed many brave actions against enemies both internal and foreign.
Through his alliance with the barbarians he had protected Placidia,
Valentinian's mother, and her son while he was a child. When Boniface
crossed from Libya with a large army, he out-generalled him so that he
died of disease as a result of his anxieties and Aetius gained possession
of his wife and property. Felix, who was his fellow general, he killed
by cunning when he learned that he was preparing to destroy him at
Placidia's suggestion. He crushed the Goths of western Gaul who were
encroaching on Roman territory, and he brought to heel the Aemorichans who were in revolt from the Romans.[131] In short, he wielded
enormous power, so that not only kings but neighbouring peoples
came at his order.[132]

   After destroying Aetius, Valentinian also killed Boethius the
prefect, who had been high in Aetius' favour. When he had exposed
their bodies unburied in the Forum, he immediately summoned the
senate and made many charges against the men out of fear that because
of Aetius it might support a revolt. After the murder of Aetius,
Maximus paid court to Valentinian hoping that he would be made
consul, and when he failed to achieve this, he wished to become
patrician. But Heracleius did not agree that he should have this
position. Acting from the same ambition and not wishing a counter-
balance to his own power, he thwarted Maximus' efforts by persuading
Valentinian that since he had freed himself from the oppression of
Aetius, he should not transfer his power to others. Thereupon
Maximus, thwarted in both his attempts, became angry. He summoned
Optila and Thraustila, Scythians and outstanding warriors who had

330     *Priscus: Text*

ἄνδρας Σκύθας καὶ κατὰ πόλεμον ἀρίστους, σὺν Ἀετίῳ δὲ στρατευ-
σαμένους καὶ Βαλεντινιανῷ προσοικειωθέντας, ἐς λόγους ἦλθε, καὶ
πίστεις δοὺς καὶ λαβὼν τὸν βασιλέα ἐν αἰτίᾳ ἐτίθετο τοῦ φόνου τοῦ     55
Ἀετίου ἔνεκα, καὶ μετιέναι αὐτὸν ἄμεινον ἐδίδασκεν· ἔσεσθαι γὰρ
αὐτοῖς τὰ μέγιστα ἀγαθὰ ἐν δίκῃ τῷ πεσόντι τιμωροῦσιν.

Ἡμερῶν δὲ διαγενομένων οὐ πολλῶν, ἐδόκει τῷ Βαλεντινιανῷ
ἱππασθῆναι κατὰ τὸ Ἄρεος πεδίον ὀλίγοις ἅμα δορυφόροις καὶ τοῖς
περὶ τὸν Ὀπτήλαν καὶ Θραυστήλαν. ὡς δὲ ἀποβὰς τοῦ ἵππου ἐπὶ τὴν     60
τοξείαν ἐχώρει, ἔνθα δὴ ἐπέθεντο Ὀπτήλας καὶ οἱ περὶ αὐτὸν καὶ τὰ
παραιωρημένα αὐτοῖς ἑλκύσαντες ξίφη ὥρμησαν. καὶ ὁ μὲν Ὀπτήλας κατὰ τοῦ κροτάφου παίει τὸν Βαλεντινιανόν, ἐπιστραφέντα δὲ
ἰδεῖν τὸν πατάξαντα δευτέραν κατὰ τῆς ὄψεως ἐπαγαγὼν κατα-
βάλλει· ὁ δὲ Θραυστήλας τὸν Ἡράκλειον καθεῖλε, καὶ ἄμφω τε τὸ     65
διάδημα τοῦ βασιλέως καὶ τὸν ἵππον λαβόντες ἐς τὸν Μάξιμον ἀπέ-
τρεχον. εἴτε δὲ πρὸς τὴν ἀδόκητον τόλμαν, εἴτε δὲ καὶ τὴν ἐν τοῖς
πολέμοις τῶν ἀνδρῶν δόξαν τῶν παρόντων ἐπτοημένων, ἀκίνδυνος
αὐτοῖς ἡ ἐπιχείρησις ἦν. δαιμόνιον δέ τι ἐπὶ τῷ Βαλεντινιανοῦ
θανάτῳ συνέβη. μελισσῶν γὰρ ἑσμὸς ἐπιγενόμενος τὸ ἐς τὴν γῆν     70
ἀπ᾽ αὐτοῦ ῥυὲν αἷμα ἀνιμήσατο καὶ ἅπαν ἐμύζησεν. τελευτᾷ μὲν οὖν ὁ
Βαλεντινιανὸς ἔτη βιώσας ἑπτὰ καὶ τριάκοντα.

Τὸ ἐντεῦθεν δὲ ἡ Ῥώμη ἐν θορύβῳ καὶ ταραχαῖς ἦν, τά τε
στρατιωτικὰ διῃρεῖτο πλήθη, τῶν μὲν τὸν Μάξιμον βουλομένων
παράγειν ἐς τὴν ἀρχήν, τῶν δὲ Μαξιμιανὸν ἐσπουδακότων χειρο-     75
τονεῖν· ὃς ἦν μὲν πατρὸς Δομνίνου Αἰγυπτίου πραγματευτοῦ, εὐημερήσαντος δὲ κατὰ τὴν Ἰταλίαν, καὶ τῷ Ἀετίῳ τὴν τοῦ δομεστίκου
διακονούμενος χρείαν. τῷ δὲ Μαιωρίνῳ ἐσπουδάκει καὶ Εὐδοξία ἡ
τοῦ Βαλεντινιανοῦ γαμετὴ γενομένη. ἀλλὰ τῇ τῶν χρημάτων
χορηγίᾳ ὁ Μάξιμος περιὼν τῶν βασιλείων ἐκράτει· οἰηθεὶς δὲ     80
βεβαίαν αὐτῷ ἔσεσθαι τὴν ἀρχὴν βιάζεται τὴν Εὐδοξίαν θάνατον
ἀπειλῶν. οὕτω μὲν οὖν Μάξιμος ἐπὶ τὴν Ῥωμαίων ἡγεμονίαν ἦλθε.

Καὶ Γιζέριχος ὁ τῶν Βανδήλων ἄρχων τὴν Ἀετίου καὶ Βαλεντινιανοῦ ἀναίρεσιν ἐγνωκὼς ἐπιτίθεσθαι ταῖς Ἰταλίαις καιρὸν
ἡγησάμενος, ὡς τῆς μὲν εἰρήνης θανάτῳ τῶν σπεισαμένων λυ-     85
θείσης, τοῦ δὲ εἰς τὴν βασιλείαν παρελθόντος μὴ ἀξιόχρεων κεκτη-
μένου δύναμιν, οἱ δέ φασι καὶ ὡς Εὐδοξίας τῆς Βαλεντινιανοῦ γαμετῆς
ὑπὸ ἀνίας διὰ τὴν τοῦ ἀνδρὸς ἀναίρεσιν καὶ τὴν τῶν γάμων ἀνάγκην
λάθρα ἐπικαλεσαμένης αὐτόν, σὺν πολλῷ στόλῳ καὶ τῷ ὑπ᾽ αὐτὸν
ἔθνει ἀπὸ τῆς Ἀφρων ἐς τὴν Ῥώμην διέβασεν. ἐπειδὰν δὲ ἐν τῷ     90

61 ἔνθα δὴ [ἐνθαδὶ de Boor     75 Μαξιμιανὸν [Μαιωρῖνον ?     78 διακονούμενος [διακονουμένου ?     86 τοῦ δὲ de Boor [τοῦδε codd. et edd.

campaigned with Aetius and were attached to Valentinian's household, and spoke with them. When they had exchanged oaths, Maximus blamed the Emperor for Aetius' murder and told them that it would be better to take vengeance upon him; for those who avenged the dead man would justly receive very great rewards.

A few days later Valentinian decided to go riding on the Campus Martius with a few guardsmen and the followers of Optila and Thraustila. When he dismounted from his horse and was walking off to practise archery, Optila and his followers made for him and, drawing the swords at their sides, attacked him. Optila struck Valentinian across the side of the head and, when he turned to see who had struck him, felled him with a second blow to the face. Thraustila cut down Heracleius, and both of them took the Emperor's diadem and horse and rode off to Maximus. Whether those present were stunned by the surprise of the attempt or frightened by the warlike reputation of the men, their attack brought them no retaliation. A divine sign appeared at Valentinian's death. For a swarm of bees settled on the blood which had run onto the ground, drank it and sucked it all up. Thus Valentinian died, having lived for thirty-seven years.[133]

Then Rome was in disorder and confusion. The armed forces were divided. Some wanted to make Maximus Emperor, others wished to proclaim Maximian. The latter was the son of Domninus, an Egyptian who had been a successful businessman in Italy, and he had been an attendant of Aetius.[134] Also, Eudoxia, Valentinian's wife, supported Majorian. But Maximus prevailed through his distribution of money and gained control of the palace. By threatening Eudoxia with death he forced her to marry him, thinking that then his position would be secure. Thus Maximus became Emperor of Rome.

Gaiseric, the ruler of the Vandals, heard of the deaths of Aetius and Valentinian and concluded that the time was right for an attack on Italy, since the peace treaty had been dissolved by the deaths of those who had made it with him and the new Emperor did not command an estimable force. They also say that Eudoxia, the wife of Valentinian, out of distress at the murder of her husband and her forced marriage,[135] secretly summoned Gaiseric, who crossed from Africa to Rome with a large fleet and the people whom he led. When

Ἀ<ι>έστῳ (τόπος δὲ οὗτος τῆς Ῥώμης ἐγγύς) τὸν Γιζέριχον ὁ Μάξιμος
ἔγνω στρατοπεδευόμενον, περιδεὴς γενόμενος ἔφευγεν ἵππῳ ἀναβὰς
καὶ αὐτῶν τῶν βασιλικῶν δορυφόρων καὶ τῶν ἀμφ' αὐτὸν ἐλευ-
θέρων, οἷς μάλιστα ἐκεῖνος ἐπίστευε, ἀπολιπόντων, οἱ ὁρῶντες
ἐξελαύνοντα ἐλοιδόρουν τε καὶ δειλίαν ὠνείδιζον· τῆς δὲ πόλεως     95
ἐξιέναι μέλλοντα βαλών τις λίθον κατὰ τοῦ κροτάφου ἀνεῖλε· καὶ τὸ
πλῆθος ἐπελθὸν τόν τε νεκρὸν διέσπασε καὶ τὰ μέλη ἐπὶ κοντῷ
φέρον ἐπαιωνίζετο. ταύτης μὲν οὖν ἐκεῖνος ἔτυχε τῆς τοῦ βίου καταστροφῆς, ἐπὶ τῇ τυραννίδι μηνῶν αὐτῷ διαγενομένων τριῶν. ἐν
τούτῳ δὲ καὶ Γιζέριχος ἐς τὴν Ῥώμην ἐσέβαλε.]     100

[2. (Theophanes Chron. a.m. 5946)
    Τούτῳ τῷ ἔτει Οὐαλεντινιανός, ὁ βασιλεὺς ἐν Ῥώμῃ, ὑφορώ-
μενος τὴν Ἀετίου τοῦ πατρικίου καὶ στρατηγοῦ δύναμιν δολοφονεῖ
τοῦτον, Ἡρακλείου τινὸς τῶν εὐνούχων συμπράξαντος αὐτῷ.]

[3. (Jordanes Rom. 334)
    Valentinianus autem occidentalis imperator dolo Maximi
patricii, cuius etiam fraude Aetius perierat, in campo Martio, per
Optilam et Thraufistilam Aetii satellites iam percusso Eraclio
spadone truncatus est. imperium quoque eius idem Maximus invasit
tertioque tyrannidis suae mense membratim Romae a Romanis     5
discerptus est. Gizericus tunc rex Vandalorum ab Eudoxia Valentiniani uxore invitatus ex Africa Romam ingressus est eamque urbem
rebus omnibus expoliatam eandem Eudoxiam cum duabus filiabus
secum in Africa rediens duxit.]

31

1. (Exc. de Leg. Rom. 7)
    Ὅτι Γεζερίχου τὴν Ῥώμην πορθήσαντος, καὶ βασιλεύοντος
Ἀβίτου, Μαρκιανὸς ὁ τῶν τῆς ἕω Ῥωμαίων βασιλεὺς παρὰ τὸν
Γεζέριχον τὸν τῶν Βανδίλων ἄρχοντα πρέσβεις ἔστελλεν, ὥστε τῆς
Ἰταλῶν ἀπέχεσθαι γῆς καὶ τὰς βασιλείους ἐκπέμπειν γυναῖκας
αἰχμαλώτους ἀγομένας, τήν τε Βαλεντινιανοῦ γαμετὴν καὶ τὰς αὐτῆς     5
θυγατέρας. καὶ οἱ πρέσβεις ἐς τὴν ἕω ἄπρακτοι ἐπανήεσαν· οὐδενὶ
γὰρ <τῶν> ἐπεσταλμένων παρὰ τοῦ Μαρκιανοῦ ὁ Γεζέριχος ὑπήκουσεν, οὐδὲ μὴν λύειν τὰς γυναῖκας ἐβούλετο. ὁ δὲ Μαρκιανὸς ἕτερα
πρὸς αὐτὸν διέπεμπε γράμματα καὶ τὸν πρεσβευσόμενον Βλήδαν· ἦν
δὲ τῆς τοῦ Γεζερίχου αἱρέσεως ἐπίσκοπος· τῆς γὰρ τῶν Χριστιανῶν     10

7 τῶν add. Niebuhr

Maximus learned that Gaiseric was encamped at Azestus (which is a place near Rome), he panicked, mounted a horse and fled. The imperial bodyguard and those free persons around him whom he particularly trusted deserted him, and those who saw him leaving abused him and reviled him for his cowardice. As he was about to leave the city, someone threw a rock, hitting him on the temple and killing him. The crowd fell upon his body, tore it to pieces and with shouts of triumph paraded the limbs about on a pole. This was the end of his life, having usurped power for three months. Meanwhile Gaiseric entered Rome.] [136]

[2. (Theophanes *Chron. a.m.* 5946)
    In this year Valentinian, the Emperor at Rome, becoming suspicious of the power of Aetius the patrician and general, killed him by treachery with the aid of Heracleius, an eunuch.] [137]

[3. (Jordanes *Rom.* 334)
    Valentinian, the western Emperor, through the treachery of Maximus (by whose contrivances Aetius had perished) was killed on the Campus Martius by Optila and Thraufistila, followers of Aetius who had already cut down the eunuch Heracleius. This same Maximus also seized the throne and in the third month of his usurpation was torn to pieces at Rome by the Romans. Then Gaiseric, the king of the Vandals, who had been summoned from Africa by Eudoxia, the wife of Valentinian, entered Rome and, when he had despoiled the city of everything, returned to Africa taking with him the same Eudoxia and her two daughters.]

## 31

1. (*Exc. de Leg. Rom.* 7)
    When Gaiseric had plundered Rome and while Avitus was Emperor, Marcian, the Emperor of the eastern Romans, sent envoys to Gaiseric, the ruler of the Vandals, telling him to keep away from the land of the Italians and to release the royal women whom he held captive, the wife of Valentinian and her daughters. The envoys returned to the East empty-handed, since Gaiseric paid heed to none of those sent from Marcian nor was he even willing to free the women. To Gaiseric Marcian sent more letters and as ambassador Bleda, a bishop of Gaiseric's own heresy (for the Vandals, too, are of the Christian faith).

θρησκείας καὶ τοὺς Βανδίλους εἶναι συμβαίνει. ὃς ἐπειδὴ παρ' αὐτὸν
ἀφίκετο καὶ ἔγνω τῇ αὐτοῦ μὴ ὑπακούοντα πρεσβείᾳ, αὐθαδεστέρων
λόγων ἥπτετο καὶ ἔφη μὴ συνοίσειν αὐτῷ, εἴπερ ὑπὸ τῆς παρούσης
εὐημερίας ἀρθεὶς καὶ τῶν κατὰ τὴν ἕω Ῥωμαίων βασιλέα πρὸς πόλεμον αὐτῷ ἀναστῆναι παρασκευάσοι τὰς βασιλείους μὴ λύων γυναῖ-    15
κας. ἀλλ' οὔτε <ἢ> τῶν προηγησαμένων ἐπὶ τῇ πρεσβείᾳ ῥημάτων
ἐπιείκεια οὔτε ὁ ἀπειληθεὶς φόβος μέτρια τὸν Γεζέριχον φρονεῖν
ἠνάγκασεν· ἄπρακτον γὰρ καὶ τὸν Βλήδαν ἀπέπεμπε καὶ ἐς τὴν Σικελίαν αὖθις καὶ ἐς τὴν πρόσοικον αὐτῇ Ἰταλίαν δύναμιν διαπεμψάμενος
πᾶσαν ἐδῄου· ὁ δὲ Ἄβιτος ὁ τῶν ἑσπερίων Ῥωμαίων βασιλεὺς    20
ἐπρεσβεύετο καὶ αὐτὸς παρὰ τὸν Γεζέριχον τῶν πάλαι αὐτὸν ὑπο-
μιμνήσκων σπονδῶν, ἃς εἰ μὴ φυλάττειν ἔλοιτο, καὶ αὐτὸν παρασκευ-
άσασθαι πλήθει τε οἰκείῳ πίσυνον καὶ τῇ τῶν συμμάχων ἐπικουρίᾳ.
ἔπεμπε δὲ καὶ παραυτὰ τὸν Ῥεκίμερ ἐς τὴν Σικελίαν σὺν στρατῷ.

16 ἢ add. Müller    24 παραυτὰ de Boor [παρὰ codd., exp. Niebuhr in textu,
in notis coni. τὸν πατρίκιον Ῥεκίμερ    Thompson (CR 1946 p.106) lac. ind.
post Σικελίαν

2. (Suda X 144)

Πρίσκος δὲ λέγει περὶ Χαρύβδεως· παραπλέουσι δὲ τὴν Σικελίαν πρὸς τῇ Μεσσήνῃ κατὰ τὸν πορθμὸν τῆς Ἰταλίας, ἐν ᾧπερ ἡ Χά-
ρυβδις, πνευμάτων ἐπιλαβόντων δυσαῶν, αὐτοῖς ἀνδράσι κατέδυσαν.

[32]
[(John of Antioch Fr. 202 = Exc. de Ins. 86)

Ὅτι Ἀβίτου βασιλεύσαντος τῆς Ῥώμης, καὶ λιμοῦ κατὰ τὸν
αὐτὸν καιρὸν γενομένου, ἐν αἰτίᾳ τὸν Ἄβιτον ὁ δῆμος ποιησάμενος
ἠνάγκασε τοὺς ἐκ Γαλατίας αὐτῷ συνεισφρήσαντας συμμάχους
ἀπάγειν τῆς Ῥωμαίων πόλεως. ἀπέπεμπε δὲ καὶ τοὺς Γότθους, οὓς
ἐπὶ τῇ σφετέρᾳ ἐπήγετο φυλακῇ, χρημάτων αὐτοῖς ποιησάμενος δια-    5
νομὴν ἐκ τῶν δημοσίων ἔργων, τοῖς ἐμπόροις χαλκὸν ἀποδόμενος· οὐ
γὰρ χρυσίον ἐν τοῖς βασιλικοῖς ταμείοις ἔτυχεν ὄν. ὅπερ τοὺς Ῥωμαίους πρὸς στάσιν διανέστησεν ἀφηρημένους τοῦ τῆς πόλεως
κόσμου.

Περιφανῶς δὲ καὶ ὁ Μαιωρῖνος καὶ ὁ Ῥεκίμερ ἐπανίσταντο τοῦ    10
ἐκ τῶν Γότθων ἀπηλλαγμένοι δέους, ὥστε αὐτὸν πῇ μὲν τὰς ἐμφυλίους ταραχὰς πῇ δὲ τοὺς τῶν Βανδήλων πολέμους ὑφοραθέντα
ὑπεξελθεῖν τῆς Ῥώμης καὶ ἔχεσθαι τῆς ἐπὶ Γαλατίαν ὁδοῦ. ἐπιθέμενοι δὲ αὐτῷ κατὰ τὴν ὁδὸν Μαιωρῖνός τε καὶ Ῥεκίμερ εἰς
τέμενος φυγεῖν κατηνάγκασαν, ἀπαγορεύοντα τῇ ἀρχῇ καὶ τὴν    15
βασίλειον ἀποδυσάμενον στολήν. ἔνθα οἱ περὶ τὸν Μαιωρῖνον οὐ

When he arrived and observed that Gaiseric was paying no heed to his embassy, Bleda adopted bolder language and said that even though he were puffed up by his current success, it would not be to his advantage also to rouse the Emperor of the eastern Romans to go to war against him by refusing to free the royal women. But neither the reasonable arguments first advanced by the embassy nor the formidable threats then made forced Gaiseric to a moderate course. He sent Bleda away unsuccessful and again despatched his forces across to Sicily and the neighbouring parts of Italy and ravaged them all. Avitus, the Emperor of the western Romans, also sent an embassy reminding Gaiseric of the old agreements and said that if he chose not to keep them, he would prepare for war relying on his own forces and the aid of his allies.[138] In addition he immediately[139] sent Ricimer to Sicily with an army.

### 2. (*Suda* X 144)

Priscus says about Charybdis: "[The ships] sailed past Sicily by Messene through the Italian Strait, where storm winds seized them and Charybdis sank them together with their crews."[140]

### [32]

[(John of Antioch *Fr.* 202 = *Exc. de Ins.* 86)

When Avitus was Emperor of Rome and there was famine at that time, the people blamed Avitus and forced him to send away from the city of Rome those whom he had brought with him from Gaul. He also dismissed the Goths whom he had brought as his own guard and gave them a money payment raised from public works through the sale of the bronze in them to the merchants, for there was no gold in the imperial treasuries. This roused the Romans to revolt, since they were robbed of the adornments of their city.[141]

Majorian and Ricimer also broke into open revolt now that they were freed from fear of the Goths. As a result Avitus, afraid both of these internal disturbances and of the attacks of the Vandals, withdrew from Rome and began to make his way to Gaul. Majorian and Ricimer attacked him on the road and forced him to renounce his throne, put off his imperial robe and flee to a shrine. Then Majorian's followers

πρότερον τῆς πολιορκίας ἀπέστησαν, πρὶν ἢ λιμῷ πιεσθεὶς τὸν βίον
ἀπέλειπε, ὀκτὼ ἐπὶ τῆς βασιλείας διαγενομένων μηνῶν· οἱ δέ φασι
ὅτι ἀπεπνίγη. καὶ τοῦτο μὲν Ἀβίτῳ τοῦ βίου τέλος καὶ τῆς βασιλείας
ἐγένετο.]                                                                                    20

## 33

1. (*Exc. de Leg. Rom.* 8)

Ὅτι τῶν Ῥωμαίων ἐς Κόλχους ἐλθόντων καὶ συμβαλόντων
πόλεμον πρὸς Λαζούς, ὁ μὲν Ῥωμαϊκὸς στρατὸς ἐς τὰ σφέτερα
ἐπανέζευξεν, καὶ οἱ ἀμφὶ τὰ βασίλεια πρὸς τὴν ἑτέραν μάχην παρε-
σκευάζοντο βουλευόμενοι, πότερον τὴν αὐτὴν ἢ τὴν δι᾽ Ἀρμενίας τῆς
Περσῶν χώρας προσοίκου πορευθέντες ὁδὸν τὸν πόλεμον ἐπάξουσι,      5
πρότερον πρεσβείᾳ τὸν μόναρχον τῶν Παρθυαίων πείσαντες· κατὰ
γὰρ θάλατταν ἄπορον αὐτοῖς πάνυ ἐνομίζετο τὰς δυσχωρίας παρα-
πλεῖν, ἀλιμένου τῆς Κόλχου τυγχανούσης. ὁ δὲ Γωβάζης ἐπρεσβεύετο
μὲν καὶ αὐτὸς παρὰ τοὺς Παρθυαίους, ἐπρεσβεύετο δὲ καὶ παρὰ τὸν
βασιλέα Ῥωμαίων. καὶ ὁ μὲν τῶν Πάρθων μόναρχος, ὡς πολέμου    10
αὐτῷ συνισταμένου πρὸς Οὔννους τοὺς Κιδαρίτας καλουμένους,
ἀπεσείσατο παρ᾽ αὐτὸν τοὺς Λαζοὺς καταφεύγοντας.

7 πάνυ Maltese (1977) [πᾶν codd. πάμπαν de Boor εἶναι Niebuhr

2. (*Exc. de Leg. Gent.* 12)

Ὅτι Γωβάζης πρεσβεύεται παρὰ Ῥωμαίους. Ῥωμαῖοι δὲ
ἀπεκρίναντο τοῖς παρὰ Γωβάζου σταλεῖσι πρέσβεσιν ὡς ἀφέξονται
τοῦ πολέμου, εἴ γε ἢ αὐτὸς Γωβάζης ἀπόθοιτο τὴν ἀρχὴν ἢ γοῦν τὸν
παῖδα τῆς βασιλείας ἀφέλοιτο· οὐ γὰρ θέμις τῆς χώρας ἀμφοτέρους
ἡγεμονεύειν παρὰ τὸν παλαιὸν θεσμόν. ὥστε δὲ θάτερον βασιλεύειν,     5
Γωβάζην ἢ τὸν αὐτοῦ παῖδα, τῆς Κολχίδος, καὶ τῇδε λυθῆναι τὸν
πόλεμον, Εὐφήμιος ἐσηγήσατο, τὴν τοῦ μαγίστρου διέπων ἀρχήν· ὃς
ἐπὶ συνέσει καὶ λόγων ἀρετῇ δόξαν ἔχων Μαρκιανοῦ τοῦ βασιλέως
τὴν τῶν πραγμάτων ἔλαχεν ἐπιτροπὴν καὶ πλείστων τῶν εὖ βουλευθέντων ἐκείνῳ καθηγητὴς ἐγένετο· ὃς καὶ Πρίσκον τὸν συγγραφέα    10
τῶν τῆς ἀρχῆς φροντίδων ἐδέξατο κοινωνόν. τῆς δὲ αἱρέσεως [τῆς]
αὐτῷ δοθείσης, ὁ Γωβάζης εἵλετο τῆς βασιλείας παραχωρῆσαι τῷ
παιδί, αὐτὸς τὰ σύμβολα ἀποθέμενος τῆς ἀρχῆς, καὶ παρὰ τὸν
κρατοῦντα Ῥωμαίων τοὺς δεησομένους ἔπεμπεν, ὡς, ἑνὸς Κόλχων
ἡγεμονεύοντος, οὐκ ἔτι δι᾽ αὐτὸν χαλεπαίνοντα ἐπὶ τὰ ὅπλα χωρεῖν.     15
βασιλεὺς δὲ διαβαίνειν αὐτὸν ἐς τὴν Ῥωμαίων ἐκέλευε καὶ τῶν αὐτῷ

11 τῆς exp. Dindorf [τῆσδε τῆς αἱρέσεως αὐτῷ de Boor    14 Κόλχων
Niebuhr [Κόλχου codd.

kept him under siege until he died of starvation, having reigned for eight months. Some say that he was strangled. Thus ended the life and the reign of Avitus.] [142]

## 33

1. (*Exc. de Leg. Rom.* 8)

The Romans went to Colchis, made war on the Lazi, and then the Roman army returned home. The Emperor's advisers prepared for a second campaign and deliberated whether in pursuing the war they should travel by the same route or through the part of Armenia close to Persian territory, having first sent an embassy to win over the monarch of the Parthians. For it was considered wholly impracticable to take the sea route along the rugged coast, since Colchis had no harbour. Gobazes himself sent envoys to the Parthians and also to the Romans. Since the monarch of the Parthians was involved in a war with the so-called Kidarite Huns, he ejected the Lazi who were fleeing to him. [143]

2. (*Exc. de Leg. Gent.* 12)

Gobazes sent an embassy to the Romans. The Romans replied to the envoys sent by Gobazes that they would refrain from hostilities if either Gobazes himself resigned his sovereignty or he deprived his son of his royalty, since it was not right that both rule the land in defiance of ancient custom. That one or the other, Gobazes or his son, should rule over Colchis and that war should cease there was the proposal of Euphemius, the master of the offices. Because of his reputation for sagacity and eloquence he was given oversight of the affairs of the Emperor Marcian and was his guide in many good counsels. He took Priscus to share in the cares of his office. [144]

When the choice was put to Gobazes, he chose to hand over sovereignty to his son and himself laid down his symbols of office. He sent envoys to the ruler of the Romans to ask that, since Colchis now had one ruler, he should not take up arms out of anger against him. The Emperor ordered him to cross to the land of the Romans and

δεδογμένων διδόναι λόγον. ὃς δὲ τὴν μὲν ἄριξιν οὐκ ἠρνήσατο, Διονύσιον δὲ τὸν εἰς τὴν Κολχίδα πάλαι διαπεμφθέντα τῆς τε αὐτοῦ Γωβάζου διαφορᾶς ἕνεκα πίστιν δώσοντα ᾔτησεν, ὡς οὐδὲν ὑποσταίη ἀνήκεστον. διὸ δὴ ἐς τὴν Κολχίδα Διονύσιος ἐστέλλετο, καὶ περὶ τῶν    20
διαφόρων συνέβησαν.

## 34
(Death of Marcian)

## Liber VI
## 35
(Leo Emperor)

## 36
### 1. (*Exc. de Leg. Gent.* 13)

Ὅτι ὁ Μαιοριανὸς ὁ τῶν ἑσπερίων Ῥωμαίων βασιλεύς, ὡς αὐτῷ οἱ ἐν Γαλατίᾳ Γότθοι σύμμαχοι κατέστησαν, καὶ τὰ παροικοῦντα τὴν αὐτοῦ ἐπικράτειαν ἔθνη τὰ μὲν ὅπλοις, τὰ δὲ λόγοις παρεστήσατο, καὶ ἐπὶ τὴν Λιβύην σὺν πολλῇ διαβαίνειν ἐπειρᾶτο δυνάμει, νηῶν ἀμφὶ τὰς πριακοσίας ἠθροισμένων αὐτῷ, πρέσβεις    5
μὲν πρότερον παρ' αὐτὸν ὁ τῶν Βανδίλων ἡγούμενος ἔπεμπε λύειν τὰ διάφορα λόγοις βουλόμενος · ὡς δὲ οὐκ ἔπειθε, τὴν Μαυρουσίων γῆν, ἐς ἣν τοὺς ἀμφὶ τὸν Μαιοριανὸν ἀπὸ τῆς Ἰβηρίας ἀποβαίνειν ἐχρῆν, πᾶσαν ἐδῄωσε καὶ ἐκάκωσε καὶ τὰ ὕδατα.

### 2. (John of Antioch *Fr.* 203 = *Exc. de Ins.* 87)

Ὅτι Μαιωρῖνος ὁ τῶν ἑσπερίων βασιλεύς, ὡς αὐτῷ οἱ ἐν Γαλατίᾳ Γότθοι σύμμαχοι κατέστησαν, καὶ τὰ παροικοῦντα τῇ ἑαυτοῦ ἐπικρατείᾳ ἔθνη τὰ μὲν λόγοις τὰ δὲ ὅπλοις παρεστήσατο, καὶ ἐπὶ τὴν Λιβύην σὺν πολλῇ διαβαίνειν ἐπειρᾶτο δυνάμει, νηῶν ἀμφὶ τὰς τ' αὐτῷ ἠθροισμένων · καὶ ἐπὶ συνθήκαις αἰσχραῖς καταλύσας τὸν    5
πόλεμον, ἐπανεζεύγνυεν. ἤδη δὲ ἐς τὴν Ἰταλίαν διαβεβηκότι ὁ Ῥεκίμερ θάνατον ἐπεβούλευσεν. ὁ μὲν γὰρ τοὺς συμμάχους μετὰ τὴν ἐπάνοδον ἀποπέμψας σὺν τοῖς οἰκείοις ἐπὶ τὴν Ῥώμην ἐπανήρχετο, οἱ δὲ περὶ τὸν Ῥεκίμερα συλλαβόντες αὐτὸν τῆς ἁλουργίδος καὶ τοῦ διαδήματος ἐγύμνωσαν, πληγάς τε ἐντείναντες τῆς κεφαλῆς ἀπε-    10
τέμνοντο. τοῦτο μὲν τῷ Μαιωρίνῳ τῆς τοῦ βίου καταστροφῆς γίνεται τὸ τέλος.

---

4 νηῶν e Prisco *Fr.* 36,1 l.5 [νικῶν codd.

give an explanation of what he had decided. Gobazes said that he was willing to come, but asked that the Emperor should hand over Dionysius, who had earlier been sent to Colchis over the disagreement with this same Gobazes, as a pledge that no harm should befall him. Therefore, Dionysius was sent to Colchis, and they composed their differences.

## 34
(Death of Marcian)

## Book VI
## 35
(Leo Emperor)

## 36

1. (*Exc. de Leg. Gent.* 13)

When the Goths in Gaul had become allies of Majorian, the Emperor of the western Romans, he subdued the peoples who neighboured upon his dominions, some in war and some by diplomacy, and was attempting to cross to Libya with a large army, having collected a fleet of about three hundred ships. Gaiseric, the ruler of the Vandals, first sent envoys to him in an attempt to settle their differences by negotiation. But when Majorian would not agree, he laid waste all the land of the Moors, to which Majorian's forces would have to cross from Spain, and also poisoned the wells.

2. (John of Antioch *Fr.* 203 = *Exc. de Ins.* 87)

When the Goths in Galatia had become allies of Majorian, the Emperor of the West, he subdued the peoples neighbouring upon his dominions, some by diplomacy and some by war, and was attempting to cross to Libya with a large army, having collected a fleet of about three hundred ships. He broke off the war on shameful terms and retreated. When he had already crossed to Italy, Ricimer plotted his death. Majorian had already dismissed his allies after his return and was on his way to Rome with his own followers when Ricimer's men seized him, stripped him of his purple and diadem, beat him and cut off his head. This was the end of Majorian's life.[145]

340     Priscus: Text

37

(Exc. de Leg. Rom. 9)

Ὅτι τοῦ Βαλάμερος τοῦ Σκύθου παρασπονδήσαντος καὶ
πολλὰς πόλεις δηωσαμένου καὶ χώρας Ῥωμαϊκάς, ἔπεμπον παρ'
αὐτὸν οἱ Ῥωμαῖοι πρέσβεις, οἳ αὐτῷ τοῦ νεωτερισμοῦ κατεμέμφοντο,
καὶ ὥστε μὴ αὖθις τὴν χώραν καταδραμεῖν τ' λίτρας φέρειν αὐτῷ
ἑκάστου ἔτους ἔταξαν· σπάνει γὰρ τῶν ἀναγκαίων ἔφραξε πρὸς     5
πόλεμον τὸ οἰκεῖον διαναστῆναι πλῆθος.

38

1. (Exc. de Leg. Rom. 10)

Ὅτι ὁ Γεζέριχος οὐκ ἔτι ταῖς πρὸς Μαιοριανὸν τεθείσαις
σπονδαῖς ἐμμένων Βανδίλων καὶ Μαυρουσίων πλῆθος ἐπὶ δηώσει
τῆς Ἰταλίας καὶ Σικελίας ἔπεμπεν, Μαρκελλίνου ἤδη πρότερον τῆς
νήσου ἀναχωρήσαντος διὰ τὸ Ῥεκίμερα παρελέσθαι αὐτὸν τῆς
δυνάμεως ἐθελήσαντα τοὺς παρεπομένους αὐτῷ Σκύθας (ἦσαν δὲ ἐν     5
πλείστοις ἀνδράσι) παραπείθεω χρήμασιν, ὥστε ἐκεῖνον μὲν ἀπολιπεῖν, ἀφίκεσθαι <δὲ πρὸς αὐτόν, καὶ Μαρκελλῖνον> εὐλαβηθέντα
τὴν ἐπιβουλήν (οὐ γὰρ ἀντιφιλοτιμεῖσθαι τῷ Ῥεκίμερος ἐδύνατο
πλούτῳ), τῆς Σικελίας ὑπονοστῆσαι. ἐστέλλετο οὖν καὶ παρὰ τὸν
Γεζέριχον πρεσβεία, τοῦτο μὲν παρὰ τοῦ Ῥεκίμερος, ὡς οὐ δεῖ κατο-     10
λιγωρεῖν αὐτὸν τῶν σπονδῶν, τοῦτο δὲ καὶ παρὰ τοῦ κρατοῦντος τῶν
ἐν τῇ ἕῳ Ῥωμαίων, ἐφ' ᾧ τῆς Σικελίας καὶ τῆς Ἰταλίας ἀπέχεσθαι
καὶ τὰς βασιλείους ἐκπέμπειν γυναῖκας. Γεζέριχος δέ, πολλῶν πρὸς
αὐτὸν πρεσβευτῶν κατὰ διαφόρους σταλέντων χρόνους, τὰς γυναῖκας
οὐ πρότερον διαφῆκε πρὶν ἢ τὴν πρεσβυτέραν τῶν Βαλεντινιανοῦ     15
θυγατέρων (Εὐδοκία δὲ ἦν ὄνομα αὐτῇ) Ὀνορίχῳ τῷ ἑαυτοῦ παιδὶ
κατενεγύησεν. τότε γὰρ καὶ τὴν Εὐδοξίαν τὴν Θεοδοσίου θυγατέρα
ἀπέπεμπε σὺν Πλακιδίᾳ τῇ ἑτέρᾳ αὐτῆς θυγατρί, ἣν ἐγεγαμήκει
Ὀλύβριος. τοῦ δὲ τὰς Ἰταλίας καὶ τὴν Σικελίαν δηοῦν ὁ Γεζέριχος
οὐκ ἀπέστη, ἀλλὰ μᾶλλον αὐτὰς ἐξεπόρθει, μετὰ τὸν Μαιοριανὸν     20
βουληθεὶς βασιλεύειν τῶν ἐν τῇ ἑσπέρᾳ Ῥωμαίων Ὀλύβριον διὰ τὴν
ἐξ ἐπιγαμίας συγγένειαν.

7 δὲ πρὸς αὐτόν, καὶ Μαρκελλῖνον addidi in lac. [δὲ πρὸς αὐτόν. τοῦτ' ἐποίησε
τὸν M. add. Niebuhr

2. (John of Antioch Fr. 204 = Exc. de Ins. 88)

Ὅτι ὁ Γιζέριχος ἐπόρθει τὰς Ἰταλίας βουλόμενος βασιλεῦσαι
τῶν ἑσπερίων Ὀλύβριον διὰ τὴν ἐξ ἐπιγαμίας συγγένειαν. οὐκ ἐποιεῖτο δὲ προφανῆ τοῦ πολέμου αἰτίαν τὸ μὴ τὸν Ὀλύβριον ἐς τὰ τῆς

## 37

(*Exc. de Leg. Rom.* 9)

When Valamir the Scythian broke the treaty and ravaged many cities and much Roman territory, the Romans sent envoys to him.[146] They upbraided him for his revolt and agreed to pay him three hundred pounds of gold each year so that he not overrun the land again. For he said that his people had turned to war because of lack of necessities.

## 38

1. (*Exc. de Leg. Rom.* 10)

Since Gaiseric no longer kept the treaty which he had made with Majorian, he sent a force of Vandals and Moors to ravage Italy and Sicily. Marcellinus had already left the island because Ricimer, wishing to drain off his strength, had won over with money his Scythian followers, who were in the majority.[147] As a result they left Marcellinus and went over <to Ricimer, and Marcellinus,> as a precaution against the plot (since he could not compete with Ricimer's wealth), withdrew from Sicily. Embassies were, therefore, sent to Gaiseric, both from Ricimer, warning him not to ignore the treaty, and from the ruler of the eastern Romans,[148] telling him to keep away from Sicily and Italy and return the royal women. Although many embassies were sent to him at various times, Gaiseric did not free the women until he had betrothed Valentinian's elder daughter, whose name was Eudocia, to his son Huneric. Then he dismissed Eudoxia, the daughter of Theodosius, and Placidia, her other daughter, who was married to Olybrius. He did not end his devastation of Italy and Sicily, but ravaged it even more, since because of his kinship by marriage he wished Olybrius to be Emperor of the western Romans after Majorian.[149]

2. (John of Antioch *Fr.* 204 = *Exc. de Ins.* 88)

Gaiseric ravaged Italy wishing Olybrius to be Emperor of the West because of his kinship by marriage.[150] He did not advertise as his reason that Olybrius had not become the Emperor of the West, but

342    Priscus: Text

ἑσπερίας διαβῆναι βασίλεια, ἀλλὰ τὸ μὴ τὴν Βαλεντιανοῦ καὶ
Ἀετίου δεδόσθαι αὐτῷ περιουσίαν, τὴν μὲν ὀνόματι Εὐδοκίας, ἣν ὁ     5
τούτου παῖς εἶχε, τὴν δὲ ὡς Γαυδεντίου παιδὸς διάγοντος παρ' αὐτῷ.
(Cf. Procopius Wars 3,6,6 = Fr. 53,3)

39

1. (Exc. de Leg. Gent. 14)
    Ὅτι οἱ ἑσπέριοι Ῥωμαῖοι ἐς δέος ἐλθόντες περὶ Μαρκελλίνου,
μήποτε αὐξανομένης αὐτῷ τῆς δυνάμεως καὶ ἐπ' αὐτοὺς ἀγάγοι τὸν
πόλεμον, διαφόρως ταραττομένων αὐτοῖς τῶν πραγμάτων, τοῦτο
μὲν ἐκ Βανδίλων, τοῦτο δὲ κἀκ Αἰγιδίου, ἀνδρὸς ἐκ Γαλατῶν μὲν
τῶν πρὸς τῇ ἑσπέρᾳ ὁρμωμένου, τῷ δὲ Μαιοριανῷ συστρατευσα-     5
μένου καὶ πλείστην ἀμφ' αὐτὸν ἔχοντος δύναμιν καὶ χαλεπαίνοντος
διὰ τὴν τοῦ βασιλέως ἀναίρεσιν· ὂν τοῦ πρὸς Ἰταλιώτας τέως
ἀπήγαγε πολέμου ἡ πρὸς Γότθους τοὺς ἐν Γαλατίᾳ διαφορά. περὶ
γὰρ τῆς ὁμόρου πρὸς ἐκείνους διαφιλονεικῶν γῆς καρτερῶς ἐμάχετο
καὶ ἀνδρὸς ἔργα μέγιστα ἐν ἐκείνῳ ἐπεδείξατο τῷ πολέμῳ. τούτων     10
δὴ ἕνεκα <οἱ> ἑσπέριοι Ῥωμαῖοι παρὰ τοὺς ἑῴους πρέσβεις
ἔστειλαν, ὥστε αὐτοῖς καὶ τὸν Μαρκελλῖνον καὶ τοὺς Βανδίλους
διαλλάξαι. καὶ πρὸς μὲν τὸν Μαρκελλῖνον Φύλαρχος σταλεὶς ἔπεισεν
αὐτὸν κατὰ Ῥωμαίων ὅπλα μὴ κινεῖν, ὁ δὲ παρὰ τοὺς Βανδίλους
διαβὰς ἄπρακτος ἀνεχώρει, τοῦ Γεζερίχου μὴ ἄλλως τὸν πόλεμον     15
καταθήσειν ἀπειλοῦντος, εἰ μή γε αὐτῷ <ἡ> τοῦ Βαλεντιανοῦ καὶ
Ἀετίου περιουσία δοθῇ. καὶ γὰρ καὶ παρὰ τῶν ἑῴων Ῥωμαίων
ἐκεκόμιστο μοῖραν τῆς Βαλεντιανοῦ περιουσίας ὀνόματι Εὐδοκίας
τῆς τῷ Ὀνωρίχῳ γεγαμημένης. διὸ δι' ἔτους ἑκάστου ταύτην τοῦ
πολέμου πρόφασιν ποιούμενος εὐθὺς ἦρος ἀρχομένου σὺν στόλῳ τὴν     20
ἐκστρατείαν ἐποιεῖτο ἐπί τε Σικελίαν καὶ τὰς Ἰταλίας· καὶ ταῖς μὲν
πόλεσιν, ἐν αἷς μάχιμον δύναμιν τῶν Ἰταλιωτῶν εἶναι συνέβαινεν,
οὐ ῥαδίως προσεφέρετο, καταλαμβάνων δὲ χωρία, ἐν οἷς μὴ ἔτυχεν
οὖσα ἀντίπαλος δύναμις, ἐδῄου τε καὶ ἠνδραποδίζετο. οὐ γὰρ πρὸς
πάντα τἀποβάσιμα τοῖς Βανδίλοις μέρη οἱ Ἰταλιῶται ἀρκεῖν ἐδύ-     25
ναντο, πλήθει τῶν πολεμίων βιαζόμενοι καὶ τῷ μὴ παρεῖναι σφίσι
ναυτικὴν δύναμιν, ἣν παρὰ τῶν ἑῴων αἰτοῦντες οὐκ ἐτύγχανον διὰ
τὰς πρὸς Γεζέριχον ἐκείνοις τεθείσας σπονδάς· ὅπερ ἔτι μάλιστα
ἐκάκωσε τὰ ἐν τῇ ἑσπέρᾳ Ῥωμαίων πράγματα διὰ τὸ διῃρῆσθαι τὴν
βασιλείαν.     30

4 κἀκ Αἰγιδίου de Boor [καὶ νεγιδίου cod. καὶ Αἰγιδίου Niebuhr     11 οἱ add.
Bekker   16 ἡ add. Müller   19 δι' Valesius [δὴ codd.

rather that he himself had not been given the property of Valentinian and of Aetius, the former in the name of Eudocia, who was married to his son, the latter because Gaudentius, Aetius' son, was living with him.[151]    (Cf. Procopius *Wars* 3,6,6 = *Fr.* 53,3)

## 39

1. (*Exc. de Leg. Gent.* 14)

The western Romans came to fear that Marcellinus, whose strength was increasing,[152] would make war upon them while their affairs were troubled in a variety of ways, both by the Vandals and by Aegidius, a man sprung from the western Gauls.[153] He had a large force and, having been a fellow soldier of Majorian's, was angry at the murder of the Emperor. In the meanwhile his disagreement with the Goths in Gaul deterred him from war against the Italians. For, being in dispute with them over some border land, he fought hard against them and in the war performed deeds of the greatest bravery. For these reasons the western Romans sent envoys to the East to reconcile Marcellinus and the Vandals to them. Phylarchus was sent to Marcellinus and persuaded him not to attack the Romans. But when he had crossed to the Vandals, he returned having achieved nothing, since Gaiseric refused to end the war unless the property of Valentinian and Aetius were given to him. (From the eastern Romans he had acquired a part of the property of Valentinian in the name of Eudocia, who had married Huneric.)[154] Therefore, using this as a reason for hostilities, every year at the beginning of spring he descended upon Sicily and Italy with his fleet. He did not readily attack the cities which the Italians had garrisoned, but seized the places in which there was no adequate force, laid them waste and enslaved them.[155] The Italians were unable to bring help to all the points at which the Vandals could land, being hampered by the numbers of their enemies and by their lack of a fleet. The latter they sought from the eastern Romans but did not receive it because of the treaty which they had with the Vandals. Because of the division of the Empire this fact resulted in great harm for the western Romans.

2. (Stephanus Byzantius *s.v.* Σαλῶναι)

Σαλῶναι, πόλις Δαλματίας, ὧν Σαλωνεὺς τὸ ἐθνικὸν, ὡς Πρίσκος ἐν ἕκτῳ.

## 40

1. (*Exc. de Leg. Gent.* 14)

Ἐπρεσβεύσαντο δὲ κατ' ἐκεῖνον τὸν χρόνον κατὰ τοὺς ἑῴους Ῥωμαίους Σαράγουροι καὶ Οὔρωγοι καὶ Ὀνόγουροι, ἔθνη ἐξαναστάντα τῶν οἰκείων ἠθῶν, Σαβίρων ἐς μάχην σφίσιν ἐληλυθότων, οὓς ἐξήλασαν Ἄβαροι μετανάσται γενόμενοι ὑπὸ ἐθνῶν οἰκούντων μὲν τὴν παρωκεανῖτιν ἀκτήν, ὥσπερ καὶ οἱ Σαράγουροι ἐλαθέντες      5
κατὰ ζήτησιν γῆς πρὸς τοῖς Ἀκατίροις Οὔννοις ἐγένοντο, καὶ μάχας πρὸς ἐκείνους πολλὰς συστησάμενοι τό τε φῦλον κατηγωνίσαντο καὶ πρὸς Ῥωμαίους ἀφίκοντο, τυχεῖν τῆς αὐτῶν βουλόμενοι ἐπιτηδειότητος. βασιλεὺς οὖν καὶ οἱ ἀμφ' αὐτὸν φιλοφρονησάμενοι καὶ δῶρα δόντες αὐτοὺς ἀπέπεμψαν.      10

1 κατὰ codd. [παρὰ de Boor      3 ἠθῶν Cantoclarius [ἐθῶν A ἐθνῶν X
5 παρωκεανῖτιν Suda [παρωκεανίτιδα A

2. (*Suda* A 18)

Ὅτι οἱ Ἀβάρις οὗτοι ἐξήλασαν Σαβίωρας, μετανάσται γενόμενοι ὑπὸ ἐθνῶν οἰκούντων μὲν τὴν παρωκεανῖτιν ἀκτήν, τὴν δὲ χώραν ἀπολιπόντων διὰ τὸ ἐξ ἀναχύσεως τοῦ Ὠκεανοῦ ὁμιχλῶδες γινόμενον, καὶ γρυπῶν δὲ πλῆθος ἀναφανέν· ὅπερ ἦν λόγος μὴ πρότερον παύσασθαι πρὶν ἢ βορὰν ποιῆσαι τὸ τῶν ἀνθρώπων γένος. διὸ δὴ ὑπὸ τῶνδε ἐλαυνόμενοι τῶν δεινῶν τοῖς πλησιοχώροις ἐνέ      5
βαλλον· καὶ τῶν ἐπιόντων δυνατωτέρων ὄντων οἱ τὴν ἔφοδον <οὐχ> ὑφιστάμενοι μετανίσταντο, ὥσπερ καὶ οἱ Σαράγουροι ἐλαθέντες πρὸς τοῖς Ἀκατίροις Οὔννοις ἐγένοντο.      (Cf. A 820, Σ 111)

1 ἐξήλασαν [ἐξῴκισαν M      3 ἀπολιπόντων AGTB [καταλιπόντων
SMB      ἀναχύσεως [ἀναλωθῆναι ὑπὸ M      7 δυνατωτέρων ὄντων AGT [ἐμ
φανισθέντων M      οὐχ add. Müller [μὴ A

## 41

1. (*Exc. de Leg. Gent.* 15)

Ὅτι στασιαζόντων τῶν φυγάδων ἐθνῶν κατὰ τοὺς κατὰ τὴν ἕω Ῥωμαίους, παρὰ τῶν Ἰταλῶν πρεσβεία ἀφίκετο λέγουσα ὡς οὐχ ὑποστήσονται, εἰ μή γε σφίσι τοὺς Βανδίλους διαλλάξοιεν. ἀφίκετο δὲ καὶ παρὰ τοῦ Περσῶν μονάρχου, τῶν τε παρ' αὐτοὺς καταφευγόντων ἐκ τοῦ σφετέρου ἔθνους αἰτίαν ἔχουσα καὶ τῶν Μάγων [καὶ] τῶν ἐν      5

5 καὶ exp. Valesius

2. (Stephanus Byzantius *s.v.* Σαλῶναι)

*Salonae*: a city of Dalmatia, the adjective from which is *Saloneus*, according to Priscus in his sixth book.

## 40

1. (*Exc. de Leg. Gent.* 14)

At this time the Saraguri, Urogi and the Onoguri sent envoys to the eastern Romans. These tribes had left their native lands when the Sabiri attacked them. The latter had been driven out by the Avars who had in turn been displaced by the tribes who lived by the shore of the Ocean. In the same way, the Saraguri, driven to search for land, came into contact with the Akatirian Huns and, after engaging them in many battles, defeated that tribe. The Saraguri then approached the Romans, wishing to win their friendship, and the Emperor and his courtiers received them in a kindly manner, gave them gifts and sent them away.[156]

2. (*Suda* A 18)

These Avars drove out the Sabinores having themselves been displaced by the tribes who lived by the shore of the Ocean. The latter had left their land on account of the mist which came from an inundation of the Ocean and because a flock of gryphons had appeared. It is said that they would not leave until they had eaten the whole race of men. Therefore, driven out by these evils, the ocean dwellers fell upon their neighbours, and since the attackers were more powerful, the Avars, who could not resist their onset, were displaced. In the same way the Saraguri were driven out and came into contact with the Akatirian Huns.[157]    (Cf. A 820, Σ 111)

## 41

1. (*Exc. de Leg. Gent.* 15)

While the fugitive peoples were at odds with the eastern Romans,[158] an embassy came from the Italians saying that they could not continue to resist unless the eastern Romans reconciled them with the Vandals. An embassy also arrived from the Persian monarch which complained to the Romans both about the Persians who were fleeing to the Romans and about the Magi who had lived from old in Roman

τῇ Ῥωμαίων γῇ ἐκ παλαιῶν οἰκούντων χρόνων, ὡς ἀπάγειν αὐτοὺς
τῶν πατρίων ἐθῶν καὶ νόμων ἐθέλοντες καὶ τῆς περὶ τὸ θεῖον
ἁγιστείας παρενοχλοῦσί τε καὶ ἐς ἀεὶ ἀνακαλεῖσθαι κατὰ τὸν θεσμὸν
οὐ συγχωροῦσι τὸ παρ' αὐτοῖς ἄσβεστον καλούμενον πῦρ· καὶ ὡς χρὴ
τοῦ Ἰουροειπαὰχ φρουρίου ἐπὶ τῶν Κασπίων κειμένου πυλῶν χρή-    10
ματα χορηγοῦντας Ῥωμαίους ποιεῖσθαι ἐπιμέλειαν ἢ γοῦν τοὺς
φρουρήσοντας αὐτὸ στρατιώτας στέλλειν, καὶ μὴ μόνους <σφᾶς>
δαπάνῃ καὶ φυλακῇ τοῦ χωρίου βαρύνεσθαι· εἰ γὰρ ἐνδοῖεν, οὐκ εἰς
Πέρσας μόνους, ἀλλὰ καὶ εἰς Ῥωμαίους τὰ ἐκ τῶν παροικούντων
ἐθνῶν κακὰ ῥᾳδίως ἀφικέσθαι. χρῆναι δὲ αὐτοὺς ἔλεγον καὶ χρή-    15
μασιν ἐπικουρεῖν ἐπὶ τῷ πρὸς Οὔννους πολέμῳ τοὺς Κιδαρίτας
λεγομένους· ἔσεσθαι γὰρ σφίσιν αὐτῶν νικώντων ὄνησιν, μὴ συγχω-
ρουμένου τοῦ ἔθνους καὶ εἰς τὴν Ῥωμαϊκὴν διαβαίνειν ἐπικράτειαν.
πάντων δὲ ἕνεκα Ῥωμαίων ἀποκρυψαμένων στέλλειν τὸν διαλεξόμενον τῷ Παρθυαίῳ μονάρχῃ· μήτε γὰρ φυγάδας εἶναι παρὰ σφίσι    20
μήτε παρενοχλεῖσθαι τοὺς Μάγους τῆς θρησκείας πέρι· τὴν φυλακὴν
δὲ τοῦ Ἰουροειπαὰχ φρουρίου καὶ τὸν πόλεμον τὸν πρὸς τοὺς Οὔννους
ὑπὲρ σφῶν αὐτῶν ἀναδεδεγμένους μὴ δικαίως χρήματα αἰτεῖν παρ'
αὐτῶν. ἐπρεσβεύετο δὲ παρὰ μὲν Βανδίλους ὑπὲρ Ἰταλῶν Τατιανὸς
ἐν τῇ τῶν πατρικίων ἀξίᾳ καταλεγόμενος, παρὰ δὲ Πέρσας Κων-    25
στάντιος, τρίτον μὲν τὴν ὕπαρχον λαχὼν ἀρχήν, πρὸς δὲ τῇ ὑπατικῇ
ἀξίᾳ καὶ τῆς πατρικιότητος τυχών.

8 ἁγιστείας παρενοχλοῦσί τε καὶ ἐς ἀεὶ ἀνακαλεῖσθαι scripsi [ἁγιστείας. παρα-
χωροῦσι δὲ καὶ ἐς ἀεὶ ἀνακαλεῖσθαι A    ἁγιστείας παρενοχλοῦσί τε ἐς ἀεὶ καὶ
ἀνακαλεῖσθαι Bekker, Niebuhr    12 σφᾶς add. Bekker    26 ὕπαρχον codd.
[ὕπατον ex Fr. 41,2 l.3 Maltese (1977)

2. (Exc. de Leg. Rom. 11)

Ὅτι ἐπὶ Λέοντος βασιλέως Ῥωμαίων ἐπρεσβεύετο παρὰ μὲν
Βανδίλους ὑπὲρ Ἰταλῶν Τατιανὸς ἐν τῇ τῶν πατρικίων ἀξίᾳ καταλεγόμενος, παρὰ δὲ Πέρσας Κωνστάντιος, τρίτον μὲν <τὴν> ὕπαρχον
λαχὼν ἀρχήν, πρὸς δὲ τῇ ὑπατικῇ ἀξίᾳ καὶ τῆς πατρικιότητος τυχών.
καὶ Τατιανὸς μὲν ἐκ Βανδίλων εὐθὺς ἄπρακτος ἀνεχώρησεν, τῶν    5
αὐτοῦ ὑπὸ τοῦ Γεζερίχου μὴ παραδεχθέντων λόγων· ὁ δὲ Κωνστάντιος τῇ Ἐδέσῃ, Ῥωμαϊκῇ μὲν πόλει, προσοίκῳ δὲ τῆς Περσῶν
χώρας, ἐγκατέμεινεν, ἐσδέξασθαι αὐτὸν ἐπὶ πολὺ διαναβαλλομένου
τοῦ Παρθυαίου μονάρχου.

3 τὴν add. Niebuhr    ὕπαρχον Müller ex Fr. 41,1 l.26 [ὕπατον codd. def.
Maltese (1977)    4 λαχὼν Dindorf [λαβὼν codd.

territory. The embassy alleged that the Romans, wishing to turn the Magi from their ancestral customs, laws and form of worship, harassed them and did not allow the fire, which they call unquenchable, to be kept burning continually according to their law.[159] It also said that the Romans, through a contribution of money, should show interest in the fortress of Iouroeipaach, situated at the Caspian Gates, or they should at least send soldiers to guard it. It was not right that the Persians alone should be burdened by the expense and the garrisoning of the place, since if they did not make these expenditures, the neighbouring peoples would easily inflict damage not only upon the Persians but upon the Romans also. They further said that the Romans should help with money in the war against the so-called Kidarite Huns, since a Persian victory would be advantageous to the Romans insofar as that people would be prevented from penetrating to the Roman Empire also. The Romans replied that they would send someone to discuss all these issues with the Parthian monarch. They claimed that there were no fugitives amongst them and that the Magi were not harassed on account of their religion, and said that since the Persians had undertaken the guarding of the fortress of Iouroeipaach and the war against the Huns on their own behalf, it was not right that they demand money from the Romans.

Tatian, who held the rank of patrician, was sent as ambassador to the Vandals on behalf of the Italians, while Constantius, who was prefect for the third time and a patrician as well as a consular, was sent to the Persians.[160]

## 2. (*Exc. de Leg. Rom.* 11)

When Leo was Emperor of the Romans, Tatian was sent as ambassador to the Vandals on behalf of the Italians, while Constantius, who was prefect for the third time and a patrician as well as a consular, was sent to the Persians. Tatian returned immediately from the Vandals having accomplished nothing since Gaiseric would not give him an audience. But Constantius waited at Edessa, a Roman city close to Persian territory, since the Parthian monarch delayed receiving him for a long time.[161]

348    Priscus: Text

3. (Exc. de Leg. Rom. 12)

Ὅτι τὸν Κωνστάντιον τὸν πρεσβευτὴν ἐν τῇ Ἐδέσῃ χρόνον
ἐπιμείναντα, ὡς εἴρηταί μοι, τῆς πρεσβείας πέρι, τότε ἐδέξατο ὁ
Περσῶν μόναρχος ἐς τὴν σφετέραν καὶ παρ᾽ αὐτὸν ἀφικέσθαι προσέταξεν, οὐκ ἐν ταῖς πόλεσιν, ἀλλὰ γὰρ ἐν τοῖς μεθορίοις αὐτῶν τε
καὶ Οὔννων τῶν Κιδαριτῶν τὰς διατριβὰς ποιούμενος, <πρὸς οὓς    5
πόλεμος> αὐτῷ συνίστατο αἰτίαν ἔχων ὡς τοὺς φόρους τῶν Οὔννων
μὴ κομιζομένων, οὓς οἱ πάλαι μὲν τῶν Περσῶν καὶ Πάρθων βασιλεύοντες ἔθεντο. οὐ ὁ πατὴρ τὴν τοῦ φόρου ἀπαρνησάμενος ἀπαγωγὴν τὸν πόλεμον ὑπεδέξατο καὶ τοῦτον μετὰ τῆς βασιλείας παρέ-
πεμψε τῷ παιδί, ὥστε ταῖς μάχαις ἐπιτριβομένους τοὺς Πέρσας    10
ἀπάτῃ ἐθελῆσαι τὴν τῶν Οὔννων λῦσαι διαφοράν, καὶ δῆτα δια-
πέμψασθαι τὸν Πειρώζην (τοῦτο γὰρ ἦν ὄνομα τῷ τότε Περσῶν
βασιλεύοντι) πρὸς τὸν Κούγχαν τὸν Οὔννων ἡγούμενον, ὡς τὴν πρὸς
αὐτὸν ἀσμενίζων εἰρήνην ἐπί τε συμμαχίᾳ σπένδεσθαι βούλοιτο καὶ
τὴν αὐτοῦ κατεγγυᾷ ἀδελφήν (νεώτατον γὰρ αὐτὸν εἶαι συνέβαινε    15
καὶ μηδέπω παίδων εἶαι πατέρα). τὸν δὲ προσδεξάμενον τοὺς
λόγους γήμασθαι οὐ τοῦ Πειρώζου ἀδελφήν, ἀλλ᾽ ἑτέραν γυναῖκα
βασιλικῶς διακοσμηθεῖσαν, ἣν ὁ Περσῶν μόναρχος ἐξέπεμψε,
παρεγγυήσας ὡς οὐδὲν μὲν ἀνακαλύπτουσα τῶν ἐσχηματισμένων
βασιλείας καὶ εὐδαιμονίας μεθέξει, ἐκλέγουσα δὲ τὴν ὑπόκρισιν    20
θάνατον ἕξει ζημίαν· οὐ γὰρ ἀνέξεσθαι τὸν Κιδαριτῶν ἄρχοντα
θεράπαιναν ἔχειν γαμετὴν ἀντὶ τῆς εὖ γενομένης.

Τούτου χάριν σπεισάμενος ὁ Πειρώζης πρὸς τὸν τῶν Οὔννων
ἡγούμενον οὐκ ἐπὶ πολὺ τῆς ἀπάτης ἀπώνατο· εὐλαβηθεῖσα γὰρ ἡ
γυνή, μήποτε ὁ ἄρχων τοῦ ἔθνους ὑπὸ ἑτέρων πυθόμενος τὴν αὐτῆς    25
τύχην χαλεπῷ αὐτὴν ὑφέξει θανάτῳ, μηνύει τὸ μελετηθέν. ὁ δὲ
Κούγχας ἐπαινέσας τὴν γυναῖκα τῆς ἀληθείας αὐτὴν μὲν ἔμεινεν
ἔχων γαμετήν, τίσασθαι δὲ τοῦ δόλου Πειρώζην ἐθέλων πόλεμον πρὸς
τοὺς ὁμόρους ἔχειν ὑπεκρίνετο δεῖσθαί τε ἀνδρῶν οὐ τῶν πρὸς μάχην
ἐπιτηδείων, (μυρίον γὰρ αὐτῷ παρεῖναι πλῆθος) ἀλλὰ τῶν στρατη-    30
γησόντων αὐτῷ τὸν πόλεμον. ὁ δὲ τ᾽ αὐτῷ ἄνδρας τῶν λογάδων
ἐξέπεμψεν. καὶ τοὺς μὲν ὁ τῶν Κιδαριτῶν ἄρχων ἀπέκτεινεν, τοὺς δὲ
λωβησάμενος παρὰ τὸν Πειρώζην ἀπέπεμψεν ἀπαγγελοῦντας ὡς
τῆς ἀπάτης ταύτην ἔδωκε δίκην. οὕτως αὖθις αὐτοῖς ὁ πόλεμος ἀνε-
ζωπυρήθη, καὶ ἐμάχοντο καρτερῶς. ἐν Γόργᾳ τοίνυν, (τοῦτο γὰρ    35
ὄνομα τῷ χωρίῳ, ἐν ᾧπερ συνέβαινε τοὺς Πέρσας στρατοπεδεύεσθαι)
τὸν Κωνστάντιον ὁ Πειρώζης ἐδέχετο καί τινας ἡμέρας φιλοφρονησάμενος διαφῆκε δεξιὸν οὐδὲν περὶ τῆς πρεσβείας ἀποκρινάμενος.

4 Περσῶν ante πόλεσιν add. de Boor      5-6 πρὸς οὓς πόλεμος add. Niebuhr
8 οὐ scripsi [ ὧν codd.    παρνησάμενος X      21 ἔξεσθαι X    26 χαλεπῶς codd.

3. (*Exc. de Leg. Rom.* 12)

When Constantius the envoy had waited for a while at Edessa, as I have said,[162] for the sake of his embassy, the Persian monarch gave him admittance to his territory. He asked Constantius to come to him while he was engaged not in the cities but on the borders between his people and the Kidarite Huns. With these a war had begun, the cause of which was that the Huns were not receiving the tribute monies which the former rulers of the Persians and the Parthians had paid.[163] The father of the monarch had refused the payment of the tribute and had undertaken the war, which his son had inherited together with the kingdom. As a result the Persians were being worn down by the fighting and wished to end the dispute with the Huns by guile. So Perozes (for this was the name of the current Persian king) sent to Kunchas, the leader of the Huns, saying that he welcomed peace with him and wished to make a treaty of alliance and betroth his sister to him, for he happened to be very young and not yet the father of children. However, when Kunchas had accepted these proposals, he married not the sister of Perozes but another woman dressed as a princess, whom the Persian king had sent, having told her that if she did not reveal the trick she would enjoy royal status and affluence, but if she told of the deceit she would suffer death as the penalty, since the ruler of the Kidarites would not endure to have a maidservant to wife instead of a noble-woman.

Having made the treaty on these terms, Perozes did not long profit from his treachery towards the ruler of the Huns. For the woman, fearing that at some time the ruler of the people would be told of her status by others and would put her to a cruel death, revealed what had been done. Kunchas praised the woman for her honesty and continued to keep her as his wife. But, wishing to punish Perozes for his trick, he pretended that he was at war with his neighbours and had need, not of fighting men (for he had an enormous number of these), but of generals to direct the war. Perozes sent him three hundred of his leading captains, and of these the ruler of the Kidarites killed some and mutilated the rest, sending them back to Perozes with the message that this was the punishment for his treachery. Thus the war between them was rekindled, and there was heavy fighting. Therefore, Perozes received Constantius in Gorga, which was the name of the place at which the Persians were encamped, and having treated him generously for a few days, dismissed him without a satisfactory reply to the embassy.[164]

[42]

[(Evagrius *HE* 2,13)

Συνηνέχθη δὲ τούτοις ὅμοια ἢ καὶ δεινότερα ἀνὰ τὴν Κωνσταντινούπολιν, ἀρχῆς τοῦ κακοῦ γενομένης ἐν τῷ παραθαλασσίῳ τῆς
πόλεως μέρει, ὅπερ βοὸς καλοῦσι πόρον. ἱστόρηται δὲ ὡς κατὰ τὰς
ἐπιλυχνίους ὥρας δαίμων τις κακοῦργος παλαμναῖος γυναικὶ εἰκασ-
θείς, εἴτε καὶ ταῖς ἀληθείαις γυνὴ χερνῆτις ὑπὸ δαίμονος οἰστρου-     5
μένη – λέγεται γὰρ ἐπ’ ἀμφότερα –, λύχνον πρὸς παντοπώλιον
ἐνεγκεῖν ὠνησομένη τι τῶν τεταριχευμένων, τεθέντος δ’ αὖ τοῦ
λύχνου τὸ γύναιον ὑπαναχωρῆσαι· τὸ δέ γε πῦρ στυππίου λαβόμενον
φλόγα μεγίστην ἐξᾶραι, λόγου τε θᾶττον ἐμπρῆσαι τὸ οἴκημα· ἐκ
τούτου δὲ τὰ παρακείμενα ῥᾴδιον ἀφανισθῆναι, τοῦ πυρὸς ἀμφι-     10
νεμομένου οὐ μόνον τὰ εὔξαπτα ἀλλὰ καὶ τὰς ἐκ λίθων οἰκοδομίας,
καὶ ἄχρι τετάρτης ἡμέρας διαμείναντος, καὶ πᾶσαν ἄμυναν ὑπερ-
βεβηκότος, τὸ μεσαίτατον ἅπαν τῆς πόλεως ἀπὸ τοῦ ἀρκτῴου μέχρι
τοῦ νοτίου κλίματος δαπανηθῆναι, ἐπὶ πέντε μὲν σταδίους τὸ μῆκος,
δεκατέσσαρας δὲ τὸ πλάτος· ὡς μηδὲν μεταξὺ καταλειφθῆναι μὴ     15
δημοσίων μὴ ἰδιωτικῶν οἰκοδομιῶν, μὴ κίονας, μὴ τὰς ἐκ λίθων
ψαλίδας, ἀλλὰ πᾶσαν ἀπεσκληκυῖαν ὕλην ὥσπερ τι τῶν εὐεξάπτων
κατακαυθῆναι. τοῦτο δὲ τὸ κακὸν γενέσθαι ἐν μὲν τῷ βορείῳ
κλίματι, ἐν ᾧ καὶ νεώρια τῆς πόλεως καθεστᾶσιν, ἀπὸ τοῦ καλου-
μένου βοὸς πόρου μέχρι τοῦ παλαιοῦ Ἀπόλλωνος ἱεροῦ, ἐν δὲ τῷ     20
νοτίῳ ἀπὸ τοῦ Ἰουλιανοῦ λιμένος μέχρις οἰκιῶν οὐ πολὺ κειμένων
τοῦ εὐκτηρίου τῆς ἐπίκλην Ὁμονοίας ἐκκλησίας, ἐν δὲ τῷ μεσαιτάτῳ
τῆς πόλεως μέρει ἀπὸ τοῦ Κωνσταντίνου προσαγορευομένου φόρου
μέχρι τῆς τοῦ Ταύρου καλουμένης ἀγορᾶς, οἰκτρὸν πᾶσι θέαμα καὶ
εἰδεχθέστατον. ὅσα γὰρ ἐπηώρητο τῇ πόλει κάλλη, ἢ πρὸς τὸ μεγα-     25
λοπρεπὲς καὶ ἀπαράβλητον ἐξησκημένα, ἢ πρὸς κοινὰς ἢ ἰδιωτικὰς
καλοῦντα χρείας, ὑφ’ ἓν ἐς ὄρη τε καὶ βουνοὺς ἀπεσχεδιάσθη δυσ-
βάτους τε καὶ δυσδιαπορεύτους καὶ παντοίων ὑλῶν πλήρεις, τὴν
προτέραν συγχέοντας ὄψιν· ὡς μηδὲ τοῖς οἰκήτορσι τὸν τόπον ἐπι-
τρέπειν εἰδέναι τί τε ἢ ὅπη τῶν προτέρων ἐτύγχανεν ὤν.     30
(Cf. Nicephorus Callistus *HE* 15,21)]

8 γε om. Pv     12-13 ὑποβεβηκότος B     15 ὡς [καὶ B     24 τοῦ σταυροῦ A
26 ἀπαράκλητον P     29 τῶν τόπων LBv     30 ὄν A

[43]

[(*Suda* B 163)

Βασιλίσκος, Βηρίνης ἀδελφὸς τῆς βασιλίδος, ἐπὶ Λέοντος τοῦ
βασιλέως ἀντὶ Ῥουστικίου στρατοπεδάρχου ᾑρέθη, εὐεπίτευκτος μὲν
ὢν ἐν μάχαις, βραδύνους δὲ καὶ φενακίζουσιν ὑπαγόμενος ῥᾳδίως.]

## [42]

[(Evagrius *HE* 2,13)

At the same time as these disasters[165] there occurred similar or even worse ones at Constantinople. The trouble began in that part of the city on the coast which they call the Bosporus. It is said that at dusk a malignant and vengeful spirit in the guise of a woman, or really a working woman possessed by a spirit (for both versions are offered), carried a lamp into a general store intending to buy some pickles. The silly woman set down the lamp and left, and the flame caught some fibres, burst into a huge conflagration and burned down the building in an instant. After this the neighbouring buildings were quickly consumed as the fire spread not only to the structures made of inflammable materials but even to stone buildings. It burned for four days and overcame every attempt to stop it. The whole core of the city from the north to the southern edge was destroyed, an area five stades deep and fourteen wide. Within this area nothing remained of any building, public or private – not even the pillars or stone vaults –, but all materials were burned up and reduced to ashes as if they had been easily combustible. In the northern quarter, where the city's dockyards are, the damage extended from the Bosporus to the old Temple of Apollo, in the southern quarter from Julian's Harbour to buildings close to the oratory of the church called Concord, and in the centre of the city from Constantine's Forum to the Agora of Taurus. To all it offered a miserable and affecting spectacle. Whatever beautiful things had graced the city, all that was built with an eye to unsurpassable magnificence, all that was put to public or private use was at one stroke reduced to hills and mounds of all kinds of rubble, impassable obstacles, the jumbled remains of former beauty. As a result the site did not even allow its inhabitants to recognise what had been there before and where it had stood.[166]

(Cf. Nicephorus Callistus *HE* 15,21)]

## [43]

[(*Suda* B 163)

Basiliscus, the brother of the Empress Verina, was during Leo's reign chosen general to replace Rusticius. He was a successful soldier but slow-witted and easily taken in by deceivers.]

## 44

(*Exc. de Leg. Gent.* 16)

Ὅτι μετὰ τὸν ἐμπρησμὸν τῆς πόλεως τὸν ἐπὶ Λέοντος ἧκεν ὁ
Γωβάζης σὺν Διονυσίῳ ἐς τὴν Κωνσταντίνου Περσικὴν ἔχων στολὴν
καὶ τῷ Μηδικῷ δορυφορούμενος τρόπῳ. ὃν οἱ ἀμφὶ τὰ βασίλεια δεξάμενοι πρότερον μὲν τοῦ νεωτερισμοῦ κατεμέμψαντο, ἔπειτα δὲ
φιλοφρονησάμενοι ἀπέπεμψαν· εἷλε γὰρ αὐτοὺς τῇ τε θωπείᾳ τῶν    5
λόγων καὶ τὰ τῶν Χριστιανῶν ἐπιφερόμενος σύμβολα.

## 45

(*Exc. de Leg. Gent.* 17)

Ὅτι Σκίροι καὶ Γότθοι ἐς πόλεμον συνελθόντες καὶ διαχωρισ-
θέντες ἀμφότεροι πρὸς συμμάχων μετάκλησιν παρεσκευάζοντο· ἐν
οἷς καὶ παρὰ τοὺς ἑῴους Ῥωμαίους ἦλθον. καὶ Ἄσπαρ μὲν ἡγεῖτο
μηδετέροις συμμαχεῖν, ὁ δὲ αὐτοκράτωρ Λέων ἐβούλετο Σκίροις
ἐπικουρεῖν. καὶ δὴ γράμματα πρὸς τὸν ἐν Ἰλλυριοῖς στρατηγὸν    5
ἔπεμπεν ἐντελλόμενος σφίσι κατὰ τῶν Γότθων βοήθειαν τὴν προσήκουσαν πέμπειν.

1 Σκίροι Cantoclar. [Σκύθαι A    3 Ἄσπαρ Cantoclar. [ἄπερ A

## 46

(*Exc. de Leg. Gent.* 18)

Ὅτι ἧκε κατὰ τοῦτον τὸν χρόνον παρὰ τῶν Ἀττήλα παίδων
ὡς τὸν βασιλέα Λέοντα πρεσβεία τὰς αἰτίας διαλύουσα τῆς προϋπαρ-
ξάσης διαφορᾶς, καὶ ὡς χρὴ αὐτοὺς ἐπὶ εἰρήνη σπένδεσθαι καὶ κατὰ
τὸ παλαιὸν ἔθος παρὰ τὸν Ἴστρον ἐς ταὐτὸν ἰόντας Ῥωμαίοις προ-
τιθέναι ἀγορὰν καὶ ἀντιλαμβάνειν, ὧν ἂν δεόμενοι τύχοιεν. καὶ ἡ μὲν    5
σφῶν αὐτῶν πρεσβεία ἐν τοῖσδε οὖσα ἄπρακτος ἐπανήει· οὐ γὰρ
ἐδόκει τῷ βασιλεύοντι Οὔννους τῶν Ῥωμαϊκῶν συμβολαίων μετέχειν
πολλὰ τὴν αὐτοῦ κακώσαντας γῆν· οἱ δὲ τοῦ Ἀττήλα παῖδες τὴν ἐπὶ
τῇ πρεσβείᾳ ἀπόκρισιν δεξάμενοι πρὸς σφᾶς διεφέροντο· ὁ μὲν γὰρ
Δεγγιζίχ, ἀπράκτων ἐπανελθόντων τῶν πρέσβεων, πόλεμον Ῥω-    10
μαίοις ἐπάγειν ἐβούλετο, ὁ δὲ Ἡρνὰχ πρὸς ταύτην ἀπηγόρευε τὴν
παρασκευήν, ὡς τῶν κατὰ χώραν ἀπαγόντων αὐτὸν πολέμων.

## 47

(*Exc. de Leg. Gent.* 19)

Ὅτι Σαράγουροι Ἀκατίροις καὶ ἄλλοις ἔθνεσιν ἐπιθέμενοι ἐπὶ
Πέρσας ἐστράτευον. καὶ πρότερον μὲν ἐπὶ τὰς Κασπίας παρεγένοντο

### 44

(*Exc. de Leg. Gent.* 16)

After the fire in the city during the reign of Leo, Gobazes came with Dionysius to Constantinople, dressed in Persian style and with a bodyguard in the Median manner. The officials at court received him and at first blamed him for his rebellion, but then treated him in a kindly manner and dismissed him. For he won them over both by his flattering words and because he brought with him the symbols of the Christians.[167]

### 45

(*Exc. de Leg. Gent.* 17)

A war broke out between the Sciri and the Goths. When the two sides separated, they prepared to call for assistance. Amongst others they came to the eastern Romans. Aspar thought that they should ally with neither, but the Emperor Leo wished to help the Sciri. He sent letters to the general in Illyricum ordering him to send the appropriate help against the Goths.[168]

### 46

(*Exc. de Leg. Gent.* 18)

At this time an embassy came to the Emperor Leo from the sons of Attila to remove the causes of previous disputes. They also said that a peace treaty should be made and that in the old manner they should meet with the Romans at the Danube, establish a market and exchange whatever they required.[169] The embassy left having achieved none of these things, since the Emperor's view was that the Huns, who had done much damage to his territory, should not have access to Roman trade. When the sons of Attila received the reply to the embassy, they fell into disagreement. Since the embassy returned unsuccessful, Dengizich wished to make war on the Romans, whereas Ernach objected to such a campaign because wars in his own territory were occupying him.

### 47

(*Exc. de Leg. Gent.* 19)

The Saraguri, having attacked the Akatiri and other peoples, invaded Persia. First they came to the Caspian gates, but when they

πύλας· καὶ φρουρὰν Περσικὴν ἐν αὐταῖς ἐγκαθεστῶσαν εὑρόντες
ἑτέραν ὁδὸν ἐτράποντο, δι᾽ ἧς ἐπὶ τοὺς Ἴβηρας ἐλθόντες τήν τε
αὐτῶν ἐδῄουν καὶ τὰ Ἀρμενίων χωρία κατέτρεχον· ὥστε Πέρσας      5
πρὸς τῷ πολέμῳ τῶν Κιδαριτῶν τῷ πάλαι αὐτοῖς συστάντι καὶ
ταύτην εὐλαβουμένους τὴν ἔφοδον παρὰ Ῥωμαίους πρεσβεύσασθαι
καὶ αἰτεῖν χρήματα σφίσιν αὐτοῖς δίδοσθαι ἢ ἄνδρας πρὸς φυλακὴν
τοῦ Ἰουροειπαὰχ φρουρίου, καὶ λέγειν, ἅπερ αὐτοῖς πολλάκις εἴρητο
πρεσβευομένοις, ὡς, αὐτῶν ὑφισταμένων τὰς μάχας καὶ μὴ συγχω-    10
ρούντων τὰ ἐπιόντα ἔθνη βάρβαρα πάροδον ἔχειν, ἡ τῶν Ῥωμαίων
ἀδῄωτος διαμένει χώρα. τῶν δὲ ἀποκριναμένων ὡς ἕκαστον ἀνάγκη
τῆς οἰκείας ὑπερμαχοῦντα γῆς τῆς σφετέρας φρουρᾶς ἐπιμελεῖσθαι,
πάλιν ἄπρακτοι ἐπανέζευξαν.

## 48

### 1. (*Exc. de Leg. Gent.* 20)

Ὅτι Δεγγιζὶχ πόλεμον ἐπὶ Ῥωμαίους ἐπενεγκόντος καὶ τῇ τοῦ
Ἴστρου ὄχθῃ προσκαρτεροῦντος, τοῦτο μαθὼν ὁ Ἀναγάστης ὁ Ὀρνι-
γίσκλου (αὐτὸς γὰρ εἶχε τὴν πρὸς τῷ Θρᾳκίῳ μέρει τοῦ ποταμοῦ
φυλακήν) ἐκ τῶν ἀμφ᾽ αὐτὸν ἐκπέμψας ἐπυνθάνετο ὅ τι βουλόμενοι
πρὸς μάχην παρασκευάζονται. ὁ δὲ Δεγγιζὶχ τοῦ Ἀναγάστου κατο-    5
λιγωρήσας τοὺς ὑπ᾽ αὐτοῦ πεμφθέντας ἀπράκτους ἠφίει, παρὰ δὲ τὸν
βασιλέα τοὺς διαλεξομένους ἔστελλεν, ὡς, εἰ μὴ γῆν καὶ χρήματα
αὐτῷ τε καὶ τῷ ἑπομένῳ δοίη στρατῷ, πόλεμον ἐπάξει. τῶν δὲ παρ᾽
ἐκείνου πρέσβεων ἐς τὰ βασίλεια ἀφικομένων καὶ τὰ αὐτοῖς ἐν-
ταλθέντα ἀπαγγειλάντων, ἀπεκρίνατο βασιλεὺς ἑτοίμως ἔχειν πάντα    10
ποιεῖν, εἴ γε ὑπακουσόμενοι αὐτῷ παραγένωνται· χαίρειν γὰρ τοῖς
ἀπὸ τῶν ἐθνῶν ἐπὶ συμμαχίᾳ ἀφικνουμένοις.

8 δοίη Dindorf [δώη A

### 2. (Evagrius *HE* 2,14)

Ὑπὸ τοῖς αὐτοῖς χρόνοις, τοῦ Σκυθικοῦ πολέμου συνισταμένου
πρὸς τοὺς ἑῴους Ῥωμαίους, ἥ τε Θρᾳκία γῆ καὶ ὁ Ἑλλήσποντος
ἐσείσθη, καὶ Ἰωνία καὶ αἱ καλούμεναι Κυκλάδες νῆσοι, ὡς Κνίδου
καὶ τῆς Κρητῶν νήσου τὰ πολλὰ κατενεχθῆναι. καὶ ὄμβρους δὲ
ἐξαισίους ὁ Πρίσκος ἱστορεῖ γενέσθαι ἀνὰ τὴν Κωνσταντινούπολιν    5
καὶ τὴν Βιθυνῶν χώραν, ἐπὶ τρεῖς καὶ τέσσαρας ἡμέρας ποταμηδὸν
τῶν ὑδάτων ἐξ οὐρανοῦ φερομένων· καὶ ὄρη μὲν εἰς πεδία κατενεχθῆναι, κατακλυσθείσας δὲ κώμας παραπολέσθαι, γενέσθαι δὲ καὶ
νήσους ἐν τῇ Βοάνῃ λίμνῃ, οὐ μακρὰν τῆς Νικομηδείας ἀφεστώσῃ, ἐκ

4 τῆς Κρητῶν νήσου [τῆς Κῶ τῶν νήσων zv      8 περιαπολέσθαι B
9 Βοάνη [Καικιανῇ A    ἀφεστώσῃ Lowth, Müller [ἀφεστώσης codd.

found that the Persians had established a fort there, they took another route, by which they came to Iberia. They laid waste this country and overran Armenia. As a result the Persians, apprehensive of this inroad on top of their old war with the Kidarites, sent an embassy to the Romans and asked that they give them either money or men for the defence of the fortress of Iouroeipaach. They repeated what had often been said by their embassies, that since they were facing the fighting and refusing to allow access to the attacking peoples, the Romans' territory remained unravaged. When the Romans replied that each had to fight for his own land and take care of his own defence, they again returned having achieved nothing.[170]

### 48

1. (*Exc. de Leg. Gent.* 20)

    Dengizich declared war on the Romans and approached close to the bank of the Danube. When Ornigisclus'[171] son Anagast, who commanded the defences of the part of the river in Thrace, learned this, he sent some of his men to ask what was their object in preparing for war. Dengizich scorned Anagast and sent his men away with nothing accomplished. He despatched men to the Emperor to announce that if he did not give land and money to himself and the army that followed him, he would make war. When his envoys came to the palace and spoke as they had been ordered, the Emperor replied that he was ready to do everything if they would remain obedient to him, for he was well-disposed to those of the foreign peoples who came into alliance with him.[172]

2. (Evagrius *HE* 2,14)

    At about the same time, when the Scythian war against the Romans was beginning, the land of Thrace and the Hellespont, Ionia and the islands called the Cyclades were hit by an earthquake. As a result most of the islands of Cnidus and Crete was devastated. The historian Priscus says that extraordinarily heavy rains fell at Constantinople and over Bithynia, and for three and four days torrents of water poured from the sky. Hills were flattened, villages were flooded and destroyed, and in Lake Boanē not far from Nicomedia

τῶν συνενεχθέντων ἐς αὐτὴν παμπόλλων φορυτῶν. ἀλλὰ ταῦτα    10
μὲν ὕστερον ἐπράχθη.    (Cf. Nicephorus Callistus *HE* 15,20)

## 49

*(Exc. de Leg. Gent.* 21)

ὅτι Ἀναγάστου καὶ Βασιλίσκου καὶ Ὄστρυος καὶ ἄλλων
τινῶν στρατηγῶν Ῥωμαίων τοὺς Γότθους ἔς τινα κοῖλον χῶρον
συγκλεισάντων καὶ πολιορκούντων, λιμῷ τε πιεζομένων τῶν Σκυθῶν σπάνει τῶν ἐπιτηδείων, πρεσβείαν παρὰ τοὺς Ῥωμαίους ποιήσασθαι, ὥστε αὐτοὺς εἰ ἐνδιδόασι νεμομένους γῆν ὑπακούειν αὐτῶν    5
ἐς ὅ τι ἂν θέλοιεν · τῶν δὲ ἐπὶ βασιλέα τὴν ἐκείνων φέρειν ἀποκριναμένων πρεσβείαν, καὶ τῶν βαρβάρων τοῦ λιμοῦ πέρι σφᾶς θέσθαι
ἐθέλειν τὰς συμβάσεις φαμένων καὶ μὴ οἵους τε εἶναι μακρὰς ποιεῖσθαι ἀνακωχάς, βουλευόμενοι οἱ τὰς Ῥωμαϊκὰς τάξεις διέποντες
τροφὰς χορηγήσειν αὐτοῖς ὑπέσχοντο ἄχρι τῆς βασιλέως ἐπιτροπῆς,    10
εἴ γε σφᾶς αὐτοὺς διέλοιεν ὥσπερ καὶ τὸ Ῥωμαϊκὸν διακέκριται
πλῆθος · ἔσεσθαι γὰρ αὐτῶν ῥαδίως οὕτως ἐπιμέλειαν, ἐς τοὺς
κληρουμένους καὶ οὐκ εἰς πάντας ἀποβλεπόντων τῶν στρατηγῶν,
οἵπερ ἐς φιλοτιμίαν ὁρῶντες πρὸς τὴν αὐτῶν πάντως ἁμιλληθή-
σονται κομιδήν. τῶν δὲ Σκυθῶν τοὺς ἀπαγγελθέντας διὰ τῶν    15
πρεσβέων προσδεξαμένων λόγους καὶ ἐς τοσαύτας σφᾶς αὐτοὺς
ταξάντων μοίρας, ἐς ὅσασπερ καὶ οἱ Ῥωμαῖοι διεκέκριντο, Χελχάλ,
τοῦ Οὔννων γένους ἀνὴρ καὶ ὑποστράτηγος τῶν διεπόντων τὰ
Ἄσπαρος τάγματα, παρὰ τὴν ἐπιλαχοῦσαν αὐτοῖς βαρβαρικὴν
μοῖραν ἐλθὼν καὶ τῶν Γότθων (πλείονες δὲ τῶν ἄλλων ὑπῆρχον)    20
μεταπεμψάμενος τοὺς λογάδας τοιῶνδε ἐποιήσατο λόγων ἀρχήν,
ὡς δώσει μὲν αὐτοῖς γῆν ὁ βασιλεύς, οὐκ εἰς σφετέραν δὲ αὐτῶν
ὄνησιν, ἀλλὰ τοῖς ἐν σφίσιν Οὔννοις. τούτους γὰρ ὀλιγώρως γεη-
πονίας ἔχοντας δίκην λύκων τὰς αὐτῶν ἐπιόντας διαρπάζεσθαι
τροφάς, ὥστε θεραπόντων τάξιν ἐπέχοντας τῆς ἐκείνων ἕνεκα    25
ταλαιπωρεῖσθαι τροφῆς, καίπερ ἐς ἀεί ποτε τοῖς Οὔννοις τοῦ Γότθων
γένους ἀσπόνδου διαμείναντος, καὶ ἐκ προγόνων τὴν αὐτῶν ἀπο-
φυγεῖν ὁμαιχμίαν ὁμοσαμένων, ἐφ' ᾧ καὶ ὅρκων πατρίων πρὸς τῇ
τῶν οἰκείων στερήσει καταφρονεῖν · αὐτὸν δέ, εἰ καὶ τὸ Οὔννων αὐχεῖ
γένος, δικαιοσύνης πόθῳ τάδε πρὸς αὐτοὺς εἰπόντα δεδωκέναι περὶ    30
τοῦ πρακτέου βουλήν.

Ἐπὶ τούτοις οἱ Γότθοι διαταραχθέντες καὶ εὐνοίᾳ τῇ πρὸς
αὐτοὺς ταῦτα τὸν Χελχὰλ εἰρηκέναι νομίσαντες, τοὺς ἐν αὐτοῖς

---

1 Ὄστρυος de Boor [Ὄστρουΐ A  Ὀστρύου Niebuhr    4-5  ποιησαμένων de
Boor ἐποιήσαντο?    17  ὅσασπερ Niebuhr [ὅσας ἄσπερ A    20  καὶ τῶν
Bekker [καὶ αὐτῶν A

islands were formed by the large amount of debris that was washed into
it. But these things happened later.[173]
(Cf. Nicephorus Callistus *HE* 15,20)

## 49

(*Exc. de Leg. Gent.* 21)
Anagast, Basiliscus, Ostrys and other Roman generals trapped the
Goths in a hollow place and held them under siege, and the Scythians
were pressed by starvation owing to their lack of supplies. They sent[174]
an embassy to the Romans to say that if they were given land upon
surrendering, they would obey whatever the Romans commanded.
When the generals replied that they would convey the embassy to the
Emperor, the barbarians said that they wanted a settlement because
they were starving and could not make a long truce. The commanders
of the Roman forces took counsel and promised that they would
supply food until the Emperor made his decision, provided they split
themselves up into as many units as the Roman force was divided into.
In this way they would be easily cared for, since the generals would be
concerned not with the whole force but with individual groups and as
a matter of honour would compete to keep them fully supplied. The
Scythians accepted the proposals brought to them by their envoys and
split themselves up into as many divisions as the Romans were in.
Chelchal, a man of the Hunnic race and a junior officer on Aspar's
staff, approached the part of the barbarians which had been assigned
to them and, summoning the chiefs of the Goths (who were more
numerous than the other peoples), began to speak to them as follows.
He claimed that the Emperor would give them land not for their own
enjoyment but for the Huns amongst them. For these men have no
concern for agriculture, but, like wolves, attack and steal the Goths'
food supplies, with the result that the latter remain in the position of
servants and themselves suffer food shortages. Yet the Gothic people
have never had a treaty with the Huns and from the time of their fore-
fathers have sworn to escape from the alliance with them. Thus, in
addition to their own hardships, they make light of their ancestral
oaths. Chelchal concluded that, although he was proud of his Hunnic
origin, out of a sense of justice he was saying these things to them and
offering advice as to what they should do.

The Goths were disturbed by these words and, thinking that
Chelchal had said them out of good will, attacked the Huns amongst

358     Priscus: Text

Οὔννους [ὡς] συστάντες διεχειρίζοντο· καὶ μάχη καρτερὰ ἀμφοτέρων συνίστατο τῶν ἐθνῶν <ὡς> ἐκ συνθήματος. οἶα οἱ Ἄσπαρος     35
πυθόμενοι, ἀλλὰ γὰρ καὶ οἱ τῶν λοιπῶν στρατοπέδων ἡγεμόνες μετὰ
τῶν οἰκείων παραταξάμενοι τὸν ἐπιτυχόντα τῶν βαρβάρων ἀνῇρουν.
τοῦ δὲ δόλου καὶ τῆς ἀπάτης οἱ Σκύθαι λαβόντες ἔννοιαν σφᾶς τε ἀνεκαλοῦντο καὶ ἐς χεῖρας τοῖς Ῥωμαίοις ἐχώρουν. ἀλλ' οἱ μὲν Ἄσπαρος
τὴν σφίσιν ἐπιλαχοῦσαν ἔφθασαν ἀναλώσαντες μοῖραν, τοῖς δὲ     40
λοιποῖς στρατηγοῖς οὐκ ἀκίνδυνος ἡ μάχη ἐγένετο, τῶν βαρβάρων
καρτερῶς ἀγωνισαμένων, ὥστε τοὺς ἐξ αὐτῶν ὑπολειφθέντας τάς
τε Ῥωμαϊκὰς τάξεις διώσασθαι καὶ τῇδε τὴν πολιορκίαν διαφυγεῖν.

34 ὡς exp. Niebuhr     35 ὡς addidi e v.34     35-36 οἶα οἱ Ἄσπαρος πυθόμενοι scripsi [οἱάπερ πειθόμενοι A  δ Ἄσπαρ πυθόμενος Bekker     43 διώσασθαι Niebuhr [δηώσασθαι aut δηώσασθαι codd.

[50]
[(Evagrius HE 2,16)
Ἐκ πρεσβείας δὲ τῶν ἑσπερίων Ῥωμαίων, Ἀνθέμιος βασιλεὺς
τῆς Ῥώμης ἐκπέμπεται· ᾧ Μαρκιανὸς ὁ πρώην βεβασιλευκὼς τὴν
οἰκείαν κατενεγγύησε παῖδα.
(Cf. Nicephorus Callistus HE 15,11; Procopius Wars 3,6,5 = Fr. 53,3)]

51
1. (Exc. de Leg. Gent. 22)
Ὅτι μεγίστης πρὸς τὸ Σουάνων ἔθνος Ῥωμαίοις τε καὶ Λαζοῖς
ὑπαρχούσης διαφορᾶς, καὶ σφόδρα ἐς τὴν τοῦ †σήματος τῶν Σουάνων συνισταμένων μάχην, καὶ Περσῶν δὲ ἐθελόντων αὐτῷ
πολεμεῖν διὰ τὰ φρούρια, ἅπερ <ὑπὸ> τῶν Σουάνων ἀφῄρηντο,
πρεσβείαν ἔστελλεν, ἐπικούρους αὐτῷ διαπεμφθῆναι παρὰ βασιλέως     5
αἰτῶν ἐκ τῶν παραφυλαττόντων στρατιωτῶν τὰ Ἀρμενίων ὅρια
τῶν Ῥωμαίοις ὑποτελῶν, ἐφ' ᾧ προσχώρων ὄντων ἑτοίμην ἔχειν
βοήθειαν, καὶ μὴ κινδυνεύειν τοὺς πόρρωθεν ἀπεκδεχόμενον, ἢ παραγενομένων ἐπιτρίβεσθαι δαπάνῃ, τοῦ πολέμου, ἂν οὕτω τύχῃ, διαναβαλλομένου, καθάπερ ἤδη πρότερον ἐγεγόνει. τῆς γὰρ σὺν Ἡρακ-     10
λείῳ ἀπεσταλμένης βοηθείας, καὶ Περσῶν καὶ Ἰβήρων τῶν αὐτῷ
ἐπαγόντων τὸν πόλεμον πρὸς ἑτέρων ἐθνῶν τότε ἀπασχοληθέντων
μάχην, τὴν συμμαχίαν ἀπέπεμψεν ἀσχάλλων ἐπὶ τῇ τῶν τροφῶν
χορηγίᾳ, ὥστε αὖθις τῶν Πάρθων ἐπ' αὐτὸν ἀναζευξάντων Ῥωμαίους ἐπικαλέσασθαι.     15

2 σήματος aut Σήματος edd. [σώματος de Boor (per errorem?)     4 ὑπὸ add.
Bekker     8 τοὺς Hoeschel [τοῖς A     14 ἐπ' αὐτὸν Hoeschel [ἐπ' αὐτῶν A

them and began to kill them; and as if at a signal, the two peoples began a fierce battle. When Aspar's staff learned this,[175] they and the commanders of the other camps drew up their own forces and killed all the barbarians who came their way. When the Scythians realised the intent of the deceit and treachery, they formed up their own forces and began to fight with the Romans. Aspar's men anticipated this and destroyed the section which had been assigned to them. But for the other generals the battle was not easy, since the barbarians fought stoutly, so that those who survived forced their way through the Roman lines and in this way escaped the blockade.

## [50]

[(Evagrius *HE* 2,16)

As a result of an embassy of the western Romans, Anthemius was sent as Emperor of Rome. To him Marcian, the previous Emperor, had betrothed his own daughter.[176]

(Cf. Nicephorus Callistus *HE* 15,11; Procopius *Wars* 3,6,5 = *Fr.* 53,3)]

## 51

1. (*Exc. de Leg. Gent.* 22)

A very serious dispute existed between the Romans and Lazi and the nation of the Suani. The Suani were making war against . . ., and the Persians wished to go to war with him because of the forts which had been captured by the Suani.[177] He, therefore, sent an embassy to the Romans, asking that reinforcements be sent by the Emperor from amongst the troops who were guarding the borders of that part of Armenia which was tributary to the Romans.[178] Thus, since these were close at hand he would have ready assistance and would not be endangered while waiting for troops to come from a distance. Furthermore, he would not be burdened with the expense of supporting them if they came and the war were postponed, as had happened earlier. For when Heracleius was sent with help and the Persians and Iberians, who were at war with him, were diverted to fighting other peoples, he dismissed the reinforcements since he was worried about supporting them.[179] As a result, when the Persians returned against him, he again called upon the Romans.

360     Priscus: Text

Τῶν δὲ στεῖλαι τὴν βοήθειαν ἐπαγγειλαμένων καὶ ἄνδρα τὸν
αὐτῆς ἡγησόμενον, παρεγένετο καὶ Περσῶν πρεσβεία ἀγγέλλουσα
τοὺς Κιδαρίτας Οὔννους ὑπ᾽ αὐτῶν καταγωνίσθαι καὶ Βαλαὰμ πόλιν
αὐτῶν ἐκπεπολιορκηκέναι. ἐμήνυον δὲ τὴν νίκην καὶ βαρβαρικῶς
ἐπεκόμπαζον τὴν παροῦσαν αὐτοῖς μεγίστην δύναμιν ἀποφαίνειν      20
ἐθέλοντες. ἀλλὰ αὐτοὺς παραυτίκα τούτων ἀγγελθέντων ἀπέπεμπε
βασιλεύς, ἐν μείζονι φροντίδι τὰ ἐν Σικελίᾳ συνενεχθέντα ποιούμενος.

20 ἐπεκόμπαζον Niebuhr [ἀπεκόμπαζον A    21 τούτων Hoeschel [τῶν codd.

[2. (John of Antioch *Fr.* 206,2 = *Exc. de Ins.* 90)
Ἐστέλλετο δὲ καὶ κατὰ Τζάνων βοήθεια ληϊζομένων τὰ περὶ
τὴν Τραπεζοῦντα χωρία.]

52
(*Exc. de Leg. Rom.* 13)
Ὅτι Λέων ὁ βασιλεὺς στέλλει πρὸς τὸν Γεζέριχον Φύλαρχον
τὴν τοῦ Ἀνθεμίου βασιλείαν μηνύσων καὶ πόλεμον ἀπειλήσων, εἰ μή
γε τῆς Ἰταλίας καὶ Σικελίας ἀφέξοιτο. ἐπάνηκε δὲ ἀγγέλλων μὴ
ἐθέλειν αὐτὸν τοὺς τοῦ βασιλέως προσίεσθαι λόγους, ἀλλὰ ἐν
πολέμου εἶναι παρασκευῇ, ὡς ὑπὸ τῶν ἑῴων Ῥωμαίων παρα-      5
σπονδούμενον.

3 Σικελίας Bekker [βασιλείας codd.    5 ἑῴων Bekker [νέων codd.

53
1. (Theophanes *Chron. a.m.* 5961)
Τούτῳ τῷ ἔτει Λέων ὁ βασιλεὺς κατὰ Γιζερίχου, τοῦ τῶν
Ἄφρων κρατοῦντος, στόλον μέγαν ἐξοπλίσας ἀπέστειλεν. ὁ γὰρ
Γιζέριχος μετὰ τὴν τελευτὴν Μαρκιανοῦ πολλὰ δεινὰ ἐνεδείξατο ἐν
ταῖς ὑπὸ τὴν τῶν Ῥωμαίων βασιλείαν χώραις ληϊζόμενος καὶ αἰχμα-
λωτίζων πολλοὺς καὶ τὰς πόλεις κατασκάπτων. ὅθεν ζήλῳ κινηθεὶς      5
ὁ βασιλεὺς ἐκ πάσης τῆς ἀνατολικῆς θαλάσσης ἑκατὸν καὶ χιλιάδα
πλοίων ἀθροίσας καὶ στρατῶν καὶ ὅπλων ταύτας πληρώσας κατὰ
Γιζερίχου ἀπέστειλεν. φασὶ γὰρ αὐτὸν ,ατ᾽ κεντηνάρια δεδαπανη-
κέναι χρυσίου ἐν τούτῳ τῷ στόλῳ. στρατηγὸν δὲ καὶ ἔξαρχον τοῦ
στόλου κατέστησε Βασιλίσκον, τὸν Βερίνης τῆς αὐγούστης ἀδελφόν,      10
τῆς ὑπάτου τιμῆς ἤδη μετασχόντα καὶ Σκύθας πολλάκις νικήσαντα ἐν
τῇ Θράκῃ. ὃς δή, συνδραμούσης αὐτῷ καὶ ἐκ τῆς ἑσπερίου οὐκ

6 ἑκατὸν καὶ χιλιάδα Müller [ρ΄χιλιάδας codd.    12 ὃς x [ὡς gy ᾧ ὡς h   αὐτῷ
[οὕτω y

When the Romans had replied that they would send help and a man to command it, an embassy arrived from the Persians which announced that they had crushed the Kidarite Huns and had taken their city of Balaam. They reported their victory and in barbaric fashion boasted about it, since they wished to advertise the very large force which they had at present.[180] But when they had made this announcement, the Emperor straightaway dismissed them, since he was more concerned about the events in Sicily.

[2. (John of Antioch *Fr.* 206,2 = *Exc. de Ins.* 90)

[Leo] also sent help against the Tzani, who were ravaging the districts around Trapezus.][181]

## 52

(*Exc. de Leg. Rom.* 13)

The Emperor Leo sent Phylarchus to Gaiseric to announce to him the sovereignty of Anthemius and to threaten war if he did not evacuate Italy and Sicily. He returned with the report that Gaiseric refused to accept the Emperor's commands and that he was engaged in preparation for war on the ground that the treaty had been broken by the eastern Romans.[182]

## 53

1. (Theophanes *Chron. a.m.* 5961)

In this year the Emperor Leo fitted out a great fleet and sent it against Gaiseric, the ruler of the Africans. For after the death of Marcian, Gaiseric had done many terrible things in the lands under Roman sovereignty, plundering, taking many prisoners and devastating the cities. As a result the Emperor was roused to anger and collected from all the sea of the East eleven hundred[183] ships, which he filled with troops and arms and sent against Gaiseric. They say that he spent one hundred and thirty thousand pounds of gold on this expedition.[184] As general and supreme commander of the force he appointed Basiliscus, the brother of the Empress Verina, who had already held the consulship and had often defeated the Scythians in Thrace. He was joined by a considerable force from the West. Engaging in frequent

362    Priscus: Text

ὀλίγης δυνάμεως, συμπλακεὶς εἰς ναυμαχίας πολλάκις τῇ Γιζερίχου
<καὶ μέγα πλῆθος> τῶν νηῶν τῷ βυθῷ παραδοὺς, εἶτα καὶ αὐτὴν
ἠδυνήθη Καρχηδόνα κρατῆσαι. ὕστερον δὲ δώροις ὑπὸ Γιζερίχου    15
καὶ πλείστοις χρήμασι δελεασθεὶς ἐνέδωκε καὶ ἡττήθη ἑκών, ὡς
Πρίσκος ἱστόρησεν ὁ Θρᾷξ.

13 πολλάκις τῇ codd. [πολλοὺς τοῦ Combefis.    14 καὶ μέγα πλῆθος add.
Dindorf pro mss μετὰ [τμ' pro μετὰ Classen    17 Περσικὸς codd.

2. (Evagrius HE 2,16)
    Ἐκπέμπεται δὲ στρατηγὸς κατὰ Γιζερίχου Βασιλίσκος, ὁ τῆς
Λέοντος γυναικὸς Βερίνης ἀδελφός, μετὰ στρατευμάτων ἀριστίνδην
συνειλεγμένων. ἅπερ ἀκριβέστατα Πρίσκῳ τῷ ῥήτορι πεπόνηται.

3. (Procopius Wars 3,6,1-2 and 5-25)
    Τῶνδε εἵνεκα τίσασθαι Βανδίλους βασιλεὺς Λέων βουλόμενος
ξυνήγειρεν ἐπ᾽ αὐτοὺς στράτευμα. τοῦδε δὲ τοῦ στρατεύματος
λέγουσι τὸ πλῆθος ἐς δέκα μάλιστα μυριάδας γενέσθαι. στόλον δὲ
νεῶν ἐξ ἁπάσης τῆς πρὸς ἕω θαλάσσης ἀθροίσας πολλὴν ἐπεδείξατο μεγαλοφροσύνην ἔς τε στρατιώτας καὶ ναύτας, δεδιὼς μή τί    5
οἱ ἐκ μικρολογίας ἐμποδὼν γένηται προθυμουμένῳ ἐς τοὺς βαρβάρους ἐπιτελέσαι τὴν κόλασιν. φασὶ γοῦν αὐτῷ τριακόσια καὶ χίλια
κεντηνάρια ἐπ᾽ οὐδενὶ ἔργῳ δεδαπανῆσθαι. ἀλλ᾽ ἐπεὶ οὐκ ἔδει
Βανδίλους τῷ στόλῳ τούτῳ ἀπολωλέναι, αὐτοκράτορα τοῦ πολέμου
ποιεῖται Βασιλίσκον, Βηρίνης τῆς γυναικὸς ἀδελφὸν ὄντα καὶ τῆς    10
βασιλείας ἐκτόπως ἐρῶντα, ἥν οἱ ἤλπισεν ἀμαχητὶ ἔσεσθαι τὴν
Ἄσπαρος προσποιησαμένῳ φιλίαν. . . .
    Λέων δὲ ἤδη πρότερον Ἀνθέμιον, ἄνδρα ἐκ γερουσίας, πλούτῳ
τε καὶ γένει μέγαν, βασιλέα τῆς ἑσπερίας καταστησάμενος ἔπεμψεν,
ὅπως οἱ τὰ ἐς τὸν Βανδιλικὸν συλλήψεται πόλεμον. καίτοι Γιζέριχος    15
ἔχρηζε καὶ πολλὰ ἐλιπάρει Ὀλυβρίῳ παραδοθῆναι τὴν βασιλείαν
Πλακιδίᾳ τῇ Βαλεντινιανοῦ παιδὶ ξυνοικοῦντι καὶ διὰ τὸ κῆδος εὐ-
νοϊκῶς αὐτῷ ἔχοντι, ἐπειδή τε τούτου ἠτύχησεν, ἔτι μᾶλλον
ὠργίζετο καὶ πᾶσαν τὴν βασιλέως γῆν ἐληΐζετο. ἥν δέ τις ἐν Δαλματίᾳ Μαρκελλιανὸς τῶν Ἀετίῳ γνωρίμων, ἀνὴρ δόκιμος, ὃς ἐπειδὴ    20
Ἀέτιος ἐτελεύτησε τρόπῳ τῷ εἰρημένῳ, βασιλεῖ εἴκειν οὐκέτι ἠξίου,
ἀλλὰ νεωτερίσας τε καὶ τοὺς ἄλλους ἅπαντας ἀποστήσας αὐτὸς εἶχε
τὸ Δαλματίας κράτος, οὐδενός οἱ ἐς χεῖρας ἰέναι τολμήσαντος. τοῦτον
δὴ τὸν Μαρκελλιανὸν τότε Λέων βασιλεὺς εὖ μάλα τιθασσεύων
προσεποιήσατο, καὶ ἐς Σαρδὼ τὴν νῆσον ἐκέλευεν ἰέναι, Βανδίλων    25
κατήκοον οὖσαν. ὁ δὲ αὐτὴν Βανδίλους ἐξελάσας οὐ χαλεπῶς ἔσχεν.

22 αὐτὸς Maury [οὗτος codd.

sea-battles with Gaiseric's force, he sent <a large number of ships> to the bottom, and at that point he could have taken Carthage itself. But later, having been won over by Gaiseric with gifts and a large sum of money, he gave in and willingly suffered defeat, as Priscus the Thracian narrates.

2. (Evagrius *HE* 2,16)
Basiliscus, the brother of Verina, Leo's wife, was sent as general against Gaiseric with excellently equipped forces. These things have been set down with the greatest accuracy by Priscus the rhetor.

3. (Procopius *Wars* 3,6,1-2 and 5-25)
The Emperor Leo, wishing to punish the Vandals for these acts,[185] collected an army against them. They say that this army numbered one hundred thousand men. He collected a fleet of ships from the whole eastern sea and he showed great generosity to the soldiers and sailors out of fear that if he was parsimonious, some obstacle would arise to his desire to punish the barbarians. Certainly, they say that he spent one hundred and thirty thousand pounds of gold to no avail. Since it was not to be that the Vandals would be destroyed by this expedition, he appointed as supreme commander Basiliscus, the brother of his wife Verina and a man extraordinarily eager to become 'Emperor, which he thought he would achieve without difficulty if he won the friendship of Aspar. . . .[186]
Earlier Leo had made Anthemius, a very wealthy senator of noble birth, Emperor of the West and had sent him off to assist in the Vandalic war. But Gaiseric desired and repeatedly asked that the sovereignty be conferred upon Olybrius, who was the husband of Valentinian's daughter, Placidia, and, because he was connected by marriage,[187] friendly towards him. When this was denied him, he became even more angry and ravaged the whole of the Emperor's territory. There was in Dalmatia a certain Marcellianus, one of Aetius' acquaintances and a man of high reputation. When Aetius died in the manner described, he refused to obey the Emperor any longer and, having revolted and having persuaded all the others to secede, he himself held power in Dalmatia, since no one dared to confront him. At this time the Emperor Leo courted Marcellianus assiduously, won him over and told him to go to the island of Sardinia, which was in the possession of the Vandals. He drove out the Vandals and held it without

Ἡράκλειος δὲ σταλεὶς ἐκ Βυζαντίου εἰς Τρίπολιν τὴν ἐν Λιβύῃ
νικήσας τε μάχῃ τοὺς ταύτῃ Βανδίλους τάς τε πόλεις ῥᾳδίως εἷλε
καὶ τὰς ναῦς ἐνταῦθα ἀπολιπὼν πεζῇ τὸ στράτευμα ἐς Καρχηδόνα
ἦγε. τὰ μὲν οὖν τοῦ πολέμου προοίμια τῇδε ἐφέρετο.                     30
Βασιλίσκος δὲ τῷ παντὶ στόλῳ ἐς πόλισμα κατέπλευσε,
Καρχηδόνος διέχον οὐχ ἧσσον ἢ ὀγδοήκοντά τε καὶ διακοσίοις
σταδίοις (Ἑρμοῦ δὲ νεὼς ἐνταῦθα ἐκ παλαιοῦ ἐτύγχανεν ὤν, ἀφ' οὗ
δὴ καὶ Μερκούριον ὁ τόπος ἐκλήθη· οὕτω γὰρ τὸν Ἑρμῆν καλοῦσι
Ῥωμαῖοι), καὶ εἰ μὴ ἐθελοκακήσας ἐμέλλησεν, ἀλλ' εὐθὺ ἐπεχείρησε     35
Καρχηδόνος ἰέναι, αὐτήν τε ἂν αὐτοβοεὶ εἷλε καὶ Βανδίλους ἐς οὐδεμίαν ἀλκὴν τραπομένους κατεδουλώσατο. οὕτω Γιζέριχος Λέοντα
ὡς ἄμαχον βασιλέα κατωρρώδησεν, ἐπεί οἱ Σαρδώ τε καὶ Τρίπολις
ἁλοῦσαι ἠγγέλλοντο καὶ τὸν Βασιλίσκου στόλον ἑώρα οἷος οὐδείς πω
ἐλέγετο Ῥωμαίοις πρότερον γεγενῆσθαι. νῦν δὲ τοῦτο ἐκώλυσεν ἡ     40
τοῦ στρατηγοῦ μέλλησις, εἴτε κακότητι εἴτε προδοσίᾳ προσγενομένη.
Γιζέριχος δὲ τῆς Βασιλίσκου ὀλιγωρίας ἀπολαύων ἐποίει τάδε.
ὁπλίσας ἅπαντας ὡς ἄριστα εἶχε τοὺς ὑπηκόους ἐπλήρου τὰς ναῦς,
ἄλλας τε κενὰς ἀνδρῶν καὶ ὡς τάχιστα πλεούσας ἐν παρασκευῇ
εἶχε. πέμψας δὲ πρέσβεις ὡς Βασιλίσκον ἐδεῖτο τὸν πόλεμον ἐς     45
πέντε ἡμερῶν ὑπερβαλέσθαι χρόνον, ὅπως μεταξὺ βουλευσάμενος
ἐκεῖνα ποιοίη ἃ δὴ μάλιστα βασιλεῖ βουλομένῳ εἴη. λέγουσι δὲ αὐτὸν
καὶ χρυσίου πολύ τι χρῆμα κρύφα τῆς Βασιλίσκου στρατιᾶς πέμ-
ψαντα ταύτην δὴ τὴν ἐκεχειρίαν ὠνήσασθαι. ἔπρασσε δὲ ταῦτα
οἰόμενος, ὅπερ ἐγένετο, πνεῦμα ἐπίφορον ἐν τούτῳ οἱ τῷ χρόνῳ     50
γενήσεσθαι. Βασιλίσκος δὲ ἢ Ἄσπαρι καθάπερ ὑπέστη χαριζόμενος
ἢ τὸν καιρὸν χρημάτων ἀποδιδόμενος, ἢ καὶ βέλτιον αὐτῷ ἐνομίσθη,
ἐποίει τε τὰ αἰτούμενα καὶ ἡσύχαζεν ἐν τῷ στρατοπέδῳ, τὴν εὐ-
καιρίαν προσδεχόμενος τῶν πολεμίων. οἱ δὲ Βανδίλοι, ἐπειδὴ σφίσι
τάχιστα τὸ πνεῦμα ἐγεγόνει, ὃ δὴ τέως καραδοκοῦντες ἐκάθηντο,     55
ἀράμενοί τε τὰ ἱστία καὶ τὰ πλοῖα ἀφέλκοντες ὅσα αὐτοῖς ἀνδρῶν
κενά, ὥσπερ μοι πρότερον εἴρηται, παρεσκεύαστο, ἔπλεον ἐπὶ τοὺς
πολεμίους. ὡς δὲ ἀγχοῦ ἐγένοντο, πῦρ ἐν τοῖς πλοίοις ἐνθέμενοι, ἃ
δὴ αὐτοὶ ἐφέλκοντες ἦγον, κεκολπωμένων αὐτοῖς τῶν ἱστίων, ἀφῆκαν
ἐπὶ τὸ τῶν Ῥωμαίων στρατόπεδον. ἅτε δὲ πλήθους ὄντος ἐνταῦθα     60
νηῶν, ὅπῃ τὰ πλοῖα ταῦτα προσπίπτοιεν, ἔκαιόν τε ῥᾳδίως καὶ αὐτὰ
οἷς ἂν συμμίξαιεν ἑτοίμως ξυνδιεφθείρετο. οὕτω δὲ τοῦ πυρὸς ἐπι-
φερομένου θόρυβός τε, ὡς τὸ εἰκός, εἶχε τὸν Ῥωμαίων στόλον καὶ
κραυγῆς μέγεθος τῷ τε πνεύματι καὶ τῷ τῆς φλογὸς βόμβῳ ἀντι-

---

41 γενομένη O   43 ἐπηκόους O   47 βεβουλομένῳ V   61 παραπίπτοιεν
O  αὐτοὶ P αὐτοῖς Grotius   62 ξυνδιεφθείρετο codd. [ξυνδιεφθείροντο Haury
63 εἶχε τὸν Ῥ. στόλον [ἦν ἐν τῷ Ῥ. στόλῳ O

difficulty. Moreover, Heracleius was sent from Byzantium to Tripolis in Libya. He conquered the Vandals there in battle and easily took the cities and then, leaving his ships there, led his army overland towards Carthage. These events were the prelude to the war.

Basiliscus put in with his whole fleet at a place over two hundred and eighty stades from Carthage. (A temple of Hermes had been there from of old, and hence the place was called Mercurium, for the Romans call Hermes 'Mercurius'.) If he had not delayed with cowardly intent, but had made straight for Carthage, he would have captured it without a fight and enslaved the Vandals without their making any resistance; so great was Gaiseric's terror of Leo as an invincible Emperor when he was told of the capture of Sardinia and Tripolis and he saw Basiliscus' fleet, such as the Romans, it was said, had never had before. But on this occasion the general's hesitation, whether the result of cowardice or treachery, prevented this conclusion.

Gaiseric, taking advantage of Basiliscus' negligence, did as follows. Arming all his subjects as heavily as possible, he manned his ships, while keeping some — the swiftest — empty but ready to sail. He sent envoys to Basiliscus and asked that the attack be deferred for a space of five days, during which he might take counsel and do those things which the Emperor most desired. They say that, without the knowledge of Basiliscus' army, he also sent a large amount of gold and thus bought his truce. He did this thinking that during this time a favouring wind would arise, as happened. Basiliscus, either as a favour to Aspar as promised, or because he had sold the opportunity for money, or because he thought it the best course, granted the request, did not stir from his camp and conceded the initiative to the enemy. As soon as the wind arose which the Vandals had been waiting for, they raised their sails and, towing the ships which, as I have said, had been made ready but left empty, they sailed against the enemy. When they came near, they set fire to the ships which they were towing and, when their sails were bellied by the wind, sent them against the Roman station. Since a large number of ships were there, wherever these fire-ships struck, they readily spread their fire and were themselves quickly destroyed along with those with which they came into contact. As the fire spread in this way, panic, as was natural, gripped the Roman fleet. A great uproar drowned out the wind and the roaring of the flames as

παταγούσης μάλιστα, καὶ τῶν στρατιωτῶν ὁμοῦ τοῖς ναύταις    65
ἀλλήλοις ἐγκελευομένων καὶ τοῖς κοντοῖς διωθουμένων τά τε
πυρφόρα πλοῖα καὶ τὰς σφῶν αὐτῶν ναῦς ὑπ᾽ ἀλλήλων διαφθειρομένας οὐδενὶ κόσμῳ. ἤδη δὲ καὶ οἱ Βανδίλοι παρῆσαν ἐμβάλλοντές τε
καὶ καταδύοντες καὶ αὐτοῖς ὅπλοις τοὺς διαφεύγοντας τῶν στρατιωτῶν ληϊζόμενοι. εἰσὶ δὲ οἳ καὶ ἄνδρες ἀγαθοὶ Ῥωμαίων ἐν τῷ    70
πόνῳ τούτῳ ἐγένοντο, καὶ πάντων μάλιστα Ἰωάννης, ὑποστράτηγός
τε ὢν Βασιλίσκου καὶ οὐδ᾽ ὁπωστιοῦν τῆς ἐκείνου προδοσίας μετα-
λαχών. περιστάντος γὰρ ὁμίλου πολλοῦ τὴν αὐτοῦ ναῦν, ἔκτεινε μὲν
ἐπιστροφάδην ἀπὸ τοῦ καταστρώματος πολύ τι τῶν πολεμίων
πλῆθος, ὡς δὲ ἁλισκομένης ᾔσθετο τῆς νεώς, ἥλατο ξὺν πάσῃ τῇ    75
τῶν ὅπλων σκευῇ ἀπὸ τῶν ἰκρίων εἰς θάλασσαν. πολλὰ μὲν οὖν
αὐτὸν ἐλιπάρει Γένζων ὁ Γιζερίχου, πιστά τε παρεχόμενος καὶ
σωτηρίαν προτεινόμενος, ὁ δὲ οὐδὲν ἧσσον ἐς θάλασσαν καθῆκε τὸ
σῶμα, ἐκεῖνο μόνον ἀποφθεγξάμενος, ὡς οὐ μή ποτε Ἰωάννης ὑπὸ
χερσὶ κυνῶν γένηται.    80
    Ὁ μὲν δὴ πόλεμος οὗτος ἐς τοῦτο ἐτελεύτα καὶ Ἡράκλειος ἐπ᾽
οἴκου ἀπεκομίσθη· Μαρκελλιανὸς γὰρ πρὸς τοῦ τῶν συναρχόντων
ἀπώλετο δόλῳ.

66 ἀλλήλους τε O    68 βάλλοντές P    75 ἥλατο Hoeschel [ἤλλατο codd.
76 ἀποσκευῇ O

[4. (Jordanes Rom. 337)
    Basiliscum cognatum suum, id est fratrem Augustae Verinae
Africam dirigens cum exercitu, qui navali proelio Chartaginem saepe
adgrediens ante ea victus cupiditate pecuniis vendidit regi Vandalorum, quam in Romanorum potestatem redigeret.]

[5. (Theophanes Chron. a.m. 5963)
    Τούτῳ τῷ ἔτει ἀπέστειλε Λέων ὁ βασιλεὺς κατὰ Γιζερίχου
Ἡράκλειον τὸν Ἐδεσηνόν, υἱὸν Φλώρου τοῦ ἀπὸ ὑπάτων, καὶ Μάρσον
Ἴσαυρον, ἄνδρας δραστηρίους, καὶ στρατὸν ἐξ Αἰγύπτου καὶ Θηβαΐδος καὶ τῆς ἐρήμου. οἵ τινες προσπεσόντες ἀδοκήτως τοῖς Οὐαν-
δήλοις Τρίπολίν τε καὶ ἄλλας παρεστήσαντο πόλεις τῆς Λιβύης    5
πολλὰς καὶ πλέον τῆς Βασιλίσκου ναυμαχίας ἠνίασαν τὸν Γιζέριχον,
ὥστε παρασκευάσαι αὐτὸν περὶ εἰρήνης πρεσβεύσασθαι πρὸς Λέοντα
τὸν βασιλέα· καὶ ταύτης τυγχάνει παρὰ Λέοντος χρῄζοντος τότε
Βασιλίσκου καὶ Ἡρακλείου καὶ Μάρσου εἰς τὴν κατὰ Ἄσπαρος ἐπιβουλήν. ὕποπτος γάρ, ὡς προέφην, γενόμενος τῷ βασιλεῖ ὁ Ἄσπαρ    10
καὶ πολλὴν περικείμενος δύναμιν δόλῳ παρὰ τοῦ βασιλέως φονεύεται

2 ἀπὸ τῶν ὑπάτων cf    7 πρεσβεῦσαι gy

the soldiers and the sailors alike shouted orders to each other and used
their poles to push away both the fire-ships and those of their own
ships which were being destroyed by each other quite unpredictably.[188]
And now the Vandals arrived, ramming and sinking and plundering the
soldiers as they fled, even those with their weapons. But there were also
some of the Romans who showed themselves brave men in this disaster,
and most of all John, a general under Basiliscus who had no part at all
in his treachery. Although a great crowd of the enemy had surrounded
his ship, from the deck he kept killing a large number of them on all
sides, and when he saw that the ship was being captured, he leaped
in full armour from the prow into the sea. Although Genzon, the son
of Gaiseric, begged him many times, offering him pledges and promising
him safety, he nonetheless threw himself down into the sea, saying
only that John would never come into the hands of dogs.

This, then, was the end of the war, and Heracleius returned home.
For Marcellianus had perished by the treachery of one of his fellow
generals.

[4. (Jordanes *Rom.* 337)
[Leo] sent his kinsman Basiliscus, the brother of the Empress
Verina, to Africa with an army. He made frequent seaborne attacks
upon Carthage, but before he conquered it he was himself overcome
by greed and sold it back to Gaiseric for money.]

[5. (Theophanes *Chron. a.m.* 5963)
In this year the Emperor Leo sent against Gaiseric Heracleius of
Edessa, the son of the consular Florus, and the Isaurian Marsus, both
men of action, with an army drawn from Egypt, the Thebaid and the
desert. They fell unexpectedly upon the Vandals, captured Tripolis
and many other cities of Libya and caused Gaiseric more trouble than
did Basiliscus' fleet. As a result he made ready to send a peace mission
to the Emperor Leo. He was granted peace by Leo, who wanted Basiliscus, Heracleius and Marsus for his plot against Aspar. As I have said,
Aspar had acquired great power and had fallen under the Emperor's
suspicion.[189] Therefore, the Emperor soon had him killed together with

μετὰ βραχὺ σὺν τοῖς αὐτοῦ παισίν, Ἀρδαβουρίῳ καὶ Πατρικίῳ, ὃν καίσαρα ὁ βασιλεὺς πεποίηκε πρότερον, ἵνα τὴν Ἄσπαρος εὔνοιαν ἔχῃ.]

**[54]**

[1. (John of Antioch *Fr.* 205 = *Exc. de Ins.* 89)
Ὅτι ἐπὶ Ἀνθεμίου καὶ Λέοντος τῶν βασιλέων Οὔλλιβος ὑπὸ
Ἀναγάστου ἀνηρέθη κατὰ τὴν Θράκην, ἀμφότεροι τοῦ Σκυθικοῦ
γένους καὶ πρὸς τὸ νεωτερίζειν ἐπιτήδειοι.]

[2. (*Suda* Υ 583)
Πορευομένων δὲ αὐτῶν καὶ γενομένων κατά τινα στενωπόν,
προῄει μὲν ὁ Οὐλίθ, ὑποστὰς δὲ ὁ Ἀναγάστης, τῷ δῆθεν ῥᾳδίως
ἑκάτερον αὐτῶν διεξελθεῖν, τὸν ἀπὸ τῆς κεφαλῆς πῖλον ἀνέλαβε.]

**[55]**

[(John of Antioch *Fr.* 206,1 = *Exc. de Ins.* 90)
Ὅτι τῶν Ἰσαύρων ἐν τῇ Ῥοδίων νήσῳ πρὸς ἁρπαγὴν τρα-
πέντων καὶ φόνους ἐργασαμένων, οἱ στρατιῶται τούτους διεχειρί-
σαντο. καὶ οἱ μὲν ἐπὶ τὰς ναῦς φυγόντες ἐπὶ τὴν Κωνσταντίνου ἅμα
Ζήνωνι τῷ ἐπὶ θυγατρὶ τοῦ βασιλέως γαμβρῷ παραγενόμενοι καὶ
τοὺς τὴν ἀγορὰν προτιθέντας διαθορυβοῦντες τὴν δῆμον εἰς λιθο-    5
βολίας διανέστησαν. ἐμφυλίου δὲ ἐντεῦθεν κινηθέντος πολέμου, νὺξ
ἐπιλαβοῦσα τὴν στάσιν διέλυσεν.]

4 τοῦ Müller [τῷ codd.    6 ἀνέστησαν S

**[56]**

[(John of Antioch *Fr.* 206,2 = *Exc. de Ins.* 90)
Καὶ κατὰ τοῦτον τὸν χρόνον Ἀναγάστης, ὁ τῶν Θρακίων
τελῶν ἔξαρχος, πρὸς τὸ νεωτερίζειν ἀρθεὶς τὰ Ῥωμαίων ἐπέτρεχε
φρούρια. αἰτία δὲ τῆς αὐτοῦ διαφορᾶς ἐλέγετο, ὡς Ἰορδάνου τοῦ
Ἰωάννου παιδός, ὅνπερ Ἀνέγισκλος ὁ Ἀναγάστου πατὴρ ἀνῃρήκει, ἐς
τὴν ὕπατον ἀνιέντος τιμήν· τὴν γὰρ ἐπ' αὐτῷ γενομένην ὁ Ἀνα-    5
γάστης οὐκ ἐδέξατο ψῆφον, ὡς ἐπιληψίαν νοσῶν τε καὶ δεδιώς,
φησί, μήποτε ἐν τῷ τῆς γερουσίας αἶσχος ἀπενέγκοιτο τῷ πάθει, ἂν
οὕτω τύχοι. ἄλλοι δέ φασι αὐτὸν χρημάτων ἐφιέμενον ἐς τὴν ἐπανάστασιν χωρεῖν. πολλῆς δὲ τῆς περὶ αὐτοῦ γενομένης ὑποψίας,
τέλος ἐκ τῆς βασιλικῆς αὐλῆς σταλέντες τινὲς ἔπεισαν αὐτὸν    10
παύσασθαι τῆς ἐπιχειρήσεως. ὁ μὲν οὖν Ἀρδαβούριον τὸν Ἄσπαρος
αἴτιον τῆς τυραννίδος ἀπέφηνε καὶ τὰ τούτου γράμματα παρὰ τὸν
βασιλεύοντα ἔπεμπεν.]

his sons Ardabur and Patricius, the latter of whom he had earlier made
Caesar in order to win Aspar's support.]

## [54]

[1. (John of Antioch *Fr.* 205 = *Exc. de Ins.* 89)

When Anthemius and Leo were Emperors, Oullibus was killed by
Anagast in Thrace. Both were of the Scythian race and ready for
rebellion.] [190]

[2. (*Suda* Υ 583)

As they were marching along they came to a defile. Ulith went
ahead, and Anagast, who had dropped behind so that, as he pretended,
the other might pass through more easily, lifted the cap from his head.]

## [55]

[(John of Antioch *Fr.* 206,1 = *Exc. de Ins.* 90)

When the Isaurians on Rhodes turned to robbery and murder,
the soldiers put them down. They fled to their ships and came to
Constantinople where they joined Zeno, the son-in-law of the Emperor.
When they harassed the merchants at the market, they aroused the
populace to attack them with stones. This would have been the start of
a civil insurrection, but night fell and ended the disorders.]

## [56]

[(John of Antioch *Fr.* 206,2 = *Exc. de Ins.* 90)

At this time Anagast, the commander-in-chief of the Thracian
forces, rose in revolt and overran the Roman fortresses. The reason for
his disaffection was said to be that Jordanes, the son of John, whom
Anegisclus, [191] the father of Anagast, had killed, was raised to the office
of consul. For Anagast had not been given the honour that had come
to Jordanes because he suffered from epilepsy and was, they say,
afraid that at some time he would be disgraced in the senate by his
illness, if it were to attack him there. Others say that he revolted
because he wanted money. When he had caused great apprehension,
envoys were sent from the palace who persuaded him to abandon his
attempt. He revealed that Ardabur, the son of Aspar, was to blame for
his revolt and sent Ardabur's letters to the Emperor.]

370     Priscus: Text

[57]
[(John of Antioch *Fr.* 206,2 = *Exc. de Ins.* 90)
Ὁ δὲ τοῦ βασιλέως γαμβρὸς Ζήνων τὴν ὕπατον ἔχων ἀρχὴν
ἔστελλε τοὺς τὸν Ἰνδακὸν ἀποστήσοντας ἀπὸ τοῦ λεγομένου Πα-
πιρίου λόφου. τοῦτον γὰρ πρῶτος Νέων ἐφώλευε· μεθ᾽ ὃν Παπίριος
καὶ ὁ τοῦδε παῖς Ἰνδακός, τοὺς προσοίκους ἅπαντας βιαζόμενοι καὶ
τοὺς διοδεύοντας ἀναιροῦντες.]                                         5

[58]
[(John of Antioch *Fr.* 206,2 = *Exc. de Ins.* 90 = *Fr.* 51,2)]

[59]
[(John of Antioch *Fr.* 206,2 = *Exc. de Ins.* 90)
Διανέστη δὲ τότε πρὸς πόλεμον καὶ τὸ Γότθων ἔθνος Γαλατίαν τὴν πρὸς ἑσπέραν νεμόμενον, οἵπερ πάλαι μὲν Ἀλλαρίχου
ὠνομάζοντο· ἔτι γε μὴν καὶ τὸ ἐν Παιονίᾳ βαρβαρικὸν πλῆθος,
πρότερον μὲν ὑπὸ Βαλίμερι, μετὰ δὲ τὴν ἐκείνου ἀναίρεσιν ὑπὸ
Θευδίμερι ταττόμενον τῷ Βαλίμερος ἀδελφῷ.]                             5

[60]
[(John of Antioch *Fr.* 206,2 = *Exc. de Ins.* 90 = *Fr.* 59)]

61
(Evagrius *HE* 2,16)
Ὅπως τε δόλῳ περιελθὼν ὁ Λέων μισθὸν ὥσπερ ἀποδιδοὺς
τῆς ἐς αὐτὸν προαγωγῆς ἀναιρεῖ Ἄσπαρα τὴν ἀρχὴν αὐτῷ περιθέντα, παῖδάς τε αὐτοῦ Ἀρδαβούριόν τε καὶ Πατρίκιον, ὃν Καίσαρα
πεποίητο πρότερον ἵνα τὴν Ἄσπαρος εὔνοιαν κτήσηται.
(Cf. Theophanes *Chron. a.m.* 5963 = *Fr.* 53,5)

[62]
[(John of Antioch *Fr.* 207 = *Exc. de Ins.* 91)
Ὅτι ὁ τῶν ἑσπερίων βασιλεὺς Ἀνθέμιος νόσῳ περιπεσὼν
ὑπὸ μαγγανείας χαλεπῇ πολλοὺς ἐπὶ τούτῳ ἁλόντας ἐκόλασε,
μάλιστα Ῥωμανὸν ἐν τῇ τοῦ μαγίστρου ἀρχῇ τελέσαντα καὶ ἐν τοῖς
πατρικίοις ἐγγεγραμμένον, ἐπιτήδειόν τε ἐς τὰ μάλιστα ὄντα τῷ
Ῥεκίμερι· δι᾽ ὃν ἀνιαθεὶς τῆς τε Ῥώμης ἐξῆλθε καὶ ἑξακισχιλίους   5
ἄνδρας ἐς τὸν κατὰ Βανδήλων πόλεμον ὑπ᾽ αὐτὸν ταττομένους
ἀνεκαλέσατο.]

[57]

[(John of Antioch *Fr.* 206,2 = *Exc. de Ins.* 90)

The Emperor's son-in-law Zeno, who was then consul, sent men to eject Indacus from the hill called Papirius.[192] First Neon made this his lair, and after him Papirius and his son Indacus, who attacked all those who lived in the neighbourhood and murdered passers-by.]

[58]

[(John of Antioch *Fr.* 206,2 = *Exc. de Ins.* 90 = *Fr.* 51,2)]

[59]

[(John of Antioch *Fr.* 206,2 = *Exc. de Ins.* 90)

At that time the Gothic people who were living in Galatia in the West[193] and who were of old named after Alaric, began hostilities, as also did the horde of barbarians in Pannonia who had earlier been ruled by Valamir and after his death by Theodemir, Valamir's brother.]

[60]

[(John of Antioch *Fr.* 206,2 = *Exc. de Ins.* 90 = *Fr.* 59)]

61

(Evagrius *HE* 2,16)

[Priscus the rhetor also tells] how Leo by the use of treachery rewarded Aspar, as it were, for his own promotion and destroyed the man who had made him Emperor together with his sons Ardabur and Patricius, the latter of whom he had earlier made Caesar in order to win Aspar's favour.   (Cf. Theophanes *Chron. a.m.* 5963 = *Fr.* 53,5)

[62]

(John of Antioch *Fr.* 207 = *Exc. de Ins.* 91)

Anthemius, the Emperor of the West, became seriously ill as the result of sorcery and punished many who were caught in this crime, especially Romanus, who had held the office of master and was enrolled amongst the patricians.[194] He was a very close friend of Ricimer who, out of anger over Romanus, left Rome and summoned six thousand men who were under his command for the war against the Vandals.][195]

372 Priscus: Text

[63]
[(John of Antioch *Fr.* 208 = *Exc. de Ins.* 92)
῞Οτι ἐπὶ Λέοντος τοῦ βασιλέως Ἰορδάνης ὁ τῆς ἑῴας στρατηγὸς καὶ ὕπατος εἰς ἔσχατον ἦλθε κινδύνου, ἅμα δὲ αὐτῷ Μισαὴλ
καὶ Κοσμᾶς τῶν βασιλείων ὄντες θαλαμηπόλοι, ὅτι τὰ βασίλεια
φυλάττειν καταλελησμένοι, τοῦ βασιλέως ἔξω διαιτωμένου, Ἰορδάνη
τὰ ἔνδον ἱστορῆσαι βουληθέντι ἐφῆκαν.]                                      5

[64]
[1. (John of Antioch *Fr.* 209,1 = *Exc. de Ins.* 93)
῞Οτι ὁ Ῥεκίμερ εἰς διαφορὰν πρὸς τὸν Ἀνθέμιον καταστὰς τὸν
βασιλέα τῶν ἑσπερίων, καὶ ταῦτα θυγατέρα αὐτοῦ κατεγγυηθεὶς
Ἀλυπίαν, ἐμφύλιον ἔνδον τῆς πόλεως συνεκρότησε πόλεμον ἐπὶ
μῆνας θʹ. καὶ Ἀνθεμίῳ μὲν συνεμάχουν οἵ τε ἐν τέλει καὶ ὁ δῆμος,
τῷ δὲ Ῥεκίμερι τὸ τῶν οἰκείων βαρβάρων πλῆθος. συνῆν δὲ καὶ       5
Ὀδόακρος, γένος ὢν τῶν προσαγορευομένων Σκίρων, πατρὸς δὲ
Ἰδικῶνος, καὶ ἀδελφὸς Ὀνοούλφου, [καὶ] Ἁρματίου σωματοφύλακός
τε καὶ σφαγέως γενομένου. καὶ ὁ μὲν Ἀνθέμιος κατῴκει ἐν τοῖς
βασιλείοις, ὁ δὲ Ῥεκίμερ τὰ περὶ τὸν Τίβεριν διαφράξας λιμῷ τοὺς
ἔνδον ἐβιάζετο. ἐντεῦθεν [τε] αὐτοῖς συμβολῆς γενομένης, πολὺ τῆς    10
Ἀνθεμίου κατέπεσε μοίρας· τοὺς δὲ λοιποὺς ὁ Ῥεκίμερ παραστησάμενος δόλῳ βασιλέα τὸν Ὀλύβριον ἀπεδείκνυσιν. πέντε γοῦν διόλου
μῆνας ἐμφύλιος τῆς Ῥώμης ἐπεκράτει πόλεμος, ἄχρις οὗ, τῶν περὶ
τὸν Ἀνθέμιον ἐνδόντων τοῖς βαρβάροις καὶ τὸν βασιλεύοντα γυμνὸν
καταλιπόντων, αὐτοῖς τοῖς πτωχεύουσιν ἀναμιχθεὶς ἐν τοῖς πρόσφυξι   15
τοῦ μάρτυρος Χρυσογόνου γίνεται· ἐκεῖ τε τῆς κεφαλῆς ἀποτέμνεται
ὑπὸ Γονδουβάνδου τοῦ Ῥεκίμερος ἀδελφοῦ βασιλεύσας ἔτη πέντε
μῆνας γʹ ἡμέρας ὀκτωκαίδεκα.]

4 θʹ [εʹ Müller   7 καὶ expunxi   10 τε exp. Müller

[2. (Theophanes *Chron. a.m.* 5964)
Ἐν Ἰταλίᾳ δὲ Ῥεκίμερ ὁ στρατηγός, οὗ καὶ πρώην ἐμνήσθην,
γαμβρὸς δὲ Ἀνθεμίου, τοῦ εὐσεβῶς ἐν Ῥώμῃ βασιλεύσαντος, ἐπανίσταται τῷ ἰδίῳ κηδεστῇ. καὶ πολέμου κρατοῦντος τὴν χώραν,
λιμώττουσιν οὕτως αἱ τοῦ βασιλέως δυνάμεις, ὡς καὶ βυρσῶν καὶ
ἄλλων ἀηθῶν ἅψασθαι βρωμάτων, αὐτὸν δὲ τὸν βασιλέα Ἀνθέμιον    5
ἕβδομον ἔτος ἔχοντα τῆς ἀρχῆς ἀναιρεθῆναι.]

[65]
[(John of Antioch *Fr.* 209,2 = *Exc. de Ins.* 93)
Ὁ δὲ Ῥεκίμερ αὐτὸν μὲν βασιλικῆς ἠξίωσε ταφῆς, τὸν δὲ

**[63]**

[(John of Antioch *Fr.* 208 = *Exc. de Ins.* 92)

During the reign of the Emperor Leo, Jordanes, the general of the East and consul, came into extreme danger together with Misael and Cosmas, who were chamberlains of the palace.[196] For when the Emperor was away, they failed to guard the palace and allowed in Jordanes, who wished to see the interior.]

**[64]**

[1. (John of Antioch *Fr.* 209,1 = *Exc. de Ins.* 93)

Ricimer became hostile towards Anthemius, the Emperor of the western Romans, and, even though he was married[197] to his daughter Alypia, fought a civil war within the city for nine months.[198] The authorities and the populace of Rome fought on Anthemius' side, while Ricimer was supported by a force of his own barbarians. Also on Ricimer's side was Odovacer, a man of the tribe called the Sciri, whose father was Edeco and whose brother was Onulf, the bodyguard and the murderer of Harmatius.[199] Anthemius resided in the palace, while Ricimer blockaded the area by the Tiber and afflicted those inside with hunger. As a result a pitched battle was fought, and many of Anthemius' party were slain. Ricimer subdued the rest by treachery and proclaimed Olybrius Emperor. Rome was gripped by a civil war of altogether five months until Anthemius, his supporters having surrendered to the barbarians and left their Emperor defenceless, mingled with the beggars and joined the supplicants at the church of the martyr Chrysogonus.[200] There his head was cut off by Gundoband, Ricimer's brother.[201] He had reigned for five years, three months and eighteen days.]

[2. (Theophanes *Chron. a.m.* 5964)

In Italy Ricimer, the general and son-in-law of Anthemius, who was ruling righteously in Rome, revolted from his own father-in-law. As war gripped the land,[202] the Emperor's forces were so hungry that they ate hides and other unwonted foods, and Anthemius was killed in the seventh year of his reign.]

**[65]**

[(John of Antioch *Fr.* 209,2 = *Exc. de Ins.* 93)

Ricimer considered him [Anthemius] worthy of a royal burial

Ὀλύβριον ἐπὶ τὴν βασίλειον ἀνήγαγεν αὐλήν. Ὀλυβρίου δὲ κατὰ τὸν
εἰρημένον τρόπον τὴν Ῥωμαίων παρειληφότος ἀρχήν, Ῥεκίμερ
ἡμερῶν εἴσω λ' καταλύει τὸν βίον, αἵματος αὐτῷ πλείστου ἐξεμε-
θέντος. Ὀλύβριος δὲ μετὰ τοῦτον ις' μόνας ἐπιβιοὺς ἡμέρας ὑδέρῳ        5
συσχεθεὶς μεταλλάττει, τοῖς βασιλεῦσιν <ἐν>αριθμηθεὶς εἰς μῆνας
ἓξ ἥμισυ. τὴν δὲ τοῦ Ῥεκίμερος τάξιν ὑπεισελθὼν Γουνδουβάλης,
ἀνεψιὸς ὢν αὐτοῦ, Γλυκέριον τὴν τοῦ ῥ ήμητος τῶν δομεστίκων ἀξίαν
ἔχοντα ἐπὶ τὴν βασιλείαν ἄγει. γνοὺς δὲ Λέων ὁ τῶν ἑῴων βασιλεὺς
τὴν τοῦ Γλυκερίου ἀναγόρευσιν ἐπιστρατεύει κατ' αὐτοῦ, Νέπωτα       10
στρατηγὸν ἀποδείξας· ὃς ἐπειδὴ τὴν Ῥώμην κατέλαβεν, ἀμαχεὶ τὸν
Γλυκέριον ἐχειρώσατο καὶ τῶν βασιλείων ἐξώσας ἐπίσκοπον τοῦτον
Σάλωνος προχειρίζεται η' μῆνας ἐντρυφήσαντα τῇ ἀρχῇ. εὐθὺς γοῦν
ὁ Νέπως βαυιλεὺς ἀναδειχθεὶς ἦρχε τῆς Ῥώμης.]

5 ις' [ιγ' edd.    6 ἐν- add. Müller    8 ἀξίαν Müller [ἀξίως codd.    12 τοῦτον
om. P et edd.

## Sedis Incertae

## [66]

[1. (Procopius Wars 6,15,16-23)

Τῶν δὲ ἱδρυμένων ἐν Θούλῃ βαρβάρων ἓν μόνον ἔθνος, οἳ
Σκριθίφινοι ἐπικαλοῦνται, θηριώδη τινὰ βιοτὴν ἔχουσιν. οὔτε γὰρ
ἱμάτια ἐνδιδύσκονται οὔτε ὑποδεδεμένοι βαδίζουσιν οὔτε οἶνον πίνουσιν
οὔτε τι ἐδώδιμον ἐκ τῆς γῆς ἔχουσιν. οὔτε γὰρ αὐτοὶ γῆν γεωργοῦσιν
οὔτε τι αὐτοῖς αἱ γυναῖκες ἐργάζονται, ἀλλὰ ἄνδρες ἀεὶ ξὺν ταῖς       5
γυναιξὶ τὴν θήραν μόνην ἐπιτηδεύουσι. θηρίων τε γὰρ καὶ ἄλλων
ζῴων μέγα τι χρῆμα αἵ τε ὗλαι αὐτοῖς φέρουσι, μεγάλαι ὑπερφυῶς
οὖσαι, καὶ τὰ ὄρη ἃ ταύτῃ ἀνέχει. καὶ κρέασι μὲν θηρίων ἀεὶ τῶν
ἁλισκομένων σιτίζονται, τὰ δέρματα δὲ ἀμφιέννυνται, ἐπεί τε αὐτοῖς
οὔτε λίνον οὔτε ὄργανον ὅτῳ ῥάπτοιέν ἐστιν, οἱ δὲ τῶν θηρίων τοῖς       10
νεύροις τὰ δέρματα ἐς ἄλληλα ταῦτα ξυνδέοντες οὕτω δὴ ἐς τὸ σῶμα
ὅλον ἀμπίσχονται. οὐ μὴν οὐδὲ τὰ βρέφη αὐτοῖς κατὰ ταὐτὰ τιθη-
νοῦνται τοῖς ἄλλοις ἀνθρώποις. οὐ γὰρ σιτίζονται Σκριθιφίνων παιδία
γυναικῶν γάλακτι οὐδὲ μητέρων ἅπτονται τιτθοῦ, ἀλλὰ ζῴων τῶν
ἁλισκομένων τοῖς μυελοῖς ἐκτρέφονται μόνοις. ἐπειδὰν οὖν γυνὴ τά-       15
χιστα τέκοι, δέρματι τὸ βρέφος ἐμβαλομένη κρεμᾷ μὲν εὐθὺς ἐπὶ δέν-
δρου τινός, μυελὸν δέ οἱ ἐπὶ τοῦ στόματος ἐνθεμένη ξὺν τῷ ἀνδρὶ ἐπὶ
τὴν εἰωθυῖαν στέλλεται θήραν. ἐπὶ κοινῇ γὰρ τά τε ἄλλα δρῶσι καὶ

8 τὰ ὄρη ἃ ταύτῃ L [ταύτῃ τὰ ὄρη K    17-18 ξὺν τῷ ἀνδρὶ ἐπὶ τὴν εἰωθυῖαν
στέλλετει θήραν K [εὐθὺς στέλλεται ἐπὶ θήραν L    18 τά τε ἄλλα δρῶσι
καὶ K [τοῖς ἀνδράσι L

and he installed Olybrius in the royal palace. When Olybrius had received the sovereignty in the manner described, Ricimer died within thirty days after vomiting up a great deal of blood. Olybrius survived him by only sixteen days, when he was attacked by dropsy and passed away, having been numbered amongst the Emperors for about six-and-a-half months. Ricimer was succeeded in his position by his nephew, Gundobaules.[203] He made Glycerius, who held the rank of count of the domestics, Emperor. When Leo, the Emperor of the East, learned of the elevation of Glycerius, he sent a force against him, appointing Nepos general. When he took Rome, he overcame Glycerius without a fight, ejected him from the palace and made him bishop of Salonae. He had enjoyed sovereignty for eight months. Nepos was straightway appointed Emperor and ruled Rome.]

## Unplaced Fragments
### [66]
[1. (Procopius *Wars* 6,15,16-23)

Of the barbarians settled in Thule, only one people, that called the Scrithifini, live a life like that of the wild beasts. For they wear neither woven garments nor shoes for walking, and they do not drink wine or eat food from the earth. They do not till the land themselves, neither do their wives work it for them, but they only hunt, always together with their women. For the vast forests and the mountains which are there produce for them a great number of wild animals and other game. They eat only the flesh of the wild animals which they kill and they dress themselves in their skins. Since they have neither flax nor sewing needles, they tie these skins together with sinews and thus cover their whole body. Even their babies are raised in a manner different from other humans. For the young of the Scrithifini are not fed women's milk and are not put to their mother's breast, but their diet is exclusively the marrow of the animals which have been killed. As soon as a woman has given birth, she places the baby in a skin, hangs it up in a tree, places some marrow in its mouth and sets off with her husband upon the usual hunt. For they perform everything together,

τὸ ἐπιτήδευμα μετίασι τοῦτο. τούτοις μὲν οὖν δὴ τοῖς βαρβάροις τὰ
ἐς τὴν δίαιταν ταύτῃ πῃ ἔχει.]    20

[2. (Jordanes *Get.* 3,21)
  Aliae vero ibi sunt gentes Screrefennae, que frumentorum non
queritant victum, sed carnibus ferarum atque ovis avium vivunt; ubi
tanta paludibus fetura ponitur, ut et augmentum prestent generi et
satietatem ad cupiam genti.]

1 sunt [tres OB        2 ovium aviumque HPVLA  ovium (*om.* aviumque) OB
4 ad [ac B


### 67

(*Suda* A 1660)
  Ὅρκοι δὲ ἐπὶ τῇ ἀμοιβαίᾳ σφῶν ἐδίδοντο πίστει, οὐ μόνον
αὐτοῖς, ἀλλὰ καὶ τοῖς παραγινομένοις ἐκ τῶν βασιλείων Ῥωμαίων
τῆς διαλλαγῆς ἕνεκα τῶν ἀνδρῶν. Πρίσκος φησίν.

2 τοῖς παραγινομένοις M Niebuhr [τοῖς τῶν παραγινομένων ceteri codd.    τῆς
post βασιλείων ceteri codd. praeter FM


### 68

(*Suda* Π 687)
  Οἱ δὲ πεμφθέντες παρόδου ἐς τὴν πόλιν οὐκ ἔτυχον ὑστερή-
σαντες. Πρίσκος φησί.

including this activity. Such is the daily life of these barbarians.]

[2. (Jordanes *Get.* 3,21)

There [i.e. on the island of Scandza] are other peoples, the Screrefennae, who do not eat vegetable food but live off the flesh of wild animals and birds' eggs. The marshes there produce such a great abundance of these that there is sufficient for an increase in population and the satisfaction of all its desires.]

## 67

(*Suda* A 1660)

Oaths were given as mutual sureties not only for themselves but also for those who had come from the Roman court to reconcile the men.[204] Priscus says this.

## 68

(*Suda* Π 687)

Those who had been sent were not allowed to enter the city when they arrived too late. Priscus says this.

# NOTES TO PRISCUS

**1.** Although here Jordanes is looking back to his earlier story on the origin of the Huns (that they were the offspring of witches expelled by the Scythians/Goths and of unclean spirits), nevertheless, at this point Procopius also, who does not include such a story on the origin of the Huns, states as his view that the hind's purpose was to bring woe to Scythia. Thus, a similar sentiment was probably found in Priscus.

**2.** The passage of Jordanes has been printed rather than that of Procopius because, although the latter is a little more diffuse, Jordanes has all the detail in Procopius and more. The list of the tribes subjugated by the Huns appears also at the beginning of *Fr.* 2, the first passage preserved in the *Exc. de Leg. Rom.* (the doublet Alpidzuros/Alcidzuros is explained in Maenchen-Helfen 1973 p.402), where they are identified as tribes living by the Danube whose members had fled to alliance with the Romans. This suggests that the preliminary material was inserted by Priscus not as part of a longish digression on the origin and early history of the Huns (the traditional view, which I accepted in vol. I p.62), but as a brief explanation both of the status vis-à-vis the Huns of the tribes named and of the Hunnic king Rua's anger at the Romans. With this interpretation the error of Procopius (*Wars* 8,5,10) or his source in dating the Hunnic crossing of Maeotis to the period after the Vandalic crossing to Africa and the Visigothic entry into Spain can be easily explained, since in Priscus the story of the crossing was closely linked with the end of Rua's reign, 434/35 A.D., a date by which the Vandals were in Africa and the Visigoths in Spain. Thus, careless condensation simply dated the crossing by the narrative context to which it was linked.

Agathias (5,11,3) and Cedrenus (I p.547) mention the same story of the crossing, but their relationship to Priscus is quite unclear. Gordon (1960 p.199 nn.2 and 3) argues that the subsequent passage of Jordanes (*Get.* 24,126-28) is also from Priscus, but the lack of parallel material in Procopius and the very close verbal parallels there with Ammianus (31,2,1-9 *passim*) make this highly unlikely.

**3.** On these tribes see Maenchen-Helfen 1973 pp.402f., 438f., 453f. Maenchen-Helfen (p.90) takes Priscus to mean that these tribes "fled into Roman territory and offered their services to Theodosius". But if the tribes of Scythia subdued at the end of this passage are the ones mentioned at the beginning (and part of the purpose of the treaty from the Huns' point of view seems to have been to secure themselves for this expedition), then it must be a case not of tribes fleeing but of substantial numbers of individuals fleeing to seek service with the Romans (a later concern of Attila). Thus, the first clause of the treaty attempted to deal with this problem.

**4.**    At this date (?435) he was not yet quaestor (which he became in 438) but one of the *magistri scriniorum* (*PLRE* II 'Epigenes'). For another example of such a reference forward see n.102.

**5.**    Since the immediate purpose of this clause would be to forestall Roman help to the tribes mentioned at the beginning of this passage, the MSS reading makes best sense and Niebuhr's emendation (αἱρομένῳ) is unnecessary.

**6.**    On the otherwise unattested Sorosgi see Maenchen-Helfen 1973 p.439. The Greek suggests that, unlike the tribes which the Huns first subdued, these were outside their immediate dominion.

**7.**    The next few lines are an almost word-for-word parallel with the previous passage of John of Antioch from the words καὶ ἐς τοσοῦτον τὰ πράγματα.

**8.**    Noviodunum was in Scythia Minor and on the Danube. The Rubi (probably Rugi) seem to have been not invaders but a people settled near to Noviodunum, some of whom revolted (see Thompson 1948 pp.217f.). The revolt can be dated no more closely than between the beginning of the History (434/5) and the fall of Naissus (442). The initial statement that Valips had earlier (πάλιν) revolted might indicate that Priscus had described the beginning of the revolt in an earlier passage and that the present passage deals with the conclusion of the revolt.

**9.**    The fort would have been the Constantia of *Fr.* 2. The phraseology imitates Thucydides 1,144,2, from Pericles' reply to the Spartan ultimatum. A comparison of these devastating Hunnic raids with the Peloponnesian War would not have been out of place, and Thucydidean reminiscences crop up frequently hereafter.

**10.**    Θήκας could mean "treasure houses", but "tombs" is the likeliest rendering since συλᾶν is common late Greek for tomb-robbing (Thompson 1947 p.62).

**11.**    The ancient name of the river Nischava, upon which Naissus stands, is unknown. The city is said by Priscus himself (*Fr.* 11,1) to be five days' journey from the Danube (which is never called Δανούβα, and always by Priscus Ἴστρος). Therefore, Δανούβας is either the ancient name of the Nischava or (as most editors think) corrupt. No satisfactory emendation has been proposed (see Thompson 1947 p.61).

**12.**    In fact, he embellished it, since it was his birthplace (Anon. Val. 2,2).

**13.**    For Thompson's criticism of the authenticity of this description and my defence of it see vol. I p.54. Gordon (1960 p.200 n.19) follows Thompson in regarding the story of the bridge as "a bad guess". For my own ordering of the fragments, which makes the building of the bridge quite likely, see vol. I p.168 n.48.

**14.** Thompson's emendation εἲν<αι οὖτ>ως seems misconceived. The point is not that wheels made the access easy, but that the easy (i.e. smooth) access made the use of wheels feasible.

**15.** This machine seems to have been a type of crane (Blockley 1972 p.22 n.12). For the Thucydidean imitations in this and the following descriptions see Thompson 1945 pp.92-94 and Blockley *art. cit.* pp.22-25.

**16.** Malalas' somewhat Christianised account of the fall of Antiochus is the fullest and the earliest which survives. It is misplaced just before the fall of the prefect Cyrus in all the sources, and Theophanes (*Chron. a.m.* 5936) specifically dates it to the preceding year, whereas Antiochus seems to have been disgraced around 421 (*PLRE* II 'Antiochus' 5). The error might have arisen out of Priscus' mention of the disgrace before the fall of Cyrus as part of a retrospective passage attacking eunuchs and specifically Chrysaphius, who replaced Cyrus (see vol. I p.117). Zonaras (13,22,14-16) confirms that Antiochus was made a priest.

**17.** The words αὐτὸν ἐπὶ τόπον, Αὔγουστε, omitted by both Theophanes and the *Paschal Chronicle*, are a studied insult to Theodosius.

**18.** The passage of Malalas has been given for the same reasons as those remarked in n.16. The passage of the *Paschal Chronicle* is usually printed as Priscus *Fr.* 3a, but its claims are no stronger than the passage of Malalas (see vol. I pp.116f.), and it omits some details which he gives. However, it does add, what is missing in Malalas, that Cyrus used to go out in the carriage of the praetorian prefect and return in that of the urban prefect (καὶ προῄει μὲν ὡς ἔπαρχος πραιτορίων εἰς τὴν καροῦχαν τῶν ἐπάρχων, ἀνεχώρει δὲ καθήμενος εἰς τὴν καροῦχαν τοῦ ἐπάρχου τῆς πόλεως) and says that, "he himself contrived that lights were set up in the workshops in the evenings as well as at night" (καὶ αὐτὸς ἐπενόησεν τὰ ἑσπερινὰ φῶτα ἅπτεσθαι εἰς τὰ ἐργαστήρια ὁμοίως καὶ τὰ νυκτερινά – perhaps a health and safety measure for the workers). Both the *Paschal Chronicle* and Theophanes (probably wrongly) give Smyrna as the place of which Cyrus was made bishop. All three sources continue with an obviously Christianised story of how Cyrus, by his wit, won over the people of the place, who had shown a marked propensity for murdering their bishops. It is possible that a similar anecdote, less obviously Christian, was found in Priscus.

**19.** Although this and the following are a little unclear, they seem to be mainly an attack on the cowardice of the Roman military establishment, to whom the Asimuntians are contrasted. Towards the end of this fragment the Roman commanders are said to be cowed (κατεπτηχότων) by their defeats.

**20.** Under the previous year, *a.m.* 5941, a passage which could be Priscan, although there is no indication of this at all. The naval expedition in question is the one against Gaiseric in 441. Its mention here reflects the fact that in this passage Theophanes is incorporating details of both Hunnic invasions (of 441/2 and 447).

**21.** The form of his name varies widely in the sources. The form preferred by modern scholars is Arnegisclus.

**22.** The immediate source of Nicephorus is not known (Eustathius?), though there are clear verbal parallels with Theophanes.

**23.** For the interpretation of this passage and its dating to 447 see Croke 1982 (against Bayless 1979).

**24.** On the reading ἀπέσταλκά σοι see Thompson 1947 p.62. I have assumed that ἔπειτα marks the transition from summary to direct quotation, whereas usually only the second quotation is treated as such.

**25.** For the translation of λίθοις Ἰνδικοῖς see Thompson *loc.cit.* at n.24 above.

**26.** The identification of Edeco as the father of Odovacer (who is called by the *Suda* K 693 the son of a Thuringian father and Scirian mother) is accepted by *PLRE* II 'Edeco' but rejected by Maenchen-Helfen 1973 p.388 n.104.

**27.** This is a reminiscence of Homer *Il.* 8,490f. (Bornmann 1974 p.116).

**28.** See lines 12f. of the present passage.

**29.** Thompson (1948 p.106) and Browning (1953 pp.143f.) both make the envoys reach (and, indeed, travel beyond) the Danube on the next day after leaving Agintheus near to Naissus. But in *Fr.* 11,1 Priscus says specifically that Naissus was five days' journey from the Danube for an unencumbered traveller, a measurement which he probably obtained from his experience on this occasion; in the present passage there is no indication of the time taken over the journey. Thus, if the envoys took five days to reach the Danube, Browning (*loc.cit.*) is wrong to argue that their crossing point was at Ratiaria, an argument which also ignores Priscus' firm statement that they were marching westwards. It seems more likely that the crossing of the Danube was near to Viminacium or Margus, a distance of over 800 stades from Naissus, a four-day journey at the Herodotean rate of 200 stades per day and just under that at the Procopian rate of 210 (*Wars* 1,1,17). The extra day might have been taken up at the beginning by the short detour to Agintheus.

**30.** De Boor here reads διαφανούσης, attributing the conjecture to Niebuhr, whose text and apparatus both offer, however, διαφαινούσης, presumably by comparison with the reading at line 400. My own reading is that of the MSS.

**31.** For ὑλῶδει Browning (*art.cit.* [at n.29] p.143) seems to read ἑλῶδει ("marshy"), of which I can find no trace in the editions I have seen. Gibbon appears to have had the same reading (cf. *Decline and Fall* [Everyman edition] III p.363).

**32.** The MSS reading ποιουμένῳ is defended by Bornmann 1974 pp.116f.

**33.**    Browning (*loc.cit.* at n.31) is wrong to regard this halt as the end of a full day's journey and therefore a useful measure of distance travelled. It is clear that the envoys had been forced to stop early, and the time of halting and the distance travelled on that day are not specified. But since on the next day it took them until the ninth hour to reach Attila's camp, they must have halted a considerable distance away; and thus, for the attendants of Edeco to gallop ahead and the two Scythians to return by late afternoon, they must have halted quite early in the day.

**34.**    The embassy which ended the 'great' invasion of 447 (*Fr.* 9,3, *init.*).

**35.**    Though usually regarded as corrupt, ταῦτα can be taken as an accusative of respect, or πρός can be inserted.

**36.**    *PLRE* II 'Rusticius' 2 distinguishes this person from the one who appears in *Fr.* 14 as a prisoner from Upper Moesia used by Attila as a secretary. They are probably identical. All Priscus indicates here is that Rusticius was returning from Italy, where he had been on business for Constantius (cf. later in this fragment, line 578, where he is called τοῦ κατὰ Κωνστάντιον).

**37.**    This Constantius is to be distinguished from another secretary of Attila of the same name, also sent by Aetius, but a Gaul who was crucified by the Huns before the death of Bleda (see the present fragment, lines 329-42).

**38.**    The date of Carpilio's sojourn as hostage with Attila cannot be fixed. Attila says that Carpilio was hostage with himself (παρ' αὐτῷ) which might mean after he had killed Bleda in 445. But perhaps the language is used more loosely and indicates merely the period after he and Bleda had become kings in 434/5 (cf. Maenchen-Helfen 1973 p.106 n.481).

**39.**    The Greek is not entirely clear here. I take Priscus to be saying that after Attila had ordered Vigilas to go immediately to Constantinople with Eslas, he then told Maximinus to remain with his court to receive the replies and finally he closed the audience by accepting the gifts and dismissing the envoys. Some of the MSS and most of the editors omit the words from δόντας to ὑπεξιέναι, but this is too easy a solution to the difficulty.

**40.**    Jordanes (*Get.* 50,262) calls him Ellac. Since Attila had more than two sons, πρεσβυτέρῳ is an example of the common late-Greek use of the comparative for the superlative.

**41.**    There is a long discussion, with bibliography, of the name and location of this people in Maenchen-Helfen (1973 pp.427-38), who would place them on the Black Sea to the West of the Crimea (cf. lines 550f. of the present fragment).

**42.**    Maenchen-Helfen's analysis of this name (1973 pp.408f.) suggests that he was a Hunnic shaman.

**43.** These rivers are called *Tisia Tibisiaque et Dricca* by Jordanes (*Get.* 34,178 = *Fr.* 11,3). They cannot be identified with any certainty, but, if one accepts the view that the envoys crossed the Danube near to Viminacium (see n.29), then the Tiphesas/Tibisia may be the Timeşul (Temes) and the Tigas/Tisia would be the Tisza (Theiss). If the journey of seven days noted at line 313 was that from Attila's encampment (which was about a day's journey from the Danube) to the village where they met the western Roman envoys, then at the standard rate of 200 stades per day, the seven-day journey (less one day lost drying out after the storm [lines 305f.], plus one day from the Danube) would have covered about 1400 stades or about 175 miles (at eight stades to the mile). If they had crossed the Tisza (which surely must be Jordanes' Tisia and thus Priscus' Tigas), they would, therefore, be to the West of that river and on a latitude well to the South of the Körös, a reasonable place to meet envoys coming from Noricum (but see n.47 and the text thereat). Attila's headquarters seem to have been a short journey further on, across some, presumably small, rivers (lines 356-58). This would put the headquarters between the Tisza and the Danube, conveniently placed not only to threaten the two parts of the Roman Empire, but also close to the part of Pannonia in his hands. (Bibliography in Thompson 1948 pp.121f., whose view is here followed.)

**44.** On the (probably) Germanic *medos* ("mead") see Gelzer 1924 pp.313f. and Thompson 1947 p.62. On *kamon*, a beer known in Pannonia, see Thompson *loc.cit.* and Maenchen-Helfen 1973 pp.424f.

**45.** Bornmann (1974 p.117) points out that this description imitates Thucydidean language, especially of 5,70,1, but also of 2,4,2 and 8,24,1.

**46.** On these three, respectively, see *PLRE* II 'Romulus' 2, 'Promotus' 1 and 'Romanus' 2. The description of Romanus' office makes it unclear whether he was *comes rei militaris* or *dux*.

**47.** The punctuation of the text, including the placing of the lacuna, is that of de Boor. The older editors place a comma after ἐγεγαμήκει and the lacuna after πόλεως. No explanations are offered for either reading.

**48.** The conjecture ἀσήμου ("bullion" or "plate") for the MSS ἀρμίου or ἀσμίου is that of Bury (1958 I p.282 n.2).

**49.** As distinct from the eastern Gauls (Γαλατοί) of Asia Minor.

**50.** Probably in the first invasion of 441-2 (see vol. I p.168 n.48).

**51.** Since Niebuhr Σκυθικῶν, which the MSS favour, has been emended to συνθηκῶν (i.e. the agreements with the bishop). But the MSS reading makes good sense, since if Constantius had spoken to the bishop during the siege (as an envoy?), whatever he received would have been regarded by the Huns as part of the common booty (as is clear from Attila's attitude towards Silvanus). Therefore, in withholding the bowls he was ignoring the rights of the Huns, whom he served.

52.   The MSS read here εἰ οὖν μὴ ... ἀποσταίη, which makes the construction of τῆς εὐλόγου προφάσεως awkward. Niebuhr would change μὴ to μετά which makes the envoys issue an unlikely threat (i.e. they would send the gold only if Attila dropped his demands for the bowls). My insertion of μετά makes the envoys' words rather more conciliatory, and is, I think, an easier correction than Bornmann's proposal (1974 pp.118f.) to read εὐλόγῳ προφάσει.

53.   On the location of this village, which is often referred to as 'Attila's headquarters', see nn.29 and 43 together. One further indication that the village was west of the Tisza/Theiss (and perhaps quite close to the Danube) and not, as has often been suggested, north of the Körös or even (as Browning [*art. cit.* at n.29] argued) much further east in Wallachia, is that the baths of Onegesius, described just below, were built of stone brought from Pannonia, which the Huns are unlikely to have transported for enormous distances across the Danube.

54.   Εὐξέστοις probably qualifies only σανίσιν (which are the boards forming the face of the building) and not ξύλοις (perhaps the timbers of the frame to which the boards were attached). My interpretation appears to differ from that of Thompson (*JHS* 1945 p.115) who translates "well-planed planks and panels." (In general I follow his interpretation of Priscus' description of Attila's headquarters, except where I specifically note disagreement.) The Gothic technique of the construction of the wooden buildings is remarked by Maenchen-Helfen 1973 p.180.

55.   As Thompson (*art. cit.* [at n.54] p.113) points out, the Greek does not mean – as it has been taken to mean – that the road passed through Onegesius' house (which would thus have been a kind of gatehouse), but that it passed between the buildings that made up his compound.

56.   Maenchen-Helfen (1973 p.382 n.57) insists that πάραλος here = *ripa* (i.e. the lands along the Danube), not "sea coast", as it is usually rendered. But the recent Hunnic invasions had swept over much of Illyricum and Thrace, and it is hard to see why Priscus would single out the peoples near to the Danube as able to speak Greek. If my rendering (which is also that of Bury 1958 I p.283) is correct, then it constitutes an interesting note on the failure of Greek to penetrate into the interior at this period.

57.   Thompson (1947 pp.63f.) points out that the description of the hairstyle uses Herodotean language (3,8,3) and that the Hunnic style is described by Procopius *Anecd.* 7.

58.   In 441-42 (see *Fr.* 6,1).

59.   The meaning of διὰ τὸ ἐπὶ πλείστοις διατίθεσθαι is unclear. Both Müller's version (*quoniam plurimum auctoritate valent*) and that of Gordon ("because they sold for the most money" – supported by Bornmann 1974 pp.119f.) strain the Greek. My own version (which is not original) assumes that in the division of spoils, the λογάδες, being

the war leaders, would be responsible for the enrichment of the men
under their command and would thus choose the prisoners who were
likely to bring the highest ransom. Clearly, as in the case of the Greek
captured at Viminacium, prisoners might also pay for their freedom
with booty earned in war.

**60.** Whether by διὰ τοὺς τυράννους the Greek is castigating the
Emperors or whether he is explaining the ban on carrying arms by fear
of usurpation, is unclear. I suspect the latter.

**61.** At this point in the Greek the direct speech changes to
indirect, which continues until a few sentences from the end. Perhaps
the indirect speech marks a part where the excerptor has condensed a
longer original.

**62.** On the form of the name see Maenchen-Helfen 1973 p.408
(with references).

**63.** See nn.40 and 41 above.

**64.** The interpretation of this passage generally follows Thompson
*JHS* 1945 pp.113f., except that I read λίθων (which is closer to the
reading of the MS), rather than his δοκῶν, since the lack of building
stone in the area remarked at lines 366f. need not indicate a lack of
stones to build piles, as he argues. While following Thompson's interpretation of ἐμβεβλημένων ... ἀποτελοῦσιν, I have taken the phrase
to qualify both σανίδων and λίθων. Thus, Priscus is saying that both
types of building were raised on piles.

**65.** On Rusticius and Constantius see nn.36 and 37.

**66.** The most recent discussion (with bibliography) of the date of
this attack is by Maenchen-Helfen (1973 pp.51-59), who identifies it
with the great invasion of the East in 395, in which case the war in
which the Romans were involved would have been the war between
Theodosius I and Eugenius. Romulus does not say, however, that the
Huns entered Roman territory, which they certainly did in 395; and the
tone of his remarks suggests to me that the attack in question is not one
well known to the eastern Empire. Gordon (1960 p.202) suggested that
the attack took place during 423-25, while there were hostilities
between the eastern Romans and the usurper John, and Thompson
(1948 p.31) advanced 415-20 "or a little later". I prefer his "little
later", specifically 420-22, when there were hostilities between the
Roman Empire and Persia. The point at which the Romans failed to
resist the Hunnic advance – indeed, the only points at which the
Romans could have resisted if the attack were not into the Empire itself
– would have been the Tauric Chersonese, or even Lazica, if the Huns
kept close to the north shore of the Black Sea.

**67.** Τοὺς διαβεβηκότας most naturally means those Huns who
came over to the Romans with Basich and Kursich, perhaps as allies
of Aetius.

**68.** Thompson (1948 p.31 and n.1), citing Marquart *Ērānšahr* p.97,
suggests that this is a reference to the oilfields of Baku in Azerbaijan on

the coast of the Caspian Sea. If this is so, the Huns took a wide sweep to the East on their way home, and the reading ὀλίγων is a considerable understatement or a bad guess on the part of an editor.

**69.** The rank would have been master of both branches of the soldiery (*magister utriusque militiae*). *PLRE* II 'Attila' points out that since Priscus heard this from the western envoys, it must have been conferred by the western Emperor, Valentinian III. But it could equally well be Priscus' parenthetical comment about Theodosius. There is no independent evidence for this (honorary) title for Attila.

**70.** I am assuming here that ἐκείνῳ refers to Theodosius and that Attila is complaining again about the fugitives amongst the eastern Romans. But since Constantiolus, the speaker, was a westerner, it could equally well refer to Valentinian III.

**71.** On these rivers see n.43.

**72.** Although it is just possible that this information is from a note in Priscus which his Byzantine excerptors omitted, it is much more likely to be an addition by Jordanes or his source. Browning (1953 pp.144f.), who appears to regard it as from Priscus, locates this ambush in Transylvania or Eastern Wallachia and uses it to support his argument that Attila's headquarters were in that area rather than in the Hungarian plain. But if it were an addition by Jordanes or his source, its value to his argument is greatly diminished.

**73.** This is a free rendering of *Fr.* 11,2 lines 358-61, although the interest in the joints is not evident in the text of Priscus which we have.

**74.** This seems to be based upon *Fr.* 13,1 lines 28-33, although the picture given by the Latin is rather different from that of the Greek.

**75.** The sentences which I have omitted are not from Priscus. For the Priscan origin of the rest of this paragraph see vol. I n.51 on p.169, and cf. the Greek form of the name Roas.

**76.** On the sword cult, common amongst peoples of the steppes and Germanic and Iranian tribes, see Alföldi 1932 pp.232-38; Maenchen-Helfen 1973 pp.278-80.

**77.** Κύλικα is a conjecture for the MSS ἐπόλικα. De Boor suggests that a line has dropped out between ἐπο- and -λικα.

**78.** The description of the seating is not entirely clear. Since Attila was placed in the centre of the (square or, more likely, rectangular) hall, I take the chairs along the walls to have been set only in front of Attila. Thus, the banquet occupied the half of the hall between Attila and the entrance. Onegesius seems to have had the most honourable seat, on the right, closest to Attila, while Attila's two sons sat at the head of the left-hand line. Berichus' distance from Attila is not made clear, since we are only told that he was one seat closer than the eastern Roman envoys.

**79.** Again, Priscus' description of this ceremony is not wholly clear, and my interpretation differs from those of Bury and Gordon.

In my view Attila as the host greets everyone in turn and offers him his own wooden cup (κισσύβιον). The guest, who has stood up, drinks from the cup and returns it to Attila's waiter, who retires (ὑπεξιόντος) to his master's side. As the waiter retires, the other waiters step forward in line, offer the metal cups (κύλικες) to the other guests, who then greet the guest whom Attila has welcomed and who has now sat down. The κύλικες are then returned to the waiters, who step back. The whole ceremony is then repeated for all the guests, first down the right-hand side, then down the left.

**80.** The usual translation of μετὰ τὴν τοῦ A. is "next to the table of Attila", but if the banquet were of any size this would have been impossible, since the guests did not leave their seats. The Greek is, in fact, stressing the order of precedence. First Attila's table was set up, then the rest were set up in order — down the right- and left-hand sides — directly in front of the guests.

**81.** This passage seems to fit exactly into this place in the *Excerpta*. The error of calling Zercon a Scythian clearly arises from failure to distinguish him from the deranged Scythian who preceded him at the banquet.

**82.** Thompson (1947 p.64) points out that ἄσβεστον γέλωτα comes from Homer *Il.* 1,599 and invokes the banquet scene there, with the lame Hephaestus bustling about.

**83.** On the correct form of the name, Ernach not Ernas, see Thompson *loc. cit.* (at n.82) and cf. Maenchen-Helfen 1973 p.415.

**84.** See n.62.

**85.** De Boor, following Dindorf, would expunge the καί, and it certainly seems intrusive in the sentence as it stands. But perhaps here, as elsewhere, the excerptor has condensed the original, omitting other things which Attila had said to or about the Emperor.

**86.** Saturnilus (elsewhere Saturninus) was a count of the domestics killed at the order of Eudocia in 444 in retaliation for his killing of two clerics in her service (*PLRE* II 'Saturninus' 3). Gordon (1960 p.203 n.58) considers that the dispute over the girl had been in progress since before Saturninus' death, but it is much more likely that Theodosius would have been able to dispose of the girl so freely after her father's death (that this was the case is suggested by τὸν δὲ Σ. ἀνῃρήκει Ἀθηναΐς). Constantius probably accompanied one of the missions sent by Attila after the peace of 447 (*Fr.* 10).

**87.** Zeno was master of the soldiers in the East from 447, succeeding Anatolius, and was consul in 448. The war in which he defended the capital was Attila's invasion of 447 (*PLRE* II 'Zenon' 6).

**88.** Τοῦ φρουρίου suggests that something has dropped out (perhaps after the remark that Athenaΐs/Eudocia was called by both names) to the effect that the girl was being kept under guard after her father's murder.

**89.** Rufus was perhaps a military count, but whether he is identical with the consul of 457 is unclear. (*PLRE* II 'Rufus' 1 denies the identity on the ground that Priscus *Fr.* 18 [=23,1 of the present edition] says that he was dead by 451. But Priscus' Greek does not make it clear whether the death of Rufus or that of Theodosius II is meant, though the former seems likely.)

**90.** De Boor obelises the words παρὰ Ῥωμαίων δέξασθαι, noting that Müller had proposed to read δῶρα παρὰ Ῥωμαίων δέξασθαι βουλόμενος. However, the simple infinitive of purpose after πέμπω is common (if usually used in the active voice and in poetry) so that δῶρα alone can be inserted.

**91.** Although ἀνασταυρόω usually indicates impaling or crucifixion, the punishment here, apparently hanging by the neck with the head (probably) inserted in the cleft of a branch set upright, seems to have been gibbetting.

**92.** The cause of Berichus' anger may, therefore, have been a discussion by the envoys, which came to him through the servants, in which the Romans explained the defeat in the war of 447 by the ineptitude of the barbarian generals in the Roman armies (cf. *Fr.* 9,4 for the role of Aspar and Areobindus). Croke (1981 p.166) has a different explanation, that Maximinus had recommended to Attila that he not accept Aspar and Areobindus as envoys. This is possible.

**93.** Thompson (1947 p.64) points out that the one hundred pounds of gold was made up of the fifty sent by Chrysaphius and the fifty demanded by Attila for Vigilas' release. Clearly the first part of this long first sentence was an introductory summary by the excerptor. John of Antioch *Fr.* 198 (= *Fr.* 15,5 of the present text) has the phrase φωραθέντα τῆς κατ' αὐτοῦ [sc. Attila] ἐπιβουλῆς, but uses it of Chrysaphius.

**94.** Called Mundzuc by Jordanes *Get.* 34,180 (= *Fr.* 11,3) and Mundius by Theophanes *Chron. a.m.* 5942 (= *Fr.* 9,4).

**95.** Presumably this was to punish Rufus, who was deprived of her wealth. Presumably, also, Zeno saw Chrysaphius' hand behind this. *PLRE* II 'Zenon' 6 is probably correct to see in this affair one aspect of a struggle at court over policy towards Attila, in which Zeno opposed appeasement. But the evidence is not as unequivocal as *PLRE* implies, since none of the sources there cited actually specifies a motive for Zeno's estrangement.

**96.** As was noted in vol. I n.90 on p.145, this remark is usually taken to be sarcastic, given Priscus' dislike of Chrysaphius. Perhaps what Priscus means, however, is that on this occasion there was general support for Chrysaphius, since it would have been hardly proper to surrender a high minister, however disliked, to the personal animosity of Zeno or the demands of Attila.

**97.** Gordon (1960 p.204 n.69) is wrong to say that Nomus succeeded Martialis (cf. *Fr.* 11,1). Nomus had been master of the offices from 443 to at least 446 and possibly later (*PLRE* II 'Nomus' 1).

**98.** On Plinthas cf. *Fr.* 2. Armatus is otherwise unknown.

**99.** Gordon (1960 p.204 n.71) wrongly suggests that by the Ausoriani Priscus meant the Vandals and the expedition of 441. The Ausoriani (or Austoriani) were a Moorish tribe on the borders of Tripolitania and Pentapolis, whose frequent raids are mentioned by Ammianus and Synesius amongst others (see 'Austuriani' in *RE* II 2 col.2592). The eastern Empire held Pentapolis, and the fighting was part of the regular defence against nomad incursions. Thus Armatus could have died any time up to the present, and probably had died fairly recently.

**100.** On this phrase see n.93.

**101.** The "greater fear" was the news of Attila's intrigue with Honoria, described by John in the next section (= *Fr.* 17,1). On the identity of Maximinus see vol. I p.48 and nn.7 and 8 thereto.

**102.** What Honoria escaped from has dropped out of the text. Herculanus was not consul until 452. Despite Bury's doubts (1958 I p.294 n.1), it seems that she was forced to marry Herculanus (cf. Priscus *Fr.* 20,1: ἐκδεδομένην), although τότε of the present passage suggests that whatever she escaped from, she was not so lucky later.

**103.** Nicephorus Callistus here reads μικρόν τι, which seems more appropriate.

**104.** This very laboured explanation of the conferring of the title Augustus does not seem likely to have come from Priscus, whose explanations are usually clearer than this.

**105.** Ardabur was master of the soldiers in the East from 453 to 466, when he was dismissed for treasonable correspondence (*PLRE* II 'Ardabur' 1). The present passage is clearly a summary of material from various parts of the narrative. With the phrase Μαρκιανοῦ . . . χρηστοῦ μὲν γεγονότος cf. Theophanes *Chron. a.m.* 5943: ἐγένετο [sc. Μαρκιανὸς] δὲ χρηστός. Jordanes, *Rom.* 336, refers to one of these successes when he notes Ardabur's killing of Bigelis, a king of the Goths.

**106.** The Visigothic king was Theoderic I. His daughter's name is unknown. She was repudiated before 446, by which date Huneric had been betrothed to Eudocia, the daughter of Valentinian III (Bury 1958 I p.256).

**107.** The identity of the dead king is uncertain, but it is probably the semi-legendary Merovech (*PLRE* II 'Merovechus'). The names of the sons are also uncertain, although one (the winner in the struggle for the throne) was probably Childeric, whose reign may, therefore, have begun a few years earlier than the date of *ca* 456 given by *PLRE* II 'Childericus'.

**108.** On the reading πρεσβευόμενον see vol. I n.7 on p.143. The adoption here mentioned is a Germanic custom.

**109.** Attila appears to be replying to a message from the western Romans, probably their repeated rejection of his demand for Honoria (cf. *Fr.* 20,3).

**110.** An error for Theoderic I. Since this error also appears in Nicephorus Callistus (see following note) it must have been in Eustathius of Epiphania.

**111.** The only certainly Priscan material in this very garbled account is on the death of Attila (cf. *Fr.* 24,1). Nicephorus Callistus (*HE* 14,57) has the same account except for the death of Attila by haemorrhage, and he appears to say that he derived it from Eustathius of Epiphania, who would thus have probably been the common intermediary (see vol. I pp.117f.).

**112.** The words on the embassy of Pope Leo, which I rejected in vol. I p.113 as not from Priscus, I have included both for the sake of the completeness of the narrative and also because I am now not so sure that they could not have been based on Priscus' account.

**113.** This obvious error probably arose from the tendency of Procopius or his source to incorporate his material in blocks of excerpts with scant respect for chronological precision, the account of Aetius here being placed first. On a related error of chronology see n.2 above.

**114.** On the episode of Saturnilus' daughter see *Fr.* 14, lines 35-46. The Greek does not specify who died, but it probably means Rufus rather than Theodosius II. It is also unclear whether Apollonius, who was *magister militum praesentalis* of the East from 443 to 451 (*PLRE* II 'Apollonius' 3), was the brother of Rufus (the usual view, e.g. of Thompson 1948 p.143) or of another person who married Saturnilus' daughter after Rufus' death (so *PLRE* II *loc. cit.*). The former view seems to me more likely, since that gives more point to Priscus' introducing the affair of Saturnilus' daughter here.

**115.** Presumably Priscus claimed to have heard this from Marcian himself, perhaps via Euphemius, the master of the offices, whose *assessor* he was (see vol. I p.48).

**116.** On the burial rites and the *strava* (which Maenchen-Helfen takes to be a Slavic word) see Maenchen-Helfen 1973 pp.274-78 and 425f., who points out that some of the elements in the account appear to be influenced by classical reminiscences, a characteristic of Priscus (see vol. I pp.54f.).

**117.** While the account of Attila's death in Theophanes parallels that in *Chron. Pasch.* and Malalas, the previous sentence remarks the death of Aetius (who is still alive in *Chron. Pasch.* and Malalas), an order of events which is also found in Procopius (= *Fr.* 22,2 *init.*). The word τάττεσθαι, which is used by Theophanes of Theodosius' agreement to pay tribute, also appears in the Priscan *Exc. de Leg. Gent.* 9 (= *Fr.* 23,1) and *Exc. de Leg. Rom.* 6 (= *Fr.* 23,3).

**118.** Cf. Theophanes *Chron. a.m.* 5946 = *Fr.* 24,2.

**119.** There may be some Priscan material in this fragment, as Mommsen thought (intro. to his text of Jordanes, p.xxxv), but much is from elsewhere (cf. especially *Fr.* 13,3, where the youngest son, Ernach, is said to be Attila's favourite). Although in the conspectus I included *Get.* 50,264-66 as possibly Priscan, it now seems to me in the light of Jordanes' references there both to himself and to the present time, that there is little, if any, Priscan material in those sections.

**120.** Procopius (*Wars* 1,19,32-33) indicates that they also continued to receive a subsidy in gold which had been instituted by Diocletian. On the Blemmyes see n.71 on p.219. When Diocletian moved the border northwards to Philae, the Nobadae were invited to settle the evacuated area as a buffer against the Blemmyes, who, however, still made raids. By the present time the Blemmyes and Nobadae were in alliance against the Romans, probably as a result of the increasing encroachment of Christianity (Snowden 1970 pp.138f.).

**121.** Perhaps, as Snowden (*loc.cit.*) suggests, Florus drove off the Blemmyes and Nobadae after the death of Maximinus. The Temple of Isis at Philae was not interfered with, however, and was not closed until the reign of Justinian (527-65).

**122.** For Christian dissension as a cause of rioting in classicising history cf. Ammianus Marcellinus 27,3,11-15. The present troubles were part of the ongoing dispute between the adherents of the Chalcedonian and Monophysite doctrines (Bury 1953 I pp.355ff.).

**123.** This dates the rioting to the summer since only the summer Etesian winds could have driven the ships from Constantinople to Alexandria so quickly.

**124.** On παροινούντων see n.128 below.

**125.** Thus Florus was both *comes Aegypti* and *praefectus Augustalis* (the latter is presumably *Alexandrinae urbis procurator* of Jordanes *Rom.* 333 = *Fr.* 27,2). He was presumably named *comes Aegypti* as an emergency measure after the death of Maximinus (*PLRE* II 'Florus' 2 connects the combined offices with the religious riots at Alexandria).

**126.** It is not clear who did the advising, but, since the sentence, like those which precede it, is dependent upon ἱστορεῖ δ᾽ οὖν Πρίσκος, the identity of αὐτοῦ is probably Priscus himself. Furthermore, since Priscus had been an (official or unofficial) advisor to Maximinus, and if Florus succeeded Maximinus, it is likely that Priscus continued in a similar relationship with him until his return to Constantinople. Nicephorus Callistus (*HE* 15,8) merely has σὺν εἰσηγήσει.

**127.** With this digression Nicephorus interrupts an account of the Alexandrian riots which is word-for-word almost identical with that of Evagrius. He has, however, transformed the temple to which the soldiers had fled into the temple of Serapis, which he seems to identify with the Serapeum. This, however, had been destroyed in 391 (see Eunapius *Fr.* 56). Thus, if this digression came from Priscus, as Valesius thought, in the original it is unlikely to have been so closely connected with the riots.

**128.** The original sense of παροινεῖν (= "to abuse drunkenly") has clearly been lost here. The word also occurs in *Fr.* 28,1, where the original sense of the word could stand.

**129.** This sentence is difficult, and my version differs radically from that of Gordon (1960 p.52). It is based upon the text as printed by de Boor, which seems to me to be rendered sound by the acceptance of his conjecture οὐκ ᾔει for the MS οἰκίει and the restoring of the MS reading ἐκβαλών, which adds weight to his conjecture. For παρελέσθαι τίνα τινος (= "to deprive someone of something") cf. Zosimus 1,7,2. For Valentinian's delay in recognising Marcian see W. Ensslin, 'Marcianus' 34, *RE* XIV 2 col.1518. The charge that Aetius had designs also on the West may rest upon the betrothal of his son, Gaudentius, to Valentinian's daughter, Placidia (Clover 1966 p.131 n.2).

**130.** Κοπίς usually = "a cleaver", although perhaps here it means a curved knife such as orientals carried (cf. Xenophon *Cyr.* 2,1,9), appropriate for an eunuch chamberlain, who was often an oriental. As a head chamberlain Heracleius would presumably not be searched for weapons.

**131.** During his ascendency Aetius had to contend with the expansion of the Visigoths in south-western Gaul. He drove them from Arles in 430, and another general, Litorius, drove them from Narbo in 436. The revolt of the Aemorichans (Armoricans) refers to the uprising of the Bagaudae in north-western Gaul (on which see Clover's commentary to Merobaudes *Paneg.* 2,8ff.).

**132.** De Boor alters the MS ἥκειν to εἴκειν wrongly. Aetius' ability to summon foreign peoples as auxiliaries was famous.

**133.** In fact Valentinian was not yet thirty-six, having been born on July 2, 419 and killed on March 16, 455.

**134.** *PLRE* II 'Maximianus' rejects the identification, sometimes made, of Maximian with Majorian. But the corruption is an easy one from Μάξιμον above, and it does seem from Sidonius Apollinaris (*Paneg. in Mai.* 116-25) that Majorian's father had been a senior financial official of Aetius. The simple change in John's text to διακονουμένου would put Domninus in the appropriate position in respect of Aetius (and, in my view, improve the balance of the sentence). Moreover, if Majorian had already been mentioned as a candidate, the καὶ before Εὐδοξία would have more point.

**135.** Maximus also married his son Palladius to a daughter of Valentinian. It is unclear whether this was Eudocia (so *PLRE* II 'Palladius' 10), who was engaged to Gaiseric's son Huneric (see n.106 above), or to Placidia, the date of whose marriage to Olybrius is uncertain. Recently, Clover (1978) has argued that Placidia was married to Palladius and that she married Olybrius later. The phrase οἱ δέ φασι might indicate that Priscus had doubts about the veracity of the report that Eudoxia summoned Gaiseric.

**136.** Gaiseric entered Rome on June 2, 455, three days after Maximus' death.

**137.** Theophanes' account of Valentinian's death and Gaiseric's attack upon Rome (*Chron. a.m.* 5947) appears to be non-Priscan and closer to John of Antioch *Fr.* 200, especially in stressing Valentinian's sexual habits. But some of the phraseology is also quite close to *Fr.* 30,1 above and perhaps derives from a common intermediary.

**138.** Avitus and the Visigoths were preparing to attack the Vandals via Spain in 456, but the Visigoths proved to be more interested in fighting the Sueves there (Clover 1966 pp.164f.).

**139.** The MS reading here, παρὰ τὸν ῾Ρεκίμερ, makes no sense. Niebuhr's conjecture τὸν πατρίκιον ῾Ρ. is unlikely since Ricimer was not made patrician until 457, after Avitus' death (*PLRE* II 'Ricimer' 2). Thompson (*CR* 1946 p.106) argues that παρά is not corrupt and that a name (ending in -ιανον) of someone sent has dropped out after Σικελίαν.

**140.** This article of the *Suda* is placed here by Müller. It could, of course, refer to any shipwreck off Messina, not necessarily one connected with Vandalic raids, though they are, perhaps, most likely.

**141.** Avitus' successor, Majorian, passed a law (*Nov. Mai.* 4) to ensure the preservation of public buildings.

**142.** Avitus actually reigned for fifteen months, from his proclamation in Gaul on July 9, 455 to his defeat at Placentia on October 17, 456. Perhaps John's source dated the beginning of his reign from his arrival at Rome. Gregory of Tours (*HF* 2,11) says that he was made bishop of Placentia and died shortly thereafter, the version which is usually accepted.

**143.** The fugitives whom the Persians ejected were perhaps Mazdaists who were still active in Lazica and who sought Persian intervention (cf. D.M. Lang, *The Georgians* New York/Washington [1966] pp.97f.). The nature of Gobazes' difficulties with the Romans is not clear, and why the Romans objected to a joint kingship (as noted in the next fragment) is not explained.

**144.** Probably as *assessor*. This is Priscus' last appearance in his History.

**145.** The first sentence repeats the first sentence of 36,1. The final sentence seems to imitate Polybius 6,8,6: τὸ τέλος αὐτῶν τῆς καταστροφῆς. Majorian was executed at Dertona in Liguria on August 7, 461.

**146.** After the break-up of the Hunnic Empire the Ostrogoths were settled by Marcian in Pannonia, those under Valamir between the rivers Scarniunga and Aqua Nigra (Jordanes *Get.* 52,268). The current fighting began in 459 and ended in 461.

**147.** Marcellinus, commander of the troops in Dalmatia (perhaps with the rank of *comes rei militaris*), had rebelled against Valentinian III over the murder of his friend Aetius, but gave his allegiance to

Majorian, who sent him to guard Sicily against the Vandals. *PLRE* II 'Marcellinus' 6 identifies the 'Scythians' whom Ricimer bought off as Huns, but perhaps they were Ostrogoths from Pannonia.

**148.** Leo. Marcian had died in 457.

**149.** After the death of Majorian at the beginning of August there was no western Emperor until Libius Severus was proclaimed on November 19. The present passage might remark the manoeuvrings during this interregnum. But since Leo and Gaiseric did not recognise Severus, a longer period could be covered. Gaiseric's support of Olybrius is also remarked by Procopius *Wars* 3,6,6 (= *Fr.* 53,3).

**150.** This is a shorter version of the final sentence of 38,1.

**151.** Gaudentius, too, had been captured in 455 at the sack of Rome. He is not heard of again.

**152.** Majorian had made him *magister militum* when he went to Sicily in 460. Upon his return to Dalmatia his title was recognised by Leo but not by Libius Severus (*PLRE* II *art.cit.* at n.147). Cf. Procopius *Wars* 3,6,7 = *Fr.* 53,3.

**153.** I.e. he was from Gaul as distinct from Galatia in Asia Minor. For eight years immediately before this time he had been the leader of the Franks during the exile of their king, Childeric (*PLRE* II 'Childericus' 1), and they were his allies in the hostilities with the Visigoths which culminated in the battle of Orleans in about 463 in which the Gothic king Frederic was killed (*PLRE* 'Aegidius').

**154.** Presumably some portion of Valentinian's eastern property, which had come to him from Theodosius I through his mother, Galla Placidia, was granted to Eudocia as her marriage portion (so Oost 1968 p.307).

**155.** In addition to holding parts of Sicily, Gaiseric also annexed Sardinia, Corsica and the Balearic Islands.

**156.** The Saraguri and Onoguri seem to have been Turkic peoples, the latter being identified with the Hunuguri of Jordanes *Get.* 5,37. The Saraguri are probably not the Sadagarii of Jordanes *Get.* 50,265 (as Gordon, 1960 p.134, thinks) since they were settled on Roman territory in Lower Moesia, whereas the Saraguri seem to have been beyond the Danube. The Sabiri are noted by Jordanes in the first passage cited as the neighbours of the Hunuguri. On the Akatiri-Akatziri see n.41. The reference to the Avars is one of the earliest notices of a people who were to trouble the European provinces of the Byzantine Empire from the end of Justinian's reign.

**157.** This passage is rather awkward, perhaps as the result of clumsy condensation. Gordon (1960 p.134) makes the Avars the ones "driven out by these evils", but since the evils are clearly the mist and the gryphons, those driven out must be the dwellers by the (Arctic) Ocean. On the gryphons see vol. I p.54, where I wrongly identified the Avars with the dwellers by the Northern Ocean.

**158.** This suggests that after *Fr.* 40,1 Priscus described other dealings between the Romans and the peoples displaced by the Avars, and that these dealings included fighting, presumably over their attempts to settle on Roman territory. Cf. 40,1 *init.*, ἐπρεσβεύσαντο ... κατά, where one would expect παρά (which de Boor proposes). Κατά suggests hostilities, and perhaps some words which mentioned such have been omitted here.

**159.** Whether "Magi" here means the priests of Zoroastrianism or is used generally for all followers of that religion, is unclear. Certainly, there had been missionary work by Zoroastrians in Roman territory, especially Cappadocia, during the early Sassanian period (R.N. Frye, *The Heritage of Persia* London [1962] p.220).

**160.** Constantius, the name which appears both here and in the following two passages, is an error (apparently Priscan) for Constantinus. His three prefectures were all of the East (*PLRE* II 'Constantinus' 22).

**161.** The protocol was that the embassy remain at the border until the ruler decided whether to receive it, whereupon a message of invitation (or refusal) was sent (cf. Const. Porph. *De Caer.* 1,89 p.403, 11ff.). Presumably Gaiseric refused to admit Tatian.

**162.** This suggests that Priscus interrupted his account of Constantius' embassy with other material, perhaps other diplomatic activity or the account of the fire at Constantinople (= *Fr.* 42).

**163.** Both Gordon (1960 p.10) and the translator in Müller misunderstand this sentence and make the Kidarites the tributaries. Not only is this intrinsically unlikely at the period, but the middle ἀπαρνησάμενος in the next sentence indicates that the Persians refused to pay. Thus κομιζομένων here = "receive" (cf. *Fr.* 38,1, ἐκεκόμιστο of Gaiseric receiving some of the property of Valentinian III) and ἔθεντο = "paid", as often elsewhere (see LSJ *s.v.* τίθημι A, II, 8), though Priscus usually uses τάσσεσθαι in this sense (see n.117).

**164.** On the basis of this story in the Herodotean tale of Amasis and Cambyses (3,1) see vol. I pp.154f.

**165.** An earthquake at Antioch was described in the previous chapter.

**166.** Although it is certain that Priscus mentioned the Great Fire (cf. *Fr.* 44), it is no more than a possibility that Evagrius' account came from him. Some of the vocabulary is uncommon and unexampled in Priscus (e.g. ἐπιλυχνίος, ἀποσκλῆναι, φόρον, ἐπαιωρέω in the sense used, δυσδιαπορευτός, εἰσδεχθέστατος). Some of it is Evagrius' own (see the *index graecitatis* at the end of the Bidez-Parmentier edition).

**167.** Τῇ τε θωπείᾳ τῶν λόγων alludes to Plato *Laws* 906B. On the role played by Daniel the Stylite in this reconciliation see vol. I p.60.

**168.** After the break-up of Attila's empire the Sciri, with other peoples, were settled in Lower Moesia and Scythia Minor (Jordanes

*Get.* 50,265). According to Jordanes (*Get.* 53,275-76) the Sciri were roused to hostilities by Hunimund, a Suevic king. In the ensuing fighting the Ostrogothic king Valamir was killed, but the Sciri were crushed.

**169.** Cf. *Fr.* 2. Marcian probably discontinued the market. Many barbarian tribes had become very dependent on Roman articles of trade.

**170.** See *Fr.* 40 for the attack upon the Akatiri. The Persian embassy noted in the present passage seems to have been another, later one than that remarked in *Fr.* 41,1.

**171.** See n.21.

**172.** The readiness to accede to the demands, which contrasts with the rejection remarked in *Fr.* 46, may have resulted from Roman preoccupation with the natural disasters described in the following passage and a projected expedition against the Vandals. However, the demands are different from the earlier ones, and the Romans seem to have been ready to treat provided that Dengizich was willing to become subject to them, which had not been proposed earlier. War soon broke out again, and Dengizich was killed fighting in 469 (Marcellinus *Chron. a.* 469).

**173.** On the dating of the earthquake to 467 see vol. I p.170 n.64. This passage is part of a longer account of disasters which Evagrius has inserted at this point (*HE* 2,12-14). Strictly speaking, Priscus is cited not for earthquake but only for the deluge, which is said to have happened later. It is usually assumed, however, that he was the source for both disasters.

**174.** A main verb appears to be lacking, although that may be the result of condensation by the excerptor. (De Boor's proposal to read ποιησαμένων for ποιήσασθαι is not good, since in that case one would expect a connective to link the clause with the one before. If an emendation is to be made, I should prefer ἐποιήσαντο.) Condensation may also have caused the lack of clarity over whether the Ostrogoths and the Scythians are identical or whether the former are one part of the latter. In the second case the entrapment of the Goths would have been the final blow in a situation already made serious by famine, which the speech of Chelchal suggests was a more general problem and not merely the result of the blockade.

**175.** The editors usually accept here Bekker's emendation ὁ ῎Ασπαρ πυθόμενος for the MS οἱάπερ πειθόμενοι, but there is no other indication that Aspar was present himself at these proceedings and, had he been, it is likely that he would have been named amongst the generals at the beginning of the fragment. Thus, I have written οἷα οἱ ῎Ασπαρος πυθόμενοι.

**176.** In the subsequent part of this chapter (= *Fr.* 53,2) Priscus is named as the source for Basiliscus' expedition in such a way that Evagrius might be deriving the whole chapter from him.

**177.** The beginning of this passage is corrupt and confused. Attempts have been made to argue that μάχην, which occurs twice in the passage, hides the name of a leader of the Suani (Classen) and to see in the phrase ἐς τὴν τοῦ σήματος the name of one Sema, a leader of the Lazi (Tillemont, followed by Gordon 1960 p.13). Both attempts seem misguided: μάχην in both cases has its usual Greek meaning, and the corrupt phrase is beyond emendation. There was probably a longer passage which identified both the object of the Suanian attacks (cf. the following passage, from John of Antioch, which speaks of Tzanian attacks upon τὰ περὶ τραπεζοῦντα χωρία) and the person who sent the embassy to the Romans. The latter would not have been a Suanian leader (as Gordon *loc.cit.*) but the ruler of the Lazi (a view supported by *PLRE* II 'Heraclius' 4). There is no difficulty with the fact that the Persians were threatening the Lazi because the Suani had taken some of their forts, since the Suani were regarded as being under the suzerainty of the Lazi (see Menander Protector *Fr.* 11 in Müller *FHG* IV p.217, where Peter, the Roman envoy to Persia, refers this suzerainty back as far as the reign of Theodosius). The διαφορά would then be one of a series of difficulties which the Lazi and the Romans had with the turbulent Suani and which continued at least to the reign of Justin II.

**178.** In about 386 Theodosius I agreed to the partition of Armenia with Persia. The part which the Romans acquired (about one-fifth of the country) was not absorbed into the Empire but left under the control of the hereditary satraps, who now received their insignia from the Emperor.

**179.** This sending of Heraclius is nowhere else mentioned. It perhaps only happened a short while ago, just before the Persians were embroiled with the Saraguri and Kidarites.

**180.** The Persian kings often had difficulty in raising and maintaining strong forces, since they did not have the large centralised military establishment of the Romans. Thus, when they had a large army, they tended to wish to use it.

**181.** In the conspectus in vol. I, I placed this item separately and dated it tentatively to 470, although in a note (n.69 on pp.171f.) I suggested that it might be placed where I have now placed it. The Suani (earlier called Macrones) are distinct from the Tzani, or Sanni (Bury 1958, II, index pp.486 and 489 and page references thereat). The former lived in the hills to the East of Colchis/Lazica (*RE* XIV, 1 col. 815 'Makrones'), the latter in the mountains south of Trapezus (Procopius *Wars* 8,1,8-9).

**182.** Cf. *Fr.* 39,1. The treaty was the one of 462 with Leo (Clover 1966 pp.186-91). Gaiseric seems to have raided the East in 467 (Clover 1966 p.193 n.2).

**183.** The MSS read ἑκατὸν χιλιάδας (100,000). The emendation to ἑκατὸν καὶ χιλιάδα is based upon Cedrenus' figure (p.613 ed. Bonn) of 1113. The MS reading gives the same number of ships as Procopius (*Wars* 3,6,1 = *Fr.* 53,3) gives of men.

**184.** This figure differs from others given. Candidus (*Fr.* 2) gives 64,000 lbs. of gold, 700,000 lbs. of silver and a substantial sum from Anthemius. John Lydus (*De Mag.* 3,43) gives 65,000 lbs. of gold and 700,000 lbs. of silver.

**185.** In the previous chapter Procopius has described the Vandals' expropriation of the African landowners and their yearly descents upon Italy and Sicily and attacks upon the East.

**186.** The next two sections describe Aspar's Arianism and sympathy to the Vandals. After his material from Priscus, Theophanes (*Chron. a.m.* 5961 = *Fr.* 53,1) continues φασὶ δέ τινες and offers a similar story.

**187.** Through the marriage of his son, Huneric, to Placidia's sister, Eudocia (*Fr.* 38,1).

**188.** I take the point of τὰς σφῶν αὐτῶν ναῦς ὑπ' ἀλλήλων διαφθειρομένας οὐδενὶ κόσμῳ to be that the fire spread so quickly and randomly through the Roman ships that the men were unable to tell where it was going and so decide which ships to push away.

**189.** At *Chron. a.m.* 5962 it is said that Aspar attempted the murder of the subsequent Emperor Zeno, who was at the time master of the soldiers in Thrace, and so incurred Leo's suspicion.

**190.** The older interpretation of this passage (cf. Gordon 1960 pp.136f.) treated the name Oullibus as corrupt, hiding possibly the name of Attila's son Dengizich, and regarded ἀμφότεροι as referring to 'Oullibus' and another Hun, possibly another son of Attila, Ernach. But Norman's linking (1953 pp.171f.) of the passage with the *Suda* Υ 583 makes it clear that Oullibus = Ulith, who was probably a Goth in Roman service, and that the other potential rebel was Anagast himself, another Goth (for his revolt see *Fr.* 56).

**191.** See n.21 above.

**192.** Upon the hill was an almost impregnable fortress, also called Cherris, in which Verina was later imprisoned and Illus sustained a siege of four years (484-88) after the failure of his revolt (Bury 1958, I pp. 397f.).

**193.** See n.49 above.

**194.** Gordon (1960 p.205 n.13) suggests that he was "not unlikely" the same as the western Roman envoy in *Fr.* 11,2 lines 319f. But since the envoy was a military man and the present Romanus is identified as *magister*, which usually means master of the offices, it is better to regard them as two persons (so *PLRE* II 'Romanus' 2 and 4).

**195.** This fragment and the next were wrongly dated to 472 in the conspectus in vol. I. The date of both should be 470 (cf. *PLRE art.cit.* 4 and 'Jordanes' 3).

**196.** The name Misael, which is attested elsewhere, should not be emended to Michael, as Müller suggested (*ad loc.*). Cosmas may be identical with the 'Cosmas' 3 of *PLRE* II, who was *praepositus sacri cubiculi* from *ca* 488-91.

**197.** For this rather loose use of κατεγγυάω cf. *Fr.* 15,3.

**198.** Müller (*ad loc.*), by comparison with the statement below, would emend ϑ' to ε'. But the passage is clumsily condensed, perhaps from two versions which gave different lengths for the fighting and varied in other details also (see n.203 below).

**199.** On Onulf and Harmatius see Malchus *Fr.* 17.

**200.** Now the church of Santa Maria in Trastevere.

**201.** Gundobad was, in fact, Ricimer's nephew (*PLRE* 'Gundobadus' 1).

**202.** With the phrase πολέμου κρατοῦντος τὴν χώραν cf. ἐμφύλιος τῆς 'Ρώμης ἐπεκράτει πόλεμος of the previous passage.

**203.** The differences in the spelling of Gundobad's name and in his relationship to Ricimer from those in the passage of John above (= *Fr.* 64,1) seem to confirm that John drew from two sources. One of these, represented by the beginning and end of *Fr.* 64,1, gave the length of the civil war as nine months and made Gundobad Ricimer's brother. The other gave five months, made Gundobad Ricimer's nephew and correctly placed the elevation of Olybrius before the blockade of Rome (note in the present passage after Anthemius' death Ricimer is said to have installed [ἀνήγαγεν] Olybrius in the palace, not made him Emperor, which he was already). This second source also carefully computed Olybrius' reign as about 6½ months, i.e. five months of the siege, plus thirty days, plus sixteen days.

**204.** The second part of this sentence is awkward and unclear, and the MSS variants reflect attempts to tidy it up. My own reading suggests that the sentence might have come from an account of an attempt by the Roman authorities to mediate a dispute between quarrelling barbarians in Roman service (cf. *Fr.* 54).

# MALCHUS

Text and Translation

# MALCHUS

## TESTIMONIA

### 1

(Photius *Bibl. Cod.* 78, I pp.160f.)

Ἀνεγνώσθη Μάλχου σοφιστοῦ Βυζαντιακὰ ἐν βιβλίοις ἑπτά. ἄρχεται μὲν ἐξ οὗ Λέοντα τὸν βασιλέα ἡ νόσος ἐπίεζε, τούτῳ δὲ τῆς βασιλείας ἔτος ἑπτακαιδέκατον παρετείνετο. διέρχεται δὲ τήν τε Ζήνωνος ἀνάρρησιν, καὶ τὴν ὑπερόριον τῆς βασιλείου δόξης διατριβήν, καὶ τὴν Βασιλίσκου ἀνάρρησιν, καὶ τὴν τῆς ἁλουργίδος ἀπό- 5
θεσιν καὶ τὴν ἐπὶ τῇ βασιλείᾳ πάλιν κάθοδον Ζήνωνος, τήν τε τοῦ προειρημένου Βασιλίσκου διὰ ξίφους ἀναίρεσιν, ἧς καὶ γυνὴ καὶ τέκνα παρανόμῳ κρίσει ἐκοινώνησαν. καὶ ὅτι Ἁρμάτος, ὁ Ζήνωνα κατάγων, τοιαύτης ἀντιμισθίας ἀπώνατο διὰ Ὀνούλφου δεξάμενος τὴν σφαγήν. 10

Διαλαμβάνει δὲ καὶ τὴν Θευδερίχου τοῦ Ὀτριαρίου στάσιν, καὶ τὴν Θευδερίχου τοῦ Μαλαμείρου φιλίαν, καὶ τὸν πρὸς τὸν τοῦ Ὀτριαρίου Θευδέριχον πόλεμον, καὶ τὴν κατὰ Ζήνωνος πάλιν στάσιν καὶ τὴν Μαρκιανοῦ ἐπανάστασιν, καὶ πρό γε τούτου τὴν τῆς πενθερᾶς Βηρίνης ἐπιβουλήν, καὶ τὴν διὰ τοῦτο φυγαδείαν τὴν ἀΐδιον, καὶ τὴν 15
κατὰ Ἰλλου πρότερον ἐπιβουλὴν Βηρίνῃ συσκευασθεῖσαν, καὶ τὴν Ἐπιδάμνου ὑπὸ Θευδερίχου τοῦ Μαλαμείρου ἐν δόλῳ κατάσχεσιν.

Ταῦτα διεξιών, διέξεισι καὶ τὰ ἐπὶ Ῥώμης καὶ τέλος τοῦ ἑβδόμου λόγου ποιεῖται τὸν Νέπωτος θάνατον, ὃς ἐκβαλὼν τῆς ἀρχῆς Γλυκέριον τήν τε Ῥωμαϊκὴν ἰσχὺν περιεβάλετο, καὶ εἰς σχῆμα κείρας 20
κληρικοῦ ἀντὶ βασιλέως ἀρχιερέα κατέστησεν· ὑφ' οὗ καὶ ἐπιβουλευθεὶς ἀνῄρηται.

Οὗτοι οἱ ζ' τῆς ἱστορίας λόγοι καὶ προηγουμένους ὑποφαίνουσιν αὐτῷ λόγους ἄλλους διαπεπονῆσθαι· καὶ ἡ ἀπαρχὴ δὲ τῶν ἑπτὰ τοῦ

6 ἐπὶ Α [ἐν Μ    8 Ἁρμάτιος Α²    13 πάλιν στάσιν Α [πάλην Μ    15 ἐπιβουλήν Α² Μ [ἐπιβολήν Α    20 τε Α [τότε Μ

# MALCHUS

## TESTIMONIA

### 1

(Photius *Bibl. Cod.* 78, I pp.160f.)

Read the *Byzantine History* of the sophist Malchus in seven books. He begins from the time when the Emperor Leo was struck by his disease. Leo had then reached the seventeenth year of his reign. He describes the proclamation of Zeno, the period he spent in exile deprived of his royalty, the proclamation of Basiliscus, his renunciation of the purple and the return of Zeno to the throne, and the execution by the sword of the aforementioned Basiliscus, whose wife and children by an unjust judgement met the same fate. He also tells how Armatus, who effected Zeno's return, enjoyed an appropriate reward, meeting his end at the hand of Onulf.

He further describes the revolt of Theoderic the son of Otriarius, the friendship of Theoderic the son of Malamir,[1] and the war against Theoderic the son of Otriarius; his second revolt[2] and the rebellion of Marcian; before this the plot of Zeno's mother-in-law, Verina, and her perpetual exile because of this;[3] the earlier plot contrived by Verina against Illus; and the capture of Epidamnus by Theoderic the son of Malamir by a trick.

During the narrative of these events he also describes events at Rome and ends the seventh book with the death of Nepos. Having deposed Glycerius, tonsured him and made him a bishop, Nepos assumed power at Rome. He was killed as the result of a plot by Glycerius.

These seven books of History show that Malchus produced other books which preceded them, as the beginning of the first of the seven

πρώτου λόγου τοῦτο παραδηλοῖ· οὐ μὴν ἀλλὰ καὶ ἑπομένους, εἰ τὸ     25
ζῆν προσῆν τῷ συγγραφεῖ, ὡς τοῦ ἑβδόμου λόγου τὸ πέρας ἐνδείκ-
νυσω. ἔστι δὲ ὁ συγγραφεὺς Φιλαδελφεύς, εἴ τις ἄλλος κατὰ συγγραφὴν ἱστορίας ἄριστος, καθαρός, ἀπέριττος, εὐκρωής, λέξεων ταῖς
ἀνθηροτάταις καὶ εὐσήμοις καὶ εἰς ὄγκον τινὰ ἀνηγμέναις χρώμενος·
οὐδὲ αἱ καινοπρεπεῖς αὐτῷ, ὅσαι τὸ ἐμφατικὸν καὶ εὔηχον καὶ μεγα-     30
λεῖον ἔχουσι, παραβλέπονται ὥσπερ τὸ ... καὶ τοιαῦτ' ἔνια. καὶ
ὅλως κανών ἐστιν ἱστορικοῦ λόγου. σοφιστὴς δ' ἦν τὸ ἐπιτήδευμα,
καὶ ῥητορικῆς εἰς ἄκρον ἐληλακώς, καὶ τὴν θρησκείαν οὐκ ἔξω τοῦ
χριστιανικοῦ θειασμοῦ.

28 εὐκρωής [εἰλικρωής Niebuhr          31 ὥσπερ ... ἔνια om. M., lac. viii
litterarum in A

2

(Suda M 120)

    Μάλχος, Βυζάντιος, σοφιστής. ἔγραψεν ἱστορίαν ἀπὸ τῆς βασι-
λείας Κωνσταντίνου καὶ ἕως Ἀναστασίου· ἐν ᾗ τὰ κατὰ Ζήνωνα καὶ
Βασιλίσκον καὶ τὸν ἐμπρησμὸν τῆς δημοσίας βιβλιοθήκης καὶ τῶν
ἀγαλμάτων τοῦ Αὐγουσταίου καὶ ἄλλα τινὰ διεξέρχεται μάλα
σεμνῶς καὶ τραγῳδίας δίκην ἀποθρηνῶν αὐτά.     5

FRAGMENTA

1

(Exc. de Leg. Gent. 1)

    Ὅτι ἐν τῷ ἑπτακαιδεκάτῳ ἔτει τῆς βασιλείας Λέοντος τοῦ
Μακέλλη, πάντων πανταχόθεν τεταράχθαι δοκούντων, ἀφικνεῖταί τις
τῶν Σκηνιτῶν Ἀράβων, οὓς καλοῦσι Σαρακηνούς, ἱερεὺς τῶν παρ'
ἐκείνοις Χριστιανῶν, ἐξ αἰτίας τοιαύτης. Πέρσαι καὶ Ῥωμαῖοι
σπονδὰς ἐποιήσαντο, ὅτε ὁ μέγιστος πρὸς αὐτοὺς ἐπὶ Θεοδοσίου     5
συνερράγη πόλεμος, μὴ προσδέχεσθαι τοὺς ὑποσπόνδους Σαρακηνούς, εἴ τις ἐς ἀπόστασιν νεωτερίσαι προέλοιτο. ἐν δὲ τοῖς Πέρσαις
ἦν ὁ Ἀμόρκεσος τοῦ Νομαλίου γένους· καὶ εἴτε τιμῆς οὐ τυγχάνων ἐν
τῇ Περσίδι γῇ ἢ ἄλλως τὴν Ῥωμαίων χώραν βελτίω νενομικώς,
ἐκλιπὼν τὴν Περσίδα εἰς τὴν γείτονα Πέρσαις Ἀραβίαν ἐλαύνει,     10
κἀντεῦθεν ὁρμώμενος προνομὰς ἐποιεῖτο καὶ πολέμους Ῥωμαίων
μὲν οὐδενί, τοῖς δὲ ἀεὶ ἐν ποσὶν εὑρισκομένοις Σαρακηνοῖς· ἀφ' ὧν
καὶ τὴν δύναμιν αὔξων προῄει κατὰ μικρόν. μίαν δὲ τῶν Ῥωμαίων
παρεσπάσατο νῆσον Ἰωτάβην ὄνομα, καὶ τοὺς δεκατηλόγους ἐκβαλὼν τῶν Ῥωμαίων αὐτὸς ἔσχε τὴν νῆσον, καὶ τὰ τέλη ταύτης     15

also indicates. Moreover, had the historian lived longer he would have written others, as the end of the seventh book shows. The author, who is from Philadelphia, is the best of all the writers of history. His style is pure, straightforward and clear, and his vocabulary is choice and intelligible and it imparts dignity. His neologisms are not to be despised since they are forceful, euphonious and elevated, such as ... and a number of similar expressions. In short the work is a paradigm of historical writing. He was a sophist by profession and reached the pinnacle of the rhetor's art. In belief he was not outside the Christian faith.

## 2

(*Suda* M 120)

Malchus, a Byzantine and a sophist. He wrote a History from the reign of Constantine to Anastasius. In it he describes the events of the reigns of Zeno and Basiliscus, the burning of the Public Library and of the statues in the Augusteum and other happenings. He laments these things in a dignified and tragic manner.

## FRAGMENTS

### 1

(*Exc. de Leg. Gent.* 1)

In the seventeenth year of the reign of Leo the Butcher, when everything everywhere seemed to be in confusion, a priest of the Christians amongst the Tent Arabs, whom they call Saracens, arrived for the following reason. When in the time of Theodosius the greatest war had broken out against the Persians, they and the Romans made a treaty to the effect that neither side would accept the Saracen allies of the other if any of them attempted to revolt. Amongst the Persians was a certain Amorkesos of the tribe of Nomalius, who, whether because he did not receive honour in the land of Persia or because for some other reason he thought the Roman Empire better, left Persia and travelled to that part of Arabia adjacent to Persia. Setting out from here he made forays and attacks not upon any Romans, but upon the Saracens whom he encountered. Building up his forces from these, he gradually advanced. He seized one of the islands belonging to the Romans, which was named Jotaba, and, ejecting the Roman tax collectors, held the island himself and amassed considerable wealth

λαμβάνων χρημάτων εὐπόρησεν οὐκ ὀλίγων ἐντεῦθεν. καὶ ἄλλας δὲ
ὁ αὐτὸς Ἀμόρκεσος τῶν πλησίον ἀφελόμενος κωμῶν ἐπεθύμει Ῥωμαίοις ὑπόσπονδος γενέσθαι καὶ φύλαρχος τῶν ὑπὸ Πετραίαν ὑπὸ
Ῥωμαίοις ὄντων Σαρακηνῶν. πέμπει οὖν πρὸς Λέοντα τὸν βασιλέα
Ῥωμαίων Πέτρον ἐπίσκοπον τῆς φυλῆς τῆς ἑαυτοῦ, εἴ πως δύναιτο      20
ταῦτα πείσας ποτὲ διαπράξασθαι. ὡς δ' ἀφίκετο καὶ διελέχθη τῷ
βασιλεῖ, δέχεται τοὺς λόγους ὁ βασιλεὺς καὶ μετάπεμπτον εὐθὺς
ποιεῖται τὸν Ἀμόρκεσον ἐλθεῖν πρὸς αὐτόν, ἀβουλότατα τοῦτο δια-
νοησάμενος καὶ ποιήσας. εἰ γὰρ δὴ καὶ φύλαρχον χειροτονῆσαι
προῄρητο, ἔδει πόρρωθεν ὄντι τῷ Ἀμορκέσῳ τοῦτο προστάξαι, ἕως      25
καὶ τὰ Ῥωμαίων ἐνόμιζε φοβερὰ καὶ τοῖς ἄρχουσιν ἀεὶ τοῖς τυχοῦσι
Ῥωμαίων ἔμελλεν ἥκειν πεπτηχὼς καὶ τήν γε προσηγορίαν βασιλέως ἀκούων αὐτήν· καὶ γὰρ διὰ πολλοῦ κρεῖττόν τι τῶν ἀνθρώπων
εἶναι τῶν ἄλλων ἐνόμιζεν. νῦν δὲ πρῶτον μὲν αὐτὸν διὰ πόλεων
ἦγεν, ἃς ἔμελλεν ὄψεσθαι τρυφῆς μόνον γεμούσας, ὅπλοις δὲ οὐ      30
χρωμένας· ἔπειτα δέ, ὡς ἀνῆλθεν ἐς Βυζάντιον, δέχεται παρὰ τοῦ
βασιλέως ἀσμένως, καὶ τραπέζης κοινωνὸν βασιλικῆς ἐποιήσατο καὶ
βουλῆς προκειμένης μετὰ τῆς γερουσίας συμπαρεῖναι ἐποίει· καὶ τό
γε δὴ αἴσχιστον ὄνειδος τῶν Ῥωμαίων, ὅτι καθέδραν αὐτῷ τὴν
πρωτοπατρικίων ἀποδοθῆναι ἐκέλευσε σχηματισάμενος ὁ βασιλεύς,      35
ὅτι δὴ Χριστιανὸς ἀνεπείσθη γενέσθαι· καὶ τέλος ἀπέπεμψεν αὐτόν,
ἰδίαν μὲν παρ' αὐτοῦ εἰκόνα τινὰ χρυσῆν καὶ κατάλιθον λαβὼν
σφόδρα τε οὖσαν πολυτελῆ, χρήματα δὲ καὶ αὐτὸς ἐκείνῳ ἐκ τοῦ
δημοσίου ἀντιδοὺς καὶ τῶν ἄλλων κελεύσας ἕκαστον εἰσενεγκεῖν,
ὅσοι ἐτέλουν εἰς τὴν βουλήν. τὴν δὲ νῆσον ἐκείνην, ἧς ἐμνήσθημεν      40
πρόσθεν, οὐ μόνον κατέλιπεν αὐτῷ ἔχειν βεβαίως, ἀλλὰ καὶ ἄλλας
αὐτῷ κώμας προσέθηκε πλείονας. ταῦτα παρασχὼν Ἀμορκέσῳ ὁ
Λέων καὶ τῶν φυλῶν ἄρχοντα, ὧν ἤθελε, ποιήσας ἀπέπεμψεν
ὑψηλόν, καὶ ὅσος οὐκ ἔμελλε τοῖς δεξαμένοις λυσιτελεῖν.

18 τῶν ὑπὸ [τῶν ἐπὶ Valesius τῶν κατὰ Bekker    37 λαβόντα Niebuhr

## 2

*(Exc. de Leg. Gent. 2)*

    Ὅτι ὁ αὐτὸς Λέων βασιλεὺς ἀπέστειλε πρὸς τοὺς ἐν τῇ Θρᾴκῃ
βαρβάρους πρεσβευτὴν Τελόγιον τὸν σελεντιάριον. οἱ δὲ βάρβαροι
τοῦτον ἀσμένως δεξάμενοι ἀντιπέμπουσι πρέσβεις πρὸς τὸν βασιλέα
φίλοι Ῥωμαίων εἶναι βουλόμενοι. ᾐτήσαντο δὲ τρία, πρῶτον [ἵνα]
Θευδέριχον τὸν κατάρχοντα αὐτῶν τὴν κληρονομίαν ἀπολαβεῖν, ἣν      5

2 Πελάγιον vel Εὐλόγιον Niebuhr    4 ἵνα exp. Niebuhr

through collecting taxes.[4] When he had seized other villages nearby, Amorkesos wished to become an ally of the Romans and phylarch of the Saracens under Roman rule on the borders of Arabia Petraea.[5] He, therefore, sent Peter, the bishop of his tribe, to Leo, the Roman Emperor, to see if he could persuade Leo and arrange these things. When Peter arrived and spoke to the Emperor, Leo accepted his proposals and immediately sent for Amorkesos to come to him.

This intention of Leo, which he carried out, was very unwise. If he wished to appoint Amorkesos phylarch, he ought to have made this appointment while keeping him at a distance and while Amorkesos held Roman power in awe, so that he would always come submissively before the Roman officials whom he encountered and give heed to the Emperor's communications. For in this case he would have thought the Emperor to be much greater than the rest of mankind. But as it was he first led him through cities which he would observe to be full of luxury and unready for war. Then, when he came to Byzantium, the Emperor readily received him in person, invited him to dine at his table and, when the senate was meeting, had him attend that assembly. The worst insult of all to the Romans was that the Emperor, pretending that Amorkesos had been persuaded to become a Christian, ordered that he be granted a chair amongst the highest-ranking patricians. Finally, Leo dismissed him, having received from him as a personal gift a very valuable ikon of gold set with precious stones,[6] while giving him in return money from the public treasury and ordering all the senators to give him gifts. The Emperor not only left him in firm control of the island which I mentioned earlier, but added to it a large number of other villages. By granting Amorkesos these things and by making him phylarch, as he desired, Leo sent away a proud man and one who would not work for the advantage of those who had received him.

### 2

*(Exc. de Leg. Gent. 2)*

The Emperor Leo himself sent Telogius the silentiary as envoy to the barbarians in Thrace.[7] The barbarians gladly received him and in turn sent envoys to the Emperor, wishing to be friends of the Romans. They had three demands: first, that Theoderic, their leader, should receive the inheritance which Aspar had left him; second, that he be

ἀφῆκεν αὐτῷ Ἄσπαρ, δεύτερον νέμεσθαι τὴν Θράκην συγχωρη-
θῆναι αὐτῷ, τρίτον καὶ στρατηλάτην γενέσθαι τῶν ταγμάτων,
ὧνπερ καὶ Ἄσπαρ ἡγήσατο. καὶ ὁ μὲν βασιλεὺς πρὸς τὰ δύο παντελῶς ἀπείπατο, μόνον δὲ περὶ τῆς στρατηγίας κατένευσεν, εἰ φίλος
αὐτοῦ γένηται ἀδόλως· καὶ οὕτω τοὺς πρέσβεις ἀπέπεμψεν.          10
Ὁ δὲ Θευδέριχος ὁ τῶν βαρβάρων ἀρχηγὸς τοὺς πρέσβεις
αὐτοῦ δεξάμενος ἐκ τοῦ βασιλέως ἀπράκτους τὸ μὲν τῆς δυνάμεως
αὐτοῦ εἰς Φιλίππους ἐκπέμπει, τῷ δὲ προσεκάθητο τὴν Ἀρκαδιούπολιν μηχανῇ πάσῃ πολιορκῶν. καὶ ταύτην παραλαμβάνει οὐχ ὅπλοις,
ἀλλὰ λιμῷ τοὺς ἔνδον τοῦ ἄστεος ἰσχυρῶς στενοχωρήσαντι· καὶ γὰρ   15
καὶ ἵππων καὶ ὑποζυγίων καὶ νεκρῶν σωμάτων ἥψαντο καρτε-
ροῦντες εἴ ποθεν αὐτοῖς ἔλθοι βοήθεια, τῆς δὲ μὴ παρούσης ἀπήλ-
πισαν καὶ συνέδωκαν. οἱ δὲ ἐκπεμφθέντες ἐπὶ Φιλίππους τὰ πρὸ τοῦ
ἄστεος ἐνέπρησαν μόνον, οὐδὲν δὲ ἄλλο δεινὸν εἰργάσαντο. καὶ
τούτων οὕτω λυμαινομένων τὴν Θράκην, ὅμως καὶ αὐτοὶ οἱ βάρβαροι   20
ὑπὸ τοῦ λιμοῦ συνεχόμενοι πρεσβείαν πέμπουσι περὶ εἰρήνης πρὸς τὸν
βασιλέα. καὶ γίνεται ἡ σύμβασις τῶν ὅρκων ἐπὶ τούτοις, τοῖς μὲν
Γότθοις δίδοσθαι κατ' ἔτος χρυσίου λίτρας δισχιλίας, τὸν δὲ Θευδέριχον καθίστασθαι στρατηγὸν <τῶν> δύο στρατηγιῶν τῶν ἀμφὶ
βασιλέα, αἵπερ εἰσὶ μέγισται, αὐτὸν δὲ τῶν Γότθων αὐτοκράτορα   25
εἶναι, καὶ μηδένας ἐξ αὐτῶν ἀποστῆναι εἰς τὴν σφετέραν γῆν
θέλοντας τὸν βασιλέα δέχεσθαι· συμμαχεῖν δὲ τῷ βασιλεῖ εἰς πᾶν ὃ
τι κελεύοι, πλὴν ἐπὶ μόνων τῶν Βανδήλων.

10 ἀδόλως Bekker [ἄδολος codd.    18 ἐνέδωκαν Niebuhr    24 τῶν ante
δύο addidi    26 εἰς τὴν σφετέραν γῆν inseruit Valesius ex εἰς τὴν ἑτέραν γῆν
quae post μέγισται (v.25) exstant in codd.

## 3

(Suda Λ 267)
Λέων, βασιλεὺς Ῥωμαίων, ὁ Μακέλλης· ὃς ἔδοξε τῶν πρὸ
αὐτοῦ βασιλέων ἁπάντων εὐτυχέστατος εἶναι καὶ φοβερὸς ἅπασι τοῖς
τε ὑπ' ἐκείνου τὴν βασιλείαν τελοῦσι καὶ τῶν βαρβάρων αὐτῶν, ὅσοις
εἰς φήμην ἀφίκετο. καὶ ταύτην μὲν τοῖς πολλοῖς καταλέλοιπε δόξαν.
ἐγὼ δέ, φησὶ Μάλχος, εὐτυχίαν οὐκ οἶμαι, εἴ τις τῶν ἀρχομένων τὰ   5
ὄντα διασυλῶν καὶ μισθούμενος ἀεὶ συκοφάντας ἐς τοῦτο καὶ κατη-
γορῶν αὐτός, ὅτε μὴ ἄλλον ἀνηύρισκε, καὶ τὸν χρυσὸν ἐξ ἁπάσης τῆς
γῆς συλλεξάμενος, ἑαυτῷ μόνῳ κατάθοιτο, ἐρήμους μὲν τὰς πόλεις
ἦσπερ ἔμπροσθεν εἶχον εὐπορίας ποιήσας, ὡς μηκέτι τοὺς φόρους,
οὓς ἐτέλουν, δύνασθαι μετ' εὐχερείας ἀπενεγκεῖν. καὶ ἁπλῶς πάσης   10
κακίας ἀπισχυρίζεται ὁ Μάλχος γενέσθαι αὐτὸν καταγώγιον. [ὅς
γε καὶ Ὑπερέχιον τὸν γραμματικὸν ἐφυγάδευσε καί ποτε καὶ τῷ

allowed to live in Thrace; third, that he receive the generalship of the forces which Aspar had led. The Emperor absolutely rejected the first two demands and agreed to the generalship only if Theoderic would become his friend with no treacherous intent. With this reply Leo dismissed the envoys.

When Theoderic, the leader of the barbarians, received his envoys, who had come empty-handed from the Emperor, he sent part of his army off to Philippi and with the rest he encamped before Arcadiopolis and besieged it by every means. He took the city not by storm but through severe starvation which wore down those within. For, as they held out in the hope that help would come to them from some quarter, they ate horses, pack animals and corpses, and only despaired and surrendered when this did not arrive. Those sent against Philippi merely burned the buildings outside the fortifications and did no other damage. Although these disasters were afflicting Thrace, the barbarians, too, were beset by famine and sent a peace embassy to the Emperor. A sworn agreement was made on these terms: that every year the Goths should receive two thousand pounds of gold; that Theoderic be appointed general of the two forces attendant upon the Emperor (which are the most important);[8] that he should be sole ruler of the Goths, and that the Emperor should not admit anyone who wished to cross to his territory; that Theoderic should fight with the Emperor against anyone whom the latter ordered, except only the Vandals.[9]

### 3

(*Suda* Λ 267)

Leo, Roman Emperor, 'The Butcher'. Of all the emperors who preceded him, he seemed to be the most successful, being feared by all those who lived under his regime and even by the barbarians whom his reputation reached. Although he left this opinion amongst many men, Malchus says, "But I do not consider it success if someone plunders the possessions of his subjects, continually pays informers to this end, himself brings accusations when he cannot find another to do it for him, collects the gold from every land and lays it up for himself alone, and so thoroughly empties the cities of their former wealth that they could no longer easily pay the taxes which were assessed". In short, Malchus asserts that he was a lodging place of every vice. [He exiled the grammarian Hyperechius and, yet again, when he said that a stipend

Εὐλογίῳ τῷ φιλοσόφῳ σιτηρέσιον εἰπὼν δοθῆναι, τινὸς τῶν εὐνούχων λέγοντος, ὅτι ταῦτα εἰς στρατιώτας προσήκοι δαπανᾶσθαι,
εἶπεν· εἴθε γένοιτο ἐπὶ τοῦ ἐμοῦ χρόνου, ὥστε τὰ τῶν στρατιωτῶν    15
εἰς διδασκάλους παρέχεσθαι.    (Cf. Photius Bibl. Cod. 78 = T.1)]

4

(Photius Bibl. Cod. 78 = T.1)

5

(Exc. de Leg. Rom. 3)
    Ὅτι Ζήνων ἀνὴρ ὢν ἀπόλεμος ἄγαν, καὶ πολλῆς πανταχόθεν
ταραχῆς ἐφεστώσης, ἔγνω πρὸς τὸν Βάνδιλον εἰς Καρχηδόνα πρεσβεύσασθαι. καὶ Σεῦρον ἐκ τῆς βουλῆς πρεσβευτὴν αἱρεῖται, ἄνδρα
καὶ σωφροσύνῃ διαφέρειν δοκοῦντα καὶ τῷ ἐθέλειν τὰ δίκαια, καὶ
πατρίκιον αὐτὸν ποιήσας ἀποπέμπει, ὅπως ἐκ τῆς ἀξίας τῆς πρεσ-    5
βείας τὸ σχῆμα κατασκευάσοι σεμνότερον. καὶ ὁ μὲν ἐξέπλευσεν, ὁ δὲ
Βάνδιλος, μαθὼν ὅτι ἥξοι πρεσβεία, φθάσας ἔκπλουν ποιεῖται καὶ
Νικόπολιν εἷλεν. ὁ δὲ πρεσβευτὴς Σεῦρος διαβὰς ἀπὸ Σικελίας εἰς
Καρχηδόνα ἀφῖκτο καὶ πολλὰ διὰ τὸν ἔκπλουν ἐμέμφετο τὸν Βάνδιλον.
ὁ δὲ τὰ μὲν ἔλεγεν ὡς πολέμιος πρᾶξαι· τὸν δὲ περὶ τῆς εἰρήνης,    10
ἐπειδὴ πρεσβεύοιτο, νῦν ἔφη λόγον προσδέχεσθαι. τοῦ δὲ Σεύρου τό
τε σῶφρον τοῦ βίου θαυμάσας καὶ τῶν λόγων ἠγάσθη, καὶ τῆς
δικαιοσύνης ἀεὶ πεῖραν λαμβάνων πᾶν ἕτοιμος ἦν ποιεῖν, ὅπερ
ἐκεῖνος προβάλλοιτο. μάλιστα δὲ ἔδοξεν αὐτῷ δίκαιος εἶναι, ὅτι, τὰ
χρήματα αὐτῷ τοῦ βαρβάρου διδόντος, καὶ τὰ πρέποντα δῶρα πρεσ-    15
βευτῇ δωρούμενος ἀπεώσατο πάντα εἰπών, ὡς ἀντὶ τούτων δῶρόν
ἐστιν εὔσχημον πρεσβεύοντι ἀνθρώπῳ τοὺς αἰχμαλώτους κομί-
σασθαι. ὁ δὲ τῆς διανοίας ἐπαινέσας τὸν ἄνδρα· οὓς μὲν ἐγώ, ἔφησεν,
σὺν τοῖς ἐμοῖς υἱέσι τῶν αἰχμαλώτων ἀπέλαχον, τούτους σοι πάντας
ἀφίημι· ἣν δὲ τὸ πλῆθος αὐτῶν κατενείματο μοῖραν, τούτους σοὶ μὲν    20
ἐξέσται παρ' ἑκόντων, εἰ βούλει, πρίασθαι τῶν ἐχόντων, αὐτὸς δ' ἂν
οὐ δυναίμην οὐκ ἐθέλοντας ταῦτα τοὺς εἰληφότας βιάσασθαι. ἐνταῦθα ὁ Σεῦρος ἀπέλυσε μὲν προῖκα οὓς αὐτὸς εἶχεν ὁ Βάνδιλος· ἃ
δὲ εἶχε χρήματα καὶ ἐσθῆτας καὶ σκεύη πάντα ὑπὸ κήρυκι δημοσίᾳ
πωλήσας τούτοις ὅσους ἴσχυσε τῶν αἰχμαλώτων ἐπρίατο.    25

4 τῷ Hoeschel [τὸ codd.    6 κατασκευάσῃ de Boor    16 ἀπεώσατο de Boor
[ἀπεσώσατο codd. ἀπεσείσατο Hoeschel    20 αὐτῶν Niebuhr [αὐτὸ codd.

should be given to the philosopher Eulogius and one of the eunuchs suggested that the money be spent on the soldiers, he replied, "I wish I might see the day when the pay of the soldiers is given to teachers". (Cf. Photius *Bibl. Cod.* 78 = T.1)]

## 4

(Photius *Bibl. Cod.* 78 = T.1)

## 5

(*Exc. de Leg. Rom.* 3)

Zeno was a very unwarlike man and, when troubles broke out on all sides, he decided to send an embassy to the Vandal at Carthage. He selected as ambassador a senator, Severus, who had a reputation for outstanding moderation and desire for justice. In order that he might cut a majestic figure in keeping with the dignity of the embassy, Zeno made him patrician before sending him off. When Severus set sail, the Vandal, learning that an embassy was to arrive, first made a raid by sea and captured Nicopolis. The ambassador Severus crossed from Sicily and when he reached Carthage complained bitterly to the Vandal over the raid. The latter said that he had done this as an enemy, but since the embassy had arrived, he would now listen to the proposals for peace. He marvelled at the moderation of Severus' lifestyle, admired his words and, while continually putting his uprightness to the test, was prepared to do everything that he proposed.[10] Severus seemed to him especially upright in that when the barbarian offered him money and was presenting him with gifts appropriate for an ambassador, he refused them all, saying that instead of these things the most fitting gift for an envoy was that the captives be handed over to him. The Vandal praised the man's attitude and said, "All of the prisoners which I and my sons obtained in the division of the spoils I hand over to you, and, as for the portion which my followers received, you are free to buy these from their owners, if you so wish and they are willing to sell. But if the owners are unwilling, I cannot force them." Thereupon Severus straightway freed as a gift those whom the Vandal held and, offering by public herald all his money, clothes and equipment, bought back those other prisoners whom he was able.[11]

6

[1. (*Suda* H 466)

Ἡράκλειος, στρατηγὸς γεγονὼς ἐπὶ Ζήνωνος, οἷος μὲν τολμῆ-
σαι καὶ πρόθυμος ἐγχειρεῖν ἐς πολέμους ἑτοίμως, οὐ μέντοι τὸ
προμηθὲς εἶχεν ἐν τοῖς κινδύνοις, οὐδὲ βουλὴν πρότερον ποιησάμενος
ὥρμα πρὸς ὃ ἔσπευδε πράττειν, ἀλλ' ἔξω τοῦ λογισμοῦ πρὸς τὰ ἔργα
ἐχώρει καὶ τὸ ἐμπλήκτως ὀξὺ ἐν ἀνδρὸς μοίρᾳ ἐτίθετο. ὅπερ δὴ καὶ      5
μάλιστα αὐτὸν ὕστερον ἔσφηλεν.]

5 δὴ A [δὲ GVM

2. (*Exc. de Leg. Rom.* 4)

Ὅτι Ζήνων ὁ βασιλεὺς πρὸς τὸν ἀρχηγὸν τῶν Γότθων πρεσβευσάμενος περὶ Ἡρακλείου τοῦ στρατηγοῦ τοῦ κρατηθέντος παρὰ
τῶν Γότθων, ὑπέσχετο ἐπὶ λύτροις ἀφήσειν καὶ τὰ λύτρα ρ' συνωμο-
λόγησε τάλαντα. ταῦτα τοὺς προσήκοντας Ἡρακλείῳ Ζήνων
ἐκέλευσε παρασχεῖν, ἵνα μὴ δοκοίη λελυμένος ὑπ' ἄλλων ἐν δούλου      5
γενέσθαι σχήματι. πέμπεται δὲ εἰς Θρᾴκην τοῖς Γότθοις τὰ χρήματα.
οἱ δὲ ἐδέξαντο μὲν καὶ δῆθεν ἐκ τῆς φρουρᾶς ἀνιᾶσιν Ἡράκλειον·
προϊόντι δὲ αὐτῷ ἐν Ἀρκαδίου πόλει προστρέχουσί τινες Γότθοι, καὶ
βαδίζοντι τῷ Ἡρακλείῳ τις ἐκ τῶν Γότθων βίᾳ τὸν ὦμον ἔπαισε.
τῶν δὲ περὶ τὸν Ἡράκλειόν τις ἐπέπληξε τῷ Γότθῳ· καὶ πῶς, εἶπεν,      10
οὔτε σαυτὸν οἶδας, ἄνθρωπε, οὔτε γιγνώσκεις ὃν ἔπληξας; ὁ δὲ πάνυ
γιγνώσκειν ἔφη τὸν ὑπ' αὐτοῦ κάκιστα ἀπολούμενον· καὶ ἅμα σπασά-
μενοι ὁ μέν τις τὴν κεφαλὴν τοῦ Ἡρακλείου, ὁ δὲ τὰς χεῖρας ἀπέτεμεν. καί φασιν ὅτι κατὰ ἀνταπόδοσιν ἔπαθεν Ἡράκλειος· ἐλέγετο
γάρ τινας τῶν ὑφ' αὐτῷ τελούντων στρατιωτῶν δόξαντάς τι πλημ-      15
μελεῖν οὐκ ἄξιον θανάτου εἰς βόθρον καταβαλὼν πᾶν τὸ στράτευμα
ἀναγκάσαι αὐτοὺς καταλεῦσαι. ἔκτοτε οὖν ἡ τοῦ θεοῦ ἀγανάκτησις
εἰς αὐτὸν ἐτηρεῖτο.

8 προστρέχουσι Niebuhr [προτρέχουσι codd.   10 ἐπέπληξε Hoeschel [ἔπληξε
codd.   15 αὐτῷ EMP

[7]

[(*Suda* E 3100)

Ἐρύθριος, ἔπαρχος γεγονὼς ἐπὶ Ζήνωνος· ὃς ἐπεὶ μήτε τὰ
κοινὰ διαρκοῦντα ἑώρα, μήτε βάρος προσθεῖναι πλεῖον τοῦ τεταγμένου τοῖς συντελέσιν ἠνείχετο, μήτε τινα ποιεῖν πονηρόν, ὡς ὢν
φιλάνθρωπος, τῶν ὀφειλομένων ἠδύνατο χάριν, αἰτησάμενος παρὰ
Ζήνωνος ταύτην τῆς ἀρχῆς ἐπαύσατο. λύπην δὲ τῇ πόλει παρέσχεν,      5
ἡνίκα ταύτην ἀπέθετο· μόνος γὰρ τῶν τελούντων τότε εἰς τὴν
πολιτείαν οὗτος ἐπὶ τῷ πάντων ἀγαθῷ ἐπεφύκει, θάττους μὲν τὰς

**6**

[1. (*Suda* H 466)

Heracleius, a general during the reign of Zeno. He was eager for deeds of daring and to rush forthwith into battle. However, he lacked forethought amidst danger and took no counsel before he set out to do what he proposed, but he went off to action without any planning. He considered frantic, headlong activity to be the mark of a man,[12] and this later caused his downfall.]

2. (*Exc. de Leg. Rom.* 4)

The Emperor Zeno sent an embassy to the leader of the Goths concerning Heracleius, who had been defeated by the Goths. [Theoderic the son of Triarius] promised to free him for ransom and agreed to the sum of one hundred talents. Zeno ordered Heracleius' relatives to pay the money lest Heracleius be thought to have been reduced to servile status if he were ransomed by others.[13] The money was sent to the Goths in Thrace. They accepted it and freed Heracleius from custody. When he was making a public appearance at Arcadiopolis, some Goths rushed up to him, and one of them struck him hard on the shoulder as he was walking along. One of Heracleius' escort rebuked the Goth, saying, "Don't you know who you are, man? Don't you know whom you've struck?" The other replied that he knew very well and was going to bring him to a nasty end. The Goths drew their swords together and one cut off Heracleius' head, another his hands. They say that Heracleius was killed in revenge. For it is alleged that when some of the soldiers under his command had committed an offence less than capital, he had them thrown into a pit and compelled the whole army to stone them to death. Thereafter God's retribution pursued him.[14]

**[7]**

[(*Suda* E 3100)

Erythrius, [praetorian] prefect under Zeno. When he saw that the treasury could not meet expenses, since he could neither bear to lay upon the taxpayers a heavier burden than the regular taxes nor bring himself, being a kindly man, to injure anyone because of unpaid debts, he sought Zeno's permission and resigned his office. When he laid down his office it caused grief to the city. For, of the high officials in the state at the time, he alone worked for the good of all, giving prompt

χάριτας παρέχων τοῖς αἰτουμένοις, οὐκ ἔχων δέ τινα παντάπασι τῶν
πρόσθεν προσκεκρουκότων ἀμύνεσθαι. τὸ δὲ κοινὸν τότε εἰς πᾶσαν
ἀπορίαν κατῆλθεν ὡς μηδὲν ἔχεω ὑπόλοιπον. ἅ τε γὰρ ἐν τῷ κοινῷ    10
ταμιείῳ Λέων κατέλιπεν ἀποθνήσκων, ὑπὸ Ζήνωνος ταχὺ ἐκεκέ-
νωτο πάντα, πολλὰ μὲν χαριζομένου τοῖς φίλοις ὡς ἔτυχεν, οὐκ ὄντος
δὲ ἀκριβοῦς, ὥστε γινώσκεω αὐτά, εἴ πη καὶ ἄλλως κλέπτοιντο.]

9 τὸ δὲ κοινὸν τότε [ὅτε τὸ κοινὸν οὕτως V    13 ὥστε [ὥς γε GIM

[8]
[(Suda Z 84)
Ζήνων, βασιλεὺς Ῥωμαίων. ὃς Ζήνωνα τὸν ἑαυτοῦ υἱὸν διά-
δοχον καταλιμπάνεω θέλων κομιδῇ νέον προῆγέ τε δι' ἀξιῶν καὶ
σωμασκεῖσθαι ἐκέλευεν εἰς ἐπίδοσω τῆς ἡλικίας. οἱ δὲ βασιλικοὶ ἐν
ἐξουσίᾳ γενόμενοι τοῦ ἄδην τὰ δημόσια καταναλίσκεω Συβαριτικῶς
τὸν νέον κραιπαλᾶν ἐνήργουν καὶ μαστροπεύοντες αὐτῷ τοὺς    5
συνήβους πρὸς τοὺς τῶν ἀρρένων ἔρωτας λυσσᾶν ἐπαίδευσαν
ἐκτόπως. διαίτης οὖν ἐν ἡδοναῖς καὶ τύφῳ τιθεμένης τὸ καλὸν ἐθὰς
γενόμενος καὶ τὴν ὑποτυφωμένην ἀλαζονείαν ἐπὶ τῇ βασιλικῇ καρα-
δοκίᾳ διὰ τῶν προσώπων ἀπεμφαίνων ἀκροβατεῶ τε ἤρξατο καὶ
μετέωρον τὸν αὐχένα αἴρεω καὶ συλλήβδην φάναι, προσέχεω πᾶσω    10
ὡς οἰκέταις ἀνθρώποις. ἀλλ' ὁ πάντων ἔφορος τὴν φυσικὴν καὶ
διδακτικὴν κακότητα αὐτοῦ τεθεαμένος, διαρρεύσαντα τῇ γαστρὶ καὶ
ἀναισθήτως ἐπὶ πολλὰς ἡμέρας ἐς τὴν εὐνὴν ἀποπατοῦντα, πρόωρον
τῶν ἀνθρωπείων ἐδικαίωσεν ἐκβῆναι.    (Cf. A 463, Δ 885, M 270)]

3 οἱ [οὐ A    6 ἐνήβους V et M 270    9 τοῦ προσώπου ὑπεμφαίων GIM

9
[1. (Suda E 1727)
Ἐξῆλθεν: ἐξέβη, ἐτελέσθη. ὅτι Ζήνωνι παρ' ἣν εἶχε δόξαν
ἐξῆλθε τὸ μάντευμα· ἀντὶ γὰρ τῆς βασιλίδος, ὡς ᾤετο, πόλεως, εἰς
λόφον συγκλεισθέντι τὸ αὐτὸ ὄνομα ἔχοντα, συνέβη τὸ πέρας τοῦ
Ἰουλίου.]

4 Ἰουλίου Müller [βίου codd.

2. (Exc. de Leg. Rom. 5)
Ὅτι ... φεύγεω τε καὶ πλανᾶσθαι καὶ μηδαμῶς δύνασθαι
τῶν κακῶν ἀναπνεῦσαι, παρ' οἷς μοι τοῦ πταίσματος ἤλπιζον εἶναι
παραψυχήν.

1 συμβαίνει μοι add. Niebuhr in lac.

relief to those who requested it and not pursuing someone for all his previous delinquencies.[15] At that time the treasury had been reduced to utter exhaustion, so that there was nothing left in it. For what Leo had left in the exchequer at his death was all quickly dissipated by Zeno, who gave much of it on impulse to his friends and took no care to learn whether other assets were being stolen.]

## [8]
[(*Suda* Z 84)

Zeno, Emperor of the Romans. Wishing to make his own son, Zeno, his successor, he promoted him through the public offices, even though he was very young, and told him to exercise in order to increase his stature. However, the imperial officials charged with utterly consuming the public funds saw to it that the young man was as drunk as a Sybarite and, procuring youths of his own age for homosexual affairs, taught him extraordinary perversions. As he became accustomed to consider as good a life dedicated to empty pleasures and displayed in his expression the arrogant pretensions of his expectation of the throne, he began to strut, to raise his neck high and, to speak briefly, to treat all men as his servants. But the Ruler of all, observing his wickedness, which was both innate and learned, decreed that he suffer an untimely death, having contracted dysentery and having lain unconscious, befouling his bed, for many days. (Cf. A 463, Δ 885, M 270)]

## 9
[1. (*Suda* E 1727)

The prophecy turned out for Zeno otherwise than he had expected. For he spent July, which was to be the limit of his exile, not in the imperial city, as he had thought, but shut up on a hill of the same name.][16]

2. (*Exc. de Leg. Rom.* 5)

... to be a fugitive and a wanderer and never be able to enjoy a respite from my sufferings even with those amongst whom I hoped to find solace for my misfortune.[17]

416    Malchus: Text

[3. (*Suda* B 164)

Βασιλίσκος· ὅτι Βασιλίσκος, ὁ Ῥωμαίων τῶν ἑῴων βασιλεύς,
τῶν ἐκκλησιῶν τοὺς ἐπισκόπους εἰσέπραττε χρήματα καὶ Ἀκάκιον
τὸν Κωνσταντινουπόλεως ἐπίσκοπον μικροῦ δεῖν ἀπώσατο, εἰ μὴ τῷ
πλήθει τῶν λεγομένων μοναχῶν ἀπεκρούσθη. πολύς τε ἦν πρὸς
ἐπιθυμίαν χρημάτων, ὡς μηδὲ αὐτῶν τῶν τὰς εὐτελεῖς καὶ βα-      5
ναύσους μετιόντων ἐπιστήμας ἀπέχεσθαι. καὶ ἦν ἅπαντα μεστὰ
δακρύων τῇ τῶν τοιούτων εἰσφορῶν εἰσπράξει. (καὶ ζήτει ἐν τῷ
Ἀρμάτος.)]

6 μετὰ AN

[4. (*Suda* A 3968)

Ἀρμάτιος· οὗτος μέγιστον ἴσχυσε παρὰ τῇ Ζηνωνίδι τῇ βασι-
λίσσῃ καὶ αὐτῷ Βασιλίσκῳ. ἐσφάγη δὲ ὑπὸ Ζήνωνος τοῦ βασιλέως,
καὶ ὑπερήσθησαν οἱ πολῖται τῇ τούτου σφαγῇ. ἐπὶ γὰρ Λέοντος πρὸς
τοὺς στασιάζοντας ὅσους λάβοι τῶν Θρακῶν τὰς χεῖρας ἐκτέμνων
ἀπέπεμπεν. Ὀνόουλφος δὲ αὐτὸν διεχρήσατο, ὄντινα ὁ Ἀρμάτιος      5
πένητα καὶ ἄρτι ἐκ βαρβάρων ἥκοντα προσλαβὼν φιλοφρόνως τὸ μὲν
πρῶτον κόμητα ἐποίησεν, ἔπειτα καὶ στρατηγὸν Ἰλλυριῶν, καὶ εἰς
ἑστίασιν ἔχειν πολὺν ἄργυρον παρέσχεν. ἀντέδωκε δὲ τούτῳ τὴν
βαρβαρικὴν ἀπιστίαν μετὰ χειρὸς μιαιφόνου.
(Cf. Photius *Bibl. Cod.* 78 = T.1; *Suda* M 120 = T.2)]

[10]

[(*Suda* E 2494)

Ἐπίνικος, ὕπαρχος τῆς πόλεως ἐπὶ Βασιλίσκου, κόρον χρημα-
τισμοῦ μὴ λαμβάνων μηδένα καὶ τὰ ἔθνη καὶ τὰς πόλεις πάσας
καπηλεύων καὶ ἀτόπων τὰς ἐπαρχίας προσταγμάτων ἐμπλήσας· ἃ
μὴ φέρουσαι ἔτι τῶν ἀρχόντων αἱ τάξεις, μηδὲ αἱ ἔξω βουλαί, φυ-
γοῦσαι κατέλιπον τὰς τῶν φόρων εἰσπράξεις. ἐκ δὲ τῆς τούτου      5
πλεονεξίας <οἳ> ἀρχόμενοι ἱκέται ἐν τοῖς κοινοῖς ἱεροῖς ἐκαθέζοντο
ἐλέγχοντες τὰ τούτου κλέμματα. ἦν δὲ πᾶσιν ἀπεχθὴς τιμὴν οὐδενὶ
νέμων προσήκουσαν. καὶ τοῦτον τῆς ἀρχῆς ἀπήλλαξαν ἀτίμως·
ἀνθαιροῦνται δὲ ἄνδρα Λαυρέντιον, ὃς ἦν ἐξ ἀρχῆς τῶν ἐπὶ τῆς
ἀγορᾶς τῆς μεγάλης ῥητόρων καὶ πρωτεύσας ἐν ταύτῃ. ὅτῳ δὲ      10
συνείποι, οὔτε τρίβειν, ὡς ἂν μᾶλλον κερδαίνοι, οὔτε διέλκειν
ἠνείχετο.]

1 ἔπαρχος A    3 πλήσας A    6 οἳ addidi    ἀγχόμενοι Bernhardy ἐρχόμενοι
Drachmann

[3. (*Suda* B 164)
Basiliscus, the Emperor of the eastern Romans, exacted money from the bishops of the churches and almost banished Acacius, the bishop of Constantinople, but was deterred by a crowd of the so-called 'monks'. He was so greedy for money that he did not leave alone even those who pursued mean and mechanical occupations. There was universal lamentation because of the imposition of such taxes. (Also look under 'Harmatus'.)] [18]

[4. (*Suda* A 3968)
Harmatius was extremely influential with the Empress Zenonis and Basiliscus himself. He was put to death by Zeno, and the citizens were overjoyed at his execution. For during the reign of Leo he cut off the hands of all the rebellious Thracians whom he caught and sent them away. He was killed by Onulf, whom Harmatius had received in a kindly manner when he was in poverty and newly arrived from amongst the barbarians. He had first made him count, then general of the Illyrians, and had given him much money to pay for his entertainment. Onulf's bloodstained hands paid Harmatius back with barbarous treachery.
(Cf. Photius *Bibl. Cod.* 78 = T.1; *Suda* M 120 = T.2)]

## [10]

[(*Suda* E 2494)
Epinicus, city prefect [19] during the reign of Basiliscus. He profiteered incessantly, selling all the provinces and the cities, and he overloaded the provincial governments with extraordinary demands. Since neither the administrators nor the local councils could endure these, they left their posts and abandoned the collection of the taxes. As a result of his profiteering the provincials sat as suppliants in the public churches attesting to his thefts. He was hated by everyone and gave to no one his due honour. He lost his office in disgrace, and in his stead they chose Laurentius, who was the senior official of the rhetors in the Great Agora. Epinicus did not allow anyone with whom he was associated to waste any time or procrastinate, so that he might make more profit.]

## [11]

[(Zonaras 14,2,22-24)

Οὗ κρατοῦντος ἐμπρησμὸς ἐν Κωνσταντινουπόλει ἐγένετο
μέγιστος, ἐκ τῶν Χαλκοπρατίων ἀρξάμενος καὶ πάντα τὰ προσεχῆ
τούτοις νεμηθεὶς καὶ ἀποτεφρώσας τάς τε τῶν δημοσίων πλατειῶν
στοὰς καὶ τὰς αὐταῖς ἐπικειμένας οἰκοδομάς, ἀλλὰ μὴν καὶ αὐτὴν
τὴν κεκλημένην Βασιλικήν, καθ' ἣν καὶ βιβλιοθήκη ἐτύγχανε δώδεκα    5
μυριάδας βιβλίων ἀποκειμένων ἐν αὐτῇ ἔχουσα· ἐν οἷς ἀναγράφεται
εἶναι καὶ δράκοντος ἔντερον, μήκους ὂν ποδῶν ἑκατὸν εἴκοσιν, ἔχον
ἐγγεγραμμένα χρυσοῖς γράμμασι τὰ τοῦ Ὁμήρου ποιήματα, τήν τε
Ἰλιάδα καὶ τὴν Ὀδύσσειαν, οὗ καὶ ὁ Μάλχος τὰ περὶ τούτων τῶν
βασιλέων συγγραφόμενος μέμνηται. διέφθειρε δὲ τὸ πῦρ ἐκεῖνο καὶ    10
τὴν ἐν τοῖς Λαύσου τῆς πόλεως ἀγλαΐαν καὶ τὰ ἐκεῖ ἐνιδρυμένα
ἀγάλματα τῆς τε Σαμίας Ἥρας καὶ τῆς Λυδίας Ἀθηνᾶς καὶ τῆς
Κνιδίας Ἀφροδίτης, τὰ κατὰ τέχνην περιβόητα ἀφιδρύματα, καὶ
μέχρι τοῦ Φόρου ἐπέδραμε.
(Cf. Cedrenus I p.618; Suda M 120 = T.2)]

## 12

(Photius Bibl. Cod. 78 = T.1; [Suda B 164 = Fr. 9,3])

## 13

[1. (Suda K 693)
Ὁ δὲ Ὀνόουλφος ἔφυ ἐξ ἐθνῶν κατὰ πατέρα μὲν Θεουρίγγων,
τῶν δὲ Σκίρων κατὰ τὴν μητέρα.]

2. (Photius Bibl. Cod. 78 = T.1; [Suda A 3968 = Fr. 9,4])

## 14

(Exc. de Leg. Gent. 3)

Ὅτι ὁ Αὔγουστος ὁ τοῦ Ὀρέστου υἱὸς ἀκούσας Ζήνωνα πάλιν
τὴν βασιλείαν ἀνακεκτῆσθαι τῆς ἔω τὸν Βασιλίσκον ἐλάσαντα,
ἠνάγκασε τὴν βουλὴν ἀποστεῖλαι πρεσβείαν Ζήνωνι σημαίνουσαν,
ὡς ἰδίας μὲν αὐτοῖς βασιλείας οὐ δέοι, κοινὸς δὲ ἀποχρήσει μόνος ὢν
αὐτοκράτωρ ἐπ' ἀμφοτέροις τοῖς πέρασι. τὸν μέντοι Ὀδόαχον ὑπ'    5
αὐτῶν προβεβλῆσθαι ἱκανὸν ὄντα σῴζειν τὰ παρ' αὐτοῖς πράγματα,
πολιτικὴν ἔχοντα σύνεσιν ὁμοῦ καὶ μάχιμον· καὶ δεῖσθαι τοῦ Ζήνωνος
πατρικίου τε αὐτῷ ἀποστεῖλαι ἀξίαν καὶ τὴν τῶν Ἰταλῶν τούτῳ
ἐφεῖναι διοίκησιν. ἀφικνοῦνται δὴ ἄνδρες τῆς βουλῆς τῆς ἐν Ῥώμῃ
τούτους εἰς Βυζάντιον κομίζοντες τοὺς λόγους, καὶ ταῖς αὐταῖς ἡμέραις    10

[11]

[(Zonaras 14,2,22-24)

While [Basiliscus] was Emperor a very serious fire broke out at Constantinople. Beginning in the quarter of the bronze merchants, it spread to all the areas nearby and reduced to ashes the colonnades of the public squares and the adjacent houses, as well as the Basilica, so-called, which contained a library of 120,000 books. Amongst these it is written that there was the intestine of a serpent, one hundred and twenty feet long, which had written on it in gold letters the poems of Homer, the *Iliad* and the *Odyssey*. Malchus, who wrote a history of these Emperors, also mentions this. The fire also destroyed the beautiful palace of Lausus and the statues therein, the Hera of Samos, the Athena of Lindos and the Aphrodite of Cnidos, famous masterpieces of art, and it spread as far as the Forum.[20]
(Cf. Cedrenus I p.618; *Suda* M 120 = T.2)]


12

(Photius *Bibl. Cod.* 78 = T.1; [*Suda* B 164 = *Fr.* 9,3])


13

[1. (*Suda* K 693)

On his father's side Onulf was descended from the Theuringi, on his mother's side from the Sciri.]

2. (Photius *Bibl. Cod.* 78 = T.1; [*Suda* A 3968 = *Fr.* 9,4])


14

(*Exc. de Leg. Gent.* 3)

When Augustus, the son of Orestes, heard that Zeno had driven out Basiliscus and regained the sovereignty of the East, he compelled the senate to send an embassy to Zeno proposing that there was no need of a divided rule and that one, shared Emperor was sufficient for both territories. They said, moreover, that they had chosen Odovacer, a man of military and political experience, to safeguard their own affairs and that Zeno should confer upon him the rank of patrician and entrust him with the government of Italy. Representatives of the Roman senate arrived at Byzantium carrying these proposals. During these same days envoys came from Nepos to congratulate Zeno on what

ἐκ τοῦ Νέπωτος ἄγγελοι τῶν τε γεγενημένων συνησθησόμενοι τῷ
Ζήνωνι καὶ δεόμενοι ἅμα ταῖς ἴσαις τῷ Νέπωτι συμφοραῖς χρησα-
μένῳ συσπουδάσαι προθύμως τῆς βασιλείας ἀνάκτησιν, χρήματά τε
καὶ στρατὸν ἐπὶ ταῦτα διδόντα καὶ τοῖς ἄλλοις, οἷς δέοι, συνεκπο-
νοῦντα τὴν κάθοδον. ταῦτά τε τοὺς λέξοντας ὁ Νέπως ἀπέστελλεν.    15
Ζήνων δὲ τοῖς ἥκουσι τοῖς μὲν ἀπὸ τῆς βουλῆς ἀπεκρίνατο ταῦτα, ὡς
δύο ἐκ τῆς ἔω βασιλέας λαβόντες τὸν μὲν ἐξεληλάκασιν, Ἀνθέμιον
δὲ ἀπέκτειναν· καὶ νῦν τὸ ποιητέον αὐτοὺς ἔφη γινώσκειν· οὐ γὰρ ἂν
βασιλέως ἔτι ὄντος ἑτέραν ἡγήσεσθαι γνώμην ἢ κατιόντα προσ-
δέχεσθαι· τοῖς δὲ ἐκ τοῦ βαρβάρου ὅτι καλῶς πράξοι παρὰ τοῦ    20
βασιλέως Νέπωτος τὴν ἀξίαν τοῦ πατρικίου δεξάμενος Ὀδόαχος·
ἐκπέμψαν γὰρ αὐτόν, εἰ μὴ Νέπως ἐπεφθάκει. ἐπαινεῖ δὲ ὡς ἀρχὴν
ἐπιδέδεικται ταύτην τοῦ τὸν κόσμον φυλάττειν τὸν τοῖς Ῥωμαίοις
προσήκοντα, καὶ πιστεύειν ἐντεῦθεν ὡς καὶ τὸν βασιλέα τὸν ταῦτα
τιμήσαντα καταδέξοιτο θᾶττον, εἰ ποιεῖν θέλοι τὰ δίκαια. καὶ βασί-    25
λειον γράμμα περὶ ὧν ἠβούλετο πέμπων τῷ Ὀδοάχῳ πατρίκιον ἐν
τούτῳ τῷ γράμματι ἐπωνόμασε. ταῦτα δὲ συνεσπούδαζε τῷ Νέπωτι
ὁ Ζήνων ἐκ τῶν ἑαυτοῦ κακῶν τὰ ἐκείνου οἰκτείρων καὶ τό γε κοινὸν
τῆς τύχης εἰς ὑπόθεσιν ἔχων τῷ δυστυχοῦντι συνάχθεσθαι. ἅμα δὲ
καὶ Βηρῖνα συνεπώτρυνε τοῦτον τῇ Νέπωτος γυναικὶ συγγενεῖ οὔσῃ    30
συσπεύδουσα.

19 εἰσηγήσεσθαι Bekker    22 ἐκπέμψαν ΑΕΧ [ἐκπέμψειν edd.    28 γε
Niebuhr [τε Α

15

(Exc. de Leg. Gent. 4)

Ὅτι ἐν τῷ ἑξῆς ἔτει ἐπὶ Ζήνωνος πρέσβεις ἦλθον ἐκ Θράκης
τῶν ὑποσπόνδων Γότθων, οὓς δὴ καὶ φοιδεράτους οἱ Ῥωμαῖοι
καλοῦσιν, ἀξιοῦντες Ζήνωνα Θευδερίχῳ σπείσασθαι τῷ παιδὶ
Τριαρίου ἥσυχον ἐθέλοντι διεξάγειν τὸν βίον καὶ μηδένα πόλεμον
τοῖς κοινοῖς αἴρεσθαι πράγμασιν. ἠξίουν δὲ καὶ σκοπεῖν ὅσα πολέμιος    5
ὢν κατέβλαψε Ῥωμαίους, καὶ ὅσα Θευδέριχος ὁ τοῦ Βαλαμείρου
παῖς στρατηγὸς ὢν καὶ φίλος ταῖς πόλεσιν ἐλυμήνατο, καὶ μὴ νῦν
ἀπεχθείας παλαιὰς ὁρᾶν μᾶλλον ἢ ὅπως τι τῷ κοινῷ γένοιτο
πάντως ὠφέλιμον.

Εὐθὺς οὖν ὁ βασιλεὺς τὴν βουλὴν συγκαλέσας γνώμην αὐτοῖς    10
προύθηκεν, ὅ τι δέοι ποιῆσαι. οἱ δὲ ἀμφοτέροις μὲν οὐκ ἔφασαν ἱκανὸν
τὸ δημόσιον εἶναι συντάξεις τε καὶ μισθὸν ἐπαρκέσαι προχείρως,
ὁπότε γε μηδὲ αὐτοῖς μόνοις τοῖς στρατιώταις ἀμέμπτους ὑποτελεῖν
τὰς χορηγίας δυνάμεθα. ὁπότερον δὲ αὐτῶν δεῖ φίλον προελέσθαι,

had transpired and to ask that he lend strong support to Nepos, who had suffered similar misfortunes, in the recovery of his throne by giving money and an army for this purpose and by offering other forms of assistance necessary to effect his return. Nepos had sent the men to say these things. To those who had come from the senate Zeno gave the following reply: they had received two Emperors from the East, one of whom they had ejected, the other, Anthemius, they had killed. Now, he said, they knew what they should do: since their Emperor was still alive, they should entertain no other thought than to welcome him on his return. To the representatives of the barbarian he replied that it was better that Odovacer had received the patriciate from the Emperor Nepos, although he would have conferred it[21] if Nepos had not done so first. Zeno added that he congratulated Odovacer in thus beginning by preserving the order of government appropriate for the Romans and that from this he was confident that, if Odovacer wished to act justly, he would quickly receive back the Emperor who had honoured him in this manner. He sent to Odovacer a royal letter concerning what he wished and in the letter addressed him as patrician. Zeno gave this support to Nepos since he pitied the latter's plight because of his own and since he held it as a principle that those in like positions should sympathise with their equals when they suffer misfortune.[22] At the same time Verina, too, joined in urging on[23] Zeno, since she was supporting Nepos' wife, who was her relative.

## 15

(*Exc. de Leg. Gent.* 4)

In the following year envoys came to Zeno from the allied Goths in Thrace, whom the Romans call *foederati*.[24] They requested that Zeno make a treaty with Theoderic the son of Triarius, who wished to live a life of peace and not to be at war with the state, and they asked the Emperor to consider how little harm the son of Triarius, though an enemy, had done to the Romans and how much damage Theoderic the son of Valamir, though a general and a friend, had done to the cities. Zeno ought not now look to old hatreds rather than how he might most advance the common good.

The Emperor, therefore, immediately convened the senate and asked its advice as to what he should do. They said that the treasury did not have the resources to furnish subsidies and pay to both parties, since "we cannot supply our own soldiers alone without difficulties". They left it to the Emperor to decide which of them should be chosen

τούτου κύριον αὐτὸν τὸν βασιλέα καθίστασαν. ὁ δὲ ἐπὶ τὴν αὐλὴν τούς    15
τε κατὰ τὴν πόλιν στρατιώτας καλέσας καὶ τὰς σχολὰς ἁπάσας,
ἀναβὰς ἐπὶ βῆμα πολλὰ τοῦ Θευδερίχου κατηγόρει, ἐν τούτοις ὅπως
τε τοῖς Ῥωμαίοις ἐχθρὸς ἄνωθεν εἴη, καὶ ὡς ἐλυμήνατο τοῖς τὴν
Θρᾴκην οἰκοῦσι χεῖράς τε ἀποτέμνων ἅμα τῷ Ἀρματίῳ καὶ τὸ
γεωργοῦν ἅπαν ποιήσας ἀνάστατον· ὅπως τε τυραννίδα πάλιν ἐπὶ    20
τοῖς κοινοῖς τὴν Βασιλίσκου ἐπήγειρε καὶ ὡς τοὺς στρατιώτας
ἐκεῖνον ἀνέπεισεν ἐκποδὼν ποιήσασθαι, ὡς τῶν Γότθων ἀρκούντων.
καὶ νῦν δὲ πρεσβεύεσθαι οὐκ εἰρήνης γε μᾶλλον ἢ στρατηγίας δεόμενον. ἢν οὖν ἔχετε γνώμην καὶ ὑμεῖς περὶ τούτων, ταύτην, ἔφη, παρ'
ὑμῶν ἀκοῦσαι βουλόμενος νυνὶ παρεκάλεσα, εἰδὼς τῶν βασιλέων    25
τούτους ἀσφαλῶς πράττειν, οἱ ἂν τὰ βουλεύματα τοῖς στρατιώταις
κοινώσουσιν. οἱ δὲ ἧς κατέτεινε κατηγορίας ἀκούσαντες καὶ ἐκ
ταύτης διδαχθέντες ὃ χρῆν ἀποκρίνασθαι πάντες ἀνεβόησαν ἐχθρὸν
εἶναι Ῥωμαίοις Θευδέριχον καὶ πάντας, εἴ τις ἐκείνῳ συνέστηκεν.
    Οὐ μέντοι τοῖς πρέσβεσι ταύτην εὐθὺς ἔδωκεν ἀπόκρισιν ὁ    30
Ζήνων, ἀλλ' ἐπεῖχεν, ἕως τι πλέον ἀκούσει τῶν ἔξωθεν. ἐν τούτῳ δὲ
γράφοντες τὰ ἔνδον γινόμενα τῶν ἐν τῇ πόλει τινὲς τῷ Θευδερίχῳ
ἑάλωσαν, Ἄνθιμός τε ἰατρὸς καὶ Μαρκελλῖνος καὶ Στέφανος, καὶ οὐ
μόνον ἑαυτῶν ἐπιστολὰς ἔπεμπον, ἀλλὰ καὶ τῶν ἐν τέλει πλαττό-
μενοι γράμματα ἐκείνῳ ἐπέστελλον θαρσύνειν βουλόμενοι, ὡς    35
ἱκανοὺς ἔχοντα τοὺς συμπράττοντας ἔνδον. καὶ τρεῖς τῶν ἀπὸ βουλῆς,
τοῦ μαγίστρου παρόντος, ἐξετάσαντες ταῦτα καὶ πληγὰς τὰ σώματα
πολλὰς ἐπιθέμενοι φυγὴν εἰς ἅπαξ ἐπέθηκαν. δῆθεν γὰρ ἀπέχεσθαι
θανάτου καὶ σφαγῶν δοκεῖν ὁ Ζήνων ἐβούλετο.

16 καλέσας Valesius [κελεύσας A    27 κοινώσωσιν Müller    31 ἀκούσειε
Dindorf

# 16

1. (Exc. de Leg. Rom. 6)
    Ὅτι τὸν ἄρχοντα Αἰγύπτου ἐπὶ μόλις χρυσίου λίτραις ν' ἐκπεμ-
πόμενον, ὥσπερ εὐδαιμονεστέρας γενομένης ἢ πρόσθεν, ἐπὶ πεντα-
κοσίαις ὁμοῦ λίτραις ἀπέστειλεν.

[2. (Suda Z 83)
    Ζήνων, βασιλεὺς Ῥωμαίων, τὴν μὲν ὠμότητα, ᾗ ἐκέχρητο
Λέων, ἐν τῇ φύσει οὐκ εἶχεν. οὐδὲ τὸ θυμούμενον ἀπαραίτητον αὐτῷ
καθειστήκει ἐσάπαξ, οἷον τοῦ Λέοντος διέμενε. καὶ τήν γε προαίρεσιν ἐν πολλοῖς εἶχε φιλότιμον· καὶ ἃ ἔπραττε δόξης ἕνεκεν καὶ
τοῦ θαυμάζεσθαι ἔπραττεν, ἐπιδεικτικῶς μᾶλλον ἢ ἀληθῶς. οὐ μὴν    5

as a friend. Zeno summoned to the palace all the soldiers in the city and the palace regiments and, ascending the tribunal, made many charges against the son of Triarius. Amongst these he recounted how from the beginning he had been hostile to the Romans; how he had harmed the inhabitants of Thrace, along with Harmatius cutting off their hands[25] and driving out all the farmers; how he had encouraged Basiliscus' usurpation against the state; and how he had persuaded him to dispose of his own troops on the ground that the Goths were sufficient for him.[26] Now he was sending an embassy seeking not peace but a generalship. "I have summoned you now", said Zeno, "wishing to hear from you your view on these matters, for I know that those Emperors who share their deliberations with the soldiers act safely". When they heard the charges which he made and learned from these the answer required, they all shouted out that the son of Triarius and all who sided with him were enemies of the Romans.

Zeno did not give this reply to the envoys straightaway but waited until he should hear more of what was happening outside the city.[27] Meanwhile, certain persons in the city (the doctor Anthimus, Marcellinus and Stephanus), who were writing to Theoderic about what was happening within, were arrested. They were not only sending letters in their own names but were also despatching to him forged letters from high officials, since they wished to encourage Theoderic to think that he had sufficient supporters within the city. Three senators, in the presence of the master of the offices, examined these matters and, having inflicted many lashes upon the bodies of these persons, condemned them to perpetual exile. Zeno, of course, wished to avoid the death penalty and bloodshed.

## 16

1. (*Exc. de Leg. Rom.* 6)

Whereas the governor of Egypt is usually appointed for a payment of fifty pounds of gold, as if the country had become richer than before, he appointed him for almost five hundred pounds.[28]

[2. (*Suda* Z 83)

Zeno, the Roman Emperor, did not have in his character the same cruel streak as Leo, nor did he have the constant, inexorable anger that was in Leo. In many matters he desired repute, and what he did, he did to win glory and cause admiration – for show rather than out of commitment. He lacked both the practical experience and the knowledge[29]

οὔτε ἔμπειρος τῶν πραγμάτων ἦν οὔτε εἶχεν ἐπιστήμην, δι' ἧς ἔστιν
ἀσφαλῶς τὰς βασιλείας ἰθύνεσθαι. πρὸς δὲ κέρδος καὶ λῆμμα οὐχ
οὕτω μὲν ἐμμανῶς ὡς ὁ Λέων διέκειτο· οὐδὲ ἔπλαττε μὴ ὄντα τοῖς
κεκτημένοις ἐγκλήματα· οὐ μὴν οὐδὲ παντελῶς κρείττων ὑπῆρχε τοῦ
πράγματος. καὶ χρηστῆς ἂν βασιλείας ἔτυχον Ῥωμαῖοι, εἰ μὴ Σε-    10
βαστιανὸς ὁ τότε παραδυναστεύων ἦγεν αὐτὸν ἐς ὅπη ἐβούλετο,
καπηλεύων ὥσπερ ἐξ ἀγορᾶς ἅπαντα καὶ μηδὲν ἄπρατον ἐῶν ἐν τῇ
βασιλέως αὐλῇ διαπράττεσθαι. ἀλλὰ τὰς μὲν ἀρχὰς ἀπεδίδοτο
πάσας, ἰδίᾳ μὲν ἑαυτῷ, ἰδίᾳ δὲ λαμβάνων τῷ βασιλεῖ τὰ τιμήματα·
καὶ εἰ προσῆλθεν ἕτερος βραχύ τι προστιθείς, ἐκεῖνος ἦν αἱρετώ-    15
τερος. τῶν δὲ ἐν τοῖς ἀρχείοις γινομένων ἁπάντων οὐδὲν ἦν, ὃ μὴ
λαβὼν ἀπεπίπρασκεν. εἰ δέ τινι ἀρχὴν τῶν περὶ αὐτὸν ὄντων ἐχαρί-
σατο Ζήνων, ὥσπερ πολιτοκάπηλος αὐτὸς ταύτην ὀλίγου παρ'
ἐκείνου λαμβάνων, ἄλλοις παρεῖχε τοῦ πλείονος, Ζήνωνι δὲ τὰ
κλέμματα παρέχων.]    20

11 ἐς ὅπη [ ὅποι V    12 καπηλεύων . . . παρέχων (v.20) [ὃς τῆς ἀρχῆς
ἅπαντα ἀπεπίπρασκε καὶ τῷ διδόντι βραχύ τι πλέον ἐκείνῳ ἐδίδου· Ζήνωνι δὲ
τὰ κλέμματα παρεῖχε καὶ οὕτως διέφθειρε τὰ Ῥωμαίων V    17 τινι ἀρχὴν
Müller (τινι post ἀρχὴν Bernhardy) [τινα ἀρχὴν codd.

17
(*Exc. de Leg. Gent.* 5)

Ὅτι τῷ αὐτῷ ἔτει πρέσβεις ἐκ Καρχηδόνος ἐς Βυζάντιον
ἦλθον, οὓς Ἀλέξανδρος ἦγεν ὁ τῆς Ὀλυβρίου γυναικὸς ἐπίτροπος· ὃς
ἐτύγχανε πεμφθεὶς ὑπὸ Ζήνωνος πάλαι, συνθελούσης καὶ αὐτῆς
τοῦτο τῆς Πλακιδίας. ἔλεγον δὲ οἱ πρέσβεις ὅτι Ὀνώριχος φίλος τε
τῷ βασιλεῖ καθεστήκοι ἀδόλως καὶ στέργοι τὰ Ῥωμαίων, καὶ ἀφίησι    5
πάντα, ἃ πρόσθεν ἐνεκάλει περί τε τῶν προσόδων καὶ τῶν ἄλλων
χρημάτων, ἃ τῆς αὐτοῦ γυναικὸς προειλήφει ὁ Λέων, καὶ ὅσα τῶν
ἐμπόρων τῶν ἐκ τῆς Καρχηδόνος ἄρτι καθισταμένου τοῦ πολέμου
ἐλήφθη, καὶ εἴ τι ἄλλο πάλαι ὁ πατὴρ πρὸς Ῥωμαίους ὁπωσοῦν
ἔσχεν αἰτίαν· τήν τε εἰρήνην ἔχειν ἀξιοίη βεβαίαν, καὶ μηδὲν εἶναι    10
λοιπὸν τοῖς Ῥωμαίοις ὕποπτος τῷ μὴ οὐχὶ γνησίως τὰς σπονδὰς
ἐμπεδώσειν καὶ ὅσα ἤδη συνέκειτο. εἰδέναι γὰρ χάριν, ὅτι τὴν
Ὀλυβρίου τετιμήκοι γυναῖκα· καὶ ταῦτα πυθόμενος πάντα ἕτοιμος
ἦν βασιλεῖ πράττειν ἃ βούλοιτο. ἦν δὲ τοῦτο πρόσχημα εὐπρεπὲς
τῷ λόγῳ, ἐπεὶ τό γε ἀληθὲς πᾶσαν ἐδεδοίκεσαν ὑποψίαν πολέμου,    15
καὶ μετὰ τὸν θάνατον Γωζιρίχου πεσόντες ἐς πᾶσαν μαλακίαν οὔτε
τὴν αὐτὴν ῥώμην ἐς πράγματα ἔσχον οὔτε τὰς αὐτὰς ἔτι συνεῖχον
παρασκευάς, ἃς ἐκεῖνος πρὸς πᾶσαν πρᾶξιν εἶχεν ἐφόρμους, ὡς

5 ἀφιεὶς Papabasileios (1896)    14 ἃ Hoeschel [ ᾧ A

through which it is possible to govern states safely. He was not so
frantically eager as Leo for wealth and profit, and he did not fabricate
false charges against wealthy men, although he was not wholly above
such activity. The Romans would have enjoyed a successful reign if
Sebastianus, who at the time had great influence with the Emperor,
had not led him into whatever he wished, selling everything as if at a
market and allowing no business to be done in the palace without
payment. He sold all government positions, taking private profit, partly
for himself and partly for the Emperor. If someone else came forward
and offered a little more, he was preferred. There was nothing in the
palace which he did not buy and sell. If Zeno bestowed a position upon
a member of his court, Sebastianus, like a trader in public offices,
bought it from him for a small price and sold it to others for more,
giving the proceeds of his robbery to Zeno.]

## 17

*(Exc. de Leg. Gent. 5)*

In the same year envoys came from Carthage to Byzantium
conducted by Alexander, the guardian of Olybrius' wife. He had been
earlier sent out by Zeno with the consent of Placidia herself. The
envoys said that Huneric had established himself as an honest friend
of the Emperor, loved everything Roman and was renouncing all claims
on the public revenues and the other monies which Leo had earlier confiscated from his wife, as well as what the Emperor had seized from the
Carthaginian merchants soon after the beginning[30] of the war, and
everything else over which his father had grievances against the Romans. He wished to enjoy a secure peace and to leave no ground remaining for the Romans to suspect that he would not honestly adhere
to the treaty and the matters already agreed upon. He was grateful that
Zeno had honoured Olybrius' wife and, learning this, was ready to do
for the Emperor whatever he wished. This was the plausible pretext for
the proposal, when, in reality, the Vandals feared any hint of war. For
after the death of Gaiseric they had fallen completely into softness
and had maintained neither the same strength for action nor the same
military establishment which he had kept ready for use, so that he

θᾶττον ἀεὶ πράττειν ἢ ὡς ἂν ἄλλοι βουλεύσαιντο. δεξάμενος δὲ
αὐτοὺς φιλοφρόνως ὁ Ζήνων τιμῆς μὲν ἠξίωσε δεούσης τοὺς πρέσ-    20
βεις, καὶ δώροις ἀπέπεμψε τοῖς πρέπουσι κοσμήσας, Ἀλέξανδρον δὲ
ποιεῖ τῶν πριβάτων κόμητα.

## 18

1. (*Exc. de Leg. Rom.* 7)

Ὅτι ἐν τῷ αὐτῷ χρόνῳ ὁ Ζήνων αἰσθόμενος ὡς τὰ μὲν
Θευδερίχου τοῦ παιδὸς Βαλαμήρου ἀεὶ ἀσθενέστερα καὶ ἐλάττονα
γίγνοιντο, ὁ δὲ τοῦ Τριαρίου ἔθνη τε συναθροίζει καὶ συστρέφει
δυνάμεις, ἐνόμισε βέλτιον ἐπὶ μετρίοις αὐτῷ, εἰ συμβῆναι βούλοιτο,
καταλῦσαι τὴν ἔχθραν. καὶ πρέσβεις ἀποστείλας ἠξίου τόν τε υἱὸν    5
παραδοῦναι ὅμηρον, ὡς πάλαι προυκαλεῖτο, καὶ ἰδιώτην ὄντα ἐν τοῖς
ἑαυτοῦ μένειν μηδὲν ἐνοχλούμενον, ὥσπερ ᾔτησε τότε, λαβεῖν τε τὴν
οὐσίαν ὁπόσης ἀφῄρητο καὶ τἆλλα ἡσυχάζειν οὐδὲν ἔχοντα κακὸν
οὐδὲ ἑτέρῳ παρέχοντα. ὁ δὲ ἀπεκρίνατο ὅτι <οὔτε> τὸν υἱὸν ἔτι
ὅμηρον δώσοι, οὔτε δύνασθαι ἔτι ἐκ μόνης τῆς οὐσίας ἰδιώτης    10
διάγειν. ἕως μὲν γὰρ ἦν μόνος μήπω ἔθνη τοσαῦτα περὶ αὑτὸν ἔχων,
μόνην ἂν τὴν οὐσίαν σφόδρα συστελλομένῳ ἴσως ἂν ἐπαρκέσαι· νῦν
δέ, ἐπείπερ αὐτὸν εἰς ἀνάγκην τοῦ ἔθνη συλλέξαι κατέστησαν, ἐκ τῆς
ἀνάγκης εἶναι ἢ τρέφειν τοὺς ἐλθόντας ἢ σὺν αὐτοῖς πολεμεῖν, ἕως
παθὼν ἢ δράσας ἐν ἀναμφισβήτητον τῷ παντὶ πέρας ἐξοίσειεν.    15

Ταῦτα ὡς ἀπηγγέλθη, ἔδοξεν εἰς ἀκριβῆ κατασκευάζεσθαι
πόλεμον. καὶ τάγματα μὲν πάντα, ὅσα τε πρὸς τῷ Πόντῳ καὶ κατὰ
τὴν Ἀσίαν καὶ ὅσα τοῖς ἑῴοις ἐνίδρυτο μέρεσι, κατὰ τάχος ἐκάλει,
καὶ παρῆν πανταχόθεν οὐκ ὀλίγον τι πλῆθος. κατεσκευάζοντο δὲ
ἅμαξαι σκευοφόροι καὶ βόες ἐωνοῦντο καὶ σῖτός τε καὶ ὅσα χρήσιμα    20
στρατοπέδῳ πάντα ἐγίνετο ἕτοιμα, ὡς αὐτοῦ γε μέλλοντος Ἰλλοῦ
ἐξιέναι.

9 οὔτε add. Valesius    9-10 ἀπεκρίνατο οὔτε ... δώσειν coni. de Boor

2. (*Exc. de Leg. Rom.* 8)

Ὅτι ὁ Ζήνων Μαρτινιανὸν προβαλόμενος στρατηγόν, καὶ τοῦ
στρατοῦ ἐς ἀταξίαν ἐλθόντος, ὡς ταῦτα καλῶς ἔχειν ἐδόκει, πέμπει
ἄνδρας αὐτίκα παρὰ τὸν Βαλαμήρου λέγοντας, ὅτι οὐ δεῖ τρίβειν ἔτι
τὴν μάχην, ἀλλ᾽ ἔργου νῦν ἔχεσθαι καὶ πληροῦν τὰς ἐλπίδας, ἐφ᾽
αἷς τῆς στρατηγίας ἠξιώθη Ῥωμαίων. ὁ δὲ ταῦτα ἀκούσας ἀντι-    5
πέμπει καὶ αὐτὸς ὡς Βυζάντιον πρέσβεις λέγων, ὡς οὐ πρότερον
ἐγχειρήσοι τῷ ἔργῳ, εἰ μὴ καὶ ὁ βασιλεὺς καὶ ἡ σύγκλητος αὐτῷ
ἐπομόσαιτο πᾶσα, ὡς οὐδέποτε ἐπὶ τῷ Τριαρίου συμβήσονται. οἱ μὲν
οὖν ἀπὸ βουλῆς καὶ οἱ ἄρχοντες ὤμοσαν μὴ συμβαίνειν, εἰ μὴ βασιλεὺς

always moved more quickly than his opponents calculated. Zeno received the envoys in a friendly manner, bestowed upon them the honour due to ambassadors, sent them away laden with the appropriate gifts and made Alexander count of the privy purse.[31]

## 18

1. (*Exc. de Leg. Rom.* 7)

At the same time Zeno learned that the position of Theoderic the son of Valamir was eroding and becoming weaker and that the son of Triarius was assembling his tribes and collecting his forces. He, therefore, thought it better to resolve the enmity with the latter on reasonable terms, if he were willing to make an agreement. He sent envoys and proposed that the son of Triarius hand over his son as a hostage, as he had earlier offered,[32] live as a private citizen amongst his own people causing no disturbances (as at the time he had requested), enjoy the possession of whatever he had seized, and otherwise live in peace, being harmed by no one and harming no one. The son of Triarius replied that he would not now hand over his son as hostage, nor could he still live off his own possessions alone. While he was on his own and did not have so many tribes with him, his own property alone would perhaps have been sufficient, if he lived very frugally. But now, since they had brought him to the necessity of gathering the tribes, out of this necessity he either had to feed those who had come to him or fight alongside them until, either defeated or victorious, he should bring the whole business to a clear and definite conclusion.

When this reply was delivered, it seemed best to make careful preparations for war. Zeno speedily summoned all the legions, both those stationed near to the Black Sea and those throughout Asia and the eastern districts. A large force assembled from all quarters; baggage wagons were prepared, cattle and grain were purchased, and all things of use to an army were made ready, since Illus himself was going to march out.

2. (*Exc. de Leg. Rom.* 8)

When Zeno appointed Martinianus general, the army fell into disorder. Since it seemed a good course of action, the Emperor immediately sent men to the son of Valamir, saying that he should put off battle no longer but take action now and fulfil the hopes for which he had been judged worthy of a Roman generalship. When the son of Valamir received this message, in reply he himself sent envoys saying that he would not take action before the Emperor and the whole senate had sworn that they would never make a treaty with the son of Triarius. The senators and the high officials swore, therefore, that they would

θέλοι, αὐτὸς δὲ ὁ βασιλεὺς μηδὲν ἀποστήσεσθαι τῶν ἤδη συγκει-    10
μένων, εἰ μὴ πρῶτον ἐκεῖνον παραβαίνοντα ἴδοι.

Τούτων δὲ ὁμοθέντων, αὐτὸν μὲν Θευδέριχον ἔδοξε κινήσαντα
τὴν αὐτοῦ δύναμιν ἐν Μαρκιανοῦ πόλει τὴν πᾶσαν ἱδρυμένην εἰς τὸ
εἴσω ἐλαύνειν· ἐπειδὰν δὲ γένηται πρὸς ταῖς πύλαις τοῦ Αἴμου, τότε
τὸν τῆς Θρᾴκης στρατηγὸν δισχιλίοις ἱππεῦσι καὶ ὁπλίταις μυρίοις    15
ἀπαντῶντα συμμίξαι· ὑπερβάντι δὲ Αἷμον ἄλλην ἀπαντήσεσθαι
δύναμιν πρὸς τῷ Ἕβρῳ καὶ Ἀδριανουπόλει, πεζοὺς μὲν δισμυρίους,
ἑξακισχιλίους δὲ μετὰ τούτων ἱππέας. ἀπὸ δὲ Ἡρακλείας καὶ τῶν
πρὸς Βυζαντίῳ πόλεων καὶ φρουρίων ἄλλην ἔλεγον εἶναι δύναμιν, εἰ
δεήσοι, ὥστε μηδὲν ἐλλείπειν τῶν εἰς ἐλπίδα χρηστὴν συντελούντων    20
τῷ ἔργῳ. ταῦτα ὑποσχόμενος ὁ Ζήνων τοῖς πρέσβεσι κατὰ τάχος
ἐκπέμπει.

Ἄρας δὲ Θευδέριχος τῷ αὐτοῦ στρατεύματι ᾔει ἐπὶ τὰς πύλας,
καθάπερ συνέκειτο. ἐρχομένῳ δὲ αὐτῷ οὔτε ὁ στρατηγὸς τῆς
Θρᾴκης ἀπήντα οὔτε οἱ πρὸς τῷ Ἕβρῳ ὑποκαθῆσθαι λεγόμενοι,    25
ἀλλὰ δι’ ἐρημίας διελθὼν τὰ ἐν μέσῳ εἰς τοὺς περὶ Σόνδιν παραγίνεται χώρους· ὄρος δέ ἐστι τοῦτο ὑψηλόν τε καὶ μέγα καὶ ἄπορον
ἐπελθεῖν, εἴ τις ἄνω κωλύοι· ἐν ᾧ στρατοπεδεύων ὁ Τριαρίου
ἐτύγχανεν. κἀντεῦθεν προσβάλλοντες ἐξ ἐφόδων ἀλλήλοις ποίμνιά
τε καὶ ἵππους καὶ λείαν ἄλλην ἀφήρπαζον. ὁ δὲ τοῦ Τριαρίου    30
συνεχῶς προσιππεύων ἐπὶ τὸ στρατόπεδον τὸ ἐκείνου ὕβριζε καὶ
ὠνείδιζε πλεῖστα ἐπίορκόν τε καλῶν καὶ παῖδα καὶ ἄφρονα καὶ τοῦ
γένους τοῦ κοινοῦ ἐχθρόν τε καὶ προδότην, ὅστις οὐ συνίησι τῆς
γνώμης τῆς Ῥωμαίων μηδὲ ὁρᾷ τὴν σκέψιν, ὅτι αὐτοὶ βούλονται
καθήμενοι ἡσυχῇ αὐτοὺς περὶ ἑαυτοὺς κατατρῖψαι τοὺς Γότθους.    35
κἀκεῖνοι μὲν τὴν νίκην ἀκονιτὶ ἔχουσιν, ὁπότεροι πέσοιμεν, ἡμῶν δὲ
ὁπότεροι τοὺς ἑτέρους φθείρουσι τὴν τοῦ λόγου Καδμείαν ἀποφέρον-
ται νίκην ἐλάττους λειπόμενοι πρὸς τὴν Ῥωμαίων ἐπιβουλήν. νῦν
γοῦν σὲ καλέσαντες καὶ ἐπαγγειλάμενοι παρέσεσθαι καὶ αὐτοὶ καὶ
κοινῇ συστρατεύειν οὔτε ἐνταῦθα πάρεισιν οὔτε ἐπὶ τὰς πύλας    40
ἀπήντησαν, ὡς εἶπον, μόνον τε ἀπέλιπον ἀπολέσθαι κάκιστα καὶ
τῆς γε θρασύτητος δοῦναι δίκην ἀξίαν ᾧ προδέδωκας γένει.

Ταῦτα ἐπακούσαντες πολλοὶ τοῦ αὐτοῦ πλήθους συνῇδον τοῖς
λόγοις καὶ τῷ σφετέρῳ αὐτῶν στρατηγῷ προσιόντες ἔλεγον ὡς
εἰκότα ὀνειδίζοι ἐκεῖνος, καὶ ὅτι οὐ προσήκοι φθείρεσθαι περαιτέρω    45

17 Ἕβρῳ Valesius [εὔρῳ codd. (item v.25)    20 δεήσοι ΒΕ [δεήσει ΜΡ
26 ἠρεμίας Valesius    Σοῦκιν Valesius    36 ἡμῶν Niebuhr [ἡμῖν codd.
37 Καδμείαν Valesius [καὶ ἐς μίαν codd.    39 αὐτοὶ Valesius [αὐτῷ codd.
42 προδέδωκας ΕΜ [προσέδωκας codd.    43 τοῦ αὐτοῦ ΜΡ edd. [τῶν ἐκ
τοῦ Ε (corr. ex τῶν αὐτοῦ) de Boor   τῶν αὐτοῦ Β    44 αὐτῶν Niebuhr [αὐτῷ
codd.

not make an agreement unless the Emperor wished it, and the Emperor himself swore that he would not abandon the agreements currently in force, unless he observed that the son of Valamir was breaking them first.

When these oaths had been sworn, it was decided that Theoderic should move his own force, which was concentrated around Marcianople, and bring it closer in. When he reached the gates of the Haemus range, the master of the soldiers of Thrace would come to join him with two thousand cavalry and ten thousand infantry. When he had crossed the Haemus range, another force of twenty thousand infantry and six thousand cavalry would meet him at the river Hebrus near to Adrianople. If he should need it, they said, there would be more men available from Heraclea and the towns and forts close to Byzantium, in order that nothing be lacking for the realisation of their high hopes. Zeno, having made these promises to the envoys, quickly dismissed them.

Theoderic set out and arrived with his army at the gates, as had been agreed. When he arrived he was met neither by the master of the soldiers of Thrace nor by the forces said to be stationed at the Hebrus. As he was crossing the central wildernesses he came to the area around Sondis, which is a huge, high mountain, impossible to cross if anyone on top should bar the way. The son of Triarius was encamped upon it. There the two sides attacked one another on the approaches and carried off herds, horses and other plunder. But the son of Triarius kept riding up to the other's camp, insulting and reproaching him and calling him a swearer of useless oaths, a child and a madman, an enemy and betrayer of his own race, who did not know the mind of the Romans nor recognise their intentions. "For they, while remaining at peace, wish the Goths to wear each other down. Whichever of us falls, they will be the winners with none of the effort, and whichever of us destroys the other side will enjoy a Cadmean victory (as they say), since he will be left in diminished numbers to face Roman treachery. Now, having summoned you and having announced that they would come and campaign along with you, they are not here nor did they meet you at the gates as they promised. They have left you alone to be destroyed most disgracefully and to pay to the people whom you have betrayed a just penalty for your rashness."

When they heard these words, many of those amongst the son of Valamir's followers agreed with them. They went to their own leader and said that the other's reproaches were just, that he should cause no

οὐδὲ τῆς συγγενείας τῆς κοινῆς ἀμελοῦντα τοῖς προδοῦσι προσέχειν.

Τῇ δὲ ὑστεραίᾳ πάλιν ἀναβὰς Θευδέριχος ἐπί τινα γήλοφον ὑπὲρ τοῦ στρατοπέδου τοῦ ἐκείνων ἐβόα· τί τοὺς ἐμοὺς συγγενεῖς, ὦ κάκιστε, ἀπόλλυς; τί τοσαύτας γυναῖκας ἐποίησας χηρεύειν; ποῦ δὲ οἱ τούτων ἄνδρες; ἢ πῶς ἐξαπόλωλε πάντων ἡ εὐπορία, ἣν ἔχοντες 50 οἴκοθεν συνεστράτευσάν σοι; καὶ σύνδυο καὶ σύντρεις ἕκαστος ἵππους ἔχων νῦν ἄνιπποι χωροῦσι καὶ πεζοὶ καὶ διὰ Θράκης ὥσπερ ἐν ἀνδραπόδων ἑπόμενοι μερίδι· ἀλλὰ καὶ ἐλεύθεροί τε καὶ γένους οὐ χείρονος· ἢ μεδίμνῳ χρυσίον ἐλθόντες ἀπομετρήσονται.

Ταῦτα ὡς ἐπήκουσε τὸ στρατόπεδον ἅπαν ἄνδρες τε καὶ 55 γυναῖκες ὁμοῦ πάντες ἦσαν ἐπὶ τὸν Θευδέριχον τὸν αὐτῶν ἡγεμόνα κραυγῇ τε καὶ θορύβῳ ἀξιοῦντες συμβαίνειν, εἰ δὲ μή, ἀπολείψειν αὐτὸν ἔφασαν πάντες ἐς τὸ συμφέρον χωρήσαντες. ἐνταῦθα ἀποστέλλει πρὸς Θευδέριχον πρέσβεις, καὶ συνέρχονται ἄμφω παρὰ ποταμόν τινα ἐφ' ἑκατέρας ὄχθης. μέσον δὲ ποιησάμενοι τὸν ποταμὸν 60 διελέγοντο, καὶ ποιοῦνται συνθήκας μὴ πολεμεῖν ἀλλήλοις, <ἄλλως δὲ πράττειν> ὅσα ἡγοῦντο συμφέροντα. καὶ ταῦτα ὀμόσαντες πέμπουσιν ἄμφω πρέσβεις ἐπὶ τὸ Βυζάντιον.

53 ἀλλὰ καὶ ἐλεύθεροί Müller [ἀλλὰ κελευθεροί codd. ἀλλὰ κ' ἐλεύθεροί Hoeschel   54 ἢ scripsi [οἱ P ἢ οἱ M ἢ edd.   χρυσίον scripsi sec. Hoeschel qui coni. χρυσίον . . . ἀπεμετρήσαντο [χρυσίου codd.   61-62 ἄλλως δὲ πράττειν addidi [καὶ add. Niebuhr ἀλλὰ κοινῇ συμπράττειν ἀλλήλοις add. de Boor 62 ἤγηντο Hoeschel

## 3. (*Exc. de Leg. Gent.* 6)

Ὅτι συνθήκας πρὸς ἀλλήλους ποιησάμενοι Θευδέριχος καὶ ὁ Τριαρίου οἱ Γότθοι μὴ πολεμεῖν ἀλλήλοις πέμπουσιν ἄμφω πρέσβεις ἐπὶ τὸ Βυζάντιον, ὁ μὲν τοῦ Βαλαμείρου τῷ βασιλεῖ ἐγκαλῶν ὅτι προδεδομένος ὑπ' ἐκείνου τυγχάνει, καὶ ὡς τῶν συντεθέντων οὐδὲν εὑρὼν ἀληθὲς Θευδερίχῳ συμβαίη, αἰτῶν δὲ χώραν αὐτῷ, ἐν ᾗ 5 μένοι, δοθῆναι καὶ σῖτον, ὅστις αὐτῷ καὶ μέχρι καρποῦ τὸν στρατὸν ἐξαρκέσει διάγειν, καὶ τοὺς προαγωγέας τῶν λημμάτων τῆς ἀρχῆς, οὓς δομεστίκους καλοῦσι Ῥωμαῖοι, ἐκπέμπειν ὡς τάχιστα, λόγον διδόντας ὧν ἔλαβον· ἢ μὴ ταῦτα ποιουμένων πρὸς αὐτὸν τῶν Ῥωμαίων οὐ δυνήσεσθαι αὐτὸς πολὺν ὄχλον κατέχειν τοῦ μὴ ὅθεν 10 δύναιντο δι' ἁρπαγῆς ἑαυτοῖς ἐπανορθοῦσθαι τὴν ἔνδειαν.

Ταῦτα μὲν ὁ ἕτερος Θευδέριχος ἔλεγεν· ὁ μέντοι Τριαρίου τά τε ἐπὶ Λέοντος συντεθέντα ἠξίου αὐτῷ πάντως γενέσθαι, καὶ τῶν προτέρων χρόνων τὰς συντάξεις λαμβάνειν, τούς τε κηδεστὰς αὐτῷ ζῶντας ἀποδοθῆναι· εἰ δὲ καὶ ἄρα τεθνήκασι, τὸν Ἰλλοῦν περὶ τού- 15 των ἐπομόσαι καὶ ἄλλους, οἷς αὐτὸς ἐπὶ τούτῳ τῶν Ἰσαύρων πιστεύει.

9 ἢ Valesius [εἰ A   10 τοῦ Niebuhr [τῷ A

more destruction and that he should not ignore their common origin and side with their betrayers.

On the following day Theoderic the son of Triarius went to a hill overlooking their camp and shouted, "Why, you criminal, are you destroying people of my race? Why have you widowed so many wives? Where are their men? How has the wealth of all been lost, which they had when they set out from home with you on campaign? Each of them had two or three horses. Now they are horseless and go on foot, following you through Thrace like slaves. Yet they, too, are free men and of origin no worse than yours. Or now that they have arrived, will they measure gold by the bushel?"[33]

When the whole army heard this, all the men and women went to their leader Theoderic and with shouting and uproar demanded that he make an agreement. They said that if he did not do so they would desert him and follow the course advantageous to themselves. Thereupon he sent envoys to Theoderic the son of Triarius, and both leaders met by a river, each standing on the opposite bank. Keeping the river between them they parlayed and made an agreement not to fight against each other <but otherwise to do>[34] whatever they thought advantageous. When they had sworn to these agreements, they both sent envoys to Byzantium.

### 3. (*Exc. de Leg. Gent.* 6)

When the Goths, Theoderic and the son of Triarius, had made an agreement not to war with one another, they both sent envoys to Byzantium. The son of Valamir accused the Emperor of betraying him and said that since he had found none of the things which had been promised, he had made a genuine agreement with the son of Triarius. He demanded that he be given land upon which to settle and sufficient grain to support his army until the next harvest and that the disbursers of the state revenues (whom the Romans call *domestici*) be sent to him as quickly as possible to render account of what they received.[35] But if the Romans did not do this for him, he himself would not be able to prevent his large force from meeting its needs by plundering wherever it could.

These were the demands of Theoderic the son of Valamir. The son of Triarius demanded that the agreements made in the reign of Leo be fulfilled to the letter, that he receive the payments of the previous years and that those of his relatives who were alive should be handed over to him. If they had actually died, Illus and others of the Isaurians whom he trusted in this matter should swear an oath concerning them.[36]

Ζήνων δὲ πυθόμενος πρὸς μὲν τὸν Βαλαμείρου ἀπεκρίνατο, ὅτι
αὐτὸς εἴη προδότης καὶ πάντα ἐναντία οἷς ὑπέσχετο δράσας, ὅστις
διαπολεμεῖν ὑποσχόμενος μόνος εἶτα καὶ βοήθειαν προσκαλέσηται
ἄλλην, πάλιν δὲ τὴν δύναμιν τῶν Ῥωμαίων καλέσας κρύφα πρὸς    20
Θευδέριχον πράττει περὶ φιλίας· οὗ δὴ καὶ αἰσθόμενον τὸν στρατηγὸν τῆς Θράκης καὶ τοὺς ἄλλους, ὁπόσοι τὰ Ῥωμαίων φρονοῦσι,
μήτε ἀπηντηκέναι μήτε συμβάλλειν αὐτῷ τὰς δυνάμεις θαρσῆσαι
φοβουμένους ἐνέδραν. νῦν τε, εἰ θελήσαι πρὸς αὐτὸν πολεμῆσαι,
ἐπαγγέλλεσθαι αὐτῷ ταῦτα δώσειν νικῶντι, χρυσίου λίτρας χιλίας,    25
μυριάδας δ' ἀργυρίου, πρόσοδόν τε πρὸς τούτοις νομισμάτων μυρίων·
καὶ γάμον αὐτῷ δώσειν τῆς Ὀλυβρίου παιδὸς ἢ ἄλλης τῶν ἐνδόξων
γυναικῶν ἐν τῇ πόλει.

Ταῦτά τε ἅμα λέγων τῶν τε ἀποσταλέντων παρ' αὐτοῦ τοὺς
πλείονας ἀξίαις ἐτίμησε καὶ πρέσβεις ἀπέστειλε πρῶτον μὲν Φιλό-    30
ξενον, εἶτα Ἰουλιανόν, εἴ πως ἄρα δύναιντο μεταπεῖσαι ξυρραγῆναι
ἐκείνῳ. ὡς δὲ οὐδὲν ἔπειθεν, πέμψας τοὺς στρατιώτας ἐς τὸν
πόλεμον ὥρμα καὶ παρεκάλει θαρσεῖν ὡς αὐτὸς ἐκστρατεύσων καὶ
κοινῇ σὺν ἐκείνοις ὅ τι ἂν δέοι πεισόμενος. οἱ δὲ ὡς ἐπήκουσαν ὅτι
αὐτὸς βασιλεὺς ἐξάγειν ἐθέλοι, οὕτως ἕκαστος αὐτῶν ἠπείγετο    35
ἑαυτὸν ἐπιδεῖξαι βασιλεῖ πολλοῦ ἄξιον ὄντα, ὥστε καὶ οἱ πρότερον
τοῖς ἡγεμόσιν αὐτῶν ἐφ' ᾧ μὴ στρατεύοιντο ἀργύριον διδόντες πάλιν
εἰς τὸ μετέχειν τῆς ἐξόδου παρεῖχον.

Καὶ πάντες ἀνθήπτοντο τούτου τοῦ πολέμου ὀργῶντες, καὶ τοὺς
τε κατασκόπους τοὺς παρὰ Θευδερίχου πεμφθέντας ἐζώγρησαν, καὶ    40
τῆς τοῦ Βαλαμείρου φυλακῆς μοῖραν ἐλθοῦσαν ἐπὶ τὸ Μακρὸν τεῖχος
οἱ ἐκεῖ φυλάττοντες διαπρεπῶς ἀπεκρούσαντο. ἐπεὶ δὲ εἰς τὴν αὐτοῦ
φερόμενος ὁ Ζήνων ἀνεχώρησε φύσω καὶ ὑπὸ τῆς συμφύτου ἀπεσ-
βέσθη δειλίας, ἐνταῦθα ὀργίζονται καὶ χαλεπῶς ἔφερον κατὰ
συστάσεις τε γινόμενοι ἐμέμφοντο ἀλλήλους τῆς ὅλης ἀτολμίας, εἰ    45
χεῖράς τε ἔχοντες καὶ βαστάζοντες ὅπλα μαλακίας τοιαύτης ἀκούειν
ἀνέχονται, δι' ἧς πόλεις ἅπασαι καὶ ἡ πᾶσα Ῥωμαίων ἰσχὺς ἐξαπόλωλε, πάντων ἐπ' ἐξουσίας περικοπτόντων ἃ βούλοιντο.

Τοῦτον ὁ Μαρτινιανὸς συναισθόμενος τὸν θροῦν πέμπει Ζήνωνι
λέγων ὅτι δεῖ τὸ στρατόπεδον ὡς τάχιστα διαλύειν, μή τι καὶ νεώ-    50
τερον συνεστηκότες ἐργάσωνται. πέμψας οὖν ἐκέλευεν ἀπιέναι
ἑκάστους ἐπὶ τὰ χειμάδια, ὡς πρὸς τὸν Θευδέριχον ἐσομένης
εἰρήνης. οἱ <δὲ> τὸν χάρακα ἔλυσαν· καὶ ἀπῆλθον οἱ πλείους τῇ
διαλύσει ἀχθόμενοι, καὶ ὅτι θᾶττον αὐτοῖς χωρισθῆναι συνέβη, πρὶν

19 προσκαλέσαιτο Dindorf    39 τούτου τοῦ scripsi [τοῦτο A τοῦ de Boor τοῦ
τε Hoeschel    45 εἰ Niebuhr [εἰς A    53 δὲ add. Niebuhr

When Zeno heard these demands, he replied to the son of Valamir that he was a traitor and had acted completely contrary to his promises. He had promised to fight the war on his own, then he had asked for further help, and again, when he had summoned the Roman forces, he had made secret overtures of friendship to Theoderic the son of Triarius. When they learned this, the general of Thrace and the others who were friendly to the Roman cause did not dare to meet him or combine their forces with his, since they feared a trap. But now, Zeno promised, if he were willing to make war on the son of Triarius, the Emperor would give him, if he were victorious, one thousand pounds of gold, forty thousand pounds of silver and an income of ten thousand *nomismata*. He would also give him as his wife the daughter of Olybrius[37] or another of the noblewomen in the city.

When he had said this, Zeno bestowed honours upon most of those sent by the son of Valamir and himself sent as envoys first Philoxenus and then Julianus to see if they could persuade him to break with the son of Triarius. When they did not succeed, Zeno sent and urged the soldiers on to war, telling the men to be in good spirits since he himself would take part in the campaign and endure along with them whatever was necessary. When they heard that the Emperor himself wished to lead the army, every man was so eager to show the Emperor his mettle that even those who had paid money to their leaders to avoid fighting now paid a second time to take part in the campaign.

All entered this war with great enthusiasm. They captured alive the scouts sent by Theoderic, and the guards on the Long Wall made a magnificent defence against a part of the son of Valamir's bodyguard which advanced against it.[38] Then Zeno's character re-asserted itself and, overcome by his innate cowardice, he withdrew from the campaign. At this the soldiers became disgusted and angry, and, gathering in groups, blamed each other for their complete lack of courage, if, while having hands and wielding weapons, they endured to hear of such feebleness, as a result of which all the cities and all the power of the Romans were being destroyed; for everyone was cutting away from their resources whatever he wished.

When Martinianus learned of these mutterings, he sent to Zeno telling him that he must disband the army as soon as possible lest they unite and start a revolt. Zeno, therefore, sent and ordered each regiment to depart to its winter quarters, since peace would be made with Theoderic the son of Triarius. They broke camp, and the majority went away angry at the disbanding, especially because they happened to be split up too quickly for them to be able to seek out and set over the

ἄνδρα σκεψαμένους τοῖς κοινοῖς ἐπιστῆσαι, ὃς τῆς παρούσης λύμης    55
ἀνακτᾶσθαι τὴν πολιτείαν ὁπωσοῦν δυνήσεται.

## 4. (*Exc. de Leg. Rom.* 9)

Ὅτι Ζήνων, ἐπεὶ διέλυσε τὴν στρατιάν, πέμπει πρὸς Θευδέριχον τὴν εἰρήνην συνθέσθαι πρὸς αὐτὸν ὅπως καὶ δύναιτο. ἐν δὲ
τούτῳ συστρέψας τὴν ἑαυτοῦ δύναμιν ὁ παῖς ὁ Βαλαμήρου ἐπὶ τὰ
πρὸς Ῥοδόπην παραγίνεται μέρη, καὶ κατατεινάμενος τὰ κάλλιστα
τῆς χώρας τῶν Θρᾳκῶν ἅπαντα [καὶ] εἴ τι ἦν κτηνικὸν ἀφαρπάξει,    5
ἐξέτριψε δὲ ἅπαν τὸ αὐτόθι γεωργοῦν, κτείνων τε καὶ εἰσπράττων
ὅσα μὴ φέρειν ἠδύναντο. Θευδέριχος δὲ ταῦτα ἀκούων γινόμενα
ἥδεσθαι μὲν ἔλεγεν ὅτι φίλος αὐτῶν καὶ υἱὸς λεγόμενος ταῦτα
αὐτοὺς δρῴη, ἄχθεσθαι μέντοι ὅτι τῆς ἐκείνων ἀνοίας ἐν τοῖς
γεωργοῖς βλέπει γινομένην τὴν δίκην, ὧν οὐδὲν φθειρομένων Ζή-    10
νωνά γε ἢ Βηρίναν οὐδ᾽ ὁπωσοῦν ἐπιστρέφεσθαι.

Ὡς δὲ ἦλθον οἱ πρέσβεις, τίθενται τὴν εἰρήνην ἐφ᾽ ᾧ τε
μυρίοις μὲν καὶ τρισχιλίοις ἀνδράσιν οἷς θέλοι Θευδέριχος συντάξεις
τε καὶ τροφὴν χορηγεῖν βασιλέα, δυοῖν δὲ αὐτὸν σχολῶν προβάλ-
λεσθαι ἄρχοντα, ἀπολαβεῖν δὲ αὐτοῦ τὴν οὐσίαν, ὅσην πρότερον    15
εἶχεν, λαβεῖν δὲ τὴν ἑτέραν τῶν δύο στρατηγιῶν τῶν περὶ βασιλέα,
καὶ ἔχειν τὰς ἀξίας, εἰς ἃς ἤδη προῆκτο ὑπὸ τοῦ Βασιλίσκου. περὶ δὲ
τῶν κηδεστῶν, εἰ μὲν ἐτελεύτησαν, ὡς ἔλεγεν ὁ Ζήνων, μηδὲν εἶναι
οἱ πρᾶγμα· εἰ δὲ ζῶσι, λαβόντας ἥνπερ εἶχον οὐσίαν οἰκεῖν πόλιν, ἣν
αὐτὸς δοκιμάσειε Ζήνων. ταῦτα ὡς συνέδοξε, παύσας τὸν Βαλαμήρου    20
τῆς ἀρχῆς ὁ βασιλεὺς στρατηγὸν ἀντ᾽ ἐκείνου Θευδέριχον ποιεῖται
καὶ χρήματα ἔπεμψεν, ὅσα ἔδει αὐτίκα διανεῖμαι τοῖς Γότθοις.

4 κατασιυάμενος Valesius [κατατέμνει μὲν de Boor    5 καὶ expunxi    6
σπαράττων Bekker    7 ἠδύναντο edd. [ἠδύναιυτο codd. ἠδύνατο Bekker
10 οὐδὲν codd. [ὧδε Valesius οὐδὲ Bekker οὐδ᾽ ἐκφθειρομένων de Boor
11 γε Bekker [δὲ codd.

## 19

(Photius *Bibl. Cod.* 78 = T.1)

## 20

(*Exc. de Leg. Rom.* 1)

Ὅτι ὁ Βαλάμηρος ὑπὸ τῶν Ῥωμαίων στρατηγῶν πολλοὺς
τῶν ἰδίων ἀποβαλών, οὐ μικρὰν ἔχων ὀργὴν τῷ πάθει ἀπέδραμεν,
ἀφειδῶς ὅ τι ἐν ποσὶν εὕροι καίων τε καὶ φονεύων· καὶ τὴν πρώτην
τῆς Μακεδονίας πόλιν τοὺς Στόβους ἐπόρθησε καὶ τῶν γε στρατιωτῶν τῶν ταύτῃ ἐμφρουρούντων τοὺς ἀντιστάντας ἀπέκτεινεν. ὡς    5

state a man who could, by some means or other, save the empire from the present outrages.

4. (*Exc. de Leg. Rom.* 9)

When Zeno had disbanded the army, he sent envoys to Theoderic the son of Triarius to make peace with him on whatever terms they could. Meanwhile, the son of Valamir formed up his forces and moved to the area near Rhodope. Spreading out over the best of all the land of Thrace, he drove off all the herds and ruined all the farmers, killing them and plundering what they could not carry off.[39] When he heard of this Theoderic the son of Triarius said that he was pleased at what was happening insofar as one who was called the 'friend' and 'son'[40] of the rulers was doing this to them, but he grieved because he observed that the punishment for their stupidity fell upon the farmers. Neither Zeno nor Verina cared a whit for them, even if they were dying.

When the envoys arrived, Theoderic the son of Triarius made peace on condition that the Emperor supply pay and food for thirteen thousand men chosen by Theoderic; that he be made commander of two *scholae*;[41] that he receive back such of his property as he had formerly held;[42] that he receive one of the two generalships in the presence; and that he enjoy the honours to which he had been already advanced by Basiliscus. Concerning his relatives, if they were dead, as Zeno alleged, that was the end of the matter; but if they were alive, they should take whatever property they had and live in whatever city Zeno thought best. When the Emperor had ratified this agreement, he removed the son of Valamir from office, appointed the son of Triarius in his stead, and sent the money which had to be distributed immediately to the Goths.

# 19

(Photius *Bibl. Cod.* 78 = T.1)

# 20

(*Exc. de Leg. Rom.* 1)

The son of Valamir, having lost many of his men at the hands of the Roman generals, retreated in great rage at his plight, mercilessly burning and killing whatever he encountered. He sacked Stobi, the first city of Macedonia, and slaughtered those of the garrison there who

δὲ τῇ Θεσσαλονίκῃ ἐγγύθεν ἐφεδρεύων ἠγγέλθη ὁ βάρβαρος, αὐτίκα
οἱ πολῖται νομίσαντες ἐκ δόλου τὰ ἐν τῇ προτεραίᾳ ἀνεγνῶσθαι
γράμματα καὶ τὴν πόλιν βούλεσθαι Ζήνωνά τε καὶ αὐτὸν ἐκείνῳ
παραδοῦναι, συστραφέντες ἐν σφίσιν αὐτοῖς τὰς τοῦ Ζήνωνος στήλας
καταβάλλουσι πάσας καὶ αὐτὸν ὁρμήσαντες τὸν ὕπαρχον ἕτοιμοι    10
διασπάσαι ἦσαν. οἱ δὲ κομισάμενοι πῦρ ἐπὶ τὸ ἀρχεῖον ἐμπιπράναι
ἔμελλον, εἰ μὴ ὑποφθάσαντες τά τε ἱερὰ γένη καὶ οἱ ἐν ταῖς ἀξίαις
ἐξήρπασάν τε αὐτὸν τῆς ὀργῆς τῆς τοῦ δήμου καὶ τὸ ἀτακτοῦν λόγοις
πραέσι κατέστειλαν, λέγοντες οὔτε αὐτὸν αἴτιον εἶναι τούτου οὔτε τὸν
βασιλέα τῇ πόλει τι δυσχερὲς ἢ κακὸν βεβουλεῦσθαι, τῆς τε πόλεως    15
χρῆναι ποιήσασθαι φυλακήν, ὅτῳ ἂν ἐθέλωσι καὶ ὃν ἡγοῦνται πιστὸν
ἐπιτρέποντες ταύτην. οἱ δὲ τὰς κλεῖς τῶν πυλῶν ἐκ τοῦ ὑπάρχου
λαβόντες τῷ ἀρχιερεῖ ἔδοσαν καὶ ἀπὸ τῶν ἐνόντων φρουρὰν ἐπε-
νόησαν ὡς ἠδύναντο πλείστην καὶ τὸν στρατηγὸν ἔστεργον.

Ἐν δὲ τούτῳ ὁ Ζήνων πυθόμενος τὸν κατέχοντα κίνδυνον καὶ    20
ἰδὼν ὡς οὐδενὸς βουλομένου μάχεσθαι ἄριστον εἴη σπονδαῖς ὡς ἐν
κακοῖς μετρίαις τῆς τῶν πόλεων φθορᾶς ἐπισχεῖν τὸν βάρβαρον,
Ἀρτεμίδωρον πέμπει καὶ Φωκᾶν τὸν ὅτε ἦν στρατηγὸς γραμματέα
αὐτῷ τῆς ἀρχῆς ὄντα. οἳ ἐλθόντες ἔλεγον ὅτι· σὲ ὁ βασιλεὺς φίλον
ἐποιήσατο καὶ ἀξίαις, αἵ εἰσι λαμπρόταται Ῥωμαίοις, σεμνῶς ἐπε-    25
κόσμησε καὶ ἄρχειν τῶν μεγίστων ταγμάτων ἐποίησεν οὐδὲν οἷάπερ
ἀνδρὶ ἀπιστήσας βαρβάρῳ. σὺ δὲ οὐκ ἴσμεν ὅπως ταῖς τῶν κοινῶν
δυσμενῶν ἀπάταις ὑπαχθεὶς τά τε ὑπάρχοντά σοι ἀγαθὰ διέφθειρας
καὶ τῆς εὐδαιμονίας τῆς σῆς ἄλλον ἐποίησας ὡς οὐκ ᾔδεις κύριον.
οὐκ ἂν δίκαιος εἴης τῷ βασιλεῖ ἐγκαλῶν ὧν εἰς ἑαυτὸν ἅμα καὶ εἰς    30
ἐκεῖνον ἐξήμαρτες. νῦν οὖν, ἐπειδὴ σαυτὸν εἰς τοῦτο κατέστησας,
ὑπόλοιπόν σοί ἐστιν ἐκ τῆς παρούσης τύχης τῆς τε κατὰ τῶν ἐθνῶν
καὶ τῶν πόλεων βλάβης ἐπισχεῖν ὡς οἷόν τε, πέμποντα δὲ πρεσβείαν
πειρᾶσθαί τι μέτριον παρὰ τοῦ βασιλέως ἀγαθοῦ ὄντος εὑρίσκεσθαι.

Ὁ δὲ πεισθεὶς ἄνδρας μὲν ἐπὶ τὸ Βυζάντιον σὺν αὐτοῖς ἀποπέμ-    35
πει, αὐτὸς δὲ τοῦ μὲν καίειν ἢ φονεύειν τοὺς ἀνθρώπους ἀνεῖργε τὸ
στράτευμα, οὐ μέντοι ἐδύνατο πάντων ὄντας ἀπόρους τὰ γοῦν ἐπιτήδεια ἐκπορίσαι κωλύειν. καὶ δὴ προϊὼν ἦλθεν ἐπὶ τὴν Ἡράκλειαν τὴν
ἐν Μακεδονίᾳ καί, τοῦ ἀρχιερέως τοῦ ἐν ταύτῃ τῇ πόλει πολλὰ καὶ
παντοδαπὰ τῇ στρατιᾷ καὶ αὐτῷ ἀποστείλαντος δῶρα, τήν τε χώραν    40
ἀπαθῆ πᾶσαν διεφύλαξε καὶ οὐδὲν τοὺς οἰκοῦντας ἐνταῦθα παραλυπῶν ἐκ τῶν ταύτῃ μοίρων τὸ πλῆθος ἐπιεικῶς ἐπειρᾶτο διάγειν.

10 ὕπαρχον Niebuhr [ἔπαρχον codd.    29 ᾔδεις de Boor ex ἥδεις Μ [ἴδεις
ΒΕΡ εἰδώς Hoeschel ἔδεις Valesius ἔδει σε Bekker    37 μέντοι ΜΡ [μέν
τι alii codd.    41-42 παραλυπῶν Hoeschel [παραλιπὼν codd.    42 μοίρων
scripsi [μόρων codd. μερῶν Hoeschel φόρων Niebuhr ὁμόρων de Boor

resisted him. When it was reported that the barbarian was lying in wait near to Thessalonika, the citizens immediately suspected that the letter read out on the previous day was a trick and that Zeno and he[43] wished to hand over the city to the son of Valamir. They gathered together, overthrew all Zeno's statues, made an attack on the prefect and were ready to tear him to pieces. They had brought fire to the prefect's palace and were intending to burn it down. But the clergy and the officials acted first, snatching the prefect away from the anger of the mob and quelling the disorder with calming words. They said that the prefect was not the cause of the trouble and that the Emperor had arranged nothing disadvantageous or harmful for the city; but they should arrange the guarding of the city for themselves, entrusting it to whomsoever they wished and considered trustworthy. The people took the keys of the gates from the prefect and handed them to the archbishop, organised as strong a guard as possible from the inhabitants and were content with the general.[44]

Meanwhile Zeno learned of the immediate danger and realised that since no one was willing to fight, it would be best to keep the barbarian from destroying the cities by offering moderate terms in view of the present difficulties. He sent Artemidorus and Phocas, who had been secretary of his office when he was general. They came to the son of Valamir and said, "The Emperor made you his friend, solemnly honoured you with the highest offices amongst the Romans and placed you in command of the greatest armies. Although you were a barbarian, he trusted you entirely. Yet somehow you were deceived by the wiles of our common enemies and, ruining your present advantages, have, as you did not know,[45] made another master of your good fortune. It would not be right to accuse the Emperor over wrongs which you have done both to yourself and to him. Now, since you have brought yourself to this state, all that remains for you in your present circumstances is to refrain as best you can from harming the provincials and the cities and by sending an embassy to try to moderate the Emperor, who is a kindly man."

The son of Valamir was persuaded and sent men with the envoys to Byzantium. He himself restrained his army from arson and murder, although he was unable to prevent them from carrying off necessities, since they were completely destitute. In his advance he came to Heraclea in Macedonia. Since the bishop of the city sent him and his army many and various gifts, he kept all the countryside unravaged, caused no grief to the inhabitants there, and supported his force modestly from the estates[46] of the area.

Εἰς δὲ τὸ Βυζάντιον ὡς ἦλθον οἱ παρ' αὐτοῦ σταλέντες πρέσβεις, ἔλεγον ὅτι δέοι ταχέως περὶ πάντων αὐτοκράτορα αὐτῷ
πρεσβευτὴν ἀποστεῖλαι, ὡς οὐχ οἷοί τέ εἰσι πλῆθος ἄπειρον εἴργειν    45
ἐπὶ πλείονα χρόνον τῆς ἐφ' ὧν ἂν δύναιντο βλάβης. ὁ δὲ Ἀδαμάντιον
τὸν Βιβιανοῦ παῖδα πατρίκιόν τε ὄντα καὶ πολιαρχήσαντα προσθεὶς
αὐτῷ καὶ τιμὴν ὑπατικὴν ἔπεμψε παραγγείλας, χώραν μὲν αὐτῷ
δοῦναι ἐν Παυταλίᾳ, ἢ τῆς μὲν Ἰλλυρικῆς μοῖρα ἐστὶν ἐπαρχίας, οὐ
πολὺ δὲ ἀπέχουσα τῶν εἰσβολῶν τῆς Θρᾴκης, ὅπως, εἴτε Θευδέριχος    50
ὁ Τριαρίου ἐγχειροίη τι κινεῖν, ἔφεδρον ἔχοι αὐτὸν ἐγγύθεν κατ'
ἐκείνου, εἴτε αὐτὸς ταράττειν τὰ συγκείμενα θέλοι, ἐν μέσῳ αὐτὸν
ἔχων τῶν τε Ἰλλυρικῶν καὶ τῶν Θρᾳκίων δυνάμεων εὐκολώτερον
αὐτοῦ περιεῖναι δύναιτο. εἰ δὲ τροφῶν ἀπορεῖν τῷ στρατεύματι λέγοι
τὸν παρόντα ἐνιαυτόν, ἅτε μήτε ἐνσπείρας μήτε καρποῦ ἐλπίδα ἔχων    55
ἐν Παυταλίᾳ, ἔδωκε λίτρας χρυσίου ἀπιόντι διακοσίας, ἃς ἐκέλευε
δόντα τῷ ὑπάρχῳ τῷ ἐκεῖ ποιῆσαι τὴν δαπάνην αὐτοῖς εἰς Παυταλίαν
χορηγῆσαι τὴν ἐπαρκοῦσαν.

Ἔτι δὲ τοῦ πρεσβευτοῦ ὄντος ἐν Βυζαντίῳ, στρατιῶται συστάντες ἐν τῇ Θεσσαλονίκῃ τὸν ὕπαρχον Ἰωάννην προϊόντα φυλάξαντες    60
ξιφήρεις ὥρμησαν· καὶ ὡρίσθη παρὰ τοῦ Ζήνωνος Ἀδαμάντιος, καὶ
ταῦτα κατέστησεν.

Ὁ δὲ [τὸν] Βαλαμήρου, ἐν ᾧ τὰ τῆς Θεσσαλονίκης ἐγένετο,
περὶ Ἡράκλειαν ἔμενεν καὶ ἐπὶ τὴν Ἤπειρον πέμπει πρὸς Σιδι-
μοῦνδον, ἐκ μὲν τῆς αὐτῆς φυλῆς τὸ ἀνέκαθεν ὄντα, δοκοῦντα δὲ τότε    65
εἶναι Ῥωμαίοις ὑπόσπονδον καὶ ἐν τῇ κατ' Ἐπίδαμνον Ἠπείρῳ
χώραν τε νεμόμενον καὶ εὐδαίμονα κλῆρον καὶ παρὰ βασιλέως
δεχόμενον συντάξεις. ἀνεψιὸς δὲ ἦν οὗτος Αἰδοΐγγου Βηρώης τε
μάλιστα ὄντος οἰκειοτάτου καὶ τὴν τῶν λεγομένων δομεστίκων
ἀρχὴν ἄρχοντος μεγάλην τινὰ οὖσαν τῶν περὶ βασιλέα. πρὸς τοῦτον    70
οὖν ἔπεμπε τῆς τε παλαιᾶς αὐτὸν συγγενείας ἀναμιμνήσκων καὶ
ἀξιῶν ἐξευρεῖν καὶ συμπρᾶξαι τρόπον, δι' οὗ τῆς τε Ἐπιδάμνου καὶ
τῆς ἄλλης Ἠπείρου δυνηθείη κρατήσας στῆναι τῆς πολλῆς πλάνης,
καὶ ἱδρύσας ἑαυτὸν ἐν πόλει καὶ τείχεσιν ἐντεῦθεν ὡς ἂν διδῷ
δέχεσθαι τὸ συμβαῖνον. Σιδιμοῦνδος δὲ ταῦτα παρ' αὐτοῦ δεξάμενος    75
καὶ βάρβαρος βαρβάρῳ συνοικεῖν ἢ Ῥωμαίοις ἡγησάμενος κρεῖττον,
ἐλθὼν εἰς Ἐπίδαμνον καὶ ἰδίᾳ μετιὼν τῶν πολιτῶν ἕκαστον ὡς
δῆθεν κατ' εὔνοιαν συνεβούλευεν αὐτοῖς, ἅ τε ἕκαστος ἔχει θᾶττον
ὑπεκτίθεσθαι καὶ αὐτοὺς ἢ εἰς νήσους ἢ πόλιν ποι σώζεσθαι, λέγων

46 ἐφ' scripsi [ἀφ' codd.    ὠφελεῖσθαι ante βλάβης add. Niebuhr et βασιλεὺς
post ὁ δὲ    49 μοῖρα ... ἐπαρχίας scripsi [μοῖρας ... ἐπαρχία codd.    61 τοῦ
Bekker [τῶν codd.    63 τὸν exp. Valesius [τοῦ de Boor    72 τε Bekker [τοῦ
codd.    73 κρατῆσαι M

When the envoys despatched by the son of Valamir reached Byzantium, they said that the Emperor must quickly send an ambassador to him to deal with everything, since they could not for long restrain a very large force from causing damage on whatever occasion it could. Zeno sent Vivianus' son, Adamantius, a patrician and ex-prefect of the city, upon whom he also conferred consular rank. He announced that he was giving Theoderic land in Pautalia, a district of the prefecture of Illyricum,[47] not far from the entrance to Thrace. His purpose was that if Theoderic the son of Triarius should attempt any disturbance, he would have the son of Valamir stationed nearby to use against him, and if the son of Valamir wished to break the agreements, he would have him between the forces of Illyricum and Thrace and be more easily able to hold him at a disadvantage. In case the son of Valamir should say that, since he had sown no seed and had no hope of a harvest in Pautalia, he lacked food for his army for the current year, Zeno gave to Adamantius as he was leaving two hundred pounds of gold, which he told him to hand over to the prefect there to cover the cost of bringing in adequate supplies to Pautalia for the Goths.

While the envoys were still at Byzantium, some soldiers stationed at Thessalonika lay in wait for the prefect John to appear in public and attacked him with drawn swords. Adamantius was told by Zeno to settle the matter, and did so.

While this was happening in Thessalonika, the son of Valamir was waiting near to Heraclea. He sent to Epirus to Sidimund, a man descended from the same tribe and apparently an ally of the Romans. He received a fertile estate and a regular stipend from the Emperor, and he lived on his lands in Epirus near to Epidamnus. He was a cousin of Aedoingus, who was a very close associate of Verina and held the command of the so-called *domestici*, which is an important position at court. The son of Valamir sent to Sidimund reminding him of their old relationship and asking him to look around and find a means whereby he could gain control of Epidamnus and the rest of Epirus and, thus, settling himself in a city with fortifications, face whatever chance might bring. Sidimund received this message from the son of Valamir and, as a barbarian, thinking it preferable to live with a barbarian than with Romans, went to Epidamnus. There he went around to each of the citizens individually and, pretending to be well-disposed to them, advised them each to gather up quickly his possessions and to take refuge on the islands or in some other city. He said that the

ὡς ὁ βάρβαρος ἐπὶ ταύτην ὥρμηται, καὶ ὅτι τῷ βασιλεῖ ταῦτα    80
δοκοῦντά ἐστιν, καὶ ὡς Ἀδαμάντιος ἐπὶ ταῦτα πεμφθείη· κρεῖττον οὖν
εἶναι αὐτοῖς, ἕως ἔτι ἄπεστιν, κατὰ πλείονα σχολὴν τὰ κατ' αὐτοὺς
διοικήσασθαι. ταῦτα καὶ τοῖς στρατιώταις τοῖς ἐκεῖ φυλάττουσιν
οὖσιν ὡς δισχιλίοις, οἱ καὶ ἀμύνασθαι ἐπιόντα πρός γε τὸ παραχρῆμα
ῥᾳδίως ἠδύναντο, ἔπεισεν ὁμοῦ πάντας ἐκλιπεῖν Ἐπίδαμνον καὶ    85
λέγων καὶ ταράττων καὶ φήμην ἀεὶ καινὴν πειρώμενος ἐμβάλλειν,
καὶ ὅτι βασιλεῖ ἀπεχθήσονται μᾶλλον ἀντιστῆναι θέλοντες· καὶ πρὸς
τὸν Βαλαμήρου εὐθέως ἐπέστελλεν ὡς τάχος ἐπείγεσθαι.
    Ὁ δὲ τὸ τοῦ Σιδιμούνδου ἐπέμενε δήλωμα καὶ τὴν αὐτοῦ
ἀδελφὴν νόσῳ κατεχομένην, ἐξ ἧς ἐτελεύτησεν. φανερὰν μέντοι τῆς    90
καθέδρας πρόφασιν ἐποιεῖτο τὴν τοῦ πρεσβευτοῦ παρὰ Ζήνωνος
ἄφιξιν καὶ τὸ βούλεσθαι μαθεῖν, ὅπως πρὸς αὐτὸν ἔχει τὰ ἐκ τοῦ
βασιλέως. ἐπεὶ δὲ τὴν μὲν ἀδελφὴν ἀποθανοῦσαν ἔθαψεν, τὰ δὲ
παρὰ Σιδιμούνδου ἀπήντησε καλοῦντα, πρὸς τοὺς Ἡρακλεώτας
ἐκλιπόντας μὲν τὴν πόλιν, ἐς φρούριον δὲ ἰσχυρὸν ἀνασκευασαμένους    95
πέμψας ἀπήτει σῖτον πολύν τινα καὶ οἶνον, ὅπως τῷ στρατῷ ἔχοι
ἀπιὼν ἐφόδια. οἱ δὲ οὐδὲν ἔφασαν αὐτῷ δύνασθαι δοῦναι ἐν
τοσαύταις ἡμέραις λέγοντες ὅσον εἶχον ἐπὶ φρουρίῳ γε μικρῷ
δεδαπανῆσθαι. ὁ δὲ πρὸς ὀργὴν τὰ πλεῖστα τῆς πόλεως ἐμπρήσας
ἀνδρῶν οὔσης ἐρήμου εὐθὺς ἀπανίσταται, καὶ κατὰ τὴν δύσοδον καὶ    100
στενὴν ὁδὸν τὴν ἐπὶ τὴν Νέαν λεγομένην Ἤπειρον ἀπάγουσαν
ἀναστήσας ἤλαυνεν, καὶ προπέμπει τοὺς ἱππεῖς τὰ ἄκρα τῇ στρατιᾷ
προκαταληψομένους, καί, ἕως ἀνέλπιστοί εἰσιν, κατ' ἐκείνων χωρήσειν ἐξ ἐφόδου ἀθρόας ἐκκρούσοντας τὴν φυλακήν, ἥτις ἦν αὐτόθι.
οἱ δὲ ὡς ἀνέβησαν, οἱ ἐπὶ τῷ τειχίῳ φρουροῦντες στρατιῶται τό τε    105
πλῆθος ἰδόντες καὶ πρὸς τὸ αἰφνίδιον αὐτῶν καταπλαγέντες οὔτε εἰς
ἀλκὴν ἔτι τραπέσθαι ὑπέμειναν οὔτε λογισμὸν ἔσχον ἀποξεῦξαι τὸ
τείχισμα, ἀλλ' ὥρμησαν φεύγειν ὑπὸ τῆς ἐκπλήξεως ἀπερίοπτοι
πάντων τῶν εἰς τὸν τότε καιρὸν ὠφελῆσαι δυναμένων.
    Οἱ δὲ κατὰ πολλὴν ἐρημίαν προσιόντες ἐχώρουν, ἐπὶ τοῦ    110
στόματος αὐτὸς ὁ Θευδέριχος, Σόας δὲ ὁ μέγιστος τῶν ὑπ' αὐτὸν
στρατηγῶν τὸ μέσον εἶχεν, Θευδιμοῦνδος δὲ ὁ ἕτερος τῶν Βαλαμήρου παίδων ἐπὶ τῆς οὐραγίας. Θευδέριχος μὲν οὖν προκαταβὰς καὶ
θαρσῶν, ὡς οὐδεὶς ἦν αὐτοῖς ἐφεπόμενος, τοῖς ἐπὶ τῶν ἁμαξῶν καὶ
τοῖς ἄλλοις σκευοφόροις εἶπε ἐπὶ σχολῆς προχωρεῖν· αὐτὸς δὲ    115
ἠπείγετο φθάσαι προκαταλαβὼν ἣν ἂν δύναιτο πόλιν. καὶ πρὸς μὲν

82 ἕως Valesius [εὖ X    83 λέγων post στρατιώταις add Niebuhr    97 δοῦναι
om. X et edd.    103 ἐκείνων Niebuhr [ἐκείνω X    107 ἀλκὴν Niebuhr [ἄλλην
codd.    110 πολλὴν Valesius [πολὺ codd.    ἠρέμα de Boor    112 κατὰ
ante τὸ X

barbarian was moving into this area, that the Emperor approved of this, and that Adamantius had been sent for this purpose; it would, therefore, be best for them to arrange their affairs at greater leisure, while he had not yet arrived.[48] He persuaded the soldiers garrisoning the place, who were two thousand in number and well able to hold off the son of Valamir's immediate assault, all to leave Epidamnus together. He told them the same story,[49] raised doubts in their minds and continually tried to add new rumours to support his contention that if they wished to resist they would anger the Emperor more. Then he immediately sent to the son of Valamir to come as quickly as possible.

The latter was waiting upon the signal from Sidimund and upon his sister, who was suffering from an illness, which proved fatal. But he gave as the excuse for his delay that he was awaiting the arrival of the Emperor's envoy and wished to learn the Emperor's arrangements regarding himself.[50] When he had buried his deceased sister and the summons from Sidimund reached him, he sent to the people of Heraclea, who had abandoned their city and taken themselves off to a strong fortress. He demanded a large supply of grain and wine so that when he left he should be able to feed his army on the journey. They claimed that what they had in the tiny fortress had been consumed and said that in such circumstances they could give nothing. In anger he burned most of the city, which was deserted, and left immediately. Upon his departure he took the difficult and narrow road[51] which led to New Epirus, so-called. He sent ahead the cavalry to secure the heights for the army and, while they had surprise on their side, to descend from there and drive out by a sudden attack whatever garrison was at the place. As they approached, the soldiers guarding the wall, when they saw the force, were panicked by their unexpected appearance. They did not dare to put up a resistance and did not think to close the gates, but in their panic took to their heels reckless of all measures[52] which could have been of help at that time.

The Goths advanced through a great wasteland.[53] Theoderic himself was at the head, Soas, the greatest of the generals under him, commanded the centre, and Theodimund, the other son of Valamir, was at the rear. When he had come down from the mountains, Theoderic, confident that no one was following them, told those in charge of the wagons and the other baggage animals to proceed at their leisure. He himself hurried on to take by surprise whatever city he could. When

τὴν Λυχνιδὸν ἐπελθὼν ἀπεκρούσθη ἐπὶ ὀχυροῦ κειμένην καὶ πηγῶν
ἔνδον πλήρη, καὶ σίτου προενόντος. ἀναστὰς δὲ ἐκεῖθεν τήν τε Σκαμ-
πίαν αἱρεῖ, τῶν οἰκητόρων αὐτὴν πάλαι ἐκλελοιπότων, καὶ ἐξ αὐτῆς
ὁρμήσας Ἐπίδαμνον λαμβάνει.                                                120
Ἀδαμάντιος δὲ ταῦτα πυθόμενος προπέμπει τῶν ἱππέων τῶν
βασιλείων τινά, οὓς μαγιστριανοὺς καλοῦσι, μεμφόμενός τε αὐτῷ
παρὰ τὴν ὑπόσχεσιν τῆς πρεσβείας ποιοῦντι καὶ κελεύων ἠρεμεῖν καὶ
μήτε πλοῖα λαβεῖν μήτ' ἄλλο τι τῶν παρόντων πλέον νεωτερίσαι,
ἕως ἂν αὐτὸς ἔλθῃ· ἀποστεῖλαι δὲ καὶ ἄνδρα, ὅστις τὰ πιστὰ δώσει    125
τῆς μετὰ τὴν πρεσβείαν αὖθις ἀναχωρήσεως καὶ τῆς ὅλης ἀδείας.

Ταῦτά τε πρὸς ἐκεῖνον ἐπέστελλε καὶ αὐτὸς ἄρας ἀπὸ Θεσσαλονίκης ἔρχεται εἰς Ἔδεσαν, ὅπου ἦν Σαβινιανός, σὺν δὲ αὐτῷ καὶ
Φιλόξενος· καὶ τάς τε δέλτους αὐτῷ παρέχουσι καὶ στρατηγὸν ἀπο-
φαίνουσι, καὶ περὶ τῶν παρόντων εὖ διεβουλεύοντο. καὶ τὸ μὲν ἐπι-    130
χειρεῖν τοῖς βαρβάροις πορευομένοις οὐκ ἀσφαλὲς ἐδόκει, ὀλίγων μὲν
συνόντων αὐτῷ Σαβινιανῷ μισθοφόρων οἰκείων· τῆς δὲ δημοσίας
στρατιᾶς καὶ τῶν κοινῶν ταγμάτων τῶν μὲν διεσπαρμένων κατὰ
πόλεις, τῶν δὲ μετὰ τοῦ στρατηγοῦ Ὀνούλφου ἀκολουθούντων,
ἐδόκει πέμπειν ἁπανταχοῦ προστάγματα συγκαλοῦντα τοὺς στρατι-    135
ώτας καὶ τὸν στρατηγὸν δηλοῦντα προπέμπειν τὸν πρεσβευτήν.

Ἤδη δὲ ὁρμωμένοις ὁ παρὰ τοῦ Ἀδαμαντίου προαπεσταλμένος
ἱππεὺς ἀπαντᾷ τὸν τῶν βαρβάρων ἔχων ἱερέα, ὃν οἱ Χριστιανοὶ
καλοῦσι πρεσβύτερον, ὡς πίστιν τῆς ἀδείας αὐτῷ ἐπιθήσοντα.
ἄγοντες οὖν αὐτὸν σὺν αὐτοῖς ἠπείγοντο καὶ ἀφικνοῦνται εἰς Λυχ-    140
νιδόν. τῶν δὲ ἐκ τῆς πόλεως τῶν ἐν ταῖς ἀξίαις (παλαιόπλουτός τε
γὰρ αὕτη καὶ εὐδαίμων ἡ πόλις) καὶ τῶν ἄλλων ἀπαντησάντων,
εἰσέρχονται ἐνταῦθα. καὶ ἀποστέλλει πάλιν Ἀδαμάντιος εἰς Ἐπίδαμνον κελεύων ἢ αὐτὸν τὸν Θευδέριχον εἴς τι τῶν περὶ Λυχνιδὸν
χωρίων ἀπαντῆσαι μετ' ὀλίγων διαλεξόμενον αὐτῷ περὶ ὧν ἀπέ-    145
σταλτο, ἤ, εἰ βούλοιτο αὐτὸν ἐλθεῖν εἰς Ἐπίδαμνον, πέμψαι ὁμήρους
εἰς Λυχνιδὸν Σόαν τε τὸν αὐτοῦ στρατηγὸν καὶ Δαγίσθεον φυλαχ-
θησομένους, ἕως ἂν αὐτὸς ἐπανέλθῃ. ὁ δὲ πέμπει μὲν τούτους,
ἐκέλευσε δὲ αὐτοὺς περιμεῖναι ἐν Σκαμπίᾳ καὶ προαποστεῖλαι ἄνδρα,
ὃς τὸν Σαβινιανὸν ὁρκώσει ἦ μὴν ἐπανιόντος σῴου τοῦ Ἀδαμαντίου    150
καὶ αὐτὸν τοὺς ὁμήρους ἀπαθεῖς ἀποπέμψαι. ὁ δὲ Σαβινιανὸς οὐκ ἂν
ἔφη ὁμεῖσθαι· οὐδὲ γὰρ ἐν τῷ πρόσθεν χρόνῳ ὀμωμοκέναι ἐπ' οὐδενὶ
πράγματι, καὶ τὸ πάλαι αὐτῷ δόξαν οὐκ ἂν νῦν καταλύσειν. καὶ τοῦ
Ἀδαμαντίου λέγοντος ὡς ἀνάγκη συγχωρῆσαι τῷ καιρῷ ἢ ἄπρακτον

---

118 παρόντος Hoeschel [προσενόντος de Boor    124 πλοῖα [πόλεις vel πλείω
de Boor    134 Ὀνούλφου Valesius [Εὐούλφου codd.    140 ἄγοντες Valesius
[λέγοντες codd. ἔχοντες Niebuhr

he made an attempt on Lychnidus, he was repulsed, for the city lies in a
strong position, it has many springs inside, and the grain had already
been gathered in.[54] Advancing from there he took Scampia, whose
inhabitants had earlier evacuated it. Then he pressed on from that place
and occupied Epidamnus.

When Adamantius learned of this, he sent ahead one of the
imperial mounted couriers (whom they call *magistriani*) complaining
to Theoderic that he was acting contrary to the promise of the embassy
and ordering him to stay where he was, seize no ships and make no
further change in the present situation until he himself should arrive.
He also told Theoderic to send a man to give pledges for his own
complete safety and his immediate return after the embassy.

Adamantius sent these instructions to Theoderic and himself
left Thessalonika and came to Edessa, where Sabinianus was. Philoxenus travelled with him. They handed to Sabinianus the codicils
appointing him general and took careful counsel about the present
circumstances. It did not seem safe to attack the barbarians while they
were on the march,[55] since Sabinianus had with him only a few of his
own mercenaries, and of the imperial army and the legions part was
dispersed through the cities and part was away with the general Onulf.
It, therefore, seemed best to send orders to all points summoning the
soldiers and to send the envoy forward to announce the appointment
of the general.[56]

As they were setting out, the courier whom Adamantius had sent
ahead met them with a priest of the barbarians (whom the Christians
call a 'presbyter') to give him a guarantee of safe conduct. Taking him
with them, they hurried on and came to Lychnidus. The men of rank –
for the city is fertile and full of old wealth – and the other inhabitants
came out to greet them, and they entered the place. Adamantius again
sent to Epidamnus bidding Theoderic, in order to discuss with him the
matters about which he had sent the message, either to come with a few
men to a place close to Lychnidus or, if he wished Adamantius to come
to Epidamnus, to send Soas, his general, and Dagistheus to Lychnidus
as hostages, to be detained there until he returned. Theoderic sent these
men, but ordered them to remain at Scampia and send forward someone to take an oath from Sabinianus that, when Adamantius had
returned safely, he would send back the hostages unharmed. Sabinianus
refused to swear, saying that he had never before sworn an oath for
anything and he would not now change his old practice. Adamantius
argued that it was necessary to accommodate himself to the situation or

εἶναι τὴν πρεσβείαν· οὐ γὰρ αὐτὸν ἀπελθεῖν μή τι καὶ ἐνέχυρον τοῦ σώ-   155
ματος λαβόντα· οὐδὲν μᾶλλον ἐπείσθη, ἀλλ' ἐκεῖνον μὲν ἔφη εἰδέναι
τὸ ἑαυτῷ πρακτέον, αὐτόν δὲ οὐδὲν ποιήσειν παρὰ τὸν αὐτοῦ νόμον.

Ἐνταῦθα Ἀδαμάντιος καταστὰς εἰς ἄπορον, λαβὼν στρατιώτας σ' δι' ὄχθων τε ἀβάτων καὶ ὁδοῦ ἀδήλου μὲν τοῖς πολλοῖς,
στενῆς δὲ καὶ ἀτριβοῦς καὶ τότε πρῶτον ἵππους, ὡς ἐλέγετο, δεξα-   160
μένης, ἀφ' ἑσπέρας ὁρμήσας καὶ κύκλῳ περιελθὼν ἔρχεται εἰς
φρούριον Ἐπιδάμνου πλησίον ἐπὶ λόφου ὑψηλοῦ κείμενον καὶ ἄλλως
ἄμαχον, ᾧ φάραγξ ὑπέκειτο βαθεῖα, καὶ παρὰ τὴν φάραγγα ποταμὸς
βαθὺς ἔρρει. ἐνταῦθα μεταπέμπεται τὸν Θευδέριχον. καὶ ὁ μὲν
ὑπακούσας ἔρχεται καὶ τὴν ἄλλην στρατιὰν πόρρω καταστήσας σὺν   165
ὀλίγοις ἱππεῦσι πρὸς τὸν ποταμὸν ἀφικνεῖται. Ἀδαμάντιος δὲ κύκλῳ
περὶ τὸν λόφον τάξας στρατιώτας, ὅπως μή τις κύκλωσις παρ'
ἐκείνου γένηται, ὑποκαταβὰς εἰς πέτραν, ἀφ' ἧς ἦν ἀκουστόν, καὶ
κελεύσας κἀκείνῳ τοὺς ἄλλους ἀποπέμψαι, μόνος διελέγετο μόνῳ.
καὶ καταστὰς ὁ Θευδέριχος κατηγόρει Ῥωμαίων, ὡς ἐδόκει, δίκαια,   170
λέγων ὅτι· ἐγὼ μὲν ἔξω τῆς ὅλης Θράκης διατρίβειν ἡρούμην
πόρρω πρὸς τὴν Σκυθίαν, ὅπου μένων οὔτε ἐνοχλεῖν ἐνόμιζον οὐδένα,
ἑτοίμως δὲ βασιλεῖ ὑπακούσεσθαι ἐντεῦθεν ἐς ὅ τι προστάξειεν.
ὑμεῖς δὲ καλέσαντες ὡς ἐπὶ τὸν πόλεμον τὸν πρὸς Θευδέριχον
πρῶτον μὲν ὑπέσχεσθε τὸν τῆς Θράκης στρατηγὸν μετὰ τῆς δυνά-   175
μεως εὐθύς μοι παρέσεσθαι, ὃς οὐδαμοῦ ἐφάνη, ἔπειτα καὶ Κλαύδιον
τὸν τοῦ Γοτθικοῦ ταμίαν σὺν τῷ ξενικῷ ἥξειν, ὃν οὐδὲ αὐτὸν εἶδον,
τρίτον καὶ ἡγεμόνας ὁδῶν μοι δεδώκατε, οἳ τὰς εὐπορωτέρας τῶν
ὁδῶν ἐάσαντες τὰς εἰς τοὺς πολεμίους φερούσας ἀπήγαγον δι' ὀρθίας
ἀτραποῦ καὶ κρημνῶν ἀμφιρρόπων, ἐν οἷς παρὰ μικρὸν ἦλθον σὺν   180
ἱππεῦσί τε ἰών, ὡς εἰκός, καὶ ἀμάξαις καὶ στρατοπέδων κατασκευῇ,
ἐπιθεμένων ἡμῖν ἄφνω τῶν πολεμίων, ἅμα τῷ ἐμῷ πλήθει παντὶ
ἀπολέσθαι καθάπαξ. ἐνταῦθα ἀναγκαίαν ἐβιάσθην σύμβασιν πρὸς
αὐτοὺς ποιήσασθαι· οἷς χρὴ πολλὴν χάριν ἔχειν, ὅτι ὑφ' ὑμῶν προ-
δοθέντα δυνάμενοι καὶ διαφθεῖραι διέσωσάν γε ὅμως.   185

Ἀδαμάντιος δὲ τῶν τε τοῦ βασιλέως τιμῶν αὐτὸν ἀνεμίμνησκε
καὶ ὅτι πατρίκιον καὶ στρατηγὸν ποιήσας, ἃ τοῖς πλεῖστα καμοῦσι
παρὰ Ῥωμαίοις γέρα ἐστί, καὶ τῶν ἄλλων δωρεῶν καὶ πλούτου
ἐνέπλησεν, ἀνθ' ὧν ἔδει μηδέποτε πρὸς αὐτὸν ἄλλως πως ἢ πρὸς
πατέρα φρονεῖν τε καὶ διατίθεσθαι· καὶ τὰ τῶν παρ' αὐτοῦ ἐγκλή-   190
σεων (ἦν γὰρ οἶμαι ἀληθῆ) διακρούεσθαι ἐπειρᾶτο· καὶ ὅτι οὐκ
ἀνεκτὰ ποιήσειεν ἐν πρεσβείας ἐλπίδι καταλαβὼν τὰ Ῥωμαίων, οἳ

157 αὐτὸν Hoeschel [αὐτοῦ codd.   αὐτοῦ Niebuhr [αὐτοῦ codd.   167 περὶ
Niebuhr [παρὰ codd.   192 καταλαβὼν τὰ Valesius [καταλαβόντα X κατα-
λαβόντας E

the embassy would be a failure, since he would not go unless he received some guarantee of his own safety. Nevertheless, Sabinianus was not persuaded and he said that he knew what he had to do and he would do nothing contrary to his own principles.

At this point Adamantius was at an impasse. Taking two hundred soldiers, he set out at nightfall through the deserted hills along a narrow, unused path, known to few and on that occasion traversed by horses for the first time, as it was claimed. By this circuitous route he came to a guard tower near to Epidamnus. It was built upon a high hill and was otherwise impregnable. Beneath it lay a deep ravine, and through the ravine flowed a deep river. To this place he summoned Theoderic, who obediently came. Stationing the rest of his army at a distance, he approached the river with a few horsemen. Adamantius posted his troops in a circle around the hill so that Theoderic should not encircle him and, descending to a rock from which he could be heard, told the other to send away the rest of his men, and they conversed alone. When Theoderic had come up, he accused the Romans, justly, as it seemed, saying, "I chose to live completely outside Thrace, far away towards Scythia. Staying there I thought that I should trouble no one, yet from there I should be ready to obey whatever the Emperor commanded. You summoned me as if to war against Theoderic the son of Triarius. First, you promised that the general of Thrace would immediately join me with his forces. He never appeared. Then you promised that Claudius, the paymaster of the Gothic soldiery, would come with the mercenaries' pay. I never saw him. Thirdly, you gave me guides who left the easier way towards the enemy and led me aside over a steep path with sheer cliffs on both sides. Here, since I was naturally travelling with the cavalry, wagons and all the army's baggage, I was not far from complete destruction with all my force, had the enemy suddenly attacked. Then I was compelled to make an agreement with them, and for this I must be very thankful. For when you had abandoned me, they could have destroyed me. Yet they spared me."

Adamantius reminded Theoderic of the honours which the Emperor had bestowed upon him: he had made him consul and patrician, which are a reward for those of the Romans who have laboured particularly hard, and had loaded him with wealth and other gifts; and for this he should never have thought and acted towards him otherwise than as to a father.[57] Adamantius also tried to refute the complaints against the Emperor (which in my view were justified). He said that Theoderic had acted intolerably in seizing the possessions of the Romans while awaiting an embassy. They had had him confined in

καὶ ἀποκεκλεισμένον ἐν Θρᾴκῃ ἔχοντες ὄρεσι καὶ ποταμοῖς καὶ περι-
βολῇ στρατοπέδων ὅμως συνεχώρησαν ἑκόντες διεξελθεῖν· οὐ γὰρ
ἂν μὴ βουλομένων αὐτὸν ἐκεῖθεν κινηθῆναι, οὐδὲ εἰ δεκαπλασίαν      195
εἶχε δύναμιν τῆς παρούσης. νῦν τε συμβουλεύειν αὐτῷ μετριώτερον
ἑαυτὸν τῷ βασιλεῖ παρέχειν· οὐ γὰρ ἂν δυνηθῆναι τὴν Ῥωμαίων εἰς
τέλος ὑπερβαλεῖ χεῖρα πανταχόθεν ἐφεστηκότων. δεῖ οὖν, εἰ αὐτῷ
πείθοιτο, ἐκλιπεῖ μὲν τὴν Ἤπειρον καὶ τὰς αὐτόθι πόλεις (οὐδενὶ
γὰρ εἶναι φορητὸν πόλεις οὕτω μεγάλας, τῶν οἰκητόρων ἐκβλη-      200
θέντων, ὑπ' αὐτοῦ κατέχεσθαι), ἐλθεῖ δὲ εἰς τὴν Δαρδανίαν, ἐν ᾗ
χώραν εἶναι πολλὴν παρὰ τὰ οἰκούμενα καλὴν μὲν καὶ εὔγειον, ἐνδεᾶ
δὲ οἰκητόρων, ἣν δύναται γεωργῶν ἐν πᾶσιν ἀφθόνοις αὐτοῦ τὴν
στρατιὰν διάγειν.

Ὁ δὲ Θευδέριχος αὐτὸς μὲν ἐπώμνυε ταῦτα βούλεσθαι, οὐ      205
μέντοι ἀνέξεσθαι αὐτοῦ τὸ πλῆθος πολλὰ μὲν προτεταλαιπωρηκός,
μόλις δὲ ἀναπαύσεως νῦν ἐπιλαβόμενον· οὓς οὐ δύνασθαι μήπω
ἀναπνεύσαντας ἄγειν μακρὰν οὕτω πορείαν. ἀλλὰ νῦν μὲν αὐτοὺς ἐᾶν
αὐτοῦ ἐπιχειμάσαι, μήτε πρόσω χωροῦντας <ὧν> ἔχουσι πόλεων
μήτε ἐπιφθείροντας· συνθέμενος δὲ περὶ πάντων ἐπὶ τούτοις ἅμα τῷ      210
ἦρι πέμψαι τὸν ἄξοντα ἐπὶ τὴν Δαρδανίαν ἀσμένως ἐπακολουθή-
σοντας. ἔλεγε δὲ ὡς ἕτοιμος εἴη τὴν αὐτοῦ κατασκευὴν καὶ τὸ
ἄμαχον πλῆθος καταθέμενος ἐν πόλει, ᾗ βούλοιτο βασιλεύς, καὶ
ὁμήρους παρασχὼν τῆς ἁπάσης πίστεως τήν τε μητέρα καὶ τὴν
ἀδελφήν, μετὰ ἑξακισχιλίων τῶν μάλιστα μαχίμων ἐλθεῖν ὡς      215
τάχιστα εἰς Θρᾴκην· καὶ ὑπισχνεῖσθαι σὺν τούτοις καὶ τοῖς Ἰλλυριοῖς
στρατιώταις καὶ ἄλλοις, ὁπόσους ἂν βασιλεὺς ἀποστείλῃ, τοὺς ἐν τῇ
Θρᾴκῃ Γότθους ἀναλώσειν ἅπαντας, ἐφ' ᾧτε, εἰ τοῦτο ποιήσοι, αὐτόν
τε ἀντὶ Θευδερίχου στρατηγὸν γενέσθαι καὶ εἰσδεχθῆναι εἰς τὴν
πόλιν τὸν Ῥωμαϊκὸν πολιτεύσοντα τρόπον· ἕτοιμος δέ, εἰ προστάξειε      220
βασιλεύς, καὶ εἰς Δαλματίαν ἀπελθεῖν ὡς Νέπωτα κατάξειν.

Ἀδαμάντιος δὲ οὐκ ἔφη κύριος εἶναι οὐδὲν αὐτῷ συνθέσθαι μέ-
νοντι ἐν τῇ χώρᾳ, ἀλλὰ δεῖν βασιλέα πρῶτον περὶ τούτων πυθέσθαι.
ἀνοίσειν οὖν ἐκείνῳ, καὶ αὐτὸς ἐπιμενεῖν, ἕως τὴν τοῦ κρατοῦντος
διαπύθηται γνώμην. ἐπὶ τούτοις διελύθησαν ἀπ' ἀλλήλων.      225

Ἐν ὅσῳ δὲ Ἀδαμάντιος ἀμφὶ ταῦτα ἦν, συνεληλύθει μὲν
πολλὰ τῶν ταγμάτων εἰς τὴν Λυχνιδὸν κατὰ τὴν τοῦ στρατηγοῦ
ἀγγελίαν, λέγει δέ τις τῷ Σαβινιανῷ, ὡς οἱ βάρβαροι καταφρονή-
σαντες σχολαίτερον κατίασιν ἀπὸ τῆς Κανδαβείας, οἵ τε σκευοφόροι
αὐτῶν καὶ τῶν ἁμαξῶν αἱ πλείους καὶ οἱ ἐπὶ τῆς οὐραγίας, ἐν οἷς καὶ      230

200-201 ἐκβληθέντων Bekker [ἐκλυθέντων codd.      209 ὧν add. Niebuhr
210 συνθέμενον Niebuhr      211 ἀσμένως Müller [ἔνβως codd. ἐπιεικῶς
Niebuhr ἑτοίμως Bekker    223 πείθεσθαι X

Thrace by mountains, rivers and a cordon of troops. Nevertheless, they had willingly allowed him to leave, although, had they not wished it, he would never have broken out of there, even if he had a force ten-fold greater than his present one. Under the circumstances he advised him to act more reasonably towards the Emperor, since he would ultimately be unable to overcome the might of the Romans, who were poised against him on every side. If Theoderic would listen to him, he should leave Epirus and the cities there (since it was intolerable to all that such great cities should be occupied by him, their inhabitants having been ejected) and go to Dardania, where, compared with their current homes, there was much land, beautiful, fertile and depopulated. This he could farm and support his army with an abundance of everything.

Theoderic swore that he himself was willing to do this, but that his army, which had already suffered many hardships and had now barely gained a respite from them, would not stand for it. They could not make such a long journey when they had not yet rested. Under the circumstances he would allow them to winter here, and they would go no further than the cities which they already occupied and cause no additional damage. When he had reached agreement on all matters in addition to these, in spring he would allow the Romans to send someone to guide them to Dardania, and they would gladly follow. He also said that he was ready to place his own baggage and all the non-combatants in any city of the Emperor's choosing, give his mother and sister as hostages for his complete trustworthiness, and with six thousand of his best soldiers go as quickly as possible to Thrace. He promised that with these and the Illyrian troops and whatever others the Emperor should send he would destroy all the Goths in Thrace, on condition that, if he did this, he would become general in place of Theoderic and be received into Byzantium to live as a citizen in the Roman manner.[58] He was even willing, if the Emperor commanded it, to go to Dalmatia to restore Nepos.

Adamantius replied that he had no authority to make an agreement with him while he remained in that land, and that the Emperor must first be informed. He would, therefore, send a report to the Emperor and himself wait until he learned the ruler's will. Upon these terms they departed.

While Adamantius was busy on this matter, many of the Roman forces had assembled at Lychnidus at the order of the general. Someone reported to Sabinianus that the barbarians, both those conveying the baggage and the majority of the wagons and the rearguard, which

Θευδιμοῦνδος ἦν ὁ τοῦ Θευδερίχου ἀδελφὸς καὶ ἡ μήτηρ ἡ τούτων,
καὶ ὅτι ἔστιν ἐλπὶς τῶν πλειόνων κρατήσειν. ὁ δὲ τό τε ἱππικὸν μεθ᾽
ἑαυτοῦ συντάξας καὶ πεζοὺς οὐκ ὀλίγους κύκλῳ διὰ τῶν ὁρῶν περι-
πέμψας καὶ προειπών, ὁπότε δεῖ καὶ πόθεν ἐκφανῆναι, δειπνήσας καὶ
ἀναλαβὼν τὸ στράτευμα ἀφ᾽ ἑσπέρας ἐχώρει, καὶ ἅμα τῇ ἡμέρᾳ          235
αὐτοῖς ἐπιτίθεται ἤδη πορευομένοις. καὶ ὁ μὲν Θευδιμοῦνδος καὶ ἡ
μήτηρ αὐτοῦ, ὡς εἶδον τὴν ἔφοδον, ταχὺ διεκπεσόντες ὑπέφυγον εἰς
τὸ πεδίον καὶ τὴν γέφυραν, καθ᾽ ἣν ὑπερέβησαν, εὐθέως ἀνελόντες,
ἣ φάραγγι βαθείᾳ ἐπέζευκτο μέσῃ οὔσῃ τῆς ὁδοῦ, τὴν δίωξιν ἐκείνοις
ἐπὶ τοὺς καταβάντας ἐποίησαν ἄπορον καὶ μέντοι καὶ τοῖς ἑαυτῶν           240
ἀδύνατον τὴν φυγήν, ὥστε πρὸς ἀπόνοιαν ὀλίγοι ὄντες ὁμόσε τοῖς
ἱππεῦσιν ἐχώρουν. ὡς δὲ ὑπὲρ κεφαλῆς οἱ πεζοὶ ἐφάνησαν κατὰ τὸ
συγκείμενον, οὕτω δὴ ἐτράποντο, καὶ οἱ μὲν εἰς τοὺς ἱππεῖς, οἱ δὲ εἰς
τοὺς ὁπλίτας ἐμπίπτοντες ἔθνησκον. καὶ τὰς ἁμάξας αὐτῶν λαβὼν
Σαβινιανὸς οὔσας ὡς δισχιλίας αἰχμαλώτους <τε> πλείους ἢ πεντα-         245
κισχιλίους καὶ λείαν οὐκ ὀλίγην, τινὰς δὲ τῶν ἁμαξῶν καὶ κατα-
καύσας ἐν τῷ ὄρει, ἃς ἦν ἔργον ἑλκύσαι διὰ κρημνῶν τοσούτων, εἰς
τὴν Λυχνιδὸν ἀφικνεῖται.

Καὶ εὑρίσκει Ἀδαμάντιον ἐκ τῆς πρὸς Θευδέριχον συνουσίας
ἐπανελθόντα· οὐ γάρ πω Θευδέριχος ἐπέπυστο οὐδὲν τῶν ὑπὸ            250
Σαβινιανοῦ ἐν τῷ ὄρει πραχθέντων. τοὺς μὲν οὖν αἰχμαλώτους τοὺς
μὲν εὖ γεγονότας ἐν φυλακῇ ποιεῖται, τοὺς δὲ ἄλλους μετὰ τῆς λείας
διέδωκε τοῖς στρατιώταις. ἁμάξας μέντοι πολλὰς κελεύσας ταῖς
πόλεσι πρὸς τὰς τοῦ στρατοπέδου κατασκευάσαι χρείας, ὡς ἐλήφ-
θησαν αὗται, ἀπεῖπε ταῖς πόλεσι μηδὲν ἐνοχλεῖσθαι, ὡς τὰς          255
ἀρκούσας ἔχων.

Μετὰ δὲ ταῦτα γράφει μὲν Ἀδαμάντιος τῷ βασιλεῖ, ὡς ὑπέσχετο, τὰ πρὸς Θευδέριχον αὐτῷ διειλεγμένα, γράφει δὲ καὶ Σαβινιανὸς καὶ Ἰωάννης ὁ ὕπαρχος τὰ γεγενημένα, ἐπὶ μεῖζον ὀγκοῦντες
καὶ λέγοντες μὴ χρῆναί τι τῷ βαρβάρῳ συνθέσθαι, ὡς ἐλπίδος            260
οὔσης ἢ κατὰ κράτος αὐτὸν ἐξελάσειν τῆς χώρας ἢ αὐτοῦ μένοντα
κατατρίψειν.

Ταῦτα δεξάμενος βασιλεὺς καὶ νομίσας πόλεμον εἰρήνης
αἰσχρᾶς εἶναι βελτίω, πέμψας ἀνεκάλεσε τὸν πρεσβευτὴν ἐκεῖθεν,
κελεύσας μηδὲν ἔτι πρὸς ἐκεῖνον συνθέσθαι, ἀλλ᾽ εἰπεῖν Σαβινιανῷ       265
καὶ Γέντονι, Γότθῳ μὲν ὄντι ἀνδρί, γυναῖκα δὲ Ῥωμαίαν τῶν περὶ
τὴν Ἤπειρον γεγαμηκότι καὶ δύναμιν ἔχοντι, ἔχεσθαι τοῦ πολέμου
πάσῃ χειρί, ὡς οὐδὲν βασιλέως πρὸς ἐκείνους συνθησομένου. καὶ
συγκαλέσας τοὺς στρατιώτας ὁ Ἀδαμάντιος ἐπήνεσεν αὐτοὺς τῆς

---

238 ἀναλύοντες coni. Niebuhr    239 μέσης οὔσης edd.    245 τε add. Niebuhr  250 πω Niebuhr [που codd.

included Theoderic's brother, Theodimund, and their mother, were overconfidently making a very leisurely descent from Candavia, and that the Romans could hope to overwhelm most of them. Sabinianus himself took command of the cavalry and sent a considerable body of infantry on a roundabout route through the mountains, telling them when and where to put in their appearance. Then he dined, assembled his army and set out at nightfall. He attacked the Goths at daybreak when they were already on the move. When Theodimund and his mother observed the attack, they quickly slipped away and fled down to the plain, immediately breaking the bridge which they had crossed and which spanned a deep ravine that crossed the road. This made it impossible for the Romans to attack them after their descent, but it also cut off the escape of their own men. They, therefore, although few, closed with the cavalry out of desperation. When the infantry appeared over their heads according to plan, they were routed. Some died attacking the cavalry, some the infantry. Sabinianus captured their wagons, two thousand in number, more than five thousand prisoners, and considerable booty. Some of the wagons, which would have been too difficult to drag through such rugged country, he also burned in the mountains. Then he returned to Lychnidus.

There he found Adamantius, who had returned from his meeting with Theoderic. For the latter had not yet learned of what Sabinianus had done in the mountains. The well-born prisoners he placed under guard, the others he handed over with the booty to the soldiers. He had ordered the cities to prepare wagons for the use of his army, but because he had those of the Goths, he told the cities not to trouble themselves, since he now had sufficient.

After this Adamantius, as he had promised, wrote to inform the Emperor of his discussion with Theoderic. Sabinianus and John, the prefect, also wrote about what had happened. They magnified the exploit and declared that there was no need to come to terms with the barbarian, since they could hope either to drive him out of the land by force or, if he remained, to wear him down.

When he received these messages, the Emperor thought that war was better than a shameful peace and he sent and recalled the ambassador from Lychnidus, ordering that no agreement be yet made with Theoderic. He told Sabinianus and Gento,[59] who was a Goth married to a Roman woman from the area of Epirus and who had a force of men, to turn all their efforts to the war, since the Emperor would make no agreement with the enemy. Adamantius assembled the troops, praised

προθυμίας καὶ ἐκέλευσε γενναίως ὥσπερ πάτριον αὐτοῖς ἔχεσθαι 270
τῶν πραγμάτων, καὶ τὸ ἐκ βασιλέως ἐπανέγνω πρόσταγμα. ταῖς τε
ἐλπίσιν αὐτοὺς μετεώρους ποιήσας, ὡς βασιλέως ἀεὶ πᾶσι τὴν προ-
θυμίαν οὐκ ἄκαρπον ἐῶντος, εὐφημίας ἔτυχε καὶ μετὰ τιμῆς παρε-
πέμφθη. καὶ ὁ μὲν ἀπηλλάγη μηδὲν πλέον ποιήσας.

## 21

(*Exc. de Leg. Rom.* 2 = *Fr.* 22; Photius *Bibl. Cod.* 78 = T.1; *Suda* Π
137 = *Fr.* 23; scholion to Evagrius *HE* 3,26)

## 22

(*Exc. de Leg. Rom.* 2)

Ὅτι ἐπὶ Ζήνωνος τοῦ βασιλέως στάσεως γενομένης παρὰ
Μαρκιανοῦ καὶ ἄλλων τινῶν, Θευδέριχος ὁ Τριαρίου μαθὼν τὰ
γεγονότα καὶ ὑπολαβὼν καιρὸν νῦν αὐτῷ παρεστάναι τῇ πόλει
ἐπιθέσθαι καὶ τῷ βασιλεῖ αὐτῷ, πᾶν εὐθὺς ἀναστήσας τὸ βαρβαρικὸν ἦκε, δῆθεν μὲν ὡς βουλόμενος αὐτῷ τε τῷ βασιλεῖ καὶ τῇ          5
πόλει ἀμῦναι, πρόδηλος δὲ ὢν πᾶσιν ἐφ' ὅτῳ ἠπείγετο. βασιλεὺς δὲ
ἀκούσας ἱππέα ἐξέπεμψε καὶ βασίλεια γράμματα τῆς μὲν προθυμίας
αὐτὸν ἐπαινῶν, κελεύων δὲ ἀπελθεῖν, ὡς οὐκ ἔτι οὔσης χρείας, μὴ
μόλις ἐκστᾶσαν ἐκ σάλου τοιούτου τὴν πόλιν αὖθις εἰς ὑπόνοιαν
ἐμβαλόντες ἑτέραν τὸ θορυβεῖσθαι φιλοῦν εἰς χεῖρω καὶ μείζονα          10
ἐκταράξωσι στάσιν. ὁ δὲ αὐτὸς μὲν ἔφη τῷ βασιλεῖ πείθεσθαι, τὸ δὲ
πλῆθος οὐκ ἔτι δύνασθαι ἀναστρέφειν τοσοῦτόν τε συλλεγὲν καὶ
μέρος τι <κάμνον> οὐ βραχὺ διαναπαύων. ὑπέρ τε γὰρ τειχῶν
οὐδένα ἐνόμιζεν αὐτῷ ἀντιστήσεσθαι, μήτε ἐπάλξεως μηδεμιᾶς μήτε
πύργου ἑστῶτος, καὶ εἰσελθόντι πάντα τὸν δῆμον προσέσεσθαι τῇ          15
τῶν Ἰσαύρων ἀπεχθείᾳ. ἃ δὴ καὶ φοβούμενος Ζήνων ἐκπέμπει
Πελάγιον χρήματα ἔχοντα πολλά, τὰ μὲν αὐτῷ Θευδερίχῳ, τὰ δὲ καὶ
τῷ Γοτθικῷ τῷ παντὶ διδόναι, καὶ ἄλλας ὑποσχέσεις δωρεῶν οὐκ
ὀλίγας. ἐλθὼν δὲ Πελάγιος καὶ τὰ μὲν ἀπειλήσας, τὰ δὲ ὑποσχόμενος, τὰ δὲ καὶ τοῖς χρήμασιν οὐκ ὀλίγοις γε οὖσι τὸ φύσει φιλάρ-          20
γυρον τοῦ βαρβαρικοῦ τρόπου μετελθών, διαπέμπει.

Καὶ ἔδοξε δὴ τοῦτο τοῦ φόβου τοῦ πλείονος ἀναφέρειν τὴν
πόλιν· οὐδὲν γὰρ ἦν ἐλπίσαι εἰσιόντος ἢ πόλεμόν τε ἔνδον καὶ τοῦ
παντὸς ἔμπρησιν. οὐδὲ γὰρ οἱ Ἴσαυροι ἁπλῶς ἀναχωρῆσαι βιαζόμενοι ἐπενόουν, ἀλλὰ κοντοὺς ὑψηλοὺς προπαρασκευάσαντες, λίνον          25

6 ὑπήγετο M     13 κάμνον addidi [lacunam post βραχὺ indicat de Boor     διαναπαύων [λίαν ἀπειθές Niebuhr     18 διδόναι Niebuhr [διδόασι codd.     20 γε
Dindorf [τε codd.

their zeal, ordered them to apply themselves nobly to their task, as was their custom, and read out the Emperor's commands. When he had raised their hopes that the Emperor allowed no-one's zeal to go unrewarded, he won acclaim and was sent off with honour. Doing nothing more, he left.

### 21

(*Exc. de Leg. Rom.* 2 = *Fr.* 22; Photius *Bibl. Cod.* 78 = T.1; *Suda* Π 137 = *Fr.* 23; scholion to Evagrius *HE* 3,26)

### 22

(*Exc. de Leg. Rom.* 2)

During the reign of Zeno, Marcian and some others broke out in revolt. When Theoderic the son of Triarius learned what had happened, he thought that now was the time for him to attack the city and the Emperor himself. He immediately raised his whole force of barbarians and came to Byzantium pretending that he wished to defend the Emperor and the city, although it was clear to all what was his real intention. When the Emperor heard of this, he sent a mounted courier and a royal letter praising his zeal but ordering him to depart (since he was no longer needed) lest they plunge the city, which had just calmed down after a considerable disturbance, into another bout of suspicion and stir up the usual restlessness into an outbreak worse and more widespread. The son of Triarius said that he would obey the Emperor, but he could not yet turn around the force which he had collected without giving it a brief rest, since a part of it was <exhausted>.[60] He thought that, since no ramparts and towers had been set up, no one would resist him from the walls and, when he entered, the whole populace would side with him out of hatred for the Isaurians. This is what Zeno feared and he sent Pelagius bearing a large sum of money, some to give to Theoderic, the rest to the whole Gothic force, as well as lavish promises of other gifts. Pelagius arrived and persuaded them to leave by a combination of threats, promises and large sums of money which worked on the greedy nature of the barbarian mind.

It appeared that this saved the city from a very serious threat, since, had Theoderic entered, fighting and a general conflagration were inevitable. For the Isaurians, who did not intend to be driven out easily, had prepared beforehand long poles with linen and brimstone

ἐπ᾽ ἄκροις αὐτοῖς προσδήσαντες καὶ θεῖον, πολλοὺς εἶχον ἑτοίμους,
εἴ ποτε βιασθεῖεν, ἅπασαν ὑφάψαι τὴν πόλιν.

Καὶ ὁ μὲν Θευδέριχος οὕτως ἀπεχώρησεν. τοὺς δὲ περὶ Προ-
κόπιον καὶ Βούσαλβον πολλάκις ἀποστέλλων παρὰ Θευδερίχου ἐξῄτει
ἔνδειγμα τῆς εὐνοίας καὶ εὐπειθείας αὐτὸν τοῦτο ἀξιῶν παρα-    30
σχέσθαι. ὁ δὲ πάντα μὲν ἔλεγε πείθεσθαι τῷ βασιλεῖ, μὴ μέντοι
ὅσιον Γότθοις, ὥσπερ οὐδὲ ἄλλοις ἀνθρώποις, ἱκέτας καὶ σωτηρίας
δεομένους ἀνθρώπους τοῖς λαβεῖν βουλομένοις ἐκδιδόναι προχείρως.
ἐᾶν οὖν αὐτοὺς ἠξίου μηδενὶ πλὴν ἢ ὅσα ζῆν ὀχληροὺς ἐσομένους. καὶ
οἱ μὲν οὕτω βραχύ τι γῄδιον νεμόμενοι παρὰ Θευδερίχῳ διῆγον.    35

## 23

(Suda Π 137)

Παμπρέπιος· οὗτος μέγα παρὰ Ζήνωνι ἐδυνήθη· γένος μὲν ὢν
Θηβαῖος τῶν κατὰ τὴν Αἴγυπτον, φύσει δὲ πρὸς ἅπαντα δεξιᾷ χρησά-
μενος ἔρχεται εἰς Ἀθήνας, καὶ παρὰ τῆς πόλεως γραμματικὸς αἱρε-
θεὶς συχνά τε ἐπαίδευσεν ἔτη καὶ ἐπαιδεύθη ὁμοῦ, ὅσα ἦν σοφώτερα,
ὑπὸ τῷ μεγάλῳ Πρόκλῳ. διαβολῆς δὲ αὐτῷ πρὸς Θεαγένην τινὰ    5
τῶν ἐκεῖ δυναμένων συστάσης, ὑβρισθεὶς ὑπ᾽ ἐκείνου καὶ μείζονος ἢ
ἐχρῆν διδάσκαλον ὑπ᾽ αὐτοῦ πειραθεὶς σκευωρίας ἦλθεν ἐς Βυζάντιον, τὰ μὲν ἄλλα ἀγαθὸς καὶ χρηστὸς φαινόμενος, ὡς δὲ ἐν Χριστια-
νοὺς πάντας ἐχούσῃ πόλει τὸ Ἑλληνικὸν αὐτοῦ τῆς θρησκείας οὐκ
ἔχον ὑπόκρισιν, ἀλλὰ μετὰ παρρησίας προδήλως δεικνύμενον, εἰς τὴν    10
τοῦ καὶ ἕτερα τῆς ἀρρήτου σοφίας εἰδέναι ὑπόνοιαν ἦγε. συσταθέντα
δὲ αὐτὸν ὁ Ἴλλους μάγιστρος ἡδέως δέχεται, καί τι καὶ δημοσίᾳ
ποίημα ἀναγνόντα λαμπρῶς τε ἐτίμησε καὶ σύνταξιν ἔδωκε, τὴν μὲν
αὐτὸς ἰδίᾳ, τὴν δὲ ὡς διδασκάλῳ καὶ ἐκ τοῦ δημοσίου. καὶ ἀπελθόντος δὲ αὐτοῦ ἐπὶ τὴν Ἰσαυρίαν, οἱ βασκαίνοντες αὐτῷ συνθέντες    15
διαβολὴν τήν τε ἐκ τῆς θρησκείας καὶ ὅτι μαγγανεύοι καὶ μαντεύοιτο
τῷ Ἴλλου κατὰ τοῦ βασιλέως, πείθουσι τὸν Ζήνωνα καὶ τὴν Βηρίναν
τότε μέγιστα δυναμένην τῆς πόλεως ἐκπέμψαι. καὶ ὁ μὲν ἐς Πέρ-
γαμον ἔρχεται τῆς Μυσίας· Ἴλλους δὲ πυθόμενος κατὰ τὴν αὐτοῦ
πρόφασιν ἐληλάσθαι τὸν ἄνδρα, πέμψας ἀναλαμβάνει αὐτὸν ἐς    20
Ἰσαυρίαν καὶ σύμβουλόν τε αὐτὸν καὶ σύνοικον ποιεῖται, καί, ἢν γὰρ
πολιτικῆς συνέσεως ἔμπλεως, καὶ τὰ τῆς ἀρχῆς αὐτῷ πρὸς ἃ μὴ
σχολὴν ἦγε διοικεῖν ἐπέτρεπεν, ἐλθών τε ἐς Βυζάντιον συμπαρέ-
λαβεν αὐτόν. καὶ ὅτε ἐγένετο ἡ Μαρκιανοῦ σύστασις, ἀποροῦντα τὸν

1 ὢν GM [ἦν V   6 δυναμένων Bekker [ἐκεῖ γενομένων VM ἐγκειμένων G
ἐκεῖ ἐλλογίμων Bernhardy ἐκεῖ εὐγενῶν M. Schmidt   17 τοῦ Ἴλλου G [τῷ
Ἴλλῳ edd.   21 τε αὐτὸν om. V   22 καὶ exp. edd.

tied to the ends and kept a large supply of these in readiness to set fire to the whole city, if they were attacked.

Thus Theoderic departed. Zeno sent frequent messages to him demanding the followers of Procopius and Busalbus and asking that in this way he demonstrate his good will and obedience. Theoderic replied that he would obey the Emperor in everything, but it would not be right for the Goths, any more than it would be for other men, to hand over readily to those who wished to arrest them persons who were suppliants seeking refuge. He, therefore, asked the Emperor to leave them alone, since they would trouble no one except insofar as they were alive. And so they lived with Theoderic farming a small plot of land.[61]

## 23

*(Suda* Π 137)

Pamprepius: he had great power with Zeno. He came from Thebes in Egypt and showed skill in all he attempted. He came to Athens, was appointed a teacher of grammar by the city and taught there for many years,[62] while he himself was instructed in the higher learning by the great Proclus. When an accusation was made against him before Theagenes, one of the authorities there, he was manhandled by him and because he had gained more recondite knowledge than was necessary for a teacher, he went to Byzantium. Although in other respects he proved himself a good and successful man, in a city that was full of Christians he did not hide that he was a Hellene by religion but declared it openly and freely, and thus caused people to suspect that he had other knowledge of secret wisdom. The master Illus received him gladly when they met, and when Pamprepius read a poem in public he rewarded him magnificently and gave him a stipend, partly from his private funds and partly, since he was a teacher, from the public monies. When Illus went off to Isauria, Pamprepius' disparagers contrived a charge against him both that he was a pagan and that he was practising witchcraft and prophecy against the Emperor on behalf of Illus' party, and they persuaded Zeno and Verina, who was then at the height of her power, to expel him from the city.

Pamprepius went off to Pergamum in Mysia. But when Illus learned that he had been driven out on account of himself, he sent and brought him to Isauria and made him his advisor and a member of his household. Moreover, since he had great political intelligence, Illus entrusted him with the administration of those duties of his office for which he did not have time, and when he returned to Byzantium took him along. When, during the revolt of Marcian, Illus was at a loss,

Ἴλλουν αὐτὸς ἐπεθάρσυνε, καὶ τοσοῦτόν γε εἰπὼν ὅτι τὰ τῆς προ- 25
νοίας μεθ᾽ ἡμῶν ἐστι τεταγμένα, παρέσχεν ὑποψίαν τοῖς τότε
ὑπακούσασιν ὡς ἔκ τινος ἀδήλου ταῦτα θειάζοι προγνώσεως. καὶ
ἐκβάντος, ὥσπερ δὴ καὶ ἐξέβη, τοῦ τέλους, πρὸς τὴν τύχην τὸν λόγον
ἐκείνου συμβάλλοντες, αὐτὸν πάντων αἴτιον, οἷα φιλεῖ ὅμιλος, μόνον
ὑπελάμβανον τῶν παραδόξως αὐτοῖς ἀποβαίνειν δοκούντων. 30
(Cf. Σ 1263*)

26 τεταγμένα om. V    27 ἀκούσασιν V    28 ὥσπερ ... ἐξέβη om. V

# 24
(Photius *Bibl. Cod.* 78 = T.1)

## Sedis Incertae

### 25
(*Suda* E 2096)
Ἐπετίμα· ἐπηύξει τὴν τιμήν. οἱ δὲ κερδαίνειν οἰόμενοι ἐπε-
τίμων ὡς λιμώττοντι τὸν σῖτον. ὁ δὲ οὐδὲν ἧττον ἠγόραζε. Μάλχος
φησίν.

### 26
(*Suda* Λ 287)
Λέπρα· εἶδος νόσου. Μάλχος · λέπρα δὲ ἐπήνθει τῷ προσώπῳ
αὐτοῦ.

### 27
(*Suda* Σ 1623)
Καὶ Μάλχος · τῶν συντάξεων στερηθέντες πολλάκις οἱ στρατιῶται καὶ παρακοπτόμενοι τῆς τροφῆς τῆς συνήθους ἐς ἀπόνοιαν
ἦλθον.

### 28
[(*Suda* Υ 534)
Τοὺς δὲ ἀντιστῆναι οἱ τολμήσαντας ὑπολαμβάνων, ὡς ἑκάσ-
τους διέφθειρε. καὶ Μάλχος ....]

Pamprepius encouraged him by saying, "The decrees of Providence are on our side", and this led those who heard him to suspect that he was divining this from some secret foreknowledge. When a thing turned out as it did, they compared his words with the outcome and considered, after the manner of the common herd, that he was the sole cause of what seemed to have happened contrary to their expectations.[63]
(Cf. Σ 1623*)


## 24

(Photius *Bibl. Cod.* 78 = T.1)


## Unplaced Fragments

### 25

(*Suda* E 2096)
Thinking to profit thereby, they raised the price of the grain for him because he was starving. He none the less bought it.


### 26

(*Suda* Λ 287)
Leprosy broke out on his face.


### 27

(*Suda* Σ 1623)
Since they were frequently robbed of their pay and defrauded of their regular rations, the soldiers become desperate.


### 28

[(*Suda* Υ 534)
"He descended suddenly upon those who dared to resist him and killed them one by one." And Malchus . . . .][64]

## NOTES TO MALCHUS

1.    More usually Theoderic the son of Triarius (or Theoderic Strabo) and Theoderic the son of Valamir.

2.    Theoderic Strabo was reconciled with Zeno in 478 but revolted again in support of Marcian in the next year.

3.    Henry (*ad loc.*) takes "perpetual exile" to refer to that of Marcian after the failure of his revolt, though it could equally well indicate the earlier imprisonment of Verina by Illus, which was one of the causes of Marcian's revolt. The Greek seems to support the latter, but it is then hard to identify the subsequently mentioned "earlier plot" of Verina. Perhaps Photius has simply produced a doublet of the same plot which was noted twice by Malchus in two contexts (the revolt of Marcian and relations between Zeno and Illus).

4.    On the Arab Amorkesos (Amir-al-Kais) and Jotaba, at the mouth of the Gulf of Aqaba, see vol. I p.152 n.36.

5.    I have restored the MS reading ὑπὸ Πετραίαν, even though it is rather awkwardly followed by a second ὑπό, since the reading makes better sense than the proposed emendations. (For ὑπό + acc. = "on the borders of" cf. Isocrates *Paneg.* 108: ὑποκειμένης τῆς Εὐβοίας ὑπὸ τὴν Ἀττικήν). It is hardly likely that Leo would have readily ceded effective control of the area around Petra to Amorkesos (which would be the case with the usually-accepted emendation κατά), since the only Roman holding which he controlled was Jotaba. It is much more likely that, as the MS reading says, Leo merely gave official recognition to Amorkesos as ruler of the allied Saracens outside the Empire.

6.    Niebuhr's emendation of λαβών to λαβόντα is unnecessary. Amorkesos gave Leo a picture as a private gift, probably an ikon to signify his conversion to Christianity. He was rewarded from public funds and others' purses. Leo is thus implicitly accused of personal profiteering at others' expense (cf. *Fr.* 3).

7.    These are a part of the Ostrogoths led by Theoderic the son of Triarius, the rival of Theoderic the son of Theodemir (usually called the son of Valamir, his uncle). The second Theoderic was of the Amal royal family and could thus claim legitimacy as ruler of the Ostrogoths. The son of Triarius was a nephew of Aspar's wife. *PLRE* II 'Telogius' remarks that the name of the Roman envoy is strange and suggests an error for 'Pelagius' (2).

8.    I follow *PLRE* II 'Theodericus' 5 in regarding this appointment as *magister utriusque militiae praesentalis*, despite John of
Antioch *Fr.* 210, which seems to make him master of the soldiers in
Thrace. (As *PLRE loc.cit.* notes, the emendation of διέπων to διέποντα
in John would remove the difficulty by making Heracleius master of
the soldiers in Thrace, a post which he is known to have held.)

9.    In this respect Theoderic declared himself the successor of
Aspar, who, after his debacle of 431-34 against Gaiseric, avoided
fighting against the Vandals (Clover 1966 pp.40ff.).

10.    A peace was apparently made on this occasion which lasted
until Justinian's reign (Procopius *Wars* 3,7,26-28).

11.    Both Gordon (1960 p.125) and the translator in Müller seem
to misunderstand this last sentence. Severus did not sell his clothes and
equipment, add the cash raised to that which he had and ransom the
prisoners. The Greek seems to indicate that he offered to buy the
prisoners for the cash, clothes and equipment which he had.

12.    This imitates Thucydides 3,82,4: τὸ δ' ἐμπλήκτως ὀξὺ ἀνδρὸς
μοίρᾳ προσετέθη, from the discussion of the *stasis* that swept Greece.

13.    That the act of buying back the prisoner and freeing him are
separate is clear also from *Fr.* 5. Even a temporary dependence would
presumably have been intolerable for the high-spirited Heracleius.

14.    The non-Malchan *Fr.* 210 of John of Antioch claims that
Theoderic Strabo had Heracleius killed.

15.    This presumably refers to tax remittances and the refusal to
force the payment of taxes owing.

16.    The MS reading βίου is clearly wrong and I have followed
Müller in emending it to Ἰουλίου. I have placed the passage with the
fragments of Malchus solely on the very weak ground that, although
it recounts the same anecdote as the non-Malchan Z 84 (printed on
p.479), it avoids the name 'Constantinople'.

17.    Almost certainly from a communication of Zeno's in which he
lamented his expulsion from Constantinople. Its inclusion in the *Exc.
de Leg. Rom.* suggests that it was from an embassy, perhaps part of the
negotiations that brought Illus back to his side.

18.    Although this article is usually attributed to Malchus, the style
and the name Constantinople suggest otherwise. The form of the name
Harmatus (Adler reports no variant) might indicate association with
A 3970, printed on p.477.

19.    It is clear from *CJ* 5,5,8 that Epinicus had been Zeno's praetorian prefect before Basiliscus' usurpation, and the activity described
in the present passage is that of the praetorian prefect. John of Antioch
(*Fr.* 201,2) says that in 478 he was removed by Zeno from the pre-
fectural throne. This suggests, as *PLRE* II 'Epinicus' points out, that
after his deposition by Basiliscus he was appointed urban prefect (a
lower-ranking position, hence, perhaps, the point of ἀτίμως), which he

remained until his second removal in 478.

**20.**    Malchus, whose name does not appear in Cedrenus, seems to be mentioned only as an alternative source for the fire.

**21.**    In preference to the usual reading ἐκπέμψεω, I have written ἐκπέμψἀν which is based upon ἐκπἐμψαν, which is the reading of the best MS. I have done so because τιμήσαντα below then makes better sense: i.e. Zeno is pretending that Nepos has already conferred the patriciate upon Odovacer. If my emendation is correct, then Zeno is making a genuine attempt to aid Nepos (which seems to have been Malchus' view, to judge from the rest of the passage) and not (as Gordon 1960 p.128) "showing typical vacillation or duplicity".

**22.**    I take τό γε κοινόν τῆς τύχης to refer to the fact that they were both Roman Emperors, so that mutual support was in order.

**23.**    Συνεποτρύνω is very rare and probably taken from Sophocles *Electra* 299. It is a good example of Malchus' tragic manner noted by the *Suda* (M 120).

**24.**    Theoderic the son of Triarius had rebelled against Zeno (cf. *Fr.* 6,2) and had supported Basiliscus, although he had become estranged from him also (Bury 1958, II pp.391f.). Although Theoderic had signed a treaty with Leo (and presumably with Basiliscus), since treaties were personal agreements between rulers, he needed to make one with Zeno to regularise his position.

**25.**    Cf. *Suda* A 3968 = *Fr.* 9,4, where Harmatius is said to have done this in the reign of Leo, presumably after the peace with Theoderic Strabo at the end of the reign.

**26.**    *PLRE* II 'Theodericus' 5 takes this to indicate suspicions that Strabo was intending to substitute Gothic for Roman rule. But since it comes from a propaganda speech by Zeno to his troops, many of whom would have been Isaurian, it is more likely that he is referring to the massacre and expulsion of the Isaurians under Basiliscus.

**27.**    From this and what follows it appears that Strabo was camped very close to the city.

**28.**    The subject of ἀπέστειλεν is usually taken to be Zeno, but it could equally well be the praetorian prefect Sebastianus, notorious for his selling of offices (*Fr.* 16,2).

**29.**    I take ἐπιστήμην to stand in contrast with "practical experience" and to be a comment on Zeno's lack of education.

**30.**    For καθίσταμαι = "commence" cf. Thucydides 1,1.

**31.**    Gordon's interpretation of this fragment (1960 pp.125f.) is erroneous. Alexander had been sent by Zeno to Huneric to win concessions for the Catholics in Africa (Victor of Vita *Hist. Pers.* 2,2). Upon his return he escorted (but did not lead) the Vandal embassy; thus there was no question of his returning with the embassy to Africa, as Gordon suggests. Huneric was clearly seeking a renewal of the treaty of 475, which could be held to have lapsed on Gaiseric's death (a position which Gaiseric had taken upon the death of western Roman Emperors [cf. Priscus *Fr.* 38]), and to this end was seeking to disassociate himself from his father's policies. Not only did he make concessions on the Catholics (Victor of Vita *loc.cit.*), but in the present passage he proposes to drop all outstanding claims against the Emperor and the Roman treasury. These claims, which Gaiseric had apparently still pursued after the treaty of 475 and which Alexander was probably sent to negotiate (hence his financial background and his connection with the sister of Huneric's wife), included the property of Huneric's wife, Eudocia, which Leo had apparently taken back, having earlier granted it to her (Priscus *Fr.* 39), and the property of the Carthaginian merchants plying between Roman ports, which would have been seized near to the beginning of the hostilities of 467-8.

**32.** Προκαλέομαι = "propose" is a common Thucydidean usage (e.g. 1,39; 5,37). Zeno is now apparently signifying acceptance of the proposals which he had earlier rejected (*Fr.* 15).

**33.** The MS reading is corrupt. Hoeschel's emendation is too radical. Malchus' phraseology appears to be imitating Xenophon *Hellenica* 3,2,27: μεδίμνῳ ἀπομετρήσασθαι τὸ ἀργύριον, and my emendation follows the sense of that passage.

**34.** De Boor marks a lacuna here. His own suggestion to fill it, which has the two leaders making an agreement to work together for their advantage, does not seem appropriate, since it seems from *Fr.* 18,3 that they only agreed not to fight each other, but otherwise acted independently. Thus, there is no firm evidence for an alliance, as is usually assumed.

**35.** I take this to refer to those in charge of issuing the supplies stored in the depots (*horrea*) of the area. Thus, Theoderic would know what was conveniently available.

**36.** Presumably these relatives were not Aspar and his sons (as Gordon 1960 p.167), whose deaths Strabo had already recognised by claiming his inheritance (*Fr.* 2), but other members of Aspar's family who might still be alive (cf. *Fr.* 18,4).

**37.** This was probably Juliana, who later married Fl. Areobindus (*PLRE* II 'Ariobindus' 1). Zeno is offering Theoderic an alliance with the imperial family.

**38.** Croke (1982 pp.66-68) plausibly argues that this wall is the defensive wall of the Chersonese, and not the Long Wall of Thrace which protected Constantinople.

**39.** The general sense of this sentence is clear, the precise meaning less so. The emendations proposed do not help much, and I suspect clumsy condensation. One would expect that after Zeno's rebuff, Theoderic would set about systematically collecting supplies for his people; and thus the general sense of κατατεινάμενος ("spreading oneself out over") seems appropriate, although I am unaware of a precise parallel for the usage. In the case of εἰσπράττων, it seems non-sensical to have Theoderic "exacting" what he could not carry, and so I take the subject of ἠδύναντο to be the farmers.

**40.**    Jordanes (*Get.* 57,289) says that Zeno adopted Theoderic in the German manner.

**41.**    Presumably two of the *scholae palatinae.*

**42.**    In the account of Strabo's settlement with Leo (*Fr.* 2) the delivery of Theoderic's property (inherited from Aspar) was requested but not, apparently, granted. Perhaps Basiliscus handed over whatever could be recovered.

**43.**    I.e. the praetorian prefect of Illyricum, John (*PLRE* II 'Ioannes' 29). He was later attacked again, this time by the soldiers (below lines 59-61).

**44.**    The course of events is not fully clear. I take it to be that a proclamation of Zeno, perhaps entrusting the guarding of the city to a contingent of non-Roman troops, caused a riot against his chief representative. To calm the riot the authorities permitted the people to guard the city themselves and to choose their own leader. They organised their own guard but accepted the regular Roman commander.

**45.**    The implication would be that Theoderic did not know that Strabo had made an alliance with the Romans. This is more to the point than the rather feeble emendation, ἔδει σε, accepted by the older editors.

**46.**    The MS reading μόρων makes no sense, and suggested emendations do not seem satisfactory. The sentence can be viewed as a variant of the one which precedes it, in that τὴν δὲ χώραν ἀπαθῆ πᾶσαν διεφύλαξε answers τοῦ μὲν καίειν ... ἀνεῖργε and οὐδὲν τοὺς οἰκοῦντας ἐνταῦθα παραλυπῶν answers τοῦ μὲν ... ἢ φονεύειν τοὺς ἀνθρώπους ἀνεῖργε. If this is so, then the final part should correspond to the statement that Theoderic could not prevent the Goths from obtaining supplies and should indicate that he took a fair measure of supplies from the area. This line of approach suggests that μοιρῶν, which is regularly used of portions of land (cf. just below), could be read here, perhaps in the sense of "estates" (though I know of no exact parallel). In this case, perhaps Malchus is indicating that Theoderic followed the Roman rules for billetting of troops (cf. *CTh.* 7,8,5). The compliance of the people of Heraclea, compared with their refusal of supplies later, is probably to be explained by the fact that they had not yet completed their harvest (cf. line 118 and n.54).

**47.**    Pautalia was on the road between Stobi and Serdica and in the province of Dardania (Procopius *De Aed.* 4,1,31). Since Pautalia was not itself a province, probably μοίρας ... ἐπαρχία should be emended to μοῖρα ... ἐπαρχίας.

**48.**    Sidimund is not claiming, as Gordon's translation indicates (1960 p.172), that the barbarian is attacking Epidamnus, but he alleges that Zeno has permitted him to settle there and that Adamantius has been sent to arrange the settlement. Presumably, in any such settlement the inhabitants of the city could expect to lose at least a portion of their movables.

**49.** Niebuhr, followed by subsequent editors, adds λέγων after τοῖς στρατιώταις, which can, however, easily be understood.

**50.** Clearly Theoderic had already been informed that he was to be settled in Pautalia, disliked the arrangements and then proposed to take Epidamnus. The delay of Adamantius in Thessalonika was, therefore, vital since it enabled Theoderic to stall long enough for Sidimund to ensure that Epidamnus would not be defended.

**51.** This was the *via Egnatia* across the Scardus mountains.

**52.** The phrase ἀπερίοπτοι πάντων imitates Thucydides 1,41.

**53.** Despite the doubts of de Boor, the reading ἐρημίαν seems to be confirmed by *Fr.* 18,2 line 26, where ἐρημίας is used of passage through barren mountains.

**54.** Thus, this journey can be dated to around harvest time (early/middle summer), and Theoderic went forward to attempt to seize badly needed supplies.

**55.** Thus, it is clear that Theoderic had not reached Epidamnus when this discussion was held.

**56.** As often in Malchus, the second sentence addresses in order the points raised in the first. Thus, the muster call was sent to the cities (ἀπανταχοῦ), while Philoxenus (who had actually brought the codicils of appointment for Sabinianus) was sent to announce to Onulf that he had been superseded and to recall the forces with him. Adamantius, of course, and Sabinianus would advance to Lychnidus.

**57.** See n.40.

**58.** He would be a Roman citizen by virtue of his adoption by Zeno (see n.40).

**59.** Presumably the leader of a band of Gothic federates (*PLRE* II 'Gento' 2).

**60.** De Boor suspects, rightly in my view, that something has fallen out of the text. I have supplied κάμνον which is suggested by διαναπαύων and the fact that Strabo is clearly making an excuse to stay near to the city for a while.

**61.** Malchus is noted as an alternative source for the revolt of Marcian by the scholiast on Evagrius *HE* 3,26, ed. Bidez-Parmentier p.244.

**62.** Four years, in fact, 473-76 (*PLRE* II 'Pamprepius').

**63.** The next few lines of this article are usually included as Malchan. I have printed them separately on p.481 for the reasons given in n.9 on p.482. Bernhardy would assign either to Malchus or to

Damascius *Suda* A 1707: ὸ δὲ Παμπρέπιος τούτοις ἀμφίβολος ὀρθεὶς βραχὺ παρεωρᾶτο ("For these reasons Pamprepius appeared unreliable and was for a short while ignored").

**64.** The reference to Malchus is attached to the words that follow. But they are from Xenophon *Anab.* 1,1,7, and, therefore, Bernhardy suggested that what precedes the name is from Malchus and that καί should be changed to φησί or ὡς. *Suda* A 1489 names Malchus as the author of a passage actually from Xenophon *Anab.* 1,2,21.

CANDIDUS
ANONYMA E *SUDA*

Text and Translation

# CANDIDUS

# FRAGMENTA

## 1

(Photius *Bibl. Cod.* 79, I pp.161-66)

Ἀνεγνώσθη Κανδίδου ἱστορίας λόγοι τρεῖς. ἄρχεται μὲν τῆς
ἱστορίας ἀπὸ τῆς Λέοντος ἀναρρήσεως, ὃς ἦν ἐκ Δακίας μὲν τῆς ἐν
Ἰλλυριοῖς στρατιωτικῷ παραγγείλας τάγματι καὶ τελῶν ἄρξας τῶν
ἐν Σηλυμβρίᾳ, τὴν βασιλείαν σπουδῇ Ἄσπαρος ἐγχειρισθείς, ὃς ἦν
Ἀλανὸς μὲν γένος, ἐκ νεαρᾶς δὲ στρατευσάμενος ἡλικίας, καὶ παιδο-         5
ποιησάμενος ἐκ τριῶν γάμων Ἀρδαβούριον, Πατρίκιον, Ἑρμενά-
ριχον, καὶ θηλείας δύο.

Ποιεῖται μὲν ὁ συγγραφεύς, ὡς εἴρηται, ἀρχὴν τῆς ἱστορίας
τὴν ἀρχὴν τῆς Λέοντος βασιλείας, τελευτᾷ δὲ εἰς τὴν ἀναγόρευσιν
Ἀναστασίου. ἔστι δὲ πατρίδος μὲν Ἰσαυρίας, ὡς αὐτός φησι, τῆς         10
Τραχείας, ἐπιτήδευμα δὲ ἔσχεν ὑπογραφεὺς τῶν ἐν Ἰσαύροις
πλεῖστον ἰσχυσάντων. τὴν δὲ θρησκείαν χριστιανὸς ἦν καὶ ὀρθό-
δοξος· τήν τε γὰρ τετάρτην σύνοδον ἐπαίνοις στέφει, καὶ τοὺς κατ᾽
αὐτῆς καινοτομοῦντας καθάπτεται δικαίως.

Τὴν δὲ φράσιν οὐκ ἔχει πρέπουσαν λόγῳ ἱστορικῷ· ταῖς τε         15
γὰρ ποιητικαῖς λέξεσιν ἀπειροκάλως τε κέχρηται καὶ μειρακιωδῶς,
καὶ ἡ συνθήκη αὐτῷ εἰς τὸ τραχύτερον καὶ δύσηχον ἐκδιθυραμ-
βοῦται, ὥσπερ αὖ πάλιν εἰς τὸ ἐκλελυμένον τε καὶ ἐκμελὲς ὑπτιάζει.
νεωτερίζει δὲ καὶ ταῖς συντάξεσιν, οὐκ εἰς τὸ γλαφυρὸν μᾶλλον καὶ
ἐπαφρόδιτον, ὥσπερ ἕτεροι, ἀλλ᾽ ὥστε δυσχερὴς ἀκοῦσαι καὶ τοῦ         20
ἡδέος ὑπερόριος. πλὴν αὐτὸς ἑαυτοῦ πολὺ βελτίων ἐνιαχοῦ τοῖς
λόγοις πάντα γενόμενος, συμμιγῆ τὴν ἱστορίαν καὶ ἐξ ἀνομοιοτάτων
ἁρμόζων ἁλίσκεται. οὗτος ἰσχυρίζεται τὴν Ἰσαυρίαν ἀπὸ τοῦ Ἡσαῦ
λαβεῖν τὴν ἐπωνυμίαν.

Διέρχεται δὲ ἐν μὲν τῷ πρώτῳ λόγῳ τὴν Ἄσπαρος καὶ τῶν         25
παίδων αὐτοῦ δυναστείαν, τὴν ἀνάρρησιν διὰ τοῦ Ἄσπαρος Λέοντος,

13-14 τῶν . . . καινοτομούντων Μ   18 ὥσπερ . . . ὑπτιάζει om. Μ

# CANDIDUS

## FRAGMENTS

### 1

(Photius *Bibl. Cod.* 79, I pp.161-66)

Read three books of the History of Candidus. He begins his History from the proclamation of Leo, a native of Dacia in Illyricum, who was a legionary tribune and commander of the troops in Selymbria. He became Emperor with the support of Aspar, an Alan by race and a soldier from his youth, who had three sons by three marriages, Ardabur, Patricius and Ermenaric, as well as two daughters.

As I have said, the historian begins his History with the beginning of Leo's reign and he ends with the proclamation of Anastasius. Candidus was, as he himself says, a native of Isauria, from Tracheia. By profession he was secretary to the most powerful men in Isauria. He was an orthodox Christian by religion, for he heaps praises upon the fourth synod[1] and justly censures those who brought in innovations contrary to it.

He does not have a style appropriate for history. He uses poetic vocabulary in a tasteless and immature manner, and his forays into compound sentences are cruder and harsher-sounding than when he falls back into his loose and dissonant style of writing. He also innovates with his syntax, which, however, does not contribute to charm and elegance in the writing, as in other authors, but makes it harsh and unpleasant to the ear. Except for some places where his writing vastly improves, we find that he has written a history that is a mixture of disparate elements. He insists that Isauria takes its name from Esau.

In his first book he describes the power of Aspar and his sons, the proclamation of Leo through Aspar's agency, the fire which damaged

466    *Candidus: Text*

τὸν συμβάντα τῇ πόλει ἐμπρησμόν, καὶ ὅσα Ἄσπαρι περὶ τούτου ἐπὶ
τὸ κοινῇ συμφέρον διαπέπρακται. καὶ περὶ Τιτιανοῦ καὶ Βιβιανοῦ καὶ
ὡς περὶ αὐτῶν διηνέχθη Ἄσπαρ καὶ ὁ βασιλευς, καὶ οἷα εἰς ἀλλήλους ἀπεφθέγξαντο. καὶ ὡς ὁ βασιλεὺς διὰ τοῦτο ἡταιρίσατο τὸ         30
Ἰσαύρων γένος διὰ Ταρασικοδίσσα Ῥουσουμβλαδεώτου, ὃν καὶ
Ζήνωνα μετονομάσας γαμβρὸν ἐποιήσατο, τὴν προτέραν γυναῖκα
θανάτου νόμῳ ἀποβαλόντα. καὶ ὡς Ἀρδαβούριος ἐς τὸ ἐναντίον
μελετῶν τῷ βασιλεῖ, καὶ αὐτὸς οἰκειοποιήσασθαι τοὺς Ἰσαύρους
διενοήθη· καὶ ὅτι Μαρτῖνος, οἰκεῖος ὢν Ἀρδαβουρίου, μηνύει Ταρα-      35
σικοδίσσᾳ ἅπερ Ἀρδαβουρίῳ κατὰ βασιλέως ἐτυρεύετο· καὶ ὡς
ἐντεῦθεν εἰς τὸ τραχύτερον τῆς ἐς ἀλλήλους ἐπινοίας προϊούσης
ἀναιρεῖ Λέων ὁ βασιλεὺς Ἄσπαρα καὶ τοὺς παῖδας Ἀρδαβούριον καὶ
Πατρίκιον τὸν Καίσαρα. ἀλλ' ὁ μὲν Καῖσαρ τῶν πληγῶν ἀνενεγκὼν
παραδόξως διεσώθη καὶ διέζησεν. ἀλλὰ καὶ ὁ ἕτερος τῶν παίδων       40
Ἀρμενέριχος οὐ συμπαρὼν τῷ φύσαντι τὸν φόνον τότε διέφυγε.

Ταρασικοδίσσαν δὲ γαμβρὸν ἐπὶ θυγατρὶ Ἀριάδνῃ Λέων ὁ
βασιλεὺς ποιεῖται, καὶ μετονομάζει Ζήνωνα, στρατηγὸν τῆς Ἕω
χειροτονήσας. καὶ τὰ κατὰ Ἀφρικὴν Βασιλίσκου εὐτυχήματα καὶ
δυστυχήματα. καὶ ὡς Λέων πολλὰ βουληθεὶς καὶ διαμηχανησάμενος      45
Ζήνωνα τὸν γαμβρὸν ἀνειπεῖν βασιλέα, τῶν ὑπηκόων μὴ παραδεχο-
μένων οὐκ ἴσχυσε, καὶ ὡς πρὸ τελευτῆς αὐτοῦ τὸν ἔγγονον μὲν αὐτοῦ
ἐκ Ζήνωνος φύντα τῇ Ἀριάδνῃ· καὶ ὡς μετὰ τελευτὴν Λέοντος ὁ παῖς
Λέων Ζήνωνα τὸν πατέρα, συναινέσει τῆς βουλῆς, βασιλέα ἔστεψε.

Λεπτομερής τε τῆς Ἰσαύρων γενεαλογίας ἀφήγησις· καὶ ὡς       50
εἴησαν ἀπόγονοι τοῦ Ἡσαῦ, πολλὴ σπουδὴ καὶ διήγησις.

Ὅπως τε Ζήνων ὑπὸ Βηρίνης ἀπατηθεὶς φεύγει γυναικὶ ἅμα
καὶ μητρὶ τῆς πόλεως καὶ τῆς βασιλείας· καὶ ὡς Βηρῖνα, ἐλπίδι τοῦ
συναφθῆναι Πατρικίῳ τῷ μαγίστρῳ καὶ βασιλεύειν αὐτόν, τὸν γαμβρὸν αὐτῆς φυγαδεύσασα ἐξ ἀπάτης, καὶ αὐτὴ τῆς ἐλπίδος ἐσφάλη,     55
τῶν ἐν τέλει Βασιλίσκον τὸν αὐτῆς ἀδελφὸν ἀνειπόντων βασιλέα.
περί τε τῆς Ἰσαύρων ἐν Κωνσταντινουπόλει ἀμυθήτου σφαγῆς. καὶ
ὡς μετὰ Νέπωτα βασιλέα Ῥώμης Αὐγούστουλον ὁ πατὴρ Ὀρέστης
Ῥώμης κατεπράξατο βασιλεύειν. ταῦτα ὁ πρῶτος λόγος.

Ὁ δὲ δεύτερος, ὅπως Πατρίκιος ὁ μάγιστρος, ὁ Βηρίνῃ συμ-       60
φθειρόμενος, ἐπαγανακτήσαντος αὐτῷ Βασιλίσκου ἀπεβίω, καὶ διὰ
τοῦτο Βηρῖνα δι' ἔχθρας πρὸς τὸν ἀδελφὸν καταστᾶσα καὶ Ζήνωνι
διὰ χρημάτων τὴν τῆς βασιλείας ἀνάληψιν συμπράττουσα, τὰ ἔσχατα ἔπασχεν ὑπὸ τοῦ ἀδελφοῦ, καὶ εἰ μὴ διέκλεψεν αὐτὴν Ἄρματος

---

37 ὑπονοίας M      41 φύσαντι scripsi sec. Gordon (1960 p.206 n.4) [φύντι
codd.      48 φύντα M [φύντι A φύντας A²      54 αὐτόν A¹ [αὐτῶν AM      55
αὐτὴ A [αὐτῆς M      64 ὕπερ M

the city,[2] and the measures which Aspar took for the public good on this occasion. He mentions Titianus and Vivianus and relates how Aspar and the Emperor disagreed over them and what they said to one another.[3] He tells how, as a result of this, the Emperor allied himself with the Isaurian people through Tarasicodissa the son of Rusumbladeotus, whose name he changed to Zeno and whom he made his son-in-law after Zeno's former wife had died; how Ardabur, who was himself plotting to oppose the Emperor, planned to bring the Isaurians over to his side;[4] how Martinus, an attendant of Ardabur, told Tarasicodissa what Ardabur was contriving against the Emperor; and how, their intentions against one another having for this reason grown more savage, the Emperor Leo destroyed Aspar and his sons Ardabur and the Caesar Patricius. But the Caesar unexpectedly survived his injuries and lived on.[5] The third son, Ermenaric, was not present with his father and so at this time escaped the massacre. The Emperor Leo married Tarasicodissa to his daughter Ariadne, changed his name to Zeno and made him general of the East.

Candidus also describes the successes and failures of Basiliscus in Africa,[6] and he tells how Leo greatly desired to proclaim his son-in-law, Zeno, Emperor and plotted to that end, although he did not succeed, since his subjects would not accept him. But before his death he did elevate his grandson by Zeno and Ariadne, and after his death Zeno, with the approval of the senate, was crowned Emperor by his son Leo.

Then follow a detailed digression upon the genealogy of the Isaurians and much earnest argument to prove that they were the descendents of Esau.

Candidus describes how Zeno, deceived by Verina, fled with his wife and his mother from the city and his throne; how Verina tricked her son-in-law into flight hoping that she would marry Patricius, the master of the offices, and that he would become Emperor; and how she herself was disappointed in her hopes when the high officials proclaimed Basiliscus, her brother, Emperor. Candidus also tells of the enormous slaughter of the Isaurians at Constantinople and how after Nepos, the Emperor of Rome, Augustulus was made Emperor by his father Orestes. These are the contents of the first book.

The second book tells how the master Patricius, Verina's adulterer, angered Basiliscus and lost his life. As a result Verina came to hate her brother and gave financial aid to Zeno in his attempts to regain his throne. She suffered very badly at her brother's hands and would probably have been killed if Armatus[7] had not stolen her

468    Candidus: Text

ἐκ τοῦ ναοῦ, τάχα ἂν καὶ διεφθάρη. ὡς Ἀρμάτος τῇ γαμετῇ συν-      65
διαφθειρόμενος Βασιλίσκου ἐπὶ μέγα δυναστείας ἤρθη, καὶ ὡς
ὕστερον τὸν κατὰ Ζήνωνος πιστευθεὶς πόλεμον, ἀπέκλινεν ἐπὶ συνθήκαις δι' Ἴλλου πρὸς αὐτόν, καὶ εὐδοκιμῶν ἐπὶ Ζήνωνος, ὡς καὶ τὸν
υἱὸν Βασιλίσκον Καίσαρα ἰδεῖν, ὕστερον ἐκρεουργήθη, καὶ ὁ παῖς ἐκ
τοῦ Καίσαρος εἰς τοὺς ἐν Βλαχέρναις ἀναγνώστας ἐτέλεσεν. ὡς πρὸ      70
τούτων Βασιλίσκος Μάρκον τὸν ἴδιον υἱὸν Καίσαρα ἀνεῖπεν, εἶτα καὶ
βασιλέα. καὶ ὡς Ἴλλους συνέβη Ζήνωνι εἰς φιλίαν, καὶ πάλιν ἀναλαβεῖν παρεσκεύασε τὴν βασιλείαν· καὶ ὡς καταστασιασθεὶς βασιλεὺς σὺν τῇ γυναικὶ Ζηνωνίδι καὶ τέκνοις καταφεύγει εἰς τὴν
ἐκκλησίαν, κἀκεῖθεν ἀπάτῃ Ἀρμάτου ἐκβληθεὶς ἐξορίζεται εἰς      75
Καππαδοκίαν, εἶτα παγγενεὶ κατασφάζεται.

Ὡς Πέτρου τοῦ δυσσεβοῦς τὰς τῆς ἀνατολῆς ταράσσοντος
ἐκκλησίας Καλανδίωνα Ζήνων ὁ βασιλεὺς εἰς τὸ ἱερᾶσθαι Ἀντιοχείας ἀπέστειλε, καὶ δεόμενος χρημάτων ἐκ μηνυμάτων ἐπέτυχε,
καὶ πολλοὶ νεωτερίσαντες κατ' αὐτοῦ καὶ ἑαλωκότες δίκην ἔδοσαν.      80
ὡς Ἴλλους πολλὰ τῇ Ῥωμαίων συνήνεγκε πολιτείᾳ ταῖς τε κατὰ
πόλεμον ἀνδραγαθίαις καὶ ταῖς κατὰ πόλιν φιλοτιμίαις τε καὶ δικαιο-
πραγίαις.

Ὡς μετὰ τὴν ἀναίρεσιν τοῦ βασιλέως Νέπωτος Ῥώμης καὶ
τὸν διωγμὸν τοῦ μετ' αὐτὸν Αὐγουστούλου Ὀδόακρος Ἰταλίας καὶ      85
αὐτῆς ἐκράτησε Ῥώμης· καὶ στασιασάντων αὐτῷ τῶν δυσμικῶν
Γαλατῶν, διαπρεσβευσαμένων τε αὐτῶν καὶ Ὀδοάκρου πρὸς Ζήνωνα, Ὀδοάκρῳ μᾶλλον ὁ Ζήνων ἀπέκλινεν.

Ὡς Ἀλανός τις Ἴλλουν ἀνελεῖν βουληθεὶς καὶ πλήξας Ἐπι-
νίκιον εἶπεν, ὃς ἦν οἰκεῖος Βηρίνῃ, τὴν ἀναίρεσιν ὑποθέσθαι· καὶ ὡς      90
ἐξεδόθη Ἐπινίκιος Ἴλλῳ καὶ ὡς ὑποσχέσει καὶ ἀμνηστίας καὶ εὐ-
εργεσιῶν ἐξεῖπε πάντα Ἐπινίκιος ὅσα ἐπεβούλευε Βηρῖνα κατὰ
Ἴλλου· καὶ ὡς Ζήνων διὰ τοῦτο Βηρῖναν ἐκδίδωσιν, ὁ δὲ αὐτὴν εἰς
φρούριον Κιλικίας ὑπερορίσας ἠσφαλίσατο. ὡς Παμπρεπίῳ τῷ
δυσσεβεῖ διὰ Μάρσου Ἴλλους φιλωθεὶς ἅπαντα κατὰ μικρὸν συνέχει      95
τὰ αὐτοῦ. ὡς ἐμφύλιος συνέστη Ζήνωνι πόλεμος ἐξάρχοντος Μαρκιανοῦ καὶ Προκοπίου υἱῶν τοῦ βασιλεύσαντος Ῥώμης Ἀνθεμίου·
καὶ κρατήσαντος Ζήνωνος δι' Ἴλλου πρεσβύτερος μὲν Μαρκιανὸς
ἐχειροτονήθη, ὁ δὲ Προκόπιος πρὸς Θεοδώριχον τὸν ἐν Θρᾴκῃ
διέφυγε. καὶ ὡς ὑπερορισθεὶς Μαρκιανὸς ἐν Καππαδοκίᾳ καὶ δια-      100
φυγὼν ἐτάραξε τὴν κατὰ Ἄγκυραν Γαλατίαν, εἶτα συλληφθεὶς εἰς
Ἰσαυρίαν διῳκίσθη. καὶ ὡς ἡ πρὸς Ἴλλουν ἔχθρα τῷ βασιλεῖ

65 γαμετῇ A [γυναικὶ M      69-70 ἐκ τοῦ A [ἀπὸ M      71 ἀνεῖπεν M [εἶπεν A
73-74 Βασιλίσκος A²      75 Ἀρμάτου edd. [Ἀρμάτος AM      76 παγγενεὶ edd.
[παγγενῇ codd.      79 ἀπέσταλκε M

away from the church. Armatus seduced the wife of Basiliscus and was raised to the height of power.[8] But when he was entrusted with the war against Zeno, he defected and came to terms with him through the mediation of Illus. Being high in Zeno's favour, he saw his son, Basiliscus, named Caesar. But later he was butchered, and his son was deposed and enrolled as a reader at Blachernae. Before this Basiliscus had proclaimed his own son, Marcus, Caesar and then Emperor. Illus sided with Zeno and prepared to restore him to his throne. The Emperor, beaten in battle, fled to the church with his wife, Zenonis, and their children. Armatus lured him out of there by a trick,[9] and he was exiled to Cappadocia and then killed along with his whole family.

When the impious Peter was troubling the churches of the East, Zeno sent Calandion to be bishop of Antioch.[10] When Zeno needed money, he obtained it through the laying of charges by informers. Many rebelled against him, were captured and paid the penalty. Illus rendered many services to the Roman state both through his bravery in war and through acts of generosity and justice in the city.

After the assassination of Nepos and the expulsion of Augustulus, Odovacer in his own person ruled Italy and Rome.[11] When the Gauls of the West revolted against Odovacer, both they and Odovacer sent an embassy to Zeno.[12] He preferred to support Odovacer.

A certain Alan attempted to kill Illus and, when he had struck him, said that Epinicius, a dependent of Verina, had instigated the attempt.[13] Epinicius was handed over to Illus and, upon a promise of amnesty and rewards, revealed all of Verina's plotting against Illus. As a result Zeno handed over Verina, and Illus exiled her to a fortress in Cilicia, thus ensuring his own safety. Through the agency of Marsus he became friendly with the impious Pamprepius and gradually caused all his own affairs to deteriorate. Zeno was faced with a civil war waged against him by Marcian and Procopius, sons of Anthemius, who had been Emperor at Rome. Zeno prevailed through Illus, and Marcian, the elder, was made a priest, while Procopius fled to Theoderic in Thrace.[14] Marcian was exiled to Cappadocia where he escaped from custody and caused disturbances in Galatia around Ancyra. Then he was recaptured and removed to Isauria. The Emperor began to regard Illus with

συνέστη καὶ ηὐξήθη. οὕτω καὶ ὁ δεύτερος.

Ὁ δὲ τρίτος ἄλλα τε περιέχει καὶ ὡς εἰς τὸ ἐμφανὲς Ἴλλους
ἐπαναστὰς Ζήνωνι βασιλέα Λεόντιον σὺν Βηρίνῃ ἀνεῖπεν, ὅπως τε    105
δυσπραγήσαντες ἐπολιορκήθησαν καὶ ἁλόντες ἀπετμήθησαν, καὶ
τἄλλα ἕως τῆς Ζήνωνος τελευτῆς.

## 2

### (Suda X 245)

Κάνδιδος ἱστοριογράφος φησὶν ὅτι ὁ Λέων ὁ Μακέλλης, ὁ μετὰ
Μαρκιανὸν βασιλεύσας, περὶ τὴν ἐκστρατείαν τὴν κατὰ Βανδήλων
ἄπειρα χρήματα δεδαπάνηκεν. ἦσαν γάρ, ὡς οἱ ταῦτα ἐφανέρωσαν
κεχειρικότες, διὰ μὲν τῶν ὑπάρχων χρυσίου λίτραι τετρακισμύριαι
πρὸς ἑπτακισχιλίαις · διὰ δὲ τοῦ κόμητος τῶν θησαυρῶν ἑπτακισ-    5
χίλιαι πρὸς μυρίαις καὶ ἀργυρίου λίτραι ἑπτακόσιαι χιλιάδες, ἄτερ
τῶν ἀνηλωμένων ἐκ τῶν δημευσίμων ἀρχόντων καὶ ἐκ τοῦ βασιλέως Ἀνθεμίου.

6 ἄτερ A [ἅτε rel. codd.

growing hatred. These are the contents of the second book.

The third book describes, among other things, how Illus broke into open revolt against Zeno and, together with Verina, declared Leontius Emperor. They failed, were placed under siege, captured and beheaded.[15] This book deals with other events up to the death of Zeno.

## 2

(*Suda* X 245)

Candidus the historian says that Leo the Butcher, the Emperor after Marcian, spent an enormous sum of money on the expedition against the Vandals. For the officials in charge of these matters revealed that 47,000 pounds of gold came through the prefects, and through the count of the treasuries an additional 17,000 pounds of gold and 700,000 pounds of silver, as well as[16] monies raised through confiscations and from the Emperor Anthemius.

## NOTES TO CANDIDUS

**1.** The Council of Chalcedon of 451, which condemned the monophysite teachings of the Alexandrian bishop, Dioscurus.

**2.** See Priscus *Fr.* 42.

**3.** Titianus is more usually Tatianus. The cause of the quarrel between Leo and Aspar is not clear. Henry (*ad Photii loc.*) suggests a dispute over policy towards the Vandals, but this is no more than a possibility. He also remarks Cedrenus' report (I p.607) of a quarrel over the appointment of an urban prefect, but this could not have been over Tatianus, who had been prefect 450-52.

**4.** On further involvement by Ardabur in plotting against Leo see Priscus *Fr.* 56.

**5.** Priscus (*Fr.* 61) and most other sources say that he was killed. In fact, Candidus first seems to indicate that he was killed. Is this careless condensation by Photius, or is it an example of συμμιγῆ τὴν ἱστορίαν καὶ ἐξ ἀνομοιοτάτων of which he has just complained? In the second case Photius would be accusing Candidus not only of stylistic heterogeneity but also of clumsily fitting together his discrepant sources.

**6.** See Priscus *Fr.* 53.

**7.** This seems to be the correct form of his name (see *PLRE* II 'Armatus'), although Malchus and others call him Harmatius.

**8.** See *Suda* A 3970, printed on p.476.

**9.** The trick being a promise that his and his family's blood would not be shed (Anon. Val. 9,43, who says that to keep the promise Zeno had them walled up in a dry cistern where they died of cold).

**10.** Peter the Fuller, a monophysite, was first consecrated bishop of Antioch in 371. He was exiled three times. Calandion was sent to replace him in 481, not by Zeno but by Acacius, the patriarch of Constantinople. Calandion was deposed in 485, and Peter returned again to his throne which he occupied until 488.

**11.** This is probably careless condensation by Photius. Nepos was not assassinated until 480, whereas Odovacer deposed Augustulus in 476.

**12.** These embassies seem to be distinct from those of the Italians, of Odovacer and of Nepos remarked by Malchus *Fr.* 14.

**13.** On Epinicius see *Suda* E 2494 (= Malchus *Fr.* 10). *PLRE* II has separate entries for Epinicius, the οἰκεῖος of Verina, and Epinicus, the praetorian prefect of 475 and the subject of the *Suda* article cited, although it admits that the two are probably identical.

**14.** Theoderic the son of Triarius (cf. Malchus *Fr.* 22).

**15.** The rebellion lasted from 484 until the capture in 488 of the fortress of Papirius (or Cherris) to which they had fled.

**16.** Adler's reading of ἄτερ on the authority of one MS seems preferable to ἄτε, read by older editors. All four sources of revenue are thus clearly specified: the chests of the praetorian prefects (of the East and Illyricum); of the count of the largesses (κόμητος τῶν θησαυρῶν); of the count of the privy purse (ἐκ τῶν δημευσίμων = confiscated estates); and Anthemius' contributions.

## ANONYMA E *SUDA*

### 1

(A 783)

Ἀκάκιος· ὁ πατριάρχης Κωνσταντινουπόλεως, αἰδέσιμος ἦν ὡς οὐκ ἄλλος τις. ὀρφανοτρόφος γὰρ γεγονὼς καὶ καλῶς τὰ τῶν ὀρφανῶν διοικῶν πᾶσιν ἐφαίνετο καθ᾽ ἡδονήν. καὶ δὴ καὶ τῷ βασιλεῖ Λέοντι συνήθης γεγονὼς ὑπερφυῶς ἤρεσκε καὶ τούτῳ πρώτῳ ἀεὶ πάντα ἀνεκοινοῦτο τά τε κοινὰ καὶ τὰ ἴδια. καὶ ὅτε τὴν βουλὴν   5
ἤθροιζε, συνεκάλει καὶ τοῦτον καὶ τῆς σκέψεως ἀρχὴν ἐξ αὐτοῦ πάσης ἐτίθετο. ὃς Ἀκάκιος τὴν τοῦ Λέοντος τοῦ Μακέλλη ὠμότητα συνιδὼν πρὸς τούς τι λυπήσαντας καὶ τὸ ἦθος ἀκριβῶς τὸ ἐκείνου φωράσας, ὅτι τοῖς ἐπαινοῦσι μόνον ὑπάρχει εὐάλωτον, ἐπετήδευε πάντα τὰ ἐκείνου θαυμάζειν. τοιγαροῦν πειθήνιον αὐτὸν εἶχεν ἑτοί-   10
μως τόν τε θυμὸν αὐτοῦ ῥᾳδίως κατέστελλε καὶ πολλοῖς προσκε-
κρουκόσι τὴν σωτηρίαν ἐπραγματεύετο καὶ τοὺς ἐξορίαν ἀΐδιον ἔχοντας ἀνεκαλεῖτο πρὸς τὴν πατρίδα. οὗτος μετὰ θάνατον Γενναδίου, πατριάρχου Κωνσταντινουπόλεως, σπουδῇ Ζήνωνος ἱερᾶσθαι προεβλήθη. ὃς ὢν ἀρχικὸς καὶ πάσας τὰς ἐκκλησίας ὑφ᾽ ἑαυτὸν   15
ποιήσας πεφροντισμένως τῶν ἐν αὐταῖς κεκληρωμένων ἐποιεῖτο τὴν κηδεμονίαν, οἱ εὐχαριστοῦντες ἐν γραφαῖς ἀνέθηκαν αὐτὸν κατὰ τοὺς εὐκτηρίους οἴκους. ἐπείπερ οὖν ἀθρόον ἐν πάσαις ταῖς ἐκκλησίαις ἐδείχθησαν αὐτοῦ εἰκόνες, ᾠήθησάν τινες κενοδοξοῦντα τὴν ἀνά-
θεσιν προστετάχεναι οὐ μικρὰν ἔχοντες τῆς ὑπονοίας πίστωσιν, τὴν   20
ἐκ ψηφίδων γραφὴν δημιουργηθεῖσαν ἐν τῇ πρὸς τῷ νεωρίῳ ἐκκλησίᾳ. τοῦ γὰρ ἔργου παντὸς ἐπὶ Γενναδίου τελεσθέντος εἰς τὸν ἐπιφανῆ τόπον ἐξετύπωσαν αὐτὸν τοῦ νεὼ καὶ μεταξὺ τοῦδε τὸν Σωτῆρα λέγοντα τῷ Γενναδίῳ, λῦσον τὸν ναὸν τοῦτον, καὶ ἐπὶ τοῦ, μετά σε ἐγερῶ αὐτόν. ἐκ τῶν τοιούτων οὖν εἰκόνων Ἀκάκιος, εἰ καὶ   25
εὐμετάδοτος ἦν καὶ προστατικός, ἀλλὰ δοξομανὴς πᾶσιν ἔδοξεν ὑπάρχειν. ζήτει περὶ τοῦτον ἐν τῷ Βασιλίσκος.

12-13 τοῖς ... ἔχουσιν AGIT

474

# ANONYMOUS ARTICLES FROM THE *SUDA*

## 1

(A 783)

Acacius, the patriarch of Constantinople. He was the most venerable of all. He cared for orphans, and all observed with pleasure how well he arranged their affairs. He became acquainted with the Emperor Leo and so greatly pleased him that he discussed his private and public business with him first of all.[1] When he convened the senate, he invited Acacius and had him begin every discussion. When Acacius observed the savagery of Leo the Butcher towards those who annoyed him at all, he studied his character carefully, learned that it was swayed only by praise and was careful to do everything to hold the Emperor's admiration. Thus he readily kept Leo docile and easily restrained his anger, ensured the safety of many who had offended him and recalled to their homeland those who had been sentenced to perpetual exile. After the death of Gennadius, the patriarch of Constantinople, with the support of Zeno he was advanced to the patriarchate. Since he was a man fit for office and gave thought for the churches under him, he took care of those holding positions in these churches, and they, out of gratitude, set up paintings of him in their oratories. When a large number of images of him had appeared in all the churches, some men thought that out of vainglory he had ordered them to be set up, and they had not a small confirmation of their suspicion in the mosaic constructed in the church by the dockyard. Although this whole building was completed during the patriarchate of Gennadius, in the most visible point in the nave they worked in a figure of Acacius and next to him the Saviour saying to Gennadius, "Free this church", and above him, "After you I shall raise up him". As a result of such depictions Acacius seemed to all to crave fame, even if he was a generous man and a champion. (You will find more on him under 'Basiliscus'.)

2

(A 3970)

Ἀρμάτος · ὅτι Βασιλίσκος ὁ βασιλεύς, ἐπείπερ ὡς συγγενεῖ τῷ
Ἀρμάτῳ ἀδεῶς ἐπέτρεπεν ἐντυγχάνειν Ζηνωνίδι τῇ βασιλίδι, τριβο-
μένης σφίσι τῆς ὁμιλίας καὶ τοῦ κάλλους αὐτῶν οὐκ εὐπαροδεύτου
ὄντος, ἄμφω ἀλλήλων ἐκτόπως ἤρων. ῥίψεις οὖν ὀμμάτων ἐπ᾿ ἀλλήλους ἐγίνοντο καὶ παρεκστροφαὶ συνεχεῖς προσώπων καὶ μειδια-        5
μάτων μεταδόσεις · πόνος τε μετὰ ταῦτα ἔρωτος ὑπ᾿ ὄψιν στεγομένου.
ἐπεὶ δὲ κοινωσάμενοι τὸ πάθος Δανιὴλ εὐνούχῳ καὶ Μαρίᾳ μαίᾳ
ἰάσαντο τοῦτο μόλις τῇ τῆς μίξεως ἰατρείᾳ, Ζηνωνὶς Βασιλίσκον διὰ
θωπείας ἦγε τοῦ τὸν ἐραστὴν ἔχειν ἐν τῇ πολιτείᾳ τὰ πρωτεῖα.
ὁρῶν δὲ Θεοδώριχος τιμώμενον ἐκ πάντων Ἀρμάτον ἤσχαλλεν ὡς     10
παρευδοκιμούμενος ἐκ νέου τριχῶν μόνον καὶ τῆς ἄλλης φροντί-
ζοντος σωμασκίας. ὁ δ᾿ Ἀρμάτος ἔκ τε φορᾶς χρημάτων καὶ τιμῆς
ἀπλέτου τυφωθεὶς οὐδένα αὐτοῦ ᾤετο διοίσειν ἐπ᾿ ἀνδρείᾳ. καὶ
τοσοῦτον αὐτοῦ ἥδε ἡ ἄλη ἐκράτει, ὡς σκευὴν ἀναλαμβάνειν Ἀχιλ-
λέως, οὕτω τε περιβαίνειν ἐς ἵππον καὶ κατὰ τὸν ἱππόδρομον φρυάτ-   15
τεσθαι τοῦ οἴκου. ἐξῆρε δὲ τοῦτον πλείω πρὸς τοιαύτην δόξαν
μαίνεσθαι τὸ ὑπὸ δήμου σύρφακος ἐν εὐφημίαις ἀνακαλεῖσθαι
Πύρρον · ὃς εἰ μὲν οὕτως ἐβόα διὰ τὸ ἐρυθροπρόσωπον εἶναι, ἔλεγεν
εἰκότα, εἰ δ᾿ ὡς πρὸς ἔπαινον ἀνδρείας, ἔθελγεν ὡς νέον. οὐ γὰρ
ἥρωας ἔβαλλεν ὡς Πύρρος, ἀλλὰ γυναιμανὴς ἦν ὡς Πάρις.        20
(Cf. A 1167, 4301, Σ 838, 1671)

13 ἐπ᾿ [ἐν A    14 ἐπεκράτει GIM    16 οἴκου [ἵππου V ἵππου τρόπον Port.
ὄχλου Toup    18 ἐρυθροπρεπὴς G

3

(E 3770)

Εὐτόκιος, ἀπὸ Θράκης ἐλθὼν οὔτε γνώμην ἐπιεικής τις ἦν
οὔτε γένους εὖ ἥκων, ἀλλὰ στρατιώτης μὲν ὁ τυχών, πολλὰ δὲ
χρήματα κοινὰ τοῦ ἰδίου τάγματος ὑποκλέψας ᾤχετο φεύγων εἰς τὴν
Παλαιστίνην. ἐπεχείρησε μὲν οὖν Ἐλευθεροπολίταις ἑαυτὸν ἐγκατα-
λέξαι, τῆς βουλῆς μετασχὼν ἐπὶ χρήμασι μεγάλοις. καὶ γὰρ ἐγ-        5
λίχετο τὴν τύχην μεταβαλεῖν ἐς τὸ εὐγενέστερον. καίτοι ἔδει
πρότερον μετατίθεσθαι τὴν προαίρεσιν εἰς τὸ κρεῖττον, ἀλλ᾿ ὅμως οἱ
Ἐλευθεροπολῖται τὸ πλῆθος ὑπειδόμενοι τῶν χρημάτων οὐ προσεδέ-
ξαντο τὸν Εὐτόκιον. ὁ δὲ μετεχώρησεν ἐς τὴν Ἀσκάλωνα. καὶ ὁ τότε
πρωτεύων Κρατερὸς εὐμενῶς αὐτὸν ὑπεδέξατο μετὰ τῶν χρημάτων    10

1 γνώμης GIFVM    2 ἀλλὰ [οὗτος V    4-5 καταλέξαι GIVM

## 2

(A 3970)

Harmatus. Since the Emperor Basiliscus confidently allowed Harmatus, as a relative, to meet with the Empress Zenonis, they spent much time in one another's company. Since the beauty of both of them was not negligible, they fell exceedingly[2] in love. They traded glances, then continually looked at each other and exchanged smiles. After this came disease – love kept hidden from view. They told Daniel, an eunuch, and Maria, a midwife, of their suffering and at last they cured it by the medicine of copulation. Thereafter, by flattery Zenonis persuaded Basiliscus to make her lover the most powerful man in the state. Theoderic[3] took it hard that Harmatus was courted by all and that he was surpassed in honour by a young man who thought only of his hair and attending to his body. Harmatus, deluded by the wealth that he was amassing and his never-ending honours, thought that no one surpassed him in manliness. This obsession so gripped him that dressed up like Achilles he would mount a horse and parade about the hippodrome of his house. When the rabble acclaimed him, calling him "Pyrrhus", this all the more aroused his craving for such glory. If the mob shouted this because of his ruddy complexion, it spoke the truth, but if it were praising his manliness, it cozened him like a boy. For he did not slay heroes like Pyrrhus, but lusted after women like Paris.
(Cf. A 1167, 4301, Σ 838, 1671)

## 3

(E 3770)

Eutocius, a native of Thrace, had no capacity for wisdom, nor was he of a good family. He was a soldier, who, having stolen a large sum of money belonging to his regiment, took to his heels and came to Palestine. He tried to persuade the people of Eleutheropolis to enrol him as a citizen since he had as much money as a town-councillor. For he longed to become a nobleman. Although they had first to change their decision for the better, the people of Eleutheropolis, being suspicious of the size of his fortune, would not enrol him. He, therefore, went off to Ascalon. The current chief magistrate, Craterus, gave a friendly reception to Eutocius and his money and made him a citizen.

πολιτικῆς τε μετέδωκεν ἐλευθερίας. οἱ δὲ Θρᾶκες ὑστέρῳ χρόνῳ κατὰ πύστιν ἥκοντες ἐπὶ τὸν Εὐτόκιον ἀπῄτουν τὸν Κρατερὸν αὐτόν τε καὶ τὰ χρήματα. ὁ δὲ οὐ μεθίει τὸν ἄνδρα. τῶν δὲ στρατιωτῶν ἐπὶ δίκην τὸ πρᾶγμα φερόντων, ὁ Κρατερὸς ὑπεραγωνίζεται τοῦ Εὐτοκίου καὶ περιγίνεται τῶν Θρακῶν· ἐφ' ᾧ καὶ χρησμὸς ἐξέπεσεν,    15 ἔχων ὧδε . . . . (Cf. E 566)

14 τὸ πρᾶγμα φερόντων A [ἐλθόντων GIVM

### 4

(Z 84)

Ὅτι Ζήνων ὁ βασιλεύς, πυθόμενος τῶν οἰκείων τὴν ἧτταν ἐς φρούριον καταφεύγει ἐπὶ λόφου κείμενον, ὃ Κωνσταντινούπολιν οἱ πρόσχωροι ἐκάλουν. ὅπερ γνούς, τοῖς συνοῦσι στενάξας, θεοῦ παίγνιον, εἶπεν, ἄρα ὁ ἄνθρωπος· εἴγε καὶ ἐμὲ οὕτω παίζειν φιλεῖ τὸ δαιμόνιον. ἐμοὶ γὰρ δὴ οἱ μάντεις τὸν Ἰούλιον μῆνα ἐξ ἀνάγκης ἐν    5 Κωνσταντινουπόλει διατεινόμενοι προὔλεγον. κἀγὼ μὲν ἐνόμιζον ἐς Κωνσταντινούπολιν ἀναβήσεσθαι· νῦν δὲ πάντων ἔρημος καὶ φυγὰς ἐς λόφον ἦλθον, εὑρηκὼς ὁ δείλαιος προσηγορίαν ὁμώνυμον.

1 πειθόμενος A    5 ἐμὲ A (infinit. desid. coni. Bernhardy)

### 5

(I 368)

Ἴνδακος: ὄνομα κύριον. ἤκμαζε δὲ ἐπὶ Λέοντος τοῦ μετὰ Μαρκιανὸν βασιλέως, λαμπρὸς τὴν τόλμαν καὶ τοῖς ποσὶ χρήσασθαι δυνατώτατος, τῶν χειρῶν τὴν ἀριστερὰν ἀμείνων, ταχύτητι ποδῶν διαφέρων. Εὐχίδου γὰρ καὶ Ἀσσάπου καὶ Χρυσομάζου καὶ Ἐχίονος καὶ εἴ τις ἕτερος ἐπὶ ποδῶν ὠκύτητι διεβοήθη, ὀξύτατος ἦν. οὗτος    5 γὰρ ἐξεφαίνετο ὁδεύων καὶ ἠφανίζετο αὖθις, οἷά τις ἀστραπή, κατὰ κρημνῶν οὐ τρέχοντι μᾶλλον ἀλλὰ πετομένῳ ἐοικώς. ἦν γὰρ κέλευθον ἀνὴρ δι' ἵππων ἀμοιβῆς αὐθημερὸν οὐκ ἔσθενε δρᾶσαι, τοῖς ἰδίοις αὐτὸν ποσὶν ἰσχυρίζοντο ἀναλγήτως διατρέχειν. ἀπὸ γὰρ τοῦ ἐρύματος Χέρεως διὰ μιᾶς ἐφοίτα ἐς τὴν Ἀντιόχειαν, καὶ πάλιν τῇ    10 ἑξῆς ἐς τὸ ῥηθὲν εὑρίσκετο φρούριον· ἐκ δὲ τούτου αὖθις μὴ ἀναπαύλης δεόμενος διὰ μιᾶς ἡμέρας εἰς Νεάπολιν ἐγίνετο Ἰσαυρίας. (Cf. E 3827, 4014, X 200)

### 6

(Λ 646)

Λογγῖνος· οὗτος ὁ Λογγῖνος καὶ Κόνων ἀδελφοὶ Ζήνωνος τοῦ

Later, the Thracians, acting on information received, came against Eutocius and demanded that Craterus hand over both him and the money. He refused to hand over the man. When the Thracians took the matter to court, Craterus defended Eutocius and prevailed over the Thracians. Upon this matter an oracle was given, as follows: . . . .[4]
(Cf. E 566)

## 4

(Z 84)

When the Emperor Zeno learned of the defeat of his own forces, he fled to a fortress on a hill which the people living nearby called Constantinople. When he learned this, lamenting he said to his companions, "Man is indeed a plaything of God, if the divinity enjoys toying even with me in this way. For the prophets insisted that I should of necessity be in Constantinople in the month of July, and I thought that I should return to Constantinople. Now, a fugitive and completely destitute, I have come to a hill which I learn in my misery bears the same name."

## 5

(I 368)

Indacus, a personal name. He flourished during the reign of Leo, Marcian's successor. He was famed for his daring and his great ability with his feet. He was better with his left hand and outstandingly fleet of foot. For he was swifter than Euchidus, Assapus, Chrysomazus, Echion and all others who were celebrated for their speed.[5] On his travels he appeared and then disappeared like a flash of lightning, coming down the cliffs like a bird rather than a man running. A journey which a man with a change of horses could not complete in a day, he could cover without any difficulty on his own feet. From the walls of Cherris he could reach Antioch[6] in one day, and on the next he would be back again at the fortress, and from here without needing a rest he could reach Neapolis in Isauria in a day.
(Cf. E 3827, 4014, X 200)

## 6

(Λ 646)

Longinus: this Longinus and Conon were brothers of the Emperor

## 480   Anonyma e Suda: Text

βασιλέως. οἱ παραδυναστεύοντες ἀθέσμως οἷον ἐν πάσαις ταῖς
πόλεσιν ἐπὶ κτήμασιν ἀλλοτρίοις ὅρους ἐτίθεσαν καὶ τοῖς γε τὰ
ἔσχατα πλημμελοῦσιν ἔνεμον τὰς βοηθείας ἐπὶ μισθῷ. Λογγῖνος δὲ
καὶ πάσης ἀκρασίας ἦν πλήρης, ἀεὶ μὲν μεθύουσι συνδιάγων ἀν-       5
θρώποις, ἀεὶ δὲ πορνοβοσκοὺς ἔνδον ἔχων ἀφθόνους, οἳ γυναῖκας μὲν
αὐτῷ τὰς τῶν πρώτων ἀρχόντων ἐπηγγέλλοντο ἄξειν· οἱ δὲ πόρνας
ἄγοντες ἀπὸ κόσμου θαυμαστοῦ καὶ δίρρων ἐπισήμων ἐξηπάτουν, ὡς
δῆθεν αὐτὰς ἐκείνας κομίσαντες. οὗτος δὲ ὁ Λογγῖνος καὶ σύστημα
ἀσκητριῶν ἔλυσε τρόπῳ τοιῷδε. ἐπὶ δείπνῳ ἐνδιαιτώμενος ταῖς      10
κληϊζομέναις πηγαῖς ἠγγέλθη τούτῳ παρὰ τῶν προαγωγευόντων,
ὡς εὐπρεπεῖς λίαν εἰσὶν αἱ γυναῖκες. καὶ ἔπεμψεν αὐταῖς ὄσπρια καὶ
ξηροὺς ἄρτους, εἶτα χιτῶνας ἄλλα τέ τινα, ὡς προνοῶν αὐτῶν
δῆθεν, ἐξ ἐπιστροφῆς τῶν φόβων· δεινοὶ γὰρ οἱ γυναικοϊέρακες
εὐπρεπεῖς αἰτίας ἐφευρίσκειν ἐς ἄγραν τῶν θηλειῶν. καὶ ἀνιὼν ἐν     15
τῷ σεμνείῳ πολλὰς τούτων πειθανάγκῃ κατήγαγεν. οὕτω γὰρ ἦν
λάγνος, ὡς καὶ ἐλευθέραις καὶ ἀρχόντων γυναιξὶ καὶ παρθένοις
ἀωρίᾳ ἐπιπίπτειν καὶ πάντα δρᾶν ἀνέδην. ἐν προόδῳ δὲ σφαίρας
ἀργυρᾶς καὶ περικάρπια ἐρρίπτει. καὶ ἄλλων δὲ πολλῶν κακῶν
αἴτιος ἐγεγόνει ὁ Λογγῖνος οὗτος.      20
(Cf. Γ 497, Π 1436)

2 οἷον post ἀλλοτρίοις (v.3) transp. Bernhardy    9 κοσμήσαντες A
10 ἐπὶ δείπνῳ Bernhardy [ἐπιδειπνῶς A ἐπισύχνως GVM    11 προσανω-
νευόντων A    12 ἐκπρεπεῖς A

## 7
(Π 137)

... Οὕτω μὲν οἱ σώφρονες περὶ αὐτοῦ εἴκαζον. εἰ δέ τι καὶ
ἄλλο ἦν, οὔτε ἰσχυρῶς ἀνελεῖν οὔτε πείθεσθαι ἔχω· ἀλλ' ὁμοίως καὶ
μέγα καὶ ἐλάχιστον αὐτῷ πρώτῳ ἀνεκοινοῦτο. καὶ τότε τοίνυν αὐτὸν
λαβὼν ἐς Νίκαιαν ἧκε χειμάσων, εἴτε τὴν ἐκ τοῦ δήμου δυσχέρειαν
ἐκκλίνων εἴτε ἐπὶ ταῖς σφαγαῖς τὸν ἔχοντα τὴν πόλιν ἐκτρέπεσθαι      5
δαίμονα πρὸς ὀλίγον ἐθέλων.

1 Οὕτω ... εἴκαζον corrupt. susp. Bernhardy

Zeno. They exercised their great authority so lawlessly that in all the cities they set a limit to the possessions of others and gave their help for money to those who committed the most serious crimes. Longinus, moreover, was wholly devoid of self-control, being forever in the company of drunkards and keeping within his establishment compliant brothel keepers, who claimed they wanted to bring him the wives of the leading officials. They brought whores wonderfully dressed up and in luxurious sedans and tricked him into thinking that they were bringing the ones whom he asked for. This Longinus also broke up a convent of nuns in the following manner. While he was dining at the famous 'Springs',[7] the panders reported to him that the women there were beautiful. He sent them pulses and dry biscuits and cloaks and other things, as if he were taking thought for them, out of consideration for their fear.[8] For the skilful hawkers after women use specious means to hunt females. And gaining entrance to the convent, he ruined many of them by force. He was so lecherous that he attacked free-born women, wives of officials and virgins at inappropriate times and acted wholly without restraint. When he appeared in public he would throw silver balls and nutshells. This Longinus was the cause of many other evils also.

(Cf. Γ 497, Π 1436)

## 7

(Π 137)

    ... Thus the wise men believed about [Pamprepius]. If there was some other explanation, I have no strong grounds for or against. But Illus likewise consulted with him first on matters great and small. He took him with him when he went to winter in Nicaea, either to avoid the hatred of the populace or because he wished for a short while to avoid the demon which was afflicting the city with massacres.[9]

# NOTES TO *ANONYMA E SUDA*

1.  For the phraseology cf. Π 137 ( = 7 below) and n.9.

2.  For this (colloquial?) use of ἐκτόπως cf. Z 84 (= Malchus *Fr.* 8).

3.  Theoderic the son of Triarius, who had supported Basiliscus.

4.  This article has been ascribed to both Eunapius (= *Fr.* 106 in Müller) and Malchus. The interest in Palestine might suggest the latter, but, although the style might pass as Malchan, there is no evidence in his fragments that he included such local anecdotes. It is best to leave it 'anonymous'.

5.  Presumably famous contemporary athletes.

6.  Possibly Antioch-on-the-Cragus, about 30 miles west of Anemurium. For a very tentative identification of Papirius/Cherris with the village of Bagdadkiri, about 25 miles north of Ermenek in southern Turkey, see G.E. Bean and T.B. Mitford, *Journeys in Roman Cilicia 1964-1968*, Vienna (1970) p.147.

7.  A suburb of Byzantium.

8.  The point is not, as Gordon (1960 p.156) appears to think, that Longinus sent them gifts to entice them, but that he sent them mean gifts, suitable for ascetics, to allay their fear so that they would admit him to the convent.

9.  This passage is usually included with the earlier part of Π 137 (= Malchus *Fr.* 23). But the direct intervention of the author jars with the style of what has gone before and with Malchus' style in general. Bernhardy had already voiced his suspicion about the words οὕτω μὲν οἱ σώφρονες περὶ αὐτοῦ εἴκαζον because they refer abruptly to sentiments just ascribed to ὅμιλος. Furthermore, the phrase καὶ μέγα καὶ ἐλάχιστον αὐτῷ πρώτῳ ἀνεκοινοῦτο is similar to one that appears in *Suda* A 783 (= 1 above): καὶ τούτῳ πρώτῳ ἀεὶ πάντα ἀνεκοινοῦτο τά τε κοινὰ καὶ τὰ ἴδια, an article which is certainly not Malchan.

# SUPPLEMENTARY BIBLIOGRAPHY

Baldwin B., 'Olympiodorus of Thebes', *Ant. Class.*, 49 (1980) pp.212-31.

Bayless W., 'The Chronology of Priscus Fragment 6', *CPh.*, 74 (1979) pp.154-56

Bijvank A.W., 'Notes batavo-romaines', *Mnemosyne*, 6 (1938) pp.380f.

Blockley R.C., 'Eunapius Fr. XIV,7: Julian as an Homéric Hero?', *Liverpool Classical Monthly*, 6 (1981) pp.213f.

Clover F.M., *Gaiseric the Statesman: A Study of Vandal Foreign Policy*, PhD. diss. Chicago (1966).

    *Flavius Merobaudes: A Translation and Historical Commentary* (Transactions of the American Philosophical Society LXI, 1), Philadelphia (1971).

    'The Family and Early Career of Anicius Olybrius', *Historia*, 27 (1978) pp.169-96.

Croke B., 'Anatolius and Nomus: Envoys to Attila', *Byzantinoslavica*, 42 (1981) pp.159-70.

    'The Context and Date of Priscus Fragment 6', to appear in *CPh.*, 78 (1983).

    'The Date of the 'Anastasian Long Wall' in Thrace', *GRBS*, 23 (1982) pp.59-78.

Cumont F., 'Un correction au texte d'Eunape à propos de la fin des mystères d'Eleusis', *Rev. de l'instr. publ. en Belgique*, 31 (1888) pp.179-81.

Gelzer H., 'Μέδος bei Priskos', *ByzZ.*, 24 (1924) pp.313f.

Goulet R., 'Sur la chronologie de la vie et des oeuvres d'Eunape de Sardes', *JHS*, 100 (1980) pp.60-72.

Haupt M., 'Analecta', *Hermes*, 1 (1866) p.30.

Maltese E.V., 'Note ed osservazioni sul testo di Prisco di Panion', *Helikon*, 17 (1977) pp.263-79.

Papabasileios G., 'Κριτικαὶ παρατηρήσεις εἰς ἱστορικῶν ἀποσπάσματα', Ἀθῆνα, 8 (1896) pp.69-80.

Penella R.J., 'Honours for Philtatius in a Fragment of Olympiodorus of Thrace [sic]', *Liverpool Classical Monthly*, 6 (1981) pp.245f.

Thompson E.A., 'The Camp of Attila', *JHS*, 65 (1945) pp.112-15.

    'A Note on Ricimer', *CR*, 60 (1946) p.106.

Vannerus J., 'La question Μουνδιακὸν Mundiacum', *Rev. belg. de phil. et hist.*, 15 (1936) pp.5-22.

# CORRELATION OF FRAGMENTS

Since my collection of the fragments differs considerably from the older ones, I have drawn up the following table of correlations with the most commonly used older editions, those of Müller (*FHG* IV), Dindorf (*HGM* I) and Niebuhr (*CSHB* XIV), although, since the numbering of Müller and Dindorf does not greatly differ, I have combined these, noting only where they do differ by the letters M and D (where only one letter occurs the passage is omitted from the other collection). The references are to fragments in Müller and Dindorf and to pages in Niebuhr.

|  |  | Blockley |  | Müller-Dindorf |  | Niebuhr |
|---|---|---|---|---|---|---|
| Eunapius | *Fr.* | 1 | *Fr.* | 1 | pp. | 56-61 |
|  |  | 2 |  | 2 |  | 106 |
|  |  | 5,1 |  | 4 |  | 99f. |
|  |  | 5,2 |  |  |  |  |
|  |  | 7,1 |  |  |  |  |
|  |  | 7,2 |  |  |  |  |
|  |  | 8 |  |  |  |  |
|  |  | 9,1 |  |  |  |  |
|  |  | 9,2 |  | 7 M, 7a D |  |  |
|  |  | 9,3 |  |  |  |  |
|  |  | 9,4 |  |  |  |  |
|  |  | 10 |  |  |  |  |
|  |  | 11,1 |  |  |  |  |
|  |  | 11,2 |  |  |  |  |
|  |  | 12 |  |  |  |  |
|  |  | 13 |  | 7a M, 7b D |  | 61 |
|  |  | 14,1 |  | 7a M, 7b D |  | 61f. |
|  |  | 14,2 |  | 14 M |  |  |
|  |  | 15 |  | 8 M, 8a D |  | 62f. |
|  |  | 16,1 |  | 8 M, 8a D |  | 63 |
|  |  | 16,2 |  | 8a M, 8b D |  |  |
|  |  | 17 |  | 9 |  | 63f. |
|  |  | 18,1 |  | 10 |  | 64f. |
|  |  | 18,2 |  | 10 |  | 64 |

| | | Blockley | Müller-Dindorf | Niebuhr |
|---|---|---|---|---|
| Eunapius | *Fr.* | 18,3 | *Fr.* 11 | pp. 116f. |
| | | 18,4 | 11 | 65 |
| | | 18,5 | 11 | 106f. |
| | | 18,6 | 12 | 41-45 |
| | | 19 | 13 | 45 |
| | | 20,1 | 14,1 | 65 |
| | | 20,2 | 7 M, 7a D | |
| | | 20,3 | | |
| | | 20,4 | 14,2 | 65f. |
| | | 20,5 | 14,3-4 | 66 |
| | | 21,1 | 14 M | |
| | | 21,2 | 14 M | |
| | | 21,3 | 14,5 | 66 |
| | | 23,1 | 14,6 | 66 |
| | | 23,2 | 14,7 | 66f. |
| | | 23,3 | 18,1 | 67 |
| | | 23,4 | 18,2 | 67 |
| | | 24 | 15 | 46 |
| | | 25,1 | 16 | 107 |
| | | 25,2 | 25 M | |
| | | 25,3 | 18,3 | 67f. |
| | | 25,4 | 19 | 100 |
| | | 25,5 | 17 | 107f. |
| | | 26,1 | 25 M | |
| | | 26,2 | 25 | 108 |
| | | 27,1 | 22,1 | 68 |
| | | 27,2 | 21 | 101 |
| | | 27,3 | 22,2 | 68 |
| | | 27,4 | | |
| | | 27,5 | 22,3 | 68 |
| | | 27,6 | 22,4 | 69 |
| | | 27,7 | 27 | 108 |
| | | 27,8 | 20 | 101 |
| | | 28,1 | 23 | 69f. |
| | | 28,2 | 24 | 71 |
| | | 28,3 | 24 | 71 |
| | | 28,4 | 24 | 71 |
| | | 28,5 | 24 | 71f. |
| | | 28,6 | 26 | 72 |
| | | 28,7 | | |
| | | 29,1 | | |
| | | 29,2 | 45 | 109 |
| | | 30 | 28 | 72f. |
| | | 31 | 29 | 46 |
| | | 34,1 | 31 | 73 |
| | | 34,2 | 31 | 73 |
| | | 34,3 | 31 | 73 |
| | | 34,4 | 33 | 73 |

| Eunapius | Blockley | Müller-Dindorf | Niebuhr |
|---|---|---|---|
| | *Fr.* 34,5 | *Fr.* 32 | p. 101 |
| | 34,6 | | |
| | 34,7 | | |
| | 34,8 | 34 | 101 |
| | 34,9 | 35 | 74 |
| | 34,10 | 35 | 74 |
| | 35 | 36 | 101 |
| | 37 | 37 | 46-48 |
| | 39,1 | 38 | 74f. |
| | 39,2 | | |
| | 39,3 | | |
| | 39,4 | 40 | 109 |
| | 39,5 | 40 | 109 |
| | 39,6 | 40 | 109 |
| | 39,7 | 39 M | |
| | 39,8 | 39 | 110 |
| | 39,9 | 38 | 75 |
| | 41,1 | 41 | 75f. |
| | 41,2 | 41 M | 105 |
| | 42 | 42 | 48-52 |
| | 43,1 | 44 and 45 | 76 |
| | 43,2 | 45 | 76 |
| | 43,3 | 45 | 77 |
| | 43,4 | 45 | 77 |
| | 43,5 | 45 M | |
| | 44,1 | 46 | 77f. |
| | 44,2 | 46 | 78 |
| | 44,3 | 47 | 110f. |
| | 44,4 | 47 | 78 |
| | 44,5 | | |
| | 45,1 | 51 | 102 |
| | 45,2 | 52 | 102 |
| | 45,3 | 43 | 101f. |
| | 46,1 | 48 | 78f. |
| | 46,2 | 49 | 102 |
| | 46,3 | 49 | 102 |
| | 46,4 | 48 | 79 |
| | 47,1 | 50 | 79 |
| | 47,2 | 50 | 79 |
| | 47,3 | 49 | 111 |
| | 48,1 | 54 | 79-82 |
| | 48,2 | 55 | 82f. |
| | 48,3 | 56 | 83 |
| | 50 | 57 | 83f. |
| | 55 | 58 | 84f. |
| | 56 | 65 M | |
| | 57 | 59 | 85 |
| | 58,1 | 53 | 111f. |

| Eunapius | Blockley Fr. | Müller-Dindorf Fr. | Niebuhr p. |
|---|---|---|---|
| | 58,2 | | |
| | 59 | 60 | 52-54 |
| | 60,1 | | |
| | 60,2 | 61 | 117 |
| | 61 | | |
| | 62,1 | 62 | 86 |
| | 62,2 | 63 | 112f. |
| | 62,3 | 64 | 102 |
| | 62,4 | | |
| | 64,1 | | |
| | 64,2 | 65 | |
| | 64,3 | 65 M | |
| | 65,1 | 66 | 102f. |
| | 65,2 | 69 | 113 |
| | 65,3 | 70 | 113f. |
| | 65,4 | 71 | 86f. |
| | 65,5 | 67 | 117 |
| | 65,6 | | |
| | 65,7 | | |
| | 65,8 | 72 | 87 |
| | 66,1 | 73 | 87-89 |
| | 66,2 | 74-75,1 | 89f. |
| | 67,1 | 75,2 | 90f. |
| | 67,2 | 75,3 | 91 |
| | 67,3 | 75,4 | 91 |
| | 67,4 | 75,4 | 91 |
| | 67,5 | 76 | 114 |
| | 67,6 | 76 | 103 |
| | 67,7 | 76 | 103 |
| | 67,8 | 77 | 114 |
| | 67,9 | 75,5 | 91 |
| | 67,10 | 75,6 | 91f. |
| | 67,11 | 75,7 | 92 |
| | 67,12 | 79 | 103 |
| | 67,13 | 79 | 117 |
| | 68 | 78 | 92 |
| | 69,1 | 78 | 92 |
| | 69,2 | 80 | 114f. |
| | 69,3 | 104 | 106 |
| | 69,4 | 82 | 92-94 |
| | 69,5 | 82 | 94 |
| | 71,1 | 84 | 117f. |
| | 71,2 | 83 | 94f. |
| | 71,3 | 85 | 95 |
| | 71,4 | 86 | 95f. |
| | 72,1 | 87 | 96-98 |
| | 72,2 | 87 | 99 |
| | 72,3 | 88 | 99 |

| | | Blockley | | Müller-Dindorf | | Niebuhr |
|---|---|---|---|---|---|---|
| Eunapius | *Fr.* | 72,4 | *Fr.* | 88 | p. | 99 |
| | | 73 | | 105 | | 106 |
| | | 74 | | 97 | | 104f. |
| | | 75 | | 95 | | 104 |
| | | 76 | | 89 | | 103 |
| | | 77 | | 90 | | 103f. |
| | | 78,1 | | 103 | | 105f. |
| | | 78,2 | | 107 M, 103 D | | 116 |
| | | 79 | | 101 | | 105 |
| | | 80 | | 96 | | 104 |
| | | 81 | | 93 | | 105 |
| | | 82 | | | | |
| | | 83 | | 92 M 91 D | | 104 |
| | | 84 | | 4 M | | 100 |
| | | 85 | | 68 | | 113 |
| | | 86 | | 3 | | 100 |
| | | 87 | | 98 | | 105 |
| | | 88 | | 94 | | 104 |
| | | 89 | | 92 | | 104 |
| | | 90 | | 68 | | 103 |
| | | 91 | | 102 | | 105 |
| | | 92 | | 93 | | 104 |
| | | 93 | | 99 | | 105 |
| | | 94 | | 91 M, 90 D | | 104 |
| | | 95 | | 105 | | 106 |
| Olympiodorus | | 1,1 | | 1,2 | | 448 |
| | | 1,2 | | | | |
| | | 2 | | 2 | | |
| | | 3 | | 1,2 | | 448 |
| | | 4 | | | | |
| | | 5,1 | | 1,2 | | 448 |
| | | 5,2 | | | | |
| | | 5,3 | | | | |
| | | 6 | | 1,3 | | 448f. |
| | | 7,1 | | 1,4 | | 449 |
| | | 7,2 | | 1,5 | | 449 |
| | | 7,3 | | 1,6 | | 449 |
| | | 7,4 | | 1,7 | | 449f. |
| | | 7,5 | | | | |
| | | 7,6 | | | | |
| | | 8,1 | | | | |
| | | 8,2 | | 1,8 | | 450 |
| | | 9 | | 1,9 | | 450 |
| | | 10,1 | | | | |
| | | 10,2 | | | | |
| | | 10,3 | | | | |
| | | 11,1 | | | | |

| | Blockley | Müller-Dindorf | Niebuhr |
|---|---|---|---|
| Olympiodorus *Fr.* | 11,2 | *Fr.* | p. |
| | 11,3 | | |
| | 11,4 | 1,10 | 450 |
| | 12 | 1,11 | 450 |
| | 13,1 | 1,12 | 450f. |
| | 13,2 | | |
| | 14 | 1,13 | 451f. |
| | 15,1 | 1,14 | 452 |
| | 15,2 | | |
| | 16 | 1,15 | 452f. |
| | 17,1 | 1,16 | 453f. |
| | 17,2 | | |
| | 18 | 1,17 | 454f. |
| | 19 | 1,18 | 455 |
| | 20,1 | 1,19 | 455f. |
| | 20,2 | | |
| | 20,3 | | |
| | 21 | | |
| | 22,1 | 1,20 | 456 |
| | 22,2 | 1,21 | 456 |
| | 22,3 | 1,22 | 457 |
| | 23 | 1,23 | 457 |
| | 24 | 1,24 | 457f. |
| | 25 | 1,25 | 458 |
| | 26,1 | 1,26 | 458f. |
| | 26,2 | | |
| | 27 | 1,27 | 459f. |
| | 28 | 1,28 | 460f. |
| | 29,1 | 1,29 | 461 |
| | 29,2 | 1,30 | 462 |
| | 30 | 1,31 | 462 |
| | 31 | 1,32 | 462 |
| | 32 | 1,33 | 462-64 |
| | 33,1 | 1,34 | 464f. |
| | 33,2 | | |
| | 34 | 1,35 | 465 |
| | 35,1 | 1,36 | 465 |
| | 35,2 | 1,37 | 465f. |
| | 36 | 1,38 | 466 |
| | 37 | 1,39 | 467 |
| | 38 | 1,40 | 467f. |
| | 39,1 | 1,41 | 468 |
| | 39,2 | | |
| | 40 | 1,42 | 468f. |
| | 41,1 | 1,43 | 469 |
| | 41,2 | 1,44 | 470 |
| | 42 | 1,45 | 470 |
| | 43,1 | 1,46 | 470f. |
| | 43,2 | | |

|  | Blockley Fr. | Müller-Dindorf Fr. | Niebuhr |
|---|---|---|---|
| Priscus | 1 |  | pp. 223f. |
|  | 2 | 1 | 166-69 |
|  | 3,1 |  |  |
|  | 3,2 |  | 226f. |
|  | 4 |  | 227 |
|  | 5 | V p.24 M, 1a D |  |
|  | 6,1 | 2 | 140f. |
|  | 6,2 | V p.25f. M, 1b D |  |
|  | 7 |  | cf. 227 |
|  | 8 | cf. 3a |  |
|  | 9,1 | 3 | 141 |
|  | 9,2 | 4 | 169 |
|  | 9,3 | 5 | 142-45 |
|  | 9,4 |  |  |
|  | 10 | 6 | 145f. |
|  | 11,1 | 7 | 146-50 |
|  | 11,2 | 8 pp.77-91 M, pp.289-314 D | 169-201 |
|  | 11,3 | 9 | 224 |
|  | 12,1 | 8 p.91 M, p.314 D | 201 |
|  | 12,2 | 10 | 224 |
|  | 13,1 | 8 pp.91f. M, pp.314-17 D | 201-05 |
|  | 13,2 | 11 | 225f. |
|  | 13,3 | 8 pp.92f. M, pp.317f. D | 205f. |
|  | 14 | 8 pp.93-95 M, pp.318-22 D | 206-11 |
|  | 15,1 | 8 p.95 M., pp.322f. D | 211f. |
|  | 15,2 | 12 | 150f. |
|  | 15,3 | 13 | 212f. |
|  | 15,4 | 14 | 213-15 |
|  | 15,5 |  |  |
|  | 16 |  |  |
|  | 17 |  |  |
|  | 18 |  | 222 |
|  | 19 | 20 | 227f. |
|  | 20,1 | 15 | 151f. |
|  | 20,2 |  |  |
|  | 20,3 | 16 | 152f. |
|  | 21,1 |  |  |
|  | 21,2 |  |  |
|  | 22,1 | 17 | 224 |
|  | 22,2 |  |  |
|  | 23,1 | 19 | 153 |
|  | 23,2 |  |  |
|  | 23,3 | 18 | 215f. |
|  | 24,1 | 23 | 225 |

| Priscus | Blockley *Fr.* | Müller-Dindorf *Fr.* | Niebuhr p. |
|---|---|---|---|
| | 24,2 | | |
| | 25 | | |
| | 26 | 20 | 153 |
| | 27,1 | 21 | 153f. |
| | 27,2 | | |
| | 28,1 | 22 | 223 |
| | 28,2 | | |
| | 29 | | |
| | 30,1 | | |
| | 30,2 | | |
| | 30,3 | | |
| | 31,1 | 24 | 216f. |
| | 31,2 | 24 | 222 |
| | 32 | | |
| | 33,1 | 25 | 217 |
| | 33,2 | 26 | 155f. |
| | 34 | | |
| | 35 | | |
| | 36,1 | 27 | 156 |
| | 36,2 | | |
| | 37 | 28 | 217f. |
| | 38,1 | 29 | 218f. |
| | 38,2 | | |
| | 39,1 | 30 | 156-58 |
| | 39,2 | 30 | 222 |
| | 40,1 | 30 | 158 |
| | 40,2 | | |
| | 41,1 | 31 | 158-60 |
| | 41,2 | 32 | 219 |
| | 41,3 | 33 | 219-21 |
| | 42 | | |
| | 43 | Malchus *Fr.* 7 | 274 |
| | 44 | Priscus *Fr.* 34 | 160 |
| | 45 | 35 | 160 |
| | 46 | 36 | 160f. |
| | 47 | 37 | 161f. |
| | 48,1 | 38 | 162 |
| | 48,2 | 43 | |
| | 49 | 39 | 162-64 |
| | 50 | | |
| | 51,1 | 41 | 164f. |
| | 51,2 | | |
| | 52 | 40 | 221 |
| | 53,1 | 42 | |
| | 53,2 | | |
| | 53,3 | | |
| | 53,4 | | |
| | 53,5 | | |

| Priscus | *Fr.* | Blockley | *Fr.* | Müller-Dindorf | p. | Niebuhr |
|---|---|---|---|---|---|---|
| | | 54,1 | | | | |
| | | 54,2 | | | | |
| | | 55 | | | | |
| | | 56 | | | | |
| | | 57 | | | | |
| | | 58 | | | | |
| | | 59 | | | | |
| | | 60 | | | | |
| | | 61 | | | | |
| | | 62 | | | | |
| | | 63 | | | | |
| | | 64,1 | | | | |
| | | 64,2 | | | | |
| | | 65 | | | | |
| | | 66,1 | | | | |
| | | 66,2 | | | | |
| | | 67 | | | | 222 |
| | | 68 | | | | |
| Malchus | | 1 | | 1 | | 231-34 |
| | | 2 | | 2 | | 234f. |
| | | 3 | | 2a | | 269f. |
| | | 4 | | | | |
| | | 5 | | 3 | | 260f. |
| | | 6,1 | | 5 | | 278 |
| | | 6,2 | | 4 | | 261f. |
| | | 7 | | 6 | | 275 |
| | | 8 | | 9 | | 277 |
| | | 9,1 | | | | |
| | | 9,2 | | 8a M, 8b D | | 262 |
| | | 9,3 | | 7 | | 274f. |
| | | 9,4 | | 8 M, 8a D | | 274 |
| | | 10 | | | | |
| | | 11 | | 7b D | | |
| | | 12 | | 7 | | 274f. |
| | | 13,1 | | 8c D | | |
| | | 13,2 | | 8 M, 8a D | | 274 |
| | | 14 | | 10 | | 235-37 |
| | | 15 | | 11 | | 237-39 |
| | | 16,1 | | 12 | | 263 |
| | | 16,2 | | 9 | | 275f. |
| | | 17 | | 13 | | 239f. |
| | | 18,1 | | 14 | | 263f. |
| | | 18,2 | | 15 | | 264-67 |
| | | 18,3 | | 16 | | 240-43 |
| | | 18,4 | | 17 | | 267f. |
| | | 19 | | | | |
| | | 20 | | 18 | | 244-58 |

| | | Blockley | | Müller-Dindorf | Niebuhr |
|---|---|---|---|---|---|
| Malchus | *Fr.* | 21 | *Fr.* | | p. |
| | | 22 | | 19 | 258-60 |
| | | 23 | | 20 | 270-72 |
| | | 24 | | | |
| | | 25 | | 21 M, 22 D | 269 |
| | | 26 | | 21 M, 22 D | 269 |
| | | 27 | | 20 | 272 |
| | | 28 | | 21 M | |
| Candidus | | 1 | | 1 | 272-77 |
| | | 2 | | 2 | 277 |
| *Suda* | *art.* | 1 | | Malchus *Fr.* 7a D | |
| | | 2 | | Malchus *Fr.* 8 | 272f. |
| | | 3 | | Eunapius *Fr.* 107 M, 106 D | 115f. |
| | | 4 | | Malchus *Fr.* 9 | 276f. |
| | | 5 | | ad Jo. Ant. *Fr.* 206,2 M | |
| | | 6 | | Malchus *Fr.* 21 D | |
| | | 7 | | Malchus *Fr.* 20 | 272 |

# INDEX OF NAMES AND PLACES

Only the translations and notes have been indexed. The following abbreviations have been used: c.s.l. = count of the sacred largesses; m.m. = master of the soldiers; p.p. = praetorian prefect; p.u. = urban prefect.

Goth (*cont.*)
195, 205, 217, 218, 281,
307, 321, 329, 335, 339,
343, 353, 357, 379, 390,
397, 399, 409, 413, 421,
423, 429, 435, 439, 441,
447, 449, 453, 460
Gothic: 189, 191, 267, 289, 309,
371, 385, 395, 445, 451,
458, 461
Gratian, Emperor: 77, 79, 85,
143
Gratian, usurper: 171
Greece: 33, 93, 95
Gundobad, nephew of Ricimer:
373, 375, 400
Guntiarius, Burgundian chief:
183

Hades: 207
Hadrian, Emperor: 47
Haemus Mountains: 429
Harmatius (Harmatus, see also
Armatus), favourite of Basi-
liscus: 373, 400, 417, 423,
457, 458, 472, 477
Harpazacius (see Arbazacius)
Hebe: 135
Hebrus, river: 429
Helena, mother of Constantine I:
15
Helena, town in Gaul: 17
Helion, master of the offices:
207
Helios: 135
Hellene (= pagan): 109, 135,
136, 153, 161-67 *passim*,
235, 453
Hellespont: 148, 229, 355
Hellespontus, province: 117
Hephaestus: 113, 388
Hera: 43, 135
Hera of Samos: 419
Heraclea (Macedonia): 437, 439,
441, 460
Heraclea (Thrace): 429
Heracleia (Perinthus): 241
Heracleius, chamberlain: 327-33
*passim*, 393

Heracleius, m.m.: 357, 365, 367,
398, 413, 457
Heracleius, philosopher: 37, 51,
134
Heracles: 49
Heraclian, usurper in Africa: 165,
185, 187, 216
Herculanus, consular: 301, 390
Hereka (Kreka), wife of Attila:
275, 291
Herennianus, vicar of Asia: 117,
119, 149
Hermes: 365
Herodorus, author: 195, 218
Herodotus: 195
Hesiod: 119
Hierax, murderer of Fravitta:
115, 119, 148, 149
Hilarius, philosopher: 57
Himilco, Punic officer: 113, 148
Hippias of Elis: 218
Hippodrome (Alexandria): 325
Hippodrome (Constantinople):
235
Homer: 35, 55, 117, 133, 136,
197, 419
Honoria, sister of Valentinian III:
197, 301-09 *passim*, 313,
390, 391
Honorius, Emperor: 3, 153-61
*passim*, 165-83 *passim*,
187, 191, 195-203 *passim*,
212, 213, 220, 309
Hormizd, general of Procopius:
51, 138
Hun: 59, 63, 71, 87, 89, 140,
141, 183, 191-216 *passim*,
223-27 *passim*, 237-41
*passim*, 249, 255, 259,
275, 277, 309, 311, 319,
321, 347, 349, 353, 357,
379, 380, 383-87 *passim*,
395, 399
Huneric, son of Gaiseric: 307,
341, 343, 390, 393, 399,
425, 458, 459
Hunimund, Suevic king: 397
Hunnic: 239, 249, 267, 289,
309, 319, 357, 379, 380,

# INDEX OF QUOTATIONS AND CITATIONS

Zosimus (*cont.*)

5,44,1 - 51,2: 212
5,48,3: 213
6,2,2: 214
6,3,2: 214
6,4,2: 214
6,7,1: 213
6,7,2: 213

Zosimus (*cont.*)

6,7,4: 213, 214
6,8,1: 213
6,8,2: 213
6,10,1: 213
6,12,1: 213
6,12,2: 213
6,13,2: 213, 214

## CORRIGENDA AND ADDENDA TO VOLUME I

p.72, 5 lines from bottom: for "Great Wall" read "Long Wall"

p.84, 14 lines from top: for "Pataulia" read "Pautalia"

p.145 n.37: for "Theodoulus" read "Theodulus"

p.176, last line: single quotation mark after Eunapius

p.183: the Anatolius of p.23 is a different person, praetorian prefect of Illyricum

p.187: for "Huns, Epthalite" read "Huns, Ephthalite"

p.191: the Symmachus on p.49 is Aurelius Memmius, historian

# Titles in ARCA on Ancient History and the Late Roman World

The Fragmentary Classicising Historians of the Later Roman Empire
R.C. Blockley
I. Eunapius, Olympiodorus, Priscus and Malchus
ARCA 6. 978-0905205-07-6. xii+196pp. 1981
II. Text, Translation and Historiographical Notes
ARCA 10. 978-0905205-15-1. x+515pp. 1983. Pb reprint 978-0905205-49-6. 2007

A Historical Commentary on Sallust's Bellum Jugurthinum
G.M. Paul
ARCA 13. 978-0905205-16-8. xxvi+276pp. 1984

Sextus Aurelius Victor: A Historiographical Study
H.W. Bird
ARCA 14. 978-0905205-21-2. x+175pp. 1984

The History of Menander the Guardsman
Introductory Essay, Text, Translation and Historiographical Notes
R.C. Blockley
ARCA 17. 978-0905205-25-X. xiii+307pp. 1985. Pb reprint 978-0905205-45-8. 2006

Herodotus and his 'Sources'. Citation, Invention and Narrative Art
Detlev Fehling (tr. J.G. Howie)
ARCA 21. 978-0905205-70-X. x+276pp. 1989

The Fifth-Century Chroniclers.
Prosper, Hydatius, and the Gallic Chronicler of 452
Steven Muhlberger
ARCA 27. 978-0905205-76-2. xii+329pp. 1990. Pb reprint 978-0905205-46-5. 2006

Greek Philosophers and Sophists in the Fourth Century A.D.
Studies in Eunapius of Sardis
Robert J. Penella
ARCA 28. 978-0905205-79-3. x+165pp. 1990

East Roman Foreign Policy.
Formation and Conduct from Diocletian to Anastasius
R.C. Blockley
ARCA 30. 978-0905205-83-X. xiv+283pp. 1992

Augustus and the Principate. The Evolution of the System
W.K. Lacey
ARCA 35. 978-0905205-91-5. x+245pp. 1996

Rome and Persia at War, 502–532
Geoffrey Greatrex
ARCA 37. 978-0905205-93-9. xvi+301pp., 14 maps. 1998.
Pb reprint 978-0905205-48-9. 2006

Caesar against Liberty? Perspectives on his Autocracy
Papers of the Langford Latin Seminar. Eleventh Volume (2003).
edd. Francis Cairns and Elaine Fantham
ARCA 43 (= PLLS 11). 978-0905205-39-7. xxii+234pp. 2003

Anastasius I. Politics and Empire in the Late Roman World
F.K. Haarer
ARCA 46. 978-0905205-43-4. xiv+351pp. 2006